Baptism of the Holy Spirit
and 9 Holy Spirit Gifts ...

CEASED?

Revelations for Charismatics, Cessationists and Roman Catholics

Don Dixon

LKM Publishing

Copyright

CEASED?
Copyright © 2020 by Don Dixon
Written by Don Dixon
Published by LKM Publishing, Abbotsford, British Columbia, Canada
First Printing: 2020

Unless otherwise indicated, scriptures are taken from the New American Standard Bible® (NASB).

Scripture taken from the NEW AMERICAN STANDARD BIBLE®, © Copyright 1960, 1962, 1963, 1968, 1971, 1972, 1973, 1975, 1977, 1995 by The Lockman Foundation. Used by permission. www.Lockman.org

Scripture quotations taken from the Amplified® Bible (AMP), Copyright © 2015 by The Lockman Foundation. Used by permission. www.Lockman.org

Scripture quotations marked ESV are from the English Standard Version, © 2001, ESV Text Edition © 2011, by Crossway Bibles, a division of Good News Publishers. Used by permission. All rights reserved.

Scripture quotations marked KJV are taken from the Holy Bible, King James Version. Used by permission. All rights reserved.

Scripture quotations marked MSG are taken from The Message © by Eugene H. Peterson 1993, 1994, 1995, 1996, 2002, 2001, 2002. Used by permission of Tyndale House Publishers, Inc.

Scripture quotations marked NLT are from the New Living Translation © 1996, 2004, 2007 Tyndale House Foundation. Used by permission of Tyndale House Publishers, Inc. Carol Stream, Illinois 60188. All rights reserved.

All emphasis in scripture citations were made by the author.

Any references to books, articles, internet addresses, websites, blogs and telephone numbers in this book are offered as a resource. Their inclusion is not intended in any way to be, or imply, an endorsement by LKM Publishing or the author, nor does the author or LKM Publishing vouch for the content and accuracy of these resources. Some names and minor details were changed to protect the identities of the persons involved. Feedback and requests to be submitted to website www.ceased.ca.

All rights reserved. No part of this publication may be reproduced, stored in a retrieval system, or transmitted in any form by any means - electronic, mechanical, photocopying, recording or any other - without the prior written permission of the author or publisher, except as provided for by Canadian or United States of America copyright law.

Cover Design: Lori Dixon and Lisa Befus
ISBN: 978-0-9949395-2-4 (Paperback, Compact)
ISBN: 978-0-9949395-4-8 (Paperback)
ISBN: 978-0-9949395-3-1 (eBook)
ISBN: 978-0-9949395-5-5 (Audio Book)
Printed in the United States of America

Dedication

I admire people who are committed to seeking the truth, even though the costs of doing so may be high, and who are willing to admit when they are wrong.

I dedicate **CEASED?** to all those who seek the truth in God's Word, and to those who stand up and share His truths in love and kindness, and for God's glory.

Please Note

After the initial publication of **CEASED?** in July 2020, a few items were modified in August 2020 to correct some typos and clarify a handful of comments and questions. Content additions were minimal.

Contents

	An Impactful Experience	iv
	Mountain Top	iv
	Acknowledgments and Thanks	v
	Introduction	vi

PART I:
SOME CONTEXT FOR CEASED?

Chapter One	Mindset and Final Authority	1
Two	9 Holy Spirit Gifts	13

PART II:
SOME BASICS ON CHRISTIANITY

Three	Spirit, Soul and Body	27
Four	Born Again/Salvation	42
Five	Holy Spirit 'Withs' [Para and Meta]	94
Six	Holy Spirit 'In' [En]	97
Seven	Holy Spirit 'Upon' [Epi]	115
Eight	'En' & 'Epi' After the Cross	131
Nine	Filled/Refilled With the Holy Spirit	153
Ten	4 Baptisms Relevant Today, 9 in Total?	163
Eleven	Tying Chapters 3 to 10 Together	186
Twelve	Link of 9 Holy Spirit Gifts to Baptism in Holy Spirit	200

PART III:
ADDITIONAL CESSATIONIST ARGUMENTS

Thirteen	Ceased by the Numbers	205
Fourteen	Did the 9 Holy Spirit Gifts Decline, then End?	210
Fifteen	Did the Purposes of Signs and Wonders End?	226
Sixteen	Did the 9 Gifts End with Specific Groups?	235
Seventeen	If the 9 Gifts Ceased, What Else Ceased?	250
Eighteen	Is all Divine Revelation in the Bible?	253
Nineteen	Charismatic Misbehaviors	261
Twenty	Summary of Cessationist Arguments	263

PART IV:
GOING FORWARD

Twenty-One	The Gift(s) of Tongues	272
Twenty-Two	Are Believers to Live in Divine Health?	291
Twenty-Three	Today's Christian Walk	301

PART V:
INSIGHTS AND QUESTIONS ABOUT ROMAN CATHOLICISM

From Previous Chapters:

Chapter Three	Mary - Sinner in need of a Savior?	36
Four	Works - Required to Gain or Keep Salvation?	51
	Water Baptism - Required for Salvation?	52
	Communion - Symbolic or Literal?	68
	Communion, Priests and Forgiveness of Sins	74
	Other Catholic Teachings on Salvation	88
Eight	Confirmation/Baptism of the Holy Spirit [epi]	145
Ten	Acts 2:38 - Water Baptism or Baptism in Holy Spirit?	180
Twenty-One	Tongues in the Roman Catholic church	290

New Chapters:

Twenty-Four	5 of 7 Catholic Sacraments, Traditions	325
Twenty-Five	Peter and Mary	337
Twenty-Six	Images, Different Ten Commandments, Saints	381
Twenty-Seven	Has a New Veil Been Created?	399
Twenty-Eight	Protestants and Catholics Together?	411

PART VI:
IN CLOSING

Twenty-Nine	Leaders: A Crazy Request	423
Thirty	In Closing	425
	Suggested Resources	
	About the Author	
	Contact Me	

An Impactful Experience

SOON after I was born again, I visited a friend in a hospice near Bellingham, Washington. Days before Tim went home to be with Jesus, his wife Jann and I went outside the hospice for some air. We started talking with a lady who asked if she could pray for Jann. Jann agreed. After a few seconds of quiet - which I found unusual - this lady asked Jann if she had unforgiveness against anyone. Jann said no. And that was totally consistent with the Jann we knew - loving, gentle and kind. The woman was silent for a few more seconds, then asked Jann if she'd let Jesus show her any unforgiveness in her heart. Jann agreed and closed her eyes. Soon, the tears started to come down Jann's face. She slowly pulled down at the neckline of her t-shirt to reveal 2 parallel scars, about an inch long each, on the top part of her chest bone. They were knife wounds from her first husband, and she couldn't forgive him.

After a short delay, the lady asked Jann if it would be ok for Jesus to show her what unforgiveness looked like. Jann agreed, closed her eyes, and soon after received some kind of picture. The lady asked Jann if she'd like Jesus to show her what forgiveness looked like. Jann agreed, closed her eyes again, received another picture, and broke down sobbing. For at least 10 minutes, this woman gently ministered to Jann as God brought healing into Jann's soul. I stood there, mesmerized on one hand and feeling absolutely useless on the other.

Afterward, I knew I had witnessed the supernatural love and power, albeit gentle power, that Almighty God brought to one believer through another. I realized there was something major missing in my personal walk with Jesus, and my ability to minister to others. That fueled the start of my journey to seek what God would make available for me. Part of my journey included writing **CEASED?**.

> ❑ *1 Corinthians 2:5 so that your faith would not rest on the wisdom of men, but on the power of God.*

Mountain Top

I love the way the movie 'Mountain Top' introduced the issue of how thoughts can hinder us. Sam Miller is in prison where he is met by a pastor/lawyer named Mike Andrews. Sam tells Mike that Papa God told him Mike and Sam are there to help each other. Mike retorts. "Help each other? You're the one in jail." Sam says "There's all kinds of jails. The worst is the prison of wrong thoughts. I was locked up there for many years until I found the key and opened the door."

My hope is **CEASED?** will open a few prison doors holding people captive.

Acknowledgments and Thanks

MANY people have helped my wife Lori and I in our Christian walk. Lori's mother, Joy, loved Jesus and God's Word with such passion. Lori remembers coming home many a late evening to see her mom fast asleep on her bed, her Bible laying open on her chest.

My Mom has lived a life filled with love, devotion, integrity and hard work. Mom went to church all her life, but didn't have a personal relationship with Jesus until her mid 80's. Now that she knows Jesus, it's even more wonderful to be in her presence. Thank you, Mom, for being such an incredible mother, supporter and friend.

Glenda Kemp is a great friend who encouraged me to attend a course at her church on dysfunctional behavior. That was one of many acts of kindness and wisdom from Glenda which led to me finally finding Christ. When in my darkest of days in Calgary, Glenda was one of the few people there for me. Thank you. I won't forget your kindness.

I met Cliff Holloway after I moved from Calgary to Abbotsford, and within days of being born again. I was in a terrible state. Cliff helped me immensely, became a valued friend and later that year, married Lori and I. Cliff prayed with me when Jesus Baptized me in the Holy Spirit, an event that dramatically changed me. Thanks for everything Cliff. You still owe me a day of fishing though.

John and Moira Hill mentored us since our early days of marriage. Thank you both!

Teachings of men who are now with Jesus - Billy Graham, Keith Green, Dave Hunt, T. L. Osborn, Derek Prince, David Wilkerson, Henry Wright, Ravi Zacharias and Chuck Smith - blessed us immensely. We look forward to meeting them one day.

Some of the other teachers who influenced us a great deal are listed below. Please note that their inclusion doesn't mean Lori or I agree with everything they say or write. To each of you, to your spouses and to each of your children, Lori and I thank you. I took out educational notations and prefixes. I mean no disrespect in doing so; it just seemed the right thing to do.

Kay Arthur	Curry Blake	Francis Chan	Ray Comfort
Robbie Dawkins	Jimmy Evans	Todd Gantt	Mike Gendron
Anne Lotz Graham	Franklin Graham	David Jeremiah	Bill Johnson
Eric Johnson	Dan Mohler	Beth Moore	Robert Morris
Tony Neal	Phil Nordin	John Piper	Joel Rosenberg
Dutch Sheets	Priscilla Shirer	Matt Slick	Lee Strobel
Fred Tarsitano	Kris Vallotton	Todd White	

I never attended Bible School, though I once enjoyed a hot chocolate and sandwich at Calvary Chapel Bible School in Murrieta, California. But don't feel sorry for my having missed out on a traditional Bible school education. I did one better. I married a Bible School. Of all my teachers of God's Word and how to walk out a Christian life, Lori has been number 1 - - by far. Thanks Babe, for everything, including all your edits and suggestions for **CEASED?**.

Introduction

<u>Apologies in Advance</u>
I seek to help the Body of Christ, not to condemn or belittle. If anything in **CEASED?** offends you, I apologize in advance. After all, apologizing is something we Canadians apparently do quite well.

<u>How CEASED? Came to Be</u>
In early 2011, a few months after I was born again, I was Baptized in the Holy Spirit. As I entered our home late that night, Lori looked at me and asked *"What happened to you?"* She saw God's presence all over me. The next day, it was evident that I was a changed person. I had a new, burning passion to share Jesus wherever I went. My biggest problem was I didn't know how to share Him. My Baptism in the Holy Spirit changed me dramatically, and marked the beginning of my researching, making notes, and routinely sharing on Baptism in the Holy Spirit.

Over the years, I've had several encounters with believers, both Charismatic and not, who misunderstood key parts of what this incredible Baptism is, and is not. The knowledge gap, and missing out on the associated blessings weighed heavily on me. More recently, I started researching the Cessationist vs Continuationist debate and was jolted. I was certainly bothered by the fact there was disagreement, but I was bothered even more by the ungodly behavior that I too often saw and heard. I wonder if Miriam would provide counsel to those strongly criticizing and condemning other servants of God today.

- ❑ *Numbers 12:1 Then **Miriam and Aaron spoke against Moses** because of the Cushite woman whom he had married (for he had married a Cushite woman); … 4 Suddenly the Lord said to Moses and Aaron and to Miriam, "You three come out to the tent of meeting." So the three of them came out. 5 **Then the Lord came down in a pillar of cloud and stood at the doorway of the tent, and He called Aaron and Miriam**. … 8 With him I speak mouth to mouth, Even openly, and not in dark sayings, And he beholds the form of the Lord. **Why then were you not afraid To speak against My servant, against Moses?"** 9 So the anger of the Lord burned against them and He departed. 10 But when the cloud had withdrawn from over the tent, behold, **Miriam was leprous, as white as snow**. As Aaron turned toward Miriam, behold, she was leprous.*

The more I researched the Cessationist vs Continuationist argument, the more frustrated I became. Finally, in April 2019, I decided to write. **CEASED?** came to be.
CEASED? started with 2 primary goals in mind.
1. Provide information on the 'with' [para], 'in' [en] and 'upon' [epi] Holy Spirit experiences, and how they relate to the Holy Spirit gifts in 1 Corinthians 12.
2. Provide evidence showing whether or not the 9 Holy Spirit gifts in 1 Corinthians 12 and Baptism of the Holy Spirit have ceased, or still apply today.

As I researched and wrote, **CEASED?** expanded to include 4 other goals.
3. Provide information related to spiritual gifts, especially tongues.
4. Provide information for new believers on some of the basics of Christianity including how 4 baptisms and 3 Holy Spirit experiences - 'with' [para], 'in' [en] and 'upon' [epi] - relate to each other, and their connection to the issue of salvation, and to our spirit, soul and body.
5. Provide personal thoughts on a few parts of our Christian walk including binding and loosing, spiritual warfare, authority and the prosperity / poverty / abundance gospels.
6. Provide insight into key issues where Protestants and Catholics have different beliefs, and whether or not it's prudent to evangelize and worship together.

Re Protestants and Catholic Charismatics

There seems to be a growing intermixing of Protestants and Roman Catholics sharing the stage, working together, and evangelizing together, especially in Charismatic circles. Consensus seems to be that there are more than 100 million Charismatic Roman Catholics - Catholics who have been Baptized in the Holy Spirit and operate to some extent in the 9 Holy Spirit gifts (tongues, interpretation of tongues, discerning of spirits, prophecy, words of wisdom, words of knowledge, faith, miracles, healing). There are varying voices on this inter-mixing ranging from very strong support to extreme disdain. Protestant Cessationists routinely chastise Protestant Charismatics for not speaking 'truth' to Catholic Charismatics about issues in Catholic teachings. To address this concern, I address some of the key issues where Protestant and Roman Catholic teachings diverge, and do so from the following perspective:

First, how significant are the differences in key beliefs between Protestants and Roman Catholics, both Charismatic and non-Charismatic? And second, should these differences prevent individuals of these denominations from worshipping and evangelizing alongside each other, even in situations where both appear to have been Baptized in the Holy Spirit and operate in one or more of the 9 Holy Spirit gifts?

Focus on the Bible, Not Behaviors

The Cessationist vs Continuationist debate has many tentacles. I will briefly speak to some behavioral issues in Chapter 19, but human behavior is often not a reliable barometer of what the Bible teaches. As a result, my primary focus is on what the Bible says about the 9 Holy Spirit gifts and the Baptism of the Holy Spirit, not on the misbehaviors that have occurred before, or are taking place today.

Please know my lack of comments on inappropriate behaviors and teachings is not evidence that I endorse them. I find many comments of some Charismatic leaders/teachers to be at the top of the cringe-worthy scale. Discussions that suggest in any way we are a small god, for instance, are horrific in my view. The same holds true for teachings that state God gives us all our heart's desires if we have enough faith, or financially support this ministry or that person. These issues are of grave concern, but I believe my role at this time is to pray for these individuals and those who hear their teachings and messages. As a result, I comment little on these topics.

Covering some Basics

The 9 Holy Spirit gifts referred to in 1 Corinthians 12 are associated with the Baptism in the Holy Spirit. To properly understand the Baptism in the Holy Spirit in the context of the Christian life requires an understanding of the 4 baptisms applicable to believers today. These baptisms in turn are linked to salvation which in turn is linked to our 3 parts - spirit, soul and body. Accordingly, I felt led to go back to some basics starting in Chapter 3 to give new believers enough background. For seasoned students of God's Word, much of Chapters 2 through 4 will be familiar and if this is you, extra strong coffee may be in order. No donuts though.

Biblical References

Unless otherwise indicated, all scriptures are taken from the NASB translation. I usually included the text of scriptures instead of just referencing the scriptures. I hope it saves time and facilitates reading. I almost always copied and pasted scriptures from www.biblegateway.com.

Many Questions

A key goal of **CEASED?** is to stimulate thought and reflection, and to facilitate dialogue. Early in my business career, a senior executive told me a key to solving problems is not to begin by searching for the answer(s), but to search for the right question or questions. This gentleman was drafted by the Detroit Red Wings, and had huge, powerful hands. I never forgot that advice, either out of fear of those hands, or out of accidental wisdom on my part. In my own adult life, I have also found we humans often react more negatively and defensively to statements than we do to fair and reasonable questions. As a result, **CEASED?** includes questions designed to stimulate thought, to challenge readers to understand why they believe what they do, and to help readers communicate by using question numbers as reference points.

Questions are indicated by the Chapter number '1' followed by a colon ':' and then the question number '5' within that chapter. For example, consider the question:

1:5 Are we more committed to a) our current beliefs or b) to seeking the truths as revealed in God's Word?

When looking at the 1:5, the number 1 identifies the question as being in the 1st Chapter. The number 5 represents the 5th question in Chapter 1.

Greek and Hebrew

I refer to several Greek Words in **CEASED?**. When I was first born again and started to read/study/meditate on God's Word, Lori kept suggesting I look at the underlying Greek and Hebrew. When she first did so, I looked at her as would a recently neutered dog who realizes it is back at the veterinary hospital where the deed was done a few days prior. My dark inner recesses went crazy thinking *"What* *are you trying to do to me woman?"*. Woman is a term of endearment between us; at the moment, I cannot recall any of Lori's terms of endearment for me. Once I started looking into the Greek and Hebrew a bit, I was surprised I had never heard a pastor use the pulpit to teach on the basics of doing so.

In **CEASED?**, looking at the underlying Greek and Hebrew words proved vital to my understanding of what the Bible says about some of the key issues at hand. Having said that, please know I'm not a Greek or Hebrew scholar. I have a layman's understanding of a few words - period. For any of you not accustomed to examining the Greek or Hebrew, there's no need to fret. I use it to a limited extent, and I try to lay out the relevant portions of definitions taken usually from Strong's Concordance and Thayer's Greek Definitions.

As an example, consider the Greek word *'en'*. It is uniquely identified in Strong's as 'G1722'. The letter G identifies 'en' as being a Greek word (letter 'H' denotes Hebrew words) while the 1722 uniquely identifies which Greek Word that it is. Thayer defines 'en' as '1. in, by, with etc.'. A Greek or Hebrew word can be standalone with no relationship to other words, or it can be linked to one or more other Greek or Hebrew words. There can be also one or more definitions or applications for each Greek or Hebrew word which is one reason why translations can read quite differently in modern-day languages including English.

Today, there are many tools for searching out the Greek and Hebrew. For **CEASED?** and in my day-to-day life, I primarily use the King James version on the MySword app on my Android, and the Interlinear Bible on www.BibleStudyTools.com. I greatly appreciate the free access provided by these top-notch services.

Inserts, Bolding and Underlining

Scriptures are identified by using the square bullet symbol and *italicizing the words*. I often **bolded** and <u>underlined</u> words to draw attention to the most relevant part of the verse relating to the issue being addressed. I sometimes inserted a comment, number, Greek or Hebrew word within a scripture to help clarify the issue being addressed.

❑ *1 Corinthians 3:16 Do you not know that you are **<u>a temple of God</u>** and that the **<u>Spirit of God</u>** dwells <u>**in [en G1722] you**</u>?*

Charismatic

When I use the word 'Charismatic' in **CEASED?**, I am referring to all believers who have been Baptized in the Holy Spirit, and in so doing have Holy Spirit coming '<u>**upon**</u>' them. The word upon is derived from the Greek word *'epi'* [G1909]. **CEASED?** will systematically reveal why this 'upon' [epi] experience is a separate and distinct experience from the 'in' [en] [G1722] experience which occurs when we're born again and Holy Spirit comes 'in' us.

As we shall see, it is Jesus who gives this Baptism of the Holy Spirit to believers which provides access to supernatural power to be more effective witnesses for Christ. This power of God manifests through believers in various ways including the 9 Holy Spirit gifts in 1 Corinthians 12. The English word *'gifts'* is derived from the Greek word *'charisma'* [G5486] which Thayer defines in part as '... 5. Grace or gifts denoting extraordinary powers, distinguishing certain Christians and enabling them to serve the church of Christ, the reception of which is due to the power of divine grace operating on their souls by Holy Spirit'. The word *'Charismatic'* evolved from charisma and associated words. Roman Catholic Charismatics often use the word 'charisms' to refer to the 9 Holy Spirit gifts.

May **CEASED?** bless you as you read it, and may God especially bless you in your personal walk with Christ.

- ❑ *1 Corinthians 13:1 If I speak with the tongues of men and of angels, but do not have **love**, I have become a noisy gong or a clanging cymbal. 2 If I have the gift of prophecy, and know all mysteries and all knowledge; and if I have all faith, so as to remove mountains, but do not have **love**, I am nothing. 3 And if I give all my possessions to feed the poor, and if I surrender my body to be burned, but do not have **love**, it profits me nothing.*

- ❑ *John 1:31 I did not recognize Him, but so that He might be manifested to Israel, I came baptizing in water." ... 33 ... 'He upon whom you see the Spirit descending and remaining upon Him, **this is the One who baptizes in the Holy Spirit**.'*

- ❑ *Acts 1:8 but **you will receive power when the Holy Spirit has come upon you**; and **you shall be My witnesses** both in Jerusalem, and in all Judea and Samaria, and even to the remotest part of the earth."*

- ❑ *1 Corinthians 14:1 Pursue love, yet **desire earnestly spiritual gifts**, but **especially that you may prophesy**.*

1

Mindset and Final Authority

INTRODUCTION

IF we're committed to our current beliefs, if our eyes, ears and minds are closed, then we have stopped growing in Christ. If seeking the truth of God's Word is truly a desire of our heart, our reactions when we encounter new insights in the Bible that contradict any of our current beliefs will be very telling. Chapter 1 tests whether we are more loyal to our beliefs, or to the truths in the Bible.

Chapter 1 concludes with some insights as to why the Bible is not just a collection of writings but a supernatural book. **CEASED?** includes some of Ivan Panin's analysis on the numbers corresponding to each of the letters of the Greek and Hebrew words in scripture. He started his work in the 1890's, long before computers came into being. His findings were amazing.

MINDSETS AND ATTITUDES

Seasoned, intelligent theologians sometimes have radically different views on key parts of God's Word. God is not the author of confusion. As a result, when leading believers disagree so fervently, it's very peculiar. Some extreme Charismatics seem to give priority to experience and/or the opinions of those they follow. But the same seems to hold true for many Cessationists who appear more loyal to the teachings of say a John Calvin or an Ellen White than to a fresh, open-minded study of the Bible. Roman Catholics have been known to put church traditions and unique teachings above scripture. When our first loyalty is to our experience, our teachers, our church or our own rigid beliefs, then any conflicting teaching or information from the Bible cannot even be considered in our hearts and minds. We end up overlooking truths of God's Word so we can stay true to our beliefs as opposed to facing the reality we may be wrong, and missing out on the blessings that can flow from pursuing God's truths.

Only you know where your heart is at - or maybe you don't know. Your reactions to some of the questions I'm about to ask may help you see your true heart. I simply ask you be open to what the Bible has to say, and to be open to renewing your mind.

- ❑ *Romans 12:2 And do not be conformed to this world, but be transformed by the renewing of your mind ...*

CEASED?

1:1   As a starter, consider the following list of potential sources of influence. What are the top 3 sources influencing you today? If you're unsure how to answer, consider some faith issues you recently thought about, and identify which influences most impacted your current thinking on those issues:
   i.   teachings of your parents;
   ii. teachings of pastor(s), priest(s), teacher(s);
   iii. teachings and traditions of your denomination/church;
   iv. stories/information about others you personally verified;
   v.   stories/information about others you have not personally verified;
   vi. personal in-depth study of the Bible giving you personal revelation or which confirmed teachings of others; or
   vii. other _____.

1:2   Of the sources influencing your view of Biblical matters, which one(s) would satan most want you NOT to have as your main influence?

1:3   Would it be surprising if the source(s) you identified in question 1:2 is/are the source(s) that should be serving as your main influence(s)?

Many believers say the Bible is their main influence, their ultimate authority. But is that truly the case? When a theological issue comes up, do we go to the Bible to get our answer, or do we go to what we already believe without questioning it, or to another person or to our church, and rely on what they teach? I did the latter for much of my early Christian walk. It seemed safe and was easy to do. Then I realized I was not getting the full story and truth on some issues, nor was I approaching the Word of God with a knife and fork … I was content on being spoon-fed.

Many cults say their teachings are based on the Bible. And to varying degrees, they are. Deceit typically wraps itself in a great deal of truth. Individuals in cults are often very sincere people. Their problem is they are deceived, and while the cult leaders teach some or even much of what is true, the false portions are ultimately fatal when it comes to one's eternal destiny. Cult teachings include modifications to Biblical salvation, and the creation of rules and practices designed to keep the person first and foremost loyal to their organization. Teachings and practices are often based on fear and emotional blackmail. Heavy emphasis is also placed on the fact they are the only organization that has the truth. Membership and faithfulness to the church is a key requirement to be a 'true follower' of Christ.

We Christians are often quick to criticize, even mock, cults for their beliefs. Pointing out false teachings certainly has its place, but how we do so is important. We need to recognize these people, while deceived, sincerely believe what they believe. Shouldn't our hearts be first and foremost ones of compassion and love for them, and to pray for them to receive a revelation of the truth of Jesus and His Word?

Within Christian churches, how many of our traditions and teachings aren't supportable by scripture? How many hang on a mighty fragile, theological thread?

What's your mindset?
If you believe the Bible is your final authority on matters of faith, let's test it out.

1: Mindset and Authority

1:4 When you're facing **credible evidence** on an important issue that conflicts with your existing beliefs, and for which you have no scriptures or theological argument to refute:
   i. Are you defensive and look to find almost any argument, even a feeble one, that can be used to negate this evidence?
   ii. Do you shut down discussions or stop reading anything that conflicts with your views, or simply ignore the evidence? (and yes, there is much that we should immediately stop reading when it's clear it has no Biblical merit)
   iii. Are you prone to stick with the teachings of a church, pastor, priest or high-profile leader, as questioning their teachings is not right, is not allowed, or even thinkable?
   iv. Are you prone to discrediting the person that brings conflicting evidence, even if the information presented has merit?
   v. Do you use isolated incidents to make blanket judgments about those you disagree with?
   vi. If evidence showed your belief on a significant faith issue could be in error, do you respond by wanting to find the truth out now, or do you let the information pass you by until a future date - such as when you die and come face to face with Jesus?

I suggest our responses to the above reflect our answer to question 1:5.

1:5 Are we more committed to a) our current beliefs or b) to seeking the truths as revealed in God's Word?

QUESTIONS FOR CESSATIONISTS

The Cessationist camp believes the 9 Holy Spirit gifts found in 1 Corinthians 12 (and which are discussed in Chapter 2) ended with the original apostles or other groups of early believers. Consider the following.

- *Acts 1:15 At this time Peter stood up in the midst of the brethren **(a gathering of about one hundred and twenty)** ...*
- *Acts 2:1 When the day of Pentecost had come, they **were all together** in one place. 2 And suddenly there came from heaven a noise like a violent rushing wind, and it filled the whole house where they were sitting. 3 And there appeared to them tongues as of fire distributing themselves, and they rested on each one of them. 4 And **they were all filled with the Holy Spirit** and **began to speak** with **other tongues, as the Spirit was giving them utterance**.*

1:6 The 'all' who were gathered in Acts 2:1 are typically viewed as being similar to the ~120 gathered in Acts 1:15. And given '... *all were filled with the Holy Spirit and spoke in tongues* ...' in Acts 2:4, doesn't that suggest many more than the original apostles were given these gifts of tongues and potentially other Holy Spirit gifts, right from the get-go? As in all of them who were there at Pentecost? If not, why not?

1:7 A prophecy involves God giving words to one person for themselves, or to speak to one or more other persons. A tongue and corresponding interpretation of tongues typically involves God giving words to one person and the interpretation of the tongue to a second person. In this way, God uses two people to deliver a message, not just one person. When there is a tongue and a corresponding interpretation of the tongue, would this constitute a form of divine revelation similar to a prophecy, word of knowledge, or word of wisdom? If not, why not?

1:8 I cannot find the specifics of one interpretation of a tongue in God's Word. Does this indicate some of God's divine revelations aren't actually in the Bible? Or does it mean that God created the gift of interpretation of tongues, but then chose not to give the gift to any believer?

❏ *1 Corinthians 14:1 Pursue love, yet **desire earnestly spiritual gifts**, but **especially** that you may **prophesy** ... 5 Now I wish that you all spoke in tongues, but even more that you would prophesy; and **greater is one who prophesies** than one who speaks in tongues, **unless he interprets**, so that the church may receive edifying.*

CEASED? provides more information on tongues in Chapter 21.

Prophesy is one of the 9 Holy Spirit gifts that Cessationists believed ended with the early church. Consensus seems to be that Paul wrote 1 Corinthians somewhere between 52-57 AD, approximately 20-25 years after the cross.

❏ *1 Corinthians 11:4 Every **man** who has something on his head while **praying or prophesying** disgraces his head. 5 But every **woman** who has her head uncovered while **praying or prophesying** disgraces her head, for she is one and the same as the woman whose head is shaved.*

1:9 Why would Paul instruct believers to be concerned about head coverings of Corinthian believers if prophesying wasn't available to the 'ordinary' believer at Corinth, or for that matter, any ordinary believer living at that time?

1:10 If women were to wear head coverings when they prophesied, doesn't this mean that women were expected to prophesy?

Let's consider Acts 21:9.

❏ *Acts 21:9 Now this man had four virgin daughters who were prophetesses.*

1:11 Translations vary with some saying the 4 women were prophetesses while others think they only prophesied a small amount and weren't real prophets. Either way, doesn't the fact these 4 women prophesied or were prophetesses mean each one of them gave at least one prophecy? And potentially many more? If not, why not?

1:12 I can't find details of a single prophecy through these 4 women. On the basis that the specifics of the prophecies given through these 4 women aren't in the Bible, does this again show the Bible contains some but not all of God's divine revelation? If not, why not?

1: Mindset and Authority

More information on Divine Revelation is provided in Chapter 18 of **CEASED?**.

QUESTIONS FOR CHARISMATICS

Many Charismatics believe God doesn't put any afflictions such as illnesses and diseases on people today. If we go back to the Old Testament, consider these scriptures.

- Genesis 12:17 But the Lord **struck Pharaoh and his house with great plagues** because of Sarai, Abram's wife.
- Exodus 15:26 And He said, "**If you** will give earnest heed to the voice of the Lord your God, and do what is right in His sight, and give ear to His commandments, and keep all His statutes, **I will put none of the diseases on you which I have put on the Egyptians**; for I, the Lord, am your healer."
- Numbers 12:9 So the anger of the Lord burned against them and He departed. 10 ... **Miriam was leprous, as white as snow** ...
- Exodus 9:10 So they took soot from a kiln, ... and **it became boils breaking out with sores on man and beast**.
- Isaiah 48:10 "Behold, I **have refined you**, but not as silver; I have tested you **in the furnace of affliction**.

God hardened Pharaoh's heart.

- Exodus 10:1 Then the Lord said to Moses, "Go to Pharaoh, for **I have hardened his heart and the heart of his servants**, that I may perform these signs of Mine among them,

1:13 When God hardened Pharaoh's heart, did God contribute to Pharaoh's sinning which in turn led to God putting afflictions on the Egyptians?

God is the same yesterday, today and forever. God also has mercy on who He chooses to have mercy. God is God after all.

- Hebrews 13:8 **Jesus Christ is the same** yesterday and today and forever.
- Amos 4:7 "Furthermore, I withheld the rain from ... Then I would send rain on one city and on another city I would not send rain ...
- Romans 9:18 ... **He has mercy on whom He desires**, and **He hardens whom He desires**.

Given God does not change, and He put sicknesses, diseases and afflictions on people and hardened hearts in the Old Testament, is there any evidence in the New Testament that shows God continues to put sicknesses, diseases or other afflictions on people? Consider the following who were afflicted after the cross. Herod, Saul/Paul and Elymas were not believers. Ananias and Sapphira were believers.

- Acts 12:21 On an appointed day Herod... began delivering an address to them. 22 The people kept crying out, "The voice of a god and not of a man!" 23 And immediately **an angel of the Lord struck him because he did not give God the glory**, and **he was eaten by worms and died**.
- Acts 9:8 Saul got up from the ground, and though his eyes were open, he could see nothing; and leading him by the hand, they brought him into Damascus. 9 **And he was three days without sight**, ...

CEASED?

- *Acts 13:8 But **Elymas** the magician (for so his name is translated) was opposing them ... 11 Now, behold, the **hand of the Lord is upon you**, and **you will be blind and not see the sun for a time**." And immediately a mist and a darkness fell upon him, and he went about seeking those who would lead him by the hand.*
- *Acts 5:1 ... **Ananias**, with his wife **Sapphira**, sold a piece of property, 2 and kept back some of the price for himself ... 5 And as he heard these words, Ananias fell down and **breathed his last** ... 10 And immediately she fell at his feet and **breathed her last** ...*

1:14 God does not change. Accordingly, if God put afflictions on people both before and after the cross, doesn't that mean He may be afflicting some individuals today, both believers and unbelievers? If not, why not?

1:15 If you still don't believe God puts afflictions on people today, isn't there some wrath coming or something called the tribulation?

- *1 Thessalonians 1:10 and to wait for His Son from heaven, whom He raised from the dead, that is Jesus, who rescues us from the wrath to come.*

In the current COVID-19 crisis, Christians often cite Psalm 91 as a reason to believe that believers won't be harmed by the virus. Actual evidence of wonderful men and women of God getting sick would say this teaching has some holes. But in addition, consider the first verses of Psalm 91.

- *Psalm 91:1 He **who dwells** in the shelter of the Most High Will abide in the shadow of the Almighty. 2 I will say to the Lord, "My refuge and my fortress, My God, in whom I trust!"*

1:16 Doesn't this suggest there is a condition to enjoying such protection? That we need to be dwelling in God's shelter in order for God to be our refuge and fortress? Chapter 23 which addresses a few other times when God puts conditions on his blessings. As a result, is there more to the story?

1:17 On the other hand, many Christians believe God uses sicknesses and diseases to teach a person something. If by chance that is the case, shouldn't we ask God what the lesson is instead of just being passive? Furthermore, don't we live in a world where sickness and disease can arise from a variety of sources including lifestyle, diet, the environment, sins, issues in our soul (fear, anxiety, anger etc.), genetic deterioration - or from controversial sources such as demonic influences and generational curses? Don't our unhealthy choices lead to sickness and disease? And in such cases, shouldn't we change what we feed our body and soul in terms of what we eat, drink, watch, listen to, or think about? And thus, when a person is not healed after prayer, is it wise/prudent to 'blame it' on God or claim God is teaching us some unspecified lesson without first seeking God and asking Him why healing isn't occurring?

CEASED? provides more information on healing in Chapter 22.

1: Mindset and Authority

QUESTIONS FOR ROMAN CATHOLICS

The Cessationist vs Continuationist debate frequently mentions the 100+ million Charismatic Catholics. Some Cessationists criticize Continuationists for not showing Charismatic Catholics the errors of Catholic teachings. While I initially had major reservations about commenting on the Protestant/Catholic divide in **CEASED?**, I eventually felt led to comment on at least a couple of key issues. As time passed, I found myself addressing more than a couple.

To begin, I don't think many Protestants are protesting against the Roman Catholic church today. That doesn't mean Protestants agree with Roman Catholics on the issues that led to the Reformation. It simply means the Roman Catholic church is viewed as one of many different organizations with their own unique Bible, traditions and teachings. Protestants agree with some Catholic teachings, but continue to disagree on several key points.

The perspective I took in **CEASED?** is whether or not Protestants and Roman Catholics should witness and evangelize alongside each other. To put the issue another way, would a Protestant be comfortable encouraging a person seeking God to go to a Roman Catholic church, and would a Roman Catholic be comfortable encouraging someone to go to a Protestant church? If there are no major differences on key issues, no problem. But if there are key differences - that's another ballgame. Hopefully **CEASED?** will bring some insights for both Catholics and Protestants on some important topics that will help clarify what God has to say.

Now back to the core of Chapter 1 - our hearts and loyalty. Let me test Roman Catholic hearts if I may. Mary is given the title *'Mother of God'* by Catholics. One common rationale I've seen for this title is something like the following: *"Because Mary is the mother of Jesus, and since Jesus is God, Mary is therefore to be viewed as the Mother of God"*. Mary is also recognized by Catholics as a creation of God. Dr. Scott Hahn who I refer to in Chapter 25, calls Mary a magnificent creation.

When pondering Mary as Mother of God, Holy Spirit reminded me of Matthew 22.

- ❑ *Matthew 22:41 Now while the Pharisees were gathered together, Jesus asked them a question: 42 "What do you think about the Christ, whose son is He?" They said to Him, "The son of David." 43 He said to them, "Then how does David in the Spirit call Him 'Lord,' saying, 44 'The Lord said to my Lord, "Sit at My right hand, Until I put Your enemies beneath Your feet"'? 45 **If David then calls Him 'Lord,' how is He his son?**" 46 No one was able to answer Him a word, nor did anyone dare from that day on to ask Him another question.*

1:18 My related question is this. Mary is a creation of God. If God created Mary, how could Mary be the Mother of God? In other words, how can Mary be the Mother of the One who created her?

Then consider Luke 1:30.
- ❑ *Luke 1:30 The angel said to her, "**Do not be afraid, Mary**, for you have found favor with God.*

1:19 If Mary was truly the Mother of God:
  i. why would Mary fear an angel of God; and
  ii. why didn't the angel acknowledge Mary's special status and use one of

CEASED?

the many titles given to Mary by the Roman Catholic church today?

When I ask the above questions on Mary, please know I recognize Mary holds a special place in the hearts of Romans Catholics. My intent is not to blindly attack. However, beliefs in our walks with Christ must be grounded in truth, and matters of faith must not be afraid of hard questions and detailed scrutiny. If our hearts aren't receptive to hard questions, isn't that evidence that our beliefs may not be true?

OUR HEART AND MINDSET

If any readers are offended or emotionally upset by any of the above questions and do not find them to be fair and reasonable, I encourage you to determine what part of the questions is not fair or reasonable. Is it because the questions aren't fair, or is it because they present information that conflicts with your current belief system? If you're offended by other reasons, I again encourage you to determine the root reason why you're offended, and if the reason(s) are healthy ones.

In addition, what was your reaction to my questions and comments if they contradicted with your beliefs? Did you react by wanting to explore the issue further, or to deny and look for ways to counteract the evidence presented? Our hearts are interesting, aren't they?

My Mindset Was Messed Up

In late 2017, a quiet but very smart and wise friend, showed me I was more committed to my beliefs than to seeking the truth. I was shocked and humbled as I realized how prone I was to believing what I was told by 'those in the know' without taking reasonable steps to verify what I was told. I also realized my ability to learn and gain new insights was being blocked by a combination of unmerited trust in others, pride, arrogance, stubbornness, foolishness, and difficulty admitting I was wrong. I realized that for years, for decades, I had been prone to try to figure out how I could neutralize opposing arguments or facts to preserve my beliefs. My commitment to seeking the truth was half-hearted at best, and a major problem.

After those discussions, I started to take notice of how other people interacted with me, and with others. In the vast majority of cases, I realized I was not alone. Loyalty to one's beliefs almost always superseded a commitment to pursuing the truth.

Loyalty to Beliefs can be Fatal

I've spoken to many adults from a variety of countries and faiths including atheists, Bahais, Catholics, Protestants, Hindus, Jehovah Witnesses, Jews, Muslims, Mormons and Sikhs. In virtually every case, their beliefs on matters of faith is not based on independent, personal search. They typically believe what their parents believe, not what they searched out. And the vast majority of the time, the thought of going against their beliefs is unthinkable as all too often it would lead to shunning and persecution.

There are many millions of believers in the Cessationist and Continuationist camps. There are many millions of believers in the Roman Catholic and Protestant camps. In both cases, one camp is wrong on certain issues or beliefs which means

1: Mindset and Authority

hundreds of millions of individuals have it wrong. Teachers and leaders must ensure that Biblical truth is being taught, and if Biblical truth is effectively being blocked, that is an extremely unfortunate state to say the least. Some individuals cannot imagine questioning their beliefs as doing so, like many of my students, would lead to persecution from families, their church and even their employer, especially if they are employed by the church. If this is you, I feel for you and pray that God guides you if you wish to truly pursue His truths.

Within the Body of Christ, loyalty to teachings of a person or their denomination all too often takes top priority over seeking the truth. I suggest four reasons are largely responsible for the fundamental differences in these various camps:
1. lack of independent study of God's Word;
2. not enough time alone with God nor being led by Holy Spirit;
3. the Bible is not the ultimate authority; and
4. loyalty to one's beliefs mixed with fear, pride, arrogance, spiritual laziness and stubbornness. We believe what we have been told without asking Holy Spirit to reveal the truth to us, and without doing our own in-depth research and study of God's Word. And when we realize we might be wrong, we often choose not to go there. After all, who likes to admit we're wrong?

1:20 Loyalty can be a wonderful thing, but loyalty to a false belief can be costly, and not just to ourselves but those we influence. Again I ask, where's your loyalty?

THE BIBLE:
WHERE IT TRULY SITS IN OUR HEARTS

Is all of the Bible really from God, and thus True

As mentioned, God does not want us to be blindly led by any person or organization. He wants us to question what we hear and read.

❑ *Acts 17:10 The brethren immediately sent Paul and Silas away by night to Berea, and when they arrived, they went into the synagogue of the Jews. 11 Now these were more noble-minded than those in Thessalonica, for they received the word with great eagerness,* **examining the Scriptures daily to see whether these things were so**.

Some 'Christians' question if the Bible is all true. Others selectively use some scriptures and disregard others so their view can be justified. This allows for all kinds of deviations. And if I have done that in any way in **CEASED?**, I apologize. My intent is to reveal the truth, not promote a view.

If you're not sure about the truthfulness of the Bible, there is extensive evidence showing it is true. Lee Strobel's book *"The Case for Christ"* greatly impacted me. And the movie which is available on YouTube is a great watch. Other quality sources include writings and teachings by believers such as Gary Habermas and Ravi Zacharias.

CEASED?

Ivan Panin

Another source of evidence supporting the Bible that got my attention more recently was the work of Ivan Panin. In the 1890's, Mr. Panin began to study the mathematical structure associated with the Greek words in the New Testament and the Hebrew words in the Old Testament.

Greek and Hebrew do not have separate symbols for numbers as we do in English. For Greek and Hebrew, letters are used to indicate a particular number. To illustrate, we could replace our numbers with letters where A = 1, B = 2, C = 3, D = 5, E = 10 etc. Roman Numerals are a modern-day example of using letters for numbers (I for 1, II for 2, III for 3, IV for 4, V for 5, X for 10 etc.), Mr. Panin replaced each letter in the Greek and Hebrew words in the Bible with its corresponding numerical value. To find the 'score' of a word, Mr. Panin simply added the numbers associated with the letters in the word. Mr. Panin looked for 'codes' which are formulas, patterns, scores and/or relationships surrounding the numbers. To illustrate, consider Genesis 1:1.

- ❑ *Genesis 1:1 In the beginning God created the heavens and the earth.*

Using the NASB translation, Genesis 1:1 has 10 English words that are derived from 7 Hebrew words. Mr. Panin found the 7 Hebrew words in Genesis 1:1 had a total of 28 letters. In studying these 7 words and 28 letters, Mr. Panin discovered 30 separate 'codes' involving just the number 7. Eight of these codes are as follows:

- ❖ Total number of Hebrew words = 7;
- ❖ Total score of first and last letters of all 7 words = 1,393 (7 * 199);
- ❖ Total number of letters = 28 (7 * 4);
- ❖ 3 key words: 'God', 'heaven' and 'earth' = 14 letters (7 * 2);
- ❖ Total letters in the four remaining words = 14 (7 * 2);
- ❖ First 3 Hebrew words translated to English as "In the beginning God created" = 14 letters (7 * 2); and
- ❖ Last 4 Hebrew words meaning "the heavens and the earth" = 14 letters (7*2).

Ok, that was a test to see if you were reading carefully. I only gave 7 codes. Mr. Panin's analysis is captured in ~40,000 pages. This copy of **CEASED?** is ~422 pages. Mr. Panin's work, if stacked, would reach the height of ~95 copies of **CEASED?,** or ~7-8 feet high. And Mr. Panin did so long before today's computers and search engines. It's almost as if Holy Spirit was guiding him. Consider these excerpts from Mr. Panin's book, *"The Inspiration of the Scriptures Scientifically Demonstrated"*. Disregard his references to 'features'; they're not provided. If math is not your strong suit, breathe deep and just take a look at the patterns Panin discovered.

> *"1. The first 17 verses of the New Testament contain the genealogy of the Christ. It consists of two main parts: Verses 1-11 cover the period from Abraham, the father of the chosen people, to the Captivity, when they ceased as an independent people. Verses 12-17 cover the period from the Captivity to the promised Deliverer, the Christ.*

Let us examine the first part of this genealogy.
Its vocabulary has 49 words, or 7 X 7. This number is itself seven (Feature 1) sevens (Feature 2), and the sum of its factors is 2 sevens (Feature 3). Of these 49 words 28, or 4 sevens, begin with a vowel; and 21, or 3 sevens, begin with a consonant (Feature 4).

Again: these 49 words of the vocabulary have 266 letters, or 7 x 2 x 19; this number is itself 38 sevens (Feature 5), and the sum of its factors is 28, or 4 sevens (Feature 6), while the sum of its figures is 14, or 2 sevens (Feature 7). Of these 266 letters, moreover, 140, or 20 sevens, are vowels, and 126, or 18 sevens, are consonants (Feature 8).

That is to say: Just as the number of words in the vocabulary is a multiple of seven, so is the number of its letters a multiple of seven; just as the sum of the factors of the number of the words is a multiple of seven, so is the sum of the factors of the number of their letters a multiple of seven. And just as the number of words is divided between vowel words and consonant words by seven, so is their number of letters divided between vowels and consonants by sevens.

Again: Of these 49 words 35, or 5 sevens, occur more than once in the passage; and 14, or 2 sevens, occur but once (Feature 9); seven occur in more than one form, and 42, or 6 sevens, occur in only one form (Feature 10). And among the parts of speech the 49 words are thus divided: 42, or 6 sevens, are nouns, seven are not nouns (Feature 11). Of the nouns 35, or 5 sevens, are Proper names, seven are common nouns (Feature 12). Of the Proper names 28 are male ancestors of the Christ, and seven are not (Feature 13)."

The mathematical complexity of the Bible is one more way by which God reveals His power and creative genius to us. The Bible is not just a collection of stories, a set of guidelines or a how-to-live manual. It is the Word of God, and one we should revere much, much higher than all other books, traditions, teachings, articles and videos . . . all of which are the opinions and interpretations of men or women.

❑ *2 Timothy 3:16 All Scripture is inspired by God and profitable for teaching, for reproof, for correction, for training in righteousness;*

Many others have done work on this amazing aspect of God's work. I haven't researched this area much but if you're so inclined, I have no doubt you will find more of God's amazing mathematical genius in many areas beyond His Word.

One more thing if I may. The validity of God, God's creation of this universe, and the Bible has much support from the world of science. The Suggested Resources section at the end of **CEASED?** lists 4 great sources.

What's Above the Bible and Jesus in Our Lives

1:21 If we put church teachings or traditions above the Bible, are we putting these teachings and traditions above Jesus Himself, who is the Word of God?

CEASED?

- ❑ *John 1:1 In the beginning was the Word, and the Word was with God, and the Word was God.*

1:22   If we put any church teaching or traditions above the Bible, or have a belief system that contradicts the Word of God, aren't we playing a bit of poker with our life, and the lives of others whom we influence, by opening the door to what may be false teachings?

TAKEAWAYS FROM CEASED?

If you have any takeaways from **CEASED?**, I hope five of them will be:
1. God loves you (and those you disagree with);
2. a decision to make The Bible your ultimate authority on matters of faith;
3. spending more time reading and meditating in God's Word;
4. spending quiet time alone with God speaking to, and hearing from Him; and
5. seeking His Kingdom first, and being led by Holy Spirit throughout each day.

As I wrote **CEASED?**, God reminded me of these items on multiple occasions in my walk. If you haven't read the Bible very much, consider starting with the books of John, Romans, Galatians and Ephesians to get a sense of His love for you, to see how amazing God is, and to experience the Bible's richness. You will be blessed.

- ❑ *Hebrews 4:12 For the word of God is living and active and sharper than any two-edged sword, and piercing as far as the division of soul and spirit, of both joints and marrow, and able to judge the thoughts and intentions of the heart.*

CLOSING POINTS TO PONDER

1:23   On contentious issues, is your process one of finding scriptures to support your view, or to seek the truth when all of scripture is considered?

1:24   What is your final authority: The Bible, the teachings of a person, your church or denomination, traditions, or your personal Book of My Opinions, a new book of the Bible our wonderful waitress playfully introduced to Lori and I?

The very day Lori and I felt **CEASED?** was finished, Holy Spirit gave a download to Lori about love. There is a widespread desire in the Body of Christ for another major move of Holy Spirit or, as some say, many new outpourings of Holy Spirit. There is also widespread desire for unity within the Body of Christ. However, the foundation for the unity that Holy Spirit wants is true love. History has shown that a common denominator of the outpourings of the Holy Spirit was love. Proper theology is vital, but without love, our theology is mere religion. Without love, our theology has no more value than the knowledge of the leaders who caused Jesus to be mocked, ridiculed and crucified. As you read **CEASED?,** if I haven't shown true love, please forgive me. And may all of us seek greater depths, widths, lengths and heights of God's love for Him and for people. May God's love for all of humanity - and God's ability to love each person where they are at - be evident in all we say, do and think.

2

9 Holy Spirit Gifts

INTRODUCTION

CHAPTER 2 begins by reviewing the 9 Holy Spirit gifts that are the focus of the Cessationist vs Continuationist disagreement. **CEASED?** shows how the gifts were a key part of the Christian life at Corinth, and elsewhere. There are many gifts and blessings from God, the most important of which is the gift of salvation. The gifts discussed herein are a small subset of God's total gifts.

9 Holy Spirit Gifts

The 9 Holy Spirit gifts are as follows:
- ❑ *1 Corinthians 12:8 For to one is given the **word of wisdom** through the Spirit, and to another the **word of knowledge** according to the same Spirit;*
- ❑ *9 to another **faith** by the same Spirit, and to another **gifts of healing** by the one Spirit,*
- ❑ *10 and to another the effecting of **miracles**, and to another **prophecy**, and to another the **distinguishing of spirits**, to another various kinds of **tongues**, and to another the **interpretation of tongues**.*

These 9 supernatural gifts are some of the tangible ways by which Holy Spirit works through believers. They are often organized into groups, such as the following:

Mind/Revealing Gifts	Power/Doing Gifts	Speaking/Proclamation Gifts
Distinguishing of Spirits	Healings	Prophecy
Word of Knowledge	Faith	Tongues
Word of Wisdom	Miracles	Interpretation of Tongues

An overly simplistic review of these gifts follows.

3 Mind/Revealing Gifts

The 3 revealing gifts reveal or make known information about a spirit, person, group or situation that a person could not know unless God revealed it to him or her.

CEASED?

1: **Distinguishing of Spirits:** supernatural ability to discern if what is spoken or occurring is from i) Holy Spirit ii) a human spirit or iii) a demonic spirit or spirits.
- ❏ *Mark 9:25 When Jesus saw that a crowd was rapidly gathering, He rebuked the unclean spirit, saying to it, "You **deaf and mute spirit**, I command you, come out of him and do not enter him again."*

2: **Word of Knowledge:** revelation from Holy Spirit of past or present information regarding one or more persons or situations.
- ❏ *Acts 5:1 But a man named Ananias, with his wife Sapphira, sold a piece of property, 2 and kept back some of the price for himself, with his wife's full knowledge, and bringing a portion of it, he laid it at the apostles' feet. 3 But Peter said, "**Ananias, why has Satan filled your heart to lie to the Holy Spirit and to keep back some of the price of the land?***

3: **Word of Wisdom:** supernatural advice or insight from Holy Spirit.
- ❏ *Acts 15:21 For Moses from ancient generations has in every city those who preach him, since he is read in the synagogues every Sabbath." 22 **Then it seemed good** to the apostles and the elders, with the whole church, to choose men from among them to send to Antioch with Paul and Barnabas - Judas called Barsabbas, and Silas, leading men among the brethren,*

3 Speaking/Proclamation Gifts
The 3 speaking/proclamation gifts help reveal God's intentions and plans.

4: **Prophecy:** supernatural revelation from Holy Spirit. The words prophecy and prophecies are nouns, whereas prophesy and prophesied are verbs. Prophecy can be revelations regarding teachings in the Bible and events here on earth. Prophecies often encourage, uplift and comfort. Some believers think prophecies can give direction; other believers don't.
- ❏ *1 Corinthians 14:3 But **one who prophesies** speaks to men for edification and exhortation and consolation.*

Prophecies can also bring less than uplifting news.
- ❏ *Acts 5:9 Then Peter said to her, "Why is it that you have agreed together to put the Spirit of the Lord to the test? Behold, the feet of those who have buried your husband are at the door, **and they will carry you out as well**." 10 And immediately she fell at his feet and breathed her last ...*
- ❏ *Acts 21:10 As we were staying there for some days, a prophet named Agabus came down from Judea. 11 And coming to us, he took Paul's belt and bound his own feet and hands, and said, "This is what the Holy Spirit says: '**In this way the Jews at Jerusalem will bind the man who owns this belt and deliver him into the hands of the Gentiles.**'"*

Whereas words of knowledge deal with information related to the past or present, prophecy is geared to the immediate or distant future.

2: 9 Holy Spirit Gifts

5: **Tongues:** words given by Holy Spirit to a person for them to speak or sing in a language they do not understand.
- ☐ *Acts 2:4 And they were all filled with the Holy Spirit and began to speak with **other tongues**, as the Spirit was giving them utterance.*

Tongues spoken at Pentecost were earthly languages unknown by the person speaking, but known by others in attendance. The tongues were a sign to unbelievers.
- ☐ *Acts 2:5 Now there were Jews living in Jerusalem, devout men from every nation under heaven. 6 And when this sound occurred, the crowd came together, and were bewildered because each one of them was **hearing them speak in his own language**. 7 They were amazed and astonished, saying, "Why, are not all these who are speaking Galileans? 8 **And how is it that we each hear them in our own language to which we were born**?*

6: **Interpretation of Tongues:** supernatural revelation from Holy Spirit that explains what the tongue that was spoken, but not understood, actually means.
- ☐ *1 Corinthians 14:13 Therefore let one who speaks in a tongue pray that **he may interpret**.*

Chapter 21 of **CEASED?** provides much more information on tongues.

3 Power/Doing Gifts
The 3 power gifts demonstrate God's power and love for humanity.

7: **Healings:** supernatural healings of physical bodies and souls by Holy Spirit.
- ☐ *Acts 3:2 And a man who had been lame from his mother's womb was being carried along ... 6 But Peter said, "I do not possess silver and gold, but what I do have I give to you: **In the name of Jesus Christ the Nazarene - walk!**" 7 And seizing him by the right hand, he raised him up; and immediately his feet and his ankles were strengthened*

8: **Faith:** extraordinary faith and trust in God as provided by Holy Spirit.
- ☐ *Mark 2:3 And they came, bringing to Him a paralytic, carried by four men. 4 Being unable to get to Him because of the crowd, they removed the roof above Him; and when they had dug an opening, they let down the pallet on which the paralytic was lying. 5 **And Jesus seeing their faith** said to the paralytic, "Son, your sins are forgiven."*
- ☐ *Mark 10:49 And Jesus stopped and said, "Call him here." So they called the blind man ... 51 And answering him, Jesus said, "What do you want Me to do for you?" And the blind man said to Him, "Rabboni, I want to regain my sight!" 52 And Jesus said to him, "**Go; your faith has made you well.**" Immediately he regained his sight and began following Him on the road.*

9: **Miracles**: events or outcomes that aren't explainable by natural causes; are only of God.

CEASED?

- *Joshua 4:23 For the Lord your **God dried up the waters of the Jordan** before you until you had crossed, **just as the Lord your God had done to the Red Sea**, which He dried up before us until we had crossed;*

The Bible is filled with miracles. Creation. Feeding thousands with 5 loaves of bread and 2 fish. People raised from the dead. A donkey speaking. Angels freeing people from prison. God's power is diverse, amazing, and beyond human comprehension, at least my comprehension.

The Cessationist vs Continuationist Disagreement

The basic disagreement on the above 9 Holy Spirit gifts has the Cessationist camp believing the gifts ended with the early church, and in many cases, with the deaths of the original apostles. The Continuationist camp believes these gifts are still in operation today and available to the Body of Christ at large. To clarify a bit further, the Cessationist camp doesn't believe that all miracles have ceased, and that some miracles such as healing continue, but are rare. The Cessationist camp is clear in its position, however, that gifts such as tongues, interpretation of tongues and prophecy are totally non-existent today. If anyone is involved in such activities, the Cessationist camp believes these individuals are not being influenced by God, but either one's flesh or the demonic realm. The remaining gifts - discernment of spirits, miracles, words of knowledge, faith, and wisdom - are mentioned relatively infrequently in debates and commentaries.

Many Topics in 1 Corinthians

To start, let's put the first letter to the Corinthians in perspective. Paul wrote 1 Corinthians in response to information received from believers at Corinth.

- *1 Corinthians 1:11 For I have been informed concerning you, my brethren, by **Chloe's people**, that there are quarrels among you.*
- *1 Corinthians 16:17 I rejoice over the coming of **Stephanas** and **Fortunatus** and **Achaicus**, because they have supplied what was lacking on your part.*

1 Corinthians covers many topics before Chapter 12, some of which are as follows:

- ❖ Chapter 1: Divisions within the church
- ❖ Chapter 2: Wisdom and power from the Spirit of God
- ❖ Chapter 3: Jesus is the foundation, our body is the temple of Holy Spirit
- ❖ Chapter 4: Being stewards, servants, fools for Christ
- ❖ Chapter 5: Sexual immorality
- ❖ Chapter 6: Disagreements between believers, all glory to God
- ❖ Chapter 7: Marriage, unmarried, widows
- ❖ Chapter 8: Idols, conscience
- ❖ Chapter 9: Self-denial
- ❖ Chapter 10: Old Testament examples, Glory to God
- ❖ Chapter 11: Head coverings, Lord's Supper, communion

2: 9 Holy Spirit Gifts

Many other topics are also covered after Chapter 12.
- ❖ Chapter 13: Love
- ❖ Chapter 14: Prophecy, tongues, interpretation of tongues
- ❖ Chapter 15: Risen Christ
- ❖ Chapter 16: Collection of monies for other saints

1 Corinthians 12 - Putting 9 Gifts in Perspective

Corinth - a City of Gods & Idols

When Paul wrote 1 Corinthians, Corinth was a city in Greece known for its many gods, goddesses and idols. When Paul visited Athens, he was grieved by what he saw.
- ❑ *Acts 17:16 Now while Paul was waiting for them at Athens, his spirit was being provoked within him as he was observing the city full of idols.*

Paul begins 1 Corinthians 12 by referring to spiritual gifts and that the Corinthian believers need to understand what is going on.
- ❑ *1 Corinthians 12:1 Now concerning **spiritual gifts**, brethren, **I do not want you to be unaware**.*

To help put issues into context, Paul reminds the Corinthian believers of the pagan idols and influences they had previously been under.
- ❑ *1 Corinthians 12:2 You know that **when you were pagans**, you **were led astray to the mute idols**, however you were led.*

Paul also taught they can identify believers by asking "Can you say Jesus is Lord?".
- ❑ *1 Corinthians 12:3 Therefore I make known to you that no one speaking by the **Spirit of God** says, "**Jesus is accursed**"; and **no one can say, "Jesus is Lord," except by the** **Holy Spirit**.*

We Worship the One and Only True God

With the backdrop of having worshipped many false gods and goddesses before they came to Christ, Paul begins 'making the Corinthian believers aware' by explaining there is only one true God, but One God who can manifest or make His presence known in a wide variety of ways.
- ❑ *1 Corinthians 12:4 Now there are varieties of gifts, but the **same Spirit**.*
- ❑ *5 And there are varieties of ministries, and the **same Lord**.*
- ❑ *6 There are varieties of effects, but the **same God** ...*
- ❑ *7 But to each one is given the manifestation of the Spirit for the common good.*
- ❑ *8 word of wisdom ... word of knowledge ... **same Spirit**;*
- ❑ *9 to another faith by the **same Spirit**, and to another gifts of healing by the **one Spirit**,*
- ❑ *10 and ... miracles ... prophecy ... distinguishing of spirits ... tongues ... interpretation of tongues. 11 But **one and the same Spirit** works all these things, **distributing to each one individually** just **as He wills**.*

CEASED?

2:1 From verses 4 through 11, is it reasonable to suggest the primary emphasis is:
   i. on the fact there is one true God, not many gods, and not
   ii. the 9 Holy Spirit gifts in verses 8 through 10? If not, why not?

Verses 12 - 27 emphasize the Body of Christ is a single body using terms such as 'body is one', 'one body', 'the body', 'whole body' or 'Christ's body'. 'One Spirit' is also mentioned twice more.

- *1 Corinthians 12:12 For even **as the body is one** and yet has many members, and all the members of the body, though they are many, are **one body**, so also is Christ.*
- *13 For by **one Spirit** we were all baptized into **one body**, whether Jews or Greeks, whether slaves or free, and we were all made to drink of **one Spirit**.*
- *14 For **the body** is not one member, but many.*
- *15 If the foot says, "Because I am not a hand, I am not a part of **the body**," it is not for this reason any the less a part of **the body**.*
- *16 And if the ear says, "Because I am not an eye, I am not a part of the body," it is not for this reason any the less a part of **the body**.*
- *17 If the **whole body** were an eye, where would the hearing be? If the whole were hearing, where would the sense of smell be?*
- *18 But now God has placed the members, each one of them, in **the body**, just as He desired.*
- *19 If they were all one member, where would **the body** be?*
- *20 But now there are many members, but **one body**.*
- *21 And the eye cannot say to the hand, "I have no need of you"; or again the head to the feet, "I have no need of you."*
- *22 On the contrary, it is much truer that the members of **the body** which seem to be weaker are necessary;*
- *23 and those members of **the body** which we deem less honorable, on these we bestow more abundant honor, and our less presentable members become much more presentable,*
- *24 whereas our more presentable members have no need of it. But God has so composed **the body**, giving more abundant honor to that member which lacked,*
- *25 so that there may be no division in **the body**, but that the members may have the same care for one another.*
- *26 And if one member suffers, all the members suffer with it; if one member is honored, all the members rejoice with it.*
- *27 Now you are **Christ's body**, and individually members of it.*

2:2 Is it fair to say the emphasis in verses 12 through 27 is to:
   i. clarify there is one Body of Christ, that all believers are part of this body, and that believers are to work together and care for each other; and
   ii. that all believers are part of His family - the Body of Christ – which is broader than a particular legal organization?

2: 9 Holy Spirit Gifts

Gifts from Father God, Jesus and Holy Spirit

Let's return to verses 4 through 6.
- *1 Corinthians 12:4 Now there are varieties of **gifts**, but the same Spirit.*
- *5 And there are varieties of **ministries**, and the same Lord.*
- *6 There are varieties of **effects**, but the same God who works all things in all persons.*

The word 'gifts' in verse 4 is commonly viewed as referring to the 9 Holy Spirit gifts in verses 1 Corinthians 12, verses 8 through 10. Because reference is made to Holy Spirit, and because Holy Spirit reveals Himself and the Godhead through such gifts, these 9 gifts are also frequently labeled as Holy Spirit gifts, gifts of the Holy Spirit or manifestations of the Spirit. The ministries in verse 5 are commonly viewed as relating to Ephesians 4:11-13 and often labeled Ascension Gifts from Jesus or simply Jesus's gifts. The gifts in Romans 12:6-8 are often labeled Motivational Gifts or Father God's gifts.

- *Ephesians 4:11 And He gave some as **apostles**, and some as **prophets**, and some as **evangelists**, and some as **pastors** and **teachers**,*

- *Romans 12:6 Since we have **gifts** that differ according to the grace given to us, each of us is to exercise them accordingly: if **prophecy**, according to the proportion of his faith; 7 if **service**, in his serving; or he who **teaches**, in his teaching; 8 or he who **exhorts**, in his exhortation; he who **gives**, with liberality; he who **leads**, with diligence; he who shows **mercy**, with cheerfulness.*

The 3 groups of gifts are summarized on the next page. Each gift is coded. Father God's gifts are preceded by an 'F:', Jesus's gifts by a 'J:' and Holy Spirit gifts by an 'HS:'. Any gifts of one list that are the same or somewhat related to a gift in another list are followed by the corresponding code. For example, the 1st gift from Father God 'F:1 Prophecy' is followed by (J:2) which stands for the 2nd gift from Jesus and then by (HS:6) which stands for the 6th Holy Spirit gift.

Prophecy or prophet is a gift from each of Father God, Jesus and Holy Spirit. There is much written on prophecy, prophetic gift and prophet. Let me simply ask:

2:3   Per 1 Corinthians 14:31, doesn't it appear all believers can hear from God and could potentially receive a prophecy from God to be shared? If not, why not?
- *1 Corinthians 14:31 For **you can all prophesy** one by one, so that all may learn and all may be exhorted;*

CEASED?

| **Father God's Gifts** | **Jesus's Gifts** | **Holy Spirit's Gifts** |
| (Romans 12:6-8) | (Ephesians 4:11) | (1 Corinthians 12:8-10) |

F:1 Prophecy (J:2 HS:6) J:1 Apostle   HS:1 Word of Wisdom
F:2 Service   **J:2 Prophet (F:1 HS:6)** HS:2 Word of Knowledge
F:3 Teaches (J:5)   J:3 Evangelist   HS:3 Faith
F:4 Exhorts   J:4 Pastor   HS:4 Healing
F:5 Gives   **J:5 Teacher (F:3)**   HS:5 Miracles
F:6 Leads   **HS:6 Prophecy (F:1 J:2)**
F:7 Mercy   HS:7 Distinguishing Spirits
                                                     HS:8 Tongues
                                                     HS:9 Interpretation of Tongues

Three other scriptures refer to some of the same gifts, and identify 3 more gifts (O:).

1 Corinthians 12:28   **1 Peter 4:9-10**
   Apostle (J:1)   **O:3 Hospitality**
   Prophet (J:2)   Service (F:2)
   Teacher (F:3 J:5)
   Miracles (HS:5)   **Romans 12:13**
   Healings (HS:4)   Hospitality (O:3)
O:1 Helps
O:2 Administrations
   Tongues (HS:8)

- 1 Corinthians 12:28 And God has appointed in the church, first **apostles**, second **prophets**, third **teachers**, the **miracles**, then **gifts of healings**, **helps**, **administrations**, various **kinds of tongues**.
- 1 Peter 4:9 Be **hospitable** to one another without complaint. 10 As each one has received a special gift, employ it in **serving one another** as good stewards of the manifold grace of God.
- Romans 12:13 contributing to the needs of the saints, practicing **hospitality**.

There are other gifts such as celibacy and poverty, discussions on which can melt an igloo.

Reasons for Gifts

Ephesians 4 identifies two of the reasons for these functions/gifts, namely to equip the saints and build up the Body of Christ.
- Ephesians 4:11 And He gave some as **apostles,** and some as **prophets,** and some as **evangelists,** and some as **pastors** and **teachers**, 12 **for the equipping of the** saints for the work of service, to the **building up of the body of Christ**;

At first glance, it might appear Father God's gift of teaching (F:3) duplicates Jesus's gift of teaching (J:5). However, there is perhaps a bit more to the story. Each and every believer is called to teach, if only to our children, to the person next door or someone else we know well. However, not all of us are called to be Bible teachers to the Body of Christ at large. In the same way, some people may have prophetic words for individuals or groups, but are not called by God to be a prophet which has a much broader scope. King Saul, for instance, prophesied but was not called a prophet though some wondered if he was.

❏ *1 Samuel 19:24 He [i.e. King Saul] also stripped off his clothes, and he too **prophesied before Samuel** and lay down naked all that day and all that night. Therefore they say, "**Is Saul also among the prophets?**"*

Gift vs Gifts of the Holy Spirit

The Bible talks of the Gift of the Holy Spirit (the singular) and of the Gifts of the Holy Spirit (the plural). To clarify, when a person is Baptized with the Holy Spirit, Holy Spirit comes upon [epi] the person to give the person access to the supernatural power of God to be witnesses for God. This is the Gift of the Holy Spirit which is covered in more detail in Chapters 7 through 12. The Gift**s** of the Holy Spirit - the plural gifts - are generally thought to be the 9 Holy Spirit gifts referenced above.

Gifts for Individual or Collective Benefit

In 1 Corinthians 12, verse 7 refers to the 9 Holy Spirit gifts as being manifestations i.e. different ways by which Holy Spirit's presence is made apparent.

❏ *1 Corinthians 12:7 But to **each one is given the manifestation of the Spirit for the common good**. 8 For to one is given the word of wisdom through the Spirit, and to another the word of knowledge according to the same Spirit; 9 to another faith by the same Spirit, and to another **gifts of healing** by the one Spirit, 10 and to another the effecting of miracles, and to another prophecy, and to another the distinguishing of spirits, to another various kinds of tongues, and to another the interpretation of tongues.*

The Greek word underlying the English word 'manifestation' is 'phanerosis' [G5321]. Strong's defines it as 'manifestation'. One of Merriam Webster's definitions of manifestations is in part 'pubic demonstration of power and purpose.' In other words, Holy Spirit manifests Himself; He makes His presence known. 1 Corinthians 12:7 also states the manifestations are for the common good.

In the scriptures listing the 9 Holy Spirit gifts, I find it interesting that the word 'gift' is only used in reference to 'healing'. Moreover, the word is 'gifts' which is in the plural, not the singular.

2:4 In terms of the 9 gifts, I wonder who actually gets the gift. If a person gets instantly healed through us, do we have the gift of healing, or did the healed person receive the gift of healing, and we were simply the delivery vehicle? In other words, are believers:
  i. given some supernatural power within themselves apart from God that enables us to heal others;
  ii. to be used by God to 'deliver' the blessings to others by having His supernatural power flow through us for the benefit of others; or

CEASED?

      iii. to receive blessings from the gifts of healing and other gifts for our own benefit;
      iv. both ii. and iii.?

Some believers teach that Holy Spirit gives specific giftings only to certain people. Others believe Holy Spirit can give any gift to any person as the situation warrants; we are simply to seek Holy Spirit and follow His leading. In other words, we don't have a special gifting; we are just to deliver the gifts. And while we may seem to primarily deliver some gifts and never deliver other gifts, or we seem better able to deliver some gifts than other believers, that doesn't mean we have a special gifting. Still other believers teach the gifts are also available directly to each of us, such as a gift of healing or tongues. Three comments:
1. First, all glory needs to be to God.
2. Second, how can we go wrong asking Holy Spirit's guidance on what to do in a given situation?
3. Third, if we do receive a special gifting such as prophecy or are used by God for miraculous healings, we need to be careful not to let it go to our head. We're all part of the Body of Christ. And while we may have a unique involvement in areas of prophecy or healing, we need to keep reminding ourselves we are just one extremely minor part of the Body of Christ who can only do such things because of God.

CEASED? is not preoccupied with whether the 9 Holy Spirit gifts are gifts for the person delivering, gifts for the person receiving or both. As a result, I will generally refer to these 9 gifts as Holy Spirit gifts/manifestations.

For Corinthians only, or all Believers
If we return to the end of 1 Corinthians 12, we find a reference to a combination of gifts from Holy Spirit (healing, tongues), Jesus (apostle, prophet, teacher), and Father God (teacher).
- ❏ 1 Corinthians 12:28 And God has appointed in the church, first **apostles** (J:1), second **prophets** (J:2), third **teachers** (J:5), then **miracles** (HS:5), then **gifts of healings** (HS:4), **helps**, **administrations**, various **kinds of tongues** (HS:8).

The Greek word underlying *'helps'* is *'antilepsis'* [G484] which Strong's defines as *'help'*. Helps could include Father God's gifts such as service (F:2), exhorting (F:4) and giving (F:5).

The Greek word underlying *'administrations'* is *'kubernesis'* [G2941] which Strong's defines in part as *'directorship or government'*. In other words, God and His Word will provide direction in terms of managing the Body of Christ including groups gathered in a particular church body.

God has given believers a wide variety of means to help the Body of Christ function. On that point, there is seldom any disagreement. As we read Paul's writing in 1 Corinthians, a key issue is whether we believe this letter is written:

2: 9 Holy Spirit Gifts

- ❖ only to believers in Corinth;
- ❖ only to early believers established by the original apostles; or
- ❖ to all believers including believers today.

2:5 As we read 1 Corinthians, is there anything to suggest that the 9 Holy Spirit gifts/manifestations will cease with the early church?

2:6 Cessationists typically agree that there is no specific verse in the Bible that says these 9 Holy Spirit gifts/manifestations from the Holy Spirit have ceased. If we say all the issues in 1 Corinthian including Jesus's and Father God's gifts are relevant today, but the 9 Holy Spirit gifts/manifestations are not, are we being selective on what is and is not relevant?

2:7 For example, one of the 9 Holy Spirit gifts/manifestations is prophecy. Prophecy is also one of Father God's gifts in Romans 12:6. If the gift of prophecy is not available today but everything else in Romans 12:6 (serving, teaching, exhorting, giving, leading, mercy) is available, do we have a major inconsistency? Are we selecting what we believe is true and fits our belief system, and then rejecting whatever does not fit our belief system?

In verses 29 and 30, Paul refers to gifts again, but provides a different combination with 3 of Jesus's gifts (apostle, prophet, teacher), 4 Holy Spirit gifts (miracles, healings, tongues and interpretation of tongues), and teaching again as the sole gift from Father God. Paul also makes it clear that not everybody will be everything or do everything.

❑ *1 Corinthians 12:29 All are not **apostles** (J:1), are they? All are not **prophets** (J:2), are they? All are not **teachers** (F:3, J:5), are they? All are not **workers of miracles** (HS:5), are they? 30 All do not have **gifts of healings** (HS:4), do they? All do not speak with **tongues** (HS:8), do they? All **do not interpret** (HS:9), do they?*

2:8 Does 1 Corinthians 12:29 suggest that, in God's kingdom, God has disciples take on one or more roles, equips us with various tools but doesn't enable any single disciple to get everything? And in so doing, doesn't that require God's children to work together?

Verse 31 ends 1 Corinthians 12 by encouraging believers to seek the greater gifts and an even better way will be shown. The better way - is love.

❑ *1 Corinthians 12:31 But earnestly desire the greater gifts. And I show you a still more excellent way.*

2:9 1 Corinthians 12 tells us that some believers will prophesy or speak in tongues and some won't. Some will be apostles or prophets, and some won't. Given these activities and roles were actively going on in Corinth when Paul wrote his first letter to the Corinthians, doesn't this mean prophecies and tongues were occurring through all groups of believers, and not just believers at Corinth + the original apostles + others who were part of the ~120 Baptized in the Holy Spirit at Pentecost? If not, why not?

CEASED?

2:10 Paul gave correction on how to use some of the Holy Spirit gifts, but not on whether or not such gifts should be used. If these believers in Corinth who were prophesying or speaking in tongues were doing something false or of the devil, wouldn't Paul have addressed that kind of issue directly along with the other issues mentioned in 1 Corinthians, and stopped any ungodly shenanigans?

2:11 Given Paul did not say these prophecies and tongues weren't of God, doesn't that mean the prophecies and tongues were of God?

2:12 Were the spiritual needs of the believers in Corinth, and the spiritual gifts given to the believers at Corinth applicable to every other group of believers living at that time? And to us today? If not, why not?

Who Experiences Holy Spirit's Presence & Gifts

Let's return to verses 7 and 11.
- ❏ *1 Corinthians 12:7 But to **each one** is given the manifestation of the Spirit for the common good.*
- ❏ *1 Corinthians 12:11 But one and the same Spirit works all these things, distributing to **each one** **individually** just as He wills.*

The Greek word underlying the English phrase *'each one'* is *'hekastos'* [G1538]. Strong's defines it in part as *'any, both, each (one), every (man, one, woman)'*.

2:13 If each believer is given the manifestation of the Spirit for the common good, does *'each one'* in verses 7 and 11 mean every believer at Corinth was to experience, the manifest, tangible, evident presence of Holy Spirit through one or more of the 9 Holy Spirit gifts/manifestations? If not, why not? And if it includes every believer at Corinth, why wouldn't it apply to all believers living at that time elsewhere? And to all believers today?

The Bible speaks of requirements to hold positions such as an elder and deacon. I can't find any unique requirements to be met before a born-again believer can receive the Baptism of the Holy Spirit, and in turn potentially be the beneficiary of the 9 Holy Spirit gifts /manifestations such as prophecy, healing or tongues.

2:14 The verses between 7 and 11 mention the 9 Holy Spirit gifts/manifestations. On the basis *'each one'* refers to every believer, doesn't verse 11 state that Holy Spirit will distribute each of these gifts, as He chooses, to:
i. every believer, even new believers; and
ii. not just a select few believers such as the original apostles?

Spiritual Gifts or Spiritual Matters

In my early review of 1 Corinthians 12 using my New King James Bible, I was surprised the first time I learned the word *'gifts'* in verse 1 was in italics. This means the word *'gifts'* was not in the original Greek, but added by the translators to provide clarity. The same holds for 1 Corinthians 13:2 and 14:1 - the word *gifts* is in italics and was added by the translators. If we remove the word 'gifts' from 1 Corinthians 12:1, it reads as follows:

2: 9 Holy Spirit Gifts

❏ *1 Corinthians 12:1 Now concerning spiritual, brethren, I do not want you to be unaware. (NASB amended)*

The English word spiritual is derived from the Greek word *'pneumatikos'* [G4152] which Strong's defines simply as 'spiritual'. The issue is what is meant by spiritual. From the list of topics in 1 Corinthians 12, I compiled a simplified topic list.

Verses **Topics**
2: Previously pagans, mute idols
3: Only those who know Jesus can call Him Lord
4-6: Various gifts of Father God (7), Jesus (5) and Holy Spirit (9)
7: Each born-again believer to experience the manifested presence of God
8-11: 9 Holy Spirit gifts/manifestations
12-27: One Body of Christ
28-31: Diversities of gifts and functions spread throughout the Body of Christ

2:15 Given all the topics mentioned in 1 Corinthians and within Chapter 12 itself, do you think 1 Corinthians 12 refers to a narrow scope of the 9 Holy Spirit gifts/manifestations or a broader scope involving several kinds of spiritual matters?

In my review, the word *'gifts'* was added to the majority of translations. Some translations, however, use words of a more general nature including *'spiritual matters'*, *'spiritual things'*, *'spiritual ways'*, *'spiritual realities'* or *'issues'*. I prefer *'spiritual matters'*.

Why Educate
Let's return to the issue of believers being unaware in 1 Corinthians 12:1.
❏ *1 Corinthians 12:1 Now concerning spiritual gifts, brethren, **I do not want you to be unaware**.*

If you don't believe the 9 Holy Spirit gifts/manifestations were available to every Corinthian believer and not just a select few - the original apostles for instance - consider the following:

2:16 Why would Paul say *"I do not want you to be unaware"*, then take steps to ensure they were aware of these 9 Holy Spirit gifts if they would only exist when an original apostle was present which was infrequent at Corinth, and for only a few more years at most?

2:17 Visualize yourself being a new believer in your early twenties. You hear the letter from Paul being read and discussed around 53-57AD. You hear about the 9 Holy Spirit gifts/manifestations and that Holy Spirit distributes these gifts. You later hear about the 4 virgin prophetesses. You hear about Agabus and others who were not original apostles but who prophesied. You hear of the healing miracles and tongues. Then somewhere along your journey, you're told the 9 Holy Spirit gifts/manifestations ended with the original apostles. Wouldn't you be rather confused, wonder why Paul wrote and taught what he did, and perhaps question other things that Paul wrote?

Summary of 1 Corinthians 12

2:18 Would the following be a reasonable summary of 1 Corinthians 12?

> *"My brothers and sisters in Corinth. You live in a city where so many people worship one or many of the multitudes of gods and goddesses. Idolatry is widespread. But there is a big difference between that spiritual world and the kingdom of God to which you now belong. The reality is that there is only one true God who exists in 3 persons - Father God, His Son Jesus and Holy Spirit. All truly born-again believers are sons and daughters of God, and part of one body, the Body of Christ. Moreover, the Body of Christ is not just those of you here in Corinth, but in the entire world.*
>
> *God helps His family function by giving a wide variety of supernatural gifts, ministries and services including the 9 gifts of the Holy Spirit. Each of us is unique in our interaction with God. We experience God's presence in our own way, including the manner and extent to which Holy Spirit manifests himself through us in His 9 gifts. Each of us is unique in the giftings, roles and responsibilities God gives to us, but we are all part of one body, and we are to come together and work together for the common good of all."*

For those who still staunchly believe that the 9 Holy Spirit's gifts/manifestations in 1 Corinthians 12 are no longer relevant, that's your right to do so. Before getting into the next few chapters, you might consider reviewing the commentary in Chapters 13 through 20 that deal with other major Cessationist issues.

CLOSING POINTS TO PONDER

2:19 Paul's first letter to the Corinthians deals with a wide variety of spiritual matters including clarifying there is one God, one Spirit and one Body of Christ to which God distributes gifts/manifestations from the Holy Spirit, the Father and Jesus. Based only on what we read in 1 Corinthians, would you say the 9 Holy Spirit gifts/manifestations have ceased, are still active and one of the many ways by which God equips us to live a full and abundant Christian life, both individually and collectively?

2:20 And if you're Roman Catholic, don't all the references to the Body of Christ indicate God's church is the Body of Christ? And that any church organization and its leaders are to support, serve, equip and build up the members of the Body of Christ?

3

Spirit, Soul and Body

INTRODUCTION

AS mentioned previously, the 9 Holy Spirit gifts/manifestations in 1 Corinthians 12 are associated with the Baptism in the Holy Spirit. To properly understand the Baptism in the Holy Spirit, it is helpful if we understand 3 other baptisms applicable to believers today. And to understand these 4 baptisms, it is beneficial to understand their association with salvation. In addition, to gain a fuller understanding of salvation, it is useful to review the impact salvation has on our 3 parts, namely our spirit, soul and body. Chapter 3 begins this review of some Christian basics by briefly looking at our 3 parts - spirit, soul and body.

- *1 Thessalonians 5:23 Now may the God of peace Himself sanctify you entirely; and may your **spirit** and **soul** and **body** ...*

The Human Spirit

When I raise the issue of humans having a spirit with 7th Day Adventist friends, discussions shut down as they believe human beings don't have their own spirit. If this is your view and you feel like using **CEASED?** to make a fire or paperweight, can you please first consider the following scriptures of people who speak about their spirit.

- *Isaiah 26:9 ... Indeed, **my spirit** within me seeks You diligently...*
- *Daniel 7:15 As for me, Daniel, **my spirit** was distressed within me ...*
- *Job 6:4 ... Their poison **my spirit** drinks ...*
- *Psalm 142:3 When **my spirit** was overwhelmed within me ...*
- *Ezekiel 3:14 ... I went embittered in the rage of **my spirit** ...*
- *Luke 1:47 And **my spirit** has rejoiced in God my Saviour.*
- *Acts 7:59 They went on stoning Stephen ... "Lord Jesus, **receive my spirit!**"*
- *Romans 1:9 For God, whom I serve in **my spirit** in the preaching ...*
- *1 Corinthians 14:14 ... pray in a tongue, **my spirit** prays ... mind is unfruitful.*
- *2 Corinthians 2:13 I had no rest for **my spirit** ...*

3:1   If you don't believe we humans have a spirit, are you perhaps being more faithful to your beliefs than to what the Bible says?

CEASED?

4 Basic Questions
I routinely ask young believers 4 questions:

1: How Many Baptisms are in the Bible, and how many apply today?
The most common answer I get is 1-2 in total, and 1 that applies today. I suggest there are at least 8-9 unique baptisms of which 3-4 are directly applicable to believers living on earth today - Baptism into the Body of Christ (at the moment one is born again), Water Baptism, Baptism of the Holy Spirit and Baptism of Fire. Chapter 10 discusses the baptisms in more detail.

2: What are the differences between the 'para', the 'en' and the 'epi' experiences of the Holy Spirit?
The most common answer is *"I don't know"*. When I respond with *"The para, en and epi refer, respectively, to three different experiences - the with, in and upon - that believers can have with the Holy Spirit"*, it seldom clears up the confusion. Hopefully **CEASED?** will do better.

3: What does born again mean in terms of our spirit, soul and body?
Again, the most common answer I get back is akin to *"I don't know"*.

4: When Were the Apostles Born Again?
Once more, the common answer is *"I don't know"*. Few have thought about it.

Those experiences are part of why I feel I needed to go back to the very beginning when God made the first human being - Adam.

Creation of Humans
God created Adam by forming dirt and breathing life into what He had formed.
- ❏ *Genesis 2:7 Then the Lord God formed man of dust from the ground, and breathed into his nostrils the breath of life; and man became a living being.*

Our triune God made humans with 3 distinct 'parts': a spirit, a soul and a body.
- ❏ *1 Thessalonians 5:23 Now may the God of peace Himself sanctify you entirely; and may your **spirit and soul and body** be preserved complete, without blame at the coming of our Lord Jesus Christ.*

Trying to comprehend 'everything' about the human spirit, soul and body, or anything else created by God in this universe, is simply not possible. Just look at the incredible complexity of His birds. I love watching videos on birds, especially starlings and hummingbirds – they are such amazing creations of God.

Human Body
The human body is an amazingly complex creation tightly interconnected with our souls and spirits. Whether it is the DNA, skin, eyes, ears, brain, blood, skeletal system or one of the other multitudes of other body parts and systems - God's creative genius is on full display in our bodies.

3: Spirit, Soul and Body

Human Spirit

We live in a spiritual world.
- ❑ John 4:24 **God is spirit**, and **those who worship Him must worship in spirit** and truth.
- ❑ Genesis 28:12 He had a dream, and behold, a ladder was set on the earth with its top reaching to heaven; and behold, the **angels of God** were ascending and descending on it.
- ❑ James 2:19 You believe that God is one. You do well; the **demons** also believe, and shudder.

3:2 Is it surprising that humans are spirits given that God is a spirit, God created angels and demons who are spirits, those who worship God do so in spirit, and humans are created in God's image?

Our spirit has multiple roles in our lives including facilitating our communications with God, seemingly working in conjunction with our soul, as our conscience to discern right from wrong, and our intuition which influences our thoughts, words, actions and decisions.
- ❑ John 4:24 **God is spirit**, and **those who worship Him must worship in spirit** and truth.
- ❑ 1 Corinthians 2:11 For who among men knows the thoughts of a man except **the spirit of the man** which is in him? Even so the thoughts of God no one knows except the Spirit of God.

3:3 Given our body goes back to dust one day and our soul and spirit go to heaven or hell, is it more appropriate to think of humans as:
   a) a spirit with a body and soul; or
   b) a body with a soul and a spirit?

How complex is our spirit? I don't know, but I suspect our personal spirits and the spiritual realm in which we live is far more complex than the physical world we live in. Reading the Bible, seeing the power of God and how He manifested through people and angels ranges from fascinating and humorous, to downright humbling and unnerving. It is also at times rather unpleasant. We also have an active spiritual enemy. If you doubt, talk with a believer who used to be heavily involved in the occult/witchcraft. It's shocking to learn what still goes on today.

Human Soul

In the beginning, God breathed the breath of life, and man became a living soul.
- ❑ Genesis 2:7 Then the Lord God formed man of dust from the ground, and breathed into his nostrils the breath of life; and man became a living being.

Theologians seem to universally agree the human soul has at least 3 core parts - mind, will and emotions. Some believe our souls have a 4th part - the conscience - referred to earlier. Whatever your view, I suggest we're only beginning to understand the complexity of our soul and its working relationship with our body and spirit.

CEASED?

God is revealing these complex interrelationships through various people such as Dr. Henry Wright who wrote *"A More Excellent Way".* His book gives insight into many of the relationships between the soul and body, and why many of our diseases - some of which are deemed incurable - arise due to deep and often long-held issues in our souls.

- ❑ *3 John 1:2 Beloved, I pray that in all respects you may prosper and be in good health, just as your soul prospers.*

Let me share just one quote from page 67 of Dr. Wright's book.
> *"In this ministry, we deal with many autoimmune diseases: lupus, Crohn's, diabetes (type 1), rheumatoid arthritis and MS, to name a few. All autoimmune diseases have a spiritual root of self-hatred, self-bitterness and guilt."*

My Psoriasis

In 2013, I had psoriasis on much of my hands, arms, face, back and legs. The area under my eyes was so discolored that when my son met me after not seeing me for a few months, he just stared at me. He didn't know what to say. My hands were so swollen, I could hardly bend my fingers. My calves and the top of hands were so raw, I bled on our bedsheets. After over a year of struggles and consultations with ~10 different doctors, after several creams and different treatments, after much prayer and few benefits, I found myself emotionally drained in a big way.

I've had prostate cancer, 2 heart attacks, a quadruple bypass, an emergency appendectomy, a hip replacement and a serious leg infection. Yet, my psoriasis was the worst affliction of all, by far. The constant itching drove me crazy.

Friends recommended I see a Christian naturopath near Bellingham, Washington. I did. Sally opened our session with prayer. Within a few seconds, Lori and I both started to weep. We were overcome with God's presence. Sally was quiet for a short while, then indicated Holy Spirit revealed to her the root cause of my psoriasis was bitterness. She prayed again and in a short time, Holy Spirit revealed to her that my bitterness was towards myself. I was filled with guilt, regrets, shame, self-hatred and more. As I began to deal with my emotional stuff, my psoriasis receded and 2 months later, it was gone.

If God had healed my psoriasis when previously prayed for, the issues in my soul would have remained hidden and would likely have manifested in other more serious illnesses. God knew I needed my soul healed before I would get lasting physical healing. The psoriasis was not the problem, but a symptom.

3:4 Was my delayed physical healing an indication as to why some people may not immediately get healed when they receive prayer?

3:5 Was my delayed healing also an example of the benefits of asking Holy Spirit how and what to pray for, instead of just praying for what we see or think is the problem?

Souls - Our Emotions

The emotional part of our soul has various emotions, both positive and negative. This is seen in relationships between Jonathan and David, and between Joseph and

3: Spirit, Soul and Body

his brothers.
- ❑ *1 Samuel 18:1 Now it came about when he had finished speaking to Saul, that the soul of Jonathan was knit to the soul of David, and **Jonathan loved him** as himself.*
- ❑ *Genesis 37:5 Then Joseph had a dream, and when he told it to his brothers, they **hated** him even more.*

Souls - Our Will

A key function of the will component of our soul is to make choices.
- ❑ *Job 7:15 So that **my soul would choose** suffocation, death rather than my pains.*

Souls - Our Mind

The mind part of our soul does many things including thinking, knowing and remembering.
- ❑ *Psalm 13:2 How **long shall I take counsel in my soul**, having sorrow in my heart all the day? How long will my enemy be exalted over me?*
- ❑ *Psalm 139:14 I will give thanks to You, for I am fearfully and wonderfully made; Wonderful are Your works, And **my soul knows it** very well.*
- ❑ *Lamentations 3:20 Surely **my soul remembers** And is bowed down within me.*

3:6 Given both our minds and wills play such central roles in our lives, is it any surprise God's Word tells us to renew our minds?
- ❑ *Romans 12:2 And do not be conformed to this world, but **be transformed by the renewing of your mind**, so that you may prove what the will of God is, that which is good and acceptable and perfect.*

Soul Is in Charge Until...

Before we're born again, our souls are in charge of our life. Our soul is boss, and our dead spirit takes a backseat. After we're born again, we start a journey of sanctification where we become more and more like Christ in our thoughts, words, decisions, behaviors and actions. In so doing, our spirit takes more and more control and our soul goes to the backseat where it goes along for the ride. And, hopefully, it doesn't operate too much as a self-serving backseat driver.

Soul - Hell or Heaven

Our souls don't vanish when we die. I believe they go to heaven or hell along with our spirits.
- ❑ *Matthew 10:28 Do not fear those who kill the body but are unable to kill the soul; but rather **fear Him who is able to destroy both soul and body in hell**.*

Complexity of Souls

How complex are our souls? Whereas we have many technologies that helps us gain a better understanding of the complexity of our body, we have relatively few tools with which we can scientifically analyze our soul. Like our spirits, I don't know how complex our soul is, but I suspect it is at least as complex as our bodies.

CEASED?

Soul Hurts and Woundings

If I can digress for a few paragraphs, Lori and I find soul hurts and issues are often viewed within the Body of Christ as secondary to physical issues. Dr. Wright's book provides great insight as to why this should not be the case. Other evidence is starting to show, for instance, how traumatic events can impact our actual DNA, and how such events can damage our brains. Trauma hits close to home for Lori and I. We've had our fair share, especially Lori who experienced extensive trauma starting at age 2. It's a major reason why Lori is involved in this area with a goal of helping equip the Christian community to better understand and minister to those dealing with trauma (www.loridixon.ca). Sources of trauma and deep hurts in souls are widespread. Abuse with its many hats including emotional, physical, sexual, financial and spiritual abuse is one source of trauma. Other sources include grief from suicides and other deaths, divorces, health problems, major financial losses, and ill-informed treatment received from religious leaders, organizations and even Christian friends and acquaintances.

When dealing with soul hurts and woundings, we need to treat them with as much respect, sensitivity and compassion as we do for physical health issues. Yes, some people wallow in their emotional pain for too long - that was me for a season and I can relate. But for many, their hurts can be so deep that it's not as simple as 'getting over it'. If we're not careful, people coming to us for prayer can leave more traumatized than when they arrived. Let me give you two examples.

> *A woman shared her experiences of going ta church wanting prayer. A leader took her hands and placed them together palm to palm, with both of his hands gently positioned around her hands. As a result of actions of kindness, she reacted very negatively because it reminded her of the way her hands were positioned when she was bound while being trafficked. At the beginning of prayer when she was seeking help, she was triggered. As Lori describes it, her amygdala was lit up. Her mind and emotions were in turmoil, she never really heard a word of the prayer. She left more traumatized than when she arrived, and never went back.*
>
> *A second situation occurs regularly in many churches when the church says something akin to "Let's stand, grab the hand of the person beside you and pray". To some people, this can be frightening as the last thing they want is a stranger grabbing their hand or touching them. Imagine a woman near a man who resembles or reminds her of someone who abused her. Contact is the last thing she wants. If someone's soul is not yet healed, seemingly loving gestures can be traumatic and cause considerable pain and angst. We seldom have any idea what another person has gone through; we need to be sensitive. What if it is their first church experience since the trauma? We never know the journey of others.*

3:7   If your church doesn't have these issues, that's great. But let me ask - how big is the opportunity for us to reach out to people in our communities who don't attend any church because they don't feel safe in doing so?

If you're dealing with deep hurts and trauma, I am so sorry. If you feel ignored, misunderstood, if the events in your life and the pain caused to you has not been validated, if your concerns have not been recognized, if justice has not adequately

3: Spirit, Soul and Body

been served, if those who hurt you are not sorry or could care less, I am truly sorry. And if church leaders have trivialized your pain or said things akin to just get over it, I apologize on their behalf. I have seen first hand the devastating, long-term impacts of deep soul wounds and trauma. For so many of us, it's not that easy to just get over it. I asked Lori to comment on this issue. This is her brief message.

> *"The good news is that there is hope. There is healing . . . wholeness. Holy Spirit is known as our Comforter and Counselor. God hates injustice and the damage it does to us - to our body, soul and spirit. In a perfect world, there would be abundant grace and wisdom in all interactions between people, but sadly this is not the case. Even leaders and other believers with the best of intentions "get it wrong". They don't know our journeys. Our story. And for some, they don't need to know, nor have they earned the right to access our deepest, most intimate secrets. Sometimes we just need to take a deep breath, close our eyes, and recognize that those who say and do the wrong things don't know what they think they know. As difficult as it may be, we need to recognize they have their weaknesses, and we need to bless them and move on to others for help. Or, if you're feeling bold, tell them why their words and/or actions were inappropriate, and then direct them to local ministries that can educate and equip them to do better.*
>
> *As for you, seek counsel from local people or organizations that are truly familiar with trauma, and will address your hurts on all three levels - body, soul and spirit. Don't give up! There is freedom and wholeness."*

A couple more comments. I've heard teachings that when we're born again, we're a new creation and all soul issues have been dealt with. We should *"never look back but only look forward"* which is *"how we get over it"*.

- ❏ *2 Corinthians 5:17 Therefore if anyone is in Christ, he is a new creature; the old things passed away; behold, new things have come.*

3:8   If healing of souls was a done deal at the moment we're born again, as mentioned in Chapter 22, why isn't every new believer's soul healed the moment they're born again?

3:9   If you had a broken leg, a dislocated vertebrae or migraine headache at the moment you were born again and not immediately healed, what would your response have been to someone telling you: *"Hey, you're a new creation now. Get over it. Let's get into the boxing ring for a round or two."*, or *"Hey, let's go practice heading the soccer ball. Show some faith man."*

In my limited experience, those who say things like *'you need to move on and just get over it'* have usually not had major traumatic personal experiences they needed to get over. As a result, they just *'don't get it'*. Or if they had very traumatic events in their life but were healed, it's often a result of a supernatural healing that occurred after their born-again experience. However, their delayed healing sometimes seems to be forgotten when they teach others to *'just get over it'*.

If you need a major healing in your soul (or body), I pray God touches you radically, and perhaps unexpectedly during your time alone with Him, during times

CEASED?

of praise and worship, reading His Word or even as you read **CEASED?**.

WE NEED A SAVIOR

In the Garden of Eden, God gave Adam a clear command that he was not to eat of the tree of the knowledge of good and evil. If Adam did, he would die.

- ❑ *Genesis 2:15 Then the Lord God took the man and put him into the garden of Eden to cultivate it and keep it. 16 The Lord God commanded the man, saying, "From any tree of the garden you may eat freely; 17 but from the tree of the knowledge of good and evil **you shall not eat, for in the day that you eat from it you will surely die**."*
- ❑ *Genesis 3:6 When the woman saw that the tree was good for food, and that it was a delight to the eyes, and that the tree was desirable to make one wise, **she took from its fruit and ate**; and she gave also to her husband with her, and **he ate**. 7 **Then the eyes of both of them were opened, and they knew that they were naked**; and they sewed fig leaves together and made themselves loin coverings.*

After Adam and Eve ate of the tree, things changed. Their eyes were opened. They knew they did wrong when they sinned. God said they would die, but they didn't die physically right away as Adam lived to 930 years of age. After they sinned, their soul was still alive as Adam admitted he was afraid (his emotions) and hid himself (his 'will' made the decision).

- ❑ *Genesis 3:10 He said, "I heard the sound of You in the garden, and I was afraid because I was naked; so I hid myself."*

While still alive in their bodies and souls, Adam and Eve died in their spirits. There was a spiritual separation between God (who is a spirit) and the spirits of Adam and Eve. Their spiritual deaths marked the end of the unhindered, intimate relationship between God and God's first two human creations. This intimate relationship was replaced by a distant relationship where Adam and Eve were separated from God as God sent them out of the Garden of Eden, out of His presence.

- ❑ *Genesis 3:23 therefore the Lord God sent him out from the garden of Eden, to cultivate the ground from which he was taken. 24 So He drove the man out; and at the east of the garden of Eden He stationed the cherubim and the flaming sword which turned every direction to guard the way to the tree of life.*

Before the fall, we should also remember Adam had a mandate, a call on his life.

- ❑ *Genesis 1:28 God blessed them; and God said to them, "Be fruitful and multiply, and fill the earth, and subdue it; and rule over the fish of the sea and over the birds of the sky and over every living thing that moves on the earth."*

When Adam and Eve were kicked out of the Garden, they lost their close, intimate relationship with God. Fast forward to today. Human beings are sinners, something that's evident at an early age. Just watch 2-year olds and behind their cute smiles are ... opportunities for practicing patience.

3: Spirit, Soul and Body

Just as Adam and Eve sinned by disobeying God and eating of that tree, humans today are also sinners. A common problem is that people don't see themselves as sinners, but as a *'good'* person. Many believe if there is a heaven, they will go there because they are good. Ray Comfort (livingwaters.com) has a unique way of evangelizing by helping people realize that maybe they aren't so good. Ray's approach is akin to the following:

3:10 *"Have you ever lied - ever?"* Few people say no to this question. Most say yes. When they do, Ray has a follow-up question of *"What does that make you?"* Ray guides them to realize, compared to the holiness of God, they sinned and are a 'liar' in God's eyes.

3:11 *"Have you ever stolen - anything - ever?"* Ray helps people realize they are a thief in God's eyes.

3:12 *"Have you ever hated anybody - ever?"* Ray relates how Jesus took the commandment of *"Do not Murder"* to a new level where if we hate someone, even for a short time, we're considered a murderer.

3:13 *"Have you ever lusted after somebody who was not your spouse at the time?"* Ray discusses how Jesus also took the commandment on adultery to a new level, and helps people realize even looking lustfully after someone other than their spouse makes them an adulterer in God's eyes.

After 4 questions, people often realize they are not so good after all. This happened to my Mom.

Mom

My Mom turned 94 as I was writing **CEASED?**. *She is an incredible mother, grandmother, great-grandmother and overall wonderful woman. Her bread and amazing cooking, if commercialized, would have been a hit. Soon after I was born again, when Mom was about 85, we started to talk regularly about faith issues. Mom went to church her entire life and believed she would go to heaven because she was a good person. And by earthly standards, she was a very good person. Over time, I shared about how all humans are sinners, need a savior and introduced Jesus, His shed blood and death on the cross, etc. Mom was interested but she kind of heard this before, and it didn't impact her.*

Then one night, I gently challenged Mom using Ray's approach. When Mom realized that according to God's standard of holiness, she was potentially a liar, thief, murderer and adulterer, she went very quiet. It was then that she began to appreciate the sin nature of all humans including herself, her need for a Savior, and the power and beauty of what Jesus did for her on the cross. Soon after, Mom gave her life to Christ and over time, I could see significant changes.

Perhaps the most memorable change involved Mom and another person in her life. A few years after Mom accepted Christ, Mom and I briefly talked about this person. Mom's attitude towards this person who had caused her much hurt was so good. Mom said something to the effect of "____ is a lost soul. I pray ____ finds peace." When Mom spoke, there wasn't an ounce of hardness - just compassion. I wept as I saw how Jesus's goodness had healed my Mom's heart, and was now using Mom to demonstrate His love and power. Thank You Jesus. Love you Mom.

MARY - A SINNER IN NEED OF A SAVIOR?

God's Word says all humans have sinned which is why we all need a savior.
- *Romans 3:23 For **all have sinned**, and fall short of the glory of God;*

3:14 The Bible is clear that Jesus did not sin. The Bible, however, does not say anything about Mary not sinning. Doesn't the phrase 'all have sinned' mean every person other than Jesus sinned, including Mary? If not, why not?
- *Hebrews 4:15 For we do not have a high priest who cannot sympathize with our weaknesses, but One who has been tempted in all things as we are, **yet without sin**.*

Roman Catholic teachings state that Mary was not a sinner which is a key reason why Mary has such lofty positions in the Roman Catholic church today. If Mary was not a sinner, it makes one wonder why Mary referred to Jesus as her savior.
- *Luke 1:45 And blessed is she who believed that there would be a fulfillment of what had been spoken to her by the Lord." 46 **And Mary said:** "My soul exalts the Lord, 47 And my spirit has rejoiced in God **my Savior**.*

The standard Protestant view as to why Mary would need a savior was because she had sinned. The Catholic view is that she did not sin. The reason commonly cited by Catholics is found in scriptures such as Jude 24, where we find Jesus is able to keep us (and thus Mary) from stumbling, from sinning.
- *Jude 24 Now to **Him who is able to keep you from stumbling**, and to make you stand in the presence of His glory blameless with great joy, (NASB)*
- *Jude 24 Now to **Him who is able to keep you from stumbling or falling into sin**, and to present you unblemished [blameless and faultless] in the presence of His glory with triumphant joy and unspeakable delight, (AMP)*

3:15 Mary was approximately 45 when Jesus started his earthly ministry, and close to 50 years old when Jesus went to the cross. After more than 4 decades of Mary living in this world, Jesus finally fulfilled the prophecies and His role as savior was established. Before the beginning of Jesus's earthly ministry and His going to the cross, what scriptural basis is there to believe Jesus served as Mary's savior and prevented her from sinning during these 4 decades? Consider the years before His conception, His 9 months in Mary's womb, His baby years, adolescent, teenage and finally His adult years. In all those periods of time, did Jesus serve as Mary's savior and prevent her from sinning?

3:16 If you still believe Mary never sinned:
   i. After you were born again, and you had Jesus in you and Holy Spirit in [en] you, did you sin afterward?
   ii. If you sinned, was it because you have a free will, a sinful nature and your mind has not been totally renewed and your soul not perfectly sanctified?
   iii. When Mary was visited by the angel, questioned the angel and then decided to do as God asked, didn't she demonstrate she had a free will?

3: Spirit, Soul and Body

And thus, on what scriptural grounds can we gain comfort that Mary, like you, me and every other human being, did not sin before or after being born again?

As we review the 'para', 'en' and 'epi' Holy Spirit experiences, we will see that even with those experiences, we're still very prone to sin. In Romans, Paul describes his ongoing challenge with sin after he was both born again (the en experience) and was Baptized in the Holy Spirit (the epi).

- ❑ *Romans 7:18 For I know that nothing good dwells in me, that is, **in my flesh**; for the willing is present in me, but the doing of the good is not. 19 **For the good that I want, I do not do**, but I practice the very evil that I do not want. 20 But if I am doing the very thing I do not want, I am no longer the one doing it, but **sin which dwells in me** ... 24 Wretched man that I am! Who will set me free from the body of this death? 25 ... on the one hand I myself with my mind am serving the law of God, but on the other, with my flesh the law of sin.*

3:17 If you believe Mary was never born again because she never sinned before or after the cross, which means she was never separated from God, which means she did not need to be born again - on what scriptural evidence is that view based? And couldn't that only happen if Mary was not a human being, but a divine being? If you say she wasn't divine, but specially protected, the only time we read of God's influence on her was when Holy Spirit came upon Mary to impregnate her. So how could Mary not have sinned before this encounter or afterward?

- ❑ *Luke 1:35 The angel answered and said to her, "The Holy Spirit will come upon you, and the power of the Most High will overshadow you; and for that reason the holy Child shall be called the Son of God.*

Sexless Marriage / No Other Biological Children

Mary ultimately married Joseph, a marriage that the Roman Catholic church teaches was sexless which is one reason why Mary never sinned after Jesus was born. Protestants view things differently and point to i) the fact she was human and ii) in addition to Jesus, had at least four other sons and more than one daughter:

- ❑ *Matthew 13:55 Is not this the carpenter's son? Is not His mother called Mary, and **His brothers [adelphos G80] James** and **Joseph** and **Simon** and **Judas**? 56 And **His sisters**, are they not all with us? Where then did this man get all these things?"*

Common Catholic teaching is that the men mentioned in Matthew 13:55 weren't biological half-brothers and the sisters weren't biological half-sisters of Jesus, but cousins or other relatives of Jesus. Consider three Greek words - 'adelphos', 'suggenes' and 'anepsios'.

- ❖ Adelphos [G80]; Strong's definition includes a biological brother, any fellow or man, or to brethren in Christ. Adelphos is used 346 times.
- ❖ Suggenes [G4773]; Thayer's definition includes in part 'related by blood, of the same nation, a fellow countryman. Suggenes is used 12 times.

CEASED?

- ❖ *Anepsios* [G431]; Strong's definition includes '1. a cousin'. Anepsios is used one time.

3:18 Adelphos is the Greek word used to describe biological brothers. If James, Joseph, Simon and Judas weren't biological brothers of Jesus, why wouldn't the Bible - a book without error - have used suggenes or anepsios instead of adelphos in Matthew 13:55?

Consider the following:
- ❑ *Matthew 12:46 While He was still speaking to the crowds, behold, **His mother and brothers [adelphos]** were standing outside, seeking to speak to Him.*
- ❑ *Luke 8:19 And His mother and **brothers [adelphos]** came to Him, and they were unable to get to Him because of the crowd.*
- ❑ *Acts 1:14 These all with one mind were continually devoting themselves to prayer, along with the women, and Mary the mother of Jesus, and **with His brothers [adelphos]**.*

3:19 Don't the above scriptures again suggest these men were biological brothers of Jesus? If these individuals were cousins or more distant relatives, why does the Bible refer to them as brothers and not a general reference more suitable for other relatives? Especially by Luke who is often viewed as the most scholarly of New Testament writers?

3:20 And wouldn't it be inconsistent to be accurate about the references to Jesus's mother and inaccurate on references in the same verse in regards to His brothers and sisters?

In terms of Mary and Joseph having a sexless marriage, I find it rather interesting when I compare the NASB version to the Catholic Public Domain Version.
- ❑ *Matthew 1:24 And Joseph awoke from his sleep and did as the angel of the Lord commanded him, and took Mary as his wife, 25 **but kept her a virgin until she gave birth to a Son**; and he called His name Jesus. (NASB)*
- ❑ *Matthew 1:24 Then Joseph, arising from sleep, did just as the Angel of the Lord had instructed him, and he accepted her as his wife. **And he knew her not, yet she bore her son, the firstborn**. And he called his name JESUS. (CPDV: Catholic Public Domain Version)*

The Word 'Until'

The NASB version clearly states Mary and Joseph had physical intimacy, but not until after Jesus was born. The Catholic Public Domain Version states Mary and Joseph never had physical intimacy before or after Mary gave birth to Jesus. In the NASB translation, the English word 'until' is derived from the Greek word 'heos' [G2193] which Strong's defines as '1. til, until'.

3:21 The Catholic Public Domain Version changed God's Word when the translators took out the Greek word 'heos' by intentionally omitting the related English word 'until'. Isn't that a rather big omission? If the word until was put back into the Catholic Bible, it would say "... he knew her not until ..." instead of the current translation "... knew her not ...". Doesn't adding the word 'until' put a totally different perspective on a sexless Mary and Joseph

3: Spirit, Soul and Body

marriage, a sinless Mary, and the entire Mother of God issue?

Second Eve

Jesus is referred to as the last Adam, the second Adam as it were, who brought life and overcame the sins of the first Adam.

- ❑ *1 Corinthians 15:45 So also it is written, "The first man, Adam, became a living soul." The **last Adam** became a life-giving spirit.*

A common Catholic view is to claim Mary is the second Eve. But is she?

- ❖ Unlike Jesus who is clearly linked to Adam in the New Testament, Mary is never explicitly linked to Eve.
- ❖ Adam and Eve were married - to each other. Jesus was never married. Mary was married, but to a different man.
- ❖ Jesus's mandate was as the Savior and Messiah; Mary's mandate did not include this. Mary's primary mandate was giving birth to Jesus and looking after Him in His early years.
- ❖ The Bible also refers to two secondary mandates with specific reference to Mary. One mandate is from the one and only scripture Mary is referred to after the cross - to be involved in prayer.
- ❑ *Acts 1:14 These all with one mind **were continually devoting themselves to prayer, along with the women, and Mary the mother of Jesus**, and with His brothers.*

- ❖ The secondary mandate for Mary does tie back to Adam and Eve - a mandate to multiply.
- ❑ *Genesis 1:27 God created man in His own image, in the image of God He created him; male and female He created them. 28 God blessed them; and God said to them, "Be **fruitful and multiply,** and **fill** the earth, and subdue it; and rule over the fish of the sea and over the birds of the sky and over every living thing that moves on the earth."*
- ❑ *Genesis 4:1 Now the man had relations with his wife Eve, and she conceived and gave birth to Cain, and she said, "I have gotten a manchild with the help of the Lord." 2 Again, she gave birth to his brother Abel ...*

3:22 Jesus came to redeem the world by addressing the sins of mankind. He did not come to father physical children. Mary, by contrast, did not come to redeem the world or address the sins of mankind. So, what was Mary's link to Eve if indeed she is the second Eve? Wouldn't it follow that Mary's mandate would be to have multiple children as well? And wouldn't that mean Mary would have had sex? And wouldn't that go directly against the argument Mary lived a sin-free life partly because she didn't engage in sex?

Mary looked after by John

Another reason the Catholic church gives for these four men not being Mary's children was because Jesus had Mary live with John after the cross. If these 4 men were Mary's biological children, the argument holds that Mary would have gone and

CEASED?

lived with one of the 4.

As the oldest son, Jesus was obliged to care for His mother, and with His passing, He was responsible to choose who would carry on that responsibility. Why Jesus didn't do this before the cross, I don't know. Purely a guess, but Jesus had some major things on his mind. In any event, Jesus was on the cross on the verge of death, exhausted and in excruciating pain. He sees His mother and John, the apostle who laid his head on Jesus's chest the previous night, and chose John.

- *John 19:26 When Jesus then saw His mother, and the disciple whom He loved standing nearby, He said to His mother, "Woman, **behold, your son [huios G5207]**!" 27 Then He said to the disciple, "Behold, **your mother**!" From that hour the disciple took her into his own household.*
- *John 21:20 Peter, turning around, saw the **disciple whom Jesus loved** following them; the one **who also had leaned back on His bosom at the supper** and said, "Lord, who is the one who betrays You?"*

The question is why John. For one, consider there's no indication Jesus's brothers believed, at that particular point in time, that Jesus was the Messiah. There's no indication they were even at His crucifixion or were with the group gathered on resurrection Sunday evening.

- *John 7:5 For not even His brothers were believing in Him.*
- *Matthew 13:57 And they took offense at Him. But Jesus said to them, "A prophet is not without honor except in his hometown and in his own household."*

Earlier, when His biological family came to see him, Jesus showed no interest in seeing them. His real 'mother' and 'brothers' were those who believed in Him.

- *Luke 8:19 And His mother and brothers came to Him, and they were unable to get to Him because of the crowd. 20 And it was reported to Him, "Your mother and Your brothers are standing outside, wishing to see You." 21 But He answered and said to them, "**My mother and My brothers are these who hear the word of God and do it**."*

3:23 Is it surprising Jesus choose John to look after Mary given:
  i. John loved Jesus, and Jesus knew it;
  ii. Jesus's 4 biological brothers did not yet believe in Him; and
  iii. no mention is made of Jesus's 4 biological brothers being at His crucifixion?

Whether Jesus had biological brothers and sisters or relatives is potentially a secondary issue in terms of why it was John who looked after Mary. I say that because why wouldn't Jesus choose John if these other individuals didn't believe Jesus was the Messiah, their Savior? After all, Jesus didn't always follow the social norms and customs of the day.

3:24 Is it also notable that when Jesus said to John "*Behold, your mother*", Jesus only spoke to John and not to all His followers? In other words, when Jesus spoke these words, wasn't He only referring to John and not to any other

3: Spirit, Soul and Body

believers who were present? That John and John alone was to view Mary as his mom until she died and went to heaven?

CLOSING POINTS TO PONDER

3:25 Human beings are 3 parts - spirit, soul (mind, will and emotion) and body. All 3 parts are tightly interwoven, amazingly complex and designed to be in a relationship with God. Modern medicine is constantly finding out new things about the human body. Isn't it prudent to also believe that while we know a bit about our souls and spirits, that their complexity is potentially even greater than our bodies? And that when we get into issues of dealing with hurts in our souls, don't we need to be careful in how we minister? And that perhaps, first and foremost, we should ask Holy Spirit to guide us? To seek God's Kingdom first in all things? To pray with thanksgiving in everything?
- ❏ Matthew 6:33 But **seek first His kingdom and His righteousness**, and all these things will be added to you.
- ❏ Philippians 4:6 Be anxious for nothing, but **in everything by prayer and supplication with thanksgiving** let your requests be made known to God.

We human beings are sinners and like Adam and Eve, because of our sins, we are separated from God. Our spirit is 'dead' as we do not have an intimate spiritual relationship with God. This separation is a problem given we are to worship God in spirit.
- ❏ John 4:24 God is Spirit: and those who worship Him must worship in spirit and truth.

So how can we enter into a personal, intimate relationship with God? Chapter 4 provides some insight.

4

Born Again/Salvation

INTRODUCTION
MANY have heard the term born again, but aren't comfortable with what it means. Chapter 4 touches on several issues related to being born again including:
1. God created humans in order to have a personal relationship (page 43);
2. basics of being born again (page 43);
3. requirements for salvation (page 46) including the issue of works (page 51);
4. whether or not water baptism is required to be saved (page 52);
5. getting saved (page 56) and the sinner's prayer (page 57);
6. what's required, if anything, to keep our salvation (page 60);
7. can we lose our salvation (page 65);
8. is communion symbolic or literal (page 68); and
9. other Catholic teachings on salvation (page 88).

God is Holy; Are We to be Holy Too
God wants us to be holy.
- 1 Peter 1:16 because it is written, "**You shall be holy**, for I am holy."

We know we're not holy based on our efforts. The solution for mankind was God sending Jesus to the cross for all our sins, enabling us to get in right standing with God. Unfortunately, while God wants all to be saved, those who don't profess Christ as Lord and don't want a relationship with Him won't make it to heaven, but will end up in hell.
- 1 John 1:7 but if we walk in the Light as He Himself is in the Light, we have fellowship with one another, and **the blood of Jesus His Son cleanses us** from **all sin**.
- 1 Timothy 2:4 **who desires all men to be saved** and to come to the knowledge of the truth.
- Romans 6:23 For the wages of sin is death, but the **free gift of God is eternal life** in Christ Jesus our Lord.

4: Born Again/Salvation

CREATED FOR PERSONAL RELATIONSHIP

A verse that always gets my attention is Matthew 7:23.
- *Matthew 7:23 And then I will declare to them, '**I never knew you**; depart from Me, you who practice lawlessness.'*

Ouch. Jesus didn't tell people to depart because they practiced lawlessness. He told people to depart because He *'never knew'* them. The word *'knew'* is derived from the Greek word *'ginoska'* [G1097] which Strong's defines in part as *'... come to know ... to become acquainted with, to know'*. God communicated with Adam and Eve in the Garden of Eden. He had a relationship with them.

Sin changed this relationship by causing a separation that plagues people to this day. Fortunately, through the cross, Jesus paid the penalty for all sins which removed the separation between human beings and God. We can now approach Him directly.

4:1 Isn't it reasonable to believe Jesus's death and shed blood enables us to have the kind of personal relationship resembling what God had with Adam and Eve? If not, why not?

4:2 When we seek salvation, doesn't that mean we want to come into an intimate, personal relationship with God starting here on earth and continuing on into heaven? And if we don't want and seek this kind of relationship, do we risk being told to depart?

BASICS OF BORN AGAIN

- *John 3:3 Jesus answered and said to him, "Truly, truly, I say to you, **unless one is born again** he cannot see the kingdom of God."*
- *John 3:7 Do not be amazed that I said to you, '**You must be born again**.'*
- *1 Peter 1:3 Blessed be the God and Father of our Lord Jesus Christ, who according to His great mercy has caused us **to be born again to a living hope through the resurrection** of Jesus Christ from the dead,*
- *1 Peter 1:23 for you **have been born again** not of seed which is perishable but imperishable, that is, through the living and enduring word of God.*

In the Greek

The English word *'born'* is derived from the Greek word *'gennao'* [G1080]. Gennao is used 97 times and usually relates to a physical birth beginning with all those begats in Matthew. Spiritual birth is referenced about 10 times including Galatians 4:29.

- *Galatians 4:28 And you brethren, like Isaac, are children of promise. 29 But as at that time he who was born according to the flesh persecuted him **who was born according to the Spirit**, so it is now also.*

The English word *'again'* is derived from the Greek word *'anothen'* [G509] which Thayer defines in part as *'1. From above, from a higher place a. of things which come from heaven or God ... 3. anew, over again'*. Being born again is something God does for us - from His heavenly place.

Without Jesus in our lives, we are spiritually dead; we have no relationship with

CEASED?

God. When saved, Jesus is in us, our spirits are born anew and come alive as we're made righteous; as we're made right with God.
- ❑ *2 Corinthians 13:5 Test yourselves to see if you are in the faith; examine yourselves! Or do you not recognize this about yourselves, that **Jesus Christ is in you** - unless indeed you fail the test?*
- ❑ *Ephesians 2:1 And you were **dead in your trespasses and sins**,*
- ❑ *Romans 8:10 If Christ is in you, though the **body is dead because of sin**, yet **the spirit is alive because of righteousness**.*

Nicodemus and Being Born Again

The state of separation between God and humans due to sin was the topic of the discussion between Jesus and Nicodemus.
- ❑ *John 3:1 Now there was a man of the Pharisees, named Nicodemus, a ruler of the Jews; 2 this man came to Jesus by night and said to Him, "Rabbi, we know that You have come from God as a teacher; for no one can do these signs that You do unless God is with him." 3 Jesus answered and said to him, "Truly, truly, I say to you, **unless one is born again he cannot see the kingdom of God**."*
- ❑ *4 Nicodemus said to Him, "How can a man be born when he is old? He cannot enter a second time into his mother's womb and be born, can he?" 5 Jesus answered, "Truly, truly, I say to you, **unless one is born of water** and **the Spirit** he **cannot enter into the kingdom of God**. 6 That which is born of the flesh is flesh, and that which is born of the Spirit is spirit.*
- ❑ *7 Do not be amazed that I said to you, 'You **must be born again**.' 8 The wind blows where it wishes and you hear the sound of it, but do not know where it comes from and where it is going; so is everyone who is born of the Spirit." 9 Nicodemus said to Him, "How can these things be?"*

Born of Spirit

Most Bible teachers believe the reference to being *'born of spirit'* relates to our spiritual birth wherein our spirit is made new - our spirit is born again. Our spirit, which was dead and separated from God due to sin, comes alive when we're saved, when we're washed clean, when we enter into a new relationship with God.
- ❑ *1 John 1:7 But if we walk in the light, as He Himself is in the light, we have fellowship with one another, and the **blood of Jesus His Son cleanses us from all sin**.*
- ❑ *2 Corinthians 5:17 Therefore if anyone is in Christ, **he is a new creature;** the old things passed away; behold, new things have come.*

The need for our spirits to be saved is supported by Paul in his first letter to the Corinthians where a man was engaged in sexual sin. Action was required.
- ❑ *1 Corinthians 5:4 In the name of our Lord Jesus, when you are assembled, and I with you in spirit, with the power of our Lord Jesus, 5 I have decided to deliver such a one to Satan for the destruction of his flesh, **so that his spirit may be saved in the day of the Lord Jesus**.*

4: Born Again/Salvation

Born of Water

Considerable disagreement exists, however, on what is meant by *'born of water'*. The two most common alternatives are physical birth and water baptism.

- ❑ *John 3:5 Jesus answered, "Truly, truly, I say to you, unless one is born of water and the Spirit he cannot enter into the kingdom of God ... 9 Nicodemus said to Him, "How can these things be?" 10 Jesus answered and said to him,* **"Are you the teacher of Israel and do not understand these things?**

4:3   When Jesus wondered why Nicodemus doesn't know these things, Jesus could have been mocking Nicodemus. However, given Nicodemus was sincerely seeking the truth, is it likely that Jesus would mock him? Is it possible that Jesus's reference to born of water was about something very obvious? Such as when one is physically born?

i: Physical birth

If *'born of water'* indeed refers to our physical birth, Nicodemus would have understood. In addition, consider verses 5 and 6.

- ❑ *John 3:5 Jesus answered, "Truly, truly, I say to you, unless* **one is born of water** *and* **the Spirit** *he cannot enter into the kingdom of God. 6 That which is* **born of the flesh is flesh**, *and that which* **is born of the Spirit is spirit**.

The English word *'water'* in verse 5 is derived from the Greek word *'hudor hudatos'* [G5204] which is defined as actual physical water. The English word *'flesh'* is derived from the Greek word *'sarx'* [G4561] which is defined in part as physical. Both water and flesh are physical elements on this earth which would be consistent with a physical birth.

4:4   If *'born of the Spirit is spirit'* in verse 6 relates to born of the spirit in verse 5, wouldn't it follow that *'born of the flesh is flesh'* in verse 6 relates closer to physical birth (flesh) than water baptism?

ii: Water Baptism

Nicodemus was most likely familiar with John the Baptist's Baptism of Repentance, although that doesn't mean he fully understood it. Nicodemus would have been familiar with the original waters on earth, the flood, the passing of the Egyptians through the Red Sea and the Jordan River.

4:5   Before Nicodemus spoke with Jesus, there had been a foreshadowing of today's water baptism. However, could Nicodemus have been expected to know what water baptism would mean after the cross given the limited information on water baptism we see in scriptures before Jesus spoke to Nicodemus?

I personally believe born of water refers to physical birth. If you believe it refers to water baptism, then shouldn't the evidence be clear that water baptism is required for salvation? Roman Catholicism and some Protestant denominations teach exactly that - water baptism is required for salvation. But is it? **CEASED?** discusses this issue later in Chapter 4. Chapter 10 also reviews Acts 2:38 - Peter's famous: *"Repent and be baptized"* - and why it may not even refer to water baptism.

CEASED?

REQUIREMENTS OF SALVATION
(1) Repentance and Conversion

So how does one get to be saved? John the Baptist, a forerunner of Jesus, gives one key indication. We need to repent.
- Matthew 3:2 "**Repent**, for the kingdom of heaven is at hand."
- Matthew 3:11 "As for me, I baptize you with water for **repentance**, but He who is coming after me is mightier than I, and I am not fit to remove His sandals; He will baptize you with the Holy Spirit and fire."

During Jesus's ministry, His message was similar - repent.
- Matthew 4:17 From that time Jesus began to preach, and say, "**Repent, for the kingdom of heaven is at hand.**"

After the cross, Peter explained what happened at Pentecost when bystanders witnessed tongues of fire and the ~120 speaking in tongues. When the Jewish people realized they had contributed to Jesus being crucified, they were deeply impacted and asked what they needed to do. The first thing Peter said was they needed to repent.
- Acts 2:37 Now when they heard this, they were pierced in their heart, and said to Peter and the rest of the apostles, "Brethren, **what shall we do**?"
- Acts 2:38 Peter said to them, "**Repent** ..."

Peter repeated the requirement to repent in Acts 3.
- Acts 3:19 Therefore **repent** and return, so that your sins may be wiped away, in order that times of refreshing may come from the presence of the Lord;

Paul also clarified every person needed to repent.
- Acts 26:20 but kept declaring both to those of Damascus first, and also at Jerusalem and then throughout all the region of Judea, and even to the Gentiles, that they **should repent and turn to God**, **performing deeds appropriate to repentance**.

At the end of verse 20, we learn true repentance leads to *'performing deeds appropriate to repentance'*. Our actions and lives will provide evidence we have truly repented, that we've been impacted by our decision to turn towards God. Inherent in that decision was our realization that we're a sinner in need of a Savior. If we don't understand that, are we able to truly repent?

Greek and Hebrew
In the New Testament:
- ❖ The English word *'repent'* is from the Greek word *'metanoeo'* [G3340] which Thayer defines in part as 'to **change one's mind for better**, heartily to amend with abhorrence one's past sins'.
- ❖ The English word *'repentance'* is from the Greek word *'metanoia'* [G3341] which Thayer defines in part as 'a **change of mind**, as it appears to one who repents'.

4: Born Again/Salvation

In the Old Testament, the Hebrew word for repent is *'nacham'* [H5162] which primarily means **to be sorry or to comfort oneself**.

4:6 When looking at both the Hebrew and Greek definitions, we see that repentance involves both a) being sorry and b) changing one's mind, one's way of thinking. And since our way of thinking influences what we say and do, would it be surprising to find true repentance changes the very way we live and that it becomes evident to those we are closest to? And as a result, shouldn't we see other changes including a greater presence of the fruits of the Spirit?

- ❏ *Galatians 5:22 But the fruit of the Spirit is **love, joy, peace, patience, kindness, goodness, faithfulness**, 23 **gentleness, self-control**; against such things there is no law.*

God Repented

In Genesis, God was sorry for creating human beings. He was sorry He created us. Isn't that a rather humbling thought?

- ❏ *Genesis 6:6 And it **repented [nacham] the Lord** that he had made man on the earth, and it grieved him at his heart. (KJV)*
- ❏ *Genesis 6:6 The Lord **was sorry [nacham]** that He had made man on the earth, and He was grieved in His heart. (NASB)*
- ❏ *1 Samuel 15:35 Samuel did not see Saul again until the day of his death; for Samuel grieved over Saul. And the Lord **regretted [nacham]** that He had made Saul king over Israel.*

God also changed his mind in the Old Testament.

- ❏ *Exodus 32:14 And the **Lord repented [nacham]** of the evil which he thought to do unto his people. (KJV)*
- ❏ *Exodus 32:14 So the **Lord changed His mind [nacham]** about the harm which He said He would do to His people. (NASB)*
- ❏ *Amos 7:5 Then I said, "Lord God, please stop! How can Jacob stand, for he is small?" 6 The Lord **changed His mind [nacham]** about this. "This too shall not be," said the Lord God.*
- ❏ *Jonah 3:9 "Who knows, God may turn and **relent [nacham]** and withdraw His burning anger so that we will not perish." 10 When God saw their deeds, that they turned from their wicked way, then God relented concerning the calamity which He had declared He would bring upon them. And He did not do it.*

4:7 Given God repented but doesn't sin, doesn't that show repentance doesn't always have to be directly linked to sin?

Sorry and Changing Wrong Thinking

Before coming to Christ, many of us are filled with many negative things in our hearts - regrets, guilt, shame etc. Many others may feel relatively good about themselves. The reality for all of us, however, is that we're all sinners. We may be sorry for our sins, but too often the reason we're sorry is that we got caught, or we're worried or fearful of the potential consequences of our sins. Oh, our selfish hearts.

4:8 Is being genuinely sorry for our sins something we should feel? And should

it be extremely disconcerting if we aren't sorry for our sins?
- ❏ *2 Corinthians 7:10 For the **sorrow** that is according to the will of God **produces a repentance** without regret, leading to salvation, but the sorrow of the world produces death.*

Godly sorrow leads to true repentance which is a changing of our hearts and minds so we do not want to sin that way again. When a person says they have repented of their sins but do so in token words only, it's like painting an old rickety fence and not replacing the rotten boards and posts. It may look good for a while, but don't lean on it too much.

With true repentance, our desire to sin changes. We often become somewhat like the reformed smoker. Reformer smokers often can't stand someone smoking, and the thought of smoking is not even on their radar. It often disgusts them. When we truly turn our hearts and ways of thinking towards God, God becomes central in our lives. We don't seek behavior modification so that we don't sin; we pursue God who changes our hearts so we have no desire to sin. For many of us, this can be a battle as our soul and body (our flesh) can have residues of desiring sin in some areas. Or when trials hit, we can resort to old habits of hiding away in our old comforts - food, alcohol, drugs, porn - instead of turning to God and reading His Word, praying, listening to teachings, entering into praise and worship or calling another believer. If we struggle, we can always ask God to change our hearts. I believe God will honor that kind of prayer. Sometimes He responds immediately or sometimes over time. Whatever way He chooses, God does respond, and in so doing, we will be changed and become more and more like Christ.

Sin separates us from God and if we don't want our relationship with God to be compromised, we will turn our attention to things that honor God.
- ❏ *Philippians 4:8 Finally, brethren, whatever is true, whatever is honorable, whatever is right, whatever is pure, whatever is lovely, whatever is of good repute, if there is any excellence and if anything worthy of praise, dwell on these things.*

4:9 I know people who sin, repent and confess their sins. In their minds, they are good. Then, they sin again. And again. I can relate; this was me for a season. Overcoming sins can be a difficult battle. But if God is a priority and we truly want to stop sinning, don't we need to take concrete, even difficult steps? And seek Him to change our hearts so that we have no desire to sin?

Be Converted

As mentioned, Peter repeated the requirement to repent in Acts 3. But Peter also states we need to be converted or to return.
- ❏ *Acts 3:19 **Repent ye** therefore, and be **converted** [epistrepho G1994], that your sins may be blotted out, when the times of refreshing shall come from the presence of the Lord. (KJV)*
- ❏ *Acts 3:19 Therefore **repent** and **return**, so that your sins may be wiped away, in order that times of refreshing may come from the presence of the Lord; (NASB)*

4: Born Again/Salvation

The Greek underpinning the English word converted in the KJV and the word 'return' in the NASB is *'epistrepho'* [G1994]. Strong's defines epistrepho in part as *'come, convert, turn or return'*.

Some may view converting as separate from repentance. To me, both reflect the same issue - changing our way of thinking from what we have to what Jesus wants.

(2) By Faith, Believing, Trusting

Through God's grace, He provides a way - namely Jesus - that enables us to be saved. But we need to have faith that Jesus is the Way. We need to believe God's Word.

- ❑ *Ephesians 2:8 For by grace you have been saved through **faith** ...*
- ❑ *Hebrews 11:1 Now **faith** is the assurance of things hoped for, the conviction of things not seen.*
- ❑ *Hebrews 11:6 And **without faith it is impossible to please Him**: for **he who comes to God must believe** that **He is**, and that He is a rewarder of those who seek Him.*

Faith is a central part of relationships with God, starting in Old Testament days and carrying on right through to today. Consider Abraham.

- ❑ *Romans 4:1 What then shall we say that Abraham, our forefather according to the flesh, has found? 2 For if Abraham was justified by works, he has something to boast about, but not before God. 3 For what does the Scripture say? "**Abraham believed God, and it was credited to him as righteousness.**"*
- ❑ *Hebrews 11:17 By **faith Abraham**, when he was tested, offered up Isaac, and he who had received the promises was offering up his only begotten son;*

Abraham's works were important to God but were not the key. It was Abraham's belief, his trusting, his having faith in God that was the key. He was willing to sacrifice Isaac, because he believed God would raise Isaac from the dead since many promises were to be fulfilled through Isaac.

- ❑ *Hebrews 11:18 it was he to whom it was said, "In Isaac your descendants shall be called." 19 He considered that God is able to raise people even from the dead, from which he also received him back as a type.*

I can't imagine what went through the minds of Abraham and Isaac on that day. While different, Romans 10:9 tells us God does gives us at least one *'faith test'* today - do we believe **in our heart** that God raised Jesus from the dead.

- ❑ *Romans 10:9 that if you confess with your mouth Jesus as Lord, and **believe in your heart that God raised Him from the dead**, you will be saved;*

Having faith *and* believing in our heart are essential. Having said that, is there a material difference between the two? The word *'faith'* in Hebrews 11:17 is based on the Greek word *'pistis'* [G4102] while the word *'believe'* in Romans 4:3 is based on the Greek word *'pisteuo'* [G4100]. Both words mean to believe and to have trust. Pisteuo is derived from pistis, and thus from the standpoint of salvation and my

CEASED?

limited brainpower, I view faith and believing as effectively meaning the same thing ... do we trust in God ... do we believe in God ... do we have faith in God?

I've heard the comment that believing in Jesus is all that is needed to be saved. One simply needs to believe God for who He is, what He did, what He says etc.

4:10   If this is your belief, consider satan and his army of demons who all believe Jesus can do anything, know what He did and who He is. Will their belief get them into heaven?

4:11   Or consider that someone says that they believe Christ was resurrected, but He is not the only way, as there are many roads to heaven. Does that work for you? It doesn't for me and these broad, universal salvation doctrines are extremely disconcerting.

English words have limitations. Greek and Hebrew words often have multiple ways of being used. In the case of believing, does it perhaps have a deeper meaning, one wherein we know in our knower that Jesus is God, our savior? Our belief in Him is not only believing several facts to be true, but we have a belief, a trust, a confidence in the person of Jesus Christ, and in the character of God. Some simplistic analogies of *'believing'* would be a parent believing in their child to do the right thing, a coach believing in her players to come through in the clutch or a foreman believing in his crew to deal with any unexpected problems that may arise on the job site. They just know, they have faith, they believe in, they trust in their child, their players, their employees. And is this perhaps why God's Word says we're to come to God as a child - filled with childlike belief and trust?

- ❑ *Mark 10:15 Truly I say to you, whoever does not receive the kingdom of God like a child will not enter it at all.*

<u>A Package Deal</u>

In my view, repenting, believing and having faith go together. In order to repent and turn, to change our way of thinking, we need to have a reason to do so. To have faith and believe in someone, means we must have a reason to believe in the person.

Without Christ, we're sinners destined for hell. God, through His Son Jesus, provided an amazing gift of salvation that enables sinners to gain eternal life. To do so, we need to change our mind (repent) and to believe and have faith in Jesus and in what He did. They're not independent steps - they're pieces that come together to create a pathway from our living on the road to a dead-end pit, to living on a new road alongside Christ, the end of which is an amazing life in heaven.

(3) <u>Confess with Our Mouths</u>

God created the universe by speaking it into existence. The spoken word was associated with power many other times in the Bible. There certainly appears to be blessings from the spoken word. Not surprisingly then, Romans 10:9 tells us we need to not only believe with our heart, but to confess/speak with our mouth that Jesus is Lord and was resurrected from the dead.

- ❑ *Romans 10:9 that **<u>if you confess with your mouth Jesus as Lord</u>**, and **<u>believe in your heart that God raised Him from the dead</u>**, you will be saved; 10 for with the heart a person believes, resulting in righteousness, and with the*

4: Born Again/Salvation

mouth he confesses, resulting in salvation. 11 For the Scripture says, "Whoever believes in Him will not be disappointed."

4:12 Notice the second word in Romans 10:9 is the word *'if'*. By itself, does that indicate that if we don't confess Jesus as Lord or we don't believe He was resurrected from the dead, that we won't be saved? More on this in a bit.

TWO CONTENTIOUS REQUIREMENTS?
(1) <u>Works</u>

A controversial aspect of salvation is whether or not we can somehow initially earn and then continue to maintain or keep our salvation through good works.

- ❑ *James 2:24 You see that a man is justified by works and not by faith alone.*
- ❑ *James 2:26 For just as the body without the spirit is dead, so also faith without works is dead.*

4:13 Some people believe the works above are required to earn or maintain one's salvation. Could the works referenced above serve not as a requirement of salvation, but as proof of salvation? In other words, when we're born again, will our works give tangible evidence that we've been impacted by God?

Other scriptures show we're saved by our faith and by accepting the gift of salvation made available by God's Grace.

- ❑ *Ephesians 2:8 For **<u>by grace you have been saved through faith</u>**; and that not of yourselves: it is **<u>the gift of God</u>**: 9 **<u>Not as a result of works</u>**, so that no one may boast.*
- ❑ *Romans 11:6 But if it **<u>is by grace</u>**, it is **<u>no longer on the basis of works</u>**, otherwise **<u>grace is no longer grace</u>**.*
- ❑ *Romans 6:23 For the wages of sin is death; but the **<u>free gift of God is eternal life</u>** in Christ Jesus our Lord.*

4:14 Based on the three scriptures, could the works concerning salvation relate in part to repenting, believing and/or confessing with our mouths? And if we sincerely repent, believe and confess, are we then positioned to receive the gift of salvation per Ephesians 2:8 and Romans 6:23?

If we think we can earn our salvation through our works, Romans 11:6 above tells us God's grace would no longer be grace.

4:15 When we believe our works will help get us to heaven, are we saying/believing we can do what God couldn't?

4:16 Are we also potentially saying what Jesus did on the cross is not enough?

4:17 Are we also potentially indicating that deep down in our soul, we may not believe what the Bible says - that we're justified and redeemed by Christ alone? That we believe the gift of salvation may apply to others, but not to me?

In Biblical times, the Jewish people were very familiar with the 613 laws of the Old Covenant. Works were central to their faith. Jesus made it clear that the key was no longer their works, but their faith in Christ and what He did on the cross.

CEASED?

4:18 For some of us, is it simply too good to be true that we can believe the framework of works in the Old Testament has been replaced with a relationship with God involving faith, belief and trust in Christ and what He did on the cross? And especially difficult to believe for those of us whose identity has been one of doing something to prove we earned it? Or that we're not good enough to get anything so good?

The Roman Catholic church is often viewed as teaching that works are required to be initially saved. My research showed inconsistent teachings in this area as some Catholics do not believe we can earn our salvation - at least initially. Some agree with Ephesians 2:8-9 that we're not saved through works - at least initially.
- *Ephesians 2:8 For by grace you have been saved through faith; and that not of yourselves, it is the gift of God; 9 not as a result of works, so that no one may boast.*

Where the issue of works comes into play in Catholic teachings is that works are deemed to be required to maintain one's salvation. More on this later.

The Bible has many teachings in various books including Romans, James and Galatians. If you've never studied this area before, consider reading Chapters 3 through 5 in Galatians a few times and ask Holy Spirit to speak to you. Amongst other things, you may gain a new appreciation of God's love and how mind-boggling it is, and He is. He gives us great things we don't deserve (i.e. by His grace, we can have eternal life) and does not give us negative things we do deserve (i.e. by His mercy, we do not automatically get eternal death).

(2) Water Baptism

As mentioned, many followers of Christ believe we need to be water baptized to be saved. Many other followers think otherwise. Acts 2:38 is a key scripture used in believing why water baptism is required for salvation.
- *Acts 2:38 Peter said to them, "**<u>Repent, and each of you be baptized</u>** in the name of Jesus Christ for the forgiveness of your sins; and you will receive the gift of the Holy Spirit.*

A full discussion on Acts 2:38 is given in the last part of Chapter 10. I deferred this discussion as I felt it would be more fruitful after the essentials of the Baptism into the Body of Christ (done by Holy Spirit when born again) and the Baptism of the Holy Spirit (done by Jesus) are clarified in Chapters 7 through 10 of **CEASED?**. With that background, I will lay out reasons why Peter's reference to baptism in Acts 2:38 is not to water baptism, but to the Baptism in the Holy Spirit. I can hear the words 'heretic' coming out now. For now, consider the following evidence as to why many believers, including myself, don't believe water baptism is required for salvation.

Original Apostles and ~120 at Pentecost

First consider the original apostles and the rest of the ~120 who were gathered together on the morning of Pentecost. There is no mention any of these individuals

4: Born Again/Salvation

were baptized in water after the cross. There is no mention on resurrection Sunday evening nor during the following 40 days leading up to Christ's ascension of their personal need to be water baptized. There is no mention in the 10 days between His ascension and Pentecost. To be fair, Jesus also did not mention repentance, believing etc., but isn't that because they were already born again on resurrection Sunday evening right after they encountered Jesus? If you don't believe that is the timing of their being born again, Chapter 6 covers this in detail.

Paul and Water Baptism

Paul baptized individuals in water. However, Paul never mentioned water baptism was required for salvation in his teachings. In fact, Paul said very clearly that water baptism was not something Jesus sent him to do. The focus was to be on what Jesus did for us on the cross.

- ❏ 1 Corinthians 1:17 **_For Christ did not send me to baptize_**, but **_to preach the gospel_**, *not in cleverness of speech,* **_so that the cross of Christ would not be made void_**.

While Peter was the first apostle to take the gospel to the Gentiles at Cornelius's home, Paul was later entrusted to take the gospel to the Gentiles.

- ❏ *Galatians 2:7 But on the contrary, seeing that I had been entrusted with the gospel to the uncircumcised, just as Peter had been to the circumcised 8 (for He who effectually worked for Peter in his apostleship to the circumcised effectually worked for me also to the Gentiles),*

4:19 Paul led the way in taking the Good News to the Gentiles. If water baptism was necessary for salvation, is it reasonable to expect Jesus would have sent Paul to baptize in water?

4:20 Would it be reasonable to expect Paul, who scribed the most books in the New Testament of any writer, would have made it abundantly clear at least once when he presented the gospel that water baptism was required?

4:21 Given Paul never once said water baptism was required to be saved, then shouldn't other scriptures make it crystal clear that water baptism is required to be saved? After all, salvation is a hugely important issue.
Consider when Paul met with the 12 disciples at Ephesus.

- ❏ *Acts 19:1 It happened that while Apollos was at Corinth, Paul passed through the upper country and came to Ephesus, and found* **some disciples**. *2 He said to them,* **"Did you receive the Holy Spirit** *when* **you believed?"** *And they said to him, "No, we have not even heard whether there is a Holy Spirit." 3 And he said,* **"Into what then were you baptized?" And they said, "Into John's baptism."** *4 Paul said, "John baptized with the baptism of repentance, telling the people to believe in Him who was coming after him, that is, in Jesus." 5* **When they heard this, they were baptized in the name of the Lord Jesus**. *6 And when Paul had laid his hands upon them,* **the Holy Spirit came on them, and they began speaking with tongues and prophesying.**

4:22 Paul never talked to the 12 disciples about God's holiness, sin, the need for a savior, the cross, repentance, believing in Christ, confession of their faith -

CEASED?

nothing of the sort. Furthermore, given Paul refers to the 12 individuals as *'disciples'* who *'believed'*, doesn't that mean the 12 individuals were already born again when he first met them, that they were already saved?

4:23 Paul's first question to the 12 was to determine if they had been Baptized in the Holy Spirit since 'you believed'. They had not received this baptism which led Paul to do two things - have the 12 disciples water baptized and then have them Baptized in the Holy Spirit. Doesn't this experience at Ephesus indicate a person should both be water baptized and Baptized in the Holy Spirit after one is saved, but that neither is required to be saved? If not, how do we view these events at Ephesus?

Peter and Water Baptism

In Acts 10, Peter was sharing the gospel with Cornelius, friends and family. As Peter talked, they received the gift of salvation where Holy Spirit came in [en] them. In addition, Holy Spirit came upon them and they received the gift of tongues.

❑ *Acts 10:44 While **Peter was still speaking these words, the Holy Spirit fell upon all those** who were listening to the message. 45 All the circumcised believers who came with Peter were amazed, because the **gift of the Holy Spirit had been poured out** on the Gentiles also. 46 For they were hearing **them speaking with tongues and exalting God**. Then Peter answered, 47 "Surely no one can refuse the water for these to be baptized **who have received the Holy Spirit just as we did**, can he?" 48 And **he ordered them to be baptized in the name of Jesus Christ**. Then they asked him to stay on for a few days.*

4:24 After Peter observed Cornelius, his family and friends speaking in tongues, Peter recognized they had received the Holy Spirit just as he and others had received at Pentecost. Peter also realized God had just given the gift of salvation to the Gentiles, and that salvation was no longer limited to just the Jews. Peter then took steps to have them water baptized. Given Peter felt Cornelius, family and friends had received the gift of salvation, before he had them water baptized, doesn't this mean Peter believed they were born again before he had them water baptized? If not, what did Peter believe?

4:25 Moreover, if the gift of tongues was for believers only, doesn't this again indicate Cornelius, family and friends were born again before they were water baptized?

Mark 16:16

Mark 16:16 is frequently used to claim water baptism is required to be saved.

❑ *Mark 16:16 He who has **believed** and **has been baptized** shall be saved; but he who has **disbelieved shall be condemned**.*

4:26 If we look at the last half of the verse, it says that those who disbelieved shall be condemned. If water baptism was required for salvation, would it be reasonable to expect Mark 16:16 to also have included water baptism in the last section? In other words, would it be reasonable for Mark 16:16 to have read something like "... *he who has disbelieved or has not been water baptized*

4: Born Again/Salvation

shall be condemned?". However, given Mark 16:16 does not state that if you're not water baptized you will be condemned, does this again support the argument that water baptism is not required to be saved?

Thief on the Cross

Many apologists cite the example of the thief on the cross as another example of a person who was saved but not water baptized. It is true, but it was also a unique setting and I'm not sure it's appropriate to use as an overall guide. So, I don't.

1 Peter 3:21

1 Peter 3:21 reveals there is a baptism that now saves us.

- ❑ *1 Peter 3:20 who once were disobedient, when the patience of God kept waiting in the days of Noah ... eight persons, were brought safely through the water.* **21 Corresponding to that, baptism now saves you** - *not the removal of dirt from the flesh, but an appeal to God for a good conscience - through the resurrection of Jesus Christ,*

4:27 When one is water baptized to be obedient, is this an indication a person may be saved? But just because one has been water baptized, is not a guarantee one is saved?

4:28 Even if water baptism was part of the salvation formula, how could water baptism be the baptism in 1 Peter 3:21 given water baptism would not be the only 'component' by which one would be initially saved?

4:29 Per Chapter 5, when we're saved, Holy Spirit baptizes us into the Body of Christ. Holy Spirit comes to live in [en] us to guide us, convict us and lead us into a life and person that pleases God. Sins in our life should decline over time, and if not, something is amiss. As a result, aren't we being saved not only from the long-term standpoint of gaining eternal salvation, but also being 'saved' or prevented in our earthly lives from sinning? And thus, is the baptism in 1 Peter 3:21 referring to the Baptism into the Body of Christ where Holy Spirit comes in [en] us to guide us, to convict us and to help enable us not to sin?

Is Water Baptism a Form of Works

4:30 Repentance, believing and confessing are central to be being born again. There is no physical act or work involved other than making a choice and confessing a desire to pursue a relationship with Jesus. On the basis that water baptism is a physical action, is water baptism a form of works which goes against Ephesians 2:8-9?

- ❑ *Ephesians 2:8 For **by grace you have been saved through faith**; and that not of yourselves, it is the gift of God; 9 **not as a result of works**, so that no one may boast.*

Examples

4:31 If water baptism was required for salvation, wouldn't it be reasonable to expect multiple scriptures making this clear including at least one or two examples after the cross?

CEASED?

As mentioned, a core scripture behind Roman Catholic teachings that water baptism is required for salvation is Acts 2:38. This scripture is reviewed at the end of Chapter 10 in **CEASED?**.

<u>My Struggle in Believing I was Saved</u>

For many years after being born again, my head knew I was saved. But in my heart, I struggled that the truths of the Bible - that salvation was a gift, that I did not need to work for my salvation, that despite what I had done or not done, or said or not said - that salvation was still applicable to me. I didn't feel I was worthy of such a gift. My head knew what scriptures said, but it was a challenge getting my heart to go along. There were so many days when I could accept the fact that Jesus did what He did for the benefit of everybody else ... but ... I doubted His sacrifice, His Gift, His amazing blessings applied to me.

My struggle was primarily because of how I had shortchanged my children as a father. If, in your heart, you struggle to accept God's goodness and His gift of salvation, you don't feel you're worthy, you're not alone. I get it. But here's the deal. None of us are worthy - not you and certainly not me. But we humans, God's creations, are precious in the eyes of God. Jesus loves you and wants to have an everlasting relationship with you, starting now just as you are. You don't need to get right; just come as you are and God will change you. It is a gift of love beyond human understanding. This may sound trite and filled with Christianese, but it is the truth. If there are deep pains, regrets, guilt in your soul, I am so sorry. But please know, you do belong. Jesus did die for you. He does want a relationship with you. He wants to heal those deep soul wounds. And there are brothers and sisters in Christ willing to come alongside you.

My wife Lori is an amazing woman. She encouraged me and frequently spoke truths over me. Lori can be gentle, but she has her voice and can be direct when needed. One day when I was struggling with accepting God's goodness, Lori asked me, gently but clearly, the following:

"Don, would you like Jesus to have taken one more lash - just for you?"

I broke down and wept. And as I first typed and later edited this discussion on multiple occasions, I wept almost every time. Picturing Jesus dying a horrific death on the cross knowing He died in part for my sins so that I could receive His gift of salvation, a gift of an eternal relationship with Him - was and is still overwhelming at times. If you struggle in accepting God's goodness, I found if I take my eyes off me, and put them on Him and think about what He has done, I appreciate these Biblical truths more and more.

PROCESS OF 'GETTING SAVED'

To recap, God's grace coupled with Jesus's death and resurrection enables the gift of salvation to be made available. Repentance, having faith/belief in Jesus and His resurrection, choosing to turn to God, and verbally confessing our commitment to Jesus are the central tenants to salvation.

Having said that, consider this. Before we're born again, few of us have much of an appreciation of sin, holiness, the cross, the crucifixion, the resurrection, or what

4: Born Again/Salvation

repentance truly means. We may have heard someone tell us about the gospel, but if new believers were to take a short test on the basics of sin, salvation, being born again or the gospel, I suggest most would fail.

More of My Story

I starting going to church in Calgary in my late 40's. I did the 'right' things that might cause another person to think I was a Christian. Looking back, I doubt I was born again. About 10 years ago, at age 56, I was broke financially, broken emotionally and spiritually dead. I was lost, didn't care about anything, and too empty to care much about myself or anyone else. I was also prideful, arrogant, stubborn and selfish. I was battling a 40-year addiction to pornography that started in my teens. I was a mess. One morning, I cried out to Jesus in desperation, and that is when I believe I was truly born again. No Biblical words. No sinner's prayer. Just a desperate cry for help. And I know I was born again because things immediately began to change inside of me. For one, I started to dislike the porn, then later hated the porn. I was a different person, a new creation in some ways. God is so good. When I truly wanted to get free of the porn, God set me totally and permanently free. He doesn't want us to have behavior modification; He wants to give us freedom and victory. He gave it to me.

So yes, while I had heard teachings for years about repentance, confession, believing and having faith and all of that, I had minimal understanding of what it really meant. My spiritual eyes and ears were closed for the most part even though I was a regular attendee at more than one church, tithed to some degree, and helped out through ushering, stacking chairs and parking cars.

Salvation in some ways can seem to be a fairly involved process. But there is also the simplicity of it being a heart issue - the broken and contrite heart of a person who is seeking after God, understanding little but wanting whatever God has to offer them.

- *Psalm 51:17 The sacrifices of God are a broken spirit; a broken and a contrite heart, O God, You will not despise.*

Sin separated us from God, but through His goodness, God provided a way that gives us new life in Christ. I believe the only reason I am alive today is because of God's gift of salvation, His ongoing pursuit of me, and His willingness to answer my cry for help.

Sinner's Prayer

Many believers focus on 'getting' a non-believer to a place where they give their heart to the Lord by reciting a form of 'sinner's prayer'. A short-form version of such a prayer is as follows.

"Lord Jesus, I know I'm a sinner, and I ask for Your forgiveness. I believe You died for my sins and that You rose from the dead. I turn from my sins and invite You to come into my heart and life. I want to trust and follow You as my Lord and Savior. Amen."

CEASED?

After a person says this prayer, they are then congratulated and welcomed into the family of Christ. We often add them to our personal salvation count. I attended a church for a season where the message could be on a non-salvation topic such as 5 steps to a better work week. Towards the end of the service, an altar call would be given inviting those who wanted to accept Jesus into their heart to raise their hand. While these individuals continued to sit in their chairs, they repeated the sinner's prayer along with the entire congregation. Once this was done, they would be welcomed into the family of Christ. No discussion on sin, repentance, the cross, shed blood, resurrection, Lordship, etc. Nothing.

I typically have no idea what is truly going on in any person's heart or mind, but it concerns me that we can automatically state that a person is born again by simply saying such a prayer. Did this prayer 'accomplish' what it intended to do, or was it more of a feel-good insurance policy against which no claim could be filed. I wonder how many people are walking around today believing they are Christians because they said a sinner's prayer, but who aren't truly saved. I have the same concern for those who profess to be Christians because *'they are good people'*, *'were raised in a Christian home'*, *'have gone to church all their life'* or *'were water baptized as a baby'*.

Believers are called to make disciples. To me, part of discipling someone starts before the 'sinner's prayer' or equivalent. I believe some elementary teachings of sin, of their need to realize they are a sinner of their need for a savior (using the Roman's Road or Ray Comfort's approach are good for this), and their need to change their minds, making Jesus central in their lives and to be their Lord. The basics of Jesus's shed blood, death, burial and resurrection, the gift of salvation, and the grace and mercy of God are all important to address, albeit very briefly. With this in mind, a discussion of what a sinner's prayer represents would then seem to be in order.

- 4:32 If the focus is getting someone to say a sinner's prayer, could doing so be potentially irresponsible if the person hasn't truly decided to change their way of thinking and want Jesus in their lives? Could they just be saying it as an insurance policy or to be polite? Could we leave the five and fly interaction (five minutes together before we fly away/leave) believing they are saved when they aren't?
- 4:33 God's word tells us we are to make disciples. Thus, when someone does accept the Lord, doesn't the person who participated in this wonderful event have a responsibility to help the new believer get started? Giving them a Bible? Helping them locate a quality church near where they live? Recommending some online Bible teachers that are solid on the basics? Praying for them?

When we do lead someone in a form of sinner's prayer, I think it's wise to help them understand that they probably understand very little about God, about what Jesus did for them, about what is involved in having Jesus as Lord and Savior - and that those limitations are perfectly ok and normal. People need to understand that God knows where they're at, and He simply wants them to come to Him just as they are, but with a sincere heart to seek and be with Him.

4: Born Again/Salvation

If you're inclined to use an expanded sinner's prayer, here's a few thoughts.

Limited Knowledge / Heart Condition:	*"Lord Jesus, I come to you today with limited understanding, but what I lack in understanding, hopefully my heart makes up for it in desire. I thank You for offering me the free gift of eternal life, the gift of having an eternal, personal relationship with You.*
Acknowledge am a sinner and need a Savior:	*Jesus, I realize I'm a sinner although I don't understand the extent to which I have sinned. I believe that You are without sin, and that my sins prevent me from have a personal relationship with You.*
Believe in Jesus:	*While I don't claim to know a whole lot, I do believe Jesus that You are God. You humbled yourself and came to earth where You paid the penalty for my sins by dying on the cross for me. I also believe that You were resurrected on the 3rd day, and as a result, I believe You are the one and only Savior, not only for me but for all of mankind. I believe in You Jesus and thank You for the gift of salvation where Your shed blood washes me clean, and enables me to enter into a relationship with You, Holy Spirit and Father God.*
Repent:	*I am truly sorry for my sins Jesus and I want to change my life so that it is built around You. I don't know what that looks like, but I trust that You will help me live a life that is new, and involves me turning from my old ways to a new life where You are central, to a life that honors You.*
Confess/Ask:	*Jesus, I come to You and ask for Your forgiveness of my sins and that You change my heart and mind, that You help me turn away from my sins and things that aren't right, things and ways that aren't of You, and towards those things and ways that are of You. I ask You to come into my life and change me so that my life honors and pleases You. Please bring people into my life to come alongside me to help me walk more closely with You. Thank You Jesus. Amen."*

Having all said the above, every person's journey and situation is different. Some individuals are born again through the intellectual study of God's Word and realizing the truth as Holy Spirit speaks to them through the Bible. Others may be like me and find God out of desperate cries for help, or seeing His presence in His Creations in this world. Others may hear the gospel and just know they have to pursue Jesus, even though they understand virtually nothing. Others may have a powerful encounter with God. The words in a prayer, in whatever form they take if any, are key but I suggest the condition of one's heart is even more key. And thus, we need to be careful not to try to follow some formula. For some, their words may

CEASED?

be very few, as in my case, and simply a desperate cry of *"Jesus, help me!"*

As part of initial discipleship, I also suggest we make it clear to a person that, if we are truly born again, there will be evidence in the days and weeks ahead. Our attitudes towards sins in our life will change, our desire to read God's Word will change, our desire to be around believers will change, our demeanor will change. Whatever our situation, God will start changing us, and there should be evidence of change. And these changes, as mentioned before, will also involve changes in the fruit of the Spirit.

- *Galatians 5:22 But the fruit of the Spirit is love, joy, peace, patience, kindness, goodness, faithfulness, 23 gentleness, self-control; against such things there is no law.*

This transformation in our heart and life is part of sanctification where there is a noticeable shift away from sin and towards holiness. A person will usually know in their knower they are saved, because some transformation will have occurred. And how can it not? After all, as discussed in Chapter 6, Holy Spirit - God Almighty - comes in [en] us when we're born again.

4:34 When we're discipling a new believer or helping someone who is seeking Jesus, again I ask, can we ever go wrong by asking Holy Spirit what He wants us to do or say?

'KEEPING' OUR SALVATION

After we're born again, many believers think we have to do good works to keep our salvation; other believers do not. Some scriptures certainly make this topic an interesting one. For instance, we are told to work out our salvation and that persevering in good works brings benefits related to immortality, to eternal life.

- *Philippians 2:12 So then, my beloved, just as you have always obeyed, not as in my presence only, but now much more in my absence, **work out your salvation** with fear and trembling;*
- *Romans 2:6 who will render to each person according to his deeds: 7 to those **who by perseverance in doing good seek** for glory and honor and **immortality, eternal life**;*

When we're born again, there is no question we're called to do good works.

- *Titus 2:14 who gave Himself for us to redeem us from every lawless deed, and to purify for Himself a people for His own possession, **zealous for good deeds**.*

The issue is whether works keeps our salvation, or only bring rewards in heaven.

- *Matthew 5:12 Rejoice and be glad, for **your reward in heaven is great**; for in the same way they persecuted the prophets who were before you.*
- *1 Corinthians 3:11 For no man can lay a foundation other than the one which is laid, which is Jesus Christ. 12 Now if any man builds on the foundation with gold, silver, precious stones, wood, hay, straw, 13 each man's work will become evident; for the day will show it because it is to be revealed with fire, and the fire itself will test the quality of each man's work. 14 **If any man's work which he has built on it remains, he will receive a reward.***

4: Born Again/Salvation

Working out our salvation is a major and often controversial topic, and a full discussion is beyond the scope of **CEASED?** A few comments though, beginning with these two scriptures:

- *Ephesians 1:13 In Him, you also, after listening to the message of truth, the gospel of your salvation -* **having also believed***, you were* **sealed in Him with the Holy Spirit of promise***,*
- *Romans 8:38 For I am convinced that* **neither** *death, nor life, nor angels, nor principalities, nor things present, nor things to come, nor powers, 39 nor height, nor depth, nor any other created thing,* **will be able to separate us from the love of God, which is in Christ Jesus our Lord***.*

4:35 Do these scriptures indicate that once we're **truly** born again and saved, we're sealed and saved permanently? Or only temporarily?

Consider Galatians 3:24-29.

- *Galatians 3:24 Therefore the* **Law has become our tutor** *to* **lead us to Christ***, so that* **we may be justified by faith***. 25* **But now that faith has come***, we are* **no longer under a tutor***. 26 For you* **are all sons of God through faith in Christ Jesus***. 27 For* **all** *of you who* **were baptized into Christ have clothed yourselves with Christ***. 28 There is neither Jew nor Greek, there is neither slave nor free man, there is neither male nor female; for* **you are all one in Christ Jesus***. 29 And* **if you belong to Christ***, then you are Abraham's descendants, heirs according to promise.*

4:36 When saved, Holy Spirit comes in [en] us. Jesus is in us. We're a new creation. We're adopted into the family of God. We're sons and daughters of Christ. We're clothed with Christ. We're joint-heirs. We're one in Christ. We're seated in heavenly places with Christ. We're Christ's sent ones, His ambassadors. We're part of the royal priesthood. If we're God's children and belong to Him, other than a direct and clear rejection of Christ, can our status with God change? Consider Revelations 3:5.

- *Revelation 3:5* **He who overcomes** *will thus be clothed in white garments; and* **I will not erase his name from the book of life***, and I will confess his name before My Father and before His angels.*

Does Revelations 3:5 suggest our name can be erased from the book of life if we don't overcome? And that all of the above and other blessings leave as well? Each of us has to decide the truth for ourselves.

4:37 If we're truly born again and a follower of Christ, shouldn't the issue be fairly simple? Shouldn't we have such a desire to follow Jesus that we don't need a theological interpretation to give us peace that once we're saved, we're always saved? Shouldn't our peace come from our desire to grow in our personal relationship with Jesus? And from a risk management standpoint, why would anyone take the chance on losing their eternal salvation? Life on earth is a matter of years while eternity is a long time, as in forever. And as

CEASED?

Paul says, pursuing Jesus is so worth it.
- *Philippians 3:7 But whatever things were gain to me, those things I have counted as loss for the sake of Christ. 8 More than that, I count all things to be loss in view of the **surpassing value of knowing Christ Jesus my Lord, for whom I have suffered the loss of all things, and count them but rubbish so that I may gain Christ.***

Spirit, Soul and Body - What Rules

When we're born again, our sins are forgiven, we're made clean, we're redeemed and our spirit is made right with God. Our souls and bodies, however, are not perfected. Our souls (mind, will, emotions) need work. Before being born again, our spirits are dead. Our souls rule. When born again, our spirits come to life and our connection with God through Holy Spirit is established. A challenge for us then becomes - what is going to rule our lives - our souls or our spirits? Our souls are used to being in charge. Holy Spirit coming in [en] a person can have a dramatic effect and major changes are sometimes immediate (per Chapter 6). Our spirits can begin to rule from the very get-go. For others, changes occur at a slower pace and we may go one day where we follow our flesh (desires of body and soul) to the next day where we follow what our spirit wants (Godly living) which is being led by Holy Spirit.
- *Romans 8:14 For all who are being led by the Spirit of God, these are sons of God.*

We know that what we watch and read greatly influences our thought life, decision making and actions. Our minds need to be renewed such that we think in alignment with God's desires.
- *Romans 12:2 And do not be conformed to this world, **but be transformed by the renewing of your mind**, so that you may prove what the will of God is, that which is good and acceptable and perfect.*

Our will needs to make choices in alignment with God's desires. And our emotions need to be influenced by God's desires. God's Word is alive and active and if we study and apply what it says, the Bible will be key in changing our lives from where our soul rules to where our spirit rules.
- *Hebrews 4:12 For the **word of God is living and active** and sharper than any two-edged sword, and **piercing as far as the division of soul and spirit**, of both joints and marrow, and able to judge the thoughts and intentions of the heart.*
- *Isaiah 55:11 So will My word be which goes forth from My mouth; it will not return to Me empty, without accomplishing what I desire, and without succeeding in the matter for which I sent it.*

On those days when our spirit rules, we're traveling on 'Route 3: Dying to Self'.
- *Galatians 5:24 Now those who belong to Christ Jesus have crucified the flesh with its passions and desires.*
- *Colossians 3:3 For you have died and your life is hidden with Christ in God.*

4: Born Again/Salvation

- *Matthew 16:24 Then Jesus said to His disciples, "If anyone wishes to come after Me, he must deny himself, and take up his cross and follow Me.*

After being born again, with Holy Spirit in [en] us, another key factor influencing whether our soul or spirit rules is the time we spend alone with God - talking, listening, giving praise, crying, worshipping, laughing - things associated with having a personal relationship with Christ.

Risk, Faith Without Works is Dead

I'd also like to touch on the issue of faith without works. To begin, we know we cannot please God without faith.
- *Hebrews 11:6 And **without faith it is impossible to please Him**, for he who comes to God must believe that He is and that He is a rewarder of those who seek Him.*

James 2 tells us without works, our faith is dead.
- *James 2:17 Even so **faith, if it has no works, is dead**, being by itself. 18 But someone may well say, "You have faith and I have works; show me your faith without the works, and I will show you my faith by my works." 19 You believe that God is one. You do well; the demons also believe, and shudder. 20 But are you willing to recognize, you foolish fellow, that faith without works is useless?*

Many view James 2:17 as meaning - if we don't have good works in our lives, we have no evidence to show we are saved. Without good works, moreover, we may not even be saved. As a result, we better do some good works. Let me try to share another perspective other believers have shared with me over the years. To start, we need to realize we can't please God without faith.
- *Hebrews 11:6 And **without faith it is impossible to please Him** …*

To have faith involves dealing with the unknown, something unseen.
- *Hebrews 11:1 Now faith is the assurance of things hoped for, the **conviction of things not seen**.*

Consider two scenarios involving Bobby and Robin, both of whom love God, and love to feed and care for the homeless. Bobby is part of a big church that provides all the resources required. Bobby and four others receive the church funds, buy the food, prepare it, and serve ~200 people every week. Does Bobby require faith to feed the homeless? Was he dealing with uncertainties, with things not seen? I suggest the answer is no.

Robin, on the other hand, is part of a small body of believers with limited resources. Robin prays and every time God tells her to purchase groceries and prepare a meal for the homeless, she does so. This one week, she believes God tells her to go and buy 1 loaf of bread, small-sized condiments, and enough meat and cheese for 10 sandwiches. After doing so, God tells her to go to an empty parking lot near a homeless camp where Robin will feed over 200 people. Ten sandwiches and 200 people doesn't add up. To feed all 200 would require God doing something supernatural including providing additional help. If God doesn't do something supernatural - if God doesn't come through - failure is inevitable.

Before going further, let me say both Bobby and Robin are doing commendable works of God. And all of us should have good works going on in our lives, and that we do so out of love for God and people. We don't keep score of what we do, nor do we keep score of what others do or don't do. I don't value one person over the other, or one ministry over the other. But let me ask:

4:38   Does Robin show faith by buying enough groceries for a few, but then going forward fully expecting to feed many more than a few?

4:39   Would this be evidence of Robin *'showing her faith by her works'*? In other words, does faith involve risk - the risk that requires us to rely on God - to trust God - for the desired outcome?

4:40   Should the lives of today's believers have elements of risk where, if God doesn't come through, we cannot succeed? If not, how do we show faith?
- *Hebrews 11:1 Now faith ... **conviction of things not seen**.*
- *Hebrews 11:6 And **without faith it is impossible to please Him** ...*
- *James 2:17 Even so faith, **if it has no works, is dead, being by itself**.*

I've not seen this kind of food multiplication first hand. However, people we met in Mexico say it occurs all the time in their orphanage. A former student told me of a dinner meeting involving about 30 individuals. He was cooking and put in one package of spaghetti before he was distracted and forgot to put in the rest of the spaghetti. Everybody was fed. When they went to clean up, they looked at all the unopened spaghetti bags and realized only 1 bag was used. That opened the door to share the gospel. A different kind of situation, but one that shows God still does unexpected stuff today. Lori was on deployment as a chaplain in Australia just as the COVID-19 virus was breaking out. She witnessed first-hand Godly multiplication of food one evening.

Should Prayer Involve Risk

Consider Peter who was key in a paralyzed man being healed.
- *Acts 3:6 But Peter said, "I do not possess silver and gold, but what I do have I give to you: In the name of Jesus Christ the Nazarene - walk!" 7 And seizing him by the right hand, he raised him up; and immediately his feet and his ankles were strengthened.*

4:41   When Peter *spoke "... In the name of Jesus Christ the Nazarene – walk!"* was he doing so in faith? Was Peter taking a risk by boldly and publicly telling this man to get up and walk? Was he taking a risk of being ridiculed if God didn't come through and heal this man?

4:42   Is this an example of the kind of risk believers are to engage in today as part of what God wants us to do?
- *Mark 16:17 These **signs will accompany those who have believed**: in My name they will **cast out demons**, they will **speak with new tongues**; 18 they will pick up serpents, and if they drink any deadly poison, it will not hurt them; they will **lay hands on the sick, and they will recover**.*

4:43   If we don't take risks doing God's works, are we limiting our walk? Have we

4: Born Again/Salvation

reduced the inherent value, and excitement, of this amazing relationship?
- ❏ *James 2:20 But are you willing to recognize, you foolish fellow, that faith without works is useless?*

4:44 On the other hand, when Peter spoke *"... In the name of Jesus Christ the Nazarene - walk!"*
   i. was he obeying what Holy Spirit was telling him to do, just as Jesus only did what He saw the Father doing?
   ii. And thus, while on the surface it may appear Peter was taking a risk, how much of a risk was he actually taking if he was simply doing what Holy Spirit told him to do?
   iii. So I ask again, how can we go wrong by asking Holy Spirit what to say or do?
   iv. One other question. Do Peter's words show the power of the spoken words of believers of Jesus, words that align with God's Word and are part of our mandate?
- ❏ *John 5:19 Therefore Jesus answered and was saying to them, "Truly, truly, I say to you, the Son can do nothing of Himself, unless it is something He sees the Father doing; for whatever the Father does, these things the Son also does in like manner.*

In What/Whom is Our Faith

Another part of faith is who or what we have faith in. Peter spoke on this in Acts 3.
- ❏ *Acts 3:16 And on the **basis of faith in His name, it is the name of Jesus** which has strengthened this man whom you see and know; and the faith which comes through Him has given him this perfect health in the presence of you all.*

4:45 Does Acts 3:16 indicate the key is i) **who** Peter had faith in, namely Jesus and His name, as opposed to ii) the amount of faith Peter had?

4:46 Many in false religions have a deep faith and belief in their leader or leaders. Does their great faith do these individuals any good from an eternal perspective? If yes, how?

CAN WE LOSE OUR SALVATION
Unforgiveness

One aspect of salvation that has much disagreement is whether or not a believer can lose their salvation. One of the contributing factors to this disagreement is what happens if we don't forgive.
- ❏ *Matthew 6:15 But if you do not forgive others, then your Father will not forgive your transgressions.*

Consider person XYZ who does something atrocious to Believer B such as assaulting B, stealing a major amount of B's money, or murdering someone B loved deeply. Three days after the atrocious event, Believer B is killed in an accident without having forgiven XYZ. A literal interpretation of Matthew 6:15 suggests B would have lost his/her salvation. But let me ask:

CEASED?

4:47 Would God have taken into consideration the nature of the offense and recognized that immediate forgiveness may have been very difficult for B?

4:48 Would B have maintained his/her salvation if he/she had said the words *'I forgive you XYZ'* without actually meaning them in his/her heart?

4:49 There are levels of forgiveness ranging from forcing the words out of one's mouth, to wanting the offender to be radically blessed by God. At what level does B's forgiveness need to reach in order to retain their salvation?

In recent times, some high-profile Christians have said they *'lost their faith'* and are no longer Christians. I don't reject the idea that it is possible to be born again and saved, but later on totally reject God and walk away from their Christian faith. But I also wonder if sometimes, losing one's faith is not an issue of losing faith and thus one's salvation, but an issue of having difficulty dealing with hurt(s) from other believer(s), or blaming God for not preventing something tragic from happening. And if this is where you're at, I am so sorry. I pray your heart will be healed.

4:50 In other cases, though, did some individuals who lost their faith have an 'intellectual' or 'religious' faith where Christianity sounded like the right thing to abide by, where Jesus represented the kind of person they could follow, where a Christian church felt like a good place to attend or even work for, but a faith where there was no actual transforming relationship with Jesus where Holy Spirit actually came in [en] them? In other words, were they saved in the first place and had a personal relationship with Jesus to lose? Was the seed not planted in good soil to begin with?

❑ *Luke 8:12 Those beside the road are those who have heard; then the devil comes and takes away the word from their heart, so that they will not believe and be saved. 13 Those on the rocky soil are those who, when they hear, receive the word with joy; and these have no firm root; they believe for a while, and in time of temptation fall away. 14 The seed which fell among the thorns, these are the ones who have heard, and as they go on their way they are choked with worries and riches and pleasures of this life, and bring no fruit to maturity.*

Ongoing Confession of Sins

Many people believe we need to regularly confess our sins to keep our salvation. James 5:16 is often cited as a key verse in this regard.

❑ *James 5:16 Therefore, **confess your sins to one another** ...*

But consider the next few words in James 5:16.

❑ *James 5:16 Therefore, confess your sins to one another, and pray for one another **so that you may be healed**. The effective prayer of a righteous man can accomplish much.*

4:51 Thus, are we to confess our faults (sins) to one another and to pray for one another so we can be healed in our souls and/or bodies? If not, why not?

If you disagree with that view, let's try to put the context of James 5:16 into perspective. Consider the scriptures immediately preceding James 5:16.

❑ *James 5:13 **Is anyone among you suffering**? Then he must pray. Is anyone*

4: Born Again/Salvation

*cheerful? He is to sing praises. 14 **Is anyone among you sick**? Then he must call for the elders of the church and they are to pray over him, anointing him with oil in the name of the Lord; 15 and **the prayer offered in faith will restore the one who is sick**, and the Lord will raise him up ...*
- *Psalm 32:3 When **I kept silent about my sin, my body wasted away** ...*

Sins impact our soul and body. Confessing sins is important for that reason. But is there more to the story? Consider Proverbs 28:13.
- *Proverbs 28:13 He who **conceals his transgressions will not prosper**, But he who confesses and forsakes them will find compassion.*

4:52 In addition, consider our relationship with God. When we're born again, Holy Spirit comes in [en] us. When we sin, and God is right there within us, doesn't that inhibit the closeness of our walk with God? Many believers struggle with habitual sins such as porn. If a person watches porn, God is there. Right there. Would there be a different response from God for a person who has a truly repentant heart and desperately wants to stop porn as compared to a person who watches porn, isn't sorry apart from a little guilt, perhaps confesses to another person but all the time knowing and expecting and perhaps looking forward to the next porn session? Won't God respond quite differently?

4:53 And if a person is engaged in habitual sin and doesn't have a strong desire to stop sinning, is there reason to be concerned:
   i. the person may be under demonic influence;
   ii. the person is motivated by soul issues that are so painful that the addiction is the one thing they can rely on to help them escape the pain right then; and/or
   iii. the person may not be born again?

In the natural, we don't know the issues a person faces which is why Holy Spirit guiding us is so essential. Issues related to one's sin(s) can be complex. Other scriptures show the importance of confessing sins.
- *1 John 1:8 If **we say that we have no sin, we are deceiving ourselves** and the **truth is not in us**. 9 If we confess our sins, He is faithful and righteous to forgive us our sins and to cleanse us from all unrighteousness.*
- *Psalm 32:5 I acknowledged my sin to You, and my iniquity I did not hide; I said, "I will confess my transgressions to the Lord"; and You forgave the guilt of my sin. Selah.*

I find it interesting that while forgiveness of sins is mentioned, the issue of eternal salvation is not. The reality is Jesus paid the penalty for all our sins. When born again, we are His bride. But ... we mess up and sin. Sinning is a given for all of us. But God gives us a way to make things right.

4:54 Thus, when truly born again and Holy Spirit is in [en] us, don't we confess our sins first and foremost because of the inherent desire to keep a close, personal relationship with God, to not have this relationship compromised by sin, to want to make things right when we do wrong? And other benefits such as healing are secondary? If not, why not?

By the way, if you struggle with habitual sin, take serious actions. Pray. Set alarms to remind you to read a scripture or speak it out loud. Print scriptures and put them in your pocket. Pray. Get apps such as *"Shut Up Devil"*. Seek God. Change friends. Move. Get a dumb phone. Get alone with God. Cancel the internet. Always have gospel music or a teaching playing in the background. Place Bibles everywhere. Wear a reminder band around your wrists. And know Jesus loves you.

COMMUNION – SYMBOLIC OR LITERAL AND FOR FORGIVENESS OF SINS, OR REMEMBRANCE ONLY

One of the goals of **CEASED?** was to address some issues making it difficult for Protestants and Roman Catholics to evangelize and worship together. Communion is one of those key issues. It's a very big issue for me, and thus I cover this issue in some depth. If you're Roman Catholic, please know I'm not questioning if you're a Christian. I'm just trying to examine the issue in detail.

Roman Catholic teachings hold that a key reason for taking communion is to gain forgiveness for 'venial' sins, lesser sins that won't cause a person to lose their salvation. Communion is not enough, however, to cover 'mortal' sins which can cause one's salvation to be lost. To gain forgiveness of mortal sins, they must be confessed to a Catholic priest. Most Protestants struggle at the get-go because we believe Jesus's one-time sacrifice was enough for all sins. We don't see the Bible differentiating between sins wherein one approach deals with one group of sins, while a different approach is required for another group of sins.

Most Protestants see communion as a way to remember what Jesus did for us on the cross, His one-time, finishing sacrifice which paid the penalty for all sins.

- ❏ *Luke 22:19 And when He had taken some bread and given thanks, He broke it and gave it to them, saying, "This is My body which is given for you; **do this in remembrance of Me**."*
- ❏ *1 Peter 3:18 For Christ also **died for sins once for all**, the just for the unjust, so that He might bring us to God, having been put to death in the flesh, but made alive in the spirit;*
- ❏ *John 19:30 Therefore when Jesus had received the sour wine, He said, **"It is finished!"** And He bowed His head and gave up His spirit.*

As a result of Jesus's one-time finishing sacrifice, most Protestants view the eating of the bread and the drinking of the juice/wine as being symbolic - a tangible act to remember what Jesus did. Many Protestants also believe that while communion is not about forgiveness of new sins, other blessings can come from communion. We also believe Jesus is present when we take communion.

- ❏ *Matthew 18:20 For **where two or three have gathered together in My name, I am there in their midst**."*

4: Born Again/Salvation

Roman Catholic teachings agree that communion is taken to remember Jesus. The key difference is that the Catholic church - some Protestant churches, notably in Anglican and Lutheran denominations - teach that eating the bread/wafer and drinking the wine/juice aren't symbolic acts, but literal acts. In other words, eating the wafer and drinking the wine involves actually eating Jesus's body and drinking His blood.

4:55 If Almighty God was 'in' the wafer and wine, wouldn't it seem logical that DNA and other scientific tests of a regular wafer and a Jesus-filled wafer would show radical differences? Catholic apologists admit there's no difference if/when such tests are done. Regardless of what arguments are used to justify that result, doesn't it seem unusual there is no change when the Creator of the entire universe is in the wafer and wine?

To examine the scriptural evidence, consider Jesus's teachings in John 6 that occurred **before** the Last Supper. Jesus is referred to as the bread who gives life.
- ❑ *John 6:33 For the **bread of God** is that which comes down out of heaven, and **gives life** to the world."*
- ❑ *John 6:35 Jesus said to them, "I am the **bread of life**; he who comes to Me **will not hunger**, and he who believes in Me will never thirst.*
- ❑ *John 6:48 I am the **bread of life**.*

4:56 Do these scriptures suggest the 'bread' is actual bread, or is symbolic of the spiritual food and spiritual life that Jesus provides all believers?

Jesus also says anyone who eats the bread will receive spiritual life on earth and into eternity.
- ❑ *John 6:51 I am the **living bread** that came down out of heaven; if **anyone eats of this bread**, he will live forever; and **the bread also which I will give for the life of the world is My flesh**."*
- ❑ *John 6:52 Then the Jews began to argue with one another, saying, "How can this man give us His flesh to eat?" 53 So Jesus said to them, "Truly, truly, I say to you, **unless you eat the flesh of the Son of Man and drink His blood, you have no life in yourselves**. 54 **He who eats My flesh and drinks My blood has eternal life**, and I will raise him up on the last day.*
- ❑ *John 6:55 For My **flesh is true food**, and My blood is true drink. 56 **He who eats My flesh and drinks My blood abides in Me, and I in him**. 57 As the living Father sent Me, and I live because of the Father, **so he who eats Me, he also will live because of Me**. 58 This is the bread which came down out of heaven; not as the fathers ate and died; **he who eats this bread will live forever**."*

No question Jesus gives life, but this teaching was unusual and led to many deciding not to walk with Jesus. And if I was there, I might have been one of them.
- ❑ *John 6:59 These things He said in the synagogue as He taught in Capernaum. 60 Therefore many of His disciples, when they heard this said, "This is a difficult statement; who can listen to it?" ... 66 As **a result of this many of His disciples withdrew and were not walking with Him anymore**.*

CEASED?

Because Jesus "Said So"

Information from the Baltimore Catechism in the Q&A section of the website: www.ewtn.com/catholicism/teachings/eucharist-gives-us-jesus-christ-150 explains the reason we should take the body and blood literally is because we should take the words of Jesus - God Almighty - literally.

"... a) Christ could not have used clearer, more explicit words than "This is My body." He did not say, "This is a sign of My body," or "This represents My body," but, "This is My body." **Catholics take Christ at His word because He is the omnipotent God. On His word they know that the Holy Eucharist is the body and blood of Christ***."*

4:57 In other words, we're to take Jesus's word's literally because Jesus is God and what God says, He means. On that basis, if we're to treat Jesus's references to the bread and wine as literal references to Christ's body and blood because Jesus spoke words to that effect, aren't we then required to treat all - as in all - of Jesus's words in a literal way? If not, why not?

Consider the following scriptures:
- ❑ *John 10:7 So Jesus said to them again, "Truly, truly, I say to you, I am the **door** of the **sheep**.*
- ❑ *John 15:1 I am the true **vine**, and My Father is the **vinedresser**. Every **branch in Me** that does not bear fruit, He takes away; and every branch that bears fruit, He prunes it so that it may bear more fruit.*

4:58 If we're to take everything Jesus said in a literal way, how do we take these descriptions of Jesus being a door and a vine in a literal way? Moreover, how do we look at ourselves since we would not only be human, but also part sheep and part branch? I don't mean to be funny or sarcastic when I ask this, but if we're to take this perspective seriously, could someone be blamed for asking if we need to feed ourselves food that sheep enjoy such as grass or wheat?

The Disciples and the Last Supper

When Jesus next taught on eating His body and drinking His blood in Mark 14, He did so at the Last Supper which occurred just before the cross. This Last Supper was a Passover meal.
- ❑ *Mark 14:22 While they were eating, He took some bread, and after a blessing* **He broke it, and gave it to them, and said, "Take it; this is My body."**

4:59 Given the Roman Catholic argument that we are to literally take Jesus's words of eating His body and drinking His blood, communion is not to be taken symbolically, let me ask.
   i. Shouldn't this literal application also apply to the Last Supper when Jesus was present and actually spoke the words to eat His body and drink His blood? If not, why not?
   ii. Furthermore, given Jesus said the bread was His body, wouldn't Catholic reasoning tell us to believe at the very moment Jesus was giving out the bread that it wasn't just bread, but bread that included the actual

4: Born Again/Salvation

           physical body of Christ? If not, why not since Jesus said it was His body?
    iii. Given that Jesus had not yet been crucified on the cross, been buried, or ascended to the right hand of Father God, how could the bread be His mangled body? And how could the wine be His shed blood, if His blood had not been shed?
    iv. Was the breaking of bread at the Last Supper thus a symbolic act?
    v. If so, per Catholic teaching, wouldn't that contradict what Jesus said when He said *"Take it; this is My body"* and cause us to be inconsistent by taking Jesus's words literally in one case but symbolically in another?

And please let me remind you, as I ask these questions, I believe it's vital we take Jesus's words seriously and to treat communion with utmost reverence and deep gratitude, and to appreciate the elements not for what they are (bread and wine/juice) but for Who and what they represent.

4:60 This first communion does not appear to involve an unbloody sacrifice/death of Christ. No priest is involved in commanding Jesus to come to earth. Jesus never indicated there would be anything different about the eating of the bread and drinking the wine in the future. As a result, don't we have a rather large gap between communion at the Last Supper and communion as per Catholic church teachings today?

Context for the Last Supper - a Passover Meal

At a Passover meal, several food items and cups of wine were used as symbols to help tell the story of the redemption of Israel, of their being set free from slavery in Egypt. Three pieces of bread covered by a cloth were on the table. One of the 4 cups of wine placed on the table was for the Prophet Elijah who would signal the arrival of the Messiah. The cup was not to be consumed.

4:61 Were the 3 pieces of bread a foreshadowing of the 3 days between Christ's crucifixion and resurrection? When Jesus raised the cup at the Last Supper, was the cup He raised and which the disciples drank from, the cup reserved for the Messiah? Was Jesus emphatically stating again that He was the Messiah, and that the Messiah had arrived?

Reaction of Disciples

❑ *Mark 14:23 And when He had taken a cup and given thanks, He gave it to them, **and they all drank from it**. 24 And He said to them, "**This is My blood** of the covenant, which is poured out for many.*

4:62 The disciples ate the bread, and then drank from the cup. If Jesus was truly saying His body was in the bread, is it reasonable to expect one or more of the disciples would have asked Jesus how could the bread be His physical body given Jesus was sitting or standing there with all His body parts intact? Or were they accustomed to the symbolism of Passover foods and drinks?

There was no apparent abnormal reaction from the disciples when they ate the bread and drank from the cup at the Last Supper. After the Last Supper was completed, Jesus washed the feet of His apostles. Peter, who had no issue eating the bread and drinking the wine, reacted strongly.

CEASED?

> ❑ *John 13:3 Jesus ... 5 Then He poured water into the basin, and began to wash the disciples' feet and to wipe them with the towel with which He was girded. 6 So He came to Simon Peter. He said to Him, "Lord, do You wash my feet?" 7 Jesus answered and said to him, "What I do you do not realize now, but you will understand hereafter." 8 Peter said to Him, "Never shall You wash my feet!" Jesus answered him, "If I do not wash you, you have no part with Me." 9 Simon Peter said to Him, "Lord, then wash not only my feet, but also my hands and my head."*

Peter expressed major reservations about Jesus washing his feet. After the cross, Peter also expressed strong reservations about eating animals and birds when God gave Peter a vision about eating animals and birds.

> ❑ *Acts 10:12 and there were in it all kinds of four-footed animals and crawling creatures of the earth and birds of the air. 13 A voice came to him, "Get up, Peter, kill and eat!" 14 But Peter said, **"By no means, Lord, for I have never eaten anything unholy and unclean**."*

4:63   Does Peter's strong and emotional reactions to having his feet washed, and eating these unclean animals and birds, seem inconsistent with his lack of reaction to partaking of bread and wine if indeed Peter believed he was consuming Jesus's body and blood?

Consider Mark 4 which tells us that Jesus used parables extensively in His teaching, and that Jesus would explain the parable to His disciples in private.

> ❑ *Mark 4:33 **With many such parables** He was speaking the word to them, so far as they were able to hear it; 34 and **He did not speak to them without a parable**; but **He was explaining everything privately to His own disciples**.*

Prior to the Last Supper, Jesus had previously talked to the crowds and His disciples about eating His body and drinking His blood.

> ❑ *John 6:55 For My **flesh is true food**, and My blood is true drink. 56 **He who eats My flesh and drinks My blood abides in Me, and I in him.** 57 As the living Father sent Me, and I live because of the Father, **so he who eats Me, he also will live because of Me**. 58 This is the bread which came down out of heaven; not as the fathers ate and died; **he who eats this bread will live forever**."*

4:64   Based on Mark 4:34, Jesus would have explained what He meant by eating His body and drinking His blood when Jesus first raised the issue. Thus, by the time the Last Supper rolled around, the apostles knew the truth on the matter. Would the lack of a reaction from Peter and the other apostles to eating the bread and drinking the wine at the Last Supper be understandable and consistent with their other behaviors if they believed they were eating the bread and drinking the wine in a symbolic act to remember Jesus?

> ❑ *Luke 22:19 And when He had taken some bread and given thanks, He broke it and gave it to them, saying, "This is My body which is given for you; **do this in remembrance of Me**."*

4: Born Again/Salvation

It's also worth noting the apostles' reaction as reported in Luke.
- *Luke 22:19 And when He had taken some bread and given thanks, He broke it and gave it to them, saying, **"This is My body which is given for you; do this in remembrance of Me."** 20 And in the same way He took the cup after they had eaten, saying, **"This cup which is poured out for you is the new covenant in My blood**. 21 But **behold, the hand of the one betraying Me is with Mine on the table**. 22 For indeed, the Son of Man is going as it has been determined; but woe to that man by whom He is betrayed!" 23 And they began to discuss among themselves which one of them it might be who was going to do this thing. **24 And there arose also a dispute among them as to which one of them was regarded to be greatest**.*

The apostles had no apparent reaction to the notion of *'eating'* Jesus's body and *'drinking'* His blood. When Jesus advises the apostles one of them will betray Him, they are most concerned. After discussing that, the disciples then talk about which apostle was the greatest.

4:65 If indeed the apostles believed they were eating the body of Jesus and drinking the blood of Jesus - the person standing right there in front of them and giving out the elements - isn't it awfully surprising that the disciples' reaction was not one of questioning, shock or concern of being involved in an act that some have labeled as getting close to cannibalism, but instead:
   i. debated who might be the one who would betray Jesus; and then
   ii. discussed which one of them was the greatest?

4:66 The discussion on the greatest was not the first time this issue had arisen. In their previous discussion, they were reluctant to admit this reality to Jesus. How could discussions about who would betray Jesus and who was the greatest - an issue they knew was not a discussion they should be having - take priority in their hearts and minds over consuming the actual body and blood of Jesus if that's what they were actually doing?
- *Matthew 18:1 At that time the disciples came to Jesus and said, "Who then is greatest in the kingdom of heaven?"*
- *Mark 9:33 They came to Capernaum; and when He was in the house, He began to question them, "What were you discussing on the way?" 34 But they kept silent, for on the way they had discussed with one another which of them was the greatest.*
- *Luke 9:46 An argument started among them as to which of them might be the greatest.*

Other Aspects of Catholic Communion

In Catholic communion, the belief is the priest commands Christ to come to earth where Jesus is sacrificed in an unbloody manner. His body and blood are transfigured into the wafer and wine, with only the appearance of the wafer and wine remaining. The process is called transubstantiation. From the Catholic Catechism, we read:

CEASED?

*1333 At the heart of the Eucharistic celebration are the bread and wine that, by the words of Christ and the invocation of the Holy Spirit, become Christ's Body and Blood. ... 1357 We carry out this command of the Lord by celebrating the memorial of his sacrifice. In so doing, we offer to the Father what he has himself given us: the gifts of his creation, **bread and wine** which, by the power of the Holy Spirit and by the words of Christ, **have become the body and blood of Christ. Christ is thus really and mysteriously made present** ... 1366 The Eucharist is thus a sacrifice because it re-presents (makes present) the sacrifice of the cross ... **But because his priesthood was not to end with his death,** ... **by which the bloody sacrifice which he was to accomplish once for all on the cross would be re-presented**, ... 1367 **The sacrifice of Christ and the sacrifice of the Eucharist are one single sacrifice**: "The victim is one and the same: the same now offers through the ministry of priests, who then offered himself on the cross; only the manner of offering is different." "**In this divine sacrifice** which is celebrated in the Mass, **the same Christ who offered himself once in a bloody manner** on the altar of the cross is contained and **is offered in an unbloody manner**."*

In the last sentence, it begins with *'in this divine sacrifice'* and ends with *'offered in an unbloody manner'*. This unbloody sacrifice is a critical part of Roman Catholic teachings. Let me ask:

4:67 The New Testament was written over a period of ~65 years following Christ's death and resurrection. If this additional sacrifice of Christ as per Roman Catholic teaching is critical, a must-do activity on a daily/weekly basis, isn't it a bit surprising no mention is made in the Bible of these ongoing sacrifices, or that there would be multiple sacrifices after Jesus's initial death, resurrection and ascension?

Communion: Forgiveness of Sins

The Roman Catholic Church teaches communion is taken in part for the forgiveness of venial sins. Most Protestants would disagree and believe Jesus paid the penalty for all sins on the cross.

4:68 On the basis that communion does result in forgiveness of the less serious venial sins, doesn't it seem extremely unusual that a sacrifice of Christ, Almighty God Himself, is not adequate to also deal with any outstanding more serious, mortal sins? And that confession of mortal sins to a sinful priest can accomplish what the death of Almighty God couldn't accomplish, and still can't accomplish to this day even for one person?

Jesus Forgave Sins During His Ministry

Jesus had the authority to forgive sins in His earthly ministry, an authority He used.

- ❑ *Mark 2:10 But so that you may know that the Son of Man has authority on earth to forgive sins" - He said to the paralytic,*
- ❑ *Luke 7:48 Then He said to her, "Your sins have been forgiven."*

God sent Jesus to earth with a mandate, and to fulfill the mandate, Jesus was given

4: Born Again/Salvation

authority. Jesus also sends us just as the Father sent Jesus.
- *John 20:21 So Jesus said to them again, "Peace be with you; **as the Father has sent Me, I also send you**."*

Various scriptures tell believers what we are to do - love all including our enemies, look after widows and orphans, heal the sick, cast out demons, raise the dead, make disciples, baptize etc.
- *Matthew 28:18 And Jesus came up and spoke to them, saying, "All authority has been given to Me in heaven and on earth. 19 Go therefore and **make disciples** of all the nations, **baptizing them** in the name of the Father and the Son and the Holy Spirit, 20 **teaching them** to observe all that I commanded you; and lo, I am with you always, even to the end of the age."*
- *Matthew 10:8 **Heal the sick, raise the dead, cleanse the lepers, cast out demons**. Freely you received, freely give.*
- *Luke 10:27 And he answered, "You shall **love the Lord your God** with all your heart, and with all your soul, and with all your strength, and with all your mind; and **your neighbor** as yourself."*

4:69 These and other scriptures collectively define the parameters around the scope of what we believers are to do today. To do these things, isn't it reasonable to conclude that God gives believers adequate authority to do the core things of Christianity that He wants us to do, but nothing more?

A point of disagreement between Roman Catholics and Protestants is whether or not believers have the authority to forgive sins as Jesus did. In Jesus's case, recall the paralytic and how the scribes were reasoning how Jesus could forgive sins as only God could forgive sins.
- *Mark 2:6 But some of the scribes were sitting there and reasoning in their hearts, 7 "Why does this man speak that way? He is blaspheming; **who can forgive sins but God alone?**" 8 Immediately Jesus, aware in His spirit that they were reasoning that way within themselves, said to them, "Why are you reasoning about these things in your hearts? 9 Which is easier, to say to the paralytic, 'Your sins are forgiven'; or to say, 'Get up, and pick up your pallet and walk'? 10 But so that you may know that the Son of Man has authority on earth to forgive sins" -He said to the paralytic, 11 "I say to you, get up, pick up your pallet and go home." 12 And he got up and immediately picked up the pallet and went out in the sight of everyone, so that they were all amazed and were glorifying God, saying, "We have never seen anything like this."*

Jesus didn't disagree with the statement that only God can forgive sins. In fact, He made it clear He did have the authority to forgive sins. Which raises the issue of whether or not Jesus was both man and God in His earthly life, or man but with authority given by God. I'll leave that aside for the moment, perhaps a long moment. Coming back to us today, what is rather interesting is that after His resurrection, Jesus tells His followers they are also supposed to forgive sins.

CEASED?

❑ *John 20:21 So Jesus said to them again, "Peace be with you; **as the Father has sent Me, I also send you**." 22 And when He had said this, He breathed on them and said to them, "Receive the Holy Spirit. 23 **If you forgive the sins of any, their sins have been forgiven them; if you retain the sins of any, they have been retained**."*

As said before, Roman Catholic teaching holds that venial or less significant sins can be forgiven during communion/mass. The mortal or more serious sins, however, need to be dealt with by confessing such sins to a priest. The need to confess to a priest is largely based on John 20:21-23 above. When Jesus appeared to the apostles on resurrection Sunday evening and stated He was sending them into the world just as Father God had sent Jesus, He followed that up by breathing on them, told them to receive the Holy Spirit, and then instructed them to forgive. The apostles were Jesus's ministers and by breathing the Holy Spirit on them, the apostles were empowered to forgive sins. This responsibility/authority given to the original apostles was passed on to succeeding generations, specifically to Catholic priests through the 7th sacrament of Holy Orders. Thus today, in ordinary circumstances, individuals confess their mortal sins to a priest, a proceeding known as the sacrament of reconciliation or confession.

4:70   Do any scriptures clearly state Jesus had human ministers before or after the cross? On the basis He did not, isn't referring to those gathered on resurrection Sunday evening as His ministers incorrect? If you believe scriptures show the apostles, and only the apostles, were Jesus's ministers - what are the New Testament scriptures supporting your view?

Priests, Forgiveness and Role of Apostle

Ephesians 4 tells us individuals will have different functions in the 5-fold ministry.

❑ *Ephesians 4:11 And He gave some as **apostles**, and some as **prophets**, and some as **evangelists**, and some as **pastors** and **teachers**, 12 for the equipping of the saints for the work of service, to the building up of the body of Christ;*

4:71   Within the Roman Catholic church:
   i.   are priests the only Catholics who can hold these five functions today?
   ii. If so, does every Catholic priest hold every one of these 5 positions?
   iii. If not, does that mean some priests don't have the function of an apostle?
   iv. If these positions are not limited to priests, does that mean the non-priest apostle in the Catholic church also has the ability to forgive sins?

4:72   If the responsibility of forgiving sins is limited to priests, and this responsibility is passed down starting from the apostles to priests, and from one generation of priests to the next, and if every priest is not an apostle, how can those priests who are not apostles today have the authorization/ability to forgive sins within the Roman Catholic church?

4: Born Again/Salvation

In addition, consider this. Earlier in John 19, we see Jesus appearing on resurrection Sunday evening to the disciples who were gathered. The word apostles was not used.

- *John 20:19 So when it was evening on that day, the first day of the week, and when the doors were shut where the **<u>disciples</u>** were, for fear of the Jews, Jesus came and stood in their midst and said to them, "Peace be with you."*

The English word *'disciple'* is based on the Greek word *'mathetes'* [G3101] which means a *'learner, pupil, disciple'*. And if we look at Luke 24, we see that the disciples gathered on resurrection Sunday evening when Jesus breathed on them and told them to forgive sins included not only the eleven apostles but also the 2 disciples Jesus met on the road to Emmaus.

- *Luke 24:13 And behold, **<u>two of them</u>** were going that very day to a village named Emmaus, which was about seven miles from Jerusalem ... 15 While they were talking and discussing, Jesus Himself approached and began traveling with them ... 30 When He had reclined at the table with them, He took the bread and blessed it, and breaking it, He began giving it to them. 31 Then their eyes were opened and they recognized Him; and He vanished from their sight ... 33 And **<u>they got up that very hour and returned to Jerusalem</u>**, and found gathered **<u>together the eleven</u>** and those who were with them, 34 saying, "The Lord has really risen and has appeared to Simon." 35 They began to relate their experiences on the road and how He was recognized by them in the breaking of the bread. 36 While they were telling these things, He Himself stood in their midst and said to them, "Peace be to you."*

4:73 Given these two disciples Jesus met on the road to Emmaus were with the eleven apostles when Jesus dropped in on resurrection Sunday evening and were part of the group that Jesus breathed on and told they needed to forgive sins, doesn't that mean forgiving sins was not limited to the original apostles? And thus, how is forgiving of sins limited to Catholic priests today?

4:74 Two original apostles weren't present - Judas and Thomas who would encounter Jesus 8 days later. Does the eleven on resurrection Sunday evening thus include Matthias, who was not yet an apostle, but was nonetheless breathed on and told to forgive sins?

Now consider verse 33 which reads 'And ... found ... **<u>those who were with them</u>**.'
- *Luke 24:33 And **<u>they got up</u>** that very hour and returned to Jerusalem, and found gathered **<u>together the eleven</u>** and **<u>those who were with them</u>**,*

Starting on page 107 in Chapter 6, I review evidence that shows the 11 apostles plus *'those who were with them'* on resurrection Sunday was essentially the same group of ~120 who were together in Acts 1:12-20 after Jesus ascended, and was again essentially the same group that was together at Pentecost. There were at least five women involved including Mary, the mother of Jesus.

4:75 With the ~120 in mind, consider the following:
  i. Per Chapter 6, when Jesus breathed on the disciples in John 20:22, I

believe that was the moment when the first disciples were born again, when Holy Spirit came in [en] them, and the first living Christians came into being. Some may argue the thief on the cross or those who rose from the graves between Jesus's crucifixion and resurrection were the first Christians. You can choose. But the key point to this issue is this: Is there any reason to believe Jesus did not breathe on all of those gathered including **'those who were with them'**?

    ii. Given Jesus breathed on all the disciples, and given all believers are sent ones called to share the Good News in words and power, don't Jesus's instructions on forgiving sins apply to all who were in attendance and upon whom Jesus breathed the Holy Spirit, and not just the 11 apostles? And doesn't that:

        a. contradict teachings that we need to confess mortal sins to priests; and

        b. support the notion that when the veil was torn from top to bottom, all people have direct access to God and can confess sins directly to God?

In the last chapter of Luke, no mention is made of Jesus telling His disciples they are to forgive sins. What Luke does mention is the following:

- ❖ Jesus proved He was the risen Jesus;
- ❖ all things written about Him must be fulfilled;
- ❖ He opened their minds to scriptures and talked about His need to suffer, He would rise again, and repentance of sins would be proclaimed;
- ❖ He is sending the promise of the Father; and
- ❖ they are to stay in Jerusalem until they are clothed with power on high. This power, we now know, is the Baptism of the Holy Spirit which they received at Pentecost.

❑ *Luke 24:40 And when He had said this, **He showed them His hands and His feet**. 41 While they still could not believe it because of their joy and amazement, He said to them, "Have you anything here to eat?" 42 They gave Him a piece of a broiled fish; 43 and He took it and ate it before them. 44 Now He said to them, "These are My words which I spoke to you while I was still with you, that **all things which are written about Me in the Law of Moses and the Prophets and the Psalms must be fulfilled**."*

❑ *45 Then He **opened their minds to understand the Scriptures**, 46 and He said to them, "Thus it is written, that the **Christ would suffer and rise again** from the dead the third day, 47 and that **repentance for forgiveness of sins** would be proclaimed in His name to all the nations, beginning from Jerusalem. 48 You are witnesses of these things. 49 And behold, I am **sending forth the promise of My Father upon you**; but you **are to stay in the city until you are clothed with power from on high**."*

4:76 Is it significant that Luke didn't address the issue of the disciples needing to forgive sins on behalf of all other believers?

4: Born Again/Salvation

So, what do we make of John 20:23?
- *John 20:23 If you forgive the sins of any, their sins have been forgiven them; if you retain the sins of any, they have been retained."*

Consider the Lord's Prayer. When Jesus taught us how to pray, one part involved forgiveness.
- *Matthew 6:12 And **forgive us** our debts, as we also **have forgiven our debtors.** (NASB)*
- *and **forgive us** our sins, as we have **forgiven those who sin against us.** (NLT)*

4:77 Sin separates a person from God. Our closeness, our intimacy, our relationship with God is hindered because of sin. Our repentance and God's forgiveness remove that gap. In a similar way, the sins of another person against us hinders our relationship with them. We can't require the other person to repent, but we can do our part by forgiving the person. And while God is the only one who can forgive sins against God which restores our relationship with God, is the forgiveness Jesus refers to in John 20:23 about us restoring our relationship with those who sinned against us?

Consider the following 7 verses.
- *Colossians 3:13 **bearing with one another, and forgiving each other**, whoever has a complaint against anyone; **just as the Lord forgave you, so also should you**.*
- *Matthew 18:21 Then Peter came and said to Him, "Lord, **how often shall my brother sin against me and I forgive him**? Up to seven times?"*
- *Matthew 18:35 My heavenly Father will also do the same to you, **if each of you does not forgive his brother from your heart**."*
- *Mark 11:25 Whenever you stand praying, **forgive, if you have anything against anyone**, so that your Father who is in heaven will also forgive you your transgressions.*
- *Luke 17:3 Be on your guard! If your brother sins, rebuke him; **and if he repents, forgive him**. 4 And if he sins against you seven times a day, and **returns to you seven times, saying, 'I repent,' forgive him**."*
- *2 Corinthians 2:5 But if any has caused sorrow, he has caused sorrow not to me, but in some degree - in order not to say too much - to all of you ... 7 so that on the contrary **you should rather forgive and comfort him**, ...*
- *Ephesians 4:32 Be kind to one another, tender-hearted, **forgiving each other**, just as God in Christ also has forgiven you.*

4:78 Collectively, humans sin against God and against each other hundreds of billions of times a day. God forgives our sins against Him. In terms of sins we commit against other human beings, do any of the above verses indicate forgiveness of our sins against another person is to come from a priest? Or is it to be given by the person against whom we sinned?

4:79 Don't all of the above 7 verses show we are to forgive those who sin against us, just as Jesus forgave us for sinning against Him? And thus, isn't John 20:23 which follows Jesus breathing on all those in attendance on

CEASED?

resurrection Sunday evening, a message that all believers are to forgive other persons for sins committed against them?

I can't find any verses stating a third party such as a pastor or priest is to forgive our sins against another person. If there is, I would appreciate you letting me know.

People involved?

Another key reason cited by Catholics for the need to confess mortal sins to a priest is that God always involves people in key issues related to salvation. Water baptism is cited as an example. In water baptism, another person is absolutely needed to baptize the person needing to be baptized. This is true. However, it should also be noted that the instruction was for all believers to water baptize, not just priests or a select few. In terms of a person always being involved, consider this.
1. Holy Spirit baptizes a person into the Body of Christ. No one else is needed.
2. As reviewed in Chapter 8, the Roman Catholic church teaches that Confirmation is very closely tied to salvation. Catholic Confirmation is centered around Baptism of the Holy Spirit and occurs at the hands of a Bishop or delegate. The Bible says otherwise. Jesus is the one who Baptizes a person in the Holy Spirit and Fire. No other person is needed.

Individuals Ordering God

Returning to the issue of communion after that road trip on confessing sins to priests, Roman Catholic teachings hold that priests can command Jesus to be sacrificed because Jesus allowed them to command Him to do so.

*"The supreme **power of the priestly office** is the power of consecrating…Indeed, it **is equal to that of Jesus Christ** … **When the priest pronounces the tremendous words of consecration, he reaches up into the heavens, brings Christ down from His throne, and places Him upon our altar to be offered up again as the Victim for the sins of man** … **The priest speaks and lo! Christ, the eternal and omnipotent God, bows his head in humble obedience to the priest's command.**"* – (John A. O'Brien, Ph.D., LL.D., The Faith of Millions, 255-256)

4:80 When a priest commands God to come to earth to be sacrificed, and Christ bows His head in humble obedience - isn't it extremely unusual that a sinful creation is telling the Holy, perfect and all-powerful Creator what to do? I personally wouldn't command God to do something. How about you?

4:81 How well would it go for priests who try commanding the Pope to do something daily?

A Scenario to Ponder

If the alternate view is accepted that Jesus is not ordered by the priest to come to be sacrificed, but voluntarily comes upon a priest's request, let me raise what may be a very delicate and perhaps painful issue for some - sexual abuse by priests. If this happened to you, I am so so sorry. But let me paint a picture. A priest involved in sexual abuse or other sexual sins for years has been leading his congregation in communion for years. He also takes communion often by himself, or with one or more other priests. After 20 years, this priest would have been involved in over

4: Born Again/Salvation

1,000 communions with the congregation and many more either by himself or with other priests.

4:82 When taking communion alone or with other priests who were also involved in sexual abuse, does it seem reasonable Jesus would allow Himself to be sacrificed over and over for this priest and/or other priests for sins which they had no intention of stopping?

As mentioned elsewhere, a verse that always gets my attention is Matthew 7:23.
- ❑ *Matthew 7:23 And then I will declare to them, 'I never knew you; depart from Me, you who practice lawlessness.'*

4:83 In situations where a priest has been engaged in ongoing sexual abuse or other sexual sins for a long time, doesn't that indicate the priest never really had a desire to repent, to change, to stop sinning? Does it perhaps indicate that priest didn't really know Jesus, that Jesus was not really His Lord, that he was not born again? And if so, would it be surprising if, upon the priest's death, the priest is told by Jesus to depart from Him?

4:84 Furthermore, if the priest is told to depart upon his death, doesn't it seem rather inconsistent of Jesus to allow Himself to be sacrificed by this priest over and over again when this priest and other priests fully intend to engage in these same sins again?

4:85 You may see this as an extreme example and not relevant. However, sexual abuse by church leaders isn't a small issue. It has occurred in large numbers, and probably far more than has been made public. Do you think Jesus would see all the communions led by priests involved in habitual sin as acts of remembrance, as acts of reverence, as acts of deep devotion to Him? Or as acts of hypocrisy on the part of priests involved as well as on the part of those priests and superiors perpetuating such ongoing hideous sins?

4:86 **IF** the Catholic view on communion is correct - which I believe it isn't but on the basis that it is - consider priests who were either repeatedly involved in sexual abuse or enabled these and other horrific sins to continue. Would it be surprising to one day learn that Jesus did not allow himself to be sacrificed during communions led by these priests? If so, wouldn't this mean Jesus's body and blood weren't in the wafer and wine received by Catholics participating in communions led by these rogue priests? And wouldn't that mean the venial sins of these people weren't forgiven? Or what about last rites led by these priests? The implications for Catholics are many.

New Believers

Consider two individuals. Person A and Person B are both born in 1980. Person A is born again on May 1, 2010 at age 30. Person B is born again 20 years later on May 1, 2030 at age 50.

- ❖ My abbreviated understanding of Roman Catholic teaching is that forgiveness for all the sins of Person A that occurred up to May 1, 2010 was provided for by the blood of Jesus. After being water baptized by a Catholic priest, the person is saved. Forgiveness for sins beyond May 1, 2010, is made possible through a combination of regularly taking

CEASED?

communion led by Catholic priests (for less serious venial sins) and repentance to Catholic priests leading to their forgiveness (for the more serious mortal sins).
- ❖ Similarly, according to Roman Catholic teaching, forgiveness for all the sins of Person B that occurred up to May 1, 2030 was provided for by the blood of Jesus. And again, after being water baptized, the person is saved according to Catholic teaching.

4:87 My questions are these.
  i. Why does the blood of Jesus cover the sins of Person B for the 20-year period from May 2, 2010 through May 1, 2030, but not the sins of Person A during that same 20-year period? If so, doesn't that mean the blessings from Jesus' shed blood, death and resurrection have an expiry date? Or get diluted?
  ii. In other words, consider Person C who is born again when he/she is 80 years old. The sins for the first 80 years of his/her life are covered by what Jesus did on the cross, but sins committed an hour after being born again aren't? Doesn't that seem a bit inconsistent?
  iii. If my understanding is wrong, and communion and a priest's forgiveness are also essential to be initially born again, doesn't that represent a new gospel?
  iv. If communion and a priest's forgiveness aren't required for a person to be initially born again, why isn't Jesus's shed blood, death and resurrection adequate to cover any and all sins - venial and mortal - that occur at any point in a person's life?

Sacrifices - Additional Deaths

I've seen Roman Catholic arguments that suggest this sacrifice during communion, this representation in a non-bloody manner, should not be viewed as an actual killing of Jesus. It's unbloody and therefore it's different. If so, I'm not sure how we should view the sacrifice. Is it 'only' torture? Regardless of the terminology and the label put on it - re-presentation, crucifixion, sacrifice, memorial gesture - the key to me is whether or not Catholic communion teaches that Christ dies again. Consider the following which is part of the material copied from the Catholic catechism and shown just before **CEASED?**'s question 4:67 above.

In this **_divine sacrifice_** which is celebrated in the Mass, the same **_Christ who offered himself once in a bloody manner_** on the altar of the cross is contained and **_is offered in an unbloody manner_**."

4:88 When I read official Roman Catholic teachings, I see Catholic communion as involving the death of Christ at the demand of a priest. When I read of the Jewish leaders who caused Jesus to be crucified, and of the Romans who carried it out, I don't have pleasant thoughts of them. I'm sorry but I don't. And I understand what they did was something that needed to happen. Is it understandable why I and others would have similar thoughts to anyone who believes they can cause our Lord and Savior, Jesus Christ, to continue to

4: Born Again/Salvation

be sacrificed over and over again when I believe it is not needed? And if you're Catholic and don't believe Jesus actually dies, then I ask what does happen. Is he tortured then? And if He isn't tortured, then what does happen during this non-bloody sacrifice? I believe Jesus is neither being sacrificed nor tortured during communion, but the mere thought that someone believes they can cause Jesus to be sacrificed when they want, with whatever that entails, over and over ... it just gets me.

Bloody vs Unbloody Sacrifice

In the Old Testament, sacrifices of animals were a core part of the Jewish life. Jesus's death on the cross and His shed blood were monumental events replacing the need for animal sacrifices. In **both** cases, the blood was key since, without shed blood, there is no forgiveness.

- *Hebrews 9:22 And according to the Law, one may almost say, all things are cleansed with blood, and **without shedding of blood there is no forgiveness**.*

4:89 How does the Catholic communion, a non-bloody sacrifice, provide for forgiveness of sins since without shedding of blood there is no forgiveness?

4:90 When a priest forgives a person's sin in a confessional booth or when the Pope gives a special indulgence for remission of temporal punishment (time spent in purgatory up to that time in a person's life), how is this **additional provision** for forgiveness of sins and remission of punishment possible without **additional shed blood**?

One Crucifixion or One Crucifixion + Billions/Trillions of Sacrifices

Let me approach the issue of the disagreement on communion in another way. Based on conservative numbers of ~220,000 Roman Catholic parishes, and an average of only 1 church per parish, and only one communion at each church every Sunday, Jesus is sacrificed in an unbloody manner ~220,000 times every Sunday around the world.

In 24 hours, there are 86,400 seconds. In other words, Christ is being sacrificed, on average, ~2.5 times every second on Sundays (~220,000 sacrifices divided by 86,400 seconds = ~2.5 sacrifices per second). And those numbers are based on each sacrifice lasting 1 second. If each sacrifice lasted an average of one minute (60 seconds), that translates to ~150 (60 * 2.5) sacrifices simultaneously going on around the world, and that assumes the sacrifices are spread out evenly over the 86,400 seconds in the day.

These ~220,000 sacrifices every Sunday translate to ~11,440,000 sacrifices per year (220,000 * 52). Over a 100-year period, that means Christ would be sacrificed over 1 billion times (11,440,000 * 100 = 1,144,000,000). And remember the 1.1 billion sacrifices are based on only 1 church per parish and only 1 communion per church per week. Many parishes have multiple churches. Many churches have multiple communions on Sundays, plus communions throughout the week. Over the centuries, per Roman Catholic practices, this analysis indicates Christ has been crucified tens, if not hundreds, of billions of times - at a minimum.

CEASED?

Simultaneous Sacrifices

Based on 24 time zones and 1 church for each of the ~220,000 parishes, on average, there are over ~9,000 communions on Sundays in the same time zone. Given most communions tend to be in the morning within a 2-3-hour window of time, that means tens if not hundreds of sacrifices are occurring at the same time in Europe and Africa, in North and South America, in Asia and Australia.

4:91 Every single Sunday, sinful human beings (i.e. priests) around the world are simultaneously commanding Almighty God, Jesus, to come down to their respective churches to be sacrificed for the forgiveness of some sins of a few people. Close your eyes and mull on that for a few seconds and ask: does that seem consistent with Christ's death on the cross where payment was made for all sins for all of humanity for all time?

4:92 Why does Jesus need to be sacrificed in every church? Isn't one sacrifice of Christ sufficient to cover the venial sins of all Catholics for at least one week?

All of Jesus in each wafer

Paragraph 1377 of the Roman Catholic Catechism states:

The Eucharistic presence of Christ begins at the moment of the consecration and endures as long as the Eucharistic species subsist. ***Christ is present whole and entire in each of the species*** *and whole and entire in each of their parts,* ***in such a way that the breaking of the bread does not divide Christ****.*

4:93 If indeed the entire body of Jesus is in each species - i.e. each wafer - does the number of sacrifices increase even more? For instance, if the average mass has 100 people taking communion, then wouldn't the above numbers need to be multiplied by 100? And thus, if we are to take Catholic teachings as presented, wouldn't that mean Christ has been sacrificed many tens if not hundreds of trillions of times since Calvary?

For One Person

The Code of Canon Law #276 encourages priests to offer the eucharist daily with others or by themselves if no one else is available. If priests do as encouraged by the Roman Catholic church, that would increase the number of sacrifices to far greater levels than previously mentioned.

4:94 Does it seem consistent with God's Word, who God is and who humans are:
   i. that a sinful priest can ask Christ to die, just for him, day after day, week after week, year after year if and when the priest so chooses?
   ii. that this sacrifice of Christ during communion is not enough, 'under ordinary circumstances', to cover the mortal sins of the one priest or the mortal sins of all those gathered together at a church, but only the less significant venial sins?
      Note: 'Under ordinary circumstances' means God doesn't do something out of the ordinary to forgive the mortal sins at that moment in time.
   iii. Doesn't it seem unusual that verbally confessing mortal sins to a priest is somehow able to do what Jesus couldn't do through His one-time death on the cross and all His unbloody sacrifices in communion?

4: Born Again/Salvation

Pain Endured by Christ
  4:95 When I think of the crucifixion of Christ, I shudder at the pain Christ endured. especially the emotional pain when He was forsaken by Father God. Based on Roman Catholic teachings, if Jesus is indeed to be sacrificed hundreds of billions/ trillions of times, wouldn't He need to be forsaken by Father God hundreds of billions/trillions of times as well - once for each sacrifice - each communion?   If not, why not?

When Peter told the Jewish people they had crucified the Lord, they were pierced to the heart.
- Acts 2:36 Therefore let all the house of Israel know for certain that God has made Him both Lord and Christ - this Jesus whom you crucified." 37 Now when they heard this, they were **pierced to the heart**, and said to Peter and the rest of the apostles, "Brethren, what shall we do?"

The English word *'pierced'* is derived from the Greek word *'katanusso'* [G2660] which Thayer defines in part as *'to prick, pierce, to pain the mind sharply, agitate it vehemently'*. The thought of being partially responsible for the killing of Christ penetrated their hearts deeply.
  4:96 If we're to accept the view that we are to kill or torture Christ billions/trillions more times after the cross, a minimum of 220,000 times on Sundays, how we do live in joy when Jesus is dying or at a minimum suffering greatly, repeatedly, virtually all day long? Shouldn't we all be pierced to the heart, all day long or longer knowing that Jesus is currently being forsaken by Father God over and over again?

Wouldn't Clarity be Warranted?
Trillions of sacrifices of Christ are based on taking a few words literally and not symbolically.
  4:97 If God knew Christ was going to be sacrificed hundreds of billions/trillions of times after His crucifixion on the cross, would it be reasonable to expect God's Word to indicate there would be a monumental amount of such sacrifices of Christ going forward?

Instead of finding scriptures showing Jesus would need to be sacrificed over and over again, we find scriptures stating Jesus died once, for all sins, for all mankind. Only one death was required.
- *Hebrews 7:27 who does not need daily, like those high priests, to offer up sacrifices, first for His own sins and then for the sins of the people, because this He **did once for all** when He offered up Himself.*
- *Hebrews 9:12 and not through the blood of goats and calves, but through His own blood, He entered the holy place **once for all**, having obtained eternal redemption.*
- *Hebrews 9:26 Otherwise, He would have needed to suffer often since the foundation of the world; but now **once at the consummation of the ages** He has been manifested to put away sin by the sacrifice of Himself.*

CEASED?

- *Hebrews 9:28 so Christ also, **having been offered once** to bear the sins of many, will appear a second time for salvation without reference to sin, to those who eagerly await Him.*
- *Romans 5:18 So then as through one transgression there resulted condemnation to all men, even so through **one act of righteousness** there resulted justification of life to all men.*
- *Romans 6:10 For the death that He died, He **died to sin once for all**; but the life that He lives, He lives to God.*
- *Hebrews 10:14 **For by one offering He has perfected for all time** those who are sanctified.*
- *1 Peter 3:18 For Christ also **died for sins once for all**, the just for the unjust, so that He might bring us to God, having been put to death in the flesh, but made alive in the spirit;*

4:98 To reiterate, if this sacrifice was to happen over and over again, wouldn't it be reasonable to expect scriptures to show Jesus's death on the cross was only the first of many sacrifices instead of the one-time sacrifice for all sins message that is shown?

4:99 When Jesus continues to be sacrificed over and over again, day in and day out, aren't we saying Jesus's shed blood is not enough, that His death on the cross only paid the price for sins that occurred up to the first communion after the cross, but none after?

4:100 With so many ongoing sacrifices, do we trivialize the cross where it represents only one of billions/trillions of sacrifices that occur at the summoning of a priest?

4:101 When Christ said *"It is finished"* just before He died on the cross, isn't the teaching of the Roman Catholic church saying *"No Jesus, it was not finished. You need to keep suffering over and over, again and again."*?

On the issue of trillions of sacrifices, consider Paul's first letter to the Corinthians.
- *1 Corinthians 11:26 For as often as you eat this bread and drink the cup, **you proclaim the Lord's death** until He comes.*

4:102 If Christ was to be crucified trillions of times:
 i. why does Paul say each time we eat the bread and drink the cup we do so to proclaim one death and not multitudes of deaths; and
 ii. given Paul wrote 1 Corinthians ~20 years after he was born again, he would have participated in ~1,040 sacrifices if he had communion once per week for 20 years. Why doesn't Paul mention this reality at least once by proclaiming and thanking Jesus for the thousands of sacrifices done in Paul's presence, and on Paul's behalf?

Death and Resurrection

We're to preach the gospel, but what exactly is the gospel? The word *'gospel'* is derived from the Greek word *'euagglion'* [G2098] which means in part *'salvation or good message'*. It is referred to 97 times in the New Testament in the NASB. There are several dimensions but the foundation of the gospel is found in 1 Corinthians 15,

4: Born Again/Salvation

namely Jesus's death, burial and resurrection.

- *1 Corinthians 15:1 Now I **make known** to you, brethren, **the gospel** which I preached to you, which also you received, in which also you stand, 2 by which also you are saved, if you hold fast the word which I preached to you, unless you believed in vain. 3 For I delivered to you as of first importance what I also received, that **Christ died for our sins** according to the Scriptures, 4 and that **He was buried**, and that **He was raised on the third day** according to the Scriptures.*

Jesus's shed blood and death on the cross are of monumental importance. However, Jesus's resurrection is vital as without His resurrection, our faith is useless.

- *1 Corinthians 15:14 **and if Christ has not been raised, then our preaching is vain, your faith also is vain**. 15 Moreover we are even found to be false witnesses of God, because we testified against God that He raised Christ, whom He did not raise, if in fact the dead are not raised. 16 For if the dead are not raised, not even Christ has been raised; 17 and **if Christ has not been raised, your faith is worthless; you are still in your sins**.*

4:103 If Catholic teaching is correct, when Christ was sacrificed the very first time that communion was taken, wouldn't that sacrifice nullify the resurrection of Jesus and put an end to the living, resurrected Christ we are waiting to see in His Second Coming?

4:104 Moreover, if Jesus's crucifixion on the cross was not enough to pay the penalty for all sins, can a one-time burial and a one-time resurrection of Christ be adequate? In other words, wouldn't these billions/trillions of sacrifices during communion warrant an equal number of burials and resurrections as well? If not, why not? And if so, when, where and how do these billions/trillions of burials and resurrections occur?

4:105 When Jesus is sacrificed during communion, doesn't He have to be resurrected before He can be sacrificed again in another communion ceremony?

4:106 However, given many communions are going on simultaneously around the world, how can a resurrection for each sacrifice be possible before the next sacrifice is made?

One Sacrifice - Ongoing Consumption?

Before the cross, the Jewish people sacrificed their Passover lambs once, but then had multiple meals of the lamb. Similarly, one Roman Catholic teaching is that the Eucharist involves a one-time sacrifice and ongoing consumption of Jesus's body and blood. If the Eucharist is about a one-time sacrifice and ongoing consumption akin to the Passover lamb:

4:107 Doesn't that conflict with teachings that each communion is its own unbloody sacrifice?

4:108 How does the act of consumption provide forgiveness of sins?

CEASED?

The English Word 'Is'
One last tidbit. The word *'is'* in Luke 22:19 is derived from the Greek word *'esti'* [G2076] which Strong's defines in several different ways including *'meaneth'*.
- Luke 22:19 And when He had taken some bread ... "This **is** *[esti G2076]* My body ..."

4:109   I'm no Greek scholar and I'm easily confused with all the tenses and rules. But consider this. If the word *'is'* is changed to a word that relates to *'meaneth'*, we get something like "And when He had taken some bread ... saying "**View this bread as meaning or representing my body** ...". It provides a different perspective doesn't it?

Two Options
In terms of our own belief about communion, we have two basic choices:
1. we take communion to remember Christ Jesus Himself, and to remember what He did on the whipping post and cross; or
2. we take communion not only to remember what Christ Jesus did on the cross, but also to sacrifice Him again and again as payment of new venial sins but not new mortal sins.

Most non-Catholics believe communion is symbolic. It is to be taken with gratitude and reverence, and to remember what Christ not only did for us on the whipping post and the cross, but also in a broader sense to thank Jesus for everything else He did back then, has already done in our own lives, and will do in our lives going forward.

There are spiritual blessings from communion, but Protestants see any blessings are a result of what Jesus did once on the cross, and not from any further, ongoing sacrifices. And thus, if you're Roman Catholic, can you see why these radical differences on communion are such a major stumbling block inhibiting Protestants from coming alongside Roman Catholics?

OTHER CATHOLIC TEACHINGS ON SALVATION

In terms of Roman Catholic teachings on salvation, my research indicates getting saved involves 3 basic steps:
1. repentance, believing in Jesus, His death, burial and resurrection;
2. believing in the teachings of the Roman Catholic church; and
3. getting water baptized, the first one of the 7 sacraments.

Roman Catholic teachings also include various 'works' need to be done to keep being saved. A simplified list includes the following:
1. fulfill the other 6 sacraments of confirmation, the eucharist, reconciliation, anointing of the sick, holy orders, and marriage;
2. be a loyal member of the Church;
3. keep the Ten Commandments; and if one sins, show sorrow, resolve not to repeat the sin, and perform penance which is a self-punishment done to try to right a wrong or to receive absolution from sins. Penances vary, but can

4: Born Again/Salvation

involve a public statement, confession to a priest and/or saying several Hail Marys;
4. go to mass preferably weekly, and at least once per year, and take communion - provided the criteria for taking communion have been met;
5. obtain special penance for mortal sins; and
6. receive prayer or penance from others if one is in purgatory; some financial contributions, climbing Sacred Steps, attending special events including online events and properly embracing the Pope's tweets are all acceptable in helping one get out or reduce the time a person spends in purgatory.

Apart from sincere repenting of sins, I don't find scriptures in the Bible supporting the above kinds of works are required to maintain salvation after the cross. And if we have to keep working to keep the gift of salvation, it raises the issue of was it actually a gift in the first place?
- ❑ *Ephesians 2:8 For by grace you have been saved through faith; and that not of yourselves, **it is the gift of God**; 9 not as a result of works, so that no one may boast.*

Purgatory
4:110 On the issue of whether or not there is purgatory, Catholic teachings say it is found in the Old Testament in 2 Maccabees 12:39-45. With respect to Maccabees being part of the Old Testament and before the cross, let me ask 3 questions.
  i. How is purgatory relevant to salvation today? Doesn't Christ's death render purgatory invalid even if it did exist at one time?
  ii. How does this Old Testament practice, even if it was valid in Old Testament days, able to do what Christ's death on the cross didn't do?
  iii. Once we die, don't truly born-again sons and daughters immediately go to heaven? While all others will go to hell immediately after meeting Jesus?
- ❑ *Luke 23:43 And He said to him, "Truly I say to you, today you shall be with Me in Paradise."*
- ❑ *2 Corinthians 5:8 we are of good courage, I say, and prefer rather to be absent from the body and to be at home with the Lord.*

To help illustrate the vast differences between how Protestants and Catholics see issues of purgatory and remission of punishment through indulgences, consider the following article *"How to pray your loved ones out of Purgatory this November"* by Mary Rezac of the Catholic News Agency dated October 31, 2017.

> *"It's the first week of November, which means it's the best time of year, liturgically speaking, for you to shave off some temporal punishment for all your loved ones in Purgatory.*
> *In case you're unfamiliar with Catholic teaching on the afterlife, there are three places for a soul to go after death: Heaven, Hell, or Purgatory.*

CEASED?

According to the Catechism of the Roman Catholic church, those who go to Heaven are "(t)hose who die in God's grace and friendship and are perfectly purified live for ever with Christ."

Those souls that go to Hell are those who have freely chosen through mortal sin "exclusion from communion with God and the blessed."

Purgatory is a place where souls go who die in grace in friendship with God but are still imperfectly purified. Purgatory is where "after death they undergo purification, so as to achieve the holiness necessary to enter the joy of heaven." These souls are ensured eventual entrance into Heaven, once they are purified.

Souls in purgatory rely on the prayers of souls still on Earth to relieve some of their temporal suffering and speed their journey to Heaven, so be sure to take advantage of these days to pray for them by gaining indulgences for them.

An indulgence is a remission before God of the temporal punishment due to sins whose guilt has already been forgiven, which the faithful Christian who is duly disposed gains under certain prescribed conditions through the action of the Church which, as the minister of redemption, dispenses and applies with authority the treasury of the satisfactions of Christ and the saints. [CCC 1471]

Here's when and how:
The first chance for gaining a plenary (or full) indulgence for the deceased is available Nov. 2 only. In a Church, recite the Creed and the Our Father for the dead, receive Communion, and pray for Pope's intentions.

The second opportunity lasts through November 8. A person can obtain one plenary indulgence for a deceased person per day if they receive Communion, pray for the deceased at a cemetery, and pray for the Pope's intentions.

Throughout the year, a person can obtain one partial indulgence for a deceased person per day if they receive Communion, pray for the deceased at a cemetery, and pray for the Pope's intentions. November is a good time to remember to do this, since the Church is praying in a special way for souls this month.

In each instance, the person obtaining the indulgences needs to receive the sacrament of confession within about a week of the indulgence act. One confession covers the person obtaining one partial indulgence per day. Additionally, the person needs to be in a state of grace when completing the indulgence act, and have detachment from all sin (which, if that sounds impossible, is more fully explained by a priest in this blog post.)

So take advantage of the month of November, and love your deceased relatives by praying them out of Purgatory!

"Let us help and commemorate them. If Job's sons were purified by their father's sacrifice [Job 1:5], why would we doubt that our offerings for the dead bring them some consolation? Let us not hesitate to help those who have died and to offer our prayers for them" – St. John Chrysostom

4:111 In my study, I struggle to see where all the comments, nuances and rules related to purgatory and indulgences correspond to what the Bible teaches. Full indulgences on November 2 only, and only if one receives communion. One indulgence per day through November 8 and again, only if one receives

4: Born Again/Salvation

communion. Partial indulgences per day through the rest of the year. None of this is in the Bible and resembles anything like what Christ or His apostles taught. Thus, if you're Roman Catholic, can you again see why many Protestants have major difficulties with Roman Catholic teachings?

If you're Roman Catholic, can I encourage you to read the New Testament yourself and let it speak to you? The Bible is God's love letter to you, and He delights when we spend time reading His Word. Compare what you find in John, Romans, Galatians and Ephesians to the above article and the 15 promises of the rosary in Chapter 25, and see if there is a connection or disconnection.

ALTERNATE VIEWS

In a broader context, there are other aspects of salvation in some Protestant churches that I don't find in the Bible or to me, are contrary to the Bible. Two include:
- ❖ 'enough' participation in church activities such as going to church, prayer meetings and Bible studies, helping out within and outside the church, tithing, going on missions etc.; and
- ❖ Baptism in the Holy Spirit (see Chapters 7-10 of **CEASED?**).

In terms of the first items, the Bible is clear they aren't related to being saved or keeping our salvation. In terms of the Baptism of the Holy Spirit, Chapters 6-11 will clearly show Baptism in the Holy Spirit is a totally separate experience from being born again.

Some believers see differences in the process of salvation as not being a big deal as long as we believe in Jesus. However, if a person influences anyone to believe in a different gospel than what's in the Bible, Paul writes that person should be accursed. And Paul says it not once, but twice.
- ❑ *Galatians 1:8 But even if we, or an angel from heaven, **should preach to you a gospel contrary** to what we have preached to you, **he is to be accursed**! 9 As we have said before, **so I say again** now, if **any man is preaching to you a gospel contrary** to what you received, **he is to be accursed**!*

The book of Revelation also gives a warning which some believe only relates to changes to the book of Revelation; others believe it pertains to the entire Bible.
- ❑ *Revelation 22:18 I testify to everyone who hears the words of the prophecy of this book: **if anyone adds to them, God will add to him the plagues** which are written in this book; 19 and **if anyone takes away from the words of the book of this prophecy, God will take away his part from the tree of life** and from the holy city, which are written in this book.*

4:112 Either way we look at Revelation 22:18-19, God warns of consequences of preaching a different gospel, or of adding to or taking away from His Word. I personally want to only teach and share the true gospel which is based on the one-time crucifixion of Christ, His one-time burial and His one-time resurrection. What's your take?

CEASED?

BY GRACE ALONE, BY FAITH ALONE

4:113 A common phrase is that we are saved by grace alone, by faith alone. It is by God's grace and by our faith in God. God's grace alone is correct, but I think there is a bit more to our side than faith alone. Repentance, believing and confessing Jesus from a heart desiring an ongoing personal relationship with God, with no one in between, are all essential.

CLOSING POINTS TO PONDER

God created humans to have a relationship. God's love is unconditional. Father God sent Jesus to die for our sins. We are saved because of God's goodness. As seen in future chapters, when we become true Christians and are truly born again, Holy Spirit comes in [en] us. We become many things. We're a child of God and a joint-heir. We're adopted. We're seated in heavenly places. We become sent ones and ambassadors with a responsibility to share the Good News. Crazy good stuff.

4:114 If salvation depends on what we do to earn it, would this align:
   i. with having a close, intimate personal relationship with God; or
   ii. with false religions where one needs to strive and perform to prove oneself worthy enough to get into heaven?

For Roman Catholics

Communion

The COVID-19 pandemic is in full swing as I write **CEASED?**. Devoted Catholics aren't able to go to mass and take communion. What are the implications for the Roman Catholic church of long delays between communions for the vast majority of Catholics? I'll let you decide. Lori and I take communion at home to remember Jesus. If you can't go to mass, consider taking a form of communion at home by eating a piece of bread/wafer/cracker and drinking a little juice to show gratitude to Jesus, to remember Jesus for who He is and for what He did for you, and me. And if eating/drinking the elements causes you angst at this point, you can also just hold your hands and hearts up to God, and give Him praise and worship. After all, it's your heart He wants.

Priests Forgiving Sins

Starting on page 76, **CEASED?** reviewed why John 20:21-23 isn't about Jesus giving the original apostles (nor today's Catholic priests) a unique authority to forgive sins on behalf of God, or on behalf of any other person. As per the Lord's prayer, just as Jesus forgives all sins we committed against Him, we are to forgive those who sin against us. If you disagree with my analysis of John 20:21-23, I have a few last questions for you.

4:119 In ancient times, transportation was slow - walking, riding a donkey, horse or camel, or taking a rowboat or sailboat. There were no telephones or internet services. In the first few years after the cross when the original apostles were still alive, believers were becoming more and more widely spread throughout the Middle East. If these believers were to meet with the original apostles regularly in order to have mass and to confess their mortal sins to the apostles, I wonder about a few things such as:

4: Born Again/Salvation

      i. How were the original apostles able to regularly meet with all the different believers in order to conduct communion and forgive all the mortal sins?
      ii. How were the original apostles able to do all the water baptisms and last rites for believers that were required?
      iii. If these issues weren't needed for all followers of Christ at that time, why are they necessary now?
      iv. If the delegation to the next generation of priests had occurred very early on and there were many, many priests elsewhere doing water baptisms, forgiving mortal sins and giving last rites, why don't we see specific examples of these extremely important events in the Bible?

God created humans for relationship with Him, something we see from the very beginning when God created Adam and Eve. Sin entered the world and created a separation between human beings and God. Thankfully, God provided a solution through Jesus's death, burial and resurrection - the most important sequence of events since creation. Wicked sinners that we are, God so loved us that Jesus was willing to die for us. And it is God's love, a love that is to flow through His children, which leads a person to want Jesus in their lives and will cause them to repent and change their ways.

❑ *Romans 5:8 But God demonstrates His own love toward us, in that while we were yet sinners, Christ died for us.*

Chapter 5 reviews how Holy Spirit is actually with [para] us, how God draws us to a relationship with Him before we're even born again. Talk about being blessed.

Chapters 6 through 12 go on to discuss aspects of our relationship with God when we're first born again, and in our walk thereafter as a blood-bought, born-again, child of God.

5

Holy Spirit 'Withs'
Temporary [Para] & Permanent [Meta]

INTRODUCTION

PRIOR to being born again, the apostles were drawn to Christ. Yes, Jesus told the apostles to follow Him. However, many others who don't appear to have been told to follow Christ, nevertheless followed Him. Chapter 5 discusses how Holy Spirit is with us in 2 ways:
1. Holy Spirit is temporarily with [para] us while He leads us to Jesus; and
2. Holy Spirit is permanently with [meta] us after we're born again.

Father God Draws us to Christ

The Bible tells us that Father God draws people to Christ.
- ❑ *John 6:44* **No one can come to Me** *unless* **the Father who sent Me draws him**: *and I will raise him up on the last day.*
- ❑ *John 6:65 And He was saying, "For this reason I have said to you, that* **no one can come to Me** *unless* **it has been granted him from the Father."**

To clarify, Father God draws people to Christ through Holy Spirit who convicts people of their sins and helps them realize their need for righteousness and a savior.
- ❑ *John 16:7 But I tell you the truth.* **it is to your advantage that I go away; for if I do not go away, the Helper will not come to you**; *but if I go, I will send Him to you. 8 And He, when He comes, will* **convict the world concerning sin** *and* **righteousness** *and judgment;*

Conviction of sin involves a renewing of our mind, a process that leads to repentance which involves not only sorrow, but a commitment to change one's way of thinking by turning towards God.
- ❑ *Ephesians 1:18 I pray that the* **eyes of your heart may be enlightened**, *so that you will know what is the hope of His calling, what are the riches of the glory of His inheritance in the saints,*

A wonderful thing about God is that He wants to grow His relationship with those who are saved, but He also wants to establish a personal relationship with those who are not saved. John 14:17 reveals Holy Spirit was **with** those who were listening

5: Holy Spirit With [Para/Meta]

to Him at that time, but one day in the future, Holy Spirit **will** also be **in** them.
- ❑ *John 14:17 that is the Spirit of truth, whom the world cannot receive, because it does not see Him or know Him, but you know Him because He abides **with [para G3844]** you and will be **in** you.*

The English word *'with'* in John 14:17 is derived from the Greek word *'para'* [G3844] which Thayer defines as 'from, of at, by, besides, near'.

5:1 Before the cross, Jesus tells His apostles they already know Holy Spirit because Holy Spirit dwells with them. And, one day, Holy Spirit shall be in them, which per Chapter 6 occurs when they are born again. Isn't it reasonable to conclude Holy Spirit is with [para] non-believers today, just as Holy Spirit was with these unsaved individuals before the cross?

'Para', a Temporary 'With'

One role played by Holy Spirit is to draw people to Jesus. There are two outcomes. The first involves individuals who don't accept Christ as their Lord and Savior and don't enter into a personal relationship with Him. These individuals will unfortunately end up in hell. At that point, Holy Spirit no longer draws them to Jesus - it's too late.

The second outcome involves those individuals who accept Christ and enter into a personal relationship with Him. In this case, they have Jesus. They no longer need Holy Spirit to be with [para] them for purposes of drawing them to Jesus. However, they do now have another variation of a 'with' experience.

'Meta', a Permanent 'With'

In John 14:16, Jesus tells the disciples He will give us another Helper - Holy Spirit. Other translations have other descriptors of Holy Spirit.
- ❑ *John 14:16 I will ask the Father, and He will give you another **Helper**, that He may be **with [meta]** you forever;* [NASB]
- ❑ *John 14:16 And I will ask the Father, and He will give you another **Helper (Comforter, Advocate, Intercessor-Counselor, Strengthener, Standby)**, to be **with [meta]** you forever.* [AMP]

A key part of John 14:16 is that Holy Spirit will not just be with us temporarily drawing us to Christ, but will be with us ... forever.
- ❑ *John 14:16 I will ask the Father, and He will give you another Helper, that He may be **with [meta]** you **forever**.*

The English word *'with'* in John 14:16 is based on a different Greek word, *'meta'* [G3326], and not *'para'* when Holy Spirit draws individuals to Jesus. Meta is defined as 'with, after, behind'.

One view of para and meta is that para indicates Holy Spirit is close by as He draws us to Christ. Whereas para is a temporary relationship, meta is a permanent relationship where Holy Spirit is with us forever after we're born again. This would be consistent with Matthew 1:23 which tells us Jesus will be also with us. This second with experience involving Jesus is also permanent, and is based on the same

CEASED?

Greek word meta.
- *Matthew 1:23 "Behold, the virgin shall be with child and shall bear a Son, and they shall call His name Immanuel," which translated means, "God **with [meta]** us."*

The very last verse in the book of Matthew also tells us that Jesus will be with [meta] us always.
- *Matthew 28:20 teaching them to observe all that I commanded you; and lo, I am **with [meta]** you **always, even to the end of the age**.*

If you haven't already done so, consider reading Chuck Smith's *"Living Water"*, Francis Chan's *"Forgotten God"* and Robert Morris's *"The God I Never Knew"*. As the latter two titles indicate, Holy Spirit is often relegated to the background. If you have never studied Holy Spirit and haven't spent time with Him in your walk with God, may I suggest doing so. It's a can't lose proposition. After all, if you're born again, He is in [en] you and has time for you.

CLOSING POINT TO PONDER

5:2 Holy Spirit, Almighty God Himself, is with us and personally leading us to Christ, and then stays in [en] and with [meta] us after we accept Christ. Chapters 6 through 8, also reveal that Holy Spirit is not only with [meta] us, He is also in [en] us after we're born again. We also see Jesus is not only with us, He is also in [en] us forever once we're saved. Are we children of God blessed, or what?

6

Holy Spirit 'In' [En]

INTRODUCTION

BEFORE we're born again, God is with [para] us as Holy Spirit draws us to Christ. Chapter 6 reviews various aspects of what happens when we're born again including:
1. the in [en] experience (page 97);
2. start of an amazing relationship (page 99); the Great Exchange (page 100);
3. the original apostles' born-again experience (page 102);
4. was Jesus's breathing on His disciples on resurrection Sunday evening symbolic, or their personal born-again experience (page 103);
5. who was actually breathed upon resurrection Sunday evening (page 107);
6. women and the resurrected Christ (page 111); and
7. Holy Spirit's baptism of believers into the Body of Christ (page 112).

<u>**Sin Separates**</u>

Before we come to Christ, we're separated from God due to sin. We're spiritually dead. Once we're saved, our spirit comes alive as Holy Spirit comes in [en] us. This revival of our spirits was prophesied in the Old Testament.
- ❑ *Ezekiel 36:26 Moreover, I will **<u>give you a new heart</u>** and **<u>put a new spirit within you</u>**; and I will remove the heart of stone from your flesh and give you a heart of flesh. 27 I will **<u>put My Spirit within</u>** you and ...*

<u>**Old Testament 'In' Experiences**</u>

While researching Holy Spirit coming *'in'* a believer, I was surprised to find Holy Spirit was also *'in'* various individuals in the Old Testament. Some of them include:
- ❑ *Numbers 27:18 ... "Take Joshua ..., a man **<u>in whom is the Spirit</u>** ...;*
- ❑ *Ezekiel 2:2 As He spoke to me **<u>the Spirit entered me</u>** ...*
- ❑ *Daniel 4:8 But finally Daniel ... **<u>in whom is a spirit of the holy gods</u>** ...*

<u>**'With' and 'In' the Disciples**</u>

Moving on to the New Testament, Chapter 5 in **CEASED?** discussed how Holy Spirit was 'with' the disciples (before the cross), but in the future (after the cross), Holy Spirit will also be 'in' them.
- ❑ *John 14:16 I will ask the Father, and **<u>He will give you another Helper</u>**, that He may be **<u>with [meta]</u>** you forever; 17 that is the Spirit of truth, whom the world cannot receive, because it does not see Him or know Him, but you know*

CEASED?

*Him because He abides **with [para]** you and **will be in [en]** you.*

It's a big deal. If a person doesn't have Holy Spirit in them, they aren't a child of God.
- *Romans 8:9 However, you are not in the flesh but in the Spirit, if indeed **the Spirit of God dwells in [en] you**. But **if anyone does not have the Spirit of Christ, he does not belong to Him**.*

However, when we're born again and Holy Spirit comes in [en] us, we become a child of God. The English word *'in'* is based on the Greek word *'en'* [G1722]. Thayer defines en in part as *'in, by, with'*.
- *1 Corinthians 3:16 Do you not know that you are a temple of God and that the Spirit of God dwells **in [en] you**?*
- *1 John 3:24 The one who keeps His commandments abides in Him, and He in him. We know by this that **He abides in [en] us, by the Spirit whom He has given us**.*

When we're born again, we enter a new way of being and living. We're adopted into God's family. Holy Spirit now lives in us. Close your eyes and contemplate how amazing it is that Holy Spirit is **IN** us. Then, we learn Jesus is also **IN** us.
- *2 Corinthians 13:5 Test yourselves to see if you are in the faith; examine yourselves! Or do you not recognize this about yourselves, that **Jesus Christ is in you** - unless indeed you fail the test?*
- *Romans 8:10 **If Christ is in you**, though the body is dead because of sin, yet the spirit is alive because of righteousness.*
- *John 15:5 I am the vine, you are the branches; he who **abides in [en] Me** and **I in [en] him**, he bears much fruit, for apart from Me you can do nothing.*

We don't worship a God who is in some far-off distant universe. He is here ... in us. God wants relationship, directly. The veil in the temple was torn, and we can go into the Holy of Holies ourselves - direct access to God. No long-distance. No megaphone or intermediary is needed to act on our behalf. We can speak to Him, and hear Him speak to us, in whatever form that takes.
- *Mark 15:37 And Jesus uttered a loud cry, and breathed His last. 38 And the **veil of the temple was torn** in two from top to bottom.*
- *Ephesians 2:18 For through Him we both **have our access** in one Spirit to the Father.*
- *John 10:27 My **sheep hear My voice**, and I know them, and they follow Me;*

6:1 With both Jesus and Holy Spirit in [en] us, does this enable us to potentially have the kind of personal, intimate relationship that Adam had with God in the Garden of Eden where they walked and talked? If not, why not?

6:2 Views vary on whether Adam lost none/some/all of the call on his life when he ate of the tree. He had children so he clearly didn't lose all of his calling. For us, however, isn't our ability to fulfill the call God has for our life greatly enhanced when we're made right with God after we're born again, and God Himself is in [en] us?

6: Holy Spirit In [En]

BEGINNING OF AN INCREDIBLE RELATIONSHIP

When we're born again, the blessings from Holy Spirit living in [en] us are many. For one, Holy Spirit is given as a down payment on our future inheritance of eternal life in heaven. He seals it.

- ❑ 2 Corinthians 1:22 who also **sealed us** and gave us the Spirit in our hearts as **a pledge**.
- ❑ Ephesians 4:30 Do not grieve the Holy Spirit of God, **by whom you were sealed** for the day of redemption.

Other blessings include Holy Spirit teaching us, helping us remember, and helping us to understand and know things.

- ❑ John 14:26 But the Helper, the Holy Spirit … will **teach you all things**, and **bring to your remembrance** all that I said to you.
- ❑ John 15:26 When the **Helper** comes … the Spirit of truth …
- ❑ 1 Corinthians 2:12 Now we have received, not the spirit of the world, but the Spirit who is from God, **so that we may know the things freely given to us by God**,

Jesus is also the one and only mediator.

- ❑ 1 Timothy 2:5 For there is one God, and **one mediator also between God and men, the man Christ Jesus**,

Romans 8 gives insight into other potential blessings we receive when born again.

- ❑ Romans 8:1 Therefore there is **now no condemnation** …
- ❑ 2 … **set you free from the law of sin and of death** …
- ❑ 6 … the mind set on the Spirit is **life and peace** …
- ❑ 11 … give **life to your mortal bodies** through His Spirit who dwells in you.
- ❑ 14 For **all who are being led by the Spirit of God, these are sons of God**.
- ❑ 15 … **received a spirit of adoption as sons** by which we cry out, "Abba! Father!"
- ❑ 16 … **we are children of God**, 17 and if children, **heirs also, heirs of God and fellow heirs with Christ, if indeed we suffer** with Him …
- ❑ 24 For **in hope we have been saved** …
- ❑ 26 In the same way the Spirit **also helps our weakness**; for we do not know how to pray as we should, but **the Spirit Himself intercedes for us** with groanings too deep for words; 27 and He who searches the hearts knows what the mind of the Spirit is, because **He intercedes for the saints** according to the will of God …
- ❑ 31 … **If God is for us, who is against us?**
- ❑ 32 He who did not spare His own Son, … will He not also with Him **freely give us all things?** …
- ❑ 35 **Who will separate us from the love of Christ?** …

The in [en] experience is primarily for the benefit of the person in whom Holy Spirit dwells, the person who is born again. Benefits will flow to other people in their sphere of influence as a result of what Holy Spirit does in the born-again person. The extent to which God blesses us is amazing. I believe Derek Prince in his book *"Divine Exchange"* first summarized what happened at the cross, burial and resurrection of Christ from the perspective of what Jesus got out of the deal and what we got in return. Others have created versions of this great/divine exchange. My version is in Figure 6:1.

Figure 6:1 The Great Exchange

What happened to Jesus?	What happened for us?
1. Enslaved in human flesh; earthly living challenges ❖ Luke 9:58; 4:1-12 ❖ Philippians 2:5-8	Blessings in heavenly places ❖ Ephesians 1:3; 2:6
2. Tempted by devil ❖ Matthew 4:1-11 ❖ Mark 1:9-13 ❖ Luke 4:1-12	Works of devil destroyed for us ❖ Colossians 2:15 ❖ 1 John 3:8 Ability to resist/be free from sinning ❖ Matthew 6:13 ❖ Romans 6:6 ❖ Galatians 2:20
3. Sold for price of a slave ❖ Matthew 26:15; 27:3	Bought with blood of Jesus ❖ Acts 20:28 ❖ 1 Corinthians 6:20 ❖ 1 Peter 1:18-19
4. Surrendered ❖ John 10:17	Given spiritual authority ❖ Matthew 28:18-20 ❖ Mark 16:15-19 ❖ Luke 10:19 ❖ John 20:21 ❖ Acts 3:6
5. Captured due to sins of the world ❖ Acts 2:23	Delivered from the sins of the world ❖ Galatians 1:4
6. Despised, shamed, tormented, mocked ❖ Isaiah 53:3 ❖ Matthew 27:35-44 ❖ Mark 14:65 ❖ Luke 18:32 ❖ Romans 8:18 ❖ Hebrews 12:2	God's glory, love, peace ❖ Matthew 27:39-44 ❖ John 3:16; 17:22 ❖ Romans 15:7 ❖ Ephesians 1:6 ❖ Philippians 4:7
7. Rejected by many Jews; abandoned by disciples ❖ Matthew 21:42 ❖ Mark 8:31; 14:50 ❖ Luke 2:34	Acceptance/fellowship with God ❖ 1 Corinthians 1:9 ❖ 1 John 1:3-4

6: Holy Spirit In [En]

Figure 6:1 The Great Exchange

What happened to Jesus?	What happened for us?
8. Fulfilled the law/made a curse ❖ Deuteronomy 21:23 ❖ Matthew 5:17 ❖ Romans 8:1-4 ❖ Galatians 3:13	Free of the law; saved by grace ❖ Romans 7:6 ❖ Galatians 3:1-3; 3:13 ❖ Ephesians 2:8-9
9. Did not sin; took on our sins ❖ 2 Corinthians 5:21 ❖ 1 Peter 2:22; 2:24	Freed from the penalty of our sins; forgiven, made righteous ❖ Acts 5:31 ❖ Romans 3:22-24; 5:17 ❖ Romans 5:8-9; 6:23 ❖ Philippians 1:11 ❖ Colossians 2:14-15 ❖ 2 Peter 1:4
10. Took our sorrows and griefs ❖ Isaiah 53:4	Gladness and joy ❖ Luke 15:10; 15:11 ❖ Acts 14:17 ❖ Hebrews 1:9
11. Body was mangled ❖ Luke 22:19	By His stripe(s), healed us ❖ Psalm 103:3 ❖ Isaiah 53:5 ❖ 1 Peter 2:24
12. Forsaken/separated from God ❖ Matthew 27:46 ❖ Mark 14:50	Adopted as a child of God ❖ John 1:12-13 ❖ 1 John 3:1 Christ in us ❖ Galatians 2:20 ❖ Ephesians 3:17-21 Holy Spirit in us; leads/ guides us ❖ John 14:17 ❖ Romans 8:14-17
13. Died a thankless, cruel death ❖ 1 Corinthians 15:3 ❖ Hebrews 2:9	Eternal life/gift of salvation ❖ Romans 6:23 ❖ 1 Corinthians 15:21-26 ❖ 2 Corinthians 5:15 ❖ 1 John 5:11
14. Died to tear the veil ❖ Matthew 27:51 ❖ Mark 15:38 ❖ Luke 23:45	Direct access to God any time ❖ Exodus 30:10 ❖ Leviticus 16:1-34 ❖ Isaiah 59:1-2 ❖ Acts 17:24-28 ❖ Hebrews 4:14-16 ❖ Hebrews 9:1-9; 10:19-20

CEASED?

Figure 6:1 The Great Exchange

What happened to Jesus?	What happened for us?
15. Died in total poverty; nothing of earthly value left ❖ 2 Corinthians 8:9	Abundant life ❖ John 10:10; 14:13 ❖ Romans 8:32 ❖ 2 Corinthians 9:8 ❖ Galatians 3:9 ❖ Philippians 4:19 Heir of God/Joint heirs with Jesus ❖ Matthew 25:34 ❖ Romans 8:17 ❖ Galatians 3:29; 4:7 ❖ Colossians 1:12; 3:24 Citizen of heaven ❖ Philippians 3:20

ORIGINAL APOSTLES' BORN-AGAIN EXPERIENCE

When a person is born again, we're told the angels celebrate.
❑ *Luke 15:10 In the same way, I tell you, there is joy in the presence of the angels of God over one sinner who repents."*

Resurrection Sunday was a very special time. Finding the empty tomb, going inside and being told by angels that Jesus had risen, then learning that the resurrected Jesus would meet them later in Galilee were some of the most exhilarating minutes in history. And the excitement didn't stop. Later on resurrection Sunday evening, the women and other disciples spent time with the resurrected Jesus after He came into that locked room, a room locked because those gathered were fearful for their lives. Jesus coming to see them Sunday evening was amazing, but to come into a room with locked doors was rather unusual. No wonder Jesus told them to have peace not once but twice.

❑ *John 20:19 So when it was evening on that day, the first day of the week, and when the doors were shut where the disciples were, for fear of the Jews, Jesus came and stood in their midst and said to them, "**Peace be with you**." 20 And when He had said this, He showed them both His hands and His side. The disciples then rejoiced when they saw the Lord. 21 So Jesus said to them again, "**Peace be with you**; as the Father has sent Me, I also send you."*

After Jesus gave evidence of His risen nature, the disciples rejoiced.
❑ *John 20:20 And when He had said this, He showed them both His hands and His side. The disciples **then rejoiced** when they saw the Lord.*

6:3   The disciples spent 3½ years with Jesus witnessing miracles, witnessing the power of God time and time again, and hearing His superb teaching. They had seen the crucifixion and the empty tomb. They had heard Jesus speak of Him raising the temple on the third day. The hours between their realizing the tomb was empty and Jesus appearing that evening must have been filled with all kinds of questions, comments, and perhaps even the odd: "*Oh, that's*

6: Holy Spirit In [En]

what Jesus meant!" Jesus appeared to them in a locked room, in person. He showed them his hands and his pierced side. The disciples were no doubt excited to realize Jesus had risen. However, I wonder if they were also still convicted for running away when Jesus was first arrested, and for not helping take Jesus down from the cross, but instead left Him hanging. On resurrection Sunday evening, do you think the disciples were ready to listen to what the resurrected Jesus had to say, were ready to follow Jesus, and were ready to do what He wanted them to do?

6:4   More specifically, do you believe the disciples were ready on resurrection Sunday evening to accept Christ into their lives as their personal Lord and Savior? If not, why not?

6:5   In particular, consider Peter. Three days before, Peter had denied Jesus 3 times. Peter had wept bitterly. Earlier that morning, Peter ran to the empty tomb. He had been waiting for several hours wondering what was going to happen next. Then Jesus appears. When Peter saw the risen Christ, what were the odds Peter would deny anything the resurrected Jesus wanted to give him or ask of him - be it good, bad or indifferent?

Jesus Breathed on the Disciples

After Jesus showed His hands and side to His disciples and said peace to them a second time, Jesus breathed on them and told them to receive the Holy Spirit.

- ❏ *John 20:21 So Jesus said to them again, "Peace be with you; as the Father has sent Me, I also send you." 22 And when He had said this,* **He breathed on them** *and said to them, "***Receive the Holy Spirit***.*

This breathing by Jesus on the disciples is the moment when many believers (including myself) think Holy Spirit came in [en] the disciples, the moment when the disciples were born again, the moment the first Christians as we understand the term today, came onto the scene, and when the Body of Christ and God's church started.

- ❏ *1 Corinthians 3:16 Do you not know that you are a temple of God and that the Spirit of God dwells* **in [en] you**?
- ❏ *1 John 3:24 The one who keeps His commandments abides in Him, and He in him. We know by this that* **He abides in [en] us**, **by the Spirit whom He has given us**.

BUT, WAS JESUS'S BREATH PURELY SYMBOLIC?

The English word *'breathed'* is derived from the Greek word *'emphusao'* [G1720] which Thayer defines in part as *'to blow or breathe upon'*. Some believers teach that Jesus breathing on the disciples was purely symbolic, that Jesus was merely breathing air, and was preparing the disciples for Pentecost when Holy Spirit would come.

6:6   Is it likely that after all Jesus went through - ministering for 3 ½ years, suffering a brutal whipping and crucifixion, being buried and then resurrected - He would follow that up by blowing air on His disciples and tell them to receive the Holy Spirit, purely for symbolic reasons?

6:7 If this breathing was symbolic of a future event, why would Jesus speak in the present tense? Why wouldn't He have said sometime in a future tense such as *"Soon, you will receive the Holy Spirit."*?

Here are 5 other reasons why I think Jesus's breathing on the disciples was not symbolic.

(1) A Precedent: God Breathed Life into Adam

First, consider that when God breathed on Adam, God breathed life into Adam.
- *Genesis 2:7 Then the Lord God formed man of dust from the ground, and **breathed into his nostrils the breath of life**; and man became a living being.*

6:8 When God breathed on Adam, didn't God give life to his body, soul and spirit?

6:9 When Jesus breathed on the disciples, would it follow that God was also breathing life into the disciples, this time spiritual life?

(2) Jesus is Sending Them

A second reason as to why Jesus breathing on the disciples was not symbolic is found in John 20. Before Jesus breathes on the disciples and tells them to receive the Holy Spirit, Jesus advises He is *'sending'* them just as He was sent.
- *John 20:21 So Jesus said to them again, "Peace be with you; as the **Father has sent Me, I also send you**." 22 And when He had said this, He breathed on them and said to them, "Receive the Holy Spirit.*

6:10 As Jesus is sending the disciples out, wouldn't it be beneficial if they were born again and had Holy Spirit in [en] them before they went out?

(3) Spiritual Understanding

A third reason why Jesus's breathing on His disciples was not symbolic is due to one of the many benefits of having Holy Spirit in [en] us - gaining spiritual understanding. The latter part of Luke 24 deals with resurrection Sunday evening. Jesus showed the disciples his hands and feet, and when they didn't believe, he ate some food.
- *Luke 24:40 And when He had said this, He showed them His hands and His feet. 41 While they still could not believe it because of their joy and amazement, He said to them, "Have you anything here to eat?" 42 They gave Him a piece of a broiled fish; 43 and He took it and ate it before them.*

After He ate, Jesus opened their minds so they could more fully understand the scriptures.
- *Luke 24:44 Now He said to them, "These are My words which I spoke to you while I was still with you, that all things which are written about Me in the Law of Moses and the Prophets and the Psalms must be fulfilled." 45 **Then He opened their minds to understand the Scriptures**,*

While Jesus appeared to the disciples on resurrection Sunday evening and told them He was sending them, He didn't send them right away. Instead, Acts 1 tells us that Jesus first taught the disciples about kingdom of God matters over a 40-day

6: Holy Spirit In [En]

period.
- *Acts 1:3 To these He also presented Himself alive after His suffering, by many convincing proofs, **appearing to them over a period of forty days** and **speaking of the things concerning the kingdom of God**.*

Having an enhanced ability to understand Christ's teachings over these 40 days would have been helpful. An issue remains on how Jesus actually accomplished this opening of their minds so they could understand. 1 Corinthians 2 provides insight.
- *1 Corinthians 2:11 For who among men knows the thoughts of a man except the spirit of the man which is in him? **Even so the thoughts of God no one knows except the Spirit of God**. 12 **Now we have received**, not the spirit of the world, but **the Spirit who is from God, so that we may know the things freely given to us by God**, 13 which things we also speak, not in words taught by human wisdom, **but in those taught by the Spirit, combining spiritual thoughts with spiritual words**. 14 But a natural man does not accept the things of the Spirit of God, for they are foolishness to him; and he cannot understand them, because they are spiritually appraised.*

6:11 Holy Spirit is key to gaining spiritual insight which is why God's Word comes alive when a person is born again. Isn't it logical to think one key reason why Jesus breathed on the disciples on resurrection Sunday night was so they would have Holy Spirit in [en] them to help them understand the Kingdom teachings Jesus would give them over the next 40 days? If not, why not?

(4) If Not Sunday Evening, When

Moving on, nowhere does Jesus tell the disciples between resurrection Sunday and His ascension 40 days later that they needed to be born again. Thus, if the disciples were not born again on resurrection Sunday evening, when were they born again? The most common response is on Pentecost. One problem with this view is that the Bible does not show Holy Spirit came in [en] the disciples at Pentecost, but instead came upon [epi] them, a totally different experience. Moreover, just before Jesus's ascension, He does not tell His disciples they needed to be born again.

6:12 If Jesus's disciples weren't born again when Jesus ascended, don't you think Jesus would have made this gap clear to them before He ascended?

(5) Resurrection Sunday is in [en]; Pentecost is upon [epi]
- *Acts 1:4 ... He commanded them not to leave Jerusalem, but to wait for what the Father had promised, "Which," He said, "you heard of from Me; 5 for John baptized with water, but you **will be baptized with the Holy Spirit** not many days from now." ... 8 but you will **receive power** when the **Holy Spirit has come upon you**; and **you shall be My witnesses** both in Jerusalem, and in all Judea and Samaria, and ... the remotest part of the earth."*

Acts 1:4-8 refers to the Baptism of the Holy Spirit when the Holy Spirit comes upon a believer. This upon [epi] experience is dealt with in detail in the next 2 chapters. In brief, the upon [epi] experience would happen in the future in order for

CEASED?

them to receive power to be witnesses for Christ. Jesus didn't say the Baptism of the Holy Spirit would occur so the original apostles and disciples would be born again.

John the Baptist provided some clarity by revealing Jesus is the One who Baptizes a person in the Holy Spirit, not another person.

- ❏ Matthew 3:11 *"As for me, I baptize you with water for repentance, but He who is coming after me is mightier than I, and I am not fit to remove His sandals;* **_He will baptize you with the Holy Spirit and fire_**.

Fast forward, and the Baptism in the Holy Spirit came 10 days later at Pentecost.

- ❏ *Acts 2:1 When the day of Pentecost had come, they were all together in one place. 2 And suddenly there came from heaven a noise like a violent rushing wind, and it filled the whole house where they were sitting. 3 And there appeared to them tongues as of fire distributing themselves, and they rested* **_on [epi]_** *each one of them. 4 And* **_they were all filled with the Holy Spirit_** *and began to speak with other tongues, as the Spirit was giving them utterance.*

Later in Acts 2, Peter clarified this Baptism of the Holy Spirit was the beginning of the pouring out of the spirit upon [epi] believers as was prophesied by Joel. Furthermore, Joel stated the pouring out of the Spirit was relevant not to a few, but all mankind, and that the sons and daughters of God would prophesy, see visions, dream dreams and would have lives filled with many wonders.

- ❏ *Acts 2:17 'And it shall be in the last days,' God says, 'That I will pour forth of My Spirit* **_on [epi] all mankind_**; *And your sons and your daughters shall* **_prophesy_**, *And your young men shall see* **_visions_**, *And your old men shall dream* **_dreams_**;
- ❏ *Acts 2:18 Even on My bondslaves, both men and women, I will in those days* **_pour forth of My Spirit_** *And they* **_shall prophesy_**. *19 'And I will* **_grant wonders in the sky_** *above And* **_signs on the earth below, Blood, and fire, and vapor of smoke_**. *20 'The sun will be turned into darkness And the moon into blood, Before the great and glorious day of the Lord shall come. 21 'And it shall* **_be that everyone who calls on the name of the Lord will be saved_**.'

Jesus told the disciples in Acts 1:8 they would be Baptized in the Holy Spirit, and Holy Spirit would come upon them to receive power to enable them to be witnesses. Ten days after Jesus's ascension, Holy Spirit was poured out at Pentecost and came on those gathered, one of whom was Peter. No mention was made of their being born again at this time. Soon afterward, Peter the fisherman, who a few weeks earlier cowardly denied Jesus, now boldly spoke. That same day, ~3,000 gave their life to Christ. Talk about powerful witnessing.

Additional Considerations

Some believers may still feel the apostles/disciples weren't born again resurrection Sunday evening. If so, there are two basic alternatives when they were saved:

i. between resurrection Sunday and Pentecost; and
ii. on Pentecost at the same time as Holy Spirit came upon the disciples.

6: Holy Spirit In [En]

No scriptures indicate the born-again experience occurred in either of these alternatives. By contrast, scriptures show Jesus breathing on the disciples and telling them to receive the Holy Spirit on resurrection Sunday evening, events which are consistent with them being born again.

Prior to the cross, the disciples had referred to Jesus as Lord. When the other disciples saw Thomas, who wasn't there on resurrection Sunday evening, they again referred to Jesus as Lord.

- ❑ *John 20:24 But Thomas, one of the twelve, called Didymus, was not with them when Jesus came. 25 So the other disciples were saying to him, "**We have seen the Lord!**" ...*

Soon after, Thomas met Jesus and not only called Jesus Lord, but "... **My** Lord and **my** God."

- ❑ *John 20:26 After eight days His disciples were again inside, and Thomas with them. Jesus came, the doors having been shut, and stood in their midst and said, "Peace be with you." 27 Then He said to Thomas, "Reach here with your finger, and see My hands; and reach here your hand and put it into My side; and do not be unbelieving, but believing." 28 **Thomas answered and said to Him, "My Lord and my God!**"*

6:13 Is it realistic to think Thomas gave his life to Jesus the first night he met the risen Jesus? If not, why not?

In Summary

When Jesus breathed on His disciples on resurrection Sunday evening, I don't believe it was symbolic. I believe the disciples were born again when Jesus breathed on them. One major benefit of being born again is that with Holy Spirit in [en] the disciples, Holy Spirit was positioned to give them spiritual understanding. This understanding was important when Jesus taught them about kingdom of God issues over the following 40 days until He ascended. After Christ's ascension, the disciples were together for 10 days as they waited for the Baptism of the Holy Spirit, an experience which occurred on Pentecost when Holy Spirit came upon [epi] them and gave them access to supernatural power to be witnesses. Soon after this outpouring of the Spirit, Peter who was once full of fear now boldly witnessed to the observers of the supernatural events at Pentecost.

WHO DID JESUS BREATHE UPON, AND WHO WAS BORN AGAIN, ON RESURRECTION SUNDAY EVENING?

Valuable insight in the Cessationist vs Continuationist debate and whether all believers or only Catholic priests are to forgive sins is provided by looking at who Jesus did breathe on, and then told to receive the Holy Spirit on resurrection Sunday evening. It also provides insight into who was Baptized in the Holy Spirit at Pentecost, and received one or more of the 9 Holy Spirit gifts.

In Principle

- ❑ *Luke 24:33 And they got up that very hour and returned to Jerusalem, and*

CEASED?

__found gathered together the eleven__ and __those who were with them__, 34 saying, "The Lord has really risen and has appeared to Simon." 35 They began to relate their experiences on the road and how He was recognized by them in the breaking of the bread.

6:14 When Jesus breathed and said *"receive the Holy Spirit"*, He could have limited this blessing to the 11 apostles or given it to all including the 11, the two disciples who encountered Jesus on the road to Emmaus plus *'those who were with them'* on resurrection Sunday evening. If Jesus only breathed on the apostles and only they were born again, what benefit was there to delay the others from being born again? And if the others weren't born again resurrection Sunday evening, when were they born again?

6:15 Wouldn't it benefit God's kingdom if all the disciples gathered on resurrection Sunday evening were born again so they could also better understand the teachings Jesus gave over the following 40-day period? Just as He taught the crowds before the cross?

6:16 Wouldn't causing all who were gathered to be born again and be involved in hearing Jesus teach during those 40 days be consistent with God's nature of using all of us to advance His Kingdom - no matter our position, age, race or gender?

- *Matthew 10:7 And as you go, preach, saying, '__The kingdom of heaven__ is at hand.' 8 Heal the sick, raise the dead, cleanse the lepers, cast out demons. Freely you received, freely give.*

Let's examine 4 groups who might have been there resurrection Sunday evening when Jesus showed up, plus others who might have been born again before Pentecost.

(1) The Eleven

When the two disciples who encountered Jesus on the road to Emmaus returned to Jerusalem, they found the eleven apostles who are generally believed to have received the breath from Jesus.

(2) Women Who Found the Empty Tomb

In terms of those who were part of the group described in Luke 24:33 as *'those who were with them'*, consider the group of women that found the empty tomb.

- *Mark 16:1 When the Sabbath was over, __Mary Magdalene__, and __Mary the mother of James__, and __Salome__, bought spices, so that they might come and anoint Him.*
- *Luke 24:10 Now they were __Mary Magdalene__ and __Joanna__ and __Mary the mother of James__; also the __other women with them__ were telling these things to the apostles.*
- *Matthew 28:8 And they left the tomb quickly with fear and great joy and __ran to report it to His disciples__. 9 And behold, Jesus met them and greeted them. And they came up and took hold of His feet and worshiped Him. 10 Then Jesus said to them, "Do not be afraid; go and __take word to My brethren to leave__*

6: Holy Spirit In [En]

*for Galilee, and **there they will see Me**."*

6:17 In Mark 16:1 and Luke 24:10, 4 women are uniquely mentioned by name - Mary Magdalene, Mary the mother of James, Joanna and Salome. Luke 24.10 mentions 3 of these same 4 women by name, and then says there were *'other women'*. If there was a total of only 4 women, then it would have been more appropriate in Luke 24:10 to speak in the singular *'another woman'*, and not in the plural *'other women'*. Doesn't that indicate there were more than 4 women who went to the tomb on resurrection Sunday?

6:18 These women ran to tell the disciples of the empty tomb and to tell them to go to Galilee where they would see Jesus.
  i. Do you believe it is reasonable these 5 or more women told *'My brethren'* to go to Galilee, then traveled with *'My brethren'* to Galilee, and then waited for Jesus alongside *'My brethren'*? If not, why not?
  ii. Moreover, isn't it likely these 5 or more women were part of *'those who were with them'* on resurrection Sunday evening? If not, why not?

Shortly after Jesus ascended in Acts 1, Peter called for the vote on Judas's replacement. In this meeting, women and men were together in prayer which is something these early believers were continually devoting themselves to doing.

❏ *Acts 1:14 These all with one mind were **continually** devoting themselves to prayer, **along with the women, and Mary the mother of Jesus**, and with His brothers. 15 At this time Peter stood up in the midst of the **brethren** (a gathering of **about one hundred and twenty persons** was there together), and said,*

6:19 Several/many of the women who had walked with Christ during His ministry were with Jesus at the cross. They got up early to look after Jesus's body on resurrection Sunday morning. They had seen the empty tomb and told the disciples of the risen Christ. There were several women gathered with male disciples in constant prayer after Christ's ascension in Acts 1. Given they were dedicated followers of Christ and were in constant prayer with the men, doesn't this further indicate these same women were some of *'those who were with them'* gathered together on resurrection Sunday evening, anxiously waiting for the resurrected Christ? If not, why not?

6:20 And if they were part of this group, isn't it reasonable to think these same women were amongst the very first, born-again Christians who Jesus told He was sending just as He had been sent, then proceeded to breathe on them and tell them to receive the Holy Spirit? If not, why not? Why would Jesus give this gift to men such as the two men Jesus met on the road to Emmaus, but not to the women who showed such passion, love, commitment, and devotion to Him?

(3) My Brethren

On resurrection Sunday morning when the women left the empty tomb and met Jesus, Jesus told them to tell His brethren to leave for Galilee where they will see Jesus.

CEASED?

❑ *Matthew 28:8 And they left the tomb quickly with fear and great joy and ran to report it to His disciples. 9 And behold, Jesus met them and greeted them. And they came up and took hold of His feet and worshiped Him. 10 Then Jesus said to them, "Do not be afraid; go and **take word to My brethren** to leave for Galilee, and **there they will see Me**."*

As per Chapter 3, the English word *'brethren'* is derived from the Greek word *'adelphos'* [G80] which can be used to refer to a limited group such as men, but is often used in a broader sense.

6:21   Given adelphos is used and not other Greek words that pertain to apostles or males only, doesn't this further indicate Jesus wanted to see all His close followers, and not just a limited few? If not, why not?

(4) 70 Jesus Sent Out Before the Cross

Before the cross, Jesus sent 70 to do certain things including healing the sick.

❑ *Luke 10:1 Now after this the **Lord appointed seventy others**, and sent them in pairs... 9 and **heal those in it who are sick**, and say to them, 'The kingdom of God has come near to you.'*

The 70, who possibly included Matthias and Barsabbas, had a very positive experience.

❑ *Luke 10:17 The seventy returned with joy, saying, "Lord, even the demons are subject to us in Your name."*

6:22   Is it reasonable to expect that some, many or even all of these 70 who were still alive, were some of the *'brethren'* and part of *'those who were with them'* on resurrection Sunday evening? If not, why not?

WERE OTHERS SAVED BETWEEN RESURRECTION SUNDAY AND PENTECOST

6:23   Fifty days passed between resurrection Sunday evening and Pentecost. Is it possible some individuals who weren't present on resurrection Sunday evening, were born again after that Sunday and before Pentecost, and were part of the group Baptized in the Holy Spirit at Pentecost?

6:24   Consider that Jesus appeared to many including a group that exceeded 500. Is it reasonable to assume that some of these may have accepted Christ, and excitedly so?

❑ *1 Corinthians 15:6 After that He appeared to **more than five hundred** brethren at one time, most of whom remain until now, but some have fallen asleep;*

6:25   For a minute, consider that some individuals gave their lives to Christ either i) between resurrection Sunday evening and His ascension, or ii) between His ascension and the outpouring of the Holy Spirit at Pentecost. In Acts 1:15, ~120 gathered after Jesus's ascension when the vote was held to replace Judas. Is it reasonable to believe:

i. the group gathered on resurrection Sunday evening may have been smaller than the ~120 gathered 40 or more days later to vote on Judas's replacement; and
ii. the group gathered at Pentecost may have been larger than the ~120 gathered when the vote was held on Judas's replacement?

WOMEN AND THE RESURRECTED CHRIST

This is a bit of a diversion but I feel an important one. Many Catholic and Cessationist leaders are adamant that women should have a limited and quiet, background role in the church. As I was writing **CEASED?**, I found situations I hadn't paid much attention to before, but feel led to share. This is one.

Several women played prominent roles in the New Testament including the 4 virgin daughters who prophesied, Priscilla who joined Aquila in correcting Apollos, Euodia and Syntyche who shared the gospel, Phoebe who Paul said was to receive whatever help she needed, and Junias who was a helper to many.

- ❑ Acts 21:8 On the next day we left and came to Caesarea, and entering the house of **Philip** the evangelist, who was one of the seven, we stayed with him. 9 Now this man had **four virgin daughters who were prophetesses**.
- ❑ Acts 18:24 Now a Jew named **Apollos**, an Alexandrian by birth, an eloquent man, came to Ephesus; and he was mighty in the Scriptures ... 26 and he began to speak out boldly in the synagogue. But when **Priscilla and Aquila heard him, they took him aside and explained to him the way of God more accurately**.
- ❑ Philippians 4:2 I urge **Euodia** and I urge **Syntyche** to live in harmony in the Lord. 3 Indeed, true companion, I ask you also **to help these women who have shared my struggle in the cause of the gospel** ...
- ❑ Romans 16:1 I commend to you our sister **Phoebe**, who is a servant of the church which is at Cenchrea; 2 that you receive her in the Lord in a manner worthy of the saints, and **that you help her in whatever matter she may have need of you**; for she herself has also been a helper of many, and of myself as well.
- ❑ Romans 16:7 Greet Andronicus and **Junias**, my kinsmen and my fellow prisoners, who are outstanding among the apostles, who also were in Christ before me.

6:26 Don't these scriptures show women played a material role in the church after the cross? Given that, why wouldn't women play similar significant and prominent roles today?

This group of initial believers had a very tight bond. They were born again on resurrection Sunday evening, or soon thereafter. They experienced to varying degrees, teachings on matters pertaining to the kingdom of God. They were told to wait for the Baptism of the Holy Spirit. Each morning after Jesus's ascension must have been an exciting day wondering - is this the day? I doubt they stayed at home sipping tea and eating croissants, but instead *'continuously gathered'* to worship, give praise, pray and wonder. In the meeting where Peter called for the vote on

CEASED?

Judas's replacement, Peter referred to the men and women gathered together as brethren.
- ❑ *Acts 1:14 These all with one mind were continually devoting themselves to prayer, **along with the women, and Mary the mother of Jesus**, and with His brothers. 15 At this time Peter stood up in the midst of the **brethren** (a gathering of **about one hundred and twenty persons** was there together), and said,*

As mentioned, the word 'brethren' is derived from the Greek word 'adelphos' which can refer to either gender of a believer. In regards to women:

6:27 is it reasonable to think the women who found the empty tomb were:
  i. some of the brethren gathered on resurrection Sunday evening;
  ii. observed the vote when Judas's replacement was selected; and
  iii. were part of the group gathered at Pentecost where everybody present was Baptized in the Holy Spirit and spoke in tongues?
  iv. If not, why not?

In Summary

6:28 Given all the above:
  i. is it fair to say that the group gathered at Pentecost was diverse, and included far more than the 11 original apostles plus Matthias?
  ii. is it also reasonable to believe the group gathered on resurrection Sunday evening fairly closely resembled i) the ~120 gathered in Acts 1:14 who prayed and voted on Judas's replacement, ii) those who were continually together in the temple praising God, and iii) those gathered on Pentecost who were Baptized in the Holy Spirit? If not, why not?

- ❑ *Luke 24:36 While they were telling these things, **He Himself stood in their midst** and said to them, "Peace be to you." ... 45 Then **He opened their minds to understand the Scriptures**, ... 49 And behold, I am sending forth the promise of My Father upon you; **but you are to stay in the city until you are clothed with power from on high**." 50 And He led them out as far as Bethany, and He lifted up His hands and blessed them. 51 While He was blessing them, **He parted from them and was carried up into heaven**. 52 And they, after worshiping Him, **returned to Jerusalem** with great joy, 53 and **were continually in the temple praising God**.*

HOLY SPIRIT'S BAPTISM OF BELIEVERS INTO THE BODY OF CHRIST AND GOD'S CHURCH

In 1 Corinthians, Paul writes that all believers are part of the Body of Christ.
- ❑ *1 Corinthians 12:22 On the contrary, it is much truer that the **members of the body** which seem to be weaker are necessary; 23 and those **members of the body** which we deem less honorable ... 24 ... But **God has so composed the body**, giving more abundant honor to that member which lacked, 25 so that*

6: Holy Spirit In [En]

*there may **be no division in the body**, but that the members may have the same care for one another. 26 And if one member suffers, all the members suffer with it; if one member is honored, all the members rejoice with it. 27 Now **you are Christ's body**, and individually members of it.*

Paul writes that Holy Spirit **baptizes us** into one body, the Body of Christ.
- *1 Corinthians 12:13 For **by one Spirit** we were **all baptized into one body**, whether Jews or Greeks, whether slaves or free, and we were **all made to drink of one Spirit**.*

The English word 'baptize' is derived from the Greek word 'baptizo' [G907] which Thayer defines in part as 'immerse, to submerge'. When born again, we're surrounded by other believers who, along with us, are immersed together into the Body of Christ. And thereafter, Jesus and Holy Spirit are both with [meta] and in [en] us.

Holy Spirit's baptism of believers into the Body of Christ is one of the four key baptisms relevant to today's believers, and which are covered in Chapter 10. The baptism into the Body of Christ is done by Holy Spirit, and done automatically when we're born again.

POWER OF GOD IN THE 'EN' AND THE 'EPI'

When we're born again and Holy Spirit comes in [en] us, God is in us, right here. In addition to any power we might have as a result of God being with [para/meta] us, we're also automatically given access to God's power through His being in [en] us. In the case of the in [en] experience, this power of God is primarily geared to God changing our hearts, convicting us, speaking to us, guiding us, teaching us, leading us etc. But make no mistake, we have the power of God in us, the same Spirit whose power raised Jesus from the dead.
- *Romans 8:11 But if the Spirit of Him who raised Jesus from the dead dwells in you, He who raised Christ Jesus from the dead will also give life to your mortal bodies through His Spirit who dwells in you.*

Chapter 7 deals with the Baptism of the Holy Spirit coming upon [epi] a believer. In so doing, we gain access to a different kind of God's power that helps us be witnesses for Christ, power that we don't have when we're born again and Holy Spirit is in [en] us and with [para/meta] us. Believers are sometimes automatically Baptized in the Holy Spirit at the same time they're born again, but most believers receive it later or not at all as we shall see in Chapters 7 and 8.
- *Acts 1:8 but you will receive power when the Holy Spirit has come upon you; and you shall be My witnesses both in Jerusalem, and in all Judea and Samaria, and even to the remotest part of the earth.*

This upon [epi] power manifests in different ways including the 9 Holy Spirit gifts.

CEASED?

CLOSING POINTS TO PONDER

6:29 Given the tremendous turmoil Peter experienced when he denied Christ 3 times and the rooster crowed, do you think Peter ever ate chicken again?

6:30 When we meet another believer, challenging personalities set aside for the moment, don't we typically feel a kind of kindship as soon as we begin talking? And isn't this kindship fostered by the fact that both of us have Holy Spirit in [en] us and our respective spirits are born again?

6:31 Jesus didn't sin while living 33 ½ years on earth. As we shall see in Chapter 7, Jesus received the *'upon'* [epi] experience at the start of His ministry. Is it possible Jesus had a variation of Holy Spirit *'with'* [para or meta] or *'in'* [en] relationship starting when He was young that enabled Him not to sin?

6:32 Some Bible teachers state it is foolish to think a believer can feel or sense God's presence. My question is this: Given Almighty God, the Creator of the universe, resides inside of us, how can we not sense His presence once in a while? And if a person never senses His presence, could it mean Holy Spirit may not be in [en] the person? That he/she may not be saved?

6:33 In my view, the first Christians were born again when Jesus breathed on them resurrection Sunday evening. When we were born again and when new believers come into God's kingdom today - and this is pure speculation on my part - is it possible Jesus welcomes each of us into the Body of Christ by breathing Holy Spirit in us and gently whispering to our heart something like *"Welcome Home. Welcome to My Family!"*?

6:34 When Peter asked Ananias why he lied to Holy Spirit, was it because Ananias was a believer and with Holy Spirit now in [en] him, Ananias's words and actions were effectively said and done to Holy Spirit?

❏ *Acts 5:3 But Peter said, "Ananias, why has Satan filled your heart to **lie to the Holy Spirit** and to keep back some of the price of the land?*

6:35 I'm not sure how Holy Spirit being with [meta] us differs from Holy Spirit being in [en] us. Is this one more mystery we'll have to wait until we get to heaven to understand?

6:36 Several women clearly played key and public roles in the early church including prophesying. Does that suggest women should perhaps be playing similar roles today?

❏ *1 Corinthians 11:5 But **every woman** who has her head uncovered **while praying or prophesying** disgraces her head, for she is one and the same as the woman whose head is shaved.*

7

Holy Spirit 'Upon' [Epi]

INTRODUCTION
BEFORE we're born again, Holy Spirit is with [para] us. After we're born again, we live with Holy Spirit in [en] us and with [meta] us. Chapter 7 deals with another experience, the [epi] experience known as the Baptism of the Holy Spirit. Chapter 7 reviews:
1. what the baptism is designed to accomplish (page 116);
2. who does the actual baptism (page 117);
3. who was Baptized in the Holy Spirit at Pentecost (page 118);
4. whether or not the in [en] and upon [epi] are the same experience (page 120);
5. 4 of the many impacts of the Baptism of the Holy Spirit (page 120);
6. how to receive our own Baptism in the Holy Spirit (page 123);
7. some of the upon experiences in the Old Testament (page 124); and
8. upon experiences in the New Testament before the cross (page 125).

BORN AGAIN, TRAINED, BUT STILL NEED MORE
By the time the events at Pentecost rolled around in Acts 2, the apostles had walked with Jesus for 3 ½ years during His ministry. They saw amazing miracles. They heard great teachings. They heard Jesus declare He was God. They saw Him call out the religious people who were filled with knowledge, but not the real truths. They had seen His gruesome death. They had seen Him after the cross - resurrected and alive. Jesus breathed on them to receive the Holy Spirit, and they were born again. They had the Holy Spirit in [en] experience. From the time of His arrest in the Garden of Gethsemane on Thursday night to His appearance on Sunday night - they had witnessed historic events of monumental importance.

In Acts 1, we learn Jesus appeared to the disciples several times over a period of 40 days teaching them about matters of the Kingdom of God. The Bible gives no indication Jesus told them they still needed to be born again, nor was there any indication the disciples needed to be water baptized. Most notably, what Jesus does tell them to do at the end of the 40-day period is ... wait.

❏ *Acts 1:3 To these He also presented Himself alive after His suffering, by many convincing proofs, appearing to them **over a period of forty days** and speaking of the things concerning the kingdom of God. 4 Gathering them*

CEASED?

> *together, **He commanded them not to leave Jerusalem, but to wait for what the Father had promised**, "Which," He said, "you heard of from Me;*

"Wait". That's what Jesus commanded them to do. *"Wait"*. Acts 1:4 tells us the reason for waiting is so they can receive the promise of Father God. There are thousands of promises in the Bible from God. In Acts 1:5, Jesus clarifies this particular promise is the Baptism of the Holy Spirit.

- ❑ *Acts 1:5 for John baptized with water, but you **will be baptized with the Holy Spirit** not many days from now."*

7:1 The word *'will'* is future tense indicating this baptism will take place in the future, as do the words *'not many days from now'*. Given they already have Holy Spirit in [en] them as a result of Jesus breathing on them on resurrection Sunday evening, doesn't Acts 1:5 demonstrate this future Baptism of the Holy Spirit where Holy Spirit comes upon [epi] a person is a distinct and separate experience from being born again? If not, why not?

WAIT FOR THE BAPTISM IN THE HOLY SPIRIT

The reason the disciples needed the Baptism in the Holy Spirit is found in Acts 1:8 when three key aspects are revealed - power, upon and witnessing.

- ❑ *Acts 1:8 but you **will receive power** when the **Holy Spirit has come upon [epi] you**; and **you shall be My witnesses** both in Jerusalem, and in all Judea and Samaria, and even to the remotest part of the earth."*

The three items - power, upon [epi] and witness - reflect the what, how and why behind the Baptism of the Holy Spirit.

- ❑ The what: **to receive power** - supernatural enablement;
- ❑ The how: Holy Spirit **comes on or upon** [epi] a believer, as opposed to Holy Spirit coming in [en] a person when born again; and
- ❑ The why: to enable the person to **be a witness** for Christ - whether locally or to the ends of the earth.

Luke confirms the disciples were to wait for the promise until they were endued with *power*.

- ❑ *Luke 24:49 And behold, I am sending forth the promise of My Father upon you; but **you are to stay in the city until you are clothed with power from on high**."*

7:2 Doesn't the fact that the Baptism of the Holy Spirit is to give disciples power to be witnesses further confirm that the Baptism of the Holy Spirit (the upon or epi) is a separate and distinct experience from being saved/born again (the in or en) when one is Baptized into the Body of Christ?

After Jesus tells his disciples to wait to be Baptized in the Holy Spirit, He ascended.

- ❑ *Acts 1:9 And after He had said these things, He was lifted up while they were looking on, and a cloud received Him out of their sight.*

7:3 Given the instructions related to the Baptism of the Holy Spirit were

7: Holy Spirit Upon [Epi]

amongst the very last words Jesus gave to His disciples before His ascension, isn't it reasonable to believe Jesus's last instructions were particularly important?

Who does the Actual Baptism in the Holy Spirit

We saw at the end of Chapter 6 that it is Holy Spirit who baptizes us into the Body of Christ when we're born again.

- ❏ 1 Corinthians 12:13 For **by one Spirit, we were all baptized into one body**, whether Jews or Greeks, whether slaves or free, and we were all made to drink of one Spirit.

So, who Baptizes believers in the Holy Spirit? John the Baptist tells us that it is Jesus who Baptizes us in the Holy Spirit.

- ❏ Matthew 3:11 "As for me, I baptize you with water for repentance, but **He who is coming after me is mightier than I**, and I am not fit to remove His sandals; **He will baptize you with the Holy Spirit and fire**.
- ❏ Mark 1:8 I baptized you with water; **but He will baptize you with the Holy Spirit**.
- ❏ Luke 3:16 John answered and said to them all, "As for me, I baptize you with water; but One is coming who is mightier than I, and I am not fit to untie the thong of His sandals; **He will baptize you with the Holy Spirit and fire**.

Talk about a personal touch and how the Father, Son and Holy Spirit not only work together so uniquely and wonderfully, but they get us involved too. When born again, Holy Spirit baptizes us into the Body of Christ. Jesus baptizes us in the Holy Spirit if and when we receive this gift. And our Almighty God is so loving, that He gets us involved when we have the privilege of baptizing another disciple in water.

The Upon 'Epi' Experience

A key distinction identifying the Baptism in the Holy Spirit experience is that Holy Spirit comes *'on'* or *'upon'* a believer. These English words *'on'* and *'upon'* are derived from the Greek word *'epi'* [G1909] which means *'on or upon, at, by or before'*.

- ❏ Acts 1:8 but you **will receive power** when the **Holy Spirit has come upon [epi] you**; and you shall be My witnesses both in Jerusalem, and in all Judea and Samaria, and even to the remotest part of the earth."

When born again, Holy Spirit comes **'in' [en]** a person to convict, guide, teach, etc. This blessing is primarily for our benefit in ways such as gaining spiritual understanding. However, our lives aren't just about ourselves, and our goal is not just about getting to heaven, but to take the Good News of Jesus to those who don't know Him. And with Holy Spirit and Christ in us, we can be a light to this world. This in [en] experience is the beginning of what God has for us - but it's not the end.

When we're Baptized in the Holy Spirit, Holy Spirit comes **'upon' [epi]** the person to give us access to power, supernatural enablement as it were, so we can be a witness for Christ. The Baptism in the Holy Spirit is primarily for the benefit of

CEASED?

others. But God is so good; as Chapter 7 will soon reveal, we can also be personally blessed from this upon [epi] Baptism.

Who was Gathered Together at Pentecost

Starting midway through Chapter 6, **CEASED?** discussed who was in the groups gathered on resurrection Sunday evening (John 20:19-24, Luke 24:13-45), 40+ days later when Judas's replacement was determined (Acts 1:14; Luke 24:46-52) and those gathered at Pentecost (Acts 2:1-2; Luke 24:50-53). For anyone involved at Pentecost, they must have had some fairly incredible moments of joy and excitement along with bewilderment and trepidation. Less than two months earlier, they had seen Jesus crucified, then resurrected. He taught them kingdom matters over 40 days, then He tells them to wait for the Baptism in the Holy Spirit so they could have power. Wouldn't that get your mind going in a few different ways? Wait - for power? Wow!!

7:4 Between Jesus's ascension and Pentecost, do you think the born-again believers were each going about their day to day routines separate and apart, or were they together excitedly awaiting this Baptism of the Holy Spirit?

❏ *Luke 24:50 And He led them out as far as Bethany, and He lifted up His hands and blessed them. 51 While He was blessing them, **He parted from them and was carried up into heaven**. 52 And they, after worshiping Him, **returned to Jerusalem** with **great joy**, 53 and **were continually in the temple praising God**.*

❏ *Acts 2:1 When the day of Pentecost had come, they were **all together** in one place.*

7:5 Doesn't the word *'all'* in Acts 2:1 suggest all the disciples - ~120 of them - were involved at Pentecost, and not just the apostles?

7:6 If this group only included the original 11 apostles plus Matthias, wouldn't scripture likely distinguish the apostles from all disciples such as *"When the twelve were together"* or *"When the apostles were gathered ..."*?

What Happened at Pentecost

❏ *Acts 2:2 And suddenly there came from heaven a **noise like a violent rushing wind**, and it **filled the whole house** where they were sitting. 3 And there appeared to them **tongues as of fire distributing themselves**, and they **rested on each one of them**. 4 And they were **all filled with the Holy Spirit** and began to **speak with other tongues**, as the Spirit was giving them utterance.*

This Baptism involved an outpouring of the Holy Spirit - a manifestation of God's power - in different ways including noise, tongues of fire, and disciples speaking in tongues.

7:7 Do these tongues of fire indicate that when God sends fire, sometimes the fire is a major blessing to people?

7:8 Isn't it reasonable to believe every person in the group gathered together

7: Holy Spirit Upon [Epi]

with one accord at Pentecost was Baptized in the Holy Spirit and spoke in tongues? If not, why weren't they?

7:9 On the basis that everyone who was gathered at Pentecost was Baptized in the Holy Spirit, wouldn't that mean every one of them received access to the upon [epi] power to witness as per Acts 1:8? If not, why not?

7:10 Acts 2:1-4 says everyone in the group at Pentecost who experienced the outpouring of the Holy Spirit spoke in tongues. Doesn't this also indicate that the 9 Holy Spirit gifts were not limited to the original apostles?

7:11 In John 20:22 when Jesus breathed and told them to receive the Holy Spirit, it seems like it was a relatively gentle experience. By contrast, the Baptism of the Holy Spirit per Acts 2 was not gentle, but a radical announcement. Does this initial demonstration of God's power in various forms (sound, tongues of fire, people speaking in tongues) again support the notion that the in [en] experience when one is born again is about helping one inside while the upon [epi] experience when one is Baptized in the Holy Spirit is about power to benefit others? And given 3,000 came to the Lord later that day, isn't that a fairly convincing testimony that God's power works?

Promise of the Father

Peter tells us Jesus received the promise of the Holy Spirit, and that Jesus in turn poured out the very same promise at Pentecost.

- ❑ *Mark 1:10 Immediately coming up out of the water, He saw the heavens opening, and the Spirit like a dove descending upon Him;*
- ❑ *Acts 2:33 Therefore having been exalted to the right hand of God, and having* **received from the Father the promise of the Holy Spirit, He has poured forth this** *which you both see and hear.*

7:12 Does Acts 2:33 confirm that Jesus is the One who does the Baptism of the Holy Spirit when Peter states *"He has poured forth this which you both see and hear"*?

7:13 Doesn't Acts 2:33 also suggest the same Holy Spirit power Jesus was given access to when He began His ministry is:
  i. the same kind of Holy Spirit power followers at Pentecost were given access to; and
  ii. the same kind of Holy Spirit power believers can have access to today?

Filled with the Holy Spirit

7:14 In Acts 2:4, the disciples who were Baptized in the Holy Spirit were *'filled with the Holy Spirit'*. Doesn't the fact the disciples were filled with the Holy Spirit suggest they were not filled before this Baptism in the Holy Spirit occurred?

7:15 Doesn't Acts 2:4 show that while a believer has Holy Spirit in [en] them after being born again, this *'filling'* is a different supernatural experience and related to the power of God? In other words, isn't this another indication the experience when Holy Spirit comes in [en] a person is different than when Holy Spirit comes upon [epi] us?

7:16 If being filled in the upon [epi] experience in Acts 2 at Pentecost is not a different experience from the in [en] experience in John 20:22 on resurrection Sunday evening, how then do we explain the 50-day time gap between the two experiences occurring?

Chapter 9 of **CEASED?** discusses being filled with the Holy Spirit more completely. A key goal of Chapter 9 is to determine if *'being filled'* is more closely associated with the experience when one is born again and Holy Spirit comes in [en] a believer, or to when one is Baptized in the Holy Spirit and Holy Spirit comes upon [epi] a believer.

Still not sure En and Epi are Separate Experiences

If you still believe the disciples did not receive the Holy Spirit in [en] them on resurrection Sunday evening, a few more questions.

7:17 Do you believe they were born again between resurrection Sunday evening and 40 days later when Christ ascended to be with the Father? If so, what scripture(s) leads you to that conclusion?

7:18 Do you believe they were born again in the 10 days between when Christ ascended to be with the Father and Pentecost? If so, what scripture(s) lead you to that conclusion?

7:19 If you believe the disciples were born again and received in [en] experience on Pentecost, the same time as the upon [epi] experience, what scripture(s) lead you to override John 20:22 where Jesus breathed on them and told them to receive the Holy Spirit?

4 IMPACTS OF A BAPTISM IN THE HOLY SPIRIT

God's blessings are so many. As it relates to blessings from being Baptized in the Holy Spirit, **CEASED?** reviews only 4 of the blessings.

(1) Power to be Witnesses - Supernatural Signs

Returning to Pentecost, others who were nearby heard and saw God's power in the form of noise and tongues of fire, then heard the disciples speaking different tongues. They were amazed.

❑ *Acts 2:6 And when this sound occurred, the crowd came together, and were bewildered because each one of them was hearing them speak in his own language. 7 They **were amazed and astonished**, saying, "Why, are not all these who are speaking Galileans?*

This supernatural act of speaking in tongues was a sign to the non-believers that God was real, was alive, and He wanted them to know it. Signs and wonders come in various flavors and are a powerful witnessing tool. Healing is a great example. For instance, when somebody has their broken foot instantly healed, they can't deny the reality. They know God touched them.

7:20 Jesus performed many signs and wonders. And aren't all believers called to do the same?

❑ *John 14:12 Truly, truly, I say to you, he **who believes in Me**, the **works that I***

7: Holy Spirit Upon [Epi]

*do, **he will do also**; and **greater works than these he will do;** because I go to the Father.*

(2) Power to be Witnesses - Speaking

Peter explains what happened at Pentecost in a powerful message. The fruit of this sermon, and by extension some of the fruit from the Baptism of the Holy Spirit that took place at Pentecost, was ~3,000 souls coming into God's family.

- ❑ *Acts 2:40 And with many other words he solemnly testified and kept on exhorting them, saying, "Be saved from this perverse generation!" 41 So then, those who had received his word were baptized; and that day **there were added about three thousand souls**. 42 They were continually devoting themselves to the apostles' teaching and to fellowship, to the breaking of bread and to prayer.*

If we recall, Jesus stated in Acts 1:8 that the reason for the Baptism of the Holy Spirit was to receive power to be witnesses for Christ.

- ❑ *Acts 1:8 but **you will receive power** when the Holy Spirit has come upon you; and **you shall be My witnesses** both in Jerusalem, and in all Judea and Samaria, and even to the remotest part of the earth."*

Peter and John were fishermen. In the eyes of the Jewish leaders, they were uneducated and untrained. Yet a short time after Pentecost, these leaders marveled at how John and Peter spoke.

- ❑ *Acts 4:6 and Annas the high priest was there, and Caiaphas and John and Alexander, and all who were of high-priestly descent. 7 When they had placed them in the center, they began to inquire, "By what power, or in what name, have you done this?" 8 Then Peter, filled with the Holy Spirit, said to them, "Rulers and elders of the people, ... 13 Now as they **observed the confidence of Peter and John and understood that they were uneducated and untrained men**, they were amazed, and began to recognize them as having been with Jesus.*

Though uneducated and untrained, Peter delivered a powerful message at Pentecost, a message that cut listeners to the core.

- ❑ *Acts 2:37 Now when they heard this, **they were pierced to the heart**, and said to Peter and the rest of the apostles, "Brethren, what shall we do?"*

The ~3,000 coming to Jesus was not only because of Peter's many words. For one, Holy Spirit was with [para] them, drawing them to Christ. In addition, Jesus's earthly ministry, His death and resurrection, Jesus being seen by more than 500 as well as by others between resurrection Sunday and His ascension, and the display of God's power earlier that day, all played a role. Having said that, however, Peter played a key role. The once frightened fisherman who denied Christ ~53 days before Pentecost, was now a passionate spokesperson for Christ. Talk about a transformation!

- ❑ *Acts 2:38 Peter said ... "Repent, and each of you be baptized ... 40 And **with***

> ***many other words*** *he solemnly testified and kept on exhorting them ...*

7:21 Is Peter's sermon consistent with the notion of Peter receiving supernatural power/equipping - Holy Spirit power - that enabled him to speak as he did?

A key role of the five-fold ministry is to equip the saints and build up the body.
- ❏ *Ephesians 4:11 And He gave some as apostles, and some as prophets, and some as evangelists, and some as pastors and teachers, 12* ***for the equipping of the saints*** *for the work of service, to the* ***building up of the body of Christ****;*

7:22 Jesus needed the upon [epi] experience for His earthly ministry. Peter was an apostle who benefited from the power of the Baptism of the Holy Spirit. Chapter 8 of **CEASED?** shows other disciples including Paul were Baptized in the Holy Spirit. If Jesus, Peter and Paul needed the Baptism of the Holy Spirit in their ministries, is there any reason to think today's believers including laypeople, pastors and teachers wouldn't benefit from a Baptism in the Holy Spirit, and having Holy Spirit come upon them with His power?

(3) Power to be Witnesses - Strength to Say No

As ambassadors, as sent ones for Christ, our very lives are to be a witness for Jesus. We all sin, but being free of sin is key, especially habitual sin.
- ❏ *1 Thessalonians 3:13 so that He may establish your hearts without blame in holiness before our God and Father at the coming of our Lord Jesus with all His saints.*
- ❏ *1 Thessalonians 5:23 Now may the God of peace Himself sanctify you entirely; and may your spirit and soul and body be preserved complete, without blame at the coming of our Lord Jesus Christ. 24 Faithful is He who calls you, and He also will bring it to pass.*
- ❏ *2 Corinthians 2:15 For we are* ***a fragrance of Christ*** *to God among those who are being saved and among those who are perishing;*

If we have a life filled with sin, we're not going to give off the fragrance of Christ. Our sin is why Christ died for us, and God strengthens us so that we can not only overcome, but we can live lives that are fairly close to being free of sin - ***if*** we want to be free. Don't think this is too radical. We can surely have lives that are dramatically less sinful than they used to be, and lives that continue to see less and less sin over time.
- ❏ *Philippians 4:13 I can do all things through Him who strengthens me.*
- ❏ *1 Corinthians 10:13 No temptation has overtaken you but such as is common to man; and God is faithful, who will not allow you to be tempted beyond what you are able, but with the temptation will provide the way of escape also, so that you will be able to endure it.*
- ❏ *Ephesians 3:16 that He would grant you, according to the riches of His glory, to be strengthened with power through His Spirit in the inner man,*

More of My Story

When I was Baptized in the Holy Spirit, I was changed. I had an addiction to porn which I had grown to really dislike after I was born again. But after my Baptism in the Holy Spirit, my dislike of this sin grew to intense hatred. Shortly thereafter, by the power of God and the truths in His Word, I was instantly, totally and permanently set free of any desire for porn, and simultaneously delivered from demonic influences that had been tormenting me.

The power of God that flows from the Baptism of the Holy Spirit is more than supernatural signs and wonders. His power helped me, and based on other people's testimonies, impacted many others who were given strength and desire to say no to sin.

7:23 How many of today's believers who struggle with habitual sins such as porn would benefit from being Baptized in the Holy Spirit?

(4) Power to be Witnesses - Increasing our Faith

Paul wrote on how personally experiencing the power of God can help our faith.
- ❑ *1 Corinthians 2:5 so that **your faith** would **not rest on the wisdom of men, but on the power of God**.*

RECEIVING OUR BAPTISM IN THE HOLY SPIRIT

The world is filled with people who don't have a personal relationship with Jesus. Some don't know anything about the true Jesus. Others know things about the true Jesus, but don't know Him personally. Those in Mormon, JW and Bahai faiths know about a Jesus, but the Jesus they know is not the Jesus of the Bible. This may seem unkind, but when their respective Jesus's are examined in-depth, and compared to the Jesus in our Bible, it's clear they have a different Jesus. One of the deceptions leading them astray is their belief our Bible has been altered over time. The truth is translations based on the original Greek and Hebrew have not changed in any material way.

7:24 Would we, as individuals, benefit from God's supernatural blessings if we share the Good News with others who, for one reason or another, don't know the true Jesus?

7:25 Luke 12 refers to Holy Spirit helping us defend our faith when confronted. Is it reasonable to expect Holy Spirit will also help when we're not confronted? And perhaps even more so if we're in touch with God throughout the day and asking Holy Spirit to guide us?
- ❑ *Luke 12:11 When they bring you before the synagogues and the rulers and the authorities, do not worry about how or what you are to speak in your defense, or what you are to say; 12 for the **Holy Spirit will teach you** in that very hour what you ought to say."*

7:26 Given Jesus is the one who baptizes a person in the Baptism of the Holy Spirit, can one go wrong by seeking Jesus and saying something akin to:

1: "Jesus, the Baptism of the Holy Spirit is true and available today, and since You are the one that gives it, I ask You to please give me this Baptism. Shield me from any schemes of the enemy, and provide help so that I use this gift the way You want it used, and for Your glory, not mine. Thank You Jesus. Amen."

7:27 Would the message Peter and John prayed in Acts 4:29-30 be the kind of prayer you would welcome prayed for you?
- ❑ *Acts 4:29 And now, Lord, take note of their threats, **and grant that Your bond-servants may speak Your word with all confidence**, 30 **while You extend Your hand to heal, and signs and wonders take place through the name of Your holy servant Jesus**."*

For those who did receive this prayer in Jerusalem, God showed up.
- ❑ *Acts 4:31 And **when they had prayed**, **the place** where they had gathered together **was shaken**, and **they were all filled** with the Holy Spirit and **began to speak the word of God with boldness**. ... 33 And **with great power the apostles were giving testimony** to the resurrection of the Lord Jesus, and abundant grace was upon them all.*

Personally speaking, Lori and I want all God has for us even though, in many ways, we understand so little. This means God will often take us out of our comfort zone. And we really, really like being in our comfort zone. But we know God is good, and what He has in store for us will be good. His unpredictable ways are part of what makes a believer's walk with Christ amazing, exciting and fulfilling. And sometimes uncomfortable. And sometimes comes with a topping of persecution.

UPON [EPI] EXPERIENCES IN THE OLD TESTAMENT

The Greek word for *'power'* is *'dunamis'* [G1411], a power for performing miracles. Holy Spirit is often cited as the 'power person' of the Godhead, and the One who blesses people through this power, starting thousands of years ago at creation.
- ❑ *Jeremiah 32:17 'Ah Lord God! Behold, You have made the heavens and the earth by Your great power and by Your outstretched arm! Nothing is too difficult for You,*

And this power continued onwards. Interestingly, God chose to co-labor with humans by placing His supernatural power upon individuals in the early days of the Old Testament. Consider the 70 elders, Eldad and Medad, Gideon and Saul.
- ❑ *Numbers 11:25 Then the Lord ... He took of the **Spirit who was upon him** and **placed Him upon the seventy elders**. And when the **Spirit rested upon them**, they **prophesied**. But they did not do it again.*
- ❑ *Numbers 11:26 ... one was Eldad and the name of the other Medad. And **the Spirit rested upon them** ... and they **prophesied** in the camp.*
- ❑ *Judges 6:34 So the **Spirit of the Lord came upon Gideon** ...*
- ❑ *1 Samuel 11:6 Then the **Spirit of God came upon Saul** mightily when he heard these words, and he became very angry.*

And then there were David, Elijah, Samson and Zechariah.
- ❑ *1 Samuel 16:13 ... the **Spirit of the Lord came mightily upon David** ...*
- ❑ *2 Kings 2:9 ... And Elisha said, "Please, let **a double portion of your spirit be upon me**."*

7: Holy Spirit Upon [Epi]

- *Judges 15:14 When he [Samson] ... the **Spirit of the Lord came upon him mightily** ... 15 He found a fresh jawbone of a donkey, so he reached out and took it and **killed a thousand men with it**.*
- *2 Chronicles 24:20 Then the **Spirit of God came on Zechariah** ...*

God equipped individuals with power for centuries before Jesus walked this earth. This power manifested in many ways. And God's power continued to show up as Holy Spirit came upon individuals in the gospels before Christ's crucifixion.

HOLY SPIRIT UPON [EPI] EXPERIENCES IN THE NEW TESTAMENT - BEFORE THE CROSS

(1) Elizabeth - the Mother of John the Baptist

- *Luke 1:41 When Elizabeth heard Mary's greeting, the baby leaped in her womb; and **Elizabeth was filled [Pletho G4130] with the Holy Spirit**.*

Some may believe Holy Spirit came in [en] Elizabeth. Others may believe Holy Spirit came upon [epi] Elizabeth. Chapter 9 of **CEASED?** discusses why the term 'filled' is closely associated with the upon [epi] experience. As a result, my vote is Holy Spirit came upon [epi] Elizabeth.

(2) Mary

The angel Gabriel prophesied Mary would experience Holy Spirit coming upon [epi] her which will enable her to become pregnant.

- *Luke 1:35 The angel answered and said to her, "**The Holy Spirit will come upon you**, and the **power of the Most High will overshadow you**; and for that reason the holy Child shall be called the Son of God.*

(3) John the Baptist

John the Baptist's ministry involving speaking of the Kingdom of God, about the Messiah coming and about the need to repent. He led many people through the baptism of repentance. There's no indication he did any miraculous signs and wonders apart from prophesying. God's Word does not mention John doing healings or casting out of demons. And yet, as the forerunner of the Messiah, John the Baptist was greater than any other man before him.

- *Matthew 11:11 Truly I say to you, **among those born of women there has not arisen anyone greater than John the Baptist!** ...*

Interestingly, the least in the kingdom of Heaven will do greater things than John.

- *Matthew 11:11 ... **Yet the one who is least in the kingdom of heaven is greater than he**.*

7:28 Are all believers living today some of the 'least in the kingdom of heaven', and thus aren't we all called to do greater things than John the Baptist did?

John may have had an in [en] type experience. There is no specific mention. However, I believe John the Baptist definitely had an upon [epi] experience due to

CEASED?

the prophecy that John the Baptist would be *'filled'* with the Holy Spirit, even from his mother's womb.

❑ *Luke 1:15 For he will be great in the sight of the Lord; and he will drink no wine or liquor, and* **he will be filled [Pletho G4130] with the Holy Spirit** *while yet* **in his mother's womb**.

As mentioned in this chapter and discussed more fully in Chapter 9, being filled with the Holy Spirit is associated with the upon [epi] experience when Holy Spirit comes upon [epi] a disciple.

7:29 Doesn't it appear that this filling of the Holy Spirit relates to a form of the upon [epi] experience - the power of the Holy Spirit - that allowed John the Baptist to boldly teach, and to prophesy about Jesus?

7:30 Is it possible/reasonable to believe that when Elizabeth was filled with the Holy Spirit, that was also when John the Baptist was Baptized in the Holy Spirit?

(4) Simeon

Simeon was at the temple when Mary and Joseph brought Jesus into the temple.

❑ *Luke 2:25 And there was a man in Jerusalem whose name was Simeon; and this man was righteous and devout, looking for the consolation of Israel;* **and the Holy Spirit was upon [epi] him**. *26 And it had been revealed to him by the Holy Spirit that he would not see death before he had seen the Lord's Christ. 27 And* **he came in [en] the Spirit** *into the temple; and when the parents brought in the child Jesus, to carry out for Him the custom of the Law, 28 then he took Him into his arms, and blessed God, and said, 29 "Now Lord, You are releasing Your bond-servant to depart in peace, According to Your word; 30 For my eyes have seen Your salvation,*

Isn't it interesting that besides Holy Spirit being upon [epi] Simeon (verse 25), Simeon *'came in [en] the Spirit'* (verse 27) when he went into the temple?

(5) Jesus

Before Jesus began His earthly ministry, John the Baptist prophesied that one greater than Him would Baptize them with the Holy Spirit.

❑ *Mark 1:8 I baptized you with water: but* **he will baptize you with the Holy Spirit**.

7:31 When John the Baptist was making this declaration that *'He will baptize you with the Holy Spirit'*, we don't know who was all in attendance and able to hear John. But if you were to make a guess, was he likely speaking to:
   i. a select few individuals; or
   ii. anyone and everyone gathered, which could have quite a few?

7:32 On the basis John the Baptist was making this declaration to anybody and everybody who was present, doesn't this provide further support that the Baptism of the Holy Spirit is available for the masses and not a select few?

7: Holy Spirit Upon [Epi]

Concerning Jesus Himself, Isaiah prophesied Jesus would receive the upon experience.
- Isaiah 61:1 The **Spirit of the Lord God is upon me**, Because the Lord has anointed me To bring good news to the afflicted; He has sent me to bind up the brokenhearted, To proclaim liberty to captives And freedom to prisoners;

Which is exactly what happened when Jesus started His earthly ministry.
- Mark 1:9 In those days Jesus came from Nazareth in Galilee and was baptized by John in the Jordan. 10 Immediately coming up out of the water, He saw the heavens opening, and the **Spirit like a dove descending upon [epi] Him;** 11 and a voice came out of the heavens: "You are My beloved Son, in You I am well-pleased."

7:33 When Holy Spirit descended upon Jesus, didn't this result in Jesus receiving access to supernatural power that enabled Him to do His earthly ministry?

7:34 If not, what was the purpose of the upon experience for Jesus?

After this upon experience, Jesus was sent into the wilderness for 40 days. Afterward, He came back into Galilee preaching the gospel.
- Mark 1:12 Immediately the Spirit impelled Him to go out into the wilderness. 13 And He was **in the wilderness forty days** being tempted by Satan; and He was with the wild beasts, and the angels were ministering to Him. 14 Now after John had been taken into custody, **Jesus came into Galilee, preaching the gospel of God**,

Luke provides additional insight when Jesus returned from the desert where he was tempted by satan, He returned ... full of the Holy Spirit ... and in the power ... of the Holy Spirit.
- Luke 4:1 Jesus, **full of the Holy Spirit**, returned from the Jordan and was led around by the Spirit in the wilderness 2 for forty days, being tempted by the devil. And He ate nothing during those days, and when they had ended, He became hungry ... 13 When the devil had finished every temptation, he left Him until an opportune time. 14 And **Jesus returned to Galilee in the power of the Spirit**, and news about Him spread through all the surrounding district.
- Acts 10:38 You know of Jesus of Nazareth, **how God anointed Him with the Holy Spirit and with power,** and how He went about doing good and healing all who were oppressed by the devil, for God was with Him.

Jesus stated Holy Spirit was upon him for various reasons.
- Luke 4:18 "The **Spirit of the Lord is upon [epi] Me, Because He anointed Me to preach the gospel** to the poor. He has sent **Me to proclaim release** to the captives, And **recovery of sight** to the blind, **To set free** those who are oppressed, 19 To **proclaim the favorable year of the Lord**."

Scriptures show Jesus's ministry was filled with signs and wonders, but even then, God's Word only contains a minuscule fraction of what Christ did.

CEASED?

- ❏ *John 21:25 And there are also many other things which Jesus did, which if they were written in detail, I suppose that even the world itself would not contain the books that would be written.*

7:35 IF, and I repeat 'IF', Jesus had truly shunned all His supernatural nature during His lifetime on earth, but still needed access to God's power, would this explain why Jesus needed to be Baptized in the Holy Spirit when Holy Spirit descended on Jesus?

Who Baptized Jesus in the Holy Spirit

7:36 Jesus baptizes believers in the Holy Spirit. In His own Baptism in the Holy Spirit, it's possible Jesus could somehow have baptized Himself. Holy Spirit could have also maybe done it unilaterally. But is it most likely that Father God was the One who Baptized Jesus in the Holy Spirit?
- ❏ *Acts 10:38 You know of Jesus of Nazareth, **how God anointed Him with the Holy Spirit and with power,** and how He went about doing good and healing all who were oppressed by the devil, for God was with Him.*

7:37 Given the importance of Christ's ministry, is it surprising to see the entire Godhead involved in Jesus's Baptism of the Holy Spirit? Father God spoke it, Holy Spirit delivered it, and Jesus received it. It must have been exhilarating to those present to hear Father God's voice from heaven declaring: *"This is my beloved Son, in whom I am well pleased".*
- ❏ *Matthew 3:16 After being baptized, **Jesus** came up immediately from the water; and behold, the heavens were opened, and he saw the **Spirit of God descending** as a dove and **lighting on Him**, 17 and behold, **a voice out of the heavens said**, "**This is My beloved Son**, in whom I am well-pleased."*

7:38 Some Christian leaders teach God is only one person, but who manifests in different ways - sometimes as the Father, sometimes as Jesus and sometimes as Holy Spirit. Isn't this 'Oneness Gospel' teaching invalidated when all three - the Father, Son Jesus and Holy Spirit - are simultaneously involved in Jesus's upon [epi] experience? In addition, when Holy Spirit not only descended upon Jesus - but then remained on Him - doesn't that suggest two persons of the Godhead are simultaneously involved?
- ❏ *John 1:32 John testified saying, "I have seen the Spirit descending as a dove out of heaven, and **He remained upon Him**.*

Jesus - Only Man, or Fully Man and Fully God

Another divisive issue within the Body of Christ deals with whether Jesus was a man only, or fully man and fully God during his 33 ½ years on earth.

7:39 If Jesus was man only:
  i. How was it possible for Jesus not to sin without some form of supernatural enablement? Was it because Holy Spirit was with [para] or in [en] Jesus in some way akin to how Holy Spirit can be with and in people today? And if so, does that give us hope that we can lives with virtually no sin in our lives?
  ii. Given that Jesus is the same yesterday, today and tomorrow, where did

the 'God Jesus' go for these ~33 ½ years + 9 months that Jesus was in the womb or walking around on earth?

7:40 If Jesus was fully man and fully God:
  i. Why did Jesus need Holy Spirit to come upon Him before His earthly ministry?
  ii. How could Jesus be tempted?
  iii. How could Jesus be forsaken on the cross?
  iv. How could Jesus send us as the Father sent Him?
  v. How could Jesus grow in favor with God?
  vi. How do we deal with the facts Jesus had emptied Himself, but later needed God to anoint and fill Him with power? If Jesus was God, why did He need to be anointed with Power by Father God?

- ❑ *Philippians 2:7 but **emptied Himself**, taking the **form of a bond-servant**, and being made in the likeness of men.*
- ❑ *John 20:21 So Jesus said to them again, "Peace be with you; **as the Father has sent Me, I also send you**." 22 And when He had said this, He breathed on them and said to them, "Receive the Holy Spirit.*
- ❑ *Acts 10:38 You know of Jesus of Nazareth, **how God anointed Him with the Holy Spirit and with power**, and how He went about doing good and healing all who were oppressed by the devil, for God was with Him.*

7:41 I don't ask the above questions to get an answer, but to highlight an issue. We believers can spend a lot of time debating an issue for which scriptures could appear to support two or more points of view. In such cases, if it isn't a salvation issue, shouldn't our focus be on what we do know - the Good News - and put our energies towards those people who don't know Christ yet, rather than getting caught up in theological debates?

IN, WITH, OF, BY

Various phrases are used to describe the 'upon' [epi] experience including 'Baptism ***in*** the Holy Spirit', 'Baptism ***of*** the Holy Spirit' and 'Baptism ***with*** the Holy Spirit'. The use of which preposition to use - 'in', 'of' and 'with' - is an English grammatical issue, not a theological one. All three prepositions are appropriate. The specific usage depends on our preferences in each situation.

The phrase 'Baptism ***by*** the Holy Spirit', on the other hand, is different because the word 'by' refers to a baptism done ***by*** or performed ***by*** Holy Spirit. The one baptism, touched on in Chapter 4, that Holy Spirit does perform is when He baptizes a new believer into the Body of Christ.

- ❑ *1 Corinthians 12:13 For **by one Spirit we were all baptized into one body**, whether Jews or Greeks, whether slaves or free, and we were all made to drink of one Spirit*

CEASED?

CLOSING POINTS TO PONDER

When born again, we're God's child and adopted into God's family. We're part of the kingdom of heaven, and those of us who are least in God's kingdom are still greater than John the Baptist and should expect to see great things done in our lifetime.

- ❑ *Luke 7:28 I say to you, among those born of women there is no one greater than John; yet he who is least in the kingdom of God is greater than he."*
- ❑ *John 14:12 Truly, truly, I say to you, he who believes in Me, the works that I do, he will do also; and greater works than these he will do; because I go to the Father.*

7:42 Do the above scriptures imply/tell us that we are also called to a ministry that will have eternal impact? Impact because we can share the Good News of Christ and play a role in people coming to know Jesus? Impact because Holy Spirit is in [en] us? Impact because we can have access to the supernatural power of God through having Holy Spirit upon [epi] us after we're Baptized in the Holy Spirit?

God's power was evident in the apostles' life. In Peter's walk, people brought the sick hoping that even Peter's shadow would fall on them so they could be healed.

- ❑ *Acts 5:14 And all the more believers in the Lord, multitudes of men and women, were constantly added to their number, 15 to such an extent that they even carried the sick out into the streets and laid them on cots and pallets, **so that when Peter came by at least his shadow might fall on any one of them**. 16 Also the people from the cities in the vicinity of Jerusalem were coming together, bringing people who were sick or afflicted with unclean spirits, and they were **all being healed.***

7:43 Was it Peter's shadow that healed the sick, or was it the presence of God upon Peter and extending beyond Peter's body to an area roughly represented by his shadow, that healed the sick? In other words, was Holy Spirit's presence on [epi] Peter so tangible that when sick people got fairly close to Peter, they encountered God and bam - they got healed?

7:44 When believers today are Baptized in the Holy Spirit, and Holy Spirit comes upon [epi] us, how can't we sense God's presence - at least once in awhile?

7:45 If we're never aware of God's presence in our midst - if we never sense He is here as in right here with us - isn't that an issue we should be concerned about? Or to at least think about?

8

'En' & 'Epi' After the Cross

INTRODUCTION

CHAPTER 8 recaps the en and epi experiences in general, then reviews:
1: 'in' [en] and 'upon' [epi] experiences of the first born-again Christians on resurrection Sunday evening and Pentecost (page 132);
2: 10 other individuals/groups and their en and epi experiences (page 134);
3: summary of 11 en and epi experiences (page 143); and
4: some Roman Catholic teachings on the in [en] and [upon] epi (page 145).

SUMMARY OF 'EN' AND 'EPI'

Figure 8:1 on the next page recaps the 'en' and 'epi' experiences covered in Chapters 6 and 7. Three scriptures related to the 'in' [en] experience are as follows:

- ❑ *1 Corinthians 12:13 For **by one Spirit we were all baptized into one body**, whether Jews or Greeks, whether slaves or free, and we were all made to drink of one Spirit.*
- ❑ *John 14:16 I will ask the Father, and He will give you another Helper ... 17 ... but you know Him **because He abides with you** and **will be in you**.*
- ❑ *Romans 8:9 ... **if anyone does not have the Spirit of Christ, he does not belong to Him**.*

Three scriptures related to the 'upon' [epi] experience are as follows:
- ❑ *Mark 1:8 I baptized you with water: but **He will baptize you with the Holy Spirit**.*
- ❑ *Acts 1:8 but **you will receive power** when the **Holy Spirit has come upon [epi]** you; and **you shall be My witnesses** both in Jerusalem, and in all Judea and Samaria, and even to the remotest part of the earth."*
- ❑ *1 Corinthians 2:4 and **my message and my preaching were not in persuasive words of wisdom**, but **in demonstration of the Spirit and of power**, 5 so that **your faith would not rest on the wisdom of men, but on the power of God**.*

CEASED?

Figure 8:1

ITEM	"EN" / IN	"EPI"/ UPON
Name	Baptism into Body of Christ	Baptism of Holy Spirit
Who does the Baptism	Holy Spirit 1 Corinthian 12:1	Jesus Matthew 3:11
Believer's encounter	Holy Spirit comes in a believer	Holy Spirit comes on or upon a believer
Greek	In = En [G1722]	Upon = Epi [G1909]
Purpose	Holy Spirit guides, convicts, teaches; overall relationship with God	Access to power to witness for Jesus
Some of the Gifts received	Gift of Salvation Romans 6:23	Access to 9 Holy Spirit gifts per 1 Corinthians 12
Main Beneficiary	Oneself	Others
When Occurs	At the moment a person is Born Again	At the same time or any time after Born Again
Frequency	Once, stays	Multiple fillings

Let's now review the *'in'* [en] and *'upon'* [epi] experiences in people's lives after the cross.

THE FIRST CHRISTIANS

Figure 8:2 provides a brief summary of the *'in'* [en] and *'upon'* [epi] experiences of the believers gathered on resurrection Sunday evening and at Pentecost.

Figure 8:2

ITEM	"EN" / IN	"EPI" / UPON
When	Resurrection Sunday evening John 20:19-22	Pentecost Acts 2:1-4
How	Jesus breathed on them & said *"Receive the Holy Spirit"*	Jesus baptized believers in the Holy Spirit
Evidence	Continued prayer and worship before Pentecost	Tongues, tongues of fire Peter's sermon Signs & wonders thru disciples

For All or a Few Believers

Some believers today teach that the Baptism of the Holy Spirit was for a select few believers, and not for everybody. Consider Peter's explanation as to what happened on Pentecost.

❑ *Acts 2:16 but this is what was spoken of through the prophet Joel: 17 'And it shall be in the last days,' God says, 'That I will **pour forth of My Spirit on all mankind;** And **your sons and your daughters** shall **prophesy**, And your*

8: En and Epi After the Cross

*young men shall **see visions**, And your old men shall **dream dreams**; 18 Even on My bondslaves, both men and women, I will in those days pour forth of My Spirit And they shall **prophesy**. 19 'And I will grant wonders in the sky above **And signs on the earth below,***

8:1 The disciples gathered at Pentecost - as well as many others who were nearby - witnessed tongues of fire, loud noises and/or people speaking in tongues. Were these events the first pouring out of the Holy Spirit as prophesied by Joel? To Holy Spirit coming upon people? To wonders in the sky and signs on the earth? To the Baptism of the Holy Spirit that John the Baptist and Jesus prophesied? If not, what were they about?

Joel's prophecy is found in Joel 2:28. Notice Joel did not say God would pour forth Holy Spirit **in** mankind, but **on** mankind.
- ❏ *Joel 2:28 "It will come about after this That I will **pour out My Spirit on all mankind** ...*

This pouring out of the Spirit was also prophesied by Isaiah.
- ❏ *Isaiah 44:3 'For I will pour out water on the thirsty land And streams on the dry ground; I will **pour out My Spirit on your offspring** And My blessing on your descendants;*

8:2 Joel and Isaiah said Holy Spirit would be poured out on all mankind, to sons and daughters, to offspring - both young and old. In your view, do the words 'all', 'sons', 'daughters' and 'offspring' represent:
   i. the original apostles only;
   ii. the original apostles + believers who the original apostles laid their hands on;
   iii. all believers gathered at Pentecost;
   iv. all believers gathered at Pentecost + any believers after Pentecost who had hands laid upon them by those who were at Pentecost;
   v. all believers who were alive at the time of Pentecost;
   vi. all believers who were alive at the time of Pentecost + all believers of all future generations; or
   vii. all believers who ask and receive the outpouring of the Holy Spirit.

There are a variety of views on who this outpouring relates to. I struggle to see how the words *'all'*, *'sons'*, *'daughters'* and *'offspring'* can be anything but vi. all believers alive at the time of Pentecost + all believers in all future generations, or vii. all who ask for the outpouring.

8:3 If Holy Spirit was to be poured out on all flesh including sons, daughters and handmaidens, do the initial events at Pentecost - noise, tongues of fire and speaking in tongues impacting ~120 disciples - meet the criteria of 'all flesh'? In other words, was this the first and last Baptism of the Holy Spirit?

8:4 If your answer is yes, wouldn't that mean there would be no more believers who would be Baptized with the Holy Spirit? Let's see what the Bible says.

After the ~3,000 people came to Christ, they were devoted to the apostles'

CEASED?

teaching, fellowship and prayer. Signs and wonders were a trademark of the apostles.
- ❑ *Acts 2:40 And with many other words he solemnly testified and kept on exhorting them, saying, "Be saved from this perverse generation!" 41 So then, those who had received his word were baptized; and **that day there were added about three thousand souls.** 42 They were continually devoting themselves to the apostles' teaching and to fellowship, to the breaking of bread and to prayer. 43 Everyone kept feeling a sense of awe; and **many wonders and signs were taking place through the apostles**.*

The signs and wonders done by the apostles should not be a surprise, because 2 Corinthians 12 tells us true apostles are identified by signs, wonders and miracles.
- ❑ *2 Corinthians 12:12 The **signs of a true apostle** were performed among you with all perseverance, by **signs and wonders and miracles**.*

8:5 In your view, were the original apostles the only true apostles?
8:6 Are there any true apostles alive and ministering today?

Let's move on in Acts to see what happened.

10 INDIVIDUALS/GROUPS AND THEIR 'EN'/'EPI'
(1) The ~3,000 on Pentecost

'In' [En]

After Peter's sermon, ~3,000 accepted Christ and had Holy Spirit come in them.
- ❑ *Acts 2:40 And with many other words he solemnly testified and kept on exhorting them, saying, "Be saved from this perverse generation!" 41 So then, **those who had received his word** were baptized; and that day **there were added about three thousand souls.***

'Upon' [Epi]

Conventional teachings hold that the ~3,000 were not Baptized in the Holy Spirit, but were water baptized. A review of Acts 2:38 in Chapter 10 suggests there may be more to the story.

(2) Stephen

Consider Stephen who was chosen to help distribute food to the widows.
- ❑ *Acts 6:1 ... widows were being overlooked in the daily serving of food ... 3 Therefore, brethren, select from among you seven men of good reputation, full of the Spirit and of wisdom ... they chose Stephen, a man full of faith and of the Holy Spirit ...*

'In' [En] / 'Upon' [Epi]

No specific scriptures identify when Stephen was born again or was Baptized in the Holy Spirit. Scriptures do show, however, that while Stephen was responsible for food, he did a whole lot more.
- ❑ *Acts 6:8 And Stephen, **full of grace and power**, **was performing great wonders and signs** among the people.*

8: En and Epi After the Cross

Many Cessationists believe the original apostles were the only true apostles. Many Cessationists also believe the apostles were the only believers after the cross through whom Holy Spirit would do great wonders and signs and miracles. Stephen is but one example of why this belief system may be flawed.

8:7 To clarify, if Stephen wasn't an apostle, the Cessationist argument would say Stephen wouldn't be able to do great signs and wonders. However, given Stephen did perform great signs and wonders, and based on the logic that only apostles could do great signs and wonders, wouldn't that logic require Stephen to be an apostle? If not, why not?

8:8 If Stephen was an apostle, wouldn't that mean the original 11 apostles plus Matthias were not the only apostles?

8:9 If Stephen was not an apostle even though he did signs and wonders, does the fact that He was filled with the Spirit and performed great signs and wonders provide evidence he did receive the Baptism of the Holy Spirit?

8:10 If Stephen was not Baptized in the Holy Spirit, on what basis was Stephen able to do such signs and wonders?

8:11 If Stephen was Baptized in the Holy Spirit but was not an apostle, doesn't that indicate Baptism of the Holy Spirit is not limited to the original apostles, but available to all believers, even those of us living today? If not, why not?

(3) Believers at Samaria

'In' [En]

When Philip came to Samaria, he taught the Good News which led some to Christ.

- ❑ Acts 8:5 Philip went down to the city of Samaria and began proclaiming Christ to them ... 12 But **when they believed** Philip preaching the good news about the kingdom of God and the name of Jesus Christ, they were being baptized, men and women alike.

'Upon' [Epi]

- ❑ Acts 8:14 Now when the **apostles in Jerusalem** heard that Samaria had received the word of God, **they sent them Peter and John**, 15 who came down and **prayed for them that they might receive the Holy Spirit**. 16 For **He had not yet fallen upon [epi]** any of them; they had simply been baptized in the name of the Lord Jesus.

When the apostles in Jerusalem heard of the new believers in Samaria, they would have known Holy Spirit was in [en] the new believers. They were concerned, however, that Holy Spirit had not yet fallen upon [epi] the new believers. Their response was to have John and Peter - two leading apostles - travel to Samaria to ensure the new disciples were Baptized in the Holy Spirit.

8:12 Jerusalem and Samaria are over 60 miles walking distance apart. It would have taken several days for the news of new believers to travel from Samaria to Jerusalem, for the apostles to discuss and decide, and then for John and Peter to travel back to Samaria. Doesn't the gap of several days provide additional evidence that the 'in' [en] and 'upon'[epi] are two distinct Holy Spirit experiences for believers?

CEASED?

8:13 Does Peter and John's trip to Samaria also provide further evidence that while Baptism in the Holy Spirit is not required for salvation, there are important benefits to being Baptized in the Holy Spirit?

8:14 Given the apostles deemed it necessary for John and Peter to go to Samaria to ensure the new believers were Baptized in the Holy Spirit, does this indicate Philip was known for not ensuring this baptism took place for new Christians?

(4) Simon the Sorcerer

'In' [En]
Samaria also saw Simon the sorcerer come to Jesus.
- ❑ *Acts 8:9 Now there was a man named Simon, who formerly was practicing magic in the city and astonishing the people of Samaria, claiming to be someone great … 13* **Even Simon himself believed; and after being baptized**, *he continued on with Philip, and as he observed signs and great miracles taking place …*

'In' [En]
After he believed, Simon stayed on with Philip, and saw signs and wonders taking place when John and Peter laid hands on believers. Simon realized the doorway to these miracles was people receiving the Holy Spirit, the 'upon' [epi] experience. And Simon wanted in on the action.
- ❑ *Acts 8:18 Now when Simon saw that the* **Spirit was bestowed through the laying on of the apostles' hands**, *he* **offered them money, 19 saying, "Give this authority to me as well**, *so that everyone on whom I lay my hands may receive the Holy Spirit."*

8:15 Notice Simon realized believers received the Holy Spirit when the apostles, not Philip, laid their hands on them. Does this provide further evidence that Philip did not take steps to ensure believers received the Baptism of the Holy Spirit? And if true, is it somewhat perplexing given Philip was used by God in many signs and wonders? A heart issue perhaps? Only God knows.

Simon was a believer who had Holy Spirit in [en] him. He had been water baptized. But he had a long history of using sorcery to bewitch and impress people. He had exploited the powers of the demonic world for his personal benefit. Now he saw something/someone even better. His desire to be involved in the supernatural was so strong that he was willing to pay money so he could help believers receive the 'upon' [epi] Holy Spirit experience. Peter said no as Simon's heart still needed some sanctifying work. I suspect some Simon type hearts are living in believers today. I say that with confidence as it wasn't too long ago when a key reason for my desire to see people instantaneously healed was because I wanted some of the glory. If you ever feel led to pray for me, please pray that I truly die to self and my heart is to live and minister only for God's glory.
- ❑ *Acts 8:20 But Peter said to him,* **"May your silver perish with you, because you thought you could obtain the gift of God with money!** *21 You have no part or portion in this matter, for your heart is not right before God. 22*

8: En and Epi After the Cross

Therefore repent of this wickedness of yours, and pray the Lord that, if possible, the intention of your heart may be forgiven you.

8:16 We don't know what was in Simon's heart. However, before he believed in Christ, his magic had astonished people and he claimed he was great. Whether he wanted glory, money or both, we don't know. However, isn't Simon's heart something all believers need to be conscious of - that we're not to use our relationship with God for personal glory, fame, status, or unbiblical wealth?

8:17 There are many 'Charismatics' who seem to be doing things for personal gain. And thus, is the core issue plaguing many Charismatics more a heart issue than a theological one?

8:18 Having said that, how many non-Charismatics are using their positions for personal gain?

(5) Ethiopian Eunuch

'In' [En]
- *Acts 8:26 But an angel of the Lord spoke to Philip saying, "Get up and go south ... 27 So he got up and went; and there was an Ethiopian eunuch ...*
- *Acts 8:36 As they went along the road they came to some water; and the eunuch said, "Look! Water! What prevents me from being baptized?" 37 [And Philip said, "If you believe with all your heart, you may." And he answered and said, "I believe that Jesus Christ is the Son of God."] 38 And he ordered the chariot to stop; and **they both went down into the water, Philip as well as the eunuch, and he baptized him.***

Philip preached Jesus to the Ethiopian eunuch. The eunuch confessed his belief in Jesus, and then expressed a desire to be water baptized. Philip responded by baptizing him in water.

8:19 Philip wasn't an apostle. Doesn't his water baptism of the eunuch show any believer can water baptize another believer, not just priests, pastors or other church leaders?

8:20 Given both the eunuch and Philip went down into the water, doesn't this indicate the eunuch's water baptism was full immersion and not a few drops of sprinkled water?

'Upon' [Epi]

8:21 Philip does not appear to have taught the eunuch about Baptism in the Holy Spirit. Does this confirm Philip had a track record of not teaching on the Baptism of the Holy Spirit? Or does it indicate Philip did not have the anointing that John and Peter had to lead others in getting Baptized in the Holy Spirit?

8:22 Doesn't the lack of mention of Baptism in the Holy Spirit again demonstrate believers don't need to be Baptized in the Holy Spirit to be saved?

CEASED?

(6) Saul / Paul

'In' [En]

The conversion of Paul en route to Damascus is a great example of God's love and somewhat unpredictable nature. The Bible doesn't say exactly when Paul was born again. When Jesus first speaks to Ananias, He tells Ananias that Paul is praying.

- *Acts 9:11 And the Lord said to him, "Get up and go to the street called Straight, and inquire at the house of Judas for a man from Tarsus named Saul, for he is praying, 12 and he has seen in a vision a man named Ananias come in and lay his hands on him, so that he might regain his sight."*

Ananias obeys and greets Saul.

- *Acts 9:17 So Ananias departed and entered the house, and after laying his hands on him said, "**Brother Saul**, the Lord Jesus, who appeared to you on the road by which you were coming, has sent me so that you may regain your sight and be filled with the Holy Spirit."*

8:23 Since Ananias referred to Saul as 'brother', and there is no discussion regarding sin, repentance, born again confessing with one's mouth etc., doesn't this indicate Paul was already born again - that Holy Spirit was already in Saul - by the time Ananias arrived?

'Upon' [Epi]

- *Acts 9:17 So Ananias departed and entered the house, and after laying his hands on him said, "Brother Saul, the Lord Jesus, who appeared to you on the road by which you were coming, has sent me so that you may regain your sight and **be filled with the Holy Spirit**." 18 And immediately there fell from his eyes something like scales, and he regained his sight, and he **got up and was baptized**; 19 and he took food and was strengthened.*

Ananias laid hands and told Paul he would regain his sight and be filled with the Holy Spirit. As per Chapter 9 of **CEASED?**, being filled with the Holy Spirit occurs when Holy Spirit comes upon [epi] a believer - when the believer is Baptized in the Holy Spirit. On this basis, verse 17 indicates Paul was Baptized in the Holy Spirit and healed physically as soon as Ananias laid hands on him.

8:24 Acts 19:18 indicates Paul was water baptized. Does the fact that Paul was Baptized in the Holy Spirit before being water baptized clarify:
  i. water baptism is not required to be saved, but is important;
  ii. water baptism can occur before or after being Baptized in the Holy Spirit; and
  iii. a non-apostle (a non-church leader) can both water baptize a person, and be involved in helping a person get Baptized in the Holy Spirit?

Soon after Paul met with Ananias, Paul was in synagogues teaching about Jesus.

- *Acts 9:19 … Now for several days he was with the disciples who were at Damascus, 20 and **immediately** he **began to proclaim Jesus** in the synagogues, saying, "He is the Son of God."*

8:25 Given Paul *'immediately'* began preaching, would this be evidence Paul

8: En and Epi After the Cross

received power to witness just as Peter had received at Pentecost in Acts 2?

(7) Cornelius, Family and Friends

'In' [En] / 'Upon' [Epi]

Cornelius was a Gentile, an Italian centurion in Caesarea. God sent an angel to Cornelius and put Peter in a trance which resulted in Peter coming to Cornelius's home and sharing the gospel.

- ❏ *Acts 10:25 When Peter entered, Cornelius met him ... 42 And He ordered us to preach to the people, and solemnly to testify that this is the One who has been appointed by God as Judge of the living and the dead.*

As Peter shared the gospel, Cornelius, family and friends were all Baptized in the Holy Spirit as Holy Spirit came upon [epi] them while they were listening.

- ❏ *Acts 10:44 **While Peter was still speaking** these words, the **Holy Spirit fell upon [epi] all** those who were listening to the message. 45 All the circumcised believers who came with Peter were amazed, because **the gift of the Holy Spirit had been poured out [epi] on the Gentiles also**. 46 For they were hearing them speaking with tongues and exalting God. Then Peter answered, 47 Surely no one can refuse the water for these to be baptized who have received the Holy Spirit just as we did, can he?" 48 And **he ordered them to be baptized in the name of Jesus Christ**. Then they asked him to stay on for a few days.*

Holy Spirit fell on **all** who were listening. No mention was made of their verbally accepting Christ and believing. However, when Peter realized Holy Spirit had fallen upon Cornelius, family and friends, he had them baptized in water.

8:26 Scriptures say a key part of the reason that Peter realized Holy Spirit had fallen upon Cornelius, family and friends, was because they were speaking in tongues and exalting God. Is it reasonable to conclude speaking in tongues can be a sign (a sign, not a guarantee) that a person has both been born again and Baptized in the Holy Spirit?

8:27 After the Cornelius group was Baptized in the Holy Spirit, they were water baptized. Is this additional evidence that water baptism is not a requirement for salvation, and that water baptism can come after one is Baptized in the Holy Spirit?

8:28 Given Jesus Baptized this group in the Holy Spirit without anyone laying their hands on them, does this demonstrate Jesus can give this Baptism to whomever He wants, whenever He wants, by Himself or in conjunction with or without others, and with or without laying on of hands?

8:29 Does there appear to be a direct link between Holy Spirit coming upon a person and the person engaging in Holy Spirit gifts such as tongues?

Acts 10:45 identifies the Baptism of the Holy Spirit as a gift of the Holy Spirit. Peter repeats this in Acts 11 when he returned to Jerusalem, and explained what happened to the other disciples.

- ❏ *Acts 11:15 And as I began to speak, the Holy Spirit fell upon them just as He did upon us at the beginning. 16 And I remembered the word of the Lord, how He used to say, 'John baptized with water, but you will be baptized with the Holy Spirit.' 17 Therefore* **if God gave to them the same gift as He gave to us also after believing in the Lord Jesus Christ,** *who was I that I could stand in God's way?" 18 When they heard this, they quieted down and glorified God, saying, "Well then, God has granted to the Gentiles also the repentance that leads to life."*

8:30 The disciples responded to Peter's information by concluding - because the Gentiles had been Baptized in the Holy Spirit and received the same gift they had received after they believed - the Gentiles must have also been born again which meant God must have also given them His gift of salvation.
    i. In other words, were they concluding that Cornelius, family and friends must have had Holy Spirit in [en] them in order for them to have been Baptized in the Holy Spirit and have Holy Spirit come upon [epi] them?
    ii. If you believe the gift of the Holy Spirit does not refer to the upon [epi] experience but the in [en] experience, on what basis can this conclusion be made as only the upon [epi] experience is referenced in Acts 11:15-18?

8:31 In Acts 8:17, John and Peter laid hands on those in Samaria one by one and they were Baptized in the Holy Spirit. Ananias laid hands on Paul which appears to be to when Paul received his Baptism in the Holy Spirit. However, at Pentecost, no one laid hands on the ~120 when they were Baptized in the Holy Spirit. For Cornelius and company, no scripture suggests Peter or anyone else laid hands on them when they were Baptized in the Holy Spirit. Jesus just did it. Is it possible therefore to be Baptized in the Holy Spirit without anyone laying hands on a person, or even being involved? And given Jesus is the one who does the Baptism in the Holy Spirit, doesn't that mean we can go to Jesus directly and ask Him to Baptize us in the Holy Spirit?

(8) <u>Believers at Antioch</u>

'In' [En] / 'Upon' [Epi]

After Stephen's murder, believers scattered from Jerusalem. Some were bold enough to preach the gospel to the Greeks at Antioch.

❏ *Acts 11:19 So then those who were scattered because of the persecution that occurred in connection with Stephen made their way to Phoenicia and Cyprus and Antioch, speaking the word to no one except to Jews alone. 20 But there were some of them,* **men of Cyprus and Cyrene, who came to Antioch and began speaking to the Greeks also, preaching the Lord Jesus.** *21 And the* **hand of the Lord** *was with them, and* **a large number who believed turned to the Lord.** *22 The news about them reached the ears of the church at Jerusalem, and they sent Barnabas off to Antioch.*

Verse 21 says the *'hand of the Lord'* was with them. The Amplified translation elaborates on this issue by saying the *'hand'* is the power and presence of God.

❏ *Acts 11:21 And the* **hand (the power and presence)** *of the Lord was with*

8: En and Epi After the Cross

them, and **<u>a great number who believed</u>** turned to the Lord [for salvation, accepting and drawing near to Jesus as Messiah and Savior]. (AMP)

8:32 Given the power of God was present and a great many believed, does this indicate these believers from Cyrene and Cypress had been Baptized in the Holy Spirit which gave them access to power to be witnesses for Christ? If not this, what is indicated?

8:33 Does this group of believers provide further evidence that the Baptism of the Holy Spirit and the associated power and giftings that come with it were not limited to the apostles, but potentially available to all believers?

(9) Believers at Iconium

'In' [En] / 'Upon' [Epi]

There are no details regarding the in [en] or upon [epi] experiences for the believers at Iconium. But it's noteworthy as the book of Acts moves along, that we see God doing miracles through His followers everywhere they went. When people at Iconium witnessed these miracles, they started to speak highly of Paul and Barnabas. And while Paul and Barnabas wanted no praise, the power of God had clearly caught the attention of the believers at Iconium.

Paul also taught the Thessalonians that the gospel isn't just about words.

❑ *1 Thessalonians 1:5 For **<u>our gospel did not come to you in word only, but also in power and in the Holy Spirit</u>** and with full conviction ...*

8:34 Wouldn't sharing the gospel today be a lot easier if non-believers have previously witnessed or experienced God's power themselves?

Testimony

I was spending time with Frank who was homeless and struggling. He had left the Jehovah Witness faith years before but still believed much of their false teachings. A lady came by limping and using a cane. She was clearly in pain. I asked if I could pray for her. She said ok. I prayed a simple prayer. She gave me a big grin. I told her Jesus loves her. She said "I know", and walked away without limping, flipping her cane around and around Charlie Chaplin style. Frank was stunned. He didn't know what to make of it, but he knew he had seen the power of the true Jesus. I only saw Frank a couple more times and don't know where he is with Christ today, but I do know he was greatly impacted by seeing the love and power of Jesus in that precious woman.

(10) 12 Believers at Ephesus

'In' [En]

Paul's ministry took him to Ephesus where he met 12 disciples.

❑ *Acts 19:1 It happened that while Apollos was at Corinth, Paul passed through the upper country and came to Ephesus, and **<u>found some disciples</u>**. 2 He said to them, "**<u>Did you receive the Holy Spirit when you believed</u>?**" And they said to him, "No, we have not even heard whether there is a Holy Spirit." 3 And he said, "**<u>Into what then were you baptized?</u>**" And they said, "Into John's baptism." 4 Paul said, "John baptized with the baptism of repentance, telling the people to believe in Him who was coming after him, that is, in Jesus." 5 When they heard this, they were **<u>baptized in the name of the Lord Jesus</u>**. 6*

141

*And when Paul had laid his hands upon them, **the Holy Spirit came on them, and they began speaking with tongues and prophesying**. 7 There were in all **about twelve men**.*

8:35 Paul did not ask if the disciples knew Jesus, what was required to be saved or what born again meant. He did not share the gospel. Instead, he asked if they had received the Holy Spirit 'when you believed'. Given they were called disciples and Paul knew they had believed, isn't it reasonable to expect Paul knew these 12 disciples would have already automatically received the Holy Spirit through the in [en] experience?

8:36 Paul did not ask if they were water baptized but if they had received the Holy Spirit 'when you believed'.
  i. If Paul wasn't asking about Baptism in the Holy Spirit, what was Paul asking?
  ii. And on the basis Paul was asking them if they had been Baptized in the Holy Spirit, doesn't this show Paul's priority for new believers?

'Upon' [Epi]

In response to being asked if they had received the Holy Spirit, the disciples advised they had not even heard of receiving the Holy Spirit. Paul then basically said (using my words) *"Well, if you haven't been Baptized in the Holy Spirit, what baptism did you receive?"* The disciples advised they had received John's baptism which Paul explained was about repentance - turning their minds and lives towards God.

The first thing Paul did was to ensure the 12 believers at Ephesus were water baptized. Secondly, Paul laid hands on them, Holy Spirit came upon [epi] them, and the 12 disciples spoke with tongues and prophesied. The two Holy Spirit gifts immediately followed their Baptism in the Holy Spirit.

❑ *Acts 19:5 When they heard this, **they were baptized** in the name of the Lord Jesus. 6 And when **Paul had laid his hands upon them, the Holy Spirit came on [epi] them**, and they began **speaking with tongues and prophesying**.*

8:37 On the basis the baptism in Acts 19:5 refers to water baptism, doesn't this provide more evidence that water baptism is not required to be born again? Doesn't it also show that even though individuals may have received the baptism of repentance before the cross, they still needed to be water baptized after the cross?

8:38 Even though Paul had the 12 disciples water baptized before they were Baptized in the Holy Spirit, again I ask: Doesn't the fact that Paul inquired first about whether or not they had received the Holy Spirit indicate Paul's first priority was Baptism in the Holy Spirit and not water baptism?

After Paul laid hands on the 12 disciples and Holy Spirit came upon [epi] them, the 12 disciples spoke in tongues and prophesied immediately, or soon thereafter.

8:39 Does there again appear to be a direct link between Holy Spirit coming upon [epi] a person and the person engaging in the Holy Spirit gifts such as tongues and prophecy?

8: En and Epi After the Cross

8:40 Acts 1:8 states the apostles were to wait for the Baptism of the Holy Spirit to receive power to be witnesses. Given these 12 disciples spoke in tongues and prophesied right after the Baptism of the Holy Spirit, are these examples of the types of power (supernatural enablement) to be used by believers who are witnessing for Christ?

❑ Acts 1:8 but you **will receive power when the Holy Spirit has come upon [epi] you**; and you shall be My witnesses both in Jerusalem, and in all Judea and Samaria, and even to the remotest part of the earth."

SUMMARY OF 11 'EN' AND 'EPI' EXPERIENCES

Figure 8:3 reviews the timing and time between 11 en and epi experiences.

Figure 8:3   Time between 11 Unique En and Epi Experiences

Individual / Group	When had in 'en' experience	When had upon 'epi' experience	Time between in [en] & upon [epi]
1. Apostles, 2 disciples and 'those who were with them'	Resurrection Sunday Evening	Pentecost	50 days
2. Thomas	8 days after resurrection Sunday	Pentecost	42 days
3. 3,000 at Pentecost	Pentecost	Pentecost?	Unknown
4. Believers at Samaria	After Philip's teaching	After John and Peter came to Samaria	Several days**
5. Simon the Sorcerer	After Philip's teaching	Unknown	Unknown
6. Ethiopian Eunuch	After Philip's teaching	Unknown	Unknown
7. Saul/Paul	After encounter with Jesus	After Ananias laid on hands	0 to 3 days
8. Cornelius, family & friends	As Peter was sharing gospel	As Peter was sharing gospel	Virtually nil
9. Antioch believers	After Stephen's persecution	Unknown	Unknown
10. Iconium believers	Unknown	Unknown	Unknown
11. Disciples at Ephesus	Unknown	After Paul laid on hands	Unknown, but unlikely zero

**Several days, at a minimum, were required for the news to travel from Samaria to Jerusalem, for the apostles to discuss and decide what to do, and for John and Peter to then travel back to Samaria.

CEASED?

Four groups or individuals - (1) the group gathered on resurrection Sunday evening, (2) Thomas, (4) the new believers at Samaria, and (11) the 12 disciples at Ephesus - clearly had varying periods of time between their in [en] and upon [epi] experiences.

8:41 Don't the varying lengths of time between the different in [en] and upon [epi] experiences make it clear the epi experience is separate from the en experience?

Figure 8:4 provides information on 5 scenarios of actual Baptisms in the Holy Spirit that occurred in the Book of Acts.

Figure 8:4 Activities Related to 5 Baptisms of the Holy Spirit

Believers receiving Baptism in the Holy Spirit	Major Noise, Signs when Occurred	Laying on of Hands Before Baptism	Baptism of Holy Spirit immediately followed by Tongues	Baptism of Holy Spirit immediately followed by Prophecy	Water Baptism before or after Baptism in Holy Spirit
Pentecost	X		X		N/A
Samaria		X			Before
Saul/Paul		X			After
Cornelius+			X		After
Ephesus		X	X	X	Before

God is the same, yesterday, today and forever. However, while God's character never changes, how God does things seems to change constantly.

❏ *Hebrews 13:8 Jesus Christ is the same yesterday and today and forever.*

8:42 The above summary doesn't reflect all the details of what happened when individuals were Baptized in the Holy Spirit. However, based on what we know, don't the variety of ways by which believers were Baptized in the Holy Spirit, the variety of ways by which Jesus healed people, and the variety of ways God demonstrated His power, all indicate we should remember God moves in mysterious and unusual ways, that we can't put God in a box, and He might do things today that haven't been done before?

8:43 And thus, when individuals say they had some crazy encounters with God, shouldn't we be careful not to condemn or criticize too quickly? After all, imagine if you were trying to explain God speaking to you in a burning bush, God parting the Mississippi River for you, God sending an axe head floating up to your boat, you catch a fish and a valuable coin is inside, or ravens or other birds bring you crispy bacon while you sit on the back porch having a coffee? Can you imagine the commentary from 'Christians' or people in general on social media?

8:44 Yes, some people experience 'miracles' that are made up or are of the enemy. But isn't the possibility of crazy things one more reason why we need to be constantly talking with God and seeking Holy Spirit's guidance and

8: En and Epi After the Cross

revelation as to what's going on?
- ❏ *1 Thessalonians 5:16 Rejoice always; 17 pray without ceasing; 18 in everything give thanks; for this is God's will for you in Christ Jesus.*
- ❏ *1 John 4:1 Beloved, do not believe every spirit, but test the spirits to see whether they are from God, because many false prophets have gone out into the world.*

ROMAN CATHOLIC TEACHINGS ON BAPTISM OF THE HOLY SPIRIT

When researching the Roman Catholic church's teachings, I found many in the main Catholic church view the 9 Holy Spirit gifts as having ceased, while others view them as existing but for Charismatic Catholics only. I found Baptism of the Holy Spirit wasn't even mentioned by name in the Catechism, while receiving power to be witnesses wasn't the first reason in Catholic teaching for this Baptism. I found no specific mention of the [en] and the [epi] experiences, no distinction between the two experiences, and no Biblically-based clarity on their respective purposes and relationship to the various Holy Spirit gifts. I found the in [en] and upon [epi] experiences were intermixed with each other and incorporated with other aspects not taught in the Bible. Let me illustrate using the following information I copied on February 11, 2020 from the link:
www.aboutcatholics.com/beliefs/catholic-confirmation-explained/.

Highlighting and numbering is mine. I inserted numbers in brackets (1), (2) etc. to facilitate linking content in the article to my questions and comments that follow, I left the text unchanged including leaving the typo "howver" in the last paragraph. And trust me. I'm not judging. I get typos; you probably saw some in **CEASED?** already.

Catholic Confirmation Explained
BY ABOUT CATHOLICS TEAM
Confirmation is a sacrament of initiation which completes baptism through sealing in Holy Spirit and anoints the recipient as priest, prophet, and king.

1: Who can receive Confirmation?
In the Catholic Church, **(1) <u>anyone that has been baptized properly</u>** *can and should be confirmed.*

2: What is Catholic Confirmation?
Confirmation is a Sacrament in the Catholic Church in which the one who is confirmed (confirmandi) **(2) <u>receives the gifts of the Holy Spirit through the imposition of hand and anointing with oils by the bishop</u>. <u>It's considered a sacrament of initiation which means that it</u> (3) <u>brings you deeper into communion with the Church</u>.**

CEASED?

3: Who administers Confirmation?
(4) <u>Bishops are the original ministers of Confirmation along with other Catholic sacraments</u> *(Lumen Gentium 26).*
"**<u>Bishops are the successors of the apostles</u>.** They have received the fullness of the sacrament of Holy Orders. The administration of this sacrament by them demonstrates clearly that **(5a) <u>its effects is to unite those who receive it more closely to the Church, her apostolic origins</u>**, and **(5b) <u>her mission of bearing witness to Christ</u>.**" *(Catechism of the Catholic Church, paragraph 1313)*

In the Eastern churches (non-Latin rites) the priest is the ordinary minister of this sacrament and performs it immediately after baptism. However, it is performed with chrism oil that has been consecrated by the bishop expressing the apostolic unity. In the Latin rite (which is the largest of all rites) the bishop is the ordinary minister. Read about the history of Confirmation.

In the west, most churches have the Bishop come and visit the local parish to confirm an entire class (age group) of students who spent the year preparing for confirmation. However, the Bishop can also 'delegate' his apostolic authority to perform the sacrament of confirmation to the local priest who is then able to administer the sacrament without the bishop having to be present.

4: How many times can one be Confirmed?
"Like Baptism which it completes, **(6a) <u>Confirmation is given only once, for</u> (6b) <u>it too imprints on the soul an indelible spiritual mark, the 'character,' which is the sign that Jesus Christ has marked a Christian with the seal of his Spirit</u>** by **(7) <u>clothing him with power from on high so that he may be his witness</u>.**" *(Catechism of the Catholic Church 1304)*
In other words, just once! **(8) <u>It's a permanent thing that is fully completed and doesn't expire</u>**.

5: What is the matter and form of Confirmation?
(9) <u>Catholic Confirmation is performed with the ordinary minister extending his hand over the one to be confirmed and anointing his/her head with the oil of chrism saying, "be sealed with the Holy Spirit</u>." The actual Confirmation ceremony is much longer than this, but this is the "meat" of the action. The oil of chrism is consecrated by the bishop at the Chrism Mass on Holy Thursday and is reserved for special things like Baptism, Confirmation, Holy Orders, blessing of tower bells, consecration of churches, altars, chalices and patens.

6: What are the effects of Confirmation?
In short it **(10) <u>Is the full outpouring of the Holy Spirit as once granted to the apostles on the day of Pentecost</u>**. Confirmation brings Catholics a deepening of baptismal grace and unites us more firmly to Christ. **(11) <u>It increases the gifts of the Holy Spirit and</u> (12) <u>leaves an indelible mark on the soul just like baptism</u>**.

8: En and Epi After the Cross

7: What are the seven gifts of the Holy Spirit?
*The **(13) <u>Seven gifts of the Holy Spirit received through Confirmation</u>** are*
1. *Wisdom,*
2. *Understanding,*
3. *Knowledge,*
4. *Fortitude or Courage,*
5. *Counsel,*
6. *Piety or Love, and*
7. *Fear of the Lord.*

Where is this sacrament found in Scripture?
*Anointing with oil is an ancient Biblical tradition originating in the old testament with the Jewish people. The Jews had a messiah and it was usually their king at the time, howver they were also awaiting a greater messiah, one that would deliver them and raise them up. This messiah happened to be Jesus. The sign of the Messiah was that he was royal and messiahs were put in their position by being anointed with oil and an appointment from God. This tradition carried on in Christianity with the teaching of the sharing in Christ's messiahship and his royal priesthood. **(14) <u>In fact, the first example of Catholic Confirmation can be found in Acts 8:14-17</u>**.*

In terms of the above, I congratulate the authors of this website for their ability to succinctly summarize the Catholic position. A few observations and questions.

Per point (10), the Roman Catholic view is that the effects of confirmation are *"... the full outpouring of the Holy Spirit as once granted to the apostles on the day of Pentecost."* Moreover, per (14), the first example of Roman Catholic Confirmation is found in Acts 8:14-17.

- ❏ *Acts 8:14 Now when the apostles in Jerusalem heard that Samaria had received the word of God, they sent them Peter and John, 15 who came down and prayed for them that they might receive the Holy Spirit. 16 For He had not yet fallen upon [epi] any of them; they had simply been baptized in the name of the Lord Jesus. 17 Then they began laying their hands on them, and they were receiving the Holy Spirit.*

8:45 The outpourings at Pentecost and Acts 8:14-17 are two examples where individuals were clearly Baptized in the Holy Spirit. And thus, I conclude that Confirmation is primarily about Baptism of the Holy Spirit. If this conclusion is not correct, my question to Catholics is - where is Baptism of Holy Spirit covered in detail in Catholic teaching?

In the Roman Catholic church, Confirmation is the second sacrament which occurs after the first sacrament of water baptism. Water baptism, according to the Catholic church, is required for a person to be born again. On the basis that water baptism is required to be saved or born again and is thus required for the in [en] experience to occur, and on the basis that Confirmation relates to the upon [epi] experience, let's see how the Confirmation teaching stands up.

8:46 Point (1) ***Anyone that has been water baptized properly*** can receive confirmation. Cornelius, family and friends were Baptized in the Holy Spirit before being water baptized. Paul's focus at Ephesus was ensuring the 12 disciples were Baptized in the Holy Spirit. Water baptism was secondary. While I think it was likely they were baptized in water, there is no mention the original apostles or others gathered with the apostles at Pentecost were baptized in water before they were Baptized in the Holy Spirit. On the basis that Confirmation is primarily about Baptism of the Holy Spirit, isn't point (1) of Catholic teaching that requires a person to be baptized in water before they can be Baptized in the Holy Spirit in error?

8:47 Point (2) **receives the gifts of the Holy Spirit through the imposition of hand and anointing with oils by the bishop**. Jesus is the one who Baptizes us in the Holy Spirit. No hands were laid on believers at Pentecost or on Cornelius, family and friends. No oils were used on any individuals Baptized in the Holy Spirit. Hands were laid on Saul/Paul, and believers at Samaria and Ephesus, but those hands of service can be - like water baptism - of any disciple such as Ananias, and not limited to a select few leaders. Point (4) refers to the fact that **Bishops are the original ministers of confirmation**. Similar to point (2), while another believer can be involved when a person is Baptized in the Holy Spirit, no other person is required for this baptism to occur. We can ask Jesus ourselves or Jesus can just do it as He did with Cornelius, family and friends. On the basis Confirmation is primarily about Baptism of the Holy Spirit, aren't points (2) and (4) of Catholic teaching inherently in error?

8:48 Point (3) ***brings you deeper into communion with the church***. Point (5a) ***its effects is to unite those who receive it more closely to the church, her apostolic origins*** and (5b) ***her mission of bearing witness to Christ***. Baptism in the Holy Spirit is given for power to be witnesses for Christ, evidenced in ways including gifts such as tongues and prophecy. While an individual Baptized in the Holy Spirit may be more united with believers who also received this baptism, there is no mention Baptism in the Holy Spirit is intended to bring a person into deeper communion with the church.

    i. On the basis Confirmation is primarily about Baptism of the Holy Spirit, aren't parts (3) and (5a) of Catholic teaching in error?

    ii. If Baptism in the Holy Spirit was intended to bring a person into a deeper communion, shouldn't the deeper communion be with God as opposed to a church? Or does the Roman Catholic church rank ahead of God? I do note that between points (10) and (11), the commentary acknowledges Baptism of the Holy Spirit can unite us more firmly to Christ, but why isn't it all about God?

    iii. Point (5b) is somewhat consistent with scripture where Baptism of the Holy Spirit is about power to witness. But isn't Baptism of the Holy Spirit about individual believers being the primary witnesses for Jesus, as opposed to an organization or church being the primary witness?

8: En and Epi After the Cross

8:49   Point (6a) ***Confirmation is given only once***. Point (8) ***it's a permanent thing that is fully completed and doesn't expire***. Per Chapter 9, Baptism of the Holy Spirit relates to being filled with the Holy Spirit. The reason is that the upon [epi] experience effectively results in God's presence coming upon us, but it's intended to flow from or through us to others for their benefit. As a result, we need fresh filling, fresh baptisms upon [epi] us. The in [en] experience happens once when we're born again and Holy Spirit comes in us. Holy Spirit does not flow out of us. On the basis Confirmation is primarily about Baptism of the Holy Spirit, aren't parts (6a) and (8) of Catholic teaching in error?

8:50   Point (6b) ***imprints on the soul an indelible spiritual mark, the 'character', which is the sign that Jesus Christ has marked a Christian with the seal of His Spirit.*** The Bible does not indicate Baptism of the Holy Spirit leaves an imprint of character. Moreover, we are sealed with the Holy Spirit when we're first born again and Holy Spirit comes in [en] us. On the basis Confirmation is primarily about Baptism of the Holy Spirit, isn't point (6b) of Catholic teaching in error?

8:51   Point (12) ***leaves an indelible mark on the soul just like baptism*** Per above, leaving a mark is not even mentioned as a result of the Baptism of the Holy Spirit. It certainly can impact one's soul - as it did mine - but those are secondary impacts. Views vary on what the impacts are from water baptism. I'll let you decide what's what.

8:52   Point (9) ***ordinary minister extending his hand over the one to be confirmed and anointing his/her head with the oil of chrism saying "be sealed with the Holy Spirit"***. Per point 6b, we are sealed with the Holy Spirit when we're born again and Holy Spirit comes in [en] us - not when Holy Spirit comes upon [epi] us. No extending of hands or anointing with oil of chrism is required. On the basis Confirmation is primarily about Baptism of the Holy Spirit, isn't point (9) of Catholic teaching in error?

8:53   Point (11) ***increases the gifts of the Holy Spirit***. Baptism of the Holy Spirit gives access to the 9 Holy Spirit gifts which are distributed to individuals as Holy Spirit chooses. Point (13) **seven gifts of the Holy Spirit received through Confirmation**. These 7 gifts are not uniquely identified in God's Word as resulting from the Baptism of the Holy Spirit. The Bible leaves no doubt that the primary reason for this baptism is receiving power to witness. And one of the key ways this power manifests is through the 9 Holy Spirit gifts which aren't even mentioned. On the basis Confirmation is primarily about Baptism of the Holy Spirit, aren't points (11) and (13) of Catholic teaching in error?

According to Roman Catholic teachings, Confirmation is not a new type of experience with the Holy Spirit (which it is), but an intensification of the presence and power of Holy Spirit received when born again after being water baptized. While the water baptism is in error, there is no doubt that the Baptism of the Holy Spirit is about power to be witnesses for Christ. As a result, there are two points (7 & 10) in the above information that, in my view, are correct to a degree.

CEASED?

8:54 Point (7) *__clothing him with power on high so that he may be his witness__*. On the basis Confirmation is primarily about receiving power to be witnesses, I view point (7) of Catholic teaching as being correct if indeed Confirmation is essentially about Baptism of the Holy Spirit. If it is, isn't point (7) essentially correct?

8:55 Point (10) *__the full outpouring of the Holy Spirit as once granted to the apostles on the day of Pentecost__*. Again, on the basis Confirmation is primarily about Baptism of the Holy Spirit, I view point (10) of Catholic teaching as being correct in terms of the apostles received the outpouring of the Holy Spirit. However, where it appears to be in error is that the outpouring was limited to the original apostles, which it wasn't. Thus, isn't point (10) correct to a degree?

Both the mainstream and Charismatic streams of the Roman Catholic church tend to associate the sacrament of Confirmation with Baptism of the Holy Spirit, and an intensification of the presence and power of Holy Spirit. However, there is no clear distinction between the in [en] and the upon [epi] experiences. Instead, there is an intermixing of the two experiences along with other aspects such as water baptism and 7 gifts other than the 9 Holy Spirit gifts.

8:56 The last command Jesus gave before His ascension was for His born-again disciples to wait for the Baptism of the Holy Spirit which they received approximately 10 days later at Pentecost. This baptism was clearly important, glimpses of which became evident at Pentecost. If indeed the information contained in **CEASED?** on the in [en] and upon [epi] is correct or considerably more correct than Roman Catholic teachings:

    i. Isn't it awfully surprising the Roman Catholic church has so many incorrect teachings on Baptism of the Holy Spirit given the Roman Catholic church's claims:
        a. it is the one true church with roots going back to the very beginning of the early church; and
        b. it has the correct teachings which are supported by the writings of early church fathers, some of whom were discipled by the original apostles?

    ii. The original apostles placed an emphasis on the Baptism of the Holy Spirit and treated the upon [epi] as distinct from the in [en] experience. Why doesn't the Roman Catholic church clearly teach that today? And why does the group of Catholics who belong to what is known as the Charismatic Catholic movement only have its roots dating back to the 1960's, instead of back to the first years after the cross - the 30's, 40's, 50's, 60's, and 70's - when the bulk of New Testament was being written, and the 9 Holy Spirit gifts were in full swing in the Body of Christ?

CLOSING POINTS TO PONDER
En and Epi Experiences

After reviewing Chapter 8, hopefully the following points became clearer.

8: En and Epi After the Cross

1. There are two very distinct experiences with Holy Spirit:
   i. the one-time in [en] experience occurs when a person is first born again and Holy Spirit automatically baptizes the person into God's church, the Body of Christ; and
   ii. the upon [epi] experience which involves Jesus baptizing a believer in the Baptism of the Holy Spirit to gain access to power in order to be a more effective witness for Christ.
2. There is no example of any believer being born again and having Holy Spirit come in [en] them as a result of being water baptized. There are examples, however, including Cornelius, family and friends, and the 12 disciples at Ephesus, who were all born again and had Holy Spirit in [en] them, but who had not yet been water baptized.
3. No verse states the original apostles were water baptized after the cross. If one argues they didn't need to be water baptized because they had received John the Baptist's baptism of repentance before the cross, that contradicts the situation at Ephesus where Paul made sure the 12 disciples were water baptized even though they had previously received the baptism of repentance.
4. For some believers, water baptism occurred before being Baptized in the Holy Spirit. For others, the order was reversed. Baptism in the Holy Spirit occurred first; water baptism took place second.
5. The original apostles ensured new believers were Baptized in the Holy Spirit as evidenced by John and Peter going to Samaria and Paul asking questions of the 12 disciples at Ephesus.
6. For the groups at Pentecost, Cornelius family and friends, and at Ephesus, supernatural gifts such as tongues and/or prophecy began for some believers immediately after they were Baptized in the Holy Spirit. Clearly, such gifts were not limited to the apostles.
7. Jesus is the one who Baptizes a person in the Holy Spirit. Jesus can do so unilaterally (Pentecost, Cornelius), as a result of another believer laying on of hands (Saul/Paul, Samaria and Ephesus), or not at all. Anointing with oil was never part of Baptism of the Holy Spirit.

Roman Catholic Considerations

8:57 The Roman Catholic church does not clearly distinguish between the in [en] and upon [epi] experiences but mixes them together. There are major errors in the teachings of the 1st sacrament (water baptism) and the 2nd sacrament (Baptism in the Holy Spirit), 2 sacraments which are the foundation of the other 5 sacraments. I won't repeat all the other issues here, but if you're Roman Catholic, do you again see why many Protestants do not accept the Roman Catholic church as the one true church with the correct teachings?

8:58 Evidence that a person has been Baptized in the Holy Spirit and having received the upon [epi] experience is provided when we see the person operating in the Holy Spirit gifts such as prophecy and tongues. As the sacrament of Confirmation is largely centered around Baptism in the Holy Spirit, then:

CEASED?

     i. Instead of a minority of Catholics operating in these gifts, why don't we see all Roman Catholics who have gone through Confirmation, and therefore have been Baptized in the Holy Spirit according to the Catholic Church, operate in these gifts instead of just the 100-125 million who are labeled as Charismatic Catholics?
    ii. Is part of the reason most Roman Catholics don't operate in these gifts because Jesus is the key for the Baptism of the Holy Spirit, not a Bishop or priest?
   iii. Even though someone may have been confirmed and words were spoken that say this Baptism occurred as part of their Confirmation, does that guarantee the Baptism actually happened given it is Jesus who Baptizes us in the Holy Spirit?
   iv. Is a second reason most Roman Catholics don't operate in these gifts because the Roman Catholic church effectively taught for centuries, much like Protestant Cessationists believe, that the 9 Holy Spirit gifts ceased?
    v. And does that mean Catholics in the pews have not been getting equipped by the Catholic priesthood and leadership to use such gifts?

My understanding of Roman Catholic teachings is that:
    i. Confirmation is required;
   ii. Confirmation is primarily about Baptism of the Holy Spirit; and
  iii. Confirmation results in a believer being sealed with the Holy Spirit.

8:59 Holy Spirit gifts such as tongues and prophecy are a good indicator that a person has been Baptized in the Holy Spirit. Given Roman Catholic teaching that Baptism of the Holy Spirit seals a person with the Holy Spirit, should Roman Catholics be concerned that individuals who don't operate in Holy Spirit gifts may not be sealed with the Holy Spirit? And thus, based on Roman Catholic teachings, such individuals may not be saved?

8:60 In my view, the lack of clarity in Roman Catholic teachings on the in [en] and upon [epi] experiences leads to many other incorrect teachings and considerable confusion. Such errors can be shown by comparing Roman Catholic teachings to what the Bible says. With such significant errors existing on fundamental issues of the in [en] and upon [epi] experiences as well as in the foundational sacraments of water baptism and confirmation, how can one be comfortable with any Roman Catholic teachings that cannot be checked against the Bible? How can they be validated as being of God, and therefore true?

Water Baptism and Baptism of the Holy Spirit are two separate events, both of which are independent of being saved. The 9 Holy Spirit gifts result from being Baptized in the Holy Spirit. Chapter 10 reviews these and other Baptisms in detail, while Chapter 11 shows how various baptisms and the para, meta, en and epi Holy Spirit experiences all fit together.

9

Filled/Refilled With the Holy Spirit

INTRODUCTION
WHEN I hear the word fill, I tend to think of something being filled on the inside, like an empty bottle being filled with water. When it's full, it overflows. The terms *'filled with the Holy Spirit'* and *'spirit-filled believer'* are often used in the context of both the in [en] experience and the upon [epi] experience. The question is do these phrases apply to both experiences, or only one. And if only one experience, which one.

16 SCRIPTURES - FILLED WITH THE HOLY SPIRIT
I found 16 New Testament scriptures related to being full of, or filled with the Holy Spirit. **CEASED?** reviews all 16 scriptures with each scripture labeled by an identifier **(1 of 16), (2 of 16)** etc. In addition to these 16 scriptures, I occasionally added a few scriptures to provide context.

In these 16 scriptures, 3 different Greek words for full or filled are used:
- *Pletho* [G4130] - to fill, to be fulfilled, to be filled;
- *Pleroo* [G4137] - to fill, make full, fill up, to influence fully; and
- *Pleres* [G4134] - full, i.e. filled up (as opposed to empty), covered in every part, full, i.e. complete, lacking nothing, perfect.

John the Baptist, Elizabeth and Zacharias
Of the scriptures using the term *'filled with the Holy Spirit'*, 3 apply to John the Baptist and his parents, Elizabeth and Zacharias.
- ❑ *(1 of 16) Luke 1:15 For he will be great in the sight of the Lord; and he will drink no wine or liquor, and he will be **filled [Pletho G4130] with the Holy Spirit** while yet in his mother's womb.*
- ❑ *(2 of 16) Luke 1:41 When Elizabeth heard Mary's greeting, the baby leaped in her womb; and Elizabeth was **filled [Pletho G4130] with the Holy Spirit**:*
- ❑ *(3 of 16) Luke 1:67 And his father Zacharias was **filled [Pletho G4130] with the Holy Spirit**, and prophesied, saying:*

The experiences that Elizabeth, John the Baptist and Zacharias had with Holy Spirit occurred before the cross. They could not have been born again as was

CEASED?

possible after the cross, and thus the permanent indwelling experience, the [en] experience, wasn't available to them in the same way we have today. They could have enjoyed the blessings of a temporary indwelling [en] of the Holy Spirit, or they could have had an upon [epi] experience as others did in the Old Testament.

9:1 John was extremely bold in his ministry. Doesn't that support the notion that John had a form of an upon [epi] experience which gives the recipient power to be a witness as Peter and Paul both demonstrated in Acts?

9:2 Zacharias prophesied. As per Chapter 7, Baptism of the Holy Spirit is linked to the 9 Holy Spirit gifts/manifestations, one of which is the gift of prophecy. Doesn't that suggest Zacharias also received an upon [epi] experience?

9:3 Elizabeth's being filled with the Holy Spirit occurred ~34 years before the cross. All of us, including Elizabeth, benefit from Holy Spirit comforting us, guiding us, etc. No doubt Elizabeth would have benefited from a temporary in [en] experience, even if it was only for the time spent raising John. On the other hand, would it be a total surprise if one day we learn Elizabeth also received an upon [epi] experience, and received power that enabled her to be a mother to an unusual son, John the Baptist, and to receive a word of knowledge from Holy Spirit that Mary was carrying her Savior in her womb?

❑ *Luke 1:41 When Elizabeth heard Mary's greeting, the baby leaped in her womb; and Elizabeth was filled with the Holy Spirit. 42 And* **she cried out with a loud voice and said***, "Blessed are you among women, and blessed is the fruit of your womb!*

Jesus

❑ *John 1:32 John testified saying, "I have seen the Spirit descending as a dove out of heaven, and He remained* **upon [epi]** *Him.*

❑ *(4 of 16) Luke 4:1 Jesus,* **full [Pleres G4134] of the Holy Spirit***, returned from the Jordan and was led around by the Spirit in the wilderness,*

❑ *Luke 4:14 And Jesus returned to Galilee in the* **power of the Spirit***, and news about Him spread through all the surrounding district.*

9:4 Holy Spirit came upon Jesus like a dove, and remained. Jesus was full of the Holy Spirit as He went into the desert. Jesus returned from the desert in power. Wasn't Jesus's upon [epi] experience directly linked to His being full of the Holy Spirit and His returning in power? If not, what was it linked to?

Group of ~120

❑ *(5 of 16) Acts 2:4 And they were all* **filled [Pletho G4130] with the Holy Spirit***, and began to speak with other tongues, as the Spirit was giving them utterance.*

9:5 On the morning of Pentecost, the group of ~120 was Baptized in the Holy Spirit. They spoke in tongues. Given the simultaneous nature of these events, doesn't both their speaking in tongues and being filled with the Holy Spirit appear to be directly related to their Baptism in the Holy Spirit when Holy Spirit came upon [epi] them, and not the in [en] experience when they were born again 50 days earlier on resurrection Sunday evening? If not, why not?

9: Filled With the Holy Spirit

Peter and John
- ☐ ***(6 of 16)*** *Acts 4:8 Then Peter,* **_filled [Pletho G4130] with the Holy Spirit_**, *said to them, "Rulers and elders ..."*
- ☐ ***(7 of 16)*** *Acts 4:31 And when they had prayed, the place where they had gathered together was shaken,* **_and they were all filled [Pletho G4130] with the Holy Spirit_** *and began to speak the word of God with boldness.*

After their release from prison, Peter and John shared their experience with other believers. They began praising God who responded by filling them with the Holy Spirit. The result was they spoke the Word of God with boldness, a chain of events quite similar to events at Pentecost.

9:6   Would Peter being filled in Acts 4:8 and all of them being filled in Acts 4:31:
    i. indicate a filling that a) just happened, or b) happened several weeks before;
    ii. be more likely the result of a) an upon [epi] experience as we see happening at Pentecost or b) the in [en] experience when the disciples were born again in John 20:22 on resurrection Sunday evening?

Stephen
- ☐ ***(8 of 16)*** *Acts 6:2 So the twelve summoned the congregation of the disciples and said, "It is not desirable for us to neglect the word of God in order to serve tables. 3 Therefore, brethren, select from among you seven men of good reputation,* **_full [Pleres G4134] of_** *the Spirit and of wisdom, whom we may put in charge of this task.*
- ☐ ***(9 of 16)*** *Acts 6:5 The statement found approval with the whole congregation; and they chose Stephen, a man* **_full [Pleres G4134] of faith and of the Holy Spirit_**, *and Philip, Prochorus, Nicanor, Timon, Parmenas and Nicolas, a proselyte from Antioch.*
- ☐ ***(10 of 16)*** *Acts 6:8 And Stephen,* **_full [Pleres G4134] of grace and power_**, *was performing great wonders and signs among the people.*
- ☐ ***(11 of 16)*** *Acts 7:55 But being* **_full [Pleres G4134] of the Holy Spirit_**, *he gazed intently into heaven and saw the glory of God, and Jesus standing at the right hand of God;*

9:7   As believers, we have Holy Spirit in [en] us. If being filled in the Holy Spirit refers to this automatic indwelling that occurs when born again, let me ask.
    i. Does Acts 6:3 suggest some believers weren't filled with the Holy Spirit?
    ii. When born again, Holy Spirit automatically comes in [en] a person. Doesn't that mean if a believer is not filled with the Holy Spirit, it must relate to something other than the in [en] experience?
    iii. Why would the 12 want someone 'full of the Holy Spirit' per Acts 6:3 unless there was a significant benefit to their being filled?

9:8   Stephen was full of faith, full of the Holy Spirit, full of grace and power, and performed great wonders and signs. Would these references to being full of the Holy Spirit be more consistent with the upon [epi] experience which results in power to be witnesses, or the indwelling 'in' [en] experience?

CEASED?

Saul/Paul

- ☐ **(12 of 16)** Acts 9:17 *So Ananias departed and entered the house, and after laying his hands on him said, "Brother Saul, the Lord Jesus, who appeared to you on the road by which you were coming, has sent me so that you may regain your sight and be **filled [Pletho G4130] with the Holy Spirit**."*

9:9 Ananias laid hands on Saul for his sight to be restored and to be filled. Ananias never mentioned anything about salvation or about Paul's need to be born again. On the basis that Paul was born again before Ananias made his visit, does Paul being *'filled with the Holy Spirit'* in Acts 9:17 more likely relate to the upon [epi] experience than the in [en] experience? If not, why not?

- ☐ **(13 of 16)** *Acts 13:8 But Elymas the magician (for so his name is translated) was opposing them, seeking to turn the proconsul away from the faith. 9 But Saul, who was also known as Paul, **filled [Pletho G4130] with the Holy Spirit**, fixed his gaze on him, 10 and said, "You who are full of all deceit and fraud, you son of the devil, you enemy of all righteousness, will you not cease to make crooked the straight ways of the Lord? 11 Now, behold, the hand of the Lord is upon you, and you will be blind and not see the sun for a time." And immediately a mist and a darkness fell upon him, and he went about seeking those who would lead him by the hand. 12 Then the proconsul believed when he saw what had happened, being amazed at the teaching of the Lord.*

9:10 Does Paul's boldness and the prophecy he gave relate more closely to the upon [epi] experience - the power experience - than the in [en] experience of the Holy Spirit? And as such, would it follow that the reference to Paul being filled with the Holy Spirit relates to his upon [epi] experience, and not to his in [en] experience?

Now consider Paul's message to the Ephesian believers.

- ☐ **(14 of 16)** *Ephesians 5:18 And do not get drunk with wine, for that is dissipation, but **be filled [Pleroo G4137] with the Spirit**.*

9:11 All believers have Holy Spirit in [en] us. If being filled with the Holy Spirit refers to this indwelling that occurs automatically when born again, why would Paul encourage them to be filled with the Holy Spirit if they were already filled?

Paul and Barnabas

- ☐ **(15 of 16)** *Acts 13:45 But when the Jews saw the crowds, they were filled with jealousy and began contradicting the things spoken by Paul, and were blaspheming. 46 **Paul and Barnabas spoke out boldly** and said, "It was necessary that the word of God be spoken to you first; since you repudiate it and judge yourselves unworthy of eternal life, behold, we are turning to the Gentiles. 47 For so the Lord has commanded us, 'I have placed You as a light for the Gentiles, That You may bring salvation to the end of the earth.'" 48 When the Gentiles heard this, they began rejoicing and glorifying the word of the Lord; and as many as had been appointed to eternal life believed. 49 And*

9: Filled With the Holy Spirit

*the word of the Lord was being spread through the whole region ... 52 And the disciples were **continually filled [Pleroo G4137] with joy and with the Holy Spirit**.*

9:12 Paul and Barnabas were witnessing boldly. The Baptism of the Holy Spirit was given to receive power to be witnesses for Christ. Does their speaking boldly and being continually filled with the Holy Spirit fit with being Baptized with the Holy Spirit? If not, what does it relate to and why?

Barnabas
- ❏ *(16 of 16) Acts 11:22 The news about them reached the ears of the church at Jerusalem, and they sent Barnabas off to Antioch. 23 Then when he arrived and witnessed the grace of God, he rejoiced and began to encourage them all with resolute heart to remain true to the Lord; 24 for he was a good man, and **full [Pleres G4134] of the Holy Spirit** and of faith. And considerable numbers were brought to the Lord ...*

9:13 Many people were added to God's kingdom, in part possibly due to Barnabas being a good man. However, in addition, was the influence Barnabas had on people partly due to his being full of the Holy Spirit, a result of being Baptized in the Holy Spirit? If not, what does it relate to and why?

- ❏ *Acts 1:8 but you will receive power when the Holy Spirit has come upon you; and you shall be My witnesses both in Jerusalem, and in all Judea and Samaria, and even to the remotest part of the earth."*

9:14 When I review the 16 scriptures above, I believe they collectively show being filled with the Holy Spirit relates to the upon [epi] experience (Baptism with the Holy Spirit) and not the in [en] experience when we're born again and baptized by Holy Spirit into the Body of Christ. If you disagree, what scriptures lead you to believe it relates to the in [en] experience? And let me remind readers that when a person is born again, they have the most important Holy Spirit experience which is when Holy Spirit comes in [en] us. I'm in no way trying to diminish the importance of this experience. I'm merely trying to clarify what Holy Spirit experience that the terms *'full of the Holy Spirit'* and *'filled with the Holy Spirit'* are primarily associated with.

Spirit-Filled Believer

Further to the above, I believe when we're Baptized with the Holy Spirit, we become a 'spirit-filled' Christian. When I make this claim, some may suggest I believe a person who hasn't been Baptized in the Holy Spirit doesn't have the Holy Spirit. This is not the case. All born-again believers have Holy Spirit in [en] them. However, we don't have Holy Spirit upon [epi] us until we've been Baptized in the Holy Spirit - by Jesus.

9:15 There are amazing ministries that are filled with love and bless so many people without relying on the power and supernatural aspects associated with Baptism of the Holy Spirit and the 9 Holy Spirit gifts/manifestations. My question is ... would such ministries be able to bless people even more if they hosted the presence of God upon [epi] them and operated with the supernatural power and associated 9 Holy Spirit gifts/manifestations functioning as a normal part of their ministry?

9:16 If Baptism of the Holy Spirit is not of value, why did the disciples feel it was imperative that the leaders of the ministry serving widows and orphans needed to be spirit-filled?
- ❑ *Acts 6:1 Now at this time while the disciples were increasing in number, a complaint arose on the part of the Hellenistic Jews against the native Hebrews, because their widows were being overlooked in the daily serving of food ... 3 Therefore, brethren, **select from among you seven men** of good reputation, **full of the Spirit** and of wisdom, whom we may put in charge of this task.*

AFTER RECEIVING THE EPI, DO WE 'LEAK'?

It's not uncommon for spirit-filled believers to say we leak where Holy Spirit's presence upon us can dissipate over time. As a result, we need a fresh filling - a fresh Baptism of the Holy Spirit. But is this so? We can gain some insight on this issue from the Old Testament. Consider Samson:
- ❑ *Judges 15:14 When he came to Lehi, the Philistines shouted as they met him. And the **Spirit of the Lord came upon him** mightily so that the ropes that were on his arms were as flax that is burned with fire, and his bonds dropped from his hands.*
- ❑ *Judges 16:20 She said, "The Philistines are upon you, Samson!" And he awoke from his sleep and said, "I will go out as at other times and shake myself free." **But he did not know that the Lord had departed from him**.*

The same thing happened to King Saul.
- ❑ *1 Samuel 11:6 Then the **Spirit of God came upon Saul mightily** when he heard these words, and he became very angry.*
- ❑ *1 Samuel 16:14 Now the **Spirit of the Lord departed from Saul**, and an evil spirit from the Lord terrorized him.*

One of the first times we read about the Baptism of the Holy Spirit, is in relationship to Jesus.
- ❑ *Luke 3:21 Now when all the people were baptized, Jesus was also baptized, and while He was praying, heaven was opened, 22 and the **Holy Spirit descended upon Him** in bodily form **like a dove**, and a voice came out of heaven, "You are My beloved Son, in You I am well-pleased."*

Doves are a delicate bird. Unlike an elephant with looks at most adversity with a shrug and maybe a swing of their trunk, doves will quickly move away when it experiences the least amount of adversity or unease. Merriam Webster dictionary defines a dove in part as any of numerous pigeons ... a gentle woman or child or one who takes a conciliatory attitude and advocates negotiations and compromise.

In many sermons, Bill Johnson teaches about this dove-like descending of Holy Spirit upon Jesus, and that not only did Holy Spirit come upon Jesus, but Holy Spirit remained on Jesus.
- ❑ *John 1:32 John testified saying, "I have seen the Spirit **descending as a dove***

9: Filled With the Holy Spirit

*out of heaven, and **He remained upon Him**.*

9:17 If a dove came upon [epi] us today, is it reasonable to expect the degree or duration to which the dove stays on us may depend to a large extent on how much peace we provide to the dove?

Perhaps that's one reason we are called to imitate Christ.
- *1 Corinthians 11:1 Be imitators of me, just as I also am of Christ.*

Jesus's ministry featured signs and wonders that displayed God's power over and over again. Jesus was in a public place a great deal of time. Jesus stood for truth. Jesus showed compassion. Jesus loved everybody. Jesus was no respecter of persons. He treated the 'least' the same as the 'greatest'. Jesus didn't play mind games though some parables were mind-numbing. Jesus didn't gossip. Jesus didn't sin. Jesus also spent much time alone in communion with Father God and only did what Father God did. Is it surprising Holy Spirit remained upon Jesus?

9:18 If we spend time with God in private, live a life that pleases God and seek Him in all things, aren't the odds higher that Holy Spirit will remain on us for longer periods?
- *Mark 1:35 In the early morning, while it was still dark, Jesus got up, left the house, and went away to a secluded place, and was praying there.*
- *Mark 6:45 Immediately Jesus made His disciples get into the boat and go ahead of Him to the other side to Bethsaida, while He Himself was sending the crowd away. 46 After bidding them farewell, He left for the mountain to pray.*

Holy Spirit and Water

Jesus refers to Holy Spirit as living water.
- *John 4:10 Jesus answered and said to her, "If you knew the gift of God, and who it is who says to you, 'Give Me a drink,' you would have asked Him, and He would have given you **living water**."*
- *John 7:38 He who believes in Me, as the Scripture said, '**From his innermost being will flow rivers of living water**.'"*

9:19 Rivers flow. When the presence of God (Holy Spirit) is upon us, is His presence to flow from us to others as part of being a witness for Christ?

Consider the woman who had been hemorrhaging for 12 years.
- *Mark 5:25 A woman who had had a hemorrhage for twelve years, 26 and had endured much at the hands of many physicians, and had spent all that she had and was not helped at all, but rather had grown worse - 27 after hearing about Jesus, she came up in the crowd behind Him and touched His cloak. 28 For she thought, "If I just touch His garments, I will get well." 29 Immediately the flow of her blood was dried up; and she felt in her body that she was healed of her affliction. 30 Immediately Jesus, **perceiving in Himself that the power proceeding from Him had gone forth**, turned around in the crowd and said, "Who touched My garments?"*

9:20 This woman was healed by the power of God, a power that was upon Jesus and 'leaked' from Him when her healing occurred. We are to imitate Jesus.

Does this mean that, like Jesus, the power upon us is intended to flow out from us so that others are blessed?

9:21 Should we seek God so much and be so filled with the Holy Spirit that His presence overflows from us into our immediate environment, in the vicinity of our 'shadow' just like it did within the vicinity of Peter's 'shadow'?
- *Acts 5:15 to such an extent that they even carried the sick out into the streets and laid them on cots and pallets, so that when Peter came by at least his shadow might fall on any one of them.*

9:22 Would this outflow of power to bless others be consistent with how the Body of Christ is also to come alongside each other, in good times and bad times?
- *1 Corinthians 12:20 But now there are many members, but one body ... 25 so that there may be no division in the body, but that the members may have the same care for one another. 26 And if one member suffers, all the members suffer with it; if one member is honored, all the members rejoice with it.*

9:23 If the power of God upon us is intended to flow to others, or is like a river that flows from us on an ongoing basis, doesn't this suggest we need to get filled up regularly? Or even better, to be plugged into the power source all the time through ongoing communication throughout our waking hours?

Are we to be Re-Baptized with the Holy Spirit

Jesus baptizes believers in the Holy Spirit which gives a person their initial filling. That is clear. No specific scripture says we are to ask Jesus to Baptize us again in the Holy Spirit. However, consider what happened to Peter and John after they were released from prison in Acts 4.
- *Acts 4:23 When they had been released, they went to their own companions and reported all that the chief priests and the elders had said to them. 24 And when they heard this, they lifted their voices to God with one accord and said, "O Lord, it is You who made the heaven and the earth and the sea, and all that is in them, 25 who by the Holy Spirit, through the mouth of our father David Your servant, said,... 31 And **when they had prayed**, the place where they had gathered together was shaken, and **they were all filled with the Holy Spirit** and began to speak the word of God with boldness.*

After the disciples gave praise and prayed, they were ALL filled with the Holy Spirit ... again.

9:24 Doesn't this suggest our filling comes primarily from spending time with God in prayer, praise and worship either individually or collectively similar to when the disciples were gathered in prayer in Acts 1 before the events of Pentecost took place?

9:25 Does this leaking explain why many Charismatics ask and pray for a fresh baptism, a fresh outpouring of the Holy Spirit so they can be filled again with the Holy Spirit?

9:26 In terms of asking for a fresh baptism, do we need to guard against getting into the habit of simply asking for a fresh baptism as opposed to daily

9: Filled With the Holy Spirit

spending time with God just for the blessings of spending time with God? And if God chooses to give us a fresh filling of the Holy Spirit, we thank Him. And if we don't receive, we thank Him for that too?

9:27 Please hear me. I'm not saying we shouldn't ask for a fresh filling. What I am saying is we need to check our hearts. If our approach is simply to ask for a fresh filling instead of first seeking to spend time with God, don't we run the risk of becoming focused on God's power instead of on Him? And is this an issue that perhaps contributed to many Charismatics going astray?

9:28 When Jesus tells us to seek first the Kingdom of God and to ask Father God for our daily bread, could one of the blessings from doing so be a fresh filling of the Holy Spirit which enables us to be a vessel out of which Holy Spirit can flow to others? Does interaction with God throughout each day keep our souls in a healthy, submitted state and strengthen us as vessels to hold and dispense Holy Spirit effectively?

- ❑ *Matthew 6:33 But seek first His kingdom and His righteousness, and all these things will be added to you.*
- ❑ *Matthew 6:9 "Pray, then, in this way: 'Our Father who is in heaven, Hallowed be Your name. 10 'Your kingdom come. Your will be done, On earth as it is in heaven. 11 'Give us this day our daily bread. 12 'And forgive us our debts, as we also have forgiven our debtors. 13 'And do not lead us into temptation, but deliver us from evil. For Yours is the kingdom and the power and the glory forever. Amen.'*

9:29 Our personal walk with Jesus has its ups and downs. If our focus changes from God's way to our way, from God's glory to our glory, can we expect to see different manifestations of God's power in our own life? And could be this be one reason why miracles happen in one season of our life but not in another?

ROMAN CATHOLIC TEACHINGS ON FILLED

Roman Catholic teachings do not associate the term *'being filled with the Holy Spirit'* as being related to the Baptism of the Holy Spirit. Rather, being filled is associated more with the born-again experience where Holy Spirit comes in [en] a believer.

9:30 Does this incorrect Catholic teaching on filled again result from incorrect teachings on the two separate experiences, the in [en] and the upon [epi]?

CLOSING POINTS TO PONDER

God is amazing. When it comes to being filled with Holy Spirit, my review shows it pertains to the Baptism of the Holy Spirit, that we leak and need to be refilled. How this all works, I don't know. A friend of mine and I had too much sugar and caffeine one night and brainstormed potential answers to a few, somewhat unorthodox questions:

- ❖ How do the in [en] and upon [epi] experiences actually work together?
- ❖ Does a believer have 'all' of Holy Spirit or just part of Him when we're born again and have the in [en] experience, but not the upon [epi] experience?

CEASED?

- ❖ Do we have 'all' of Him, or just access to Him?
- ❖ How can all believers have all of Holy Spirit? Can't just one have all of Him?
- ❖ If believers have all of Holy Spirit, does part of Holy Spirit leave us and go into a new believer when they enter the scene?
- ❖ Elisha wanted a double portion of Elijah's spirit 'upon' himself. How does one measure a double portion, especially if we leak?

We were clearly off kilter that night. God's complexity is way beyond human understanding. One part - His Word - is so complex. One aspect - the Great Exchange - has so many dimensions. And yet, in some ways, God is not complex. His core messages are not complex. We can come to Him as little children. We are to love Him and others. So complex. So simple. My head hurts.

The spiritual world God created is also very complex. I don't have much of a clue as to what goes on when we're filled or have the para, meta, en and epi experiences. I don't understand much of how the supernatural, spiritual world actually works, which more and more makes me realize why faith is so central to our Christian walk, why we need constant communication with God, and why we need to be led by Holy Spirit in so much of our lives.

I'm not sure who first said it, but I love the notion that evangelizing and sharing the great news of Christ is not something we do, it's who we are. If you're not comfortable in evangelizing, I've been there and get it. But ... I encourage you to make it a priority. Loving people all the way to hell does no good from an eternal standpoint. At some point, they must hear the gospel. There are several approaches. Building relationships at work and elsewhere, loving them, being real and letting them see Christ in you, are all key steps. Then, when opportunities arise such as when they want prayer, you're there for them with the love and power of Jesus. Adopting teachings from evangelists such as Billy, Franklin and Will Graham are impactful as is the approach taught and used by Ray Comfort. No question. However, 'power' evangelism where God's power manifests through a miraculous healing or a word of knowledge, impacts people in a different way. When these events occur, people know they experienced or observed a supernatural event, and it opens the door to share the truth of Jesus. If you've never been involved in these kinds of amazing experiences, don't worry. You can do it. Holy Spirit is with you and other believers will come alongside to help you.

And - for those who like to share theological knowledge - my experience is that intellectual debates/discussions seldom yield much fruit, unless the other person is being drawn by Holy Spirit and is truly open to listening. After all, most of us are often more loyal to our beliefs than to seeking the truth.

10

4 Baptisms Relevant Today, 9 in Total?

INTRODUCTION

WHEN researching baptisms in the Bible, I was surprised to find there were 3-4 baptisms related to today's believer, another 3 that Jesus experienced, and at least two other baptisms. In addition to reviewing each of these 9 baptisms, Chapter 10 examines whether Peter's statement *"Repent and be baptized ..."* in Acts 2:38 refers to water baptism or Baptism in the Holy Spirit (page 180).

REVIEW OF THE 9 BAPTISMS

When I ask believers if they have been Baptized in the Holy Spirit. believers who have received this baptism usually know what I mean because they were impacted in a tangible way. And for those who haven't received this baptism, a very common answer is still *"Yes, I have"*. When I ask when they received this baptism, the most common response is *"When I was water baptized"*. This kind of confusion was one of the catalysts that led to my writing **CEASED?**.

The Bible speaks of several baptisms. The exact count depends on how one groups and differentiates the baptisms. While **CEASED?** discusses 9 baptisms, there may be more, or less, depending on how you view scripture. Of these 9 baptisms in **CEASED?**, 4 apply to believers today. Before getting into these 4, let's look at the other 5.

#1: BAPTISM INTO MOSES

Figure 10:1 Baptism into Moses

#	Name of Baptism	Purpose	Who Baptized Who	When Occurred
1	Baptism into Moses	Deliverance of Israel through the Red Sea	God 'baptized' people of Israel with Moses	40 Years of Exodus

After Moses returned from his 40-year exile to set Israel free, God put 10 plagues on Egypt. The last plague involved killing the firstborn of Egypt, both human and animal.

CEASED?

> ❑ *Exodus 12:12 For I will go through the land of Egypt on that night, and will strike down all the firstborn in the land of Egypt, both man and beast; and against all the gods of Egypt I will execute judgments - I am the Lord. 13 The blood shall be a sign for you on the houses where you live; and when I see the blood I will pass over you, and no plague will befall you to destroy you when I strike the land of Egypt.*

Fortunately for Israel, their eldest children were saved at Passover through the shed blood of many lambs. Moses and the rest of the Israelites began their exodus from Egypt by going to, and then through, the Red Sea. After that, Moses led Israel through the desert for 40 years with the protection and guidance of the cloud by day and the fire by night.

> ❑ *Exodus 13:21 The Lord was going before them in a **pillar of cloud** by day to lead them on the way, and in **a pillar of fire** by night to give them light, that they might travel by day and by night.*

10:1 Doesn't this pillar of fire indicate that when God sends fire, sometimes the fire is actually a major blessing?

During this 40-year journey, Moses and the people of Israel had many 'interesting' situations. They were inextricably linked on this journey.

> ❑ *1 Corinthians 10:1 For I do not want you to be unaware, brethren, that our fathers were all under the cloud and all passed through the sea; 2 and **all were baptized into Moses** in the cloud and in the sea; 3 and all ate the same spiritual food; 4 and all drank the same spiritual drink, for they were **drinking from a spiritual rock** which followed them; and **the rock was Christ**.*

Compared to a baptism where a person is fully submerged under water, I liken part of this 'baptism into Moses' as being submerged together in the presence of God for 40 years. They were immersed together as one body, with Moses as their earthly leader being led by Almighty God.

10:2 Was this 40-year journey of individuals living totally dependent on God a foreshadowing of the way that God wants each of us to have a personal relationship with Him today - depending on Him, being led by Him etc., but without the whining and the excess meat coming out of our nostrils?

> ❑ *Numbers 11:18 Say to the people, 'Consecrate yourselves for tomorrow, and you shall eat meat; for you have wept in the ears of the Lord, saying, "Oh that someone would give us meat to eat! For we were well-off in Egypt." Therefore the Lord will give you meat and you shall eat. 19 **You shall eat**, not one day, nor two days, nor five days, nor ten days, nor twenty days, 20 but a whole month, **until it comes out of your nostrils** ...*

10:3 Besides showing us that our requests may sometimes have unintended consequences, does the journey of Moses and the Jewish people, the Baptism into Moses as it were, serve as a foreshadowing of Jesus's life, death, burial and resurrection and His being the spiritual rock from which we drink?

10: 4 Baptisms Relevant Today

#2: BAPTISM OF REPENTANCE

Figure 10:2 Baptism of Repentance

#	Name of Baptism	Purpose	Who Baptized Who	When Occurred
2	Baptism of Repentance	Sign of repentance; foreshadowing righteousness of Christ & water baptism	John the Baptist, and followers of Jesus baptized Jews	A limited number of years before the cross

A core part of John the Baptist's ministry was telling the Jewish people they needed to repent. They needed to change their way of thinking and turn their hearts back to God because the kingdom of heaven was coming. Or, as the words *'at hand'* indicated, it was already there.

- ❑ Matthew 3:1 *Now in those days John the Baptist came, preaching in the wilderness of Judea, saying, 2 "**Repent**, for the kingdom of heaven is at hand."*

One way that the people of Israel displayed their repentance was by undergoing a baptism of repentance in the Jordan River.

- ❑ Mark 1:4 *John the Baptist appeared in the wilderness **preaching a baptism of repentance** for the forgiveness of sins. 5 And all the country of Judea was going out to him, and all the people of Jerusalem; and they were being baptized by him in the Jordan River, confessing their sins.*
- ❑ Luke 3:2 *in the high priesthood of Annas and Caiaphas, the word of God came to John, the son of Zacharias, in the wilderness. 3 And he came into all the district around the Jordan, **preaching a baptism of repentance** for the forgiveness of sins;*
- ❑ Acts 13:24 *after John had proclaimed before His (i.e. Jesus) coming a **baptism of repentance** to all the people of Israel.*

While John the Baptist is the person primarily associated with the baptism of repentance, disciples of Jesus also led people through this baptism before the cross.

- ❑ John 4:1 *Therefore when the Lord knew that the Pharisees had heard that Jesus was making and baptizing more disciples than John 2 (although **Jesus Himself was not baptizing**, but **His disciples were**), 3 He left Judea and went away again into Galilee.*

10:4   Given disciples of Jesus carried out the baptism of repentance per John 4:1, isn't it rather likely these disciples received the baptism of repentance themselves?

John the Baptist's ministry hit the mark as many people from Judea, Jerusalem and around the Jordan were baptized.

- ❑ Mark 1:4 *John the Baptist appeared in the wilderness preaching a baptism of repentance for the forgiveness of sins. 5 And **all the country of Judea** was going out to him, and **all the people of Jerusalem;** and they were being*

CEASED?

> *baptized by him in the Jordan River, confessing their sins.*
- *Luke 3:3 And he came into **all the district around the Jordan**, preaching a baptism of repentance for the forgiveness of sins;*

In addition, as discussed before, believers as far away as Greece were baptized.
- *Acts 19:1 It happened that while Apollos was **at Corinth**, Paul passed through the upper country and came to **Ephesus**, and found some disciples. 2 He said to them, "Did you receive the Holy Spirit when you believed?" And they said to him, "No, we have not even heard whether there is a Holy Spirit." 3 And he said, "Into what then were you baptized?" **And they said, "Into John's baptism."** 4 **Paul said, "John baptized with the baptism of repentance**, telling the people to believe in Him who was coming after him, that is, in Jesus."*

10:5 Was this spreading out of the baptism of repentance, in part, due to not only John the Baptist performing this baptism, but Jesus's disciples as well?

10:6 In a similar way, is the sharing of the gospel today:
  i. to be the focus of a few, select leaders; or
  ii. what a few believers 'do', or who a few believers 'are'; or
  iii. what all believers are called to do, and what all believers are called to be?

In terms of individuals identified by name who were baptized by John the Baptist, the only one I can find is Jesus. His baptism is unique and is reviewed in baptism #3.
- *Luke 3:21 Now when all the people were baptized, **Jesus was also baptized**, and while He was praying, heaven was opened,*

The baptism of repentance involves changing one's way of thinking and the turning of one's heart and life back towards God.

10:7 Does this mean the baptism of repentance was related to individuals who were old enough to make an informed decision by themselves or do you believe it also applied to all Jewish people including babies? In other words, how likely is it that John the Baptist and disciples of Jesus baptized babies and young children in a baptism of repentance?

10:8 When doing this baptism, John the Baptist was in the river. Do you think John sprinkled water on the head of the person or immersed the person in water? If the former, why did he need to go into the river?

#3-#5: THREE BAPTISMS EXPERIENCED BY JESUS

Figure 10:3 Baptisms Experienced by Jesus

#	Name of Baptism	Purpose	Who Baptized Jesus	When Occurred
3	Jesus's Baptism in Water	Anointing to start ministry	John the Baptist	Beginning of Jesus's Ministry
4	Jesus's Baptism in the Holy Spirit	Power to witness	Father God	Beginning of Jesus's Ministry
5	Baptism of Cup/Cross/Suffering	To take all sins on behalf of humans	Father God	On the Cross

#3: Jesus's Baptism in Water

- *Luke 3:21 Now when all the people were baptized, **Jesus was also baptized**, and while He was praying, heaven was opened,*

As mentioned earlier, the baptism of repentance was related to changing one's way of thinking and turning one's heart back to God. But as Jesus had no sins and had not walked away from God, Jesus did not need to repent. As a result, I see Jesus's baptism in water as different than #2.

There are different views on what John the Baptist's baptism of Jesus represented. Some assert John's baptism of Jesus resulted in *"fulfilling all righteousness"*, by fully immersing Jesus into His priesthood. Others see the baptism as a form of hand-off from John the Baptist to Jesus. Others believe His water baptism had nothing to do with purifying Jesus, but the opposite - that Jesus purified the water, a foreshadowing of the cleansing power of His blood and/or the cleansing associated with water baptism. Others view John's baptism of Jesus as a means by which Jesus identified with sinful humans who need to be washed clean. Still others view the baptism of Jesus as being symbolic, modeling what future believers should do, and/or a foreshadowing of water baptism identifying with Christ's death and resurrection. I'm not trying to complete an exhaustive study of this issue, but I do have a couple of comments.

John the Baptist spoke of the kingdom of heaven being at hand and that One greater than him (Jesus) will baptize the Jews with the Holy Spirit and Fire.

- *Matthew 3:2 "Repent, for the **kingdom of heaven is at hand**."*
- *Matthew 3:11 "As for me, I baptize you with water for repentance, but **He who is coming after me is mightier** than I, and I am not fit to remove His sandals; He **will baptize you with the Holy Spirit and fire**.*

A tell-tale sign revealing the identity of the Messiah would be provided when John sees Holy Spirit descending and remaining. In John 1:32, we see John testify to that reality.

CEASED?

- *John 1:32 ... "I have seen the Spirit descending as a dove out of heaven, and He remained upon Him. 33 I did not recognize Him, but **He who sent me to baptize in water said to me**, 'He **upon whom you see the Spirit descending and remaining upon Him**, this is **the One who baptizes in the Holy Spirit**.' 34 I **myself have seen**, and **have testified that this is the Son of God**."*

10:9 After John baptized Jesus in water, Holy Spirit came upon [epi] Jesus which highlighted the start of Jesus's earthly ministry. In addition to John playing a key role in this start to Jesus's ministry, John also revealed that Jesus is the one who Baptizes a person in the Holy Spirit. Does the declaration by John that Jesus would Baptize individuals in the Holy Spirit serve to indicate this future Baptism was an important one? And just as important or perhaps even more important than water baptism?

#4: **Jesus's Baptism in the Holy Spirit**

Holy Spirit came upon [epi] Jesus as He came out of the water after being baptized by John the Baptist. Whether or not we view Holy Spirit coming upon Jesus as unique and distinct from the Baptism of the Holy Spirit received by followers of Christ (Baptism #8) is not a critical theological issue for me. However, for those who are more detailed by nature, I share some thoughts. To start, as just mentioned, Jesus is the one who Baptizes believers with the Holy Spirit.

- *Matthew 3:11 "As for me, I baptize you with water for repentance, but He who is coming after me is mightier than I, and I am not fit to remove His sandals; **He will baptize you with the Holy Spirit and fire**.*

In the case of Jesus's own Baptism with the Holy Spirit coming upon [epi] Him, the choices as to who baptized Jesus are Father God, Jesus himself or Holy Spirit. Yes, John the Baptist immersed Jesus in water but I don't think John was able to tell Holy Spirit "Now Holy Spirit, come upon Jesus." If John did this, I suspect God's Word would say so. Consider Acts 10:38 and Matthew 3:17.

- *Acts 10:38 You know of Jesus of Nazareth, **how God anointed Him** with the **Holy Spirit and with power** ...*
- *Matthew 3:16 After being baptized, Jesus came up immediately from the water; and behold, the heavens were opened, and he saw the **Spirit of God descending as a dove and lighting on Him**, 17 and behold, a voice out of the heavens said, "**This is My beloved Son, in whom I am well-pleased**."*

I don't see any scriptures that Jesus baptized Himself or that Holy Spirit unilaterally carried out this baptism. As a result, I believe it was Father God who baptized Jesus. And on the basis that Father God baptized Jesus in the Holy Spirit while Jesus baptizes believers in the Holy Spirit, I treat Jesus's Baptism of the Holy Spirit as a unique baptism. If you disagree, that's fine - it's not a salvation issue.

John 1 adds another dimension to Jesus's Baptism with the Holy Spirit by stating that Holy Spirit not only came on Jesus, but as mentioned previously, Holy Spirit remained on Jesus.

- *John 1:33 I did not recognize Him, but He who sent me to baptize in water said to me, 'He upon whom you see the **Spirit descending and remaining***

10: 4 Baptisms Relevant Today

upon Him, *this is the One who baptizes in the Holy Spirit.'*

10:10 Given Holy Spirit remained upon Jesus, does it follow that a key to the miracles done by Jesus, including physical healings, was not only Holy Spirit coming upon Jesus but remaining and not leaving?

10:11 If not, what was the purpose of Holy Spirit coming upon Jesus, and where did the supernatural power come from when Jesus returned from the desert 40 days later?

- *Luke 4:14 And **Jesus returned** to Galilee **in the power of the Spirit**, and news about Him spread through all the surrounding district.*

10:12 Without Holy Spirit coming upon [epi] Jesus, wouldn't Jesus have had similar power as the ordinary person - virtually none? If earthly Jesus had divine power, or 24/7 access to divine power, before He was Baptized with the Holy Spirit:
   i. why did Jesus need to be Baptized with the Holy Spirit if He already had the power; and
   ii. how could Jesus serve as a role model for believers today if He had divine power, or had access to God's power, that we can't access?

10:13 On the basis that Holy Spirit coming upon Jesus enabled Him to access Holy Spirit power, doesn't that mean we can also access the same kind of power from the Holy Spirit when Holy Spirit comes upon [epi] us?

10:14 Is this access to power a key reason why Jesus states that those who believe in Jesus will do greater works than He did?

- *John 14:12 Truly, truly, I say to you, **he who believes in Me**, the **works that I do, he will do also; and greater works than these he will do**; because I go to the Father.*

10:15 Are you seeing greater works in your life than those Jesus did in His life? Or in the lives of other believers that you're associated with, such as at your church? If not, isn't it reasonable to ask why not and to take steps to equip yourself and any saints you influence so these greater works do occur?

If you find questions such as 10:15 to be irrelevant because you still believe the Baptism of the Holy Spirit and the 9 Holy Spirit gifts have ceased, consider checking out Chapters 13 through 20. They provide much more evidence showing why these blessings from God haven't ceased.

#5: Baptism of the Cup/Cross/Suffering

All humans are sinners and deserve separation from God. Jesus was sin-free, but loved us so much that He was willing to pay the penalty for all our sins on the cross.

- *2 Corinthians 5:21 He made Him who knew no sin **to be sin on our behalf**, so that we might become the righteousness of God in Him.*

Jesus had previously forewarned His disciples of the suffering He would endure.

- *Mark 10:32 ... And again He took the twelve aside and began to tell them what was going to happen to Him, 33 ... Son of Man will be delivered to the*

CEASED?

*chief priests and the scribes; and they will condemn Him to death and will hand Him over to the Gentiles. 34 **They will mock Him and spit on Him, and scourge Him and kill Him**, and three days later He will rise again."*

This overflowing, this immersion by Jesus in our sins, His suffering for us, is the 5th baptism.
- ❑ *Mark 10:38 But Jesus said to them, "You do not know what you are asking. Are you able to drink the cup that I drink, or to **be baptized with the baptism** with which I am baptized?"*
- ❑ *Matthew 26:39 And He went a little beyond them, and fell on His face and prayed, saying, "My Father, if it is possible, **let this cup pass from Me; yet not as I will, but as You will**."*
- ❑ *Luke 22:42 saying, "Father, **if You are willing, remove this cup from Me; yet not My will, but Yours be done**."*

After the cross, Peter warned believers we will also suffer as we take up our cross daily.
- ❑ *1 Peter 4:12 Beloved, do not be surprised at the fiery ordeal among you, ... 13 **but to the degree that you share the sufferings of Christ** ...*
- ❑ *Matthew 16:24 Then Jesus said to His disciples, "If anyone wishes to come after Me, **he must deny himself, and take up his cross** and follow Me.*
- ❑ *Mark 10:39 They said to Him, "We are able." And Jesus said to them, "The **cup that I drink you shall drink**; and **you shall be baptized with the baptism with which I am baptized**.*

We're all called to be ready to suffer for the Kingdom of God, and thus to some extent, this baptism might be considered as something we also participate in today, albeit in a way that differs from what Jesus endured. Suffering and persecution will vary, and if you're going through a difficult time right now, I pray God's grace, mercy and peace will flood your being and life.

One last comment on this baptism: *"Thank You Jesus! I can't imagine the physical, emotional and spiritual pain you endured for us."*

#6-#9: FOUR BAPTISMS FOR BELIEVERS TODAY

Before I make any comments on the 4 baptisms summarized in Figure 4 on the next page, I recognize some readers may already be sharpening your theological weapons. I ask for your patience. I think patience is mentioned somewhere in the Bible. When I started my review, I thought there were only two baptisms relevant today so I had my own share of 'oh gosh' moments. And when I shared the notion of 4 baptisms relevant for today's believers and 9 in total, I received a taste of what is likely to come my way. However, I digress.

When a person is born again, the blessings received are much more than just eternal salvation and getting a ticket into heaven. Figure 6:1, the Great Exchange, highlights some of them. One key blessing is Holy Spirit coming into the new believer, the in [en'] experience. Take a few seconds again and think about that. Almighty God ... resides in each of us for the rest of our earthly lives. For me, it's

10: 4 Baptisms Relevant Today

hard to grasp what that really means. I look at the stars, the sun and moon, and the vastness of the ocean, forests and mountains near where I live. God created all of that, and so much more. And God Almighty resides in me. I shake my head at times in absolute awe at the goodness of God.

Figure 10:4   Baptisms for Today's believers

#	Name of Baptism	Purpose	Who Baptizes Believer	When Occurs
6	Baptism into Body of Christ	Become a child of God; part of God's family	Holy Spirit	Automatically when born again
7	Water baptism	Symbolic of dying to self, new life, various blessings	Another believer	On request by believer. After born again
8	Baptism in/of/with the Holy Spirit	Power to be a witness	Jesus	After born again, often on request, sometimes Jesus just does it; repeatable?
9	Baptism of Fire	Zeal, desire to witness Refining	Jesus	Separate or in conjunction with Baptism of Holy Spirit? Spontaneous or on request.

#6: Baptism into Body of Christ

The baptism of believers into the Body of Christ is, by far, the most important baptism a person can receive, and it happens automatically. God is so good. Allow me to explain to a small degree.

In addition to Holy Spirit coming in [en] us when we're born again, we also receive the amazing blessing of becoming children of God.

- ❑ *Romans 9:8 That is, it is not the children of the flesh who are **children of God**, but the children of the promise are regarded as descendants.*
- ❑ *1 John 3:1 See how great a love the Father has bestowed on us, that **we would be called children of God**; and such we are. For this reason the world does not know us, because it did not know Him.*

Other scriptures show that we're adopted sons and daughters, and heirs of God.
- ❑ *Galatians 4:5 so that He might redeem those who were under the Law, that we might receive **the adoption as sons**. 6 Because you are sons, God has sent forth the Spirit of His Son into our hearts, crying, "Abba! Father!" 7 Therefore you are no longer a slave, but **a son**; and if a son, then **an heir** through God.*

The blessings are many. As believers, we're part of one family - the Body of Christ.
- ❑ *Romans 12:5 so we, who are many, **are one body in Christ**, and individually members one of another.*

CEASED?

- *Ephesians 3:6 ... **Gentiles are** ... **fellow members of the body** ...*
- *Ephesians 5:23 ... as **Christ also is the head of the church**, He Himself **being the Savior of the body**.*
- *Colossians 1:18 He is also **head of the body, the church**...*
- *Colossians 1:24 ... my share **on behalf of His body, which is the church** ...*

An associated blessing is that Holy Spirit automatically baptizes us into this body.
- *Galatians 3:27 For all of you who were **baptized into Christ** have clothed yourselves with Christ.*
- *1 Corinthians 12:13 For **by one Spirit are we all baptized into one body**, whether we be Jews or Gentiles, whether slaves or free; and we were all **made to drink of one Spirit**.*

Holy Spirit automatically baptizes us into Christ and the Body of Christ. This baptism isn't talked about much, and some may think it isn't really a true blessing. If that's you, that's ok. But for me, it as a direct result of being born again and the single most important baptism in our lives.

Given the Baptism into the Body of Christ receives little attention, it made me wonder about some teachings as they relate to the words 'baptism' and 'baptisms'.

10:16 To begin, given we automatically belong to God's church - the Body of Christ - when we're born again, is requiring a believer to 'officially' become a member of a church or denomination a requirement of God, or man?

10:17 Given Holy Spirit baptizes new believers into the Body of Christ, is the Baptism into the Body of Christ the *'one baptism'* referred to in Ephesians 4:4?
- *Ephesians 4:4 There is one body and one Spirit, just as also you were called in one hope of your calling; 5 one Lord, one faith, **one baptism**, 6 one God and Father of all who is over all and through all and in all.*

10:18 Similarly, is the baptism in Mark 16:16 referring to the Baptism into the Body of Christ?
- *Mark 16:16 He who has **believed** and **has been baptized** shall be saved; but he who has **disbelieved shall be condemned**.*

10:19 Finally, consider Galatians 3:27 and Romans 6:3. Do they refer to when we're baptized into the Body of Christ, or when we're water baptized?
- *Romans 6:3 Or do you not know that all of us who have been **baptized into Christ Jesus** have been baptized into His death?*
- *Galatians 3:27 For all of you who were **baptized into Christ** have clothed yourselves with Christ.*

I'll let you decide. But if we're both born again and water baptized, it's a done deal one way or the other. The key is we're saved, and we can turn to the lost and hurting.

#7: Water Baptism for Believers

Few topics have a greater diversity of views than water baptism. Let me put my 2 cents into the water baptism pool.

10: 4 Baptisms Relevant Today

Is Water Baptism Symbolic Only, or Does it Come with Blessings
To begin, consider Jesus's command:
- *Matthew 28:19 Go therefore and **make disciples** of all the nations, **baptizing** them in the name of the Father and the Son and the Holy Spirit:*

10:20 Jesus tells us to be baptized as well as to go and baptize. Are there blessings through just being obedient and getting water baptized ourselves? Are there also benefits in educating and then helping other believers to be baptized, either by ourselves or by other believers? In other words, are there heavenly benefits to discipling others?

- *Luke 11:28 But He said, "On the contrary, blessed are those who hear the word of God and observe it."*

Look at the Israelites going through the Red Sea. Bill Johnson has some great teachings on this issue. Many believe this event is a foreshadowing of water baptism today. The Jewish people had a choice. They could follow Moses or stay in Egypt. Pharaoh's army was in pursuit and getting close which probably made a few hearts pump faster than normal. They chose to follow Moses, and God's parting of the Red Sea allowed the people of Israel to get through to the other side. Shortly thereafter, the Egyptian army was wiped out. The people of Israel were free of that threat which brought several blessings - no doubt an immediate sense of peace being one of them.

10:21 On the basis going through the Red Sea is a foreshadowing of water baptism, is it reasonable to expect that *'some army or armies of Pharaoh'* that have been pursuing us in our life may get buried when we're water baptized?

10:22 I also wonder to what extent the blessings associated with water baptism are linked to the condition of our heart. For instance, could there be different blessings if our hearts view water baptism as a religious obligation we need to do versus having a passionate desire to obey God and to please Him?

This condition of the heart is no small issue. I wonder how many people have said a version of the sinner's prayer as a *'Get into Heaven'* insurance policy, not realizing that claims on some insurance policies are denied. The scariest words for a person who believes they're saved but aren't, are found in Matthew 7.

- *Matthew 7:23 And then I will declare to them, 'I never knew you; depart from Me, you who practice lawlessness.'*

Historically speaking, I haven't been a fan of the Message translation, but recently the Lord has opened my eyes and heart so that I treat it as a friend speaking to me to get a point across using their own words. Consider what Mr. Peterson had to say.

- *Matthew 7:21-23 "Knowing the correct password - saying 'Master, Master,' for instance - isn't going to get you anywhere with me. What is required is serious obedience - doing what my Father wills. I can see it now - at the Final Judgment thousands strutting up to me and saying, 'Master, we preached the Message,*

CEASED?

we bashed the demons, our God-sponsored projects had everyone talking.' And do you know what I am going to say? 'You missed the boat. All you did was use me to make yourselves important. You don't impress me one bit. You're out of here.' 24-25 "These words I speak to you are not incidental additions to your life, homeowner improvements to your standard of living. They are foundational words, words to build a life on. If you work these words into your life, you are like a smart carpenter who built his house on solid rock. Rain poured down, the river flooded, a tornado hit - but nothing moved that house. It was fixed to the rock. 26-27 "But if you just use my words in Bible studies and don't work them into your life, you are like a stupid carpenter who built his house on the sandy beach. When a storm rolled in and the waves came up, it collapsed like a house of cards." (MSG)

Rather sobering words.

Is Water Baptism Required for Salvation

Per Chapter 4 of **CEASED?,** I don't believe water baptism is required for salvation. Acts 2:38 is often cited as evidence that we need to be water baptized to be saved.

- ❑ Acts 2:38 Peter said to them, "**Repent, and each of you be baptized** in the name of Jesus Christ for the forgiveness of your sins; and you will receive the gift of the Holy Spirit.

I now believe Acts 2:38 does not refer to water baptism, but the Baptism in the Holy Spirit. If you're climbing up the wall at this moment, grab a coffee and another donut if you need to. A detailed review of Acts 2:38 is provided at the end of this chapter.

Who does the Water Baptism
- ❑ *Matthew 28:19 **Go** therefore and **make disciples** of all the nations, **baptizing** them in the name of the Father and the Son and the Holy Spirit,*

10:23 Does Matthew 28:19 mean any true believer can baptize, not just pastors, priests, elders, deacons and other leaders of churches? If not, why not?

10:24 If only pastors, priests, elders, deacons and other leaders are to water baptize another believer, then are these same pastors, priests, elders, deacons and other leaders the only ones who are supposed to *'go therefore and make disciples'*? And if so, what do the rest of us do - sit back and watch?

10:25 Some believers baptize babies in water and believe this guarantees their salvation even though it bypasses their free will to choose to follow Christ, or not. I can't find a teaching on baptizing babies after the cross in the Bible though I certainly acknowledge there are general references to everybody in families getting saved and baptized. But there's an assumption that babies were part of the group who were baptized. And to me, basing a key teaching on an assumption is risky. I wonder how many adults today believe they are saved because they were water baptized as

a baby? And as such, do they run the risk of Jesus telling them that He never knew them per Matthew 7:23?
- ❏ *Matthew 7:23 And then I will declare to them, 'I never knew you; depart from Me, you who practice lawlessness.'*

<u>Can/Should we be Water Baptized More than Once</u>
The Bible is silent on whether we can or should be water baptized more than once. Both Lori and I felt led in recent years to be baptized a second time. In Lori's case, she felt Holy Spirit prompting her to do so because she had recently come out of a prolonged period of willful disobedience. In my case, it was because my first water baptism occurred before I was born again.

#8: <u>Baptism of the Holy Spirit for Believers</u>

- ❏ *Matthew 3:11 "As for me, I baptize you with water for repentance, but He who is coming after me is mightier than I, and I am not fit to remove His sandals;* **<u>He will baptize you with the Holy Spirit</u>** *and* **<u>fire</u>**.

As touched upon at length already, the Baptism of the Holy Spirit results in Holy Spirit coming upon a believer - the epi experience. This baptism results in a believer being immersed in Holy Spirit to receive power to be a witness for Christ's kingdom. Many in the Old Testament, Jesus himself and many believers in the New Testament also had this upon [epi] type experience.

In Jesus's upon experience, Holy Spirit descended on Him like a dove ... and remained.
- ❏ *John 1:31 I did not recognize Him, but so that He might be manifested to Israel, I came baptizing in water." 32 John testified saying, "I have seen the* **<u>Spirit descending as a dove out of heaven</u>**, *and* **<u>He remained upon Him</u>**.

Another point worth noting about Baptisms in the Holy Spirit is that they vary. While Holy Spirit descended like a dove on sinless Jesus - the one who took the sins of the world - Pentecost was radically different when Holy Spirit came upon flawed believers in power.
- ❏ *Acts 2:2 And suddenly there came from heaven* **<u>a noise like a violent rushing wind,</u>** *and it filled the whole house where they were sitting. 3 And there appeared to them* **<u>tongues as of fire</u>** *distributing themselves, and they rested on each one of them. 4 And they were all filled with the Holy Spirit and began to* **<u>speak with other tongues</u>**, *as the Spirit was giving them utterance.*

10:26   At Pentecost, God was making a rather emphatic statement to the world that the Good News has arrived and people are to take note of God's actions, but also to take note of how God is revealing Himself through His children. Could we use more of God's presence, His evident power, in the world today? Could Holy Spirit be hovering over His children today waiting for Jesus to Baptize them in the Holy Spirit, just as Holy Spirit hovered over the waters in creation?

CEASED?

Receiving the Baptism in the Holy Spirit

Jesus baptizes believers in the Holy Spirit. Some received this baptism with hands laid on and with prayer, while others received it from Jesus with no other believers involved. Receiving this Baptism can be in the quiet of your home when alone, in the presence of another believer or with a group of believers. There are no perfect words to say in seeking this gift. The following three examples are provided merely to illustrate alternatives we can use to ask Jesus for this baptism.

Example Prayer for Another Person's Baptism in the Holy Spirit
"Lord Jesus, we come before to You today as Your children. We are so blessed and thank You for all that You have done in our lives. I now ask You Lord Jesus to Baptize (name) with the Holy Spirit. I also ask You Lord Jesus to shield (name) from any schemes of the enemy, and bring other believers alongside (name) to assist (him/her) in their walk and to help (name) use this gift in the way and ways You intend it to be used. Thank You Jesus."

Example Prayers for Our Personal Baptism in the Holy Spirit
1: "Jesus, the Baptism of the Holy Spirit is true and available today, and since You are the one that gives it, I ask You to please give me this Baptism. Shield me from any schemes of the enemy, and provide help so that I use this gift the way You want it used, and for Your glory, not mine. Thank You Jesus. Amen."

2: "Lord Jesus, thank You for all that You have done in my life. Without You, I don't know where I would be today. Your Word says that You baptize Your children in the Holy Spirit. There are no other requirements than to be Your son or daughter. I meet that requirement and I come to You now seeking the blessing of being Baptized with the Holy Spirit. I want to receive all of the blessings You have for me, including those that come with this baptism. I trust that what I receive is from You. I receive, by faith, the gift of the Baptism of the Holy Spirit and all the supernatural blessings including any and all of the 9 Holy Spirit gifts, if and when Holy Spirit chooses to give them to me. I ask that You shield me from any false gift and tactics of the enemy, that You bring people into my life that will help me grow in the proper use of these supernatural blessings. I also ask that You will reveal anything in my heart that is not right. Thank You Jesus! In Your mighty name, I pray. Amen."

#9: **Baptism with/in/of Fire**

Two of the 4 Gospels write of John the Baptist prophesying that Jesus would Baptize believers with the Holy Spirit.

- *John 1:33 I did not recognize Him, but He who sent me to baptize in water said to me, 'He upon whom you see the Spirit descending and remaining upon Him,* **this is the One who baptizes in the Holy Spirit**.'
- *Mark 1:8 I baptized you with water; but* **He will baptize you with the Holy Spirit**.

The other two Gospels write of John prophesying that Jesus would Baptize

10: 4 Baptisms Relevant Today

believers with both the Holy Spirit and Fire.
- ❑ *Matthew 3:11 "As for me, I baptize you with water for repentance, but He who is coming after me is mightier than I, and I am not fit to remove His sandals; He will **baptize you with the Holy Spirit and fire**.*
- ❑ *Luke 3:16 John answered and said to them all, "As for me, I baptize you with water; but One is coming who is mightier than I, and I am not fit to untie the thong of His sandals; He will **baptize you with the Holy Spirit and fire**.*

Many believers treat the Baptism of the Holy Spirit and Fire as one Baptism. In **CEASED?**, I separate them to address what I see as two separate issues - power and fire.

On the Day of Pentecost, tongues showed up, and so did fire.
- ❑ *Acts 2:1 When the day of Pentecost had come, they were all together in one place. 2 And suddenly there came from heaven a noise like a violent rushing wind, and it filled the whole house where they were sitting. 3 And there appeared to **them tongues as of fire [pur] distributing [diamerizo G1266] themselves**, and they rested on each one of them. 4 And they were **all filled with the Holy Spirit** and began to **speak with other tongues**, as the Spirit was giving them utterance.*

The reference to *'tongues as of fire distributing themselves'* is translated in various ways including but not limited to *'i) flames of fire coming to rest on every one of them, ii) small separate fires ... touched every person, iii) cloven tongues like as of fire ... one rested on each of them and iv) tongues like fire and it sat upon each of them.'*

The Greek word underlying *'distribution'* is *'diamerizo'* [G1266]. Diamerizo means to *'cut into pieces, to be divided into parts or to distribute'*. In other words, each of the ~120 were given their own piece of Holy Spirit Fire.

So, was this fire good or bad? The English word *'fire'* is derived from the Greek word *'pur'* [G4442] which Strong's defines as *'... fiery, fire'*. A common reaction to the word 'fire' is to think of judgment which has negative, even horrible, connotations. With that belief, many of us would tend to be cautious of receiving this baptism, or even take steps to avoid receiving it.
- ❑ *Matthew 3:12 His winnowing fork is in His hand, and He will thoroughly clear His threshing floor; and He will gather His wheat into the barn, but **He will burn up the chaff with unquenchable fire [pur]**."*
- ❑ *Luke 17:29 but on the day that Lot went out from Sodom it **rained fire [pur] and brimstone from heaven and destroyed them all**.*

That kind of begs the question - does fire associated with Acts 2 have one or more purposes other than judgment? To begin, God used fire to display His presence.
- ❑ *Exodus 3:2 The angel of the **Lord appeared to him in a blazing fire** from the midst of a bush; and he looked, and behold, the bush was burning with fire, yet the bush was not consumed.*

Fire is also used to provide comfort and protection.
- ❑ *Exodus 13:21 The Lord was going before them in a pillar of cloud by day to*

CEASED?

> lead them on the way, and in a **_pillar of fire by night to give them light_**, that they might travel by day and by night.
> ❏ *John 18:18 Now the slaves and the officers were standing there, having made a **charcoal fire**, for it was cold **and they were warming themselves**; and Peter was also with them, standing and warming himself.*

Fire is also used for refining and testing.
> ❏ *Zechariah 13:9 "And I will **_bring the third part through the fire_**, **_Refine them_** as silver is refined, And test them as gold is tested ..."*
> ❏ *Isaiah 48:10 "Behold, I **have refined you**, but not as silver; I have tested you **in the furnace of affliction**.*

10:27 Some believers are critical of believers asking for fire to come down. But do we need to consider the kind of fire being requested before criticizing those seeking it? And doesn't Jesus - who Baptizes us with the Holy Spirit and Fire - know our heart and intent?

10:28 If you're critical of requests such as *'fire come down'*, would you have advised the ~120 to avoid the Baptism of Fire Jesus gave at Pentecost?

Fiery, not Fire

I played a few sports in my younger years. I recall teammates and opponents who had a real desire to win. They had a passion, a fire in their belly, a zeal as it were.

10:29 Are we believers also called to have a zeal, a fire in our belly?
> ❏ *John 2:17 His disciples remembered that it was written, "**Zeal** for Your house will consume me."*
> ❏ *2 Corinthians 7:11 For behold what earnestness this very thing, this godly sorrow, has produced in you: what vindication of yourselves, what indignation, what fear, what longing, what **zeal**, what avenging of wrong ...*

10:30 If God desires to give disciples power as per the Baptism of the Holy Spirit, would Jesus want God's supernatural power to sit idle, or would He want us to also have a strong desire to use this power to advance His Kingdom? Would Jesus want us to have a fire in our belly to witness for Him just as He had for His Father's house?

10:31 Strong's defines the Greek word *'pur'* [G4442] in part as *'... fiery, fire'*. Is it reasonable that 'fiery' just might be an appropriate description of the word *'fire'* in Baptism of Fire?

My Baptism in the Holy Spirit and Fire

As I shared previously, I was Baptized in the Holy Spirit a few months after I was born again. When I got home late that night after this baptism, Lori looked at me and asked what the heck happened to me - or words to that effect. She could see God's presence all over me. I didn't know what she meant; I was kind of out of it. The next morning, I couldn't stop sharing Jesus even though I didn't know how to do so. Everywhere I went, I had to talk about Jesus one way or another. I had the zeal, the fire in my belly. Was this a result of the Baptism of

10: 4 Baptisms Relevant Today

Fire? I believe it was.

The other thing that happened to me was that I began to really hate a major addiction in my life - pornography. After I was born again, I disliked it. But after my Baptism in the Holy Spirit, the temperature gauge went way higher. I hated it, I learned more about spiritual warfare, and I soon got totally and permanently free of porn. I didn't learn how to cope. I got set free, and Lori and I took steps to ensure temptations were minimized so I could stay free. Was this change in attitude to the porn a result of the Baptism of the Holy Spirit, the Baptism of Fire, or both? I'm not exactly sure, but Acts 1:8 offers some insight.

<u>Witnesses vs Witnessing</u>

Jesus told His disciples in Acts 1:8 to wait in Jerusalem so they could be Baptized in the Holy Spirit, and receive power to be witnesses. The English word *'witnesses'* is derived from the Greek word *'martus'* [G344] which means in part *'those who have proved the strength and genuineness of their faith in Christ'*. Martus is a noun, not a verb, and thus the word *'witnesses'* is a noun. As a result, the power to be a witness (noun) - in my view - is more than having access to supernatural power to do signs and wonders. No question, these signs and wonders are central to the Baptism of the Holy Spirit; scripture is clear on that. But I suggest there is another dimension to this power - a dimension that helps enable us to be a witness for God. The way we live - notably our attitudes, countenance, words and behavior - should give reasons to non-believers to want the same life.

> 10:32 Doctors ... doctor. Runners ... run. Teachers ... teach. We born-again Christians are to be witnesses (noun). Doesn't that mean born-again Christians who are witnesses of and for Jesus should ... witness (verb). And if born-again Christians need Baptism of the Holy Spirit to be witnesses, how can we effectively witness without receiving the Baptism of the Holy Spirit?

<u>Timing of Baptism of the Holy Spirit and Fire</u>

Do I believe that when a person is born again, we should immediately ask Jesus to have the person Baptized in the Holy Spirit? For me, the answer is 'Yes'.

Scriptures support that argument as various new believers including Cornelius, his family and friends were Baptized in the Holy Spirit at virtually the same time as they were born again. Paul was Baptized in the Holy Spirit within 3 days of his encounter with Jesus. New believers at Ephesus were prayed over to receive the Baptism of the Holy Spirit. John and Peter made it a point to go to Samaria to ensure new believers were Baptized in the Holy Spirit. Clearly, there is scriptural evidence for the Baptism of the Holy Spirit right after we're born again. But there's another important reason - Jesus. Jesus is the One who baptizes believers in the Holy Spirit, and I believe Jesus will give this baptism to a believer whenever He wants, and His *'whenever'* is way better than my whenever. If Jesus wants to delay giving this gift, or not give this gift at all, that's His choice. Jesus knows best, and I trust Jesus. Having said that, I believe it's worth asking Jesus, and then trusting by faith we have received it.

CEASED?

Where the responsibility of other believers comes into play is to help the new recipient understand what is going on, and how to use the power and blessings that come with this baptism. When a person starts to use one of the 9 Holy Spirit gifts, coming alongside them is hugely valuable - provided of course we know what we're doing. We especially need to help believers remember the importance of using the power in a way that benefits and doesn't hurt God's kingdom, and to use it for God's glory and not ours. If signs and wonders become our identity, changes are needed.

If the Baptism of Holy Spirit and/or Fire involves refining, and God wants to refine us, then isn't it best to get refined, even if it's difficult? And if the Baptism of Fire is about receiving a deep zeal to share the gospel, then shouldn't we want that as well?

ACTS 2:38 – WHICH BAPTISM?

Acts 2:38 is often used as evidence that we need to be water baptized to be saved.

- ❑ *Acts 2:38 Peter said to them, "**Repent, and each of you be baptized** in the name of Jesus Christ for the forgiveness of your sins; and you will **receive the gift of the Holy Spirit**.*

To begin, keep in mind there are 3 baptisms to which Peter could be referring:
   i.   Water baptism, done by disciples;
   ii. Baptism in the Holy Spirit (or Baptism in the Holy Spirit and Fire), done by Jesus; or
   iii. Baptism into the Body of Christ, done automatically by Holy Spirit when born again.

There are 5 key reasons why I believe the baptism in Acts 2:38 is about Baptism in the Holy Spirit (or Baptism in the Holy Spirit and Fire if you think they are one).

Reason 1: Peter tells the crowd to repent, but does not share what's involved in salvation before telling them to repent and be baptized. He does not say anything about believing, converting, confessing with one's mouth etc. He may well have done so later in the day and before the 3,000 came to the Lord, but Peter didn't do so by the time he said *'be baptized'*. Peter also made no mention of water baptism being required in Acts 3:19.

- ❑ *Acts 3:17 And now, brethren, I know that you acted in ignorance, just as your rulers did also. 18 But the things which God announced beforehand by the mouth of all the prophets, that His Christ would suffer, He has thus fulfilled. 19 **Therefore repent and return, so that your sins may be wiped away**, in order that times of refreshing may come from the presence of the Lord; 20 and that He may send Jesus, the Christ appointed for you,*

Reason 2: Acts 2:38 says we're to repent and be baptized in the name of Jesus ... I found six verses that spoke of being *'baptized in the name of'*. Four of them derive the English word 'in' from the Greek preposition *'eis'* [G1519] which means *'into, unto, to, towards, for, among'*.

10: 4 Baptisms Relevant Today

- *Matthew 28:19 Go therefore and make disciples of all the nations, baptizing them **in [eis] the name** of the Father and the Son and the Holy Spirit,*
- *Acts 19:5 When they heard this, they were baptized **in [eis] the name** of the Lord Jesus.*
- *1 Corinthians 1:13 Has Christ been divided? Paul was not crucified for you, was he? Or were you baptized **in [eis] the name** of Paul?*
- *Acts 8:16 For He had not yet fallen upon any of them; they had simply been baptized **in [eis] the name** of the Lord Jesus.*

One verse derives the word in from the Greek preposition 'en' [G1722], the same word used when one is born again and Holy Spirit comes in [en] us.

- *Acts 10:48 And he ordered them to be baptized **in [en] the name** of Jesus Christ. Then they asked him to stay on for a few days.*

The 6th verse - Acts 2:38 - uses the Greek word for upon 'epi' [G1909]. Does this indicate Peter was saying something like *"Repent and you need to receive this epi Baptism, the baptism where Holy Spirit comes upon [epi] you"*? After all, Peter had just experienced the upon [epi] baptism personally and seen ~120 others receive the gift they had been waiting expectantly for 10 days after Jesus ascended - 10 long, exciting days. I suspect Peter was still reeling from the impact of His Baptism, and wanted others to be touched in the same, amazing way he and ~120 others had been touched.

- *Acts 2:38 Peter said to them, "Repent, and each of you be baptized **in [epi] the name** of Jesus Christ for the forgiveness of your sins …*

Reason 3: Both Acts 2:38 and Acts 10:45 refer to the Gift of the Holy Spirit which Peter clearly stated in Acts 10 referred to Baptism of the Holy Spirit, not water baptism nor being Baptized into the Body of Christ when we're born again.

- *Acts 2:38 Peter said to them, **"Repent, and each of you be baptized** … you will **receive the gift of the Holy Spirit**.*
- *Acts 10:45 All the circumcised believers who came with Peter were amazed, because the **gift of the Holy Spirit had been poured out on the Gentiles** also.*

Reason 4: The 4th reason involves putting Acts 2:38 into context. As water baptism is a major salvation issue, please be patient with me as I address this 4th reason in some detail.

3 1/2 years prior to Peter speaking the words in Acts 2:38 at Pentecost, Peter left fishing to follow Jesus. He heard Jesus teach in ways not heard before. He saw Jesus stand up to the religious people of the day. Peter saw Jesus do amazing miracles. Jesus empowered the 70 to go and do miracles. Peter called Jesus Lord. Peter briefly walked on water to get to

CEASED?

Jesus. 53 days before Pentecost, Peter could not stay awake to pray with Jesus. He ran from the scene when Jesus was arrested. Peter denied Jesus 3 times. He wept when the rooster crowed. Peter didn't help take Jesus down from the cross, but left Jesus hanging on it. Peter didn't help with the burial, and didn't go with the women to help deal with Jesus's body early on resurrection Sunday morning.

However, after the women reported the empty tomb on resurrection Sunday morning, Peter ran to see for himself that the tomb was empty. Later that day on resurrection Sunday evening, Peter saw the resurrected Christ. Jesus proved who He was, and then told the disciples to receive Holy Spirit when he breathed on Peter and the others. Peter was now born again and gained, amongst other things, spiritual understanding. The group returned to Jerusalem on an emotional high.

- *Luke 24:52 And they, after worshiping Him, returned to Jerusalem with great joy, 53 and were continually in the temple praising God.*

Over the following 40 days, Jesus showed Peter forgiveness and love. He healed Peter's heart and ensured Peter knew all was good between them. Jesus taught Peter and the other disciples about the kingdom of God. Peter knew his mandate, which like the other disciples, was focused on sharing the Good News in words and power.

- *John 21:15 … Jesus said to Simon Peter, "Simon, son of John, do you love Me more than these?" … 16 He said to him again a second time, "Simon, son of John, do you love Me?" … 17 He said to him the third time, "Simon, son of John, do you love Me?" …*
- *Matthew 28:19 Go therefore and make disciples of all the nations, baptizing them in the name of the Father and the Son and the Holy Spirit,*

Before Jesus's ascension, Jesus tells the disciples they aren't yet ready to share the Good News, that they needed to wait for the Baptism in the Holy Spirit to receive power to be more effective witnesses for Christ. Those 10 days waiting must have been emotionally charged as Peter and the other disciples waited in anticipation. Pentecost finally comes around and Holy Spirit comes upon the ~120 including Peter.

- *Acts 2:1 When the day of Pentecost had come, they were all together in one place. 2 And suddenly there **came from heaven a noise** like a violent rushing wind, and it **filled the whole house** where they were sitting. 3 And there appeared to **them tongues as of fire distributing themselves**, and they rested on each one of them. 4 And they were **all filled with the Holy Spirit** and **began to speak with other tongues**, as the Spirit was giving them utterance.*

Holy Spirit shows up with a bang - a noise from heaven filling the whole house, tongues of fire, and believers speaking in tongues.

Approximately 120 people were Baptized in the Holy Spirit, Peter included, in a radical way. Observers see and hear the events unfold. Some wonder while others mock. Peter, the emotional and excitable fisherman, responds with a passionate speech starting with an explanation that these events resulted from an outpouring of Holy Spirit in fulfillment of an ancient prophecy.

- ❏ *Acts 2:15 For these men are not drunk, as you suppose, for it is only the third hour of the day; 16 but **this is what was spoken of through the prophet Joel**:*
- ❏ *Acts 2:17 'And it shall be in the last days,' God says, 'That I **will pour forth of My Spirit on all mankind**; And your **sons and your daughters shall prophesy**, And your **young men shall see visions**, And your **old men shall dream dreams**; 18 **Even on My bondslaves, both men and women, I will in those days pour forth of My Spirit And they shall prophesy**.*

Peter goes on to explain the reality to the observers - that they had been responsible for the crucifixion of the Messiah. The crowd was crushed, and asked what to do?

- ❏ *Acts 2:37 Now when they heard this, they were pierced to the heart, and said to Peter and the rest of the apostles, **"Brethren, what shall we do?"***

10:33   Do you think this question - *"Brethren, what shall we do?"* was asked in:
   i. a bland, emotionless tone as seen while ordering for the 2,345th time, a large coffee misto, medium blend, skinny, 3 pumps of white chocolate, 3 pumps of pumpkin spice, 145 degrees, to go; or
   ii. a highly-charged tone filled with confusion, regret, distress and fear?

Peter responds:
- ❏ *Acts 2:38 Peter said to them, **"Repent, and each of you be baptized** ...*

10:34   On the basis the question *'What shall we do?"* was asked in a mindset 'filled with confusion, regret, distress and fear' - did Peter respond with:
   i. a controlled monotonic, low-key *'Repent and each one of you be baptized'* tone like a well-rested mom would speak to her 6-month old baby; or
   ii. a hyper, excited **'REPENT AND EACH ONE OF YOU BE BAPTIZED!!!'** tone?

To come at this from another angle, consider which baptism makes the most sense after considering Peter's time with Jesus during His earthly ministry, Peter's denial of Jesus, Jesus's death, the empty tomb, the events of resurrection Sunday evening, Peter's time with Jesus over the 40 days following His resurrection, Jesus's ascension, 10 days of waiting after Jesus's ascension until Pentecost, and the events at Pentecost which happened minutes before.

CEASED?

10:35 Given all the above, which baptism would excitable Peter likely refer to:
   i. **Water baptism** which is never reported as having a major impact on anybody when first baptized. There is also no mention of Peter, the other apostles and the rest of the ~120 at Pentecost even being water baptized;
   ii. **Baptism by Holy Spirit into the Body of Christ** which happens automatically when a person is born again and happened to Peter 50 days previously. No significant and visible impact was reported; or
   iii. **Baptism in the Holy Spirit and Fire** which just occurred in an amazing way featuring some of God's amazing power including an outpouring of God's Spirit on the ~120 including Peter himself?

Reason 5: Consider the 4 parts of Acts 2:38.
- ❏ *Acts 2:38 Peter said to them, "**Repent**, and each of you **be baptized** in the name of Jesus Christ for the **forgiveness of your sins**; and you will receive the **gift of the Holy Spirit**.*
   i. repent;
   ii. be baptized;
   iii. forgiveness of your sins; and
   iv. receive the gift of the Holy Spirit.

There are 2 actions *(repent; be baptized)* and 2 results *(forgiveness; receive the gift of Holy Spirit)*. As mentioned above, I believe the baptism in Acts 2:38 refers to Baptism in the Holy Spirit. On the basis I am right (which happens occasionally), and if I was involved in translating Acts 2:38, I might suggest something along the lines of:
- ❏ *Acts 2:38 Peter said to them, "First, repent in order to be forgiven of your sins. Secondly, get Baptized in the Holy Spirit in order to receive the gift of the Holy Spirit so you can be filled with the Holy Spirit and receive power that enabled us to speak in unknown languages like you have just seen, and much more."* (DD)

In this way, Peter would be telling people to repent - to change their way of thinking and turn to God - so they can be forgiven of their sins. And once saved, they are then able to receive the gift of the Holy Spirit by getting Baptized in the Holy Spirit. As a result, for the above reasons, I don't believe Acts 2:38 refers to water baptism.

What about the Baptism into the Body of Christ

I don't believe Peter was referring to the baptism into the Body of Christ in Acts 2:38 due to 4 considerations.
1. The Bible isn't clear if Jesus talked about this baptism before Pentecost.
2. This baptism is not done in the Name of Jesus.
3. This baptism does not refer to the gift of the Holy Spirit (reasons #3 and #5 above).
4. Up to that point in time, this baptism is not identified in the Bible as having

10: 4 Baptisms Relevant Today

an immediate and major impact on individuals, whereas individuals were significantly and immediately impacted after being Baptized in the Holy Spirit (reason #4 above).

<u>One Catch</u>

The one scripture that makes me wonder a bit about whether Peter was referring to water baptism or Baptism in the Holy Spirit in Acts 2:38, is Acts 2:41.

❑   *Acts 2:41 So then, those who had received his word were baptized; and that day there were added about three thousand souls.*

10:36   If Acts 2:41 does refer to water baptism, that makes sense as it's similar to other situations. However, even if Acts 2:41 does refer to water baptism, does that mean Acts 2:38 must also refer to water baptism? I don't think so, but it is a chin scratcher.

CLOSING POINTS TO PONDER

Chapter 10 covered 9 baptisms that are unique in one way or another. You may agree there are 4 baptisms relevant today. You may believe we can also be baptized in the Cup of Suffering which makes it five. You may believe Baptism of the Holy Spirit and Baptism of Fire is one baptism, not two. You may believe there are other baptisms. My objective was not to cover all baptism-related issues, but to try to help clear up some of the confusion surrounding the word 'baptism'. I hope I accomplished that goal.

The most important baptism for any individual is, by far, is when Holy Spirit automatically baptizes us into the Body of Christ as a result of being born again. We can then choose to be water baptized, or not. We can choose to ask Jesus to Baptize us in the Holy Spirit, or not. Jesus has the final say, however, and He may not Baptize us in the Holy Spirit when we ask. He may Baptize us in the Holy Spirit when we don't ask, or don't even know about it. It's His choice. My desire, however, is that many more believers will seek and receive this wonderful gift.

11

Tying Chapters 3 to 10 Together

INTRODUCTION

CHAPTERS 3 through 10 touch on issues of spirit, soul and body (Chapter 3), salvation (Chapter 4), the 'para', 'meta', 'en' and 'epi' experiences with Holy Spirit (Chapters 5-9), and the 9 baptisms (Chapter 10). Chapter 11 ties the various components together using two different frameworks.

1. Framework 1 (Figures 11:1 through 11:10) deals with the interaction of our spirit, soul and body with Father God, Jesus and Holy Spirit (page 187).
2. Framework 2 (Figure 11:12) addresses the path of unbelievers on the road to hell as well as 3 paths of believers on their journey to heaven (page 193).

In addition, Figure 11:11 provides a brief summary of what happens to our spirit, soul and body when various experiences with God occur (page 192).

GOD AND OUR SPIRITS, SOULS AND BODIES

First up is the framework on spirit, soul and body. Figures 11:1 through 11:10 collectively, but very briefly, touch on issues related to how the human spirit, soul and body were designed to interact with God at creation, and then what this relationship looks like in a variety of situations after the fall of Adam and Eve. Situations include Jesus's ministry before the cross and at the cross, after our salvation, our walk as a Christian before and after being Baptized in the Holy Spirit, and ultimately, what happens after our earthly death and our heavenly life begins. Three Figures, 11:4, 11:5 and 11:6, relate to Jesus during His earthly life.

Figures 11:1 through 11:10 are not intended to be perfect representations of what happens. Some Figures help illustrate the relationships, or lack thereof, at various points in time between God and a human being's spirit, soul and body. Other Figures are intended to help illustrate, to some extent, what happened to Jesus before, during and after His earthly ministry.

11: Tying Chapters 3-10 Together

FRAMEWORK #1:
OUR SPIRIT, SOUL AND BODY

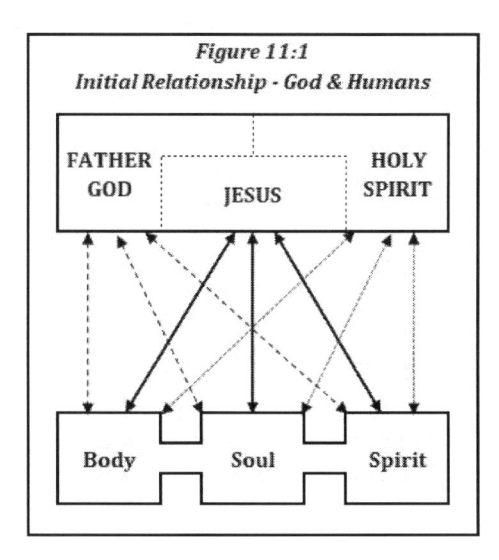

1: God and Humans - Both 3 in 1

Figure 11:1
Initial Relationship - God & Humans

God is 3 persons - Father God, Jesus and Holy Spirit. Humans are 3 parts - spirit, soul and body. God's design enables humans and God to communicate in many ways. We can talk with The Father, Jesus and Holy Spirit. They hear us. God knows our thoughts, and can communicate with or touch our spirit, soul or body in any way He chooses. However, scriptures reveal a unique link between our spirit and Holy Spirit. And as opposed to our 'physical person', it is through our spirit person that we gain spiritual understanding.

❑ *1 Corinthians 2:12 Now we have received, not the spirit of the world, but the Spirit who is from God, so that we may know the things freely given to us by God, 13 which things we also speak, not in words taught by human wisdom, but in those taught by the Spirit, combining spiritual thoughts with spiritual words. 14 But a natural man does not accept the things of the Spirit of God, for they are foolishness to him; and he cannot understand them, because they are spiritually appraised.*

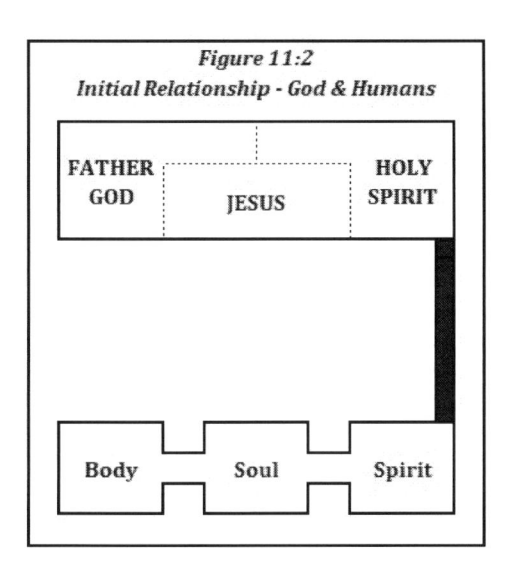

Figure 11:2
Initial Relationship - God & Humans

2: Communicating Spirit to SPIRIT

A simplistic version of God's design of our relationship with Him is in Figure 11:2. Figures 11:2 and beyond illustrate how we humans connect through our spirit with God through Holy Spirit.

❑ *Matthew 10:20 For it is not you who speak, but it is the Spirit of your Father who speaks in you.*

CEASED?

Figure 11:3
Fallen State of Human Beings

FATHER GOD — JESUS — HOLY SPIRIT

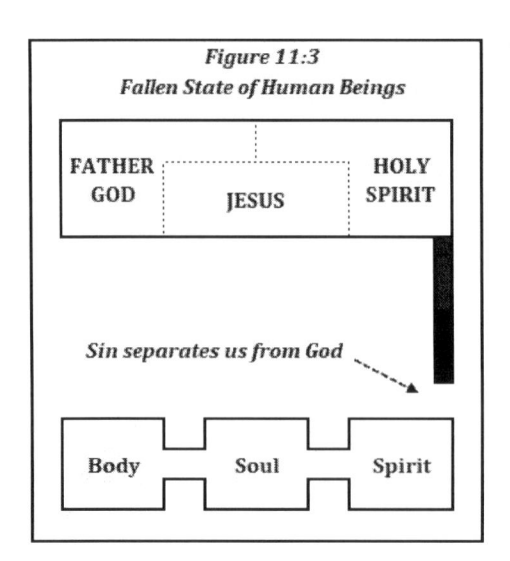

Sin separates us from God

Body | Soul | Spirit

3: The Fall

Adam and Eve had an intimate relationship with God. When they ate of the tree, they disobeyed God; they sinned. Their sins separated them from God. Their bodies and souls remained alive, but their spiritual relationship died. God still loved them, but the close intimacy was gone - because of sin.

❑ *Romans 6:23 For the wages of sin is death, but the free gift of God is eternal life in Christ Jesus our Lord.*

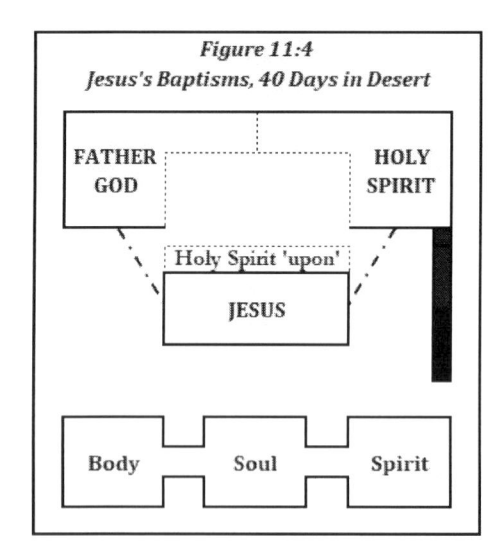

Figure 11:4
Jesus's Baptisms, 40 Days in Desert

FATHER GOD — HOLY SPIRIT

Holy Spirit 'upon'

JESUS

Body | Soul | Spirit

4: Two of Jesus's Baptisms

As Jesus didn't sin, the relationship per Figure 11:4 is shown for Jesus during his earthly ministry. To begin His ministry at age 30, Jesus went to John the Baptist who baptized Him in water. As Jesus came out of the water, Father God baptized Jesus in the Holy Spirit. Holy Spirit came upon [epi] Jesus. Jesus spent 40 days in the desert, then began His ministry.

❑ *Luke 3:22 and the Holy Spirit descended upon Him in bodily form like a dove, and a voice came out of heaven, "You are My beloved Son, in You I am well-pleased."*

11: Tying Chapters 3-10 Together

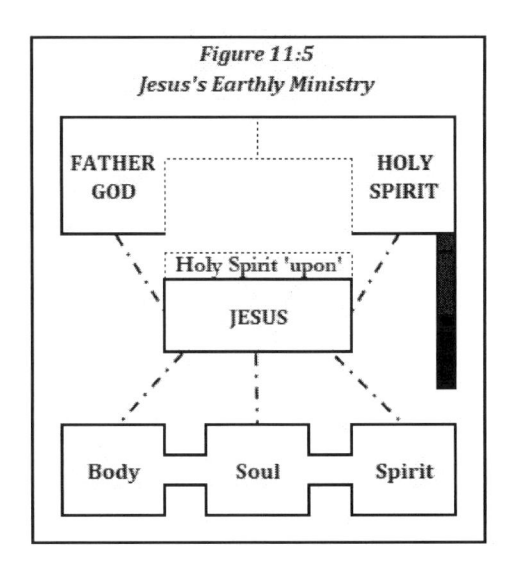

5: Jesus's Earthly Ministry

For the next 3/12 years, Jesus fulfilled His earthly ministry. Empowered by Holy Spirit who remained upon [epi] Him, Jesus did what He saw the Father do, and said what He heard the Father say. He impacted mankind in all three parts of their beings – bodies, souls and spirits.

Figure 11:5 – Jesus's Earthly Ministry

❑ *Luke 4:14 And Jesus returned to Galilee in the power of the Spirit, and news about Him spread through all the surrounding district.*

❑ *John 5:19 Therefore Jesus answered and was saying to them, "Truly, truly, I say to you, the Son can do nothing of Himself, unless it is something He sees the Father doing; for whatever the Father does, these things the Son also does in like manner.*

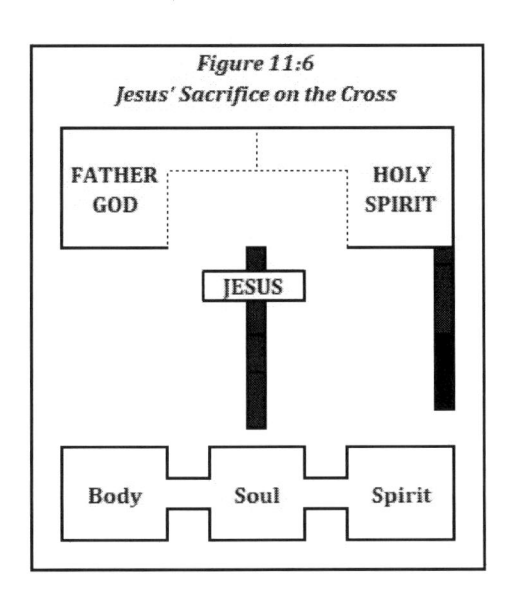

6: Jesus's Crucifixion; 3rd Baptism

Jesus died after He took on all the sins of the world, and the consequences of those sins. He was baptized in His Cup of Suffering. Our sins caused Jesus to be separated from God; Jesus was forsaken because of you and me.

Figure 11:6 – Jesus' Sacrifice on the Cross

❑ *Mark 15:34 At the ninth hour Jesus cried out with a loud voice, "Eloi, Eloi, lama sabachthani?" which is translated, "My God, My God, why have You forsaken Me?"*

CEASED?

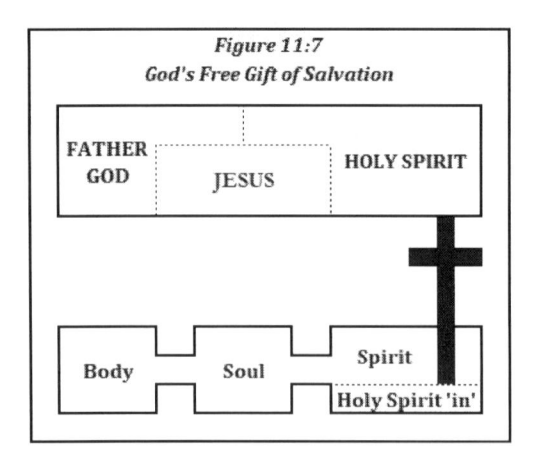

7: Free Gift of Salvation

After Jesus's death, burial and resurrection, God provided a way for people to be redeemed, for our spirit to again have an intimate relationship with God just as Adam and Eve had in the garden. Each person decides whether to accept, or reject, this gift from God.

❏ *Ephesians 1:7 In Him we have redemption through His blood, the forgiveness of our trespasses, according to the riches of His grace*

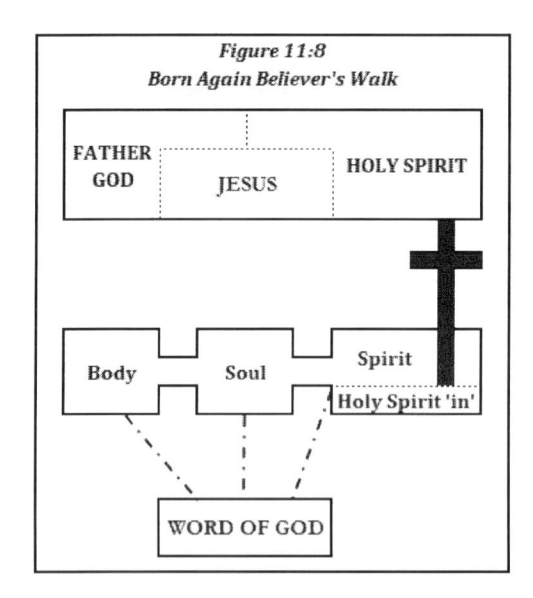

Figure 11:7 God's Free Gift of Salvation

8: Born-Again Believer's Walk

When we're born again, we receive many divine blessings - a Divine Exchange was made. The best and biggest blessings are eternal life and having Holy Spirit come in [en] us. We now have direct access to Holy Spirit, Jesus and Father God. We also gain spiritual understanding. God's Word becomes alive to us, and becomes central to our lives.

❏ *Ephesians 2:18 for through Him we both have our access in one Spirit to the Father.*

Figure 11:8 Born Again Believer's Walk

❏ *Hebrews 4:12 For the word of God is living and active and sharper than any two-edged sword, and piercing as far as the division of soul and spirit, of both joints and marrow, and able to judge the thoughts and intentions of the heart.*

11: Tying Chapters 3-10 Together

9: Born-Again Believer after Baptism with the Holy Spirit

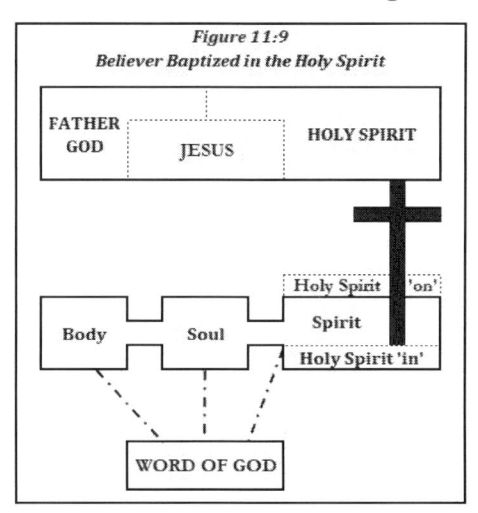

Figure 11:9 Believer Baptized in the Holy Spirit

When born again, Holy Spirit automatically baptizes us into the Body of Christ. We can be water baptized, or not. We can ask Jesus to baptize us with the Holy Spirit, or not. If we are Baptized in the Holy Spirit, Holy Spirit comes on/upon [epi] us. We can ask Jesus to baptize us with Fire, or not. It's all up to Jesus.

❑ *John 1:33 I did not recognize Him, but He who sent me to baptize in water said to me, 'He upon whom you see the Spirit descending and remaining upon Him, this is the One who baptizes in the Holy Spirit.'*

❑ *Acts 10:44 While Peter was still speaking these words, the Holy Spirit fell upon all those who were listening to the message. 45 All the circumcised believers who came with Peter were amazed, because the gift of the Holy Spirit had been poured out on the Gentiles also.*

10: When Believers Die

Figure 11:10 Believers' Earthly Death & Heavenly Life

When believers die, our earthly bodies go back to 'dust' until our resurrection. Our spirit and soul go on to heaven where we are surrounded by, and immersed in, God's presence. We will receive a transformed body.

❑ *John 14:2 In My Father's house are many dwelling places; if it were not so, I would have told you; for I go to prepare a place for you.*

❑ *Philippians 3:21 who will transform the body of our humble state into conformity with the body of His glory, by the exertion of the power that He has even to subject all things to Himself.*

11: God and Our Spirit, Soul, Body

I've heard the flesh described as the combination of body and soul (mind, will and emotions), while our heart is the combination of soul and spirit. Before we're born again, our flesh/soul rules. After we're born again, there is a battle in our heart between our spirit which is aligned with God, and our soul which still often likes the fleshly and worldly desires. Figure 11:11 is a **very simplistic summary** of what happens to our spirit, soul and body when various experiences with God occur.

Figure 11:11 Impacts on Body, Soul and Spirit from Different Encounters

Time / Event	Spirit	Soul	Body
Before Born Again	Dead / separated from God	Led by fleshly desires, some good, many aren't. Vulnerable to demonic	Aligned with worldly activities, some of which can be good, many are not
After Born Again; Holy Spirit in [en]	Redeemed, made right with God; Sealed with Holy Spirit	Changes may be dramatic or minimal at first; should see major changes over time re holiness and fruits of the Spirit	Changes may or may not be evident; usually nothing dramatic
Baptized in the Holy Spirit; Holy Spirit upon [epi]	Enhanced closeness to God; Access to power to witness for God; Increased desire for holiness		Countenance can change in a major way for a time
Baptism of Fire	Zeal to share Jesus and/or a refining		Unsure
Water Baptized	Different views	Different views	Usually little
Walking out the Christian Life	Who rules: a) Holy Spirit leading our spirit, soul & body; or b) flesh (desires of body & soul)	Changes over time through the sanctification process; Working out the salvation of our soul	May be dramatic healings; All of us deteriorate over time with aging
Death	Heaven, if born again; Hell, if not saved	Heaven, if born again; Hell, if not saved	To 'dust' until the resurrection; Unsure if have a body in hell

11: Tying Chapters 3-10 Together

FRAMEWORK #2:
TYING CHAPTERS 3 TO 10 TOGETHER

Figure 11:12 which is found a couple of pages further on, builds on Figures 11:1 through 11:10 to illustrate:
- ❖ the 4 baptisms in Chapter 10 impacting believers; and
- ❖ the parallels between the journeys of believers today and the people of Israel when they followed Moses out of Egypt - plus - how all 9 baptisms in Chapter 10 align with both journeys.

The idea for this second framework has its roots from Bill Johnson's teaching in his book *'Face to Face with God'*. I remember looking at my friend when he gave me Bill's book and wondering why on earth would he give me a book from an off the wall guy like Bill. I shelved it. A few months later, I decided to peruse the book. I soon found myself thinking *"Hey, wait a minute; this guy has some really good things to say. What are people talking about?"* My eyes had been so tainted by what I had heard about Bill and Bethel, I almost missed what turned out to be a life-impacting book and season. Don't get me wrong, I don't believe everything Bill and Bethel teach. Nor do I believe everything anybody teaches. Lori and I disagree on a few things. But we are open to examining any teacher of depth, take what we believe is right, and leave the rest behind. So, if you think Bill and Bethel are heretics, and you haven't personally taken a comprehensive look, but base your belief on what others say or on a select few seconds or minutes of videos or teachings, you might want to reconsider your approach before rendering judgment, and certainly before speaking out. Lori and I went to Bethel in the summer of 2018. We had never experienced more love and more passion for Christ or His Word. We were blown away.

While some are totally against Bill and Bethel, others will say teachers such as John MacArthur are off the rails. If this is you, I encourage you to listen to John's interview with Ben Shapiro. Neither Bill, John or anyone else have it all figured out. The reality is the Body of Christ needs the Bill Johnsons, the John MacArthurs, the Robert Morris's, the Justin Peters, the Tony Evans, the Kay Arthurs and the Beth Moores. All are friends of God, and we might be wise to recall what Miriam endured by speaking against Moses.

Lori and I have learned many lessons in our day. Some lessons seemed to take too many tries and too much time to understand. Hopefully, we'll get them easier and quicker as we season. I now realize we have to be so careful how we think and speak about our brothers and sisters. Unless we know for sure, and God is calling us to speak out, we could easily find ourselves speaking partial or even total, divisive untruths. We need to watch our tongues. No wonder God's Word has so many scriptures about the tongue.

- ❑ *Romans 14:4 Who are you to judge the servant of another? To his own master he stands or falls; and he will stand, for the Lord is able to make him stand.*
- ❑ *Ephesians 4:29 Let no unwholesome word proceed from your mouth, but only such a word as is good for edification according to the need of the moment, so that it will give grace to those who hear.*
- ❑ *James 4:11 Do not speak against one another, brethren. He who speaks against*

CEASED?

> *a brother or judges his brother, speaks against the law and judges the law; but if you judge the law, you are not a doer of the law but a judge of it.*
> ❏ *Proverbs 17:27 He who restrains his words has knowledge, And he who has a cool spirit is a man of understanding. 28 Even a fool, when he keeps silent, is considered wise; When he closes his lips, he is considered prudent.*

With that said, in Chapter 4 of his book *"Face to Face with God"*, Bill Johnson talks about how our Christian walk today was foreshadowed in the Old Testament by the people of Israel and their exodus from Egypt through to the Promised Land. The night after I had completed the first draft of the 9 baptisms, I felt it was incomplete. Soon after, God gave me a revelation on the framework seen in Figure 11:12. I'm a computer guy who prefers drawing using Excel; I seldom draw by hand. But that night ... for some reason ... I felt like drawing by hand. So I did. A short time later with an eraser reduced to pieces, I had the framework. However, I also felt something was missing. Then I listened to various YouTube teachings by Derek Prince and felt I needed to beef up the information on spirit, soul and body. This led to Figures 11:1 through 11:10, and 21:1. God's goodness is beyond measure and His timing of things, large and small, is impeccable.

Figure 11:12

When reviewing Figure 11:12, there are 3 sections - A, B and C. Each will be discussed in turn. The 9 baptisms discussed in Chapter 10 are identified ① by a heptagon with the baptism number recorded within. The legend for the 9 baptisms is found on the bottom left-hand side of Figure 11:12.

Top Section A of Figure 11:12 Old Testament Exodus from Egypt

The top section shows the seasons faced by the people of Israel as they moved from being in bondage in Egypt to the Promised Land. On the far right is eternity, which in the Old Testament, was considered to be part of God's blessings and wrath. In the New Testament, specific reference is made to heaven and hell. The first baptism, the Baptism of Moses, pertains to two seasons beginning with the Passover and ending up in the desert next to the Jordan River.

Middle Section B of Figure 11:12: Ministry of Jesus

John the Baptist's ministry paved the way for Jesus. His Baptism of Repentance, baptism #2 is on the far left. When Jesus entered the scene, He received two baptisms - #3 His Baptism in Water and #4 His Baptism in the Holy Spirit. As Jesus carried out His ministry, His disciples also led people through the same Baptism of Repentance that John was doing. On the cross, Jesus endured the 5th baptism, His Baptism of Suffering.

Bottom Section C of Figure 11:12: For Believers and Non-Believers Today

The bottom section relates to believers and non-believers today, and their walk starting as sinners and ending up spending eternity in either heaven - or hell.

11: Tying Chapters 3-10 Together

Figure 11:12   9 Baptisms in Bible and How 4 Baptisms Fit In Today

A: Old Testament Exodus from Egypt

Bondage in Egypt	Follow Moses through Passover & to Red Sea	Follow Moses through Red Sea into Desert	Follow Joshua through Jordan River into Promised Land	Eternal Blessings or Wrath

(1)   (1)

B: Ministry of Jesus

John the Baptist	Jesus's ministry starts	Jesus and His disciples	JESUS	40 days with disciples; Ascension	Seated in Heavenlies; Our Lord, Savior, Master, Friend, Mediator, Shepherd, Head of Church, High Priest, Prince of Peace

(2) (3) (4)   (2)   (5)

C: For Believers and Non-Believers Today

In Bondage to Sin	Life on Earth without Jesus			Hell
Living in Kingdom of Darkness	*Holy Spirit with [para]*			
We choose our path	JESUS	Accept Jesus as Lord and Savior (6)	Core of Christian Walk — Life on Earth with Jesus — To know and worship God — Led by Holy Spirit — Fruit of Holy Spirit	"Living by Red Sea"
Holy Spirit with (para)			*Holy Spirit in [en] & with [meta]*	
		Water Baptism (7)	Additional blessings from God	"Living in Desert"	Heaven
		Baptisms of Holy Spirit & Fire (8)(9)	Refining, zeal, power, spiritual gifts — Going, being witnesses — *Holy Spirit upon [epi]*	"Living in Promised Land"

Legend of Baptisms:
1: Moses
2: Repentance
3: Jesus in Water
4: Holy Spirit upon Jesus
5: Jesus Cup of Suffering
6: Body of Christ [in/en]
7: Water
8: Holy Spirit [upon/epi]
9: Fire

Starting at the top left corner of Section C, all of us are sinners and living in the kingdom of darkness. If we don't change our ways and begin a personal relationship with Christ, we will live without Jesus here on earth, and forever afterward. That's not an opinion; that's what the Bible teaches. And since the Bible is the inerrant Word of God, it is the Truth. The harsh reality is people who don't accept Christ here on earth will one day face the reality they are going to hell - forever. Before accepting Jesus, Holy Spirit draws people to Christ by being with them - the 'para' experience.

CEASED?

When Born Again

For those who choose to follow Jesus, we leave the kingdom of darkness thanks to what Jesus did on the cross. Numerous blessings occur including baptism #6, which is Holy Spirit Baptizing us into the Body of Christ. We begin a new life with no barrier between us and God. We're saved, our spirit is born again and we have received the gift of eternal, heavenly life with God.

If we look at the journey the people of Israel had in comparison to our walk, we see the foreshadowing that Bill Johnson talks about. When the people of Israel followed Moses to the Red Sea, they didn't know what was going to happen. Similarly, when we're first born again, many/most of us don't have a clue as to what our life with Jesus is going to be about. I sure didn't.

Red Sea and Water Baptism

After reaching the Red Sea, the people of Israel chose to go through the Red Sea. They certainly had a strong incentive to do so as Pharaoh's army was closing in on them. Nonetheless, they made a choice. They were able to get through the Red Sea and Pharaoh's army did not. Blessings flowed.

The parallel to going through the Red Sea, a body of still water, is when believers choose to get water baptized, which also typically occurs today in a body of still water.

When a believer is water baptized - baptism #7 - there may well be blessings associated with i) being obedient in getting baptized and ii) from the baptism itself. Like the drowning of Pharaoh's Army, one or more 'things' attacking or tormenting us could be 'drowned'. Spiritual blessings flow.

We can also choose not to get water baptized and forego potential blessings. However, whether we get water baptized or not, I believe we're still saved as discussed in Chapter 4.

In the Desert

Once through the Red Sea, the people of Israel followed Moses through the desert for 40 years. The people of Israel had many blessings from God including, but not limited to, manna, clothing, a cloud by day and a pillar of fire by night. They received many provisions for sure.

Even though they were cared for, their walk to the Promised Land ended up short of their destination. The distance from the Red Sea to the Jordan River was only a few days walk using the shortest route available, but yet the people of Israel wandered 40 years. Obedience and gratitude were not their strong points.

Moses was a man of humility. A dedicated leader. Yet, disobedience resulted in Moses not being allowed to lead the people through the Jordan into the Promised Land.

If believers get water baptized, the parallel is that we are out of the Red Sea and into the desert. Like the people of Israel, we have access to many of God's blessings. But the question remains: are we still in a desert of some kind? Is our Christian life dry in comparison to what God intended it to be?

11: Tying Chapters 3-10 Together

The Promised Land

When Joshua led the people of Israel into the Promised Land, incredible things continued to happen. They conquered the land with amazing victories. I love the battle of Jericho.

The water in the Red Sea is still. By contrast, the Jordan River is a river that flows. Holy Spirit is often referred to as living water, and like the Jordan River, His living water is to flow from Him, to upon us, and from us to others.

- *Isaiah 44:3 'For I will pour out water on the thirsty land And streams on the dry ground; I will pour out My Spirit on your offspring And My blessing on your descendants;*
- *John 7:37 Now on the last day, the great day of the feast, Jesus stood and cried out, saying, "If anyone is thirsty, let him come to Me and drink. 38 He who believes in Me, as the Scripture said, 'From **his innermost being will flow rivers of living water**.'"*

When born again, Holy Spirit comes in [en] us. We have the living water to guide, comfort, teach, etc. However, we're called to share the Good News, to heal the sick, to cleanse the lepers, to cast out demons. Such supernatural events in our lives will be a sign that shows we are believers.

- *Mark 16:17 These signs will accompany those who have believed: in My name they will **cast out demons**, they **will speak with new tongues**; 18 they will pick up serpents, and if they drink any deadly poison, it will not hurt them; they **will lay hands on the sick, and they will recover**.*

Jesus told His disciples in Acts 1 to do many supernatural things. However, after 3½ years of walking with Him followed by another 40-day teaching after the resurrection, they were still not ready. They were not yet adequately equipped. They were told to wait, to wait until they were Baptized with the Holy Spirit.

- *Acts 1:4 Gathering them together, He **commanded them not to leave Jerusalem**, but **to wait** for what the Father had promised, "Which," He said, "you heard of from Me; 5 for John baptized with water, but **you will be baptized with the Holy Spirit** not many days from now."*

If you recall, the reason for the Baptism of the Holy Spirit was receiving power to be witnesses.

- *Acts 1:8 but you **will receive power when the Holy Spirit has come upon [epi] you**; and **you shall be My witnesses** both in Jerusalem, and in all Judea and Samaria, and even to the remotest part of the earth."*

The Jordan River flows. Going through the Jordan River was the way for the people of Israel to move into, and then live in, the Promised Land. Similarly, after being born again, we are on 'this' side of the Baptism of the Holy Spirit. Our form of the Promised land - whatever that looks like - is found on the other side of the Baptism in the Holy Spirit. To get to the other side, we need to be Baptized in the Holy Spirit. And when we do, we may experience additional blessings. And perhaps the first will be some walls of Jericho coming down.

CEASED?

Our Walk with Jesus

The bottom right-hand side of Figure11:12 shows the two baptisms, #8 Baptism of the Holy Spirit and #9 Baptism of Fire. For many believers, the notion of supernatural, miraculous events being part of our life - tongues, prophecy and immediate, miraculous healings - is a disconcerting, if not a downright scary thought. And it's understandable to a degree. There are and have been many frauds. There are many over the top individuals whose words and actions raise questions to their authenticity or motives.

I don't know the extent to which these individuals are motivated by pride, greed, deep hurts, or a need to be recognized and have attention and/or fame. Still others may have been impacted by poor teaching or by influences from the demonic world. I don't know. None of us know what is truly in another person's heart. But what I do know is that God's Word is truth, and neither the experiences of others nor the teachings of others are my final guide or my final authority. God's Word is my final guide, my final authority. One of God's teachings is He wants us to be Baptized in the Holy Spirit in order to have access to power to be more effective witnesses for Jesus.

Additional Foreshadowing

To enter the Holy of Holies, the priest would come into the outer court through the only entrance - akin to Jesus being the only Way. After entering into this outer court, three things were required before the priest was able to safely go into the Holy of Holies, and into God's presence:
  i. sacrifice a lamb on the alter - akin to the sacrifice and shed blood of Jesus;
  ii. wash in the laver with water - akin to water baptism;
  iii. be anointed with oil - akin to being anointed in the upon experience through the Baptism of the Holy Spirit.

While only one priest went behind the veil in the Holy of Holies once per year, Jesus's death tore the veil allowing believers today to be in direct contact with God, at any time, on every day, in every year. As if to eliminate all doubt about wanting this contact, God makes it pretty easy. Holy Spirit comes in [en] us when we're born again. He's right here.
  ❑ *Matthew 27:51 And behold, the veil of the temple was torn in two from top to bottom; and the earth shook and the rocks were split.*

God's Word tells us that believers are to be water baptized and to be Baptized in the Holy Spirit. We can do so, or not. It's our choice. If we choose not to, we still have personal, direct access to Almighty God. But if we choose not to receive these baptisms - most notably the baptism of the Holy Spirit - we might want to know if our decision is because of misbehaviors of other believers, contrary teachings, long-held beliefs, fear of being judged by others in our church and the Christian community for engaging in such activities, or perhaps deep down, not fully trusting God nor believing all of His Word? If that's where you're at, that's ok. That's where you're at. But that doesn't mean God wants you to stay where you're at. He doesn't, and He will do things over time - often in unusual ways and in unexpected timing – that will lead to changes. The Christian life doesn't mean there won't be challenges.

11: Tying Chapters 3-10 Together

However, God has good things for you, and when you truly come to know God personally, you will want God fully in your life.

CLOSING POINTS TO PONDER

I don't believe in compromising God's Word for the sake of unity. Sometimes unity is simply not possible. In areas such as the Baptism of the Holy Spirit and the 9 Holy Spirit gifts, there has been extremely strong and vocal disagreement, and some fairly nasty disunity. Hopefully **CEASED?** will help overcome some of this unwarranted disunity by revealing the truth in God's Word. Not through compromise, but through truth. I hope **CEASED?** has shown:

- ❖ there is a scriptural foundation that Baptism of the Holy Spirit and the 9 Holy Spirit gifts are relevant today;
- ❖ the upon [epi] experience - the Baptism of the Holy Spirit - is a separate experience from the in [en] experience when a person is born again, and Holy Spirit baptizes the new believer into the Body of Christ;
- ❖ the in [en] and upon [epi] experiences can occur at virtually the same time or there can be a significant amount of time between the two experiences;
- ❖ that being Baptized into the Body of Christ done by Holy Spirit, that water baptism done by another believer, and Baptism of the Holy Spirit done by Jesus are three distinct and separate events; and
- ❖ neither water baptism nor Baptism of the Holy Spirit is required to be born again/become a Christian.

I also hope **CEASED?** has shown:
- ❖ there are blessings for those who are water baptized; and
- ❖ there are additional blessings for those who are Baptized in the Holy Spirit and Fire. Blessings include, but are not limited to, receiving access to a different form of power than we receive when we're born again. Power than can help refine us, give us a zeal to share Jesus and the gospel, and enable us to be used to deliver one or more of the 9 Holy Spirit gifts.

11:1 If we choose not to pursue the Baptism of the Holy Spirit, shouldn't our hearts be to support and pray for those who do seek it? And if we do receive it, shouldn't our hearts be that it's ok if someone else doesn't want to seek this gift? As we do so, shouldn't we expect many blessings to flow, one of which would be increased unity between the Cessationist and Charismatic groups of the Body of Christ?

12

Link of 9 Holy Spirit Gifts to Baptism of the Holy Spirit

INTRODUCTION

WHEN Baptized in the Holy Spirit, a believer receives access to supernatural power. Chapter 12 briefly reviews:
1: some ways God demonstrated His power (page 200);
2: how Holy Spirit gifts and Baptism in the Holy Spirit are linked (page 201);
3: whether or not Christians should regularly see supernatural signs (page 203).

GOD'S DIVERSE DEMONSTRATIONS OF POWER

God's power manifested in the Bible in wide-ranging and very unusual ways.
- Creation of heavens and earth;
- Building of Noah's ark and the global flood;
- 10 plagues on Egypt including frogs, lice, flies, boils, hail and locusts;
- Burning bush where God speaks to Moses;
- Parting of the Red Sea and Jordan River;
- Walls of Jericho tumbled down;
- Ravens bring Elijah bread and meat for breakfast and dinner;
- Peter finds a coin in a fish while Jonah spends 3 days in a whale;
- Floating axe head;
- Darkening of the sky, splitting of rocks, tearing of the veil when Christ died;
- Individuals who died before the cross had their tombs opened, were raised, and walked around Jerusalem; and
- Resurrection and ascension of Christ.

12:1 Given the wide variety of ways in which God's power was displayed in the Bible, and the fact this power was seldom repeated in the same way, would it be surprising if God displays His power today in ways not seen before?

12: Link of 9 Gifts to Baptism of Holy Spirit

LINK BETWEEN 9 HOLY SPIRIT GIFTS AND BAPTISM OF THE HOLY SPIRIT

The 9 Holy Spirit gifts/manifestations per 1 Corinthians 12 are as follows:
- 1 Corinthians 12:8 *For to one is given the **word of wisdom** through the Spirit, and to another the **word of knowledge** according to the same Spirit;*
- 9 *to another **faith** by the same Spirit, and to another **gifts of healing** by the one Spirit,*
- 10 *and to another the effecting of **miracles**, and to another **prophecy**, and to another the **distinguishing of spirits**, to another various kinds of **tongues**, and to another the **interpretation of tongues**.*

Figure 8:4 in Chapter 8 summarized various aspects of 5 different settings where people experienced a Baptism of the Holy Spirit.

Figure 8:4 Activities Related to 5 Baptisms of the Holy Spirit

Believers receiving Baptism in the Holy Spirit	Major Noise, Signs when Occurred	Laying on of Hands Before Baptism	Baptism of Holy Spirit immediately followed by Tongues	Baptism of Holy Spirit immediately followed by Prophecy	Water Baptism before or after Baptism in Holy Spirit
Pentecost	X		X		N/A
Samaria		X			Before
Saul/Paul		X			After
Cornelius+			X		After
Ephesus		X	X	X	Before

At the outset, note that on some, but not all occasions, speaking in tongues and/or prophesying immediately followed the Baptism of the Holy Spirit. Both Peter and Paul immediately began to share the gospel after they were Baptized in the Holy Spirit. The related scriptures are as follows:

Pentecost
- Acts 2:1 *When the day of Pentecost had come ... 2 And suddenly there came from heaven a noise like a violent rushing wind, and it filled the whole house where they were sitting. 3 And there appeared to them tongues as of fire distributing themselves, and they rested on each one of them. 4 And **they were all filled with the Holy Spirit** and **began to speak with other tongues**, as the Spirit was giving them utterance.*

Cornelius, family and friends
- Acts 10:44 *While Peter was still speaking these words, **the Holy Spirit fell upon all those** who were listening to the message. 45 All the circumcised believers who came with Peter were amazed, because the **gift of the Holy***

CEASED?

Spirit had been poured out on the Gentiles also. 46 **For they were hearing them speaking with tongues** and exalting God …

12 Disciples at Ephesus
- ❑ Acts 19:6 And when Paul had laid his hands upon them, **the Holy Spirit came on them**, and they **began speaking with tongues and prophesying**. 7 There were in all about twelve men.

Peter and Paul

After Peter and Paul were Baptized in the Holy Spirit, they both immediately began to share the Good News - with boldness.
- ❑ Acts 2:14 But Peter, taking his stand with the eleven, **raised his voice and declared to them**: "Men of Judea and all you who live in Jerusalem, let this be known to you and give heed to my words.
- ❑ Acts 9:17 So Ananias departed and entered the house, and after laying his hands on him said, "Brother Saul, the Lord Jesus, who appeared to you on the road by which you were coming, has sent me so that you may regain your sight and **be filled with the Holy Spirit**." 18 And immediately there fell from his eyes something like scales, and he regained his sight, and he got up and was baptized; 19 and he took food and was strengthened. Now for several days he was with the disciples who were at Damascus, 20 **and immediately he began to proclaim Jesus in the synagogues**, saying, "He is the Son of God."

12:2 Doesn't the timing of these events demonstrate Baptism of the Holy Spirit is the doorway to gifts such as prophecy and tongues, and to a supernaturally enabled ability to powerfully preach? If not, how do we explain the prophecies, tongues and emboldened teaching occurring immediately after individuals were Baptized in the Holy Spirit? Coincidence?

Jesus's Teaching

Jesus told His disciples in Acts 1 that they would be Baptized in the Holy Spirit to receive power to witness. The sights and sounds plus speaking in tongues at Pentecost caught the attention of many. When Cornelius, family and friends started speaking in tongues, that caught the attention of Peter and those with him. The tongues confirmed to Peter and his colleagues that Cornelius, family and friends were not only born again, but they had also received the gift of the Holy Spirit - the Baptism of the Holy Spirit. Some time later, other believers were also involved in these supernatural gifts including Stephen, and four daughters of Philip, the evangelist.
- ❑ Acts 6:8 And Stephen, full of grace and power, was **performing great wonders and signs** among the people.
- ❑ Acts 21:8 On the next day we left and came to Caesarea, and entering the house of Philip the evangelist, who was one of the seven, we stayed with him. 9 Now this man had **four virgin daughters** who were **prophetesses**.

12: Link of 9 Gifts to Baptism of Holy Spirit
POWER OF GOD IN BELIEVER'S LIVES

Paul was very clear that the power of God was central to his sharing of the gospel.
- 2 Corinthians 12:12 The **signs of a true apostle** were performed among you with all perseverance, **by signs and wonders and miracles**.
- 1 Corinthians 2:4 and **my message and my preaching were not in persuasive words of wisdom**, but **in demonstration of the Spirit and of power,** 5 **so that your faith would not rest on the wisdom of men, but on the power of God.**
- 1 Thessalonians 1:4 knowing, brethren beloved by God, His choice of you; 5 for **our gospel did not come** to you **in word only,** but **also in power and in the Holy Spirit** ...
- Philippians 3:10 that I may know Him and **the power of His resurrection** and the fellowship of His sufferings, being conformed to His death;

Paul tells us we are to be imitators of Christ just as he was.
- 1 Corinthians 11:1 Be imitators of me, just as I also am of Christ.

12:3 Over the 40 days following His resurrection, Jesus taught the disciples about the kingdom of God. If we don't have the power of God in our lives, how can we share the full gospel and adequately explain/demonstrate the kingdom of God?
- 1 Corinthians 4:20 For the **kingdom of God does not consist in words but in power.**
- Romans 15:18 For I will not presume to speak of anything except what Christ has accomplished through me, resulting in the obedience of the Gentiles by word and deed, **19 in the power of signs and wonders, in the power of the Spirit**; so that from Jerusalem and round about as far as Illyricum **I have fully preached the gospel of Christ.**

Jesus did many miracles, and tells us we will too.
- Mark 16:17 **These signs will accompany those who have believed**: in My name they will **cast out demons,** they will **speak with new tongues**; 18 they will pick up serpents, and if they drink any deadly poison, it will not hurt them; **they will lay hands on the sick, and they will recover.**
- John 14:12 Truly, truly, I say to you, **he who believes in Me, the works that I do, he will do also**; and **greater works than these he will do**; because I go to the Father.

Some of the very last words from Jesus before His ascension were telling His disciples not to go, but to wait for the Baptism of the Holy Spirit.
- Acts 1:4 Gathering them together, He **commanded them not to leave Jerusalem,** but to wait for what the Father had promised, "Which," He said, "you heard of from Me; 5 for John baptized with water, but **you will be baptized with the Holy Spirit** not many days from now." ... 8 but **you will receive power** when the Holy Spirit has come upon you; and you shall be My witnesses both in Jerusalem, and in all Judea and Samaria, and even to the

CEASED?

remotest part of the earth."
- 12:4 If Jesus was walking amongst us today and knew we weren't Baptized in the Holy Spirit, would He tell us we need this baptism to be better witnesses for Him? If not, why not?

<u>*To Leaders of our Ministries and Churches*</u>
- 12:5 Pastors, teachers and other leaders have difficult jobs. If this is you, I don't know how you do everything that's on your plate, especially dealing with all of us people. But let me ask. If leaders haven't been equipping the sheep they influence on how to access the power of God and how to properly use the 9 Holy Spirit gifts associated with the Baptism of the Holy Spirit, doesn't a wonderful opportunity exist for them to do so going forward? Can many leaders now begin to experience more of God's blessings in their own lives, and then help those they influence to also begin experiencing new blessings?
  - ❏ *Ephesians 4:11 And He gave some as apostles, and some as prophets, and some as evangelists, and some as pastors and teachers, 12 for the equipping of the saints for the work of service, to the building up of the body of Christ.*

If this is your situation, the enemy may try to tell you that you have fallen short in your walk, hindered your family, or failed your congregation. Those are lies from the pit of hell. For whatever reason, God reveals things in His timing, and now is a time of revelation for some of His children. It's not a time of regret, but a time of expectation and celebration.

God's ways are not our ways. He didn't need to use believers to advance His kingdom. He chose to. He gives us amazing support including His Word and Holy Spirit coming in [en] us when we're born again. But God offers more to us, including access to Holy Spirit's power that enables us to live a life where the supernatural is central to our lives - but all for God's glory. If you still don't believe Baptism of the Holy Spirit and the 9 Holy Spirit gifts are relevant today, but have ceased, consider the evidence in the next few chapters.

CLOSING POINT TO PONDER

- 12:6 Jesus is our role model. The original apostles and other believers after the cross are role models. They were all sent ones. We're today's sent ones. Several indicators reveal who is a follower of Christ. Love for God and our neighbor, and a desire to proclaim Jesus are some. Changes in our life, our attitudes, our responses to problems are additional signs. But signs and wonders are also an indicator. If supernatural signs and wonders aren't a regular part of our life, are we missing out, and potentially causing other believers to miss out too?
  - ❏ *Mark 16:17 These signs will accompany those who have believed: in My name they will cast out demons, they will speak with new tongues; 18 they will pick up serpents, and if they drink any deadly poison, it will not hurt them; they will lay hands on the sick, and they will recover.*

13

Ceased by the Numbers

INTRODUCTION
PAUL'S teachings in 1 Corinthians include encouragement to pursue spiritual gifts. Chapter 13 briefly examines how many believers were living when Paul wrote these words of encouragement, and the significance of these numbers.

Encouraging Pursuit of Spiritual Gifts
Consensus seems to be that Paul wrote 1 Corinthians somewhere between ~52 and 57 AD, some 20 to 25 years after the cross. In 1 Corinthians, Paul made several comments regarding the 9 Holy Spirit gifts including prophecy and tongues.

- ❏ *1 Corinthians 12:31* **But earnestly desire the greater gifts** ...
- ❏ *1 Corinthians 14:1 Pursue love, yet desire earnestly spiritual gifts, but* **especially that you may prophesy**.
- ❏ *1 Corinthians 14:5 Now I* **wish that you all spoke in tongues**, *but even more that you would* **prophesy**; *and greater is one who prophesies than one who speaks in tongues,* **unless he interprets**, *so that the church may receive edifying.*
- ❏ *1 Corinthians 14:39 Therefore, my brethren,* **desire earnestly to prophesy**, *and* **do not forbid to speak in tongues**. *40 But all things must be done properly and in an orderly manner.*

Given the above, let me ask:

13:1 Is it reasonable to expect Paul would only be encouraging believers to prophesy and speak in tongues if indeed it was God's will for them to pursue such gifts? If not, why would Paul have encouraged them to do so?

Number of Believers
So how many believers were living when Paul wrote 1 Corinthians? In other words, in ~52-57 AD, how many believers were being encouraged by Paul to pursue these gifts? Starting in Acts 1, the book of Acts provides considerable insight into this issue.

- ❏ *Acts 1:15 In those days Peter stood up among the brothers (the company of persons was in all about 120) and said,*
- ❏ *Acts 2:41 So those who had received his word were baptized, and that day there* **were added about three thousand souls**.

CEASED?

- Acts 2:47 praising God and having favor with all the people. And the Lord **added to their number day by day** those who were being saved.
- Acts 4:4 ... the number of the men came **to about five thousand**.
- Acts 5:14 And all the more believers in the Lord, multitudes of men and women, were **constantly added** to their number.

John MacArthur, a high-profile Bible teacher and staunch Cessationist, writes about the early church growth in a 2010 message entitled *"A Biblical Response to the Church-Growth Movement"*. Mr. MacArthur writes:

> "You come to (Acts) chapter 5 and verse 14, "And all the more believers in the Lord, multitudes of men and women, were constantly added to their number, or to the church." Now it's in the **multitudes of thousands and tens of thousands**."

Another perspective is provided by Vance Pitman who wrote in a November 2018 article '*4 Things That Caused the Early Church to Spread Like Wildfire*':

> "... historians and scholars go on to tell us that **within six months of Pentecost, there were over one hundred thousand new Christians in the city of Jerusalem**."

The growth continued into Acts 6.
- Acts 6:7 The word of God kept on spreading; and the **number of the disciples continued to increase greatly in Jerusalem**, and a **great many of the priests were becoming obedient to the faith**.

Now consider Paul's conversion and his initial efforts in sharing the gospel.
- Acts 9:4 ... "Saul, Saul, why are you persecuting me?" 5 And he said, "Who are you, Lord?" And he said, "I am Jesus, whom you are persecuting ... 20 **and immediately he began to proclaim Jesus in the synagogues** ...
- Acts 9:31 So the church throughout all Judea and Galilee and Samaria enjoyed peace, being built up. And going on in the fear of the Lord and in the comfort of the Holy Spirit, it **continued to increase**.

Peter takes the gospel to the Gentiles starting with Cornelius, family and friends.
- Acts 11:15 ... **Holy Spirit fell on them just as on us at the beginning** ... 18 When they heard these things they fell silent. And they glorified God, saying, "Then to the Gentiles also God has granted repentance that leads to life."

Stephen was murdered which led to a scattering of believers, some of whom shared Jesus with both the Jews and the Greeks.
- Acts 11:19 So then those who were scattered **because of the persecution** that occurred in connection with Stephen made their way to Phoenicia and Cyprus and Antioch, speaking the word to no one except to Jews alone. 20 But there were some of them, men of Cyprus and Cyrene, who came to Antioch and began **speaking to the Greeks also**, preaching the Lord Jesus. 21 And the hand of the Lord was with them, and a **large number who believed turned to the**

13: By the Numbers

> **Lord**. 22 The news about them reached the ears of the church at Jerusalem, and they sent Barnabas off to Antioch ... 24 ... a good man, and full of the Holy Spirit and of faith. And **considerable numbers were brought to the Lord**.

As Acts moves on, the number didn't just increase; the numbers multiplied.
- Acts 12:24 But the word of the Lord continued to grow and to be **multiplied**.
- Acts 13:47 For so the Lord has commanded us, "I have placed You as a light for the Gentiles, That You may bring salvation to the end of the earth." 48 When the Gentiles heard this, they began rejoicing and glorifying the word of the Lord; and as many as had been appointed to eternal life believed. 49 **And the word of the Lord was being spread through the whole region**.
- Acts 16:4 Now while they were passing through the cities ... 5 So the churches were being strengthened in the faith, and were **increasing in number daily**.
- Acts 17:12 Therefore **many** of them therefore **believed**, **along with** a **number of prominent Greek women and men**.

Paul's travels took him to Athens and then to Ephesus in ~52 AD.
- Acts 19:1 It happened that while Apollos was at Corinth, Paul passed through the upper country and came to Ephesus, **and found some disciples** ... 6 And when Paul had laid his hands upon them, the **Holy Spirit came on them, and they began speaking with tongues and prophesying**. 7 There were in all about twelve men.

13:2 Given i) John and Peter traveled to Samaria to ensure the new believers were Baptized in the Holy Spirit and ii) Paul also made an effort to ensure believers at Ephesus were Baptized in the Holy Spirit, is it consistent to conclude:
  i. Steps were taken by all church leaders to ensure all believers up to that point in time were being Baptized in the Holy Spirit? If not, why not?
  ii. On the basis that steps were being taken to ensure all believers were being Baptized in the Holy Spirit, wouldn't that also mean all believers living at that time were in a position to potentially receive gifts such as prophecy and speaking in tongues? If not, why not?

Paul took the gospel to not just part of Asia, but all of Asia.
- Acts 19:8 And he entered the synagogue and continued speaking out **boldly for three months**, reasoning and persuading them about the kingdom of God. 9 But when some were becoming hardened and disobedient, speaking evil of the Way before the people, he withdrew from them and took away the disciples, **reasoning daily in the school of Tyrannus**. 10 This took place for two years, **so that all who lived in Asia heard the word of the Lord, both Jews and Greeks**.

To Recap the Numbers

By Acts 5, believers numbered in the tens of thousands. Tens of thousands before Paul's coming to Christ in Acts 9. Tens of thousands before the gospel was taken to the Gentiles in Acts 10. Tens of thousand before believers were scattered in Acts 11

CEASED?

due to persecution following Steven's murder. Tens of thousands before it was taken to Asia in Acts 19. More than ten times, the book of Acts mentions the number of believers increased, increased daily, or multiplied.

In my way of thinking, if the number of believers was doubling, God's Word would say they doubled, but it doesn't. The Bible uses the word 'multiply' which suggests more than doubling. For illustrative purposes only, consider the following. **IF** there were 40,000 believers by the end of Acts 5 and **IF** the number of believers increased by multiples of 3 by Acts 9 and another 3 times by Acts 12, that would equate to 120,000 born-again Christians by Acts 9 (40,000 * 3 = 120,000) and 360,000 born-again Christians by Acts 12 (120,000 * 3 = 360,000). By the time Acts 19 rolls around when Paul was in Ephesus, there were considerably more.

Or consider this simplistic approach. Approximately 20 years passed between the cross and Paul's going to Ephesus. 20 years equates to ~7,300 days (365 days per year * 20 years). If the Body of Christ grew, on average, at a rate of only 10 believers per day from Pentecost to the time Paul visited Ephesus, that amounts to 73,000 believers. 100 new believers per day would equate to 730,000 believers.

These two mathematical approaches aren't intended to be theologically sound or statistically valid estimates of actual numbers of believers. Their inclusion is purely to illustrate how quickly the number of believers can add up and provide further support there were many tens of thousands, if not many hundreds of thousands of believers when Paul visited Ephesus in Acts 19 in ~52 AD. There were even more believers when Paul wrote 1 Corinthians in ~53 to 57 AD.

Consider again the following scriptures,
- 1 Corinthians 12:31 But **earnestly desire the greater gifts** ...
- 1 Corinthians 14:1 Pursue love, yet **desire earnestly spiritual gifts**, but **especially** that you may **prophesy**.
- 1 Corinthians 14:5 Now I **wish that you all spoke in tongues**, **but even more that you would prophesy** ...
- 1 Corinthians 14:39 Therefore, my brethren, **desire earnestly to prophesy**, and **do not forbid to speak in tongues** ...

A core issue related to the Cessationist/Continuationist debate is identifying who Paul was encouraging to pursue the Holy Spirit gifts. Alternatives include:
　i.　Original apostles only;
　ii.　Original apostles + believers at Pentecost + believers at Corinth;
　iii.　Original apostles + all believers living when Paul wrote 1 Corinthians; or
　iv.　All believers including those of us living today.

13:3　Given Paul was encouraging the believers at Corinth to pursue gifts such as prophecy and tongues, doesn't this mean, at a minimum, that all believers living at that point in time could potentially receive one or more of the 9 Holy Spirit gifts? If not, why not?

13:4　If you have a Cessationist view and your answer to question 13:3 is something like "*No, Paul's words of encouragement do not change anything. No believers living at Corinth could be given one or more of the 9 Holy Spirit*

13: By the Numbers

gifts", why would Paul encourage them to pursue something they couldn't have? And if this teaching was not true, wouldn't that mean other messages in 1 Corinthians and Paul's other letters also weren't relevant for other believers living at that time? Or for believers living today? If not, why not?

13:5 If your answer to question 13:3 is *"Yes, Paul's words of encouragement do mean believers living at Corinth could be given one or more of the 9 Holy Spirit gifts"*, doesn't that mean the hundreds of thousands of other believers living elsewhere at that time were also in a position to receive one or more of the 9 Holy Spirit gifts? If not, why not?

13:6 And if your answer to question 13:5 is *"Yes, Paul's words of encouragement do mean the other believers living at the time Paul wrote 1 Corinthians could be given one or more of the 9 Holy Spirit gifts"*, doesn't that mean all other believers including those of us living today could also receive such Holy Spirit gifts? If not, why not?

Some Cessationists believe the 9 Holy Spirit gifts were limited to a select few after the cross. If that's still your view, Chapter 16 deals with the issue in more detail.

CLOSING POINT TO PONDER

There were hundreds of thousands of believers living when Paul wrote 1 Corinthians and encouraged believers to seek spiritual gifts including tongues and prophecy. Imagine encouraging all those people to pursue such gifts when they couldn't actually get them.

13:7 God is love. God is truth. All Scripture is inspired by God. Given these scriptures written by Paul are from God, how can they not be true? And thus, how can they not apply to all believers including those living today?

❑ *2 Timothy 3:16 All Scripture is inspired by God and profitable for teaching, for reproof, for correction, for training in righteousness; 17 so that the man of God may be adequate, equipped for every good work.*

14

Did the 9 Holy Spirit Gifts Decline, then End?

INTRODUCTION

CHAPTER 1 in combination with Chapter 18 reviews a key reason Cessationists believe the 9 Holy Spirit gifts have ceased - all divine revelation is found in the Bible. Another key reason Cessationists believe the 9 Holy Spirit gifts including prophecy and tongues have ended is the apparent decline in these gifts in the latter Chapters of Acts, and the virtual non-existence of such gifts in the books following Acts. Chapter 14 analyzes whether not this perspective is accurate.

Chapter 14 Analysis includes only 9 Holy Spirit Gifts

In terms of gifts, **CEASED?** deals with whether or not the Holy Spirit gifts as per 1 Corinthians 12 declined, and then ended. As a result, Chapter 14 does not deal with all signs and wonders, but only with the 9 Holy Spirit gifts. In so doing, it excludes other supernatural events such as casting out demons or angels freeing disciples from jail.

Many For the Start, and None for the End

Multiple scriptures prophesy the Baptism of the Holy Spirit including prophetic words from John the Baptist and Jesus. In contrast, Cessationists and Continuationists both agree there is not one scripture explicitly stating the Baptism of the Holy Spirit and the 9 Holy Spirit gifts ended at a specific time or with a specific group.

14:1   If the Baptism of the Holy Spirit and the 9 Holy Spirit gifts were to exist for only a short time after the cross, doesn't it seem a bit unusual several scriptures prophesy the Baptism of the Holy Spirit will occur, but there isn't one scripture saying the Holy Spirit gifts were for a short time, or were limited to a select few people?

LACK OF MENTION IN NEW TESTAMENT BOOKS

Before getting into the book of Acts itself, I want to first touch on the Cessationist claim that says the decline and ultimate cessation of the 9 Holy Spirits is made clear by the fact there is virtually no mention of any of the 9 Holy Spirit gifts in the New Testament books following Acts. This statement has much truth. There is virtually no mention of any specific gifts. However, is there more to the story?

To begin, an inherent assumption in this Cessationist claim is that the lack of

14: Did Gifts Decline, then End?

mention of the 9 Holy Spirit gifts is because there were very few signs and wonders occurring. In other words, the Cessationist argument is based on the premise there is a direct relationship between the extent to which the Holy Spirit gifts are taking place, and the extent to which they are mentioned in the Bible. The more that occur, more mention is made. The less that occur, less mention is made.

14:2 Cessationists usually agree that the 9 Holy Spirit gifts were in full operation up to and including Acts 19 - 21 which is part of Paul's 3rd missionary journey. Given that, if the Cessationist argument is valid that the 9 Holy Spirit gifts declined because there is little or no mention of them after Acts 21, shouldn't we see much more written on the gifts before Acts 19? In other words, shouldn't there be considerably more mention of the 9 gifts in the books written between Pentecost and Paul's travels in Acts 19-21, than in the books written after Paul's journeys in Acts 19-21?

Which Books to Examine

To analyze the evidence in the other New Testament books, I excluded the 4 Gospels as very little of their content deals with events after Pentecost. I also excluded Revelation as it is filled with prophecy and/or symbolism, as opposed to day-to-day events going on at that time. The evidence in the other 21 books should be more than enough for our needs.

The 21 Books

For the remaining 21 books (27 New Testament books in total less the 4 Gospels, Acts and Revelation), there are at least 2 'reasonable' ways to examine the contents:
- ❖ examine the 21 books according to the order they are listed in the Bible which is the basis of the standard Cessationist analysis;
- ❖ examine the books in chronological order according to whether they were written before or after Paul's travels in Acts 19-21. Again, to be clear, this time was chosen as the reference point because it is when Cessationists commonly argue was the beginning of the decline of the 9 Holy Spirit gifts.

When using the first approach, we find all 21 books follow the book of Acts.

14:3 Is it reasonable to expect many readers would tend to think the order of these books is also the chronological order by which these events actually occurred? In other words, is there a tendency to think the first of the 21 books would contain details on the earliest events, and the latter of the 21 books would contain details that happened later on?

Consider the book of James. In order of the appearance of the 21 books in the New Testament found after Acts, James is 15th of the 21 books. In terms of when it was written, however, James is often considered to be the first of the 21 books to be written in ~45 AD, ~7 years before Paul's journeys in Acts 19-21. The position of the book of James in the Bible does not help explain what happened over time. And to be fair to Cessationists, looking at the books in terms of their order in the Bible should not be used. The reason is because the Holy Spirit gifts were in full operation when James was written, James should have extensive mention of the gifts.

CEASED?

Extensive mention of a book positioned late in the Bible would infer the gifts had not ceased, when they may have.

14:4 As a result, isn't it prudent to split the books into two periods - those written before Paul's travels in Acts 19-21, and those written after? If not, why not?

14:5 The Cessationist view contends that the 9 gifts were in full operation before Acts 19-21 but were on the decline afterward. On that basis, shouldn't:
  i. the books written before Paul's travels in Acts 19-21 provide extensive information on signs and wonders;
  ii. the books written afterward show limited if any mention of the 9 Holy Spirit gifts? If not, why not?

Figure 14:1 on the next page provides a brief summary of these 21 New Testament books including the estimated year they were written and one or more of their key themes. I also included the dates of a few events to provide context. The dates for the books and events are a topic of much debate. My review included articles, websites and study Bibles. Let me just say, it was an interesting exercise. The dates shown are what 'seem' to be reasonably accepted dates or close to it. If you disagree, put in your own dates and adjust my analysis as you see fit.

When examining the 21 books, we find 4 books - James and Galatians, and likely 1 and 2 Thessalonians - were written before Paul's travels in ~52-55AD (which could have been as late as 58AD). Given these 4 books were written before Paul's travels in Acts 19-21 when the 9 Holy Spirit gifts were occurring big time, then according to the Cessationist argument, we should find extensive mention of the Holy Spirit gifts in at least 2, if not all 4 of these books. The following are the number of times these books give details about the 9 Holy Spirit gifts occurring after the cross and before Paul's travels in Act 19-21:

James:	None
Galatians:	None
1 Thessalonians:	None
2 Thessalonians:	None

14:6 The four books - James, Galatians, 1 and 2 Thessalonians - were written before Paul's travels in Acts 19-21, at a time when the Holy Spirit gifts were very active. Doesn't the fact there is not a single mention or record (that I could find) of any of the 9 gifts described in these 4 books invalidate the view/assumption there is a direct correlation between the amount of the gifts occurring, and the extent to which they're mentioned in God's Word?

14:7 And thus, isn't it an invalid argument to claim the 9 Holy Spirit gifts were on the decline after the events of Acts 19-21 because there is no specific mention of them occurring? If not, why not?

14: Did Gifts Decline, then End?

Figure 14:1 Did 9 Holy Spirit Gifts Decline in 21 Books Following Acts?

Book	~Year	Primary Themes of Book / Events
	~30 AD	Pentecost
	34 AD	Paul encounters Jesus
	late 30's	Acts 10: Peter takes the gospel to Gentiles
	43	James (brother of John) martyred
	46 – 47	Acts 13-14 Paul's 1st missionary journey
1. James	44 – 62	Christian living
2. Galatians *	48 - 57	True/false Gospels, faith/life in Christ
	49 – 51	Acts 15-18 Paul's 2nd missionary journey
3. 1 Thessalonians *	51	Mentoring new believers
4. 2 Thessalonians *	51 - 52	Correction in teachings/standing firm
	52 - 58	Acts 18-21 Paul's 3rd missionary journey
	52 – 57	Acts 19: Paul and 12 disciples at Ephesus
5. 1 Corinthians *	55 – 57	Conduct, gifts to edify & unify
6. 2 Corinthians *	55 - 57	Confirm disciples; defends character, explains his authority
7. Romans *	56 – 58	Theology: sin/righteousness/ faith etc.
	57 – 58	Acts 20: Eutychus brought back to life
	58 – 60	Acts 23: Paul imprisoned at Caesarea
	58 – 60	Acts 25-26: Paul appears before Agrippa
	60 – 61	Acts 27: Paul goes to Rome; Malta miracles
	61 – 63	Acts 27-28: Paul under house arrest
8. Ephesians *	61 - 63	Grace/justification/conduct
9. Philippians *	61 - 63	Joy-filled life serving/experiencing God
10. Philemon *	61 – 63	Forgiveness
11. Colossians *	61 - 63	Supremacy of Christ
12. Acts	61 – 64	Early church in word and power
13. 1 Timothy *	64 - 65	Proper conduct, duties/advice for leading
14. Titus *	64 - 65	Need for good works/purity/kindness
15. 1 Peter	64 - 65	Some keys to Christian living
16. 2 Timothy *	66 - 67	Endurance amid difficulties
17. 2 Peter	67 - 68	Holiness/perseverance/false teachers
18. Hebrews *	65 – 68	Superiority of Christ
	67 – 68	Paul martyred
19. Jude	68 – 70	Contend for faith/love; deceivers warned
20. 1 John	90 - 95	Time with God/true & false teachings
21. 2 John	90 - 95	Expose false teachings
22. 3 John	90 - 95	Christian hospitality in love

* Books identified with an asterisk ' * ' are generally believed to be written by Paul.

14:8 When I reviewed the 17 books written after Paul's journeys in Acts 19-21, there were no details of specific signs or wonders. In that regard, this supports the Cessationist argument. However, I found more than 60 general references to the 9 Holy Spirit gifts or related items such as the office of the prophet. Don't these general references which were written after the events

CEASED?

of Acts 19-21, provide concrete evidence that the 9 Holy Spirit gifts haven't ceased? If you believe these general references don't support their existence, then shouldn't these dozens of general references support your belief that the gifts have ceased? And if so, how exactly do they do that? Or do we just ignore them?

14:9   Given there was considerable mention of signs and wonders in the 4 Gospels and Acts, is it surprising that the focus of these 21 books is on various themes and not historical events? And thus, given the focus in these books is on themes and not events, doesn't that make the lack of details of signs and wonders in these 21 books an unreliable indicator as to whether or not the 9 Holy Spirit gifts were increasing or decreasing?

Book of Hebrews

Of these 21 books, Paul is frequently viewed as having authored 9 of the 11 books written before Luke wrote Acts, and 3 of the 10 books written after Luke wrote Acts. Paul frequently wrote about the importance of sharing the gospel not only in words, but in power. Hebrews, the last book that many (but not all) Christians believe was written by Paul in ~65-68 AD, was written ~10-15 years after Paul's travels in Acts 19-21, and ~10 years after Paul wrote 1 and 2 Corinthians. And yet, in Hebrews, we find the author reaffirming that signs and wonders are to be central to our sharing of God's kingdom.

❑ *Hebrews 2:4 God also testifying with them, both by __signs__ and __wonders__ and by various __miracles__ and by __gifts of the Holy Spirit__ according to His own will.*

14:10   Doesn't Hebrews 2:4 support the Continuationist argument that the 9 Holy Spirit gifts were continuing, and expected to continue? If not, why not?

FREQUENCY OF HOLY SPIRIT GIFTS IN ACTS

To begin the numerical review of the decline in the 9 Holy Spirit gifts that Cessationists believe is revealed in Acts, let's examine Acts from beginning to end.

- ❖ Acts 1: Jesus teaches over 40 days, tells disciples to wait for the Baptism in the Holy Spirit, Matthias voted to replace Judas;
- ❖ Acts 2: Pentecost, initial Baptism of the Holy Spirit, tongues of fire, speaking in tongues, 3,000 are born again;
- ❖ Acts 3: Lame man healed;
- ❖ Acts 4: After confronted by Jewish leaders, Peter was filled with Holy Spirit, courageously preached Word of God;
- ❖ Acts 5: Apostles performed many signs and wonders, healing through Peter's 'shadow';
- ❖ Acts 6: Stephen performed great wonders;
- ❖ Acts 8: Many paralyzed and lame healed, miracles and signs;
- ❖ Acts 9: Saul encounters Jesus, born again, Baptized in the Holy Spirit, Aeneas healed, Dorcas resurrected;
- ❖ Acts 10: Cornelius plus family and friends are born again, Baptized in the Holy Spirit, spoke in tongues;
- ❖ Acts 11: Agabus prophecy;

14: Did Gifts Decline, then End?

- ❖ Acts 14: Signs and wonders, the lame man at Lystra healed, Paul potentially healed/brought back to life after stoned and left for dead;
- ❖ Acts 18: Paul in Corinth for 18 months; no signs and wonders other than God speaking to Paul in a vision.

14:11 Does the lack of mention of the 9 Holy Spirit gifts (or any signs and wonders for that matter) while Paul spent 18 months in Corinth per Acts 18 indicate one way or another:
  i. that the 9 Holy Spirit gifts had ceased or were on a major decline during these 18 months; or
  ii. that the Holy Spirit gifts were still occurring during these 18 months and later as per Acts 19 but there was no mention of them in the Bible?

Acts 19-21 show more miracles occurring although these chapters are viewed by some Cessationists as the beginning of the decline of the 9 Holy Spirit gifts.
- ❖ Acts 19: 12 believers at Ephesus are Baptized in the Holy Spirit, spoke in tongues and prophesied, people are healed by touching Paul's handkerchiefs and aprons;
- ❖ Acts 20: Paul arrived in Troas, brought Eutychus back to life;
- ❖ Acts 21: Paul sails to Tyre, Agabus prophecies Paul will be bound and handed over to the Gentiles. It happened.

14:12 Do the above indicate the 9 Holy Spirit gifts were declining or continuing?

14:13 If the events in Acts 19 through 21 occurred in the same length of time in your life, would you view that as ho-hum, or significant and exciting?

The last part of Acts 21 and the next 5 chapters deal with Paul's legal battles.
- ❖ Acts 21: Jewish people spoke against Paul. Paul was beaten amidst efforts to kill him. Paul was taken into custody but then asked to speak to the crowd, a request that was granted.
- ❖ Acts 22: Paul gives a lengthy testimony leading to his appearing before the Sanhedrin;
- ❖ Acts 23: Paul speaks, jailed, moved to Caesarea due to a plot to kill him;
- ❖ Acts 24: Paul appears before Felix who defers judgment. Paul is retained in Caesarea for 2 years until Festus replaces Felix;
- ❖ Acts 25: Paul appears before both Festus and King Agrippa;
- ❖ Acts 26: Paul provides his defense to Festus and King Agrippa.

14:14 Acts 22 through 26 deal with Paul being imprisoned. Considerable detail is given on this part of Paul's journey in these chapters. Given there's no mention of any of the 9 Holy Spirit gifts, does this indicate:
  i. the 9 Holy Spirit gifts had ended, or were well on their way to ending; or
  ii. there is no indication of change one way or another, and the lack of mention is similar to there being no mention of the gifts when Paul was in Ephesus for 18 months in Acts 18?

CEASED?

14:15 Furthermore, does the lack of mention of the 9 Holy Spirit gifts while Paul was in Caesarea mean signs and wonders weren't occurring through the other apostles? Or is it simply a situation of no mention being made of the 9 gifts that were occurring?
- ❏ *Acts 5:12 At the hands of the apostles many signs and wonders were taking place among the people; and they were all with one accord in Solomon's portico.*

Consider the last two chapters of Acts.
- ❖ Acts 27: Paul is put on a boat to Rome. Paul states the voyage is going to end in disaster, which is either a message from his flesh or he prophesies a word received from God. Paul later advises an angel of God told him not to be afraid and that all 276 onboard would survive. The trip does end in disaster, all survive, all cargo is lost and the boat sinks.
- ❖ Acts 28: Paul arrives on Malta, is bitten by a viper but isn't harmed to the amazement of all. The father of the island's chief officer, Publius, was healed through Paul as were many of the people on the island who were sick. Major miracles occur. Paul reaches Rome where he lived for 2 years with a soldier guarding him. No mention of supernatural miracles is made during these 2 years.

14:16 Do the miracles in the last two chapters of Acts - 2 prophecies fulfilled, Publius's father healed, Paul unaffected by the viper's bite, and many sick people on the island healed - suggest the 9 Holy Spirit gifts were continuing, or on the decline and en route to ceasing?

14:17 If you believe the 9 Holy Spirit gifts are on the decline because of the lack of mention, consider the following:
   i. there is also no specific mention in these verses of faith, love, heaven, hell, demons, sick people, or sin in these chapters. Does their lack of mention indicate they were on the decline as well?
   ii. There is also no mention of Peter or any of the other apostles being involved in miracles. Does that mean God had stopped using all of them to perform signs and wonders as well? That God's presence in Peter's shadow was no longer there?

By the Numbers

Figures 14:2 and 14:3 summarize the number of times the Holy Spirit gifts are referenced in general, or are specifically identified in each chapter of Acts starting with Acts 2, after Pentecost morning. The numbers or counts:
- ❖ include references to the general term *'signs and wonders'*, and to specific references of the 9 gifts, notably *'tongues'*, *'prophecy'* and *'healings'*.
- ❖ exclude references to supernatural events that don't involve one of the 9 Holy Spirit gifts such as casting out of demons and God setting people free from jail.

14: Did Gifts Decline, then End?

In terms of Figure 14:2 which covers Chapters 2 through 21, let me explain.

- ❖ Starting with the 1st row of numbers (bolded) in Figure 14:2, a general reference to the 9 Holy Spirit gifts and/or at least one of the gifts is referenced on 3 different occasions (Column A) in only one chapter (Column B) which equals 3 total occurrences (Column C which equals A* B). The one chapter in which gifts are referred to 3 times (Column D) is Chapter 5.
- ❖ In the 2nd row, the gifts are mentioned twice (Column A) in 6 different chapters (Column B) for a total of 12 occurrences (Column C). The 6 chapters are 2, 8, 9, 14, 19, and 21.
- ❖ Row 3 of Figure 14:2 above shows the 9 Holy Spirit gifts are referred to once in 5 chapters (3, 6, 10, 11, 20).
- ❖ Row 4 shows the 9 gifts are not referenced at all in the other 8 chapters.

Figure 14:2 Counts for 20 Chapters, Acts 2-21

A # Times Occurred in Same Chapter	B # Chapters with that Frequency	C Total Occurrences (C = A * B)	D Chapter Numbers
3 times	**1**	**3**	**5**
2 times	6	12	2, 8, 9, 14, 19, 21
1 time	5	5	3, 6, 10, 11, 20
0 times	8	0	4, 7, 12, 13, 15, 16, 17, 18
Total Occurrences	20	20	
I: Average # of occurrences per chapter if count all 20 chapters 20 / 20 = 1.0		20 occurrences divided by 20 chapters = 1.0 occurrence per chapter. In other words, a general or specific reference to the gifts is mentioned, on average, once per chapter when all 20 chapters are considered.	
II: Average # of occurrences if only count the 12 chapters (first 3 rows of data above) where gifts are mentioned 20 / 12 = 1.7		20 occurrences divided by 12 chapters = 1.7. In other words, a general or specific reference to one of the 9 Holy Spirit gifts is mentioned, on average, 1.7 times per chapter when we only count the 12 chapters where gifts are referenced.	

- ❖ In total, per the second last row (I:), there are 20 references to the gifts which equates to an average of once per chapter (20 occurrences divided by 20 chapters).
- ❖ If we examine the frequency of the gifts (last row, II:) by only looking at chapters where they are referenced at least once (12) - thus excluding the 8 chapters where no mention is made - the average frequency of mention increases to 1.7 times per chapter.

CEASED?

Figure 14:3 below shows the results when we examine the frequency of the 9 Holy Spirit gifts in the last 7 chapters of Acts, Chapters 22 through 28.

Figure 14:3 Counts for 7 Chapters, Acts 22-28

A # Times Occurred in the Same Chapter	B # Chapters with that Frequency	C Total Occurrences (C = A * B)	D Chapter Numbers
3 times	1	3	28
2 times	1	2	27
1 time	0	0	
0	5	0	22, 23, 24, 25, 26
Total	7	5	
I: Average # of occurrences per chapter if we count every one of the last 7 chapters of Acts 5 / 7 = 0.7		5 occurrences divided by 7 chapters = .7 times per chapter. In other words, a general or specific reference of one of the 9 Holy Spirit gifts is mentioned, on average, less than 1 time per chapter when all 7 chapters are counted.	
II: Average # of occurrences if we only count the 2 chapters (first 2 rows of data above) where the gifts are mentioned 5 / 2 = 2.5		5 occurrences divided by 2 chapters = 2.5 times per chapter. In other words, general or specific reference of one of the 9 Holy Spirit gifts is mentioned, on average, 2.5 times per chapter when the chapters to Paul's legal issues are excluded and only the last 2 chapters of Acts are counted.	

Comparing Results of Figure 14:2 to Figure 14:3

Two key findings found in the numbers of Figures 14:2 and 14:3 are as follows.
- ❖ When comparing results of I: (average occurrences per chapter when using all chapters), there was a small decline in the frequency that gifts were referenced, from 1.0 time per chapter (per Figure 14:2) to .7 times per chapter (per Figure 14:3).
- ❖ When comparing results using II: (average occurrences when we only include chapters in which gifts were mentioned), we find the average frequency of mention increased from 1.7 times per chapter (per Figure 14:2) to 2.5 times per chapter (per Figure 14:3). More insight on these numbers is provided below when we consider the time frames involved (below).

Further analysis of Chapters 2 through 21 also shows the following:
- ❖ no two consecutive chapters combined have a higher rate of occurrence than the average 2.5 times per chapter that the gifts were referenced in Acts 27 and 28;
- ❖ only once do two consecutive Chapters (8 and 9) mention the 9 gifts at the

14: Did Gifts Decline, then End?

same average rate of 2.5 times per chapter in Acts 27 and 28; and
- ❖ all other combinations of two chapters back to back in Chapters 2 through 21 have the 9 gifts mentioned less than the 2.5 times per chapter they are mentioned in Acts 27 and 28.

14:18   When we eliminate the chapters related to Paul's legal troubles, don't the numbers indicate there was no decline in the 9 Holy Spirit gifts? If not, why not?

14:19   Furthermore, isn't there an argument that the focus on Paul's legal issues warrant excluding those 5 chapters from any numerical analysis? There is no similar argument warranting exclusion of chapters between Chapters 2 to 21. On that basis, wouldn't it be even more appropriate to compare the average results of 1.0 times in Figure 14:2 to the 2.5 times in Figure 14:3? And doesn't that suggest, if we follow the Cessationist line of argument wherein frequency of mention is an indication of the frequency of occurrence, that signs and wonders were actually on the increase as Acts winds down?

CONSIDER THE TIME FRAMES INVOLVED

As mentioned, Paul's legal issues at Jerusalem and Caesarea are addressed in 6 chapters in Acts - the last part of Chapter 21, and Chapters 22 through 26. In Acts Chapters 22, 23 and 24, everything but the last 2 verses in Chapter 24 of Acts occurred in a matter of days. The time frames included the *'next day'* (Acts 22:30), the *'night immediately following'* and *'day'* (Acts 23:11-12)', the *'by night'* and *'next day'* (Acts 23:31-32), and *'some days'* (Acts 24:24).

- ❑ *Acts 22:30 But on **the next day**, wishing to know for certain why he had been accused by the Jews, he released him and ordered the chief priests and all the Council to assemble, and brought Paul down and set him before them.*
- ❑ *Acts 23:11 But on the **night immediately following**, the Lord stood at his side and said, "Take courage; for as you have solemnly witnessed to My cause at Jerusalem, so you must witness at Rome also."*
- ❑ *Acts 23:31 So the soldiers, in accordance with their orders, took Paul and brought him by night to Antipatris. 32 **But the next day**, leaving the horsemen to go on with him, they returned to the barracks.*
- ❑ *Acts 24:24 But **some days later** Felix arrived with Drusilla, his wife who was a Jewess, and sent for Paul and heard him speak about faith in Christ Jesus.*

14:20   Given that the proceedings of Paul's legal issues in Chapters 22- 24 took place over a matter of days, is that a long enough period to know whether or not the 9 Holy Spirit gifts were increasing, decreasing or had ceased?

The last 2 verses in Chapter 24 make a general reference to what happened in the following 2 years with Paul and Felix.

- ❑ *Acts 24:26 At the same time too, he was hoping that money would be given him by Paul; therefore he also used to send for him quite often and converse with him. 27 **But after two years had passed**, Felix was succeeded by Porcius Festus, and wishing to do the Jews a favor, Felix left Paul imprisoned.*

14:21   Does the lack of mention of the 9 Holy Spirit gifts while Paul was in

CEASED?

Caesarea for 2 years indicate the 9 gifts had ceased or were on a major decline during this time? If yes, how?

Chapters 25 and 26 review Paul's dealings with Festus and Agrippa which again take place over a relatively short period. Events in Chapter 25 take *'three days'* (Acts 25:1), *'eight or ten days'* (Acts 25:6), the *'next day'* (Acts 25:6), *'several days'* (Acts 25:13), *'many days'* (Acts 25:14), the *'next day'* (Acts 25:17) and *'tomorrow'* (Acts 25:22).

- *Acts 25:1 Festus then, having arrived in the province, **three days** later went up to Jerusalem from Caesarea.*
- *Acts 25:6 After he had spent **not more than eight or ten days among them**, he went down to Caesarea, and on **the next day** he took his seat on the tribunal and ordered Paul to be brought.*
- *Acts 25:13 Now when **several days** had elapsed, King Agrippa and Bernice arrived at Caesarea and paid their respects to Festus.*
- *Acts 25:14 While they were spending **many days** there ...*
- *Acts 25:17 So after they had assembled here, I did not delay, but on the **next day** took my seat on the tribunal ...*
- *Acts 25:22 Then Agrippa said to Festus, "I also would like to hear the man myself." "**Tomorrow**," he said, "you shall hear him."*
- *Acts 25:23 So, on the **next day** when Agrippa came together with Bernice ...*

Acts 26 is entirely based on Paul's defense ending with Agrippa and Festus discussing that Paul was probably innocent. Acts 26 covers one day.

- *Acts 26:1 Agrippa said to Paul, "You are permitted to speak ..." Then Paul ... proceeded to make his defense ... 30 The king ... and the governor and Bernice, and those who were sitting with them, 31 and when they had gone aside, they began talking to one another, saying, "This man is not doing anything worthy of death or imprisonment." 32 And Agrippa said to Festus, "This man might have been set free if he had not appealed to Caesar."*

165 verses deal with Paul's legal issues beginning with the last 14 verses in Acts 21 and through the following 5 chapters, Acts 22 through 26. A total of 163 verses cover events that occurred over a matter of days. By contrast, only 2 verses make general reference to what happened over the 2 years while Paul was in jail in Caesarea.

14:22 Does this combination of dramatically different verse counts and time periods make these chapters less than ideal when trying to identify whether or not gifts were continuing or decreasing? If not, how can they be used in a meaningful way?

Acts 2-21 Compared to Acts 22-28

Figures 14:2 and 14:3 compared the frequency that the Holy Spirit gifts were mentioned between Acts 2 to 21 in relation to Acts 22 to 28. A variation of this methodology involves looking at the frequency of mention of the gifts based on the number of years these chapters covered. Figure 14:4 shows the results.

14: Did Gifts Decline, then End?

- ❖ ~20-25 years passed between Acts 2 and Acts 21 when Paul's legal troubles began. To be conservative, I only use 20 years in my calculations to ensure the frequency per year calculations work in favor of the Cessationist camp. Based on 20 years and Holy Spirit gifts being referenced 20 times in these '20' years, that equates to ~1 time per year that the gifts per mentioned (point III in Figure 14:4).
- ❖ The period from Acts 22 to 28 covers ~3 years. Given the gifts were referenced 5 times, that equates to the gifts being mentioned ~1.7 times per year (point III Figure 14:4).
- ❖ Once again, no decline is observable.

Figure 14:4 Summary of Frequency of Occurrence

	Description of Analysis	Acts 2-21	Acts 22-28
I:	Average # of occurrences per chapter if count all the chapters	20 / 20 = 1.0	5/7 = .7
II:	Average # of occurrences per chapter if only count the chapters where the gifts are mentioned	20 / 12 = 1.7	5/2 = 2.5
III:	Average # of occurrences per year based on the number of years covered by chapters	20 / 20 = 1	5/3 = 1.7

Data for I: and II: are taken from Figures 14:2 and 14:3.

14:23 In the last chapters of Acts, once Paul's legal issues were resolved, I see additional documented instances of Holy Spirit moving through Paul in the form of signs and wonders. Miracles occur 5 times in Acts 27 and 28. I look at the frequency that the 9 gifts were mentioned after the events of Acts 19-21, and fail to see no decline. As a result, I struggle to see the validity of Cessationist claims that a decrease is occurring in the 9 Holy Spirit gifts as the book of Acts comes to a close. If you see a decrease, where is it?

THE 9 GIFTS: A CRITERION FOR APOSTLES

As discussed in Chapter 16, 1 of 3 criteria cited by Cessationists for a believer to be considered a true apostle was that they must have performed signs and wonders and miracles.

❑ *2 Corinthians 12:12 The **signs of a true apostle** were performed among you with all perseverance, by **signs and wonders and miracles**.*

As it relates to the apostles, Cessationists and Continuationists would typically agree that signs and wonders would have included the 9 Holy Spirit gifts such as prophecy and tongues. The Bible mentions specific details of individual healings through Peter and John (lame man) and to Peter alone (Dorcas/Tabitha). However, none of the other 10 original apostles are mentioned by name as having been used by God for a specific sign or wonder.

14:24 Does the fact only two of the original 12 apostles had signs and wonders attributed to them mean the remaining 10 apostles weren't involved in

CEASED?

them? Or does it simply mean the other 10 apostles were involved, but the Bible simply excludes the details?

Acts 5:12 makes a general comment indicating the other apostles were indeed involved in performing signs and wonders.
- ❏ *Acts 5:12 At the hands of the apostles many signs and wonders were taking place among the people; and they were all with one accord in Solomon's portico.*

GIFTS PERFORMED BY OTHER EARLY BELIEVERS

Mark 16:17 reveals that signs of a believer are casting out demons, speaking in new tongues, and laying hands on the sick who will recover.
- ❏ *Mark 16:17 **These signs will accompany those who have believed**: in My name they will **cast out demons**, they will speak with **new tongues**; 18 they will pick up serpents, and if they drink any deadly poison, it will not hurt them; **they will lay hands on the sick, and they will recover**.*

14:25 Some non-apostles such as Stephen and Philip's 4 daughters are referenced as doing miracles. But if such signs and wonders are a sign for all believers, and there were hundreds of thousands of believers by the time Acts 19 rolled around, wouldn't it be consistent with God's Word to see these hundreds of thousands of believers collectively performing hundreds of thousands of miracles regularly. If not, why not?

14:26 And wouldn't these multitudes of miracles be more examples of the 9 Holy Spirit gifts occurring, but not being documented in God's Word? If not, why not?

14:27 Would the lack of mention of 9 Holy Spirit gifts performed by these 10 apostles and other believers be consistent with Jesus's life where a tiny fraction of the miracles He performed are mentioned in the Bible?
- ❏ *John 21:25 And there are also many other things which Jesus did, which if they were written in detail, I suppose that even the world itself would not contain the books that would be written.*

14:28 In addition, would the lack of specific examples of the 9 Holy Spirit gifts by the 10 original apostles and other early believers also be consistent with the information presented in Chapters 1 and 18 where hundreds of individuals had prophesied, but whose prophecies are not described in the Bible?

WHAT ELSE DECLINED/CEASED?

If you still believe that considerable mention of the 9 Holy Spirit gifts should have been provided in the books written after Paul met with the 12 disciples in Ephesus in Acts 19 to substantiate the gifts were not declining and on their way to cessation, consider Figure 14:5 on the next page. Using www.Biblegateway.com's website and the NASB translation, I counted the number of books in which 10 different Biblical words appeared at least one time. To clarify, if a word such as 'hell' occurred 4 times

14: Did Gifts Decline, then End?

in the same book, I counted it as 1. If the word 'hell' occurred in 4 different books, I counted it as 4. The analysis excludes the 4 Gospels and Acts.

14:29 As an example, the English word 'cross' (# 7 in the table) appears in 5 of the 11 books (45%) written before Acts was written, but in only 2 of the 11 books (18%) written after Acts was written. If we use frequency of being mentioned as an indicator of importance, does the decline in mention of the cross mean its importance has declined?

14:30 Does the fact that mentions of love, faith and hope all declined also mean they were on the way to cessation? If not, why is the lack of mention of the 9 Holy Spirit gifts in the books written after Paul's trip to Ephesus reason to believe they ceased?

The above analysis of these words is very simplified. My stats professor's head would be shaking if he saw it. The analysis is merely used to show that, just because an issue isn't mentioned in some books, doesn't mean it's no longer relevant or has lesser value. If this analysis doesn't accomplish that limited goal and has been a waste of your time, well - coffee is on me if we meet.

Figure 14:5 Frequency of Some Key Biblical Words

Word	11 Books Written Before Acts	11 Books Written After Acts
1. Agapao love	9 / 82%	7 / 64%
2. Faith	11 / 100%	10 / 91%
3. Hope	10 / 91%	7 / 64%
4. Sin	10 / 91%	9 / 82%
5. Heaven	10 / 91%	5 / 45%
6. Salvation	6 / 55%	8 / 73%
7. Cross	5 / 45%	2 / 18%
8. Resurrection	3 / 27%	4 / 36%
9. Sanctification	5 / 45%	4 / 36%
10. Hell	2 / 18%	4 / 36%

SELF-FULFILLING DECLINE/CESSATION

Related to the Cessationist view that the 9 Holy Spirit gifts have ended is the argument there were no valid outpourings of Holy Spirit since the early church. Any outpourings of the Holy Spirit including Azusa Street in Los Angeles in the early 1900's are viewed by most Cessationists as fraudulent. I'm not adequately trained to be able to academically review the literature to determine if such reports of Holy Spirit outpourings are valid or not. And thus, I won't. However, I do ask four questions:

14:31 When we look at historical literature on any Biblical topic, how many of us have such strongly held views that we tend to ignore or otherwise minimize the value or credibility of any information that contradicts our belief on this issue?

14:32 Is a key reason many believers today don't see the 9 Holy Spirit gifts occurring in their lives or the lives of people with whom they associate because God caused them to cease, or because these believers choose not to seek them?

14:33 North American denominations including but not limited to the Reformed, 7th Day Adventist, Mennonite and Baptist churches have typically taught the 9 Holy Spirit gifts have ceased. However, given a belief system that the 9 Holy Spirit gifts have ceased, isn't it understandable that believers in these denominations wouldn't seek or expect such gifts? And if they don't seek the gifts, isn't it reasonable to expect that the gifts don't occur? In other words, is it a situation of *"we have not because we ask not"*?

- ❏ *James 4:2 You lust and do not have; so you commit murder. You are envious and cannot obtain; so you fight and quarrel.* ***You do not have because you do not ask.***
- ❏ *Matthew 21:22 And all things you ask in prayer, believing, you will receive.*
- ❏ *1 John 5:14 This is the confidence which we have before Him, that, **if we ask anything according to His will**, He hears us.*

14:34 And thus, isn't the Cessationist belief system prone to be self-fulfilling for believers who don't believe in the 9 Holy Spirit gifts? And is it even more likely to be self-fulfilling for those who view such activities as being heretical, or who criticize and mock other believers who are involved in these gifts?

CLOSING POINTS TO PONDER

There is no scripture specifically stating the Baptism of the Holy Spirit and 9 Holy Spirit gifts were to exist for a short time and/or for a select few individuals. If we look at the entire Bible, we find prophecies and other supernatural manifestations of Holy Spirit have been going on since creation. We see items such as prophecy occurring from Genesis through to Revelation. Cover to cover.

Chapter 14 analyzed the frequency of mention of the Holy Spirit gifts by comparing them to the number of Chapters involved and the time spans involved. As summarized in Figure 14:4, we see extensive evidence they have not declined or ended.

Figure 14:4 Summary of Frequency of Occurrence

	Description of Analysis	Acts 2-21	Acts 22-28
I:	Average # of occurrences per chapter if count all the chapters	20 / 20 = 1.0	5/7 = .7
II:	Average # of occurrences per chapter if only count the chapters where the gifts are mentioned	20 / 12 = 1.7	5/2 = 2.5
III:	Average # of occurrences per year based on the number of years covered by chapters	20 / 20 = 1	5/3 = 1.7

14:35 God hasn't changed. Why would God's demonstrations of power through

14: Did Gifts Decline, then End?

means such as the 9 Holy Spirit gifts end right after He had delivered His gift of salvation and was just starting to use His children to take the Good News to the entire world?

14:36 Many signs and wonders occurred but were not documented. Was one reason for this possibly because God is to receive all glory? And that documenting such signs and wonders might inappropriately elevate attention and credit to humans?

15

Did The Purposes of Signs and Wonders End?

INTRODUCTION
MY understanding of a commonly held Cessationist view is the two primary reasons the 9 Holy Spirit gifts/manifestations came into being were to help:
1. prove Jesus was the Messiah; and
2. powerfully launch the gospel.

With these two items fulfilled, many Cessationists now believe the 9 Holy Spirit gifts including prophecy and tongues are no longer needed. But is this so?

OTHER REASONS FOR SIGNS AND WONDERS
To begin, the two reasons given in the Introduction are not in dispute. But are there more key reasons for signs and wonders?

(1) Spreading the Gospel
Signs and wonders were beneficial in launching the gospel. But are they also beneficial to help spread the gospel after the initial launch? God's Word tells us that believers are called to share the Good News. Paul emphasized we need to share the gospel in words, but even moreso in power.

- ❑ *1 Corinthians 4:20* For the **kingdom of God does not consist in words but in power.**
- ❑ *Romans 15:18 For I will not presume to speak of anything except what Christ has accomplished through me, resulting in the obedience of the Gentiles by word and deed, 19* **in the power of signs and wonders, in the power of the Spirit**; *so that from Jerusalem and round about as far as Illyricum* **I have fully preached the gospel of Christ**.

15:1 Paul shared the gospel in words and power. Paul fully preached the gospel. If signs and wonders aren't evident in our lives today, are we able to fully preach the gospel? If yes, how can we do so when Paul couldn't?

When Peter explained events at Pentecost, he related them to Joel's prophecy.
- ❑ *Joel 2:28 "It will come about after this That I will pour out My Spirit on* **all mankind**; *And* **your sons and daughters** *will prophesy, Your old men will*

15: Did Purposes of Signs and Wonders End?

dream dreams, Your young men will see visions. 29 "Even on the **male and female servants** I will pour out My Spirit in those days.

15:2 Given there was an outpouring of the Holy Spirit at Samaria, at Cornelius's home with his family and friends, and again at Ephesus, doesn't that mean Joel's prophecy was not completely fulfilled at Pentecost?

15:3 Mark 16 has been quoted several times in **CEASED?**. Wouldn't it be beneficial today to have outpourings of Holy Spirit with tongues, casting out of demons and healings of bodies serving as signs for unbelievers?
- ❑ *Mark 16:16 He who has believed and has been baptized shall be saved; but he who has disbelieved shall be condemned. 17 These **signs will accompany those who have believed**: in My name they **will cast out demons**, they will **speak with new tongues**; 18 they will pick up serpents, and if they drink any deadly poison, it will not hurt them; they **will lay hands on the sick, and they will recover**.*

15:4 I can't find one scripture that says signs and wonders are only for launching the gospel and not for additional spreading of the gospel. If signs and wonders helped in the launch, wouldn't they help in the spreading too?

(2) Making it Easier to Share the Gospel

In Mark 2:12, God was glorified. In verse 13, we learn 'all the people' were coming to Jesus where He was teaching them.
- ❑ *Mark 2:12 And he got up and immediately picked up the pallet and went out in the sight of everyone, so that they were all amazed and were glorifying God, saying, "We have never seen anything like this." 13 And He went out again by the seashore; and **all the people were coming to Him**, and He was teaching them.*

15:5 Do you believe Jesus was able to teach so many people in large part because of the signs and wonders that He performed?

Consider what gave Herod the desire to see Jesus.
- ❑ *Luke 23:8 Now **Herod** was very glad when he saw Jesus; for he had wanted to see Him for a long time, **because he had been hearing about Him and was hoping to see some sign performed by Him**.*

Peter healed the lame man which allowed him to share the Good News of Jesus. The result of the miracle and Peter's teaching was many believed.
- ❑ *Acts 3:6 Then Peter said, "**Silver or gold I do not have, but what I do have I give to you. In the name of Jesus Christ the Nazarene - walk!**" ... 10 ... and **they were filled with wonder and amazement at what had happened to him**.*
- ❑ *Acts 4:4 **But many of those who had heard the message believed**; and the number of the men came to be about five thousand.*

Consider what happened when Aeneas and Tabitha were healed.

CEASED?

- *Acts 9:34 Peter said to him, "**Aeneas**, Jesus Christ heals you; get up and make your bed." Immediately he got up. 35 And **all who lived at Lydda and Sharon saw him, and they turned to the Lord**.*
- *Acts 9:36 Now in Joppa there was a disciple named **Tabitha** ... 37 And it happened at that time that **she fell sick and died**; and when they had washed her body, they laid it in an upper room ... 40 But Peter sent them all out and knelt down and prayed, and turning to the body, he said, "Tabitha, arise." And she opened her eyes, and when she saw Peter, she sat up. 41 And **he gave her his hand and raised her up; and calling the saints and widows, he presented her alive**. 42 **It became known all over Joppa, and many believed in the Lord**.*

The apostles performed many signs and wonders, events which impacted many.

- *Acts 5:12 At the hands of **the apostles many signs and wonders were taking place** among the people; and they were all with one accord in Solomon's portico. 13 But none of the rest dared to associate with them; however, the people held them in high esteem. 14 And **all the more believers in the Lord, multitudes of men and women, were constantly added** to their number, 15 to such an extent that they even **carried the sick out into the streets** and laid them on cots and pallets, so that when Peter came by at least his shadow might fall on any one of them. 16 Also the people from the cities in the vicinity of Jerusalem were coming together, bringing people who were **sick or afflicted with unclean spirits**, and **they were all being healed**.*

These signs and wonders got people's attention and were key in leading more people to Jesus.

15:6 As believers share the Good News of Jesus today, wouldn't their efforts be helped by signs and wonders of God?

15:7 Where are the most accessible opportunities to share the Good News with non-believers: in our churches or the streets, grocery stores, gas stations, offices and malls of our communities? And what would be the most impactful way of sharing the gospel:
   i. in love, words, works; or
   ii. in love, words, works and the power of God; or
   iii. sitting in a pew and waiting for the pastor(s) to do it?

15:8 Many ministries today do good works that impact many lives. They are an essential part of what the Body of Christ brings to the world. But which is more evident in the Bible:
   i. good works impacting people to consider Christ; or
   ii. signs and wonders impacting people to consider Christ?

I encourage you to take a minute and answer the following question:

15:9 *"If God used me to miraculously heal people, to give them supernatural wisdom or some other obviously supernatural gift that would bless them, would that make my witnessing not only more fruitful but also more exciting?"*

15: Did Purposes of Signs and Wonders End?

Testimony

After prayer one night, Lori and I stopped by our grocery store. On the way into the store, we paused and started to speak to a Sikh security guard. As I talked, Lori listened and prayed quietly. A couple of minutes later, she asked the guard what was wrong with his knee. He was startled and initially said there was nothing wrong. Lori briefly paused, then repeated her question. He somewhat reluctantly responded by telling us he hurt his knee about ten years before. Lori asked him if she could pray for his knee. He said yes in a somewhat hesitant and confused state. Lori prayed a simple "Knee, in the name of Jesus, pain go and knee be healed." He was instantly healed - and shocked. We told him Jesus loved him, and then felt led to leave him and go into the store. As we exited the store a short time later, he followed us to our truck. He wanted to give Lori praise which she quickly shut down, but it opened the door for Lori to more fully share the good news about Jesus. A week later, we came back to the store after another prayer meeting and talked to him again. His knee was still healed. Once again, he wanted to worship Lori which she gently but clearly refused, then took the opportunity to once again share Jesus with him.

15:10 Our respective Baptisms in the Holy Spirit have emboldened both Lori and I to share the Good News. It was God's power that gave this man indisputable, lasting and personalized evidence that Jesus is real and loves him.
   i. Sharing the gospel can often be a challenge, but wasn't sharing the gospel with this individual made much easier when God's power showed up?
   ii. And doesn't our experience with this man show why Paul talks about the importance of being able to share the gospel in words and power?
   iii. If God did such miracles through you, wouldn't that make sharing the gospel a different ball game than by using words only?

When Lori and I first started to share the gospel in power as well as words, we were nervous. Our mustard seeds were pretty small. We had both been Baptized in the Holy Spirit and Fire long before, but I think we had leaked quite a bit. We had a desire to see people healed, but we were unsure as to what to do. Fortunately, we found some people to teach us. We first looked at scriptures on authority and healing. We were then taught some words and one simple approach to pray for the sick. With that background knowledge, we then witnessed actual, real-time healings being done in our presence. No scam, no fakes. We watched, then went and did it. Jesus healed over 20 strangers through us in one weekend. And it was, and still is, so exciting to see Jesus heal people. It was life-changing. Until believers actually experience God healing someone through them, one can't really understand it. Even afterward, it's still a wonderful mystery.

(3) <u>Confirm God's Word</u>

In Acts 16, we learn the disciples *'went out and preached everywhere'* and the

word they preached was confirmed by the signs that followed.
- *Mark 16:19 So then, when the Lord Jesus had spoken to them, He was received up into heaven and sat down at the right hand of God. 20 And **they went out and preached everywhere**, while the Lord worked with them, and **confirmed the word by the signs that followed**.*
- *Hebrews 2:2 For if **the word** spoken through angels proved unalterable, and every transgression and disobedience received a just penalty, 3 how will we escape if we neglect so great a salvation? After it was at the first spoken through the Lord, **it was confirmed to us by those who heard, 4 God also testifying with them, both by signs and wonders and by various miracles and by gifts of the Holy Spirit** according to His own will.*

15:11 Would signs and wonders such as healing miracles help us today in confirming that God's Word is still true? And help refute the many lies that God's Word has been changed or is out of date?

God is so good. He gives us children access to incredible power. And when signs and wonders happen as per Hebrews 2:4, God is right there testifying with us.

(4) Glorify God

John 2:11 reveals that the miracles Jesus performed not only confirmed that Jesus was who He claimed to be, but also served to glorify God.
- *John 2:11 This beginning of His signs Jesus did in Cana of Galilee, and **manifested His glory**, and **His disciples believed** in Him.*
- *Mark 2:3 … bringing to Him a paralytic, carried by four men. 4 Being unable to get to Him because of the crowd, they removed the roof above Him; and when they had dug an opening, they let down the pallet on which the paralytic was lying. 5 And Jesus **seeing their faith** said to the paralytic, "Son, your sins are forgiven." … 10 But **so that you may know that the Son of Man has authority on earth to forgive sins**" -He said to the paralytic, 11 "I say to you, get up, pick up your pallet and go home." 12 And he got up and immediately picked up the pallet and went out in the sight of everyone, so **that they were all amazed and were glorifying God, saying, "We have never seen anything like this**."*

(5) Signs for Unbelievers and Believers

At Pentecost, Jesus baptized ~120 in the Holy Spirit and enabled them to speak in tongues in the form of earthly languages they didn't know.
- *Acts 2:7 They were **amazed and astonished**, saying, "Why, are not all these who are speaking Galileans? 8 And how is it that we each hear them in our own language to which we were born?*

At Pentecost, tongues were a sign for unbelievers. When Cornelius, family and friends were Baptized in the Holy Spirit and started speaking in tongues, it caused Peter to realize God had granted eternal life to both Gentiles and Jews. In this case, tongues were a sign for believers, namely Peter and the Jews that had joined Peter.
- *1 Corinthians 14:22 So then **tongues are for a sign**, not to those who believe*

15: Did Purposes of Signs and Wonders End?

but **to unbelievers**; but prophecy is for a sign, not to unbelievers but to those who believe.

There are many benefits of tongues, some of which are reviewed in Chapter 21.

(6) Demonstrate the Power of the Name of Jesus

The original apostles walked with Jesus for 3½ years. They heard His teachings. They witnessed many signs and wonders. People of that time knew about spiritual matters. They weren't surprised by demons, only that demons had to obey Christ.
- ❑ Luke 10:17 *The seventy returned with joy, saying, "Lord, even the demons are subject to us in Your name."*

The English phrase *'in my name'* comes from three Greek words *'eis'* [G1519], *'emos'* [G1699] and *'onoma'* [G3686].
- ❖ *'Eis'* is defined as *'into, unto, to, towards, for, among'.*
- ❖ *'Emos'* is defined as *'my, mine, etc.'*
- ❖ *'Onoma'* refers to name in different contexts including *'the name, i.e. for one's rank, authority, interests, pleasure, command, excellences, deeds'.*

Jesus's name matters. Everything in this universe was created through Him. All authority has been delegated to Jesus. And thus, understandably, His Name is not any name, but the Name above all names, the Name that carries all authority.
- ❑ Philippians 2:9 *For this reason also, God highly exalted Him, and bestowed on Him **the name which is above every name**,*

Jesus has all authority, authority which is associated with His Name. And as sent ones, as ambassadors for Christ, we have not only the right, but the responsibility, to use Jesus's Name to advance the Kingdom of God.
- ❑ Acts 4:7 *When they had placed them in the center, they began to inquire, "**By what power, or in what name, have you done this**?" 8 Then Peter, filled with the Holy Spirit, said to them, "Rulers and elders of the people, 9 if we are on trial today for a benefit done to a sick man, as to how this man has been made well, 10 let it be known to all of you and to all the people of Israel, **that by the name of Jesus Christ the Nazarene**, whom you crucified, whom God raised from the dead - by **this name this man stands here before you in good health**.*

In the world, we hear the phrase *'by the authority vested in ...'.* People generally recognize the authority they have, and the authority given to others. Given *'in the name'* refers to authority, when Peter healed the paralytic using the words *'in the name of Jesus'*, he effectively was saying *'by the authority Jesus has delegated to me'.*

After the rulers asked *'in what name was Peter able to heal the paralytic'*, Peter was very clear that it was by the name of Jesus Christ the Nazarene - by the authority of Jesus - that the man was healed. Signs and wonders demonstrated the authority of the Name of Jesus, the same authority we believers today have been given as well.

(7) Demonstrate and Use the Authority over Demons

Believers are told to heal the sick, cleanse the lepers and cast out demons. Scriptures show that the demonic world and sickness are sometimes related.

- *Job 2:7 Then **Satan** went out from the presence of the Lord and **smote Job with sore boils** from the sole of his foot to the crown of his head.*
- *Mark 9:25 ... Jesus ... rebuked the unclean spirit, saying to it, "**You deaf and mute spirit**, I command you, come out of him and do not enter him again."*
- *Luke 13:11 ... **for eighteen years had had a sickness caused by a spirit**; and she was bent double, and could not straighten up at all.*
- *Acts 5:16 Also the people from the cities in the vicinity of Jerusalem were coming together, **bringing people who were sick or afflicted with unclean spirits, and they were all being healed**.*

15:12 Would healings arising from casting out demons have significant impacts on people today, just as they did 2,000 years ago? If not, why not?

There are many diverse views on the issue of demons and whether or not believers today are to be involved. Chapter 23 provides some insights.

(8) Showed God's Compassion

Another purpose for signs and wonders is to show Jesus's compassion.

- *Matthew 14:14 When He went ashore, He saw a large crowd, and **felt compassion for them and healed** their sick.*

Father God sent Jesus, and just as Father God sent Jesus, Jesus is in turn sending us.

- *John 20:21 So Jesus said to them again, "Peace be with you; **as the Father has sent Me, I also send you**."*

15:13 As we go out as Jesus's sent ones, wouldn't miraculous healings occurring through believers still be considered an act of compassion today?

(9) Sending People a Message

Some of God's signs and wonders got people's attention. Peter prophesied to Ananias and Sapphira they would die because of their lies. They died very soon after these prophetic words were spoken. As a result of their death and the prophetic word being fulfilled - fear came over many.

- *Acts 5:1 But a man named Ananias, with his wife Sapphira, sold a piece of property, 2 and kept back some of the price for himself, with his wife's full knowledge, and bringing a portion of it, he laid it at the apostles' feet. 3 But Peter said, "Ananias, **why has Satan filled your heart to lie to the Holy Spirit** and to keep back some of the price of the land? ... 5 And as he heard these words, **Ananias fell down and breathed his last**; and great fear came over all who heard of it ... 10 And immediately **she fell at his feet and breathed her last**, and the young men came in and found her dead, and they carried her out and buried her beside her husband. 11 And **great fear came over the whole church, and over all who heard of these things**.*

15: Did Purposes of Signs and Wonders End?

(10) <u>Forewarning Believers</u>

❑ *Acts 11:28 One of them named Agabus stood up and began to indicate by the Spirit that there **would certainly be a great famine all over the world**. And this took place in the reign of Claudius.*

15:14 If a famine or major hardship such as a virus or market meltdown was coming that would greatly impact you and others you care about, wouldn't it be beneficial to hear that reality from God in advance?

15:15 If such warnings were given today by believers who have a credible track record in the prophetic, how many Christians would dismiss the warnings at first? And then when the prophecy came true, dismiss it or blame the individuals for not being clearer or not being bolder in proclaiming the prophecy? In other words, do many of us tend to deflect and blame others, as opposed to taking responsibility for our own shortcomings?

NOT EVERYBODY APPROVES

The Bible shows people didn't like the miracles and teachings of the apostles.

❑ *Acts 5:17 But the high priest rose up, along with all his associates (that is the sect of the Sadducees), and they were filled with jealousy.*

15:16 As people hear the truth about God in word, signs and wonders, would it be surprising to learn of some people responding negatively, even though they saw them firsthand or were told of miracles by people they trust?

15:17 Per Acts 5:17, are there elements of fear, discomfort or jealousy today by some who perhaps wish to have signs and wonders in their lives, but don't?

CLOSING POINTS TO PONDER

15:18 Signs and wonders were used for many reasons. Just like helping launch the gospel is one reason, wouldn't these other reasons still be beneficial today?
1. spreading the gospel;
2. making it easier to share the gospel;
3. confirming God's Word;
4. glorifying God;
5. providing signs for believers and unbelievers;
6. demonstrating the power of the Name of Jesus;
7. demonstrating and using authority over demons;
8. showing God's compassion;
9. getting people's attention; and
10. providing forewarnings.

15:19 Many who claim to be followers of Christ mock efforts by other believers who are involved in casting out demons or who try to raise someone from the dead. Let me ask: Don't scriptures state that all believers are to do those things? And if we haven't done it or even tried to do it - how are we in a position to tell someone else that they are not to do it, or how they are to do it, or that they're doing it wrong? If we have concerns, shouldn't we

CEASED?

pray that God will guide them, and give them revelation and wisdom?

15:20 When it comes to raising the dead, casting out demons or seeking instantaneous healing miracles, how many of us haven't seen these miracles occur in our lives simply because we haven't tried? In my case, I haven't yet tried to raise someone from the dead in person. And the result (which is due in part to my not fully trusting God, and not fully seeking God when situations occur), is that - no surprise - no one has come back to life from my prayers.

16

Did the 9 Gifts End with Specific Groups?

INTRODUCTION

ANOTHER reason some Cessationists believe the 9 Holy Spirit gifts/manifestations have ceased is because the need for the gifts ended once the gospel was taken to the 4 different gatherings at the 4 locations mentioned in Acts 1:8 (Group 1 - page 235).

❑ *Acts 1:8 but you will receive power when the Holy Spirit has come upon you; and you shall be My witnesses both in **Jerusalem**, and in all **Judea** and **Samaria**, and even **to the remotest part** of the earth."*

Other Cessationists believe the 9 Holy Spirit gifts/manifestations ended when the group of believers charged with launching the gospel had passed on and gone home to heaven. Opinions vary as to who exactly is in this group. Three commonly cited alternatives are as follows:

Group 2: original apostles + other believers gathered at Pentecost (page 240);
Group 3: original apostles + others at Pentecost + believers upon whom the apostles laid hands (page 241); and
Group 4: original apostles only (page 241).

GROUP 1
GATHERINGS IN 4 LOCATIONS PER ACTS 1:8

The 4 Groups and Baptisms in the Holy Spirit

As mentioned, a common Cessationist view is that after the gospel was taken to the first gathering at Pentecost and the 3 subsequent Pentecost-like gatherings, the 9 Holy Spirit gifts declined and ceased soon thereafter.

❑ *Acts 1:8 but you will receive power when the Holy Spirit has come upon you; and you shall be My witnesses both in **Jerusalem**, and in all **Judea** and **Samaria**, and even **to the remotest part** of the earth."*

This Cessationist view typically matches the gatherings and locations as follows:

Scriptures	Who's there	Location	# Believers
Acts 2	Jews	Jerusalem	~120
Acts 8	Samaritans	Samaria*	Unknown
Acts 10	God-fearers	Caesarea**	Cornelius, family, friends
Acts 19	Gentiles	Ephesus***	12

* Samaria was both a city and territory in Israel
** Caesarea was the capital of a Roman province in Judea
*** Ephesus was a city in ancient Greece/modern-day Turkey, the 'remotest part' on earth

Literal or Symbolic

Contradicting this Cessationist view is the belief that the 4 locations in Acts 1:8 - Jerusalem, Judea, Samaria, and the remotest part of the earth - are symbolic. One interpretation is the locations represent the following geographic areas:

Jerusalem: Take the gospel to the town or city where we live;
Judea: Take the gospel beyond our town or city into the rest of our state or province, and those states and provinces nearby;
Samaria: Take the gospel to the rest of our country; and
Remotest part: Take the gospel to the rest of the world, countries furthest away.

Remotest part of Earth

In the phrase *'the remotest part of the earth'*, the English word *'part'* is derived from the Greek Word *'eschatos'* [G2078] which Thayer defines in part as *'extreme, the last, the uttermost part, the end, of the earth'*. Strong's defines it in part as *'ends of, last, latter end, lowest, uttermost'*.

Acts 15 discusses Paul taking the gospel to the Thessalonians prior to his trip to Ephesus in Acts 19. When he did, the gospel did not come just in words, but *'in power and in the Holy Spirit'*.

- ❑ *1 Thessalonians 1:1 Paul and Silvanus and Timothy, To the church of the Thessalonians ... 5 for **our gospel** did not come to you in word only, but also **in power** and in the **Holy Spirit** and with full conviction...*

16:1 When Paul met the 12 disciples at Ephesus, his first priority was to ensure they were Baptized in the Holy Spirit. At Thessalonica, Paul took the gospel *'in power and in the Holy Spirit'*. Doesn't that indicate Paul likely taught the Thessalonians about the Baptism of the Holy Spirit and took steps to ensure they were Baptized in the Holy Spirit? If not, why not? Why would Paul not do at Thessalonica what was a priority to do at Ephesus?

16:2 Doesn't the fact the Thessalonians became imitators of Paul, Silvanus and Timothy and an example to other believers, indicate they were indeed Baptized in the Holy Spirit?

- ❑ *1 Thessalonians 1:6 You also **became imitators of us** and **of the Lord**, having received the word in much tribulation with the joy of the Holy Spirit, 7 so that **you became an example to all the believers** in Macedonia and in Achaia.*

16:3 If believers at Thessalonica were Baptized in the Holy Spirit, doesn't that represent an outpouring of the Holy Spirit wherein Holy Spirit came upon believers? If not, why not? How is it different than what happened at Ephesus?

16:4 Thessalonica was further away from Israel than Ephesus. On the basis an outpouring - a Baptism of the Holy Spirit - occurred at Thessalonica, doesn't that invalidate the argument Ephesus was the remotest part on earth to

16: Did Gifts End with Specific Groups?

receive an outpouring?

16:5 Rome was further away from Israel than Ephesus. There were many other cities, towns and/or inhabited regions further away from Israel than Rome. Ephesus was not the uttermost part of the earth when Jesus told His disciples they would be witnesses to the remotest part of the earth. As a result, doesn't this invalidate the argument that we should take the locations in Acts 1:8 literally, and instead validate the opposing argument that we should take the locations symbolically? If not, why not?

16:6 If we're to take Ephesus as being the symbolic representation of the remotest part, then shouldn't we take Jerusalem, Judea and Samaria symbolically as well?

16:7 And if we can't take all 4 locations in Acts 1:8 literally, doesn't that invalidate the Cessationist argument that the Baptism of the Holy Spirit ended when Pentecost and the 3 Pentecost-like events happened at these 4 locations?

After Ephesus

16:8 If the 9 Holy Spirit gifts/manifestations were no longer required once the Baptism in the Holy Spirit had occurred at the last location - Ephesus - why would they be needed in the future for anyone including the apostles? With this initial mission accomplished, wouldn't the apostles and others simply stop engaging in such signs and wonders? And do we just ignore the fact that Paul most likely made it a priority to have the believers at Thessalonica Baptized in the Holy Spirit, just as he had done for the 12 believers at Ephesus?

16:9 If there was no longer a need for the 9 Holy Spirit gifts, why would Paul encourage believers to pursue these gifts/manifestations after he met the 12 believers in Ephesus? Why would Paul even write of his sharing the gospel in both words and power in the form of supernatural gifts after his trip to Ephesus, if there was no need for such power?

- ❑ *1 Corinthians 14:1 Pursue love, yet **desire earnestly spiritual gifts**, but especially that you may **prophesy**.*
- ❑ *1 Corinthians 2:4 and my **message and my preaching** were **not in persuasive words of wisdom**, but **in demonstration of the Spirit and of power**,*
- ❑ *1 Corinthians 4:20 For the **kingdom of God does not consist in words but in power**.*

Fulfill Joel's Prophecy

Cessationists typically acknowledge that all of the believers at these 4 locations were Baptized in the Holy Spirit. But in so doing, the Cessationist argument goes on to say that the outpourings at these 4 locations collectively fulfilled the prophecy as per Joel 2:28-29.

- ❑ *Joel 2:28 "It will come about after this That I will pour out My Spirit on **all mankind**; And **your sons and daughters** will prophesy, Your old men will dream dreams, Your young men will see visions. 29 "Even on the **male and female servants** I will pour out My Spirit in those days.*

CEASED?

16:10 Do these 4 outpourings upon a small number of believers equate to:
  i. *'all mankind'*
  ii. + *'your sons and daughters'*
  iii. + *'old men (who) will dream dreams'*
  iv. + *'young men (who) will see visions'*
  v. + *'male and female servants (upon whom) I will pour out My Spirit'*?

16:11 If the groups at Jerusalem, Samaria, Caesarea and Ephesus do not refer to all believers including us believers living today, then who does *'all mankind, sons, daughters, old men, young men, male and female servants'* <u>specifically</u> refer to?

No Mention of Partial or Total Fulfillment

When the Baptisms in the Holy Spirit took place at Pentecost, Samaria, Cornelius's home, and Ephesus, no scripture mentions these baptisms were in partial or full fulfillment of the four locations in Acts 1:8.

16:12 If this baptism marked the fulfillment of part of the prophecy given in Acts 1:8, wouldn't it be reasonable to expect Peter (who spoke about the Joel prophecy) or another apostle to have noted every partial fulfillment as well as the final fulfillment in Ephesus?

4 Locations or 2 Groups

The Bible takes the gospel to two groups - the Jews and the Gentiles. When Cornelius, family and friends were Baptized in the Holy Spirit, Peter had them immediately water baptized.

❑ *Acts 10:46 For they were hearing them speaking with tongues and exalting God. Then Peter answered, 47 "Surely no one can refuse the water for these to be baptized who have received the Holy Spirit just as we did, can he?" 48 And he **<u>ordered them to be baptized in the name of Jesus Christ</u>**. Then they asked him to stay on for a few days.*

In Acts 11, Peter tells disciples in Jerusalem what happened to Cornelius, family and friends.

❑ *Acts 11:15 And as I began to speak, the Holy Spirit fell upon them just as He did upon us at the beginning. 16 And I remembered the word of the Lord, how He used to say, 'John baptized with water, but you will be baptized with the Holy Spirit.' 17 Therefore **<u>if God gave to them the same gift as He gave to us also after believing</u>** in the Lord Jesus Christ, who was I that I could stand in God's way?" 18 **<u>When they heard this, they quieted down and glorified God, saying, "Well then, God has granted to the Gentiles also the repentance that leads to life."</u>***

Judging by the responses, the major significance for Peter (verse 17) and the other Jerusalem disciples (verse 18) when it comes to the experiences of Cornelius, family and friends, was not the fact they had been Baptized in the Holy Spirit, or that they spoke in tongues, or that this was a partial fulfillment of Joel's prophecy. The major issue for them was God had given eternal life to Gentiles as well as Jews.

16: Did Gifts End with Specific Groups?

16:13 Given the disciples at Jerusalem were most amazed at God bringing the gift of eternal life to the Gentiles, does that suggest the key issue surrounding Acts 1:8 was not the fulfilling of Jesus's words they would be witnesses to the 4 different locations, but that there were 2 key groups for the outpouring of the Holy Spirit and God's gift of salvation - the Jews first and then the Gentiles?

Saul/Paul

Saul was Jewish. To align with the Cessationist argument, Saul would be considered part of the first location/gathering - the Jewish believers who were at Pentecost in Jerusalem. However, as Saul was born again after Pentecost and was Baptized in the Holy Spirit after Ananias laid his hands upon him in Damascus, Saul was not part of the Jewish gathering of believers at Pentecost.

16:14 Based on the argument that the 9 Holy Spirit gifts ceased with the gatherings at these 4 locations, does Saul's Baptism in the Holy Spirit mean there were 4 gatherings or groups ... plus one person? Is it ok to ignore exceptions? Or are exceptions allowed for those with special callings such as Paul had?

16:15 But if so, don't all believers have a special calling?

16:16 If the 9 Holy Spirit gifts ceased with the 4 gatherings plus perhaps Saul, are we to believe that none of the 3,000 who came to Christ at Pentecost were Baptized in the Holy Spirit, even though they had witnessed the disciples receiving this Baptism?

Baptized into one Body

This Cessationist argument that the gifts ended when the gospel was taken to the four groups is also partially based on the fact that all believers are baptized into one body.

❑ *1 Corinthians 12:12 For even as the body is one and yet has many members, and all the members of the body, though they are many, are one body, so also is Christ. 13 For **by one Spirit we were all baptized into one body**, whether Jews or Greeks, whether slaves or free, and we were all made to drink of one Spirit.*

The Cessationist argument goes on to say that i) since the outpouring of the Holy Spirit deals with power for witnessing, and ii) since this outpouring has occurred in full once the gospel had been taken to the groups, and iii) since all believers are baptized together into one body, all believers have the power of the Holy Spirit for witnessing and ministry. No further Baptisms of the Holy Spirit are required.

To backtrack just a bit, Jesus is the one who baptizes believers in the Baptism of the Holy Spirit (the 'upon' or 'epi') which is done to receive power to witness. Holy Spirit, on the other hand, is the one who baptizes believers into the Body of Christ when a person is born again and has Holy Spirit come in [en] them. While the in [en] experience is automatic and given to all believers when born again, the upon [epi] experience is not automatic and does not happen to all believers, and not always at the same time as they are born again. The in [en] and upon [epi] experiences are two different baptisms, two different experiences.

16:17   Isn't it a major problem when one baptism - the upon [epi] experience (Baptism in the Holy Spirit) - is merged/intermixed with a second baptism - the in [en] experience (Baptism in the Body of Christ) - and treated as the same baptism, when they aren't?

16:18   Without this merging of the two baptisms, the in [en] experience would not have the power that comes from the upon [epi] experience. Doesn't that invalidate the portion of the Cessationist argument 'because we're born again, we're fully empowered to be witnesses for Christ'?

16:19   If the in [en] experience is adequate for witnessing and we don't need the upon [epi] experience:
   i.   why did Jesus tell the group of believers in Acts 1 they were not ready to share the gospel but needed to wait for the Baptism of the Holy Spirit: and
   ii. why was it such a priority for John and Peter to go to Samaria to ensure those new believers were Baptized in the Holy Spirit; and
   iii. why was Paul's first concern for the 12 disciples at Ephesus to find out whether or not they had been Baptized in the Holy Spirit?

In Summary

There are several reasons to question the argument that the Baptism of the Holy Spirit and the associated Holy Spirit gifts ended with the 4 outpourings of the Holy Spirit at Pentecost, Samaria, Ephesus, and with Cornelius, family and friends.

- ❖ The last of the four locations, Ephesus, was not even close to being the remotest part of the earth that was populated at that time.
- ❖ Paul most likely had believers Baptized in the Holy Spirit at Thessalonica prior to his travels to Ephesus, a city that was also further away than Ephesus.
- ❖ The people at the 4 locations do not represent all the types/groups of people prophesied in Joel 2:28.
- ❖ Signs and wonders continued after the gospel was taken to these 4 locations.
- ❖ Treating the 'in' [en] and 'upon' [epi] baptisms as one baptism is flawed. They are two separate baptisms with different purposes.
- ❖ Treating the indwelling of the Holy Spirit when we're born again as being adequate empowerment for believers to be witnesses contradicts Biblical teaching where the upon [epi] experiences, not the 'in' [en] experience, is needed for witnessing.
- ❖ Jesus, Paul, and the original apostles notably John and Peter, all made it a priority to ensure believers were Baptized in the Holy Spirit.

GROUP 2
THOSE GATHERED AT PENTECOST

This second group serves as kind of a catch-all group because due to a lack of specifics as to who was at Pentecost, one can try to argue almost any person who performed a sign and wonder after Pentecost was Baptized in the Holy Spirit at Pentecost.

16:20   Saul/Paul, the 12 disciples at Ephesus, and Cornelius, friends and family

16: Did Gifts End with Specific Groups?

were all involved in signs and wonders including tongues and/or prophecy. However, none of them were Baptized in the Holy Spirit at Pentecost? As a result, don't these two facts invalidate this second group? If not, why not?

GROUP 3
THOSE UPON WHOM APOSTLES LAID HANDS

This expanded group includes the original apostles + others at Pentecost + believers upon whom believers at Pentecost laid hands. This third group includes, if you will, the last 'ordinary' believers to be involved in the 9 Holy Spirit gifts.

Consider the experiences of Cornelius, family and friends who began speaking in tongues immediately after being Baptized in the Holy Spirit.

- ❏ *Acts 10:44 While Peter was still speaking these words, the Holy Spirit fell upon all those who were listening to the message. 45 All the circumcised believers who came with Peter were amazed, because the gift of the Holy Spirit had been poured out on the Gentiles also. 46 For they were hearing them speaking with tongues and exalting God ...*

16:21 No believer laid hands upon Cornelius, family and friends when they were Baptized in the Holy Spirit and immediately began to speak in the gift of tongues. Given no one laid hands on them, doesn't that invalidate the argument that the Baptism of the Holy Spirit and the associated spiritual gifts ended with individuals upon whom the earliest believers laid hands?

16:22 I can't find a Biblical reason showing the gifts would end with those upon whom the apostles laid their hands. Thus, is the rationale for this group Biblical in nature, or is it an example of efforts to find a reason to support a belief, even if the reason is lacking?

GROUP 4
ORIGINAL APOSTLES

The 4th group that Cessationists commonly associate with the ending of the 9 Holy Spirit gifts/manifestations, and thus the Baptisms in the Holy Spirit, is the original group of apostles.

The original 12 apostles were as follows:

- ❏ *Mark 3:14 And **He appointed twelve**, so that they would be with Him and that He could send them out to preach, 15 and to have authority to cast out the demons. 16 And He appointed the twelve: [1] **Simon** (to whom He gave the name Peter), 17 and [2] **James**, the son of Zebedee, and [3] **John** the brother of James (to them He gave the name Boanerges, which means, "Sons of Thunder"); 18 and [4] **Andrew**, and [5] **Philip**, and [6] **Bartholomew**, and [7] **Matthew**, and [8] **Thomas**, and [9] **James** the son of Alphaeus, and [10] **Thaddaeus**, and [11] **Simon** the Zealot; 19 and [12] **Judas Iscariot**, who betrayed Him.*

A common Cessationist definition of a true apostle is that the person met 3 criteria:

CEASED?

1. witnessed with their own eyes the physical, resurrected Christ;
2. was personally/directly appointed by Christ; and
3. was able to work miracles such as tongues, healings and prophecy.

If the three criteria were Biblical, the criteria would hold up under any circumstance. Do they?

Criterion 1: Personally Witnessed the Resurrected Jesus

Paul was cited as an apostle in the Bible.
- *1 Corinthians 1:1* **Paul called to be an apostle of Jesus Christ** *through the will of God, and Sosthenes our brother,*
- *Romans 1:1* **Paul, a bond-servant of Christ Jesus, called as an apostle,** *set apart for the gospel of God,*

Paul was a devout man of God whose coming to Christ was unexpected.
- *Acts 9:3 As he was traveling, it happened that he was approaching Damascus, and* **suddenly a light from heaven flashed around him; 4 and he fell to the ground and heard a voice** *saying to him, "Saul, Saul, why are you persecuting Me?" 5 And he said, "Who are You, Lord?" And He said, "I am Jesus whom you are persecuting, 6 but get up and enter the city, and it will be told you what you must do." 7* **The men who traveled with him stood speechless, hearing the voice but seeing no one.** *8* **Saul got up from the ground, and though his eyes were open, he could see nothing**; *and leading him by the hand, they brought him into Damascus. 9 And he was three days without sight, and neither ate nor drank.*

Acts 9 revealed Paul experienced God's light, fell to the ground, heard a voice, and was blinded.

16:23 in Acts 9, I don't see any verse indicating Paul actually saw the physical, resurrected Jesus. If Paul didn't see the resurrected Christ, wouldn't that invalidate the first condition of being a true apostle which is the apostle must have personally seen the physical, resurrected Jesus?

In 1 Corinthians 15, Paul talks about the time Jesus appeared to him.
- *1 Corinthians 15:7 then He* **appeared to James**, *then to* **all the apostles**; *8 and last of all, as to one untimely born,* **He appeared to me also.**

16:24 In terms of Paul's description of Jesus appearing to him, the Greek word underlying the English word 'appeared' is 'optanomai' [G3700] which Strong's defines as '... appear, look, see, shew self'. One may argue the word appear indicates Paul saw the physical, resurrected Jesus. But given Luke's description in Acts 9, was it a situation where Jesus revealed himself to Paul through His presence - the light, His voice - but not in a physical way as He did to the other disciples on resurrection Sunday evening? Or was it a situation where the light coming from Jesus was so bright Paul couldn't see anything? And thus, is it highly likely that Paul did

16: Did Gifts End with Specific Groups?

not see the resurrected physical Jesus in the same way the other disciples saw Him on resurrection Sunday evening?

16:25 If in the future, the criterion for being a true apostle changes from physically seeing the resurrected Christ to something akin to experiencing the resurrected Christ, would that show a mindset that seeks truth first, or a mindset that first supports an existing view?

Criterion 2: Directly Appointed By Christ

In Acts 1, the original disciples voted for Judas's replacement. This individual, who turned out to be Matthias, was part of the initial ministry that launched the gospel.

❑ *Acts 1:14 These all with one mind were continually devoting themselves to prayer, **along with the women**, and **Mary the mother of Jesus**, and with His brothers. 15 At this time Peter stood up in the midst of the brethren (a gathering of about **one hundred and twenty persons** was there together), and said ... 23 So they put forward two men, Joseph called Barsabbas (who was also called Justus), and Matthias. ... 26 And they drew lots for them, and the lot fell to Matthias; and he **was added to the eleven apostles**.*

Matthias was added to the eleven making it twelve. Acts 6:2 confirms Matthias is one of the 12 which, to me, shows there is no distinction between Matthias and the other 11.

❑ *Acts 6:2 **So the twelve summoned the congregation** of the disciples and said, "It is not desirable for us to neglect the word of God in order to serve tables.*

16:26 Matthias was appointed by the ~120 disciples of Jesus. Does this invalidate the Cessationist definition where an apostle must be appointed by Jesus? If not, why not?

16:27 The voting to replace Judas was a significant event. Given some of the ~120 were women, and given it appears all of the ~120 were involved in voting to select Barsabbas or Matthias, does this again indicate women played a central role in the early church?

Criterion 3: Performed Signs and Wonders

The third criterion cited by Cessationists for being an apostle was they must have been able to perform signs and wonders.

❑ *2 Corinthians 12:12 The **signs of a true apostle** were performed among you with all perseverance, by **signs and wonders and miracles**.*

On that point, there is little debate as to whether or not the apostles were involved in signs and wonders. They were.

❑ *Acts 5:12 At the hands of the apostles many signs and wonders were taking place among the people; and they were all with one accord in Solomon's portico.*

A question arises, however, as to whether or not signs and wonders were limited

CEASED?

to these apostles. They weren't. Consider others who gathered at Pentecost and spoke in tongues, Stephen who did great wonders, Cornelius, family and friends who spoke in tongues, Agabus who prophesied, the 12 disciples at Ephesus who spoke in tongues and prophesied, and Philip's 4 virgin daughters who were prophetesses.

- ❑ *Acts 2:1 When the day of Pentecost had come, they were all together in one place ... 4 And they were **all filled** with the Holy Spirit and began to **speak with other tongues**, as the Spirit was giving them utterance.*
- ❑ *Acts 6:8 And Stephen, full of grace and power, was **performing great wonders and signs** among the people.*
- ❑ *Acts 10:24 .... Now **Cornelius** ... **his relatives and close friends**... 46 For they were hearing them **speaking with tongues** and exalting God ...*
- ❑ *Acts 11:27 Now at this time **some prophets** came down from Jerusalem to Antioch. 28 **One of them named Agabus** stood up and began to **indicate by the Spirit that there would certainly be a great famine all over the world**. And this took place in the reign of Claudius.*
- ❑ *Acts 19:1 ... Paul passed through the upper country and came to Ephesus, and found some disciples ... 6 And when Paul had laid his hands upon them, **the Holy Spirit came on them, and they began speaking with tongues and prophesying**. 7 There were in all about **twelve men**.*
- ❑ *Acts 21:8 On the next day we left and came to Caesarea, and entering the house of Philip the evangelist, who was one of the seven, we stayed with him. 9 Now this man had **four virgin daughters who were prophetesses**.*

16:28 Doesn't the fact that signs and wonders were done by many believers who were not apostles demonstrate that signs and wonders were for all believers, and not just a few - something that coincides with Mark 16.

- ❑ *Mark 16:17 These **signs will accompany those who have believed**: in My name they will **cast out demons**, they will **speak with new tongues**; 18 they will pick up serpents, and if they drink any deadly poison, it will not hurt them; **they will lay hands on the sick, and they will recover**.*

Who were all the Apostles

In regards to this 4th group being the ones with whom the 9 Holy Spirit gifts both started and ended, a common Cessationist view is the apostles consisted of the original 11 plus Matthias and, in some cases, Paul. But were there other apostles besides the 13?

James, the Brother of Jesus
- ❑ *Galatians 1:19 But I did not see any other of the apostles except James, the Lord's brother.*

16:29 Does Galatians 1:19 suggest James, the brother of Jesus, was also an apostle? Making it 14 apostles? If not, why not?

16: Did Gifts End with Specific Groups?

Barnabas
- ❑ *Acts 14:14 But when the **apostles Barnabas and Paul** heard of it, they tore their robes and rushed out into the crowd, crying out*
- 16:30 Does Acts 14:14 suggest Barnabas was also an apostle? Making it 15 apostles? If not, why not?
- 16:31 Some Cessationists say the original 11 apostles plus Matthias and Paul had a special calling that no other apostles had. Given Barnabas and James were also apostles, what evidence is there to suggest every one of the original 13 had a calling that was above Barnabas and James?

Other Possible Apostles

Were there were even more apostles in the early church? Consider the following:
- ❑ *1 Corinthians 15:4 and that He was buried, and that He was raised on the third day according to the Scriptures, 5 and that **He appeared to Cephas**, then to **the twelve**. 6 After **that He appeared to more than five hundred brethren at one time**, most of whom remain until now, but some have fallen asleep; 7 then He **appeared to James**, then to **all the apostles**; 8 and last of all, as to one untimely born, He **appeared to me also**. 9 For I am the least of the apostles, and not fit to be called an apostle, because I persecuted the church of God*
- 16:32 After His resurrection, Jesus appeared to Peter, to the 12, to more than 500, to James, to 'all *the apostles*' and finally - in one way or another - to Paul. If Jesus was seen by the twelve as per verse 5, then doesn't the phrase 'then to all the apostles' in verse 7 indicate there were other apostles other than the 12 (original 11 plus Matthias), James and Paul?

Timothy and Silvanus

Per the above, the English word *'apostle'* in the Greek is *'apostolos'* (G652) which Strong's defines in part as *'applied to other eminent Christian teachers - Barnabas, Timothy and Silvanus'.*
- ❑ *Romans 16:7 Greet Andronicus and Junias, my kinsmen and my fellow prisoners, who are outstanding among the **apostles**, who also were in Christ before me.*
- ❑ *1 Thessalonians 1:1 **Paul and Silvanus and Timothy**, To the church of the Thessalonians in God the Father and the Lord Jesus Christ: Grace to you and peace.*
- ❑ *Acts 14:14 But when the **apostles Barnabas and Paul** heard of it, they tore their robes and rushed out into the crowd, crying out*
- 16:33 Paul and Barnabas were clearly apostles. Why would Strong's definition of apostle include Timothy and Silvanus as being examples of apostles - if they weren't?

Andronicus and Junia
- ❑ *Romans 16:7 Greet **Andronicus and Junias**, my kinsmen and my fellow prisoners, **who are outstanding among the apostles**, who also were in Christ before me. [NASB]*

CEASED?

- *Romans 16:7 Greet Andronicus and Junia, my kinsmen and my fellow prisoners. They are **well known to the apostles**, and they were in Christ before me. [ESV]*
- *Romans 16:7 Greet Andronicus and Junias, my kinsmen and [once] my fellow prisoners, **who are held in high esteem in the estimation of the apostles**, and who were [believers] in Christ before me. [AMP]*

16:34   There is disagreement over whether Andronicus and Junia were apostles, or 'ordinary believers' who were well known by the apostles. Consider Junia who was female.
   i. If Junia was indeed an apostle that clearly shows the function of apostle did not cease with the original 12 apostles; and
   ii. If Junia was not an apostle, doesn't the fact she was highly regarded by the apostles provide more substantive evidence that women were centrally involved in the early church, and to be centrally involved in the Body of Christ going forward?

The 70

Before the cross, Jesus appointed 70 individuals who were sent, among other things, to heal the sick and tell the people that the kingdom of God is upon them.
- *Luke 10:1 Now after this **the Lord appointed seventy others**, and sent them in pairs ahead of Him to every city and place where He Himself was going to come … 3 **Go; behold, I send you out as lambs in the midst of wolves** … 9 **and heal those in it who are sick, and say to them**, 'The kingdom of God has come near to you.' … 17 The seventy returned with joy, saying, "Lord, **even the demons are subject to us in Your name**."*

Consider the similarity in their mandate to the mandate Jesus gave the original 12 apostles.
- *Mark 3:14 And **He appointed twelve**, so that they would be with Him and **that He could send them out to preach**, 15 and to have **authority to cast out the demons**.*

16:35   Would these 70 individuals, already experienced in serving as sent ones, be logical candidates to be sent out after the cross, potentially as apostles?

16:36   Would it be all that surprising if they were part of the group referred to as 'all the apostles' in 1 Corinthians 15:7?
- *1 Corinthians 15:4 and that He was buried, and that He was raised on the third day according to the Scriptures, 5 and that **He appeared to Cephas**, then to **the twelve**. 6 After that **He appeared to more than five hundred brethren at one time**, most of whom remain until now, but some have fallen asleep; 7 then He **appeared to James**, then to **all the apostles**;*

Other Considerations

Messengers/Sent Ones

The English word *'apostle'* in the Greek is *'apostolos'* (G652) meaning in part *'a delegate, messenger, one sent forth with orders a) specifically applying to the twelve*

16: Did Gifts End with Specific Groups?

apostles of Christ, and b) applied to other eminent Christian teachers - Barnabas, Timothy and Silvanus'.

Apostolos originates from the Greek word *'apostello'* [G649] which means in part *'1. to order (one) to go to a place appointed, to send away or dismiss.'*

An associated Greek word is *'apostole'* [G651] which means in part *'a sending away of the sending off of a fleet, consuls with an army'.*

The 3 Greek words all refer to a person who has been sent to accomplish a task. These Greek words were not only used in reference to the original disciples, but also to Paul, Barnabas and James, the brother of Jesus.

- *Acts 2:43 Everyone kept feeling a sense of awe; and many wonders and signs were taking place through the **apostles [apostolos G652]**.*
- *Acts 14:14 But when the **apostles [apostolos G652]** Barnabas and Paul heard of it, they tore their robes and rushed out into the crowd, crying out*
- *Galatians 1:19 But I did not see any other of the **apostles [apostolos G652]** except James, the Lord's brother.*

The related Greek Word *'apostello'* [G649] was also used in reference to the 70, Silas, Epaphroditus, Titus and those with Titus.

- *Luke 10:1 Now after this the Lord appointed seventy others, and **sent [apostello G649]** them ...*
- *Acts 15:27 "... we have **sent [apostello G649]** Judas and Silas, ...*
- *Philippians 2:25 But I thought it necessary to send to you **Epaphroditus**, my brother and fellow worker and fellow soldier, who is also your **messenger [apostolos G652]** and minister to my need;*
- *2 Corinthians 8:23 As for **Titus**, he is my partner and fellow worker among you; as for our brethren, they are **messengers [apostolos G652]** of the churches, a glory to Christ.*

When we look at the group labeled apostles, it is useful to consider them in the broader context as being part of the Body of Christ. Ephesians 4 advises of 5 functions - apostles, prophets, evangelists, pastors and teachers.

- *Ephesians 4:11 And He gave some as apostles, and some as **prophets, and some as evangelists, and some as pastors and teachers**, 12 for the **equipping of the saints for the work of service**, to the building up of the body of Christ; 13 **until we all attain to the unity of the faith, and of the knowledge of the Son of God**, to a mature man, to the measure of the stature] which belongs to the fullness of Christ.*

16:37 In terms of equipping the saints *'until we all attain to the unity of the faith and of the knowledge of the Word of God'*, was that finished by the time the original apostles died? If so, why are there so many indicators today showing this is not the case?

16:38 Do we have a need today for sent ones, some of whom would do things similar to the original apostles in sharing the gospel and helping plant churches, equip the saints and when necessary - bring correction? If not, am I missing something?

CEASED?

Would it be Inconsistent of God to Limit the Gifts
Let's go back to Cornelius, his family and friends.
- ❏ *Acts 10:24 On the following day he entered Caesarea. Now **Cornelius** was waiting for them and had called together **his relatives and close friends** … 44 While Peter was still speaking these words, the Holy Spirit fell upon all those who were listening to the message. 45 All the circumcised believers who came with Peter were amazed, because the gift of the Holy Spirit had been poured out on the Gentiles also. 46 For they were hearing them **speaking with tongues** and exalting God …*

16:39 Some Cessationists argue that signs and wonders ended with the gospel going to the Gentiles as represented by Cornelius, family and friends. If so, why would God give the gift of tongues to this small group and no other Gentiles, especially when supernatural miracles are to be signs that show one is a believer?
- ❏ *Mark 16:17 These signs will accompany those who have believed: in My name they will **cast out demons**, they will **speak with new tongues**; 18 they will pick up serpents, and if they drink any deadly poison, it will not hurt them; **they will lay hands on the sick, and they will recover**.*

Summary on Apostles

Cessationists commonly cite three criteria to be a true apostle:
1. the person witnessed with their own eyes the physical, resurrected Christ;
    - Scriptures suggest Paul did not actually see the resurrected Christ, but was acutely aware of His presence.
2. the person was personally / directly appointed by Christ:
    - Matthias was not appointed by Jesus but by the believers gathered in Acts 1;
    - There is no certainty one way or another that Jesus personally appointed apostles such as Barnabas or James or appointed them in the same way He appointed the original 11 or Paul.
3. the person was involved in gifts such as tongues, healings and prophecy:
    - The original apostles were certainly involved in the Holy Spirit gifts, but so were many other non-apostles. Thus, signs and wonders do not make an apostle unique.

The Cessationist argument holds that the apostles included the original 11 plus Matthias and Paul. Scriptures indicate otherwise.
1. James, a brother of Jesus, and Barnabas weren't part of the original apostles, but were clearly cited as apostles.
2. A reference to *'all the apostles'* in 1 Corinthians 15:7 indicates there could have been other apostles including Timothy, Silvanus, Andronicus, Junia, the 70, Judas, Silas, Epaphroditus and Titus.

The Cessationist argument also holds that signs and wonders in the form of the 9 Holy Spirit gifts ended with the apostles. However, as cited many times, scriptures

16: Did Gifts End with Specific Groups?

show many believers other than the apostles performed signs and wonders. These include the others who were part of the ~120 gathered at Pentecost, Cornelius and his family and friends, Stephen, Agabus, the 12 disciples at Ephesus, and Philip's 4 daughters.

The Bible also makes it clear that signs and wonders are to be the norm, and an indication that a person is a follower of Christ.

- ❏ *Matthew 10:8 **Heal the sick, raise the dead, cleanse the lepers, cast out demons**. Freely you received, freely give.*
- ❏ *Mark 16:17 **These signs will accompany those who have believed**: ... **cast out demons**, ... **speak with new tongues**; 18 ... **they will lay hands on the sick, and they will recover**.*
- ❏ *1 Corinthians 14:1 Pursue love, **yet desire earnestly spiritual gifts**, but **especially that you may prophesy**.*

Apostolic Gifts

16:40 Because the 9 Holy Spirit gifts/manifestations were viewed by some believers as being limited to the original apostles, these 9 Holy Spirit gifts are often referred to as the *'apostolic gifts'*. However, given some of these 9 gifts were active in many other believers besides apostles - Stephen, 4 daughters who prophesied, Cornelius, family and friends, Agabus, and the 12 believers at Ephesus - isn't it inaccurate to label them as apostolic gifts?

CLOSING POINTS TO PONDER

16:41 Chapter 16 of **CEASED?** addressed 4 groups that are commonly cited by different Cessationists as being the last disciples to be used by God for signs and wonders. Evidence shows each group was not the last involved in the 9 Holy Spirit gifts. Each of the 3 criteria cited by Cessationists as required to be a true apostle is lacking. Other scriptures indicate all believers are to be involved in gifts. If you still believe gifts such as prophecy and tongues have ceased - how much of your view is based on loyalty to your beliefs versus what the Bible teaches?

Some individuals believe the 9 Holy Spirit gifts are still relevant, but keep their views private. Some speak in tongues but can't share their use of this gift for fear of being shunned, persecuted, and in the case of church employees, fear of losing one's job. I wonder - how extensive is this issue? I have no data, but I suspect it may be fairly significant. Survey anyone?

17

If the 9 Gifts Ceased, What Else Ceased?

INTRODUCTION

CHAPTER 17 focuses on the issue: If the 9 Holy Spirit gifts such as prophecy and tongues, and roles such as prophets and apostles have ceased, what else has ceased?

- *1 Corinthians 12:8 For to one is given the **word of wisdom** through the Spirit, and to another the **word of knowledge** according to the same Spirit; 9 to another **faith** by the same Spirit, and to another **gifts of healing** by the one Spirit, 10 and to another the effecting of **miracles**, and to another **prophecy**, and to another the **distinguishing of spirits**, to another various kinds of **tongues**, and to another the **interpretation of tongues**.*

Jesus's Gifts: Now a 3-Fold, not a 5-Fold Ministry?

As mentioned before, Ephesians 4 discusses 5 functions often called the 5-fold ministry. A key role of these functions is to equip the saints for service and to build up the Body of Christ.

- *Ephesians 4:11 And He gave some as **apostles**, and some as **prophets**, and some as **evangelists**, and some as **pastors** and **teachers**, 12 **for the equipping of the saints** for the **work of service**, to the **building up of the body of Christ**;*

17:1 If the functions/positions of prophet and apostle have ceased, why would the other 3 functions of evangelists, pastors and teachers continue?

17:2 Ephesians was written in ~60-62 AD, ~30 years after the cross. By that time, there were even more Christians than when Paul visited Ephesus in ~52-55AD. Why would Paul speak about these functions if they were going to be phased out in a few years when the original apostles died? Or, if some of the functions were temporary, why wouldn't he at least clarify which functions were temporary and which were permanent?

17:3 Without prophets and apostles, how can today's saints be adequately equipped or the Body of Christ adequately built up?

What Other Gifts Ceased

Consider 1 Corinthians 12:28.

- *1 Corinthians 12:28 And God has appointed in the church, first **apostles**,*

17: If Gifts Ceased, What Else Ceased?

second **_prophets_**, third **_teachers,_** then **_miracles_**, then **_gifts of healings_**, **_helps, administrations_**, various kinds of **_tongues_**.

17:4 Again, if the functions/positions of prophet and apostle have ceased, doesn't that mean other items such as teachers, helps, and administrations also ceased? If not, why not?

17:5 Further, if functions of prophets and apostles and the 9 Holy Spirit gifts were going to cease in the very near future, why wouldn't 1 Corinthians 12:28 exclude apostles, prophets, miracles and gifts of healings and only include things that wouldn't be ceasing, namely teachers, miracles, helps and administrations?

And how about Romans 12 which speaks of the Father's gifts.
- ❑ *Romans 12:6 Since we have gifts that differ according to the grace given to us, each of us is to exercise them accordingly: if **prophecy**, according to the proportion of his faith; 7 if **service**, in his serving; or he who **teaches**, in his teaching; 8 or he who **exhorts**, in his exhortation; he who **gives**, with liberality; he who **leads**, with diligence; he who shows **mercy**, with cheerfulness.*

17:6 Once again, if the 9 Holy Spirit gifts including prophecy have ceased, why wouldn't issues such as service, teaching, exhortation, giving, leading and showing mercy have also ceased? And why would prophecy be mentioned if it was going to cease very soon?

17:7 Some Cessationists say 'normative' gifts (love, good works etc.) continue but 'non-normative' gifts - the supernatural gifts - such as prophecy, words of knowledge, healings and tongues have ceased. But isn't everything about God supernatural? And as children of God who are sent ones, who are told to heal the sick, to cast out demons and to raise the dead, shouldn't the supernatural be a regular occurrence in our lives?

17:8 If the supernatural 'non-normative' gifts were a daily occurrence in our lives as we co-labor with God, wouldn't the supernatural become normative, and thus show we're a believer?
- ❑ *Mark 16:17* **_These signs will accompany those who have believed_**: ... **_cast out demons_**, ... **_speak with new tongues_**; 18 ... **_they will lay hands on the sick, and they will recover_**.

17:9 Whose definition of normative should we use - God's, or man's?

Special Knowledge

Finally consider:
- ❑ *1 Corinthians 13:8 Love never fails; but if there **_are gifts of prophecy, they will be done away_**; if **_there are tongues, they will cease_**; if **_there is knowledge, it will be done away_**.*

17:10 If gifts such as prophecy and tongues have already ceased, wouldn't knowledge have ceased by now as well? If not, why not?

17:11 There is no question that one day, gifts of prophecy and tongues and human knowledge as we understand these items today, will all cease when we are home, and living face to face with Jesus. The love of God and the presence of God, however, will never cease. Isn't this the point that Paul was trying to make in 1 Corinthians 13:8?

Some Cessationists argue that the knowledge that has gone away in 1 Corinthians 13:8 refers to *'special knowledge'*. Interestingly, Bible translators didn't write it that way. The English word *'knowledge'* is derived from the Greek word *'gnosis'* [G1108] which means in part as 'general knowledge of the Christian religion, things lawful and unlawful for Christians, moral wisdom'.

17:12 When I consider the above definition of 'knowledge', I struggle to see the specifics of the 'special knowledge' that have ceased. If you believe such special knowledge has ceased, can you provide more specific details on the 'special' nature of this knowledge, rather than just making a general claim that special knowledge has ceased?

CLOSING POINT TO PONDER

17:13 Chapter 2 of **CEASED?** provided lists of the Father God's gifts, Jesus's gifts and Holy Spirit's gifts. If the 9 Holy Spirit gifts such as prophecy and tongues have ceased, and roles such as prophets and apostles have ceased, and these gifts and functions are all listed and intermingled with other gifts and functions, the core issue raised in Chapter 17 is why haven't all the functions and gifts ceased? And why haven't these and other functions ceased in churches that loudly support Cessationism? Especially the gift of giving?

❑ *Romans 12:6 Since we have gifts that differ according to the grace given to us, each of us is to exercise them accordingly: if prophecy, according to the proportion of his faith; 7 if service, in his serving; or he who teaches, in his teaching; 8 or he who exhorts, in his exhortation; he who **gives**, with liberality; he who leads, with diligence; he who shows mercy, with cheerfulness.*

18

Is All Divine Revelation in the Bible?

INTRODUCTION

A central reason why many Cessationists believe the Baptism in the Holy Spirit and the 9 Holy Spirit gifts have ceased is because all necessary divine revelation is in the Bible. Nothing more from God is required. No more prophecies or messages from God are needed. Chapter 1 briefly touched on the topic when we tested our hearts. Chapter 18 expands on this issue further.

Divine Revelation and Prophecy

Divine revelation is God's supernatural revealing of information to one or more persons. The 66 books of the Bible are filled with divine revelation. Even though ~40 men wrote the Bible, the contents are inspired by God through Holy Spirit.

- ❑ *2 Timothy 3:16 All Scripture is inspired by God and profitable for teaching, for reproof, for correction, for training in righteousness; 17 so that the man of God may be adequate, equipped for every good work.*

Per Chapter 2, prophecies are divine revelations given to individuals by God for the benefit of that person, for one or more other persons, or for all of humanity. Prophecies often encourage, uplift and comfort. However, some prophecies in the Old Testament show prophecies can also be negative. Some believers think prophecies can give direction to a person; other believers think the opposite. I'm not that well versed in this area, and thus will abstain on that particular issue.

- ❑ *1 Corinthians 14:3 But **one who prophesies** speaks to men for edification and exhortation and consolation.*

Prophecies not in the Bible

As mentioned, many Cessationists believe that all divine revelation is found in the Bible. If this is your belief, let me ask a few questions.

18:1 The Bible contains many prophecies. Do you consider all prophecies given by God, and spoken and/or written down by individuals, to be divine revelation? If not, why not?

Consider 2 Peter 1:21.

- ❑ *2 Peter 1:20 But know this first of all, that no prophecy of Scripture is a matter* *of one's own interpretation, 21 for **no prophecy was ever made by an act of human** will, **but men moved by the Holy Spirit spoke from God.***

18:2 If prophecies from God are part of God's divine revelation and all divine revelation is in the Bible, doesn't it follow that one or more details of all prophecies from God will be found in either the Old Testament or the New Testament? If not, why not?

Women and Prophecies

Chapter 1 discussed Philip's four virgin daughters who prophesied.
- *Acts 21:9 Now this man had four virgin daughters who were prophetesses.*

Question number 1:12 reads as follows: *"I can't find details of a single prophecy of these 4 women. On the basis that the specifics of the prophecies given through these 4 women aren't in the Bible, does this mean the Bible contains some but not all of God's divine revelation? If not, why not?"*

Consider other implications presented by these 4 women who prophesied.

18:3 Given these 4 individuals who prophesied are women and were not part of the original group of apostles, doesn't this mean the gift of prophecy was not limited to the original apostle, but was also given by Holy Spirit to other individuals - both male and female?

18:4 To clarify, if these 4 women prophesied, does this mean God's use of people to deliver prophecies – divine revelations - did not cease with the original male apostles? And thus, doesn't that suggest that God continues to give divine revelations today not only through males, but also through females?

Here are scriptures referring to 5 other women identified as prophetesses.
- *Exodus 15:20 **Miriam the prophetess**, Aaron's sister....*
- *Judges 4:4 Now **Deborah, a prophetess**, the wife of Lappidoth ...*
- *2 Kings 22:14 So Hilkiah ... went to **Huldah the prophetess** ...*
- *Isaiah 8:3 So I **approached the prophetess** ...*
- *Luke 2:36 And there was a **prophetess, Anna** the daughter of Phanuel ...*

Here are ~585 individuals – including 15 after the cross - who prophesied or who were referred to as prophets, but the details of whose prophecies aren't in God's Word.
- *Numbers 11:25 Then the Lord came ... and He took of the Spirit who was upon him and placed Him upon the **seventy elders**. And when the Spirit rested upon them, **they prophesied**. But they did not do it again.*
- *1 Kings 18:4 for when Jezebel destroyed the prophets of the Lord, Obadiah took a **hundred prophets** and hid them by fifties in a cave ...*
- *1 Kings 22:6 ... **prophets together, about four hundred men** ...*
- *Acts 15:32 **Judas** and **Silas**, also being prophets themselves ...*
- *Acts 19:1 ... Paul ... came to Ephesus ... 6 ... the Holy Spirit came on them ... speaking with tongues **and prophesying**. 7 ... **about twelve men**.*
- *Titus 1:12 One of themselves, **a prophet of their own**, said, "Cretans are*

18: Is All Divine Revelation in the Bible?

always liars, evil beasts, lazy gluttons."

Chapter 1 raised the issue of women's heads being uncovered while prophesying.
- *1 Corinthians 11:4 Every **man** who has something on his head while **praying or prophesying** disgraces his head. 5 But every **woman** who has her head uncovered while **praying or prophesying** disgraces her head, for she is one and the same as the woman whose head is shaved.*

Let my repeat question 1:10.

1:10 If women were to wear head coverings when they prophesied, doesn't this mean that women were expected to prophesy?

18:6 As per various scriptures mentioned earlier, several women prophesied both before and after the cross. Doesn't that suggest God will continue to give prophecies through women today as well as through men? If not, why not?

18:7 And given Philip's 4 daughters who prophesied were virgins, and thus in their teenage or early twenties, doesn't that suggest that God may be giving prophetic words to younger believers as well?

Others who Prophesied

The following scriptures refer to unspecified numbers of individuals who prophesied. Note that 1 Kings 18:4 is referred to both above and below. 1 Kings 18 above relates to 100 prophets hid by Obadiah; the reference below relates to an untold number of prophets destroyed by Jezebel.
- *1 Samuel 10:10 ... **a group of prophets** ...*
- *1 Samuel 19:20 ... the **messengers of Saul**; and **they also prophesied**.*
- *1 Kings 18:4 for when Jezebel **destroyed the prophets** of the Lord, Obadiah took a hundred prophets and hid them by fifties in a cave ...*
- *2 Kings 2:5 The **sons of the prophets who were at Jericho** ...*
- *Acts 11:27 Now at this time **some prophets** came down from Jerusalem to Antioch. 28 One of them named Agabus stood up ...*

Several other individuals are mentioned as being prophets or who had prophesied, but the details of their prophecies aren't in the Bible. King Saul was one of them.
- *1 Samuel 19:24 He [i.e. King Saul] also stripped off his clothes, and he too **prophesied before Samuel** and lay down naked all that day and all that night. Therefore they say, "**Is Saul also among the prophets?**"*

18:8 If details of prophecies of hundreds - perhaps thousands - of individuals aren't recorded in the Bible, doesn't this mean not all of God's revelations are in the Bible? If not, how do we explain away this issue?

A Big Assumption?

18:9 There are hundreds of specific prophecies from many different prophets in the Bible. A common assumption is that every single prophecy given by every single one of these individuals is contained in the Bible. However, if prophecies of hundreds of individuals who prophesied aren't in the Bible, does this mean - for individuals who have the specifics of at least one prophecy recorded in the Bible - that they may have had other prophecies that aren't mentioned in the Bible? In other words, is it potentially a false assumption to believe that every single prophecy of prophets such as Isaiah, Jeremiah, Ezekiel, Daniel, Hosea, Joel, Amos, Obadiah, Jonah, Micah, Nahum, Habakkuk, Zephaniah, Haggai, Zechariah, and Malachi can be found in the Bible?

18:10   And if so, would it be surprising if, one day, we learn there were hundreds, even thousands of prophecies given, but not recorded in the Bible?

18:11   Again I ask, doesn't the evidence show not all prophecies are in the Bible? As a result, isn't the argument that prophecies received from God today are automatically invalid because all divine revelation is found in God's word - an argument without merit?

Tongues and Interpretation of Tongues

Cessationists believe the 9 Holy Spirit gifts in 1 Corinthians 12 have ceased. Two of the 9 gifts are tongues and interpretation of tongues.

- *1 Corinthians 14:1 Pursue love, yet **desire earnestly spiritual gifts**, but **especially** that you may **prophesy** ... 5 Now I wish that you all spoke in tongues, but even more that you would prophesy; and **greater is one who prophesies** than one who speaks in tongues, **unless he interprets**, so that the church may receive edifying.*

18:12   We see the gift of tongues occurring in the early church at Pentecost *(Acts 2)*, with Cornelius, family and friends *(Acts 10)*, and again with the 12 disciples at Ephesus *(Acts 19)*. Paul mentioned he spoke in tongues *(1 Corinthians 14)*. If the gift of tongues was being used, is it reasonable to expect the gift of interpretation of tongues was also used at that time? Or did God create this gift, but then decided not to give it to anyone?

18:13   On the basis a tongue and its corresponding interpretation constitute a form of divine revelation, does the fact that no details of even one interpretation of a tongue are found in God's Word show once again that not all of God's divine revelations are in the Bible?

Are additional Prophetic Revelations from God Possible

18:14   God doesn't change. Prophets were vital in the Old Testament and the New Testament including John in the book of Revelation. Wouldn't it be consistent of God to continue using prophets to reveal important information impacting the lives of people today?

- *Amos 3:7 Surely the Lord God does nothing Unless He reveals His secret counsel To His servants the prophets.*
- *Luke 24:25 And He said to them, "O foolish men and slow of heart to believe in all that the prophets have spoken!*
- *Revelation 1:3 Blessed is he who reads and those who hear the words of the*

18: Is All Divine Revelation in the Bible?

prophecy, and heed the things which are written in it; for the time is near.

18:15 Holy Spirit is inside us when we're born again and communicates to us. Is this a form of divine revelation? If it is, and if all divine revelation is in the Bible, wouldn't that mean one or more details of virtually every discussion between God and humans would be in the Bible? If not, why not?

18:16 If some of these discussions between God and human beings are not a form of divine revelation, doesn't that mean many communications could have taken place in ancient times between people and God that weren't recorded in the Bible? And doesn't that mean such discussions between God and people could also be going on today?

18:17 In terms of so-called prophecies given today, if the message is aligned with God's Word or does not contradict God's Word, then it might be from God. But even then, it might not be. Isn't that why we should seek God's help to identify what spirit any prophetic word is coming from – to know for sure whether it's from Holy Spirit, a demonic spirit, or the speaker's own spirit/soul?

- *1 Thessalonians 5:19 Do not quench the Spirit; 20 do not despise prophetic utterances. 21 But examine everything carefully; hold fast to that which is good;*
- *1 John 4:1 Beloved, do not believe every spirit, but test the spirits to see whether they are from God, because many false prophets have gone out into the world.*

18:18 In terms of true and false prophets:
   i. If there are false prophets, doesn't that mean there are true prophets?
   ii. If there were only false prophets, why would the Bible encourage believers to listen to any prophet, or to distinguish between true and false prophets? Why wouldn't God's Word say there will be no more prophets, and anyone claiming to be a prophet is automatically a false prophet?

Alignment, not Contradiction

As indicated, we can receive a prophetic word from either a false prophet or a true prophet. One way that God helps us know if such words are of God or not, is through His Word. If a prophetic word does not align with the Bible, or contradicts the Bible, we know for sure it is not of God.

- *1 Thessalonians 5:21 But **examine everything carefully**; **hold fast to that which is good**;*
- *Romans 12:2 And do not be conformed to this world, but be transformed by the renewing of your mind, so **that you may prove what the will of God is**, that which is good and acceptable and perfect.*

Prophetic Word for Myself

In early 2019, a pastor from Oregon was speaking near where we live. As he was preaching, he walked over to where I was seated and started to speak directly to

CEASED?

me. He told me God was reversing some of the decay in my body and that I would be writing. I never thought much of it. 3 months later, a short while after an extremely frustrating conversation, I stood up and told Lori: "That's it; I'm going to write a book." Me. No Bible school. Born again only a few years earlier. Writing a book on a topic where there is no shortage of teachings. Really? A few months later, my annual checkup showed my ever-rising cholesterol was down to where it was 3 years prior. I told my Muslim cardiologist Jesus was healing me. He didn't know what to think. I did.

I received a prophetic word that blessed me. God sees me and used another person to speak to me. Prophetic words come in various forms. Many times, they are for more than one person. Other times, prophetic words are personal and for only one individual.

Can we Personally Hear from God

In Chapter 5, we saw how Holy Spirit is **with** [para in the Greek] a person as He draws them to Jesus. Chapters 6 and 8 reviewed how Holy Spirit comes **in** [en in the Greek] us when we are born again. Chapters 7 and 8 reviewed the Baptism of the Holy Spirit where Holy Spirit comes **upon** [epi in the Greek] a believer to receive power to be witnesses.

- ❑ *John 14:17 that is the Spirit of truth, whom the world cannot receive, because it does not see Him or know Him, but you know Him because He abides **with [para]** you and will be **in [en]** you.*
- ❑ *Acts 1:8 but you will receive power when the Holy Spirit has come **upon [epi]** you; and **you shall be My witnesses** both in Jerusalem, and in all Judea and Samaria, and even to the remotest part of the earth."*

As believers, Holy Spirit will lead us.
- ❑ *Romans 8:14 For **all who are being led by the Spirit of God**, these are sons of God.*

Jesus also tells us believers will know His voice.
- ❑ *John 10:27 My sheep hear My voice, and I know them, and they follow Me;*

18:19 If we are believers, and God Almighty is in [en] us and leading us, how can we not sense His presence from time to time? And shouldn't we be able to hear God's voice today, in whatever form that may be - even a still, small voice? If not, why not?

18:20 If we don't hear from Holy Spirit when He is in [en] us, then is it fair to ask 'what's the point of Holy Spirit coming in [en] us?'

18:21 And if we don't 'hear' Holy Spirit when He is in [en] us, are we only being led by what we believe God's Word says? And how do we actually do that on the many issues of life that are not specifically addressed in the Bible?

18:22 God spoke with Adam and Eve in the garden. God spoke directly with many others in the Bible. Did God all of a sudden stop talking to people on earth once John finished writing Revelation? If God did stop speaking, wouldn't that contradict the teaching that God does not change?

18: Is All Divine Revelation in the Bible?

18:23 When God's Word tells us to pray without ceasing, does that mean there is a one-way conversation where we do all the talking and thinking, or a two-way conversation where we both speak to God, and also hear from Him?
- *1 Thessalonians 5:16 Rejoice always; 17 **pray without ceasing**; 18 in everything give thanks; for this is God's will for you in Christ Jesus.*

Today's Prophets aren't 100% Accurate

Prophecies in the Bible were 100% accurate, and because 'prophets' today usually aren't 100% accurate, Cessationists often use this as evidence that modern-day prophets aren't of God.

As believers, we can 'hear' multiple voices. We have our own thoughts, thoughts from the enemy, and messages from God in various forms. Differentiating which voice we're hearing can be difficult. This can result in prophecies that aren't of God, but which are from the enemy or ourselves.

18:24 That being said, is the accuracy of today's prophets and prophecies a separate issue from whether or not the 9 Holy Spirit gifts including prophecy ceased? And does it also help explain why God's Word tells us to test all things?
- *1 Thessalonians 5:21 But examine everything carefully; hold fast to that which is good;*

18:25 We also need to remember God changes His mind. And could that explain why <u>some</u> prophecies given in recent years, do not appear to have come true?
- *Exodus 32:14 So the Lord changed His mind about the harm which He said He would do to His people.*
- *Jonah 3:10 When God saw their deeds, that they turned from their wicked way, then God relented concerning the calamity which He had declared He would bring upon them. And He did not do it.*

Another Type/Level of Prophecy

18:26 In regards to the hundreds if not thousands of prophecies from prophets mentioned in the Bible but the specifics of which aren't actually recorded in the Bible, some believers view them as another kind or type of prophecy, or as being of a different level of value/importance. If these explanations aren't acceptable, what's your explanation?

Consider two of Jesus's prophecies related to a donkey and a room for Passover.
- *Matthew 21:2 saying to them, "**Go into the village opposite you, and immediately you will find a donkey** tied there and a colt with her; untie them and bring them to Me.*
- *Mark 14:12 ... "Where do You want us to go and prepare for You to eat the Passover?" 13 And He sent two of His disciples and said to them, "Go into the city, and **a man will meet you carrying a pitcher of water; follow him**; 14 and **wherever he enters, say to the owner of the house, 'The Teacher says, "Where is My guest room in which I may eat the Passover with My***

disciples?'" 15 And **_he himself will show you a large upper room furnished and ready_**; *prepare for us there." 16 The disciples went out and came to the city, and **_found it just as He had told them_**; and they prepared the Passover.*

18:27   Are these two prophecies of Jesus, while significant in the events of Jesus's life, on the same level as the prophecy of Jesus being born of a virgin, or that Jesus would be resurrected? Are they examples of different levels, values, or scope of prophetic words?

An Issue of Comfort

When it comes to issues of prophecy, words of knowledge and gifts of healing, I wonder if some believers don't want to get involved in such gifts out of discomfort or even fear - fear of being wrong, fear of looking foolish, fear of the unknown, fear of being criticized and judged by one's denomination that doesn't believe in the gifts, fear of having to leave one's church where family and friends attend, and/or fear of being shunned by family, friends, church leaders and co-workers? After all, shunning is not limited to the JW, Mormon, Islamic and other religions/faiths.

18:28   When it comes to divine revelations not found in the Bible, do you think:
      i.   some believers are apprehensive about the idea of needing to hear from Holy Spirit in addition to relying on what the scriptures have to say; and
      ii.   some believers will not even consider the idea that we can receive new divine revelations today. I wonder how much of this is because that would require them to admit they have been wrong? In such cases, is pride and loyalty to current beliefs greater than a commitment to seeking the truth found in God's Word?

CLOSING POINT TO PONDER

18:29   There are many hundreds, if not many thousands, of prophecies from God that aren't recorded in the Bible. If all of God's prophecies aren't in the Bible, how can the Bible be viewed as containing all of God's divine revelation?

19

Charismatic Misbehaviors

INTRODUCTION

ONE more reason why many Cessationists believe Baptism in the Holy Spirit and the 9 Holy Spirit gifts have ceased is due to inappropriate behaviors of some Charismatic leaders. An extension of this issue is a belief that other Charismatic leaders are not adequately dealing with those who are misbehaving. Chapter 19 briefly addresses these issues.

Misbehaviors

From my limited vantage point and research, the three most common types of inappropriate behaviors cited by Cessationists are sexual indiscretions, exploiting others financially, and engaging in teachings and activities that are not Biblical. In many cases, I think God would agree with the concerns. Moreover, there are probably many more inappropriate things that have gone on, or are currently going on. So many of these things make one shudder. But let me ask.

19:1 How many inappropriate behaviors are going on in non-Charismatic circles that are hidden away to protect pastors, churches, and the donation box? Even little things, such as how many expenses are charged to the church when they are personal? Or major things such as sexual harassment and spiritual abuse which we now know are not limited to Charismatic circles, but rather plagues virtually every denomination?

19:2 What are non-Charismatic leaders doing to address the ungodly judgments, criticisms and mocking of Continuationists that are made by Cessationists or by other non-Charismatic leaders? And why aren't non-Charismatic leaders speaking out against critics of Charismatics who base their criticisms on small samples of inappropriate behaviors or incorrect teachings of Charismatics to make blanket statements - often using mocking words and gestures - about hundreds of millions of Charismatics?

19:3 Further, when we see one believer mocking another, be it a Cessationist doing so to a Continuationist, or any other believer doing so to any other believer, shouldn't this kind of behavior set off alarm bells? Shouldn't all our hearts - assuming we're born again - be filled with concern and words that are filled with love and prayer?

❑ *Matthew 7:4 Or how can you say to your brother, 'Let me take the speck out of your eye,' and behold, the log is in your own eye?*

CEASED?

If you think I'm off base, consider Smith Wigglesworth. George Spormont was a close friend of Mr. Wigglesworth and wrote a book *"Wigglesworth, A Man Who Walked with God"*. The book reveals God did many miracles through Mr. Wigglesworth. He sought to live a holy life. He had great compassion for the hurting and the unsaved. He was a man of passionate prayer. He would not allow newspapers in his home because they didn't contain the truth. He shared the gospel with words and power for many decades. He didn't like being viewed as having any special gifts. All glory was to go to God. However, Mr. Wigglesworth is also known for unusual behaviors, one of which was having punched some people when praying for them to be healed and/or set free.

19:4 Why do we only see the perceived negative behaviors of individuals such as Mr. Wigglesworth being mentioned by the Cessationist movement while the amazing things done through him and other Charismatics are basically ignored? Is it because our heart and loyalty are first and foremost to our beliefs and comfort zones?

19:5 I don't know if everybody got healed after such behaviors, but the indication is they were. If not, wouldn't Mr. Wigglesworth likely have been imprisoned? A core issue is whether or not God told him to do those things. From my vantage point, I can't comprehend God telling Mr. Wigglesworth to punch somebody, but then again, I don't get God killing Ananias and Sapphira, God causing worms to eat Herod, God inflicting plagues on the Egyptians, or God flooding the earth in the time of Noah. It's often a challenge to know what is of God and what may be sinful nature that is being influenced by the demonic world. Is that perhaps one more reason why we need to seek Holy Spirit for revelation and guidance, and not rely on our thoughts or thoughts of others?

19:6 If Mr. Wigglesworth's inappropriate behavior is reason to believe the gifts have ceased, wouldn't that mean any shortcomings of non-Charismatics (lack of love, kindness, patience) is reason to believe that love, kindness and patience are also invalid now? If not, why the double standard?

19:7 If we saw inappropriate behaviors by someone today, I wonder what percentage of believers would respond by mocking or criticizing, and what percentage would seek revelation from God as to how to pray for the person, and then actually pray for them?

19:8 If we attack someone publicly - verbally or in writing - when God hasn't directly called us to do so, are we doing the devil's work, an issue Derek Prince raised in his book *'Experiencing God's Power'*?

CLOSING POINT TO PONDER

19:9 When individuals say they had a crazy encounter with God, shouldn't we be slow to criticize or condemn? After all, imagine if you were trying to explain how God spoke to you in a burning bush that didn't burn, God sent an axe head floating up to you, or birds brought you tasty meat while you sat on the back porch having a coffee? Can you imagine the comments from Christians if those things happened today? And yet, God did these and many more unusual things. Is that perhaps why God's Word recommends we're to pray - to speak to God and to hear from Him - throughout our waking hours?

20

Summary of Cessationist Arguments

INTRODUCTION

THE Cessationist/Continuationist disagreement is centered around whether or not the Baptism of the Holy Spirit and the 9 Holy Spirit gifts/manifestations including tongues and prophecy have ceased. Chapter 20 summarizes key parts of evidence presented in previous chapters of **CEASED?**.

FROM CHAPTER 1 OF CEASED?

<u>**Argument 1**</u>

Chapter 1 does a bit of a heart check on readers by asking a few questions of Cessationists, Charismatics and Roman Catholics. Chapter 1 touches on the Cessationist view that the 9 Holy Spirit gifts found in 1 Corinthians 12 ended with the original apostles or other groups of early believers. The *'all'* in Acts 2:4 shows many more believers than the original apostles were given the gifts of tongues, and potentially other Holy Spirit gifts, right from the get-go.

- ❑ *Acts 1:15 At this time Peter stood up in the midst of the brethren **(a gathering of about one hundred and twenty)** ...*
- ❑ *Acts 2:1 When the day of Pentecost had come, they **were all together** in one place ... 4 And **they were all filled with the Holy Spirit** and **began to speak** with **other tongues, as the Spirit was giving them utterance**.*

Tongues and the corresponding interpretation of tongues are similar to other Holy Spirit gifts such as prophecy, word of knowledge or word of wisdom.

20:1   I cannot find the specifics of one interpretation of a tongue in God's Word. Does this indicate some of God's divine revelations aren't actually in the Bible? Or does it mean that God created the gift of interpretation of tongues, but then chose not to give the gift to any believer?

- ❑ *1 Corinthians 14:1 Pursue love, yet **desire earnestly spiritual gifts**, but **especially** that you may **prophesy** ... 5 Now I wish that you all spoke in tongues, but even more that you would prophesy; and **greater is one who prophesies** than one who speaks in tongues, **unless he interprets**, so that the church may receive edifying.*

Consensus seems to be that Paul wrote 1 Corinthians somewhere between 52-

CEASED?

57 AD, 20-25 years after the cross. I asked two questions - 1:9 and 1:10 - on 1 Corinthians 14.
- ❏ *1 Corinthians 11:4 Every **man** who has something on his head while **praying or prophesying** disgraces his head. 5 But every **woman** who has her head uncovered while **praying or prophesying** disgraces her head, for she is one and the same as the woman whose head is shaved.*

20:2   Why would Paul tell believers they should be concerned about head coverings of Corinthian believers if prophesying was not available to the 'ordinary' believer at Corinth, or for that matter, any ordinary believer living at that time?

20:3   If women were to wear head coverings when they prophesied, doesn't this mean that women were expected to prophesy?

FROM CHAPTER 13 OF CEASED?
<u>Argument 2</u>

A second reason Cessationists believe the Holy Spirit gifts ended is the gifts were given to a limited number of early believers. Once they died, the gifts ceased. Chapter 13 of **CEASED?** shows there were hundreds of thousands of believers existing when Paul visited Ephesus in ~52-55AD. There were even more believers when Paul wrote 1 Corinthians in ~53-57AD. On several occasions, Paul encouraged all of these believers - not just a select few - to seek the 9 Holy Spirit gifts.
- ❏ *1 Corinthians 12:31 **But earnestly desire the greater gifts** ...*
- ❏ *1 Corinthians 14:1 Pursue love, **yet desire earnestly spiritual gifts**, but **especially that you may prophesy**.*
- ❏ *1 Corinthians 14:5 Now I **wish that you all spoke in tongues**, **but even more that you would prophesy** ...*
- ❏ *1 Corinthians 14:39 Therefore, my brethren, **desire earnestly to prophesy**, and **do not forbid to speak in tongues**. ...*

20:4   If these gifts didn't apply to all believers at that time, why would the Corinthians be treated differently than any other believers living at that time? Or living today for that matter?

20:5   If signs and wonders were limited to a select few individuals for a relatively short period of time, why would Paul write the above scriptures in the way he did? Wouldn't it be not only reasonable, but also responsible, for Paul to have made it clear there were limitations? That the gifts were only for a select few, and for a very short period of time?

FROM CHAPTER 14 OF CEASED?
<u>Argument 3</u>

A third reason Cessationists believe the 9 Holy Spirit gifts have ceased is that signs and wonders were already declining in the latter verses of Acts.

Considerations
Signs and wonders were mentioned frequently from Acts 2 through to Acts 21.

20: Summary of Cessationist Arguments

The next 5 chapters, 22 through 26, were focused on Paul's legal issues. Acts 27 reviews Paul's sailing adventure which included 2 prophecies that were fulfilled. Acts concludes with Paul's arrival on Malta where he is bitten by a viper but not harmed to the amazement of all who were present. The father of the island's chief officer, Publius, was healed as were many others on the island.

20:6 Isn't the lack of mention of the Holy Spirit gifts in the 5+ chapters (21-26) where Paul was effectively imprisoned a reasonable outcome given the focus on Paul's legal issues?

20:7 163 of the 165 verses from Acts 21:27 through Acts 26:32 relate to Paul's legal issues. Given the events in these verses occur over a period of time covering only a few weeks or months, doesn't this short period of time make these 5+ chapters an unreliable indicator as to whether or not the 9 Holy Spirit gifts were declining at the end of Acts?

20:8 Paul spent 2 years imprisoned in Caesarea (Acts 24:27) until Festus replaced Felix. Does the fact there was no mention of signs and wonders in the one and only verse related to these 2 years, automatically mean the 9 gifts weren't actually happening through a) Paul nor b) any of the other apostles/disciples? Or is it more reasonable to expect some/all of the 9 gifts were continuing, but there was simply no mention?

20:9 The average frequency of mention of the 9 Holy Spirit gifts in the last 2 chapters of Acts is equal to, or greater than, the average frequency of mention in any 2 consecutive chapters in all of Acts. Doesn't this show that the frequency of occurrence was not decreasing? And if anything, the frequency of occurrence was perhaps increasing?

Chapter 14 of **CEASED?** analyzes the frequency of mention of the Holy Spirit gifts by comparing them to the number of Chapters involved and the time frames involved.

Figure 14:4 Summary of Frequency of Occurrence

	Description of Analysis	Acts 2-21	Acts 22-28
I:	Average # of occurrences per chapter if count all the chapters	20 / 20 = 1.0	5/7 = .7
II:	Average # of occurrences per chapter if only count the chapters where the gifts are mentioned	20 / 12 = 1.7	5/2 = 2.5
III:	Average # of occurrences per year based on the number of years covered by chapters	20 / 20 = 1	5/3 = 1.7

Analysis 'I' in Figure 14:4 shows a slight decline in the frequency of gifts occurring in the latter chapters of Acts as compared to earlier chapters. Analysis 'II', however, shows an increase in the latter chapters of Acts if we remove the 5+ chapters that covered a few months at most, and which were focused on details surrounding Paul's legal issues. Analysis 'III' which is based on the frequency of signs and wonders occurring on average per calendar year, shows there is a notable

CEASED?

increase in the latter chapters of Acts.

20:10   Doesn't Chapter 14 of **CEASED?** demonstrate the 9 Holy Spirit gifts had not declined, and that they were not on their way to ceasing? If not, what does the evidence show?

Argument 5

Chapter 14 of **CEASED?** also discusses the 5th Cessationist argument for the 9 Holy Spirit gifts ceasing - the minimal mention of the gifts in the 21 New Testament books after Acts (27 total New Testament books excluding 4 Gospels, Acts and Revelation) means the gifts were declining and all but ceased.

Considerations

The Cessationist argument inherently assumes there is a direct correlation between the frequency of the 9 Holy Spirit gifts being mentioned, and their actual rate of occurrence. This Cessationist argument contends that signs and wonders were regularly occurring up to the time Paul traveled to Ephesus and other locations in Acts 19-21, but declined noticeably thereafter. Based on this argument, the New Testament books written before Paul went to Ephesus should make frequent mention of signs and wonders. So how often do we see the gifts mentioned in the 4 books written before Paul went to Ephesus - James, Galatians, 1 & 2 Thessalonians? Not once.

20:11   Doesn't this result invalidate the Cessationist assumption that frequency of occurrence will be validated by a corresponding frequency of mention?

In terms of the books written after Paul's travels in Acts 19-21, the Cessationist argument contends that since we see no mention in these books, that is proof that signs and wonders were declining and on their way to cessation. The first part of the argument has considerable truth. These 17 books provide few specific examples on signs and wonders. However, does this lack of mention mean they weren't occurring? More than 60 times in the 17 books, general references to signs and wonders and associated issues such as the office of prophet were recorded.

20:12   Given the 4 books written before Paul's travels in Acts 19-21 make no mention of specific occurrences of the gifts, and given these 4 books were written when the gifts were in full operation, how can one conclude the lack of specific examples of the gifts in the 17 books written after Paul's travels in Acts 19-21 means signs and wonders were declining or had ended?

The 4 Gospels and Acts record historical events, and made frequent mention of signs and wonders, many of which involved one or more of the 9 Holy Spirit gifts in action. Revelation is a revealing of Jesus with considerable prophecy and symbolism. As stated, none of the other 21 New Testament books written either before or after Paul's travels in Acts 19-21, make much mention of signs and wonders including the 9 Holy Spirit gifts. What these 21 books do address, however, is a wide variety of themes.

20:13   Isn't the absence of examples of signs and wonders a realistic result in

20: Summary of Cessationist Arguments

these books when one considers their focus is different?

20:14 When the author of Hebrews talks about signs and wonders, doesn't that further indicate signs and wonders were expected to continue?

Chapter 14 also raised the issue of whether the Cessationist belief held by many believers makes the lack of signs and wonders a self-fulfilling outcome. I copy questions 14:34 and 35.

14:34 North American denominations including but not limited to the Reformed, 7th Day Adventist, Mennonite and Baptist churches have typically taught the 9 Holy Spirit gifts have ceased. However, given a belief system that the 9 Holy Spirit gifts have ceased, isn't it understandable that believers in these denominations wouldn't seek or expect such gifts? And if they don't seek the gifts, isn't it reasonable to expect that the gifts don't occur? In other words, is it a situation of *"we have not because we ask not"*?

- *James 4:2 You lust and do not have; so you commit murder. You are envious and cannot obtain; so you fight and quarrel.* ***You do not have because you do not ask.***
- *Matthew 21:22 And all things you ask in prayer, believing, you will receive.*
- *1 John 5:14 This is the confidence which we have before Him, that,* ***if we ask anything according to His will***, *He hears us.*

14:35 And thus, isn't the Cessationist belief system prone to be self-fulfilling for believers who don't believe in the 9 Holy Spirit gifts? And is it even more likely to be self-fulfilling for those who view such activities as being heretical, or who criticize and mock other believers who are involved in these gifts?

FROM CHAPTER 15 OF CEASED?

Argument 5

Cessationists often argue there were two primary purposes for signs and wonders in the New Testament - proving Jesus was the Messiah, and to launch the gospel. Once the gospel was launched through the apostles, there was no more need for signs and wonders. And thus, Cessationists often use this 5th argument as a reason to believe the 9 Holy Spirit gifts have ceased.

Considerations

Chapter 15 outlines several other reasons for signs and wonders including:
1. spreading the gospel, not just launching it;
2. making it easier to share the gospel;
3. confirming God's Word;
4. glorifying God;
5. providing signs for believers and unbelievers;
6. demonstrating the power of the Name of Jesus;
7. demonstrating and using authority over demons;
8. showing God's compassion;
9. getting people's attention; and
10. providing forewarnings.

20:15 Don't all the above reasons still have merit today? And thus, wouldn't signs and wonders be of immense help in advancing God's kingdom today?

FROM CHAPTER 16 OF CEASED?

Argument 6

As per the summary of Chapter 13, many Cessationists believe signs and wonders ended when a group of early disciples died. Cessationists do not agree on who was actually in the group. The four most common groups cited are as follows:
1. Group 1: believers Baptized in the Holy Spirit at the 4 locations in Acts 1:8;
2. Group 2: believers Baptized in the Holy Spirit at Pentecost;
3. Group 3: original apostles + the other believers who were Baptized in the Holy Spirit at Pentecost + those upon whom these individuals laid hands;
4. Group 4: original apostles, or else the original apostles + Paul.

Considerations: Group 1 - People Baptized in the Holy Spirit at 4 locations per Acts 1:8

Other Cessationists believe signs and wonders were not needed once the Holy Spirit had been poured out to the 4 gatherings at the 4 locations as per Acts 1:8:

❑ *Acts 1:8 but you will receive power when the Holy Spirit has come upon you; and you shall be My witnesses both in **Jerusalem**, and in all **Judea** and **Samaria**, and even to the **remotest part of the earth**.*

Scriptures	Who's there	Location	# Believers
Acts 2	Jews	Jerusalem	~120
Acts 8	Samaritans	Samaria*	Unknown
Acts 10	God-fearers	Caesarea**	Cornelius, family & friends
Acts 19	Gentiles	Ephesus***	12

* Samaria was a city and territory in Israel
** Caesarea was the capital of Roman province in Judea
*** Ephesus was a city in ancient Greece/modern-day Turkey, the 'remotest part' on earth

Acts 15 shows Paul took the gospel to the Thessalonians *'in power and in the Holy Spirit'*, a trip that occurred prior to his trip to Ephesus in Acts 19.

20:16 When Paul met the 12 disciples at Ephesus, his first priority was to ensure they were Baptized in the Holy Spirit. At Thessalonica, Paul took the gospel *'in power and in the Holy Spirit'*. The Thessalonians became imitators of Paul. Doesn't that indicate Paul likely taught the Thessalonians about the Baptism of the Holy Spirit and took steps to ensure they were Baptized in the Holy Spirit? If not, why would Paul not do at Thessalonica what was a priority for him to do at Ephesus?

20:17 Thessalonica was further away from Israel than Ephesus. On the theory an outpouring - a Baptism of the Holy Spirit - occurred at Thessalonica, doesn't that invalidate the argument Ephesus was the remotest part on earth to receive an outpouring?

20: Summary of Cessationist Arguments

20:18 Rome was further away from Israel than Ephesus. There were many other cities, towns and/or inhabited regions further away from Israel than Rome. Ephesus was not the uttermost part of the earth when Jesus told His disciples they would be witnesses to the remotest part of the earth. As a result, doesn't this invalidate the argument that we should take the locations in Acts 1:8 literally, and instead validate the opposing argument that we should take the locations symbolically? If not, why not?

20:19 In addition, isn't the argument that the 9 Holy Spirit gifts were limited to those who were Baptized in the Holy Spirit at these 4 locations further invalidated given that:
   i. the Bible only identifies two groups the Good News was for - Jews and Gentiles;
   ii. Peter and the other apostles were ecstatic when the first Gentiles - Cornelius, family and friends - were Baptized in the Holy Spirit, and they realized God had given the gift of eternal life to both the Gentiles and Jews, but that no such excitement was recorded when groups in Samaria, Caesarea or Ephesus were Baptized in the Holy Spirit;
   iii. no mention was made of a prophecy being fulfilled in part, or in full when individuals were Baptized at the 3 locations after Jerusalem?

Group 2 - Original Apostles + those gathered at Pentecost

20:20 Isn't this second group invalid because Paul, Cornelius, family and friends, and the 12 believers at Ephesus all spoke in tongues and/or prophesied, but were not at Pentecost?

Group 3 - Original Apostles + others at Pentecost + those on whom hands were laid

20:21 Isn't the argument for this group invalidated by the fact no one laid hands:
   i. on the non-apostles gathered at Pentecost who spoke in tongues; nor
   ii. on Cornelius, family and friends when they were Baptized in the Holy Spirit and started to speak in tongues?

Group 4 - Original Apostles Only

20:22 Isn't the argument for this fourth group invalidated given:
   i. several individuals besides the original 11, Matthias and Paul, were labeled as apostles including James (Jesus's brother), Barnabas, and possibly Timothy, Sylvanus, Andronicus, Junia, the 70, Judas, Silas, Epaphroditus and Titus;
   ii. Holy Spirit gifts occurred through individuals other than apostles including Stephen, Cornelius, family and friends, the 12 disciples at Ephesus, Agabus and other prophets who went to Antioch, and Philip's 4 daughters who prophesied;
   iii. Mark 16 states signs and wonders are signs of all believers, not a select few; and
   iv. at the time Paul wrote 1 Corinthians, there were hundreds of thousands if not millions of believers who Paul encouraged to

pursue gifts, especially prophesy and tongues, especially if there was an interpretation?

20:23 Given many individuals performed signs and wonders after Pentecost, but who weren't identified as apostles, isn't it invalid to claim that the 9 Holy Spirit gifts of 1 Corinthians 12 (tongues, prophecy etc.) ceased with the death of the original apostles?

20:24 If the signs and wonders such as tongues and prophecy were to end when the various individuals in these groups were Baptized in the Holy Spirit, doesn't the fact that Paul tells believers in 1 Corinthians to pursue gifts, especially prophecy, negate that argument?

Related to the above is the view that, after the cross, only true apostles were used by God for signs and wonders. True apostles, according to Cessationists, are identified using three criteria:
1. witnessed with their own eyes the physical, resurrected Christ;
2. was personally/directly appointed by Christ; and
3. was able to work miracles such as tongues, healings and prophecy.

20:25 Aren't these 3 criteria invalid given:
i. it is questionable if Paul actually saw the physical, resurrected Jesus;
ii. no scriptures show Matthias, Barnabas and James, the brother of Jesus, were appointed as apostles by Jesus directly; and
iii. many other believers performed signs and wonders besides the apostles?

FROM CHAPTER 17 OF CEASED?
Argument 7

A summary of gifts from Father God (Romans 12:6-8), Jesus (Ephesians 4:11) and Holy Spirit (1 Corinthians 12:8-10) is found on page 20 in Chapter 2. Chapter 17 focuses on the question:

20:26 If the 9 Holy Spirit gifts such as prophecy and tongues, and roles such as prophets and apostles have all ceased, and these functions and gifts are all listed and intermingled with other gifts and functions in God's Word, then why haven't all the other gifts and functions ceased? Do we get to pick and choose what has continued, and what hasn't?

FROM CHAPTER 18 OF CEASED?
Argument 1

Chapter 18 of **CEASED?** builds on comments made in Chapter 1, and deals with the Cessationist view that all divine revelation is contained in the Bible. The Bible mentions hundreds of individuals who prophesied, but details of their prophecies are not in the Bible. The combination of a tongue and the corresponding interpretation of tongues is similar to a gift of prophecy, word of knowledge, or word of wisdom in that they are a form of divine revelation. However, there is not a single instance where the details of an interpretation of a tongue are given in God's

20: Summary of Cessationist Arguments

Word. Major and minor prophets of the Bible gave one or more prophecies. However, it is potentially a false assumption to believe all of their prophecies, and thus all the associated divine revelations God gave to them, are actually in the Bible.

FROM CHAPTER 19 OF CEASED?
Argument 8
Another reason Cessationists believe the 9 gifts ended are misbehaviors of some Charismatics.

Considerations

No question, lives of a limited number of Charismatics appear to be heavily rooted in sin. Some appear to be under demonic influence at times, with manifestations eerily similar to the kundalini spirit. Focus often appears to be on money and fame. Fake healings have occurred and are probably still occurring. Teachings on uncomfortable truths in God's Word are pushed to the side. These and other concerns are valid. But we should also remember God had many people in the Bible do some unusual things. And in every denomination, there are sin-filled people and leaders with sins hidden away to avoid harming reputations, and to keep the tithes and offerings flowing.

20:27 If sinful behaviors, thoughts and words of some Charismatics are reason to invalidate the corresponding parts of God's Word for all believers, in this case the Baptism of the Holy Spirit and 9 Holy Spirit gifts, how much of God's Word would remain valid today if we also considered the sinful behaviors, thoughts and words of all believers?

CLOSING POINTS TO PONDER

20:28 Chapter 20 of **CEASED?** concludes the discussion of material in the Cessationist vs Continuationist disagreement. If you still believe Cessationism is true, let me ask. God spoke to many people between Adam at creation and John on Patmos. God doesn't change. If God stopped speaking to people in ~75-95AD and hasn't spoken to any person for over 1,900 years, isn't that a radical change? And especially so since God created humans to be in relationship with Him?

If you're still a Cessationist but see holes in Cessationism, keep digging and ask the tough questions. Seek God. He will guide you. And if you're Roman Catholic, consider the Holy Spirit gifts weren't core teachings of the mainline Catholic church from ~33AD to the 1960's. Since the 1960's, over 100 million Charismatic Catholics agree the 9 Holy Spirit gifts haven't ceased. Let me ask:

20:29 How can the Roman Catholic church be God's true church if it excluded such fundamental parts of the Bible for ~1,900 years, and does not include the 9 Holy Spirit gifts as a core teaching for all of the Catholic church today?

20:30 What are the primary reasons why the vast majority of Catholics are not being encouraged to pursue the 9 Holy Spirit gifts? Chapters 24 through 27 gives some insight.

21

The Gift(s) of Tongues

INTRODUCTION

BY this point, I hope readers realize Baptism of the Holy Spirit and the 9 Holy Spirit gifts haven't ceased. In the Cessationist vs Continuationist debate, tongues, healing and prophecy are the Holy Spirit gifts most commonly discussed. I'll leave prophecy to those more qualified and experienced than myself. I will, however, share some comments on healing in Chapter 22, while this chapter will deal with tongues and interpretation of tongues. I will continue to make heavy use of scripture, but will have a larger than normal emphasis on personal experience and observations.

Chapter 21 deals with a variety of issues but is primarily focused on the issue of whether or not tongues involves a personal prayer language, also commonly referred to as a heavenly language. Cessationists frequently view such tongues as gibberish or demonic. While some people who speak in tongues may be speaking in a demonic tongue, tongues spoken by most Charismatics are a gift from God, one of the 9 Holy Spirit gifts. I have no comprehensive survey results to back up my claim. It's my opinion based on experience and what well-known teachers say.

Primary topics addressed in Chapter 21 include:
  i. Cessationist view of tongues (page 272);
  ii. some basics about tongues (page 274);
  iii. false tongues (page 279);
  iv. personal prayer language (page 280);
  v. 10 of the benefits of praying in a personal prayer language (page 282);
  vi. who can have a personal prayer language (page 286);
  vii. 7 unique scenarios involving different kinds of tongues (page 287);
  viii. praying in the Spirit (page 288);
  ix. how to start praying in tongues (page 289); and
  x. tongues and the Roman Catholic church (page 390).

CESSATIONIST VIEW OF TONGUES

My understanding of the Cessationist view of tongues, in general, is as follows:
- ❖ tongues, as per the other 8 gifts in 1 Corinthians 12:8-10, have ceased;
- ❖ true tongues were only spoken in earthly languages;
- ❖ the person didn't know the earthly language he/she was speaking;

21: Tongues

- if no person was present who knew the earthly language being spoken, an interpretation of tongues occurred;
- tongues were a sign for unbelievers; and
- there were never any personal prayer languages way back then, or today.

4 Questions to Start

If your view corresponds somewhat close to that just described, let me ask a few questions to get the ball rolling. To start, consider 1 Corinthians 14:2.

- *1 Corinthians 14:2 For one who speaks in a tongue does not speak to men but to God; **for no one understands**, but in his spirit he speaks mysteries.*

21:1 When speaking in a tongue, the person speaking does not understand what he or she is saying. It's a mystery to them. However, if all tongues are in an earthly language, why would 1 Corinthians 14:2 say that 'no one understands'. If no person can understand what's being said, how can it be an earthly language? Is there perhaps more to the story?

Now consider Peter when he shared the gospel with Cornelius, family and friends. Holy Spirit fell upon all who were listening and they started speaking in tongues.

- *Acts 10:44 While Peter was still speaking these words, the **Holy Spirit fell upon all** those who were listening to the message. 45 All the circumcised believers who came with Peter were amazed, because **the gift of the Holy Spirit had been poured out on the Gentiles also**. 46 **For they were hearing them speaking with tongues** and **exalting God**. Then Peter answered, 47 "Surely no one can refuse the water for these to be baptized who have received the Holy Spirit just as we did, can he?" 48 And he ordered them to be baptized in the name of Jesus Christ. Then they asked him to stay on for a few days.*

21:2 As soon as Peter saw/heard them speaking in tongues, he knew they had received the Baptism of the Holy Spirit. In addition, given Peter responded by immediately having them water baptized, doesn't this mean Peter also realized Cornelius, family and friends were also born again? And thus, didn't their speaking in tongues serve as a sign to Peter? And doesn't that mean tongues can be a sign for believers, not just unbelievers? Which is interesting because that seems to contradict 1 Corinthians 14:22.

- *1 Corinthians 14:22 So then **tongues are for a sign, not to those who believe but to unbelievers;** but prophecy is for a sign, not to unbelievers but to those who believe.*

21:3 For a tongue to meet the Cessationist criteria, every one of Cornelius, family and friends must have spoken in an earthly language they did not personally know. For Peter to know that every person was speaking in an earthly language they didn't personally know, wouldn't Peter have needed to know all the languages each person did know? If so, how would this be possible given Peter had just met them in a group setting?

21:4 One could argue Peter found out afterward that each person had spoken in an earthly language they didn't know. However, isn't that argument negated

CEASED?

by Peter's witnessing the tongues, and then immediately deciding to have them all water baptized, something Peter would only have done if he believed they had been born again?

Given the above, if you have been a staunch opponent of tongues as being relevant today, is there perhaps more to the story such as the existence of a heavenly language for each believer?

SOME BASICS ABOUT TONGUES - MY PERSPECTIVE
What is a Tongue?

A tongue is a supernatural enablement allowing a believer to speak in a language not known to the person speaking. There are 3 broad types or groups of tongues.

1: Earthly Language

A tongue can be in an earthly language as at Pentecost.
- Acts 2:6 *And when this sound occurred, the crowd came together, and were bewildered because each one of them was hearing them speak in his own language. 7 They were amazed and astonished, saying, "Why, are not all these who are speaking Galileans? 8 **And how is it that we each hear them in our own language to which we were born**?*

2: Languages Only God Knows

Consider 1 Corinthians 14:2 again and notice it states a tongue is spoken to God, not human beings, and no human being can understand what is being said.
- *1 Corinthians 14:2 For **one who speaks in a tongue does not speak to men but to God; for no one understands**, but in his spirit he speaks mysteries.*

21:5 If no one can understand but God, doesn't that mean those tongues weren't spoken in an earthly language? If not, what does it mean?

21:6 If speaking in tongues involves words only God can understand, is the term *'personal prayer language'* perhaps a reasonable one?

3: Tongues of Angels

Paul also indicates that he might have spoken in languages of angels.
- *1 Corinthians 13:1 If I speak with the **tongues** of men and **of angels**, but do not have love, I have become a noisy gong or a clanging cymbal.*

21:7 Does 1 Corinthians 13:1 again indicate that tongues can sometimes be in a language other than an earthly language - a heavenly language as it were?

What Happens to Our Body, Soul and Spirit when Speaking in a Tongue

Figure 11:9a below is a copy of Figure 11:9 from page 191 of Chapter 11. When we're born again and Baptized in the Holy Spirit, Holy Spirit is in [en] us and upon [epi] us. When born again, our spirit is made right with God. On the other hand, our souls are far from perfect and can still be heavily influenced by our flesh, the world, and the kingdom of darkness. What our bodies end up doing, and our tongues end up speaking, can still be largely determined by our mind, a part of our soul. Consider two scriptures:

21: Tongues

- ❑ *1 Corinthians 14:2 For one who speaks in a tongue does not speak to men but to God; for no one understands, but **<u>in his spirit he speaks mysteries</u>**.*
- ❑ *1 Corinthians 14:14 For if I pray in a tongue, my spirit prays, but **<u>my mind is unfruitful</u>**.*

As per Figure 21.1 below, when we speak in tongues, our mind/soul is largely bypassed. Holy Spirit which is intimately connected to our spirit, gives us the language and words to speak - i.e. a tongue. Our spirit communicates directly with our mouth and our soul/mind is largely on the sidelines. In so doing, we speak mysteries our mind doesn't understand or may think are unfruitful.

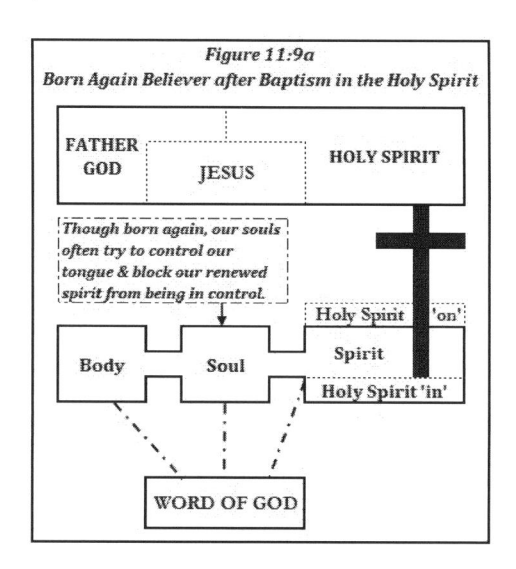

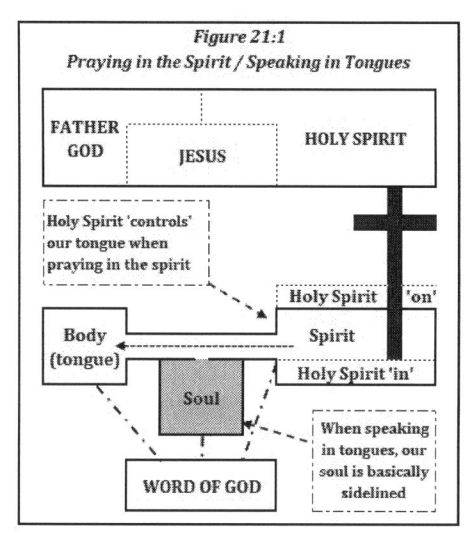

Figure 11:9a
Born Again Believer after Baptism in the Holy Spirit

Though born again, our souls often try to control our tongue & block our renewed spirit from being in control.

Figure 21:1
Praying in the Spirit / Speaking in Tongues

Holy Spirit 'controls' our tongue when praying in the spirit

When speaking in tongues, our soul is basically sidelined

When we pray with our minds, such prayers are often referred to as soulish prayers.

When speaking in tongues, we pray *"in the Spirit"*. Through our spirit, Holy Spirit gives us the words to pray which is one of the ways by which Holy Spirit helps us when we don't how to pray.

- ❑ *Romans 8:26 In the same way the Spirit also helps our weakness; **<u>for we do not know how to pray as we should</u>**, but the Spirit Himself intercedes for us with groanings too deep for words;*

A New York Times article *"A Neuroscientific Look at Speaking in Tongues"* by Benedict Carey on November 7, 2006, includes some rather interesting comments.

"The passionate, sometimes rhythmic, language-like patter that pours forth from religious people who "speak in tongues" reflects a state of mental possession, many of them say. Now they have some neuroscience to back them up.

Researchers at the University of Pennsylvania took brain images of five women while they spoke in tongues and found that their frontal lobes - the thinking, willful part of the brain through which people control what they do - were

CEASED?

relatively quiet, as were the language centers. The regions involved in maintaining self-consciousness were active. The women were not in blind trances, and it was unclear which region was driving the behavior."

Contrary to what may be a common perception, studies suggest that people who speak in tongues rarely suffer from mental problems. A recent study of nearly 1,000 evangelical Christians in England found that those who engaged in the practice were more emotionally stable than those who did not. Researchers have identified at least two forms of the practice, one ecstatic and frenzied, the other subdued and nearly silent.

The new findings contrasted sharply with images taken of other spiritually inspired mental states like meditation, which is often a highly focused mental exercise, activating the frontal lobes.

Speaking in tongues involves Holy Spirit guiding us and effectively taking our mind and fleshly thinking out of the picture in terms of what we are praying. Which for me, is often very beneficial.

Tongues = Praying and Singing in the Spirit

Speaking in tongues engages our spirit. Scriptures describe tongues as praying 'in the Spirit'.
- ❑ *Ephesians 6:18 With all prayer and petition **pray at all times in the Spirit**, and with this in view, be on the alert with all perseverance and petition for all the saints,*
- ❑ *Jude 1:20 But you, beloved, building yourselves up on your most holy faith, **praying in the Holy Spirit**,*

We can not only speak in tongues; we can also sing in tongues.
- ❑ *1 Corinthians 14:15 What is the outcome then? I will **pray with the spirit** and I **will pray with the mind also**; I **will sing with the spirit** and I **will sing with the mind also**.*

Tongues at other Outpourings of Holy Spirit

After Pentecost, there were 2 other outpourings of the Holy Spirit where tongues were immediately spoken - when Peter was speaking to Cornelius, family and friends, and when Paul was ministering to the 12 believers at Ephesus.
- ❑ *Acts 10:1 ... a man at Caesarea named Cornelius ... 44 ... the Holy Spirit fell upon all those who were listening ... 46 For they were hearing them **speaking with tongues** and exalting God ...*
- ❑ *Acts 19:1 ... Paul passed through the upper country and came to Ephesus ... 6 When Paul placed his hands on them, the Holy Spirit came on them, and they **spoke in tongues** and **prophesied**. 7 There were about twelve men in all.*

21:8 There is no indication in either of these situations as to whether it was earthly or heavenly languages being spoken by these two groups of believers. Some Cessationists argue that these outpourings of the Holy Spirit

21: Tongues

were mirror images of Pentecost, and thus only earthly languages were involved. However, the two events were different. No one at Pentecost prophesied whereas believers at Ephesus not only spoke in tongues, they also prophesied. In addition, while Pentecost had major noise and signs in the skies, there is also no evidence of these or other supernatural signs in the other two post-Pentecost events. Given these differences, couldn't the nature of the languages also be different?

21:9 Interestingly, there is also no apparent supernatural interpretation of tongues at any of those outpourings. Some Cessationists argue that a tongue must always have an interpretation. If that were so:
  i. would the lack of interpretation of the tongues given by the disciples at Ephesus and the tongues given by Cornelius, family and friends, mean these tongues were not valid? And if they weren't valid, wouldn't that mean the Bible is in error? or
  ii. does the lack of interpretation show some tongues don't need an interpretation?

21:10 The tongues spoken at Pentecost were in earthly languages not known by any of the individuals speaking, but which were known by other persons who were present. For those who were present and knew the language spoken, their understanding of what was being said was not a supernatural interpretation. Doesn't that again suggest tongues from God don't always require a supernatural gift of interpretation? Doesn't that again suggest interpretations are not mandatory when one speaks in a private prayer language?

Are Tongues the Least Valuable Gift

Some Cessationists suggest the gift of tongues was the least valuable gift because it is the last of the 9 gifts/manifestations mentioned in 1 Corinthians 12:8-10 and 1 Corinthians 12:28.

- ❑ *1 Corinthians 12:8 For to one is given the **word of wisdom** through the Spirit, and to another the **word of knowledge** according to the same Spirit; 9 to another **faith** by the same Spirit, and to another **gifts of healing** by the one Spirit, 10 and to another the effecting of **miracles**, and to another **prophecy**, and to another the **distinguishing of spirits**, to another various kinds of **tongues**, and to another the **interpretation of tongues**.*
- ❑ *1 Corinthians 12:28 And God has appointed in the church, first **apostles**, second **prophets**, third **teachers**, then **miracles**, then gifts of **healings**, helps, administrations, various **kinds of tongues**.*

21:11 Tongues and interpretation of tongues are indeed mentioned last. However, only 3 of the 9 Holy Spirit gifts in 1 Corinthians 12:8-10 are also mentioned in 1 Corinthians 12:28 (miracles, healings, tongues). The gift of tongues is one of the 3 Holy Spirit gifts mentioned; 6 other gifts aren't mentioned. As a result, don't these two scriptures suggest tongues is not the least valuable, but perhaps one of the 3 most valuable Holy Spirit gifts?

CEASED?

1 Corinthians 14 also reveals that Paul preferred - in a church environment - to speak a few words with his mind than 10,000 words in a tongue.
- ❑ *1 Corinthians 14:18 I thank God, I speak in tongues more than you all; 19 **however, in the church** I desire to speak five words with my mind so that I may instruct others also, rather than ten thousand words in a tongue.*

21:12   In a church - a public environment - Paul would sooner speak 5 words with his mind (i.e. an earthly language he and others in attendance knew) than a whole lot more words (i.e. 10,000 words) in tongues, a language his mind and the minds of others in attendance did not understand. Doesn't that suggest Paul did speak many words in tongues, but was not inclined to do so in the church or other public places, but in other settings such as when he was spending time alone with God?

In terms of the 9 Holy Spirit gifts, Paul encouraged believers to seek gifts especially prophesy.
- ❑ *1 Corinthians 14:1 Pursue love, yet desire earnestly spiritual gifts, but especially that you may prophesy.*

4 verses later, Paul appears to say prophecy is clearly of more value than a tongue.
- ❑ *1 Corinthians 14:5 Now I wish that you all spoke in tongues, but even more that you would prophesy; and **greater is one who prophesies** than **one who speaks in tongues** ...*

However, Paul goes on to add the caveat 'unless he interprets'.
- ❑ *1 Corinthians 14:5 Now I wish that you all spoke in tongues, but even more that you would prophesy; and greater is one who prophesies than one who speaks in tongues, **unless** he **interprets**, so that the church may receive edifying.*

21:13   Doesn't 1 Corinthians 14:5 suggest:
     i. tongues that are interpreted are close to, if not equal to, the value of prophecy?
     ii. the combination of tongues and interpretation of tongues are two of the more special gifts? If not, why not?

Paul also wrote in 1 Corinthians that he spoke in tongues more than anyone.
- ❑ *1 Corinthians 14:18 I thank God, I speak in tongues more than you all;*

21:14   When Paul compared the amount of tongues he spoke to the amount of tongues spoken by others, doesn't this mean that others at Corinth also spoke in tongues? If not, what is the point of making a comparison if the other believers didn't speak in tongues at all? If they didn't speak in tongues at all, why wouldn't Paul simply say something like *"I wish you all spoke in tongues just as I do"?*

21:15   I find it interesting that while Paul spoke in tongues more than others, he never mentions interpretation of tongues. Does that mean Paul received interpretations automatically, or does it possibly reveal that the tongues

21: Tongues

Paul was speaking were personal between him and God, and other believers didn't need to know what was said?

21:16 Paul was incredibly hungry for God and, like Jesus, probably spent considerable time alone with God. If Paul had a personal prayer language, could this partly explain why Paul believed that he spoke in tongues more than anyone?

21:17 When we receive any supernatural gift from God, isn't it an incredibly special gift regardless of what it is? And highly likely to be more valuable than any earthly gift or possession we can ever receive? And thus, shouldn't we be incredibly thankful to be able to receive a gift such as tongues?

Two Somewhat Perplexing Scriptures

It's interesting when Paul says that if someone speaks in a tongue, they are to pray that they will be able to interpret the tongue, or they need to know an interpreter is present before they speak the tongue.

- *1 Corinthians 14:13 Therefore let one who speaks in a tongue pray that he may interpret.*
- *1 Corinthians 14:28 but if there is no interpreter, he must keep silent in the church; and let him speak to himself and to God.*

21:18 Holy Spirit gives the believer the tongue to speak. Isn't it reasonable to expect Holy Spirit would only give someone a tongue if that believer or another believer would be given the interpretation? And how exactly would you find out in advance if somebody had the interpretation? Do you ask the group before you give the tongue (which I've never personally witnessed)? Do you ask God if someone will be given the interpretation before you give the tongue (again, I've never seen this)? Or is this a situation where we trust God when He tells us to speak, obey Him, and speak?

21:19 If we do speak a tongue but there is no interpretation given afterward, does that automatically mean we were out of line giving the tongue?

If it's a tongue from God to be spoken, the answer to Question 21:19 is no. My experience is that God always gives an interpretation, but sometimes the person who is initially given the interpretation did not share it for various reasons such as shyness, doubt, fear of judgment and/or fear of being wrong. But in such situations, God then seems to almost always give the interpretation to another person, or to the person who initially spoke the tongue.

FALSE TONGUES

Are there false tongues? Absolutely. The enemy is a master counterfeiter. People of other faiths speak in tongues. These tongues are not of God, but of demonic origin. I saw a YouTube video where an individual was teaching people how to speak in tongues. His approach involved encouraging those watching him to simply repeat a series of sounds he made. There was no mention of needing to be born again, or to be Baptized in the Holy Spirit. There was no discussion of tongues being a Holy Spirit

CEASED?

gift, something Holy Spirit gives as He chooses to give. And thus, I suspect this man was not being influenced by Holy Spirit, but by a demon. I wouldn't be surprised if people who did what this man said to do would soon be speaking in tongues. And in doing so, they were most likely speaking a false, demonic tongue.

21:20   Some Cessationists argue any instances of false tongues means all tongues are false. If that is true and all tongues are false because some tongues are false, does that mean because some individuals teach false things about Jesus and Christianity, that all teachings of Jesus and Christianity are false? If not, why the double standard?

PERSONAL PRAYER LANGUAGE
'TONGUES FOR PERSONAL USE'

On whether or not tongues include a personal prayer language, consider 1 Corinthians 14:4.

❑   *1 Corinthians 14:4 **One who speaks in a tongue edifies himself**; but one who prophesies edifies the church.*

The English word *'edify'* is derived from the Greek word *'oikodomeo'* G3618 and means in part *'to promote growth in Christian wisdom, affection, grace, virtue, holiness, blessedness and/or to grow in wisdom and piety (reverence for God)'*.

21:21   There is no mention of an interpretation of the tongue in verse 4, but yet a person still benefits when they speak in a tongue. Does that indicate there may be something more going on with tongues than simply speaking in an earthly language one doesn't know?

21:22   Given the tongue edifies/builds up the person speaking the tongue, doesn't that indicate tongues aren't always for the good/benefit of others, but sometimes are intended to be only beneficial for the person speaking the tongue?

In Chapter 2, **CEASED?** discussed the issue of who receives the spiritual gifts (prophecy, healings, tongues etc.) as listed in 1 Corinthians 12:
1. the person used by Holy Spirit to give or deliver the prophecy, healing, tongue etc.; or
2. the person receiving the prophetic word, healing or tongue.

21:23   When Paul encouraged the believers in Corinth to pursue the gifts, is it possible that one reason Paul did so was because the gifts could also be for their personal growth/benefit?

❑   *1 Corinthians 14:1 Pursue love, **yet desire earnestly spiritual gifts**, but especially that you may prophesy.*

21:24   When a believer has spoken in tongues involving 2 different earthly languages he or she doesn't know, would you describe each of these tongues as being:
   i.   two different kinds or types of tongues: or
   ii. one kind or type of tongue, but which were a bit unique?

21:25   If we say they are the same kind or type of tongue, how do we deal with 1

21: Tongues

Corinthians 12:28 which states there are various kinds of tongues?
- *1 Corinthians 12:28 And God has appointed in the church, first apostles, second prophets, third teachers, then miracles, then gifts of healings, helps, administrations, **various kinds of tongues**.*

21:26 Would tongues involving heavenly languages represent another kind or type of tongue?

Mark 16:17 states that followers of Jesus will speak with new tongues.
- *Mark 16:17 These signs will accompany those who have believed: in My name they will cast out demons, **they will speak with new tongues**; 18 ... they will lay hands on the sick, and they will recover.*

21:27 If one believer has already spoken in a tongue in earthly language ABC, would a second believer speaking in a tongue based on language ABC constitute speaking in a 'new tongue'? To expand on this, once a tongue has been spoken by someone in each and every earthly language, how could there be any new tongues left to be spoken?

21:28 Would God's creation of a unique, personal prayer language for each believer mean there is an 'unlimited' number of new tongues? And wouldn't that make all the new tongues mentioned in Mark 16:17 relevant for Biblical times as well as for today?

21:29 Based on the NASB translation, the word tongues is mentioned 23 times in the New Testament. Interpretation of tongues is referred to eight times. The word language as it refers to tongues and an earthly language is used once - in Acts 28. Would the one-time reference to earthly language be consistent with the thought that tongues include multitudes of personal, non-earthly, prayer languages that only God can understand?

The topic of tongues is controversial, and can get a bit confusing. Rather than trying to figure everything out, sometimes we just need to speak our heart. *"God, I trust you. Lead me into the truth and let me use these gifts as you want me to. But I ask this Lord ... can You please make it really clear!".*

Summary - Personal Prayer Language

Is a personal prayer language legitimate? Consider some comments made so far in Chapter 21.

1. In the natural, Peter could not have known what earthly language(s) were known by every person in the group of Cornelius, family and friends at the moment Peter realized they were speaking in tongues, and decided to immediately have them water baptized.
2. There is no mention that the tongues spoken by those at Cornelius's home, or by the 12 disciples at Ephesus, were in heavenly or earthly languages.
3. There are no details of any interpretation of a tongue anywhere in the Bible.
4. Paul spoke in tongues more than anyone else in Corinth, with no interpretation of tongues mentioned.
5. Paul spoke in tongues outside the church.
6. Paul encouraged speaking in tongues.

CEASED?

7. When we speak in heavenly tongues, we speak to God, not mankind.

If you're still not sure of the notion of a personal prayer language, seek God. If you're sincere in your seeking the truth and all that He has for you, I suspect He'll answer.

10 BENEFITS OF PRAYING IN A PERSONAL PRAYER LANGUAGE

Before getting into the 10 benefits, let me clarify two points.
1. This discussion on benefits does not include the benefits of tongues and corresponding interpretation of tongues which are intended for other believers or non-believers.
2. Tongues related to speaking in a personal prayer language, like tongues and interpretation of tongues, is available after we're born again and have been Baptized in the Holy Spirit. The teaching that we must speak in a private prayer language, or must have been Baptized in the Holy Spirit in order to be saved is false. The original apostles were born again on resurrection Sunday evening but were not Baptized in the Holy Spirit and did not speak in tongues until Pentecost, 50 days later. Speaking in a personal prayer language can serve as a confirmation of being saved as well as having been Baptized in the Holy Spirit, but tongues are not a requirement to be saved.

In terms of the benefits of speaking in a personal prayer language, a search of the internet will yield dozens of benefits. A few of the primary benefits I'm personally familiar with, follow below.

1: In line with God's Will

Since Holy Spirit gives us the words to pray in our personal prayer language, we can take comfort our prayers are in line with God's will. The reality is sometimes we don't know what to pray. Let me requote one paragraph from Benedict Carey's article referred to on page 275.

> *Researchers at the University of Pennsylvania took brain images of five women while they spoke in tongues and found that* **_their frontal lobes - the thinking, willful part of the brain through which people control what they do - were relatively quiet, as were the language centers_**. *The regions involved in maintaining self-consciousness were active. The women were not in blind trances, and it was unclear which region was driving the behavior."*

In brief, we let Holy Spirit guide our prayers which is beneficial, especially when we don't know how to pray. If you're a new believer, an example of such a time is when our child or friend is making a decision that, in our way of thinking, causes us concern. However, rather than praying in our earthly language and praying what we think is right, or voicing our opinion - our soulish view (which could be wrong) - we can ask Holy Spirit for guidance, and/or we pray in tongues. Either way helps ensure we pray according to God's will, according to what God wants.

❑ *Romans 8:26 In the same way the Spirit also helps our weakness;* ***for we do***

21: Tongues

not know how to pray as we should, *but the Spirit Himself intercedes for us with groanings too deep for words;*

21:30 To clarify, is praying in our personal prayer language recommended in part because we often don't know how best to pray with our minds in a given situation, but Holy Spirit does?

2: Control when to Start and Stop, and Quietly or Out Loud

Starting and stopping of speaking in our personal prayer language is almost always at our total discretion. I say almost always because there have been times where I felt I really had no choice. In such cases, I wasn't sure why or for who, but I just knew I had to pray. Yes, I had free will and I could have chosen not to pray, but the prompting was so strong that not praying would be akin to disobeying God. After a while, I sensed God was telling me it was ok to stop. In most cases, I had no clue what was going on. Sometimes I asked what it was about. Typically, I don't.

I've also been in gatherings where I felt prayer was needed. I began to pray in tongues - in my personal prayer language - quietly with my tongue moving somewhat, but in silence (hopefully).

3: Quieting our Minds; Peace to our Souls

When speaking in our personal prayer language, our mind is largely still. We can speak in tongues when doing every day things such as driving and household chores, just as we can pray in our earthly language while doing such things. But fundamentally, our mind is essentially forced to go relatively quiet with respect to thinking on what or how to pray. This is very helpful when experiencing tormenting, negative and/or ungodly thoughts because praying in the Spirit essentially pushes the stop button in the spin cycle of unproductive thoughts. One result of this is peace. As our mind quiets, we're also better able to enter into a time with God, and to hear from Him. Speaking in tongues is also great when our minds are active and we can't sleep. For myself, speaking in tongues settles my mind and usually enables me to go back to sleep quite quickly.

4: Part of the Process of Renewing our Minds

Paul tells us we're to renew our minds. Given that praying in our personal prayer language can help us from thinking ungodly thoughts, it is one of the tools that can help us stop our old ways of thinking, and better enable us to start building new ways of thinking, a renewing of our minds.

❑ *Romans 12:2 And do not be conformed to this world, but be transformed by the renewing of your mind, so that you may prove what the will of God is, that which is good and acceptable and perfect.*

5: Health to our Bodies

In an article by Mark Virkler, *"Health Benefits of Speaking in Tongues"*, he writes: *"He who speaks in a tongue edifies himself" (1 Corinthians 14:4). Dr. Carl Peterson, M.D. conducted a study at ORU in Tulsa, Oklahoma. Being a brain specialist, he was doing research on the relationship between the brain and praying or speaking in tongues. He found that as we pray in the Spirit or worship in the Spirit (our*

CEASED?

heavenly language), the brain releases 2 chemical secretions that are directed into our immune systems giving a 35 to 40 percent boost to the immune system. This promotes healing within our bodies. Amazingly, this secretion is triggered from a part of the brain that has no other apparent activity in humans and is only activated by our Spirit-led prayer and worship!

21:31   As mentioned before, each of our 3 parts - spirit, soul and body - is extremely complicated and intertwined with the other. Does this evidence of the benefits of speaking in our personal prayer language not only show the benefits of this blessing, but once more show God's creative genius?

6: Pray without Ceasing

God wants us to seek Him first and to walk with Him throughout our waking hours. Praying in our personal prayer language helps make that happen. With tongues, we don't have to worry about what to pray. We simply make ourselves available, and Holy Spirit gives us the words to pray.

- *Matthew 6:33 But seek first His kingdom and His righteousness, and all these things will be added to you.*
- *1 Thessalonians 5:16 Rejoice always; 17 pray without ceasing;*

7: Edification

1 Corinthians 14:4 tells us that speaking in our personal prayer language edifies ourselves.

- *1 Corinthians 14:4 One **who speaks in a tongue edifies himself**; but one who prophesies edifies the church.*

This edification is reiterated in Jude 1:20.

- *Jude 1:20 But you, beloved, **building yourselves up on your most holy faith, praying in the Holy Spirit,***

As a reminder, per above, the English word *'edify'* is derived from the Greek word *'oikodomeo'* [G3618] which means in part to *'promote growth in Christian wisdom, affection, grace, virtue, holiness and blessedness'*.

8: Spiritual Power

On June 2, 2012 Robert Morris gave a very interesting sermon called *'The Pure Language'* which is available on gatewaypeople.com. A key part of the message dealt with the power that may be associated with speaking in tongues. Here's my abbreviated understanding of this issue.

When Adam and Eve were created, God gave them a language so they could communicate with God and with each other.

- *Genesis 11:1 Now the whole earth used the same language and the same words.*

Inhabitants at Babylon built a city and tower towards heaven to make a name for themselves in order to avoid being scattered over the earth.

21: Tongues

- *Genesis 11:4 They said, "Come, let us build for ourselves a city, and a tower whose top will reach into heaven, and let us **make for ourselves a name**, **otherwise we will be scattered abroad** over the face of the whole earth."*

God stated that with one language, this first language from heaven, *'nothing they purpose to do will be impossible for them."*

- *Genesis 11:6 The Lord said, "Behold, they are one people, and they all have the same language. And this is what they began to do, and now **nothing which they purpose to do will be impossible for them**.*

'Nothing will be impossible for them' means quite a bit was possible. God responded by confusing their language, creating other languages, and then scattering people all over the earth to stop their ungodly construction and stubborn independence.

- *Genesis 11:7 Come, let Us go down and there **confuse their language**, so that they will not understand one another's speech." 8 So the Lord scattered them abroad from there over the face of the whole earth; and they stopped building the city. 9 Therefore its name was called Babel, because there **the Lord confused the language of the whole earth**; and **from there the Lord scattered them abroad over the face of the whole earth**.*

21:32 It's fairly clear a key reason for God confusing the language was to prevent the people from doing anything they purposed to do. Does that suggest there was a degree of unusual power associated with this first language?

21:33 The power of the spoken word is evident from the beginning of God's creative genius in Genesis. Believers are called to go and share the Good News in words and power. Baptism of the Holy Spirit gives power to believers to be witnesses for Christ. This power manifests itself in different ways including the 9 Holy Spirit gifts, one of which is tongues. Keeping that in mind, and considering our personal prayer language involves Holy Spirit giving us the words to speak, is there perhaps more spiritual power associated with speaking in our personal prayer language than we may recognize?

9: Armor of God

God's Word tells us to put on the armor of God which is often viewed as having 6 components: i) belt of truth, ii) breastplate of righteousness, iii) feet covered in peace, iv) shield of faith, v) helmet of salvation and vi) God's Word, the sword of the Spirit.

- *Ephesians 6:13 Therefore, take up **the full armor of God**, so that you will be able to resist in the evil day, and having done everything, to stand firm. 14 Stand firm therefore, having **girded your loins with truth**, and having put on the **breastplate of righteousness**, 15 and having **shod your feet with the preparation of the gospel of peace**; 16 in addition to all, taking up the **shield of faith** with which you will be able to extinguish all the flaming arrows of the evil one. 17 And take the **helmet of salvation**, and **the sword of the Spirit**, which is the word of God.*

But look at the next verse - verse 18 - where we're told to pray.
- *Ephesians 6:18 With all prayer and petition **pray** at all times in the Spirit, and with this in view, be on the alert with all perseverance and petition for all the saints,*

Prayer is powerful and adding prayer to our list of armor is certainly understandable. But if we look at verse 18 closer, it goes on to say we're to pray **'at all times'**. In its entirety, we should **'pray at all times in the Spirit'** which - to me - is speaking in our personal prayer language.

21:34 If speaking in our personal prayer language is part of our armor, does that lend further evidence to the notion that Holy Spirit gifts - in this case tongues - can be for personal benefit? Is this another reason why Paul said we should earnestly seek spiritual gifts?

10: Does/Doesn't Enemy Understand?

Since praying in our personal prayer language is between a person and God, I don't believe the enemy can understand all of what is being said - unless God wants him to know. To the extent God wants the enemy to know what we're saying/singing in tongues, I suspect our tongues would have significant benefits in the area of spiritual warfare.

As an example, in the first sentence of the third paragraph of Mr. Carey's article on page 306 of **CEASED?**, the article stated *"studies suggest that people who speak in tongues rarely suffer from mental problems"*. This is pure speculation on my part, but I wonder if such results occur in part because, in addition to our mind being sidelined/silenced by speaking in tongues, the enemy is also sidelined/silenced. In other words, the enemy is effectively prevented from giving us tormenting, negative, destructive and/or sinful thoughts while we're speaking in tongues.

I also wonder if some of the other words given to us by Holy Spirit when praying in tongues impact the demonic realm in other ways including hindering/preventing the enemy from attacking us for a time even when we're not speaking in tongues.

21:35 Are these multi-faceted benefits of speaking in tongues perhaps why Paul also cautioned anyone from stopping others from speaking in tongues? Because in doing so, we could be depriving others of the benefits and blessings they need? And would it again help explain why Paul spoke in his personal prayer language more than others?
- *1 Corinthians 14:39 Therefore, my brethren, desire earnestly to prophesy, and **do not forbid to speak in tongues**.*
- *1 Corinthians 14:18 I thank God, **I speak in tongues more than you all**;*

WHO CAN HAVE A PERSONAL PRAYER LANGUAGE, SPEAK IN TONGUES OR INTERPRET TONGUES?

Paul writes that not everyone will speak in tongues.
- *1 Corinthians 12:29 **All are not apostles**, are they? **All are not prophets**, are they? **All are not teachers**, are they? **All are not workers of miracles**, are they? 30 **All do not have gifts of healings**, do they? **All do not speak***

21: Tongues

*with tongues, do they? **All do not interpret**, do they?*

21:36 Is one reason why some believers will not speak in tongues because they will not consider being Baptized in the Holy Spirit, and thus do not have access to this gift?

21:37 The answer to the above question is certainly yes in some cases, but in other cases where a person wants to speak in tongues, could it be that God has chosen to either delay giving the gift, and/or will be giving these individuals other Holy Spirit gifts?

In terms of a private prayer language, this blessing is between God and each person. No one else is involved. Per the above, there are many benefits to a personal prayer language including ensuring that we pray in alignment with God's will.

21:38 Approximately 9 years ago, I was baptized in the Holy Spirit and immediately started speaking in my personal prayer language. I've never given a public tongue that was interpreted, nor have I ever had an interpretation to give that I know of. Could it be that while not everybody will be involved in the Holy Spirit gifts of 'tongues and interpretation of tongues', that many/most believers can nonetheless receive a personal prayer language if they want? Especially since it's a personal gift facilitating communication with God?

21:39 If the tongues spoken by Cornelius, family and friends, and by the 12 disciples at Ephesus were in their personal prayer language, would that explain why there was no interpretation of tongues, and why neither Peter nor Paul pursued interpretations?

21:40 If we want to have a personal prayer language, but don't have it at present, what harm can it do if we keep on asking Holy Spirit for this blessing?

- ❏ *Matthew 7:11 If you then, being evil, know how to give good gifts to your children, how much more will your Father who is in heaven give what is good to those who ask Him!*
- ❏ *Luke 11:13 If you then, being evil, know how to give good gifts to your children, how much more will your heavenly Father give the Holy Spirit to those who ask Him?"*

<u>Testimony</u>

God is sovereign. He may give us a personal prayer language immediately after we're Baptized in the Holy Spirit as He did for me, or after He has been asked time and time again. I have a good friend who was Baptized in the Holy Spirit, but did not speak in a personal prayer language for several years. Then, one day while worshipping, started to speak in a heavenly language without asking. Holy Spirit simply gave the gift out of the blue.

7 UNIQUE SCENARIOS INVOLVING TONGUES

As mentioned earlier, there are 3 potential types or groups of tongues:
  i. earthly language;
  ii. languages only God knows; and
  iii. tongues of angels.

CEASED?

In my experience, these three types materialize in seven different situations. Three situations occur in private where the believer talks or sings in a personal prayer language. Believers can ask Holy Spirit for an interpretation of the tongue which Holy Spirit may, or may not, give.
1. praying for oneself;
2. intercessory prayer for others; and
3. singing in the Spirit as part of praise and worship.

The other four situations occur in a more public setting such as when 2 or more believers gather in a home, or in gatherings at bricks and mortar churches.
4. praying in an earthly language not known by the believer speaking, but one or more other individuals who are present do understand;
5. praying in a heavenly language where an interpretation is to be given by the believer speaking, or by one or more other believers who are present;
6. corporate (group) prayer where all (virtually all) in attendance pray in the Spirit in their personal prayer language. Interpretation may occur in part, or may not occur at all;
7. corporate (group) singing in the Spirit in each believer's personal prayer language as part of corporate praise and worship. Interpretation may occur in part, or not at all.

I have witnessed each of the above situations except #4, and been directly involved in all but #4 and #5. The last two scenarios may seem strange to anyone not familiar or comfortable with tongues. That's a key reason why the Bible gives guidelines on speaking in tongues in public.

Some believers teach speaking in a personal prayer language is a different gift than what is talked about in 1 Corinthians 12. That may be the case, but I personally lean towards the view that personal tongues are one of the *'various kinds of tongues'* referred to in 1 Corinthians 12:10. And whatever it is, I'm glad God gave it to me.
- ❑ *1 Corinthians 12:10 and to another the effecting of miracles, and to another prophecy, and to another the distinguishing of spirits, to another **various kinds of tongues**, and to another the interpretation of tongues.*

PRAYING IN THE SPIRIT
- ❑ *Ephesians 6:18 With all prayer and petition pray at all times **in [en G1722] the Spirit**, and with this in view, be on the alert with all perseverance and petition for all the saints,*
- ❑ *Jude 1:20 But you, beloved, building yourselves up on your most holy faith, praying **in [en G1722] the Holy Spirit**,*

Three commonly held views on what praying in the Spirit means are as follows:
1. speaking in one's earthly language, guided by one's spirit and soul;
2. speaking in one's earthly language, but inspired by Holy Spirit as to what to pray; and
3. speaking in one's personal prayer/heavenly language.

21: Tongues

My understanding is that Cessationists typically see the first and maybe the second alternative as praying in the Spirit. Charismatics and Pentecostals see the third alternative as praying in the Spirit, with the second alternative a possibility. A couple of considerations.

1. In both Ephesians 16:8 and Jude 1:20, praying in the Spirit refers to Holy Spirit. The English word *'in'* is derived from the Greek word *'en'*, the same Greek word used to describe Holy Spirit coming in a newly born-again follower of Jesus.
2. Jude 1:20 also states praying in the Spirit builds ourselves up, a notion also discussed in 1 Corinthians 14:4 where speaking in our personal prayer language edifies ourselves.

❑ *1 Corinthians 14:4 One **who speaks in a tongue edifies himself**; but one who prophesies edifies the church.*

21:41 Given Ephesians 16:8 and Jude 1:20 both show Holy Spirit is involved when praying in the Spirit, is it understandable why many believers believe praying in the Spirit involves a believer's soul being quiet, and Holy Spirit taking charge?

21:42 If a believer has not yet received the gift of a personal prayer language and prays exclusively in his/her earthly language, that person can (and should) still seek and be led by Holy Spirit in his/her prayers. As a result, if indeed Holy Spirit is speaking to the person while praying in their earthly language, wouldn't this still represent a form of praying in the Spirit or, if not, something close to it?

When I gather with other believers who are comfortable with everybody praying or singing in their personal prayer language, we do so. Holy Spirit leads each person independently. Other times, we pray only in English when someone is present who is uncomfortable with tongues.

HOW TO START PRAYING IN OUR PERSONAL PRAYER LANGUAGE

My suggestion for someone who wants to speak in tongues is fairly straightforward.

1. Ask Jesus to Baptize you in the Holy Spirit. Here's an example prayer from page 176 in Chapter 10.

   "Jesus, the Baptism of the Holy Spirit is true and available today, and since You are the one that gives it, can You please give me this Baptism. Shield me from any schemes of the enemy, and provide help so that I use this gift the way You want it used, and for Your glory, not mine. Thank You Jesus. Amen."

2. Believe, in faith, that you have been Baptized in the Holy Spirit.
3. Ask Holy Spirit to give you the gift of tongues and to keep you from anything not of God.
4. Try to shut your mind off from thinking about anything except God. Think of

some of the things He has done for you. Open your mouth and thank Him. Praise Him. After some time, stop speaking, and start to make a sound just like a new baby trying to learn how to speak a new language - which you are. Over time, your vocabulary will increase. And, down the road, you might even get what may seem like another new language or two.

TONGUES AND THE ROMAN CATHOLIC CHURCH

The Charismatic movement within the Catholic church started in the 1960's, and has been recognized since the early 1970's by the mainline Roman Catholic church. However, my understanding is that to date, the Roman Catholic church has no formal position on whether or not tongues includes earthly languages only, or earthly languages plus heavenly languages including personal prayer languages.

21:43   If any followers of Christ would know whether or not tongues included personal prayer languages, wouldn't it be the original apostles?

21:44   Given the Roman Catholic church places heavy emphasis on the writings of early church fathers, some of whom were discipled by the original apostles, isn't it reasonable to expect those early church fathers should have known whether or not tongues included personal prayer languages?

21:45   Given the Roman Catholic church claims it is the one true church with origins from before the cross (i.e. with Peter) - before the first gift of tongues was given - and has teachings of early church fathers who were discipled by the original apostles who would have been familiar with all aspects of tongues, shouldn't the Roman Catholic church have absolute clarity on all aspects of tongues? If not, why not?

21:46   As the Catholic church does not have clarity on all aspects of tongues, isn't that reason to question other key claims of the Roman Catholic church?

CLOSING POINT TO PONDER

Hundreds of millions of Christians believe tongues, interpretation of tongues and speaking in a private prayer language are all supernatural blessings from God. If you believe a personal prayer language is gibberish and any form of tongue today is of the devil, that's your prerogative. However, if you teach that position, I encourage you to ensure you have clear scriptural evidence that refutes the evidence herein. I don't think it would be wise for anyone to mock and undermine something that is a wonderful gift from God.

And if you want the gift of a personal prayer language, talk to God. After all, you are His child.

21:47   If Christians doubt we can actually hear from God today, is speaking in tongues evidence we can? And that there is much more power and intimacy available if and when we seek God?

22

Are Believers to Live in Divine Health?

INTRODUCTION

THE issue of healing is a very controversial topic with many dimensions. **CEASED?** will only discuss a few. Chapter 1 of **CEASED?** touched on whether or not God still puts afflictions on people today. I believe He may still do so, and it shouldn't be ruled out. Chapter 22 raises questions related to a few healing issues, questions for both Charismatics and Cessationists to ponder.

We'll soon see scriptures that show signs and wonders including healings should be the norm in the lives of believers. The reality, however, is not everyone will be healed. Sometimes, the kindest, nicest, most godly, sincerest believers and loved ones die too young. Their death may seem so unfair, and made all the more difficult when we don't understand the why. Many others live today with extensive physical issues and have not been healed even after extensive prayer. If this is something you're currently dealing with, I am so sorry for your pain. And if you have anxiety at the mere thought of reading about miraculous healings, consider skipping Chapter 22 for now. But so you know in advance, I don't believe it is neither prudent nor Biblical to expect 100% of people will be healed. Vast majority healed - yes. 100% healed - no.

Heart Check: Pray or Heal the Sick

God's Word tells us to heal the sick, not to just pray for the sick (apart from a church gathering where we can ask elders to anoint and pray for the sick).

- ❑ Matthew 10:8 **Heal the sick**, raise the dead, cleanse the lepers, cast out demons. Freely you received, freely give.
- ❑ Luke 10:9 and **heal those in it who are sick**, and say to them, 'The kingdom of God has come near to you.'
- ❑ James 5:14 Is anyone among you sick? Then he must call for the elders of the church and they are to **pray over him**, anointing him with oil in the name of the Lord;

22:1   Doesn't heal the sick sound somewhat like a command, and not a request?

Defining Divine Health

To those readers who believe born-again Christians are to live in divine health, let's begin by addressing the term 'divine health'. When I think of phrases such as divine revelation or divine health, the word 'divine' brings to mind words such as

CEASED?

godly, perfect, pure, truth, clean, holy and even permanency. When I think of people who might have lived the closest to divine health (excluding Jesus), the first 2 individuals that come to mind are Adam and Eve.

22:2 When we use the term 'divine health', was the health Adam and Eve enjoyed before the fall, the level of health we should expect born-again believers to have today? Or should it be closer to the 900+ years Adam and others lived after the fall, but before the flood?

22:3 If the health/lifespan of Adam is not to be our benchmark, what are the parameters of divine health that ordinary believers can relate to? Abraham who lived to ~175? 120 per Genesis 6:3? 70-80 years per Psalm 90? Does divine health mean no sickness or disease? If so, how do we deal with prominent advocates of divine health suffering from very challenging diseases from time to time and who sometimes, unfortunately, die from such diseases?

22:4 If our expectations of health and lifespan are less than what Adam and Eve had before the fall, should a term other than divine health be used to describe the physical health available to believers because of what Jesus did - by whose wounds we were healed?

❑ *1 Peter 2:24 and He Himself bore our sins in His body on the cross, so that we might die to sin and live to righteousness;* **_for by His wounds you were healed_**.

Are All to be Healed

Besides 1 Peter 2:24, two other scriptures supporting divine health are as follows:

❑ *Psalm 103:3 Who pardons all your iniquities,* **_Who heals all your diseases;_**
❑ *Isaiah 53:4 Surely our griefs He Himself bore, And our sorrows He carried; Yet we ourselves esteemed Him stricken, Smitten of God, and afflicted. 5 But He was pierced through for our transgressions, He was crushed for our iniquities; The chastening for our well-being fell upon Him, And* **_by His scourging we are healed_**.

22:5 Divine health and sins are often lumped together because just as Jesus took 'all' our sins, He also took *'all our sicknesses and diseases'*. When I see words such as all, none, forever or never - I usually take them with reservation. Absolutes are quite rare. In the case of Psalm 103:3 for instance, the word 'all' is not in the Hebrew. The original Hebrew reads *'forgives sins, heals diseases'*. While other scriptures confirm God forgives all our sins except the one unforgiveable sin, does that inclusivity of sins automatically mean God will also heal all our diseases while we are living on earth?

When we are born again, we are cleansed; our sins are washed away and we are justified. We're a new creation, and as the old saying goes, *"I am justified 'just as if I'd' never sinned in the first place"*. Our spirits, once separated from God, are born again and come alive. Jesus came to destroy the works of the enemy. Some believers think some of the *'works to be destroyed'* are situations where the enemy contributed to people getting sicknesses or diseases.

22: Divine Health

- *1 John 3:8 the one who practices sin is of the devil; for the devil has sinned from the beginning. The Son of God appeared for this purpose, to **destroy the works of the devil**.*

There are many scriptures on healing, but for now, let me address those who believe it is God's will that all believers are to be fully healed and to live in divine health.

22:6 If sickness and disease are to be viewed in the same light as our sins, why are most believers not healed in their bodies and souls when first born again?

22:7 Why are many people not healed after they have been prayed for, even by those who have witnessed thousands of other healing miracles?

22:8 While sins are instantly forgiven and our spirits instantly made right when born again (an event), are we more accurate in viewing healing of our souls and bodies as something that can be instant, but can also be more of a process that occurs in different ways and at different speeds for each person? And sometimes, not at all?

Jesus Healed Everyone - Or did He

Another core argument of those who believe in divine health is that Jesus healed everyone He prayed for. This indeed appears to be true, but did He heal everyone who was sick? Consider what happened in Nazareth, Bethesda, and Capernaum. At Nazareth, Jesus only healed a few people.

- *Mark 6:3 Is not this the carpenter, the son of Mary, and brother of James and Joses and Judas and Simon? Are not His sisters here with us?" **And they took offense at Him**. 4 Jesus said to them, "A prophet is not without honor except in his hometown and among his own relatives and in his own household." 5 And **He could do no miracle** there **except that He laid His hands on a few sick people and healed them**. 6 And **He wondered at their unbelief**. And He was going around the villages teaching.*

22:9 Does Jesus's experience at Nazareth indicate Jesus refused to heal, or was it a case where people remained sick because they didn't believe in Jesus, and therefore didn't ask Jesus for healing?

At Bethesda, Jesus healed one person, but it's not clear if He healed others. The most common view is He did not, even though there were many others in need of healing.

- *John 5:5 A man was there who had been ill for thirty-eight years. 6 When Jesus saw him lying there ... He said to him, "Do you wish to get well?" 7 The sick man answered Him, "Sir, I have no man to put me into the pool when the water is stirred up, but while I am coming, another steps down before me." 8 Jesus said to him, "Get up, pick up your pallet and walk." 9 **Immediately the man became well, and picked up his pallet and began to walk.** ... 13 But the man who was healed did not know who it was, **for Jesus had slipped away while there was a crowd in that place**.*

CEASED?

Now consider Capernaum which was early in Jesus's earthly ministry.
- ❏ *Mark 1:34* **And He healed many who were ill with various diseases**, *and cast out many demons; and He was not permitting the demons to speak, because they knew who He was. 35 In the early morning, while it was still dark, Jesus got up, left the house, and went away to a secluded place, and was praying there. 36 Simon and his companions searched for Him; 37 they found Him, and said to Him,* "**Everyone is looking for You.**"
- 22:10 Given Jesus had healed many who were ill, is it reasonable to expect some of the group 'looking' for Jesus were afflicted and seeking healing?

However, instead of staying and healing all of the sick who were looking for Him, Jesus moved on so that He could preach - because that's what He came for.
- ❏ *Mark 1:38 He said to them, "Let us go somewhere else to the towns nearby, so that I* **may preach there** *also; for* **that is what I came for**.*" 39 And He went into their synagogues ... preaching and* **casting out the demons**.
- 22:11 Jesus's primary focus during His earthly ministry was dealing with eternal matters. Apart from that, however, do the three situations at Nazareth, Bethesda and Capernaum indicate that while Jesus can heal all, some people may not get healed for other reasons? Such as unbelief that existed in Nazareth? Or as in not right now, but in God's timing?
- 22:12 Doesn't Jesus make it clear that our priority focus is to be on eternal matters, and that signs and wonders are secondary?
- 22:13 In order to have a focus on eternal matters isn't it important for all believers to know how to share the gospel? In order to do so, wouldn't an instantaneous healing miracle get people's attention? When people have seen the gospel in power, aren't they more likely to be receptive to hearing the gospel in words?

Jesus gives more insight into why He did what He did during His earthly ministry.
- ❏ *John 8:28 So Jesus said, "When you lift up the Son of Man, then you will know that I am He, and* **I do nothing on My own initiative**, *but I speak these things* **as the Father taught Me**. *29 And He who sent Me is with Me; He has not left Me alone, for I always do the things that are pleasing to Him."*
- ❏ *John 12:49 For I did not speak on My own initiative, but the Father Himself who sent Me has given Me a commandment as to what to say and what to speak. 50* **I know that His commandment is eternal life**; *therefore the things I speak, I speak just as the Father has told Me.*
- ❏ *John 5:19 Therefore Jesus answered and was saying to them, "Truly, truly, I say to you,* **the Son can do nothing of Himself, unless it is something He sees the Father doing; for whatever the Father does, these things the Son also does in like manner**.

- 22:14 Jesus had a limited amount of time on earth. He had to keep the big picture in mind which perhaps explains why Jesus didn't take the time to heal everybody. However, given most believers today aren't limited by a 3½ year time frame, and there are hundreds of millions of us, don't we

collectively have enough time to pray for each person that is sick? Is this one reason perhaps why we will do greater works than Jesus?
- ❏ *John 14:12 Truly, truly, I say to you, he who believes in Me, the works that I do, he will do also; and **greater works than these he will do; because I go to the Father.***

22:15   I once analyzed all the healing scriptures looking for the one true healing formula, the one true sequence of steps. I didn't find it. I know some believers who seem to believe laying on of hands and anointing of oil is essential. Scriptures such as those above show there isn't one perfect format or formula.
   i. Is this because God wants us to come to Him in all things, and by not having a one and only method, we are more inclined to come to Him?
   ii. And really, can we ever go wrong by going to God with a grateful heart and asking Holy Spirit what to pray for? God can respond pretty quickly i.e. seconds or less. It's not like we need 2 hours to talk.

Commandments for Today's Believers

Since Jesus healed everybody He prayed for, since Jesus is our role model, and since believers are commanded to heal the sick, one Charismatic view is that everybody who is prayed for should be healed.
- ❏ *Matthew 10:8 **Heal the sick**, raise the dead, cleanse the lepers, cast out demons. Freely you received, freely give.*
- ❏ *Luke 9:1 And He called the twelve together, and gave them power and authority over all the demons and to **heal diseases**. 2 And He sent them out to **proclaim the kingdom of God and to perform healing**.*

This view is supported by the fact supernatural signs will identify us as believers.
- ❏ *Mark 16:17 **These signs will accompany those who have believed**: in My name they will cast out demons, they will speak with new tongues; 18 they will pick up serpents, and if they drink any deadly poison, it will not hurt them; they will **lay hands on the sick, and they will recover**.*
- ❏ *1 Thessalonians 1:5 for **our gospel did not come to you in word only, but also in power** …*

Associated with this view is the belief that it's God's will for all to be healed. Matthew 8:2-3 is another verse often cited in support of this belief.
- ❏ *Matthew 8:2 And a leper came to Him and bowed down before Him, and said, "**Lord, if You are willing**, You can make me clean." 3 Jesus stretched out His hand and touched him, saying, "**I am willing**; be cleansed." And immediately his leprosy was cleansed.*

22:16   There is scriptural evidence for the view that God wants all to be healed. However, is one reason why everybody Jesus prayed for got healed, a result of Jesus only praying for individuals who Father God told Jesus to pray for?

CEASED?

- *John 5:19 Therefore Jesus answered ... "Truly, truly, I say to you, the Son can do nothing of Himself, unless it is something He sees the Father doing; for whatever the Father does, these things the Son also does in like manner.*

22:17 Since earthly Jesus is our best role model, some believers don't pray for people unless God tells them to. Totally understandable. If we're the equivalent of a FedEx driver who is authorized to deliver packages - in this case Holy Spirit gifts including gifts of healing - we should be like the FedEx driver who only delivers to the specified recipient. In other words, we only deliver a gift of healing to who God tells us to deliver a gift. And thus, if we ask God about healing a person but don't receive any delivery instructions, we may thus be inclined to stop and do nothing. However, isn't it still beneficial to offer to pray, and to try to encourage and bless the person?

Did the Disciples Heal Everybody

In the Bible, there are many more examples of people getting healed than not. We don't know the extent to which people were not healed, but we get a few glimpses.

Paul left Trophimus sick. It's unclear if Trophimus stayed sick, or was healed later.

- *2 Timothy 4:20 ... but Trophimus I left sick at Miletus.*

Paul encouraged Timothy to take wine for his stomach and ailments. We're not sure of the cause for the ongoing ailments. Some wonder if it was a lack of clean water.

- *1 Timothy 5:23 No longer drink water exclusively, but use a little wine for the sake of your stomach and your frequent ailments.*

Some believe Paul's thorn was physical; others believe it was a demonic influence.

- *2 Corinthians 12:7 ... there was given me **a thorn in the flesh, a messenger of Satan to torment me** - **to keep me from exalting myself**!*

There are many teachings on why people don't get healed. Unbelief, unforgiveness, curses, generational sins and not understanding God's grace or our authority are some of the reasons cited by teachers experienced with miraculous healings. Other teachers believe the only hindrances to healing are those we think are hindrances.

In terms of specific examples today, consider two experiences I learned about at a recent meeting in Vancouver. One dealt with a soul issue, and one with a body issue. First, I met a young lady who had emigrated from the Philippines via Hong Kong. She had no family in Canada and was extremely lonely. In her emotional pain, she cried out and encountered Jesus. She became born again. She told me Jesus told her that by isolating her from family, He was able to turn her heart towards Him. She was thankful for the trial, as tough as it was, because she found Christ.

At the same meeting, another believer shared how she had struggled to

22: Divine Health

understand why her born-again sister was not healed. Much prayer had occurred and yet the cancer prevailed and she died. The surviving sister cried out to God wanting to know why. After a lengthy time, God finally said to her something akin to: *"You were not privy to all the conversations your sister had with me".*

22:18   Is it possible that her sister - deep down in her heart and despite whatever words came from her mouth - did not want to be healed, but was ready to go home and be with Jesus?

Then consider Lois Evans who was a Jesus-loving woman who died of cancer. She received prayers from around the world. At her funeral in early 2020, her son Jonathan gave a wonderful eulogy I encourage you to find online. Part of his eulogy revealed God's message to Jonathan:

"... Just because I didn't answer your prayer your way doesn't mean that I haven't already answered your prayer anyway. Because victory was already given to your mom ... There was always only two answers to your prayers - either she was going to be healed or she was going to be healed. Either she was going to live or she was going to live ..."

We worship a mighty God whose ways are way beyond our ways. We might be wise to avoid putting God in a box we think we can define, or control.

Are Instantaneous Healing Miracles Rare

While some believers teach everybody should be healed, others teach healing miracles are rare. If you think healing miracles are scarce today, consider the following:

- *Matthew 10:8* **Heal the sick, raise the dead, cleanse the lepers**, *cast out demons. Freely you received, freely give.*
- *Mark 16:17* **These signs will accompany those who have believed**: *in My name they will* **cast out demons, they will speak with new tongues**; *18 they will pick up serpents, and if they drink any deadly poison, it will not hurt them;* **they will lay hands on the sick, and they will recover**.
- *1 Corinthians 4:20 For the* **kingdom of God** *does* **not consist in words but in power**.

22:19   What's your take on the above three scriptures?
       i.   Do they apply to believers living today? If not, why not?
       ii.   Do they suggest that healing miracles should be commonplace in the lives of believers today? If not, what do they suggest?

Empirical Evidence

I've frequently heard the comment there is no evidence of healing miracles, any documentation is fake and almost all healings are staged, psychosomatic or imagined.

22:20   If someone publicly claims that virtually all instantaneous healings are fake, doesn't this person have the responsibility to personally validate their claims, or can they voice their opinion based on a few bad apples?

CEASED?

Without question, some/many claims of healing are fake. But I have personally seen dozens of virtually instantaneous physical healing miracles first hand. I saw my wife Lori get radically healed. Years after a man hurt his legs when jumping from a building while evading police, he was instantly healed in prayer. He jumped around the foyer like a kid in a candy store. Our nurse had her fractured foot healed immediately - much to our doctor's surprise. A teenage girl had her fractured arm instantly healed. I've witnessed healings over time such as a teenager who had an irreversible heart condition that required surgery. Just before surgery, the doctor ran another test. The medical technician at the British Columbia Children's Hospital reading the echocardiogram was confused by the change in the young man's condition and wrote "procedure done?" on the analysis. No surgery was required. The answer by the way is yes; the procedure was done - by God.

If you're interested in seeing documented evidence of healing, consider going to ministries such as Healing Room Ministries (healingrooms.com) in Spokane Washington and Bethel Church in Redding California. Dr. Henry Wright's book *'A More Excellent Way'* is another good source with dozens of testimonies of healing miracles.

Heal or Pray for the Sick

In my research on healing, I found methods such as laying on of hands and anointing with oil were only in a few of the healing scriptures. In various teachings I read or listened to, I was told to take note of the fact that individuals in the Bible did not pray to God asking Him to heal the person. Rather, I was advised to note that believers spoke directly to the person/issue. And they did so with authority. In so doing, the person was healed or the demon(s) cast out.

- *Acts 3:6 But Peter said, "I do not possess silver and gold, but what I do have I give to you: **In the name of Jesus Christ the Nazarene - walk!**" 7 And seizing him by the right hand, he raised him up; and immediately his feet and his ankles were strengthened.*
- *Acts 9:34 Peter said to him, **"Aeneas, Jesus Christ heals you; get up and make your bed.**" Immediately he got up.*
- *Acts 28:8 And it happened that the father of Publius was lying in bed afflicted with recurrent fever and dysentery; and Paul went in to see him and after he had prayed, he laid his hands on him and **healed him**.*
- *Acts 16:16 ... a slave-girl having a spirit of divination ... 17 Following after Paul and us, she kept crying out, saying, "These men are bond-servants of the Most High God, who are proclaiming to you the way of salvation." 18 ... But Paul was greatly annoyed, and turned and said to the spirit, **"I command you in the name of Jesus Christ to come out of her!**" And it came out at that very moment.*

At first, I was quite taken back. Authority to heal? Me? And then I was shown scriptures dealing with authority given to believers, a topic I discuss in Chapter 23.

And no. I don't think a believer does the healing. God does. We humans are simply vessels God often uses to heal - and often by using authority He gives to His children.

22: Divine Health

Our Expectations

Each born-again Christian has to decide if supernatural manifestations of the power of God such as healing of people, are to be commonplace in our life or not.

22:21   If such events are to be commonplace, but currently aren't in our own life, in the lives of other believers around us, or in the lives of those we heavily influence – don't we have an issue that needs to be addressed? Or can we simply look the other way, and ignore it?

22:22   The Bible tells us to heal the sick. Given we're commanded to heal the sick, given the Bible indicates a very high percentage of people 'prayed for' in the Bible are healed, and given God's Word would not misrepresent what happened, then going forward:
  i. shouldn't our standard be to expect the vast majority of people we minister to will get healed? If not, why not?
  ii. if we criticize others for not going to hospitals and not healing everybody, are we ignoring the log in our own eyes, and using perceived shortcomings of others to deflect attention from our responsibilities?

Some Charismatics claim every person should get healed and if not, it's the fault of either the person praying, or the person being prayed for. That may be true in some cases, but I disagree with such blanket claims. I believe some people will not be healed no matter what is done or who is praying. And we may never know why the person was not healed. Others people may only get healed partially, or may get healed over time.

22:23   When we pray, however:
  i. is it consistent with scripture for us to expect a person who is prayed for will get healed, but to recognize there is a chance they may not?
  ii. Would it be somewhat consistent with expecting our car to start even though we know sometimes it won't? Or expecting that we will have our job tomorrow even though we know we may lose it?

The Cessationist camp believes the healing gifts of the Holy Spirit have ceased, and that instantaneous healing miracles are rare. If this is you, Chapter 22 of **CEASED?** may seem irrelevant. And if this is the case, I encourage you to consider the arguments again in Chapters 13 through 20. And perhaps consider how strong your loyalty is to your current beliefs.

In contrast to the Cessationist camp, the Continuationist camp believes the Holy Spirit gifts such as healing are to be a regular part of the Christian life. Only one perspective is true. If the truth was known by all, hundreds of millions of believers and non-believers would be impacted. May we all get the truth - and before Jesus returns.

❏   *John 8:32 and you will know the truth, and the truth will make you free."*

CEASED?

CLOSING POINTS TO PONDER

22:24 God tells His followers to do many supernatural things including casting out demons and healing the sick. If these kinds of supernatural events aren't a regular part of our life, and the lives of people we influence, aren't we/they missing out? And as a further consideration, are we/they potentially disobeying God?

22:25 Doesn't the possibility of many more believers sharing the gospel in words and power, just as the believers did in 1 Thessalonians 1, give reason to celebrate, to get excited about what God will do through His children?

22:26 After all, don't we all want to demonstrate the Kingdom of God not just in words, but in power and love?

- *Luke 9:2 And He sent them out to proclaim the kingdom of God and to perform healing.*
- *1 Corinthians 13:2 If I have the gift of prophecy, and know all mysteries and all knowledge; and if I have all faith, so as to remove mountains, but do not have love, I am nothing.*

23

Today's Christian Walk

INTRODUCTION

THERE are so many diverse aspects to the Christian walk. Much has been written by much more experienced believers than I on how to live the Christian life. I leave you to seek them out. However, I have a few comments on the following:
1. seeking God in our private space (page 303);
2. living active, supernatural-filled lives (page 303);
3. binding and loosing on earth or in heaven (page 303);
4. spiritual warfare (page 306);
5. spiritual authority (page 311); and
6. prosperity, poverty or abundant gospel (page 318).

FIGURE 23:1 FRAMEWORK

During the early days of my Christian walk, I often found myself getting overwhelmed trying to figure everything out. My nature is to try to put things in boxes, and then try to figure out how the boxes can fit together. I like diagrams and lists. I like to be organized. One night when I was wrestling with how to organize all the different topics and issues related to Christianity, I tried to put an Excel diagram together as per Figure 23:1 on the next page. Everything needs to be based on God's Word, or otherwise aligned with God's Word, which is why I put God's Word in the center. I then tried to position important topics in some kind of simple, clear, logical order. I tried different approaches, but in the end, I 'failed'. Our Christian walk involves so many issues with so many moving pieces that are so interwoven that I couldn't come close to putting a complete and proper diagram together. One thing it did help me understand a bit better is why God's Word tells us we need to trust God, and to be led by Holy Spirit.

If you're a new Christian, don't try to understand the layout of Figure 23:1. Simply view it as a diagram that lists some of the key issues that impact your walk or the lives of those you may be trying to disciple. Over time, these terms and issues as well as many more, will become second nature to you.

CEASED?

Figure 23:1

Cross and Resurrection	Salvation Born Again	Para, Meta, En, Epi	Spirit, Soul & Body	Sanctification, Glorification	Position, Authority, Identity In Christ				Holy Spirit
Enemy and Spiritual Warfare	Hearing from God	Being Led by Holy Spirit	Heart and Flesh	Fruits of the Spirit	Renewing of Mind				Old & New Covenants
Occult	Water Baptism				Great Exchange				Reliability of Bible
False Teachings & Religions	Baptism in the Holy Spirit		**God's Word**		Living in the Supernatural				Creation Science
Financial	Other Baptisms				Spiritual Gifts from Father, Jesus & Holy Spirit				False Teachings Religions
Health	Spouse	Family	Other Relationships	Greek and Hebrew	God's Promises				Heaven, Hades, Hell
Father God	Prayer	Praise & Worship	Great Commission	Discipleship	End Times				Jesus

23: Today's Christian Walk

SEEKING GOD IN OUR PERSONAL, QUIET PLACE

My view of myself and my 'performance' in my early Christian walk is probably best described as feeling like I was usually falling short, and was a failure. Perhaps that's why, of all the scriptures and counsel given to me, the one aspect that will help me most is - like Clara Williams in the movie War Room - spending time alone with God and in His Word. I'm a work in progress in this area, but know from experience it makes a huge difference. Some believers may mock this as 'too spiritual' but how can we go wrong? Isn't time spent alone with God a key part of being a Christian?

- ❏ *Matthew 6:33 But **seek first His kingdom** and **His righteousness**, and all these things will be added to you.*
- ❏ *Matthew 6:6 But you, **when you pray, go into your inner room, close your door and pray to your Father who is in secret**, and **your Father who sees what is done in secret will reward you**.*

LIVING ACTIVE, SUPERNATURAL-FILLED LIVES

Many scriptures show the children of God are to be involved in the supernatural.

- ❏ *Romans 8:14 For all who are being **led by the Spirit of God**, these are sons of God.*
- ❏ *John 14:12 ... **he who believes in Me**, the **works that I do, he will do** also; and **greater works than these he will do**; because I go to the Father.*
- ❏ *1 Corinthians 14:1 ... **yet desire earnestly spiritual gifts** ...*
- ❏ *Mark 16:17 These **signs will accompany those who have believed**: ... **cast out demons**, they **will speak with new tongues**; 18 ... they **will lay hands on the sick, and they will recover**.*

23:1 With Holy Spirit in [en] us and leading us, the supernatural is to be part of our life. Jesus commanded the disciples to wait until they were Baptized in the Holy Spirit. If we don't seek this Baptism as well, aren't we disobeying God? And potentially missing out on something special in our Christian walk?

23:2 When God heals a person, the person who was healed cannot deny the power of God. Is there one evangelistic 'tool' better than the power of God touching someone? If so, what is it? And if not, shouldn't we pursue such gifts with vigor? If not, why not?

BINDING AND LOOSING ON EARTH OR HEAVEN

An often-cited scripture in support of miraculous healings is Matthew 16:19.

- ❏ *Matthew 16:19 I will give you the keys of the kingdom of heaven; and **whatever you bind on earth shall have been bound in heaven**, and **whatever you loose on earth shall have been loosed in heaven**."*

Since heaven has no sickness or disease, binding a sickness or disease that is tormenting a person here on earth and loosing healing over the person changes the situation so they would experience what is in heaven - health. Heaven invades earth; God's kingdom has come.

- ❏ *Luke 10:9 and heal those in it who are sick, and say to them, 'The **kingdom of God has come near to you**.'*

CEASED?

Many believers disagree on the issue of binding and loosing, and a key reason behind much of the disagreement is directional.

Heaven to Earth, or Earth to Heaven
The NASB translation of Matthew 16:19 considers **what has previously been** bound and loosed in heaven (past tense) **can now be** bound and loosed on earth (present tense). Other translations give a different perspective. ESV effectively states **what is being** bound and loosed on earth (present tense) **will also be** bound and loosed in heaven (present/future tense).
- ❑ *Matthew 16:19 I will give you the keys of the kingdom of heaven; and whatever you bind on earth **shall have been bound** in heaven, and whatever you loose on earth **shall have been loosed in heaven**. (NASB)*
- ❑ *Matthew 16:19 I will give you the keys of the kingdom of heaven, and whatever you bind on earth **shall be bound in heaven**, and whatever you loose on earth **shall be loosed in heaven**. (ESV)*

23:3 Returning to the issue of healing, the ESV version suggests that if we bind sickness on earth, we will bind sickness in heaven. Furthermore, if we loose healing on earth, we will loose healing in heaven. But isn't heaven already free of sickness? And thus, why would we need to bind sickness in heaven if sickness isn't there, and why would we try to loose healing into heaven if there is no need for healing in heaven?

23:4 Further, why would we want to loose or bind anything on earth and take it to heaven?

Clearly, it matters where we are *'starting from'* and which direction we are *'going'*.

23:5 Heaven is eternal; the earth is temporary. Heaven is filled with holiness, joy and peace; the earth is filled with sin, emotional pain and strife. Heaven has no sickness or disease; the earth is filled with sickness and disease. Which direction is more likely?
   i. Whatever is on temporary earth, we take action so it goes to heaven permanently.
   ii. Whatever is in eternal heaven, we take action so it comes to temporary earth.
- ❑ *2 Corinthians 4:18 while we look not at the things which are seen, but at the things which are not seen; for the things which are seen are temporal, but the things which are not seen are eternal.*

Consider the first half of the Lord's prayer, or as some prefer to call it - the believers' prayer - since Jesus didn't need forgiveness of sins:
- ❑ *Matthew 6:9 Pray then like this: "Our Father who is in heaven, Hallowed be your name. 10* ***Your kingdom come, Your will be done, on earth as it is in heaven****.*

23:6 Doesn't the phrase *'Your will be done on earth as it is in heaven'* suggest the direction is from heaven to earth, and not earth to heaven? And doesn't

23: Today's Christian Walk

Revelation 1:27's *"nothing unclean ... will enter it"* again suggest the direction is heaven to earth, and not earth to heaven?

❏ *Revelation 21:25 In the daytime (for there will be no night there) its gates will never be closed; 26 and they will bring the glory and the honor of the nations into it; 27 and **nothing unclean**, and no one who practices abomination and lying, **shall ever come into it**, but only those whose names are written in the Lamb's book of life.*

<u>Church Discipline Only</u>

Binding and loosing are also referred to in Matthew 18:18.

❏ *Matthew 18:18 Truly I say to you, **whatever you bind on earth shall have been bound in heaven; and whatever you loose on earth shall have been loosed in heaven.***

One Cessationist view of binding and loosing is that it doesn't relate to healing and sickness, but to church discipline which is addressed just prior to Matthew 18:18.

❏ *Matthew 18:15 "**If your brother sins, go and show him his fault in private**; if he listens to you, you have won your brother. 16 But **if he does not listen to you, take one or two more with you**, so that by the mouth of two or three witnesses every fact may be confirmed. 17 **If he refuses to listen to them, tell it to the church**; and **if he refuses to listen even to the church, let him be to you as a Gentile and a tax collector**.*

Church discipline may indeed be relevant, but what about the other issues addressed between Matthew 16:19 when binding and loosing is first mentioned, and Matthew 18:18 when binding and loosing is mentioned a second time? Consider the following items that are found between Matthew 16:19 and Matthew 18:18.

❏ *Matthew 16:24 ... If anyone wishes to come after Me, he must **deny himself and take up his cross** and follow me.*

❏ *Matthew 17:1 Six days later Jesus took with Him Peter and James and John his brother, and led them up on a high mountain .... 2 **And He was transfigured before them** ...*

❏ *Matthew 17:18 And **Jesus rebuked him, and the demon came out of him, and the boy was cured at once**.*

❏ *Matthew 17:19 Then the disciples came to Jesus privately and said, "Why could we not drive it out?" 20 And He said to them, "**Because of the littleness of your faith** ...*

❏ *Matthew 17:26 When Peter said, "From strangers," Jesus said to him, "Then the sons are exempt. 27 However, so that we do not offend them, go to the sea and throw in a hook, and **take the first fish that comes up; and when you open its mouth, you will find a shekel. Take that and give it to them for you and Me."***

❏ *Matthew 18:1 At that time the disciples came to Jesus and said, "**Who then is greatest in the kingdom of heaven?**"*

❏ *Matthew 18:8 "**If your hand or your foot causes you to stumble, cut it off***

and throw it from you ...
- ❏ Matthew 18:12 *"What do you think?* ***If any man has a hundred sheep, and one of them has gone astray, does he not leave the ninety-nine on the mountains and go and search for the one that is straying?***

23:7 If church discipline is relevant to binding and loosing, aren't the other issues sandwiched between Matthew 16:19 and Matthew 18:18 also relevant to the issue of binding and loosing? If not, why not?

23:8 And given these other issues are also relevant, doesn't that mean binding and loosing is relevant to healing of sickness and disease? If not, why not?

Some clarity

I struggled for a long time in understanding what is meant by binding and loosing. The Amplified version helped me considerably.
- ❏ *Matthew 18:18 I assure you and most solemnly say to you, whatever you bind [forbid, declare to be improper and unlawful on earth shall have [already] been bound in heaven, and whatever you loose [permit, declare lawful] on earth shall have [already] been loosed in heaven. (AMP)*

Using sickness as an example, I view binding and loosing as taking action against the sickness by using the authority given to me as a child of God. When I feel led to pray according to binding and loosing, I first forbid (bind, stop that which is not of God) the sickness from remaining in the person. Second, I declare healing to replace the sickness (loosing or releasing of God's goodness). In terms of words, I lean towards this kind of statement:

> *"Father God, I thank you for the gifts of healing that are available for us. And now, In the name of Jesus, I forbid this sickness (disease, virus, infection, etc.) of _____ from staying in JD's body just as this sickness is forbidden in heaven. I tell this sickness and all pain in this body to go now. I release the healing of heaven into JD's body, and ask Father God that You restore every cell in JD's body that has been harmed by this sickness, or by treatments associated with it. In the mighty name of Jesus, I pray. Amen."*

SPIRITUAL WARFARE IN LIVES OF BELIEVERS

Satan hates God's creations and will do whatever he can to cause damage.
- ❏ John 10:10 *The **thief comes only to steal and kill and destroy** ...*

Two of the reasons Jesus came to earth were a) to destroy the works of the enemy, and b) to bring abundant life.
- ❏ *1 John 3:8 ... The Son of God appeared for this purpose,* ***to destroy the works of the devil***.
- ❏ *John 10:10 The thief comes only to steal and kill and destroy;* ***I came that they may have life, and have it abundantly***.

Jesus accomplished what He came to do. But does that mean the battle is over?
- ❏ *Ephesians 6:12 For our struggle is not against flesh and blood, but against the*

23: Today's Christian Walk

rulers, against the powers, against the world forces of this darkness, against the spiritual forces of wickedness in the heavenly places.

Ephesians was written in ~60-62AD, ~30 years after the cross. At that time, there were many, many hundreds of thousands of believers. God's Word tells believers to cast out demons. In fact, casting out demons should be a sign that we're a believer.
- ❑ *Matthew 10:8 Heal the sick, raise the dead, cleanse the lepers, **cast out demons** ...*
- ❑ *Mark 16:17 These **signs will accompany those who have believed**: in My name they will **cast out demons**, they will speak with new tongues;*

23:9 Does the fact that believers are to cast out demons (even though Jesus had already come to destroy the works of the devil), suggest that while Jesus did His part, the battle against the devil still goes on and we're to play a part by enforcing the victory? If not, what do scriptures such as Ephesians 6:12 and Mark 16:17 call believers to be doing today?

Beginning of Jesus's Earthly Ministry

After John the Baptist baptized Jesus in water, Holy Spirit came upon [epi] Jesus.
- ❑ *Matthew 3:16 After being baptized, Jesus came up immediately from the water; and behold, the heavens were opened, and he saw the **Spirit of God** descending as a dove and **lighting on Him**,*

Jesus then went to the desert. After fasting 40 days, He was tempted by the devil.
- ❑ *Matthew 4:1 Then was Jesus led up by the Spirit into the wilderness to be tempted by the devil. 2 And **after He had fasted forty days** and forty nights, He then became hungry. 3 And the **tempter came and said to Him**, "If You are the Son of God, command that these stones become bread."*

23:10 Jesus's 40-day fast was part of the equipping God gave Jesus to prepare Him for His earthly ministry. After the disciples were born again on resurrection Sunday evening, isn't it interesting they also went through an additional 40-day equipping period between resurrection Sunday and Jesus's ascension when He taught the disciples about matters related to the kingdom of God?

After His fast, Jesus's first activity was dealing with satan. After satan was done tempting Jesus, satan left. But satan didn't leave permanently. Per Luke 4:13, satan left Jesus alone until there was an opportune time to attack Jesus. One of those times was attacking Jesus indirectly through Judas.
- ❑ *Luke 4:13 When the **devil had finished every temptation**, **he left Him until an opportune time**.*
- ❑ *Luke 22:3 And Satan entered into Judas who was called Iscariot ...*

23:11 Is this an indicator that when we begin our Christian journey, we can also expect to encounter the enemy? And that while satan's demons may leave us alone for a period of time, they will attack when we're vulnerable - when we're sad, sick or lost hope?

CEASED?

23:12   Is this also perhaps why Paul tells us that our real battle is not against other human beings, but against satan and his army of demons? And doesn't that mean we need to be equipped on how to deal with the enemy?

- ☐ *Ephesians 6:12 For our struggle is not against flesh and blood, but against the rulers, against the powers, against the world forces of this darkness, against the spiritual forces of wickedness in the heavenly places.*

Spirit, Soul and Body

Many Christians believe that once a person is born again, they are free of demonic influence. When we're first saved, our spirits are *'born again'* and are made right with God. Our spirits are tightly linked to - and sealed by - Holy Spirit. Our spirits are *'off limits'* to the enemy. However, our souls and bodies aren't all made perfect when first born again. Our bodies may get healing(s) after we're born again, but over time, we age and deteriorate. Meanwhile, our souls are a work in progress, but rather than deteriorate, they should become more and more like Christ as we're sanctified. During our Christian life here on earth, neither our body or soul is automatically set free from attacks of the enemy. And that's why we have a battle today as per Ephesians 6:12 above.

23:13   Given we can expect to wrestle with the enemy, doesn't it make sense that such battles with the enemy are waged through our souls and bodies? If not in our souls and bodies, then where does the battle take place against us?

23:14   On the basis a major battleground is in our soul which includes our minds, is this another key reason why it's so important to focus on heavenly things and to renew our minds through things of God, such as studying His Word?

- ☐ *Romans 12:2 And do not be conformed to this world, but **be transformed by the renewing of your mind**, so that you may prove what the will of God is, that which is good and acceptable and perfect.*
- ☐ *Colossians 3:1 Therefore if you have been raised up with Christ, keep seeking the things above, where Christ is, seated at the right hand of God. 2 **Set your mind on the things above**, not on the things that are on earth.*

The How To's

The spiritual world is very complex. Speak to someone who was formerly involved in witchcraft and the occult, and you start to get an appreciation of the evil nature and capabilities that satan and his army of demons still have. Terms such as *'rulers of the darkness', 'principalities and spiritual wickedness in high places'* are not idle words with no application to believers today.

There are various individuals and ministries actively involved in spiritual warfare, and helping set people free from demonic forces. Approaches vary, but a central part of these ministries is helping individuals understand a) their identity in Christ, and b) the authority they have as a born-again follower of Christ.

Some churches incorporate spiritual warfare as a fundamental part of discipling new believers. Equipping their congregation is a fundamental part of discipling. By contrast, many other believers and churches ignore the issue of spiritual warfare.

23: Today's Christian Walk

Terms such as deliverance and demons are taboo. Let me share some of the advice given to me over the years that I find helpful.

1. Jesus, His blood, and His Name are so powerful. We must never forget them.
2. Apart from some time spent here or there on education or dealing with specific issues, never let the enemy become the focal point of our attention.
3. Asking for revelations from Holy Spirit is extremely helpful.
4. The spiritual world has a complex legal framework. As alluded to in satan's talks with God about Job, things in our lives can give the enemy rights to do some things but not others. When I was first exposed to teachings on the courts of heaven by Elizabeth Nixon and Robert Henderson, it was an eye-opener and very helpful. I'm not saying I agree with everything taught by Elizabeth, Robert and others who teach on this issue, but it's absolutely an issue worth studying. There is a surprising amount of references to courts and legalities in the Bible.
5. Be careful what spiritual forces you go against. It's one thing to cast out a lower demon from yourself or another person you're ministering to; it's another thing to go against higher powers and principalities that are over our cities, regions and nations.
6. Sin is one of the doorways that enables the enemy to torment and oppress believers. Confession of sins is central to freeing ourselves from tormenting accusations and thoughts of the enemy. Dealing with root causes leading to the sins or other issues brings hidden stuff' into the light, and closes the door on the enemy. Unforgiveness is often a big issue that keeps doors open for the enemy, and which needs to be dealt with. If someone refuses to deal with unforgiveness against people or God, I won't do deliverance.
7. If a demon is cast out and the sin that opened the door for the demon to oppress us in the first place remains active, our house is not clean as the sin has not been swept out and the door has not been closed to the enemy. Our house is not 'full of God' unless we sweep our house clean, and we take steps to keep our house clean. If we don't, we potentially face the problem of not just one demon, but seven stronger demons coming against us, and we can have a bigger battle against demonic forces after deliverance than before.

- *Matthew 12:43 "Now when the unclean spirit goes out of a man, it passes through waterless places seeking rest, and does not find it. 44 Then it says, 'I will return to my house from which I came'; and when it comes, **it finds it unoccupied**, swept, and put in order. 45 Then it goes and takes along with it **seven other spirits more wicked than itself**, and they go in and live there; and the **last state of that man becomes worse than the first**. That is the way it will also be with this evil generation."*

8. This issue of potentially leaving a person worse off after deliverance than before deliverance is one reason why I get nervous when I see individuals casting out demons of new believers without discipling them first. Leading a new believer through deliverance right after they're born again may seem like the right thing to do initially, but without some basic training and education, the person delivered from the demonic force(s) may be in for

even more serious demonic attacks in the future. And in so doing, the door to their new faith can be blown open for the enemy to come in and torment their souls and bodies, to create doubts and to limit the new believer's life. The ripple effect can be significant as others can be impacted negatively as well. As a result, before going through deliverance, a believer must be taught the basics of self-deliverance - how to deal with demonic attacks when they're alone.
9. The issues in #8 are also why believers should rarely cast demons out of non-believers. One exception is if the person is so demon-possessed, he/she can't function. But if they are functioning, the odds of them being worse off after deliverance than before are high. As a result, I wouldn't do it. If a non-believer is led through deliverance, however, they need to be immediately discipled in the gospel, and on the basics of fending off future demonic attacks.

Example prayer

On April 5, 2020, Jimmy Evans of Gateway (www.gatewaypeople.com) spoke on fear. As part of his message, Jimmy gave an example of a prayer he uses when the spirit of fear tries to attack him. I share it below to help illustrate the authority all believers have, and how we can begin to use some of this authority for our benefit in the area of self-deliverance.

> *"Spirit of fear, I break all agreement with you. And I expose you. I will not let you come into my life and hide inside of me and torment me anymore. You're not me. You're a demon from hell. And I bind you by the authority of the name of Jesus, and the blood of Jesus, and I command you to leave me now in Jesus's name. Amen."*

23:15   In terms of spiritual warfare and casting out demons, my research often showed individuals critiquing others when they don't appear to have been involved in casting out demons themselves. Isn't that like a parent who never played the sport, but willingly and frequently gives advice to the coach who actually played the sport?

I ask the above question from personal experience. I played a few sports in my day. When coaching my children's teams, the most challenging parents were typically the ones who never played the sport, or never played any team sports. They were often clueless. And if you're wondering, I have forgiven those parents. Two last questions.

23:16   As mentioned, many believers think Christians can't be impacted by demons. Would satan want to hinder the lives of believers and efforts to share the Good News by promoting that very idea - that satan and his army of demons can't influence believers today? After all, why fight an enemy that doesn't exist?

23:17   I've heard it said: *"If we're not battling the enemy in our own lives to some extent, is that a sign we're not much of a threat to satan's kingdom?"* Is there merit to that statement?

23: Today's Christian Walk
SPIRITUAL AUTHORITY GIVEN TO BELIEVERS

For this section, please note the issue of authority is primarily in reference to carrying out the Great Commission which includes casting out demons and delivering supernatural gifts such as healing.

The words power and authority are often used interchangeably, but are two different things.

- *Luke 9:1 And He called the twelve together, and gave them **power [dunamis G1411]** and authority **[exousia G1849]** over all the demons and to heal diseases.*

The English word *'power'* is derived from the Greek word *'dunamis'* [G1411] which Thayer defines in part as *'power residing in a thing by virtue of its nature, power for performing miracles, power consisting in or resting upon armies, forces, hosts'*.

Previous chapters discussed Baptism of the Holy Spirit wherein Holy Spirit comes upon [epi] a believer to give access to power [dunamis] to witness. God's power manifests in many diverse ways including, but not limited to, the 9 Holy Spirit gifts.

The English word *'authority'* is based on the Greek word *'exousia'* [G1849] which Thayer defines in part as *'the power of rule or government (the power of him whose will and commands must be submitted to by others and obeyed)'*.

Lori explained the difference between power and authority to me using a police officer analogy. Police officers have responsibilities that are critically important. Officers have clearly defined purposes and roles. To do their job, they are given authority which gives them the right and responsibility to do certain things. They are also equipped to do the job. One part of their equipping is giving officers power in various ways including use of force training and provision of items including guns, batons and handcuffs. Police officers are given both authority and power to enable them to do their job. Their power is limited by the authority to apply the rules of law found in their criminal codes. In other words, authority rules over power in a law-abiding world. If a police officer is told to stand down by a superior officer, the officer obeys, even if the officer still has his/her power in the form of a gun, baton and handcuffs available. In a world where properly approved and properly applied law is not respected, corrupt power is the authority.

CEASED? has talked fairly extensively about the power portion of the Christian walk; now it's time to review the authority portion.

Original Authority - Adam and Eve

After Adam and Eve were formed by God, God gave them instructions to be fruitful and to multiply so that people would fill and subdue the earth.

- *Genesis 1:27 God created man in His own image, in the image of God He created him; male and female He created them. 28 God blessed **them**; and God said to **them**, "**Be fruitful** and multiply, and fill the earth, and **subdue** it; and **rule** over the fish of the sea and over the birds of the sky and over every living thing that moves on the earth."*

23:18 Doesn't this suggest both Adam and Eve had authority, and that God wanted human beings - both male and female - to play a pivotal role in God's management of earth? If not, what do these verses mean?

Authority in Jesus's Earthly Ministry

During Jesus's earthly ministry, ordinary people recognized God had given Jesus authority. For instance, consider the Centurion whose servant was paralyzed.

❑ *Matthew 8:5 And when Jesus entered Capernaum, a centurion came to Him, imploring Him, 6 and saying, "Lord, my servant is lying paralyzed at home, fearfully tormented." 7 Jesus said to him, "I will come and heal him." 8 But the centurion said, "Lord, I am not worthy for You to come under my roof,* **but just say the word, and my servant will be healed**. *9* **For I also am a man under authority [exousia]** *…*

Crowds acknowledged Jesus's authority after they saw the paralytic healed, a miracle supporting Jesus's claim that He had the authority to forgive sins.

❑ *Matthew 9:6 But so that you may know that the Son of Man* **has authority [exousia]** *on earth* **to forgive sins**" *- then He said to the paralytic, "Get up, pick up your bed and go home." 7 And he got up and went home. 8 But when the* **crowds saw this**, *they were awestruck, and glorified God, who had* **given such authority [exousia] to men**.

As the miracles at the hands of Jesus became more and more extensive, the Jewish leaders recognized Jesus must have had authority as they asked Him to identify what authority He was under, and who gave the authority to Him.

❑ *Matthew 21:23 When He entered the temple, the chief priests and the elders of the people came to Him while He was teaching, and said,* "**By what authority [exousia]** *are You doing these things, and* **who gave You this authority [exousia]**?"

23:19   Don't the questions posed by the Jewish leaders indicate the leaders believed there must have been a higher spiritual authority that enabled Jesus to perform such miracles?

23:20   The Jewish leaders knew the scriptures, but didn't realize God gave this authority to Jesus. But weren't there only two supernatural alternatives - God and satan? And given that, doesn't the response of the scripturally learned Jewish leaders show how blinded we can be if we're more loyal to our beliefs than to seeking God's truths?

Authority Delegated during Jesus's Ministry

During His earthly ministry which was before the cross, Jesus delegated authority to His twelve disciples and 70 others. Jesus told them to heal and cast out demons.

❑ *Luke 9:1 And He called the twelve together, and gave them* **power [dunamis]** *and* **authority [exousia]** *over all the demons and to heal diseases.*

❑ *Luke 10:1 Now after this the* **Lord appointed seventy others** *… 9 and* **heal

23: Today's Christian Walk

__those__ in it who are sick, and say to them, 'The kingdom of God has come near to you...17 The seventy returned with joy, saying, "Lord, even the demons are subject to us in Your name." ... 19 __Behold, I have given you authority [exousia]__ to __tread on serpents and scorpions, and over all the power [dunamis] of the enemy__ ...

23:21 When Jesus sent out these 82 men, was it a foreshadowing of Jesus sending out all disciples to fulfill the Great Commission? And with proper authority?

Authority Jesus had after His Ascension

After Jesus ascended, Father God seated Jesus at His right hand in heavenly places.

❏ *Ephesians 1:20 which He brought about in Christ, when He __raised Him from the dead and seated Him at His right hand in the heavenly places__,*

The phrase *'right hand'* is derived from the Greek word *'dexios'* [G1188] which is defined as *'the right, the right hand or metaphorically, a place of honor or authority'*.

Father God gave Jesus authority over all things, not some things.

❏ *Ephesians 1:21 __far above all rule and authority__ [exousia] and power [dunamis] and dominion, and every name that is named, not only in this age but also in the one to come. 22 And He __put all things__ in subjection under His feet, and gave Him as head __over all things__ to the church, 23 which is His body, the fullness of Him who fills all in all.*

Believers - Where are We

After we're born again, we're raised and seated with Jesus in heavenly places.

❏ *Ephesians 2:5 even when we were dead in our transgressions, made us alive together with Christ (by grace you have been saved), 6 and __raised us up with Him, and seated us with Him in the heavenly places in Christ Jesus__,*

23:22 As per Ephesians 1:20-21, Jesus is in heavenly places *'far above all rule and authority and power and dominion'*. Since we're seated with Jesus Christ in the heavenly places, aren't we properly positioned to receive authority as well?

23:23 And like law enforcement officers who have varying types and levels of authority depending on the requirements, is it reasonable to believe the spiritual authority given to individual believers can vary depending on the calling and the type of work God has called each person to do - above and beyond what every believer is called to do - share the Good News, heal the sick, raise the dead, cast out demons and cleanse lepers?

Sent Ones / Messengers / Ambassadors

After Jesus tells His disciples that He has been given all authority, His next message is to *'Go therefore and make disciples'*.

❏ *Matthew 28:18 And Jesus came up and spoke to them ... "__All authority__ has been given to Me in heaven and on earth. 19 __Go therefore__ and __make disciples__ ...*

Not only does Jesus tell believers to go, Jesus tells us that just as Father God sent Jesus, Jesus is sending us. We are His *'sent ones'*, His *'Ambassadors'*.
- ❏ *John 20:21 So Jesus said to them again, "Peace be with you; **as the Father has sent Me, I also send you**."*
- ❏ *2 Corinthians 5:20 Therefore, **we are ambassadors for Christ** ...*

The word *'ambassador'* is derived from the Greek word *'Presbeuo'* [G4243]. Presbeuo means older according to age, or to serve as ambassador. Merriam Webster defines an ambassador as:
> *'an official envoy especially: a diplomatic agent of the highest rank accredited to a foreign government or sovereign as the resident representative of his or her own government or sovereign or appointed for a special and often temporary diplomatic assignment'.*

As Ambassadors for Christ, we represent Jesus. Jesus did all kinds of supernatural things. Incredibly, those who believe in Him will do even greater things than Jesus did.
- ❏ *John 21:25 And there are also many other things which Jesus did, which **if they were written in detail, I suppose that even the world itself would not contain the books that would be written**.*
- ❏ *John 14:12 Truly, truly, I say to you, he who believes in Me, the works that I do, he will do also; and **greater works than these he will do**; because I go to the Father.*

Police officers are assigned responsibilities and given authority to carry out their duties. Health food inspectors are assigned certain responsibilities and given authority to carry out their duties. Same for those in fire departments, finance, manufacturing etc.

23:24   When Jesus states He is sending believers, both today and yesterday, just as Father God sent Him, that we are ambassadors for Christ, that we will do more miracles than Jesus did, doesn't this mean Jesus would give believers both the appropriate authority (seated in heavenly places alongside Christ) and access to power (Baptism in the Holy Spirit, Holy Spirit gifts) to fulfill what we are called to do as His sent ones, His ambassadors?
- ❏ *John 20:21 So Jesus said to them ... **as the Father has sent Me, I also send you**."*
- ❏ *Matthew 10:8 Heal the sick, raise the dead, cleanse the lepers, cast out demons. Freely you received, freely give.*

Authority for Believers Then and Now

Some believers may be uncomfortable thinking such authority, with its privileges and responsibilities, is for believers today. After all, receiving authority from Almighty God is pretty far out there in the natural. If we go back to Chapter 6, recall that the group gathered on resurrection Sunday evening included 10 of the original apostles, the 2 disciples Jesus met on the road to Emmaus plus *'those that were with*

23: Today's Christian Walk

them'. Evidence was provided showing *'those that were with them'* included at least 5 women, 4 of whom - Mary Magdalene, Mary the mother of James, Joanna and Salome - were mentioned by name. This group of male and female disciples is the same group Jesus told: *"as the Father has sent Me, I also send you"*.

  23:25   This group of *'sent ones'* is larger than the original apostles. Doesn't this indicate all believers, including all born-again believers living today, have been given authority to go out and share the Good News? If not, why not?

Also consider that many people were given power when they were Baptized in the Holy Spirit including the ~120 at Pentecost, the new believers in Samaria, Cornelius, family and friends, and the 12 disciples at Ephesus.

  23:26   Why would Jesus baptize these believers in the Holy Spirit to give them power if He wasn't going to give them the associated authority to use the power? Would doing so be comparable to giving police officer guns, handcuffs and batons, but then telling them to sit at their desks and talk about the problems in the world outside?

Authority over the Enemy

Dealing with the enemy is a given. To do so, Jesus gave his disciples authority over demons.

- ❑ *Mark 3:14 And He **appointed twelve**, so that they would be with Him and that He could send them out to preach, 15 and **to have authority to cast out the demons**.*

Today, Jesus wants His followers to not only preach the gospel, but to take action on many fronts including casting out demons.

- ❑ *Matthew 10:8 Heal the sick, raise the dead, cleanse the lepers, **cast out demons**. Freely you received, freely give.*
- ❑ *Mark 16:15 And He said to them, "Go into all the world and preach the gospel ... 17 These signs will accompany those who have believed: in My name they **will cast out demons** ...*

  23:27   Doesn't the command to cast out demons mean we have the authority to do exactly that? And that while the enemy still has power, our authority supersedes his power provided we know how to use it?

Who Am I, and Where Am I

John and Moira Hill have blessed Lori and I in many ways through teachings, counsel and prayer. John discipled me almost every Tuesday evening for well over a year. One evening, John asked me: *"Who are you, and where are you?"* He smiled, but I was ready for him. I responded with something deep like: *"Can I have another cup of tea please."* The simple answer to John's question is that, when we're born again, we're a blood-bought child seated in heavenly places who has been given spiritual authority. Lori taught me a simple way to remember the answers: *"Sheep say BAH".*

_B:_ I am a **B**lood **B**ought Child of the Most-High God.
- *Acts 20:28 Be on guard for yourselves and for all the flock, among which the Holy Spirit has made you overseers, to shepherd the church of God which **He purchased with His own blood**.*

_A:_ I have been given **A**uthority.
- *Luke 10:19 Behold, I have **given you authority** to tread on serpents and scorpions, and over all the power of the enemy, and nothing will injure you.*

_H:_ Just as a police officer handcuffs the guilty who oppress our society, we can **H**andcuff those thoughts that try to put us back into a broken, tormented mindset by replacing these ungodly thoughts with godly ones, and thereby pass on or 'handcuff' the ungodly thoughts to Jesus.
- *2 Corinthians 10:5 We are destroying speculations and every lofty thing raised up against the knowledge of God, and we are **taking every thought captive** to the obedience of Christ,*

In the Name of Jesus

As discussed in Chapter 15 beginning on page 231, there is authority in the Name of Jesus.
- *Acts 3:6 But Peter said, "I do not possess silver and gold, but what I do have I give to you: **In the name** of Jesus Christ the Nazarene - walk!"*
- *Acts 3:16 And on the basis of faith in His name, it is **the name of Jesus** which has strengthened this man whom you see and know; and the faith which comes through Him has given him this perfect health in the presence of you all.*
- *Acts 4:1 As they were speaking to the people, the priests and the captain of the temple guard and the Sadducees came up to them... 7 When they had placed them in the center, they began to inquire, "**By what power**, or **in what name, have you done this**?"*

Peter didn't have money, but he had the authorization to use Jesus's Name. He also had access to power as a result of being Baptized in the Holy Spirit. The result was Holy Spirit used Peter to distribute the gift of healing to this paralytic man.

The power of the Name of Jesus is also well illustrated in Matthew 7.
- *Matthew 7:21 "Not everyone who says to Me, 'Lord, Lord,' will enter the kingdom of heaven, but he who does the will of My Father who is in heaven will enter. 22 Many will say to Me on that day, 'Lord, Lord, did we not **prophesy in Your name**, and **in Your name cast out demons**, and **in Your name perform many miracles**?' 23 And then I will declare to them, '**I never knew you; depart from Me, you who practice lawlessness**.'*

The name of Jesus has such power that even non-believers can do miracles by relying on His name. Some individuals who do such miracles believe they are Christians, but aren't. They will get a terrible shock when they hear the words *"depart from me"*. When it's too late, they will realize they weren't born again, and

23: Today's Christian Walk

they aren't headed to heaven, but to hell. Tragic.

When it comes to issues such as baptizing another believer in water, we baptize the person in the name of the Father, the Son and Holy Spirit.

- ❑ *Matthew 28:18 And Jesus came up and spoke to them, saying, "**All authority has been given to Me** in heaven and on earth. 19 Go therefore and **make disciples** of all the nations, **baptizing them in the name of the Father and the Son and the Holy Spirit**,*

23:28 Water baptizing a believer *'in the name of ...'* is to baptize using the authority we've been given. It's part of being God's ambassador. Being an ambassador for a country is a big honor. As ambassadors for Christ, don't we have a far bigger honor with all our rights and responsibilities, including our right and responsibility to baptize other believers?

In Acts 2:38, Peter tells his listeners they need to be baptized in the name of Jesus. He didn't say they needed to be baptized in the Name of the Father, Son and Holy Spirit.

- ❑ *Acts 2:38 Peter said to them, "Repent, and each of you **be baptized in the name of Jesus Christ** for the forgiveness of your sins; and you will receive the gift of the Holy Spirit.*

In my review of the Baptism of the Holy Spirit in Chapter 10, I presented evidence showing why Acts 2:38 is not referring to water baptism, but instead to the Baptism of the Holy Spirit. In this case, an expanded version of the highlighted middle portion of Acts 2:38 might then read along the lines of '... **ask Jesus to baptize you in the Holy Spirit by the authority given to Jesus** ... '.

23:29 Consider for a minute that Acts 2:38 does refer to Baptism of the Holy Spirit. Given Jesus has been delegated all authority, and given Jesus is the one who baptizes believers in the Holy Spirit, would this explain why only the name of Jesus was mentioned in Acts 2:38, and not all three of The Father, Jesus and Holy Spirit?

One Final Issue on Authority

After Adam and Eve were created, God commanded them to multiply and subdue the earth.

- ❑ *Genesis 1:28 God blessed them; and God said to them, "**Be fruitful and multiply**, and **fill the earth**, and **subdue it**; and **rule over** the fish of the sea and over the birds of the sky and over every living thing that moves on the earth."*

Adam and Eve sinned, and the enemy took on a significant role on earth. He offered Jesus the earth, an offer that Jesus didn't dispute was the devil's to give.

- ❑ *Matthew 4:8 Again, the devil took Him to a very high mountain and showed Him all the kingdoms of the world and their glory; 9 and he said to Him, "All these things I will give You, if You fall down and worship me."*

Jesus said no to satan. Jesus didn't come to worship him; He came to destroy

CEASED?

satan's works.
- ☐ *1 John 3:8 the one who practices sin is of the devil; for the devil has sinned from the beginning. The Son of God appeared for this purpose, to destroy the works of the devil.*

Jesus was sent to earth by Father God. After the cross, Jesus declared that He had been given all - as in all - authority. Now, Jesus sends us into the world.
- ☐ *Matthew 28:1 Now after the Sabbath, as it began to dawn toward the first day of the week, Mary Magdalene and the other Mary came to look **at the grave** ... 18 And Jesus came up and spoke to them, saying, "**All authority** has been given to Me in heaven and **on earth**.*
- ☐ *John 20:21 So Jesus said to them again, "Peace be with you; **as the Father has sent Me, I also send you**."*

23:30 Do the above scriptures show that authority over our earth was passed from Adam and Eve to the enemy, then to Jesus? And after the cross, to believers? If today's believers don't have this authority, who does have it? And what portion, if any, do believers have?

Authority through Relationship

God is active in believer's lives. He can do anything He wants. He doesn't need human beings to do anything. However, He chooses to use us - the sinful, limited creatures that we are. When it comes to authority, many teachers believe the degree of authority is often related to:
1. the closeness of our personal relationship with God; and
2. how we use the authority we've already been given.

Humbly using authority for God's glory and the benefit of God's kingdom and other people as opposed to our benefit and glory, for instance, will lead to ever-increasing authority. But having said that, we always need to remember God is God, and He can do whatever He wants. And sometimes, He doesn't want us to do anything other than to sit still, and be with Him, for a minute, hour, day or season or two. But then, we need to go and be His arms and legs to the world.

PROSPERITY, POVERTY OR ABUNDANT GOSPEL

Cessationists have expressed considerable concern about the Charismatic movement over money. And rightly so in cases where a focus is on money and payments are specifically made to ministries for miracles of healing. Many ministries are involved in healing people and funds are needed. No question. They're legitimate and needed. But in other cases, instead of the ministry being there first and foremost to help people, it seems the healing ministry is more of a business where healing is a service that is sold to make considerable money.

Other cases include what I witnessed at a church where people were screaming *"Give and you will receive ten-fold back"*. I recall wondering if God was an ATM or a rigged casino. Even though I wasn't saved at the time, and constantly looking to make lots more money, I was shocked. Money is not a small issue for many believers, and has a larger hold in many of our hearts than it should.

23: Today's Christian Walk

❑ *Matthew 19:16 And someone came to Him and said, "Teacher, what good thing shall I do that I may obtain eternal life?" ... 20 The young man said to Him, "All these things I have kept; what am I still lacking?" 21 Jesus said to him, "If you wish to be complete, go and sell your possessions and give to the poor, and you will have treasure in heaven; and come, follow Me." 22 But when the young man heard this statement, he went away grieving; for he was one who owned much property.*

23:31 How about you? If God clearly and directly asked you to give up all your material wealth and existing sources of income, what would your response be? Where would your heart be?

Teachers of Prosperity Gospel

Leaders in God's kingdom have a major responsibility to properly equip the saints.

❑ *Ephesians 4:11 And He gave some as apostles, and some as prophets, and some as evangelists, and some as pastors **and teachers, 12 for the equipping of the saints for the work of service**, to the building up of the body of Christ;*

❑ *James 3:1 Let not many of you become teachers, my brethren, knowing that as such we will incur a stricter judgment. 2 For we all stumble in many ways. If anyone does not stumble in what he says, he is a perfect man, able to bridle the whole body as well.*

So, let me ask those who teach or promote the prosperity gospel.

23:32 Of the individuals you're equipping and leading, how many of those who are unrelated and unaffiliated with you, have accumulated as much or more wealth than you?

23:33 On your website, how pronounced is your 'Give' button relative to other menu items?

23:34 If you routinely have an offering and tell people they will be blessed if they give, what percentage of the time do you:
　i. ask God who He would like this offering to be given to; and/or
　ii. encourage people to give to a ministry which neither you nor any of your family members have an affiliation or financial connection?

Those Against the Prosperity Gospel

If you teach and speak against the prosperity gospel, I share your views in many ways. I shudder to think of the damage to people's lives and to the kingdom of God by those who deceive and fleece people financially. But let me ask you two questions.

23:35 How would you answer questions 20:32, 20:33 and 20:34?

23:36 How many Christians would gladly exchange their wealth and income for yours?

Poverty Gospel

I know a pastor who believes a friend of his was very godly because his friend lived with virtually no worldly possessions apart from a few clothes and his Bible. This pastor and others effectively promote a poverty gospel. If you believe Christians are to live with no excess (a just enough gospel?), let me ask a couple things.

23:37   Wouldn't this just enough gospel mean that believers who get by on less than we do, or own less than we do, are automatically godlier? If not, why not?

23:38   Wouldn't this just enough gospel mean that when we have excess, we shouldn't consider giving any excess to another person out of concern it may make them less godly?

23:39   And if we're the one lacking, should we avoid seeking assistance and even refuse assistance offered by others in order to remain as godly as possible?

23:40   This pastor's friend often lived in the home of another believer. Isn't there something inconsistent with the view that he was godlier because he had less than others (including the believer who owned the home), even though he was willing to receive the generosity of the homeowner who would be classified as less godly for owning a home?

23:41   Wealth can be used for evil, but it can also be used for good. Without excess, how do we look after widows and orphans, send missionaries, or do all we're commanded to do?

❑ *James 1:27 Pure and unblemished religion [as it is expressed in outward acts] in the sight of our God and Father is this:* **to visit and look after** *the fatherless and the widows in their distress, and to keep oneself uncontaminated by the [secular] world. (AMP)*

Abundance Gospel

Many Cessationists comment on the number of Charismatics in places like Africa who have been led astray and taken advantage of by proponents of the prosperity gospel. That is true to some degree. But is there more to the story? Here's some of what I experienced.

When I studied in Egypt in the 1970's, I saw extreme poverty. I have also seen extreme poverty in Canada, USA and Mexico. I was part of a team that built a 2-room house of ~400 square feet outside Ensenada, Mexico. Electricity was hooked up, but there was no running water. We built an outdoor toilet; no more walking up the hill adjacent to where they lived. Our team bought bunk beds and bedding, kitchen table and chairs, a stove and refrigerator, kitchen hardware - the basics. I'll never forget the mother standing outside looking at her new home getting built. Tears were rolling down her face in absolute joy, as she anxiously waited for her new dream home to be completed. We were able to bless her because we had excess to travel and buy things for her, her husband and children. If we had a poverty mindset, how could we have blessed her?

❑ *John 10:10 The thief comes only to steal and kill and destroy; I came that they* **may have life, and have it abundantly**.

23: Today's Christian Walk

Jesus came to do many things. Abundance is one of many blessings He provides, and I find it hard to believe God wants to give us abundance in things such as a, b, c, d ... z but never an abundance of finances. Prosperity is a relative thing. In the west, prosperity typically means things and lifestyles that are excessive. But elsewhere, for so many, prosperity is having basics such as clean water, reasonable sewage management, enough food, access to medical services, a good bike to ride and a warm, dry home with a bed. I think God wants people to have these basics.

23:42   I wonder if a core question for those who teach the excessive prosperity gospel, either locally or abroad, is this: is our heart one of giving to give, or giving to get?

That Darn Word 'If'

We humans like the blessings of God. It's mind-boggling Jesus is our friend.
- ❑   *John 15:14 **You are My friends** ...*

I've heard many messages on the blessings of God. And oftentimes, the messages forget to point out that the word *'if'* was involved. In the case of being a friend of Jesus, for instance, the *'if'* - the condition by which we are His friend - is 'if' we do what Jesus commands.
- ❑   *John 15:14 You are My friends **if you do what I command you**.*

I've heard it said many times that God will give us the desires of our hearts. True, but isn't there a condition that we're to first trust in the Lord, to do good, to cultivate faithfulness, and to delight ourselves in God?
- ❑   *Psalm 37:3 **Trust in the Lord** and **do good**; Dwell in the land and **cultivate faithfulness**. 4 **Delight yourself in the Lord**;   And   **He will give you the desires of your heart**.*

There are many ifs, conditions or requirements in the Bible both before and after the cross.
- ❑   *Exodus 19:5 Now then, **if you will** indeed obey My voice and keep My covenant, then you shall be My own possession among all the peoples, for all the earth is Mine;*
- ❑   *Deuteronomy 11:26 "See, I am setting before you today a blessing and a curse: 27 the blessing, **if you listen** to the commandments of the Lord your God, which I am commanding you today; 28 and the curse, **if you do not listen** to the commandments of the Lord your God, but turn aside from the way which I am commanding you today, by following other gods which you have not known.*
- ❑   *Malachi 2:2 **If you do not listen**, and **if you do not take it to heart** to give honor to My name," says the Lord of hosts, "then I will send the curse upon you and I will curse your blessings; and indeed, I have cursed them already, because you are not taking it to heart.*
- ❑   *Isaiah 48:18 "**If only you had paid attention** to My commandments! Then your well-being would have been like a river, And your righteousness like the waves of the sea.*

CEASED?

- Luke 6:37 "**Do not judge**, and you will not be judged; and **do not condemn**, and you will not be condemned; **pardon**, and you will be pardoned. 38 **Give**, and it will be given to you ...
- John 9:31 We know that God does not hear sinners; **but if anyone is God-fearing and does His will**, He hears him.
- Galatians 6:7 Do not be deceived, God is not mocked; **for whatever a man sows, this he will also reap**.
- James 4:3 **You ask and do not receive, because you ask with wrong motives**, so that you may spend it on your pleasures.
- 1 Thessalonians 5:18 **in everything give thanks;** for this is God's will for you in Christ Jesus.

23:43   When it comes to finances, shouldn't we consider Psalm 37:3-4 above, and first get our walk right with Christ before we begin to think of any financial blessings God will give us? And - if we're truly finding delight in the Lord - won't the desires of our heart be first and foremost to have more of Him?

Testimony

A friend of mine and I were meeting with a pastor. Before we parted, the pastor felt he was supposed to give all the money in his pocket to my friend. My friend is retired and doing fine financially. He didn't need the money but agreed as he believed he needed to take the gift in order for The Lord to bless the pastor for being obedient. My friend and I didn't know at the time that the pastor was short rent for the upcoming month. Within 24 hours, a woman showed up at the pastor's door with a check for more than 10 times what the pastor had given my friend, and just enough to pay the rent.

23:44   Is that situation part of a faulty prosperity gospel, or an example of God not only blessing them financially in the short term, but also building the faith and testimonies of two of His children who were being obedient?

Teachings About Money

Some of the best Biblically based teachings on tithing and giving that I found are Robert Morris's books, *'The Blessed Life'* and *'Beyond Blessed'*. If you're a Cessationist whose immediate reaction is along the lines *'There is zero chance I'm reading teachings of any of those high-profile Charismatics"*, you might be surprised. Robert's books aren't hype. They're biblical, with personal testimonies that align with scripture.

In regards to the rich man who struggled to leave his riches, there is a bit more to the story. Jesus states for those who left house, family and farms for Jesus's sake (a form of IF), God will bless them a hundred-fold in this age, and the next.

- Mark 10:23 And Jesus, looking around, said to His disciples, "How hard it will be for those who are wealthy to enter the kingdom of God!" ... 25 It is easier for a camel to go through the eye of a needle than for a rich man to enter the kingdom of God." ... 28 Peter began to say to Him, "Behold, we have left everything and followed You." 29 Jesus said, "Truly I say to you, there is no

23: Today's Christian Walk

one who has **<u>left house or brothers or sisters or mother or father or children or farms</u>**, for **<u>My sake and for the gospel's sake</u>**, 30 but that he **<u>will receive a hundred times</u>** as much **<u>now</u>** in the present age, houses and brothers and sisters and mothers and children and farms, **<u>along with persecutions</u>; <u>and</u> <u>in the age to come</u>**, eternal life.

23:45 Doesn't the 100-fold blessing in verse 30 suggest - for those seeking God - we can expect blessings which may include financial ones? If not, why not?

23:46 If we're blessed financially, we can bless others. We can do things or help fund ministries to advance the kingdom of God that we couldn't otherwise do. However, along with blessings, aren't we also forewarned to expect persecution not only when we stand up for the gospel, but from other believers who criticize us for having excess, even when the excess(es) are a blessing from God? I know this one well; I was one of those critics for a long time.

❑ *Matthew 5:10 Blessed are those who have been persecuted for the sake of righteousness, for theirs is the kingdom of heaven.*

One last note on money. I do find it interesting God tells us to test Him on money.

❑ *Malachi 3:10 Bring the whole tithe into the storehouse, so that there may be food in My house, and **test Me now** in this," says the Lord of hosts, "if I will not open for you the windows of heaven and pour out for you a blessing until it overflows.*

CLOSING POINTS TO PONDER

23:47 The Christian walk is not a cake-walk. We're told to work out our salvation. Wouldn't it be so simple if we could just take a God pill that enables us to trust God, seek God first, totally die to self, communicate with God throughout the day, allow Holy Spirit to lead us in all things, share the Good News, and always heal the sick, cleanse lepers, raise the dead and cast out demons ... and in all that we accomplish, give all glory to God with humility, praise and thanks?

❑ *Philippians 2:12 So then, my beloved, just as you have always obeyed, not as in my presence only, but now much more in my absence, **<u>work out your salvation</u>** with fear and trembling;*

❑ *Matthew 6:33 But **<u>seek first His kingdom and His righteousness</u>**, and all these things will be added to you.*

❑ *1 Thessalonians 5:16 **<u>Rejoice always</u>**; 17 **<u>pray without ceasing</u>**;*

❑ *Proverbs 3:5 **<u>Trust in the Lord with all your heart</u>** And **<u>do not lean on your own understanding</u>**. 6 **<u>In all your ways acknowledge Him</u>** ...*

❑ *Romans 8:14 For all who are being **<u>led by the Spirit of God</u>**, these are sons of God.*

❑ *Matthew 10:8 **<u>Heal the sick</u>, <u>raise the dead</u>, <u>cleanse the lepers</u>, <u>cast out demons</u>**. Freely you received, freely give.*

❑ *Psalm 100:4 **<u>Enter His gates with thanksgiving</u>** And **<u>His courts with praise</u>**. **<u>Give thanks to Him, bless His name</u>**.*

CEASED?

It's much easier to talk or read about the Christian life than to walk it out. If I have implied in any way that I've got it all figured out, rest assured I haven't. I often feel my Christian walk is on the same treadmill as when I try to figure out what to think when I ask Lori how she's doing and she responds with *'fine'*. God continues to reveal things in my heart, some of which are rather humbling to admit and face. I struggle in putting God first to start my day, and yet my life right now is so much easier than situations faced by others. Lori and I are empty nesters. We don't have the demands of raising children. We don't have major physical or financial issues. We work part-time and have considerable discretionary time. And yet, walking the Christian life remains a struggle at times.

If you struggle in your walk and thoughts, you're not alone. And please also know, if you feel alone in your journey, you're not. There is a body of believers ready to help. Reach out to them. And with the recent explosion in online equipping and services, access is virtually anywhere on earth. Just make sure the Bible, worship and prayer are a priority in any teaching and mentoring given to you.

If you're a Roman Catholic, I ask you to please consider these scriptures.
- *Ephesians 2:6 and raised us up with Him, and **seated us with Him in the heavenly places** in Christ Jesus,*
- *John 10:27 **My sheep hear My voice**, and I know them, and they follow Me;*
- *Romans 8:14 For all who are being **led by the Spirit of God**, these are sons of God.*

23:48   All believers are seated with Christ in heavenly places. We've been given authority to go as Christ's ambassadors to do many things including healing the sick and casting out demons. Nowhere in the New Testament do we see deceased saints – and that includes Mary - actively assisting living saints. Shouldn't we just obey God and do what He says to do which is to follow Him, to seek His kingdom first, and to be led by His Holy Spirit?

23:49   Finally, satan, his demons and the antichrist - whoever or whatever that is - are masters of deception. If we don't know Jesus's voice, how will we know what is truth and what is not?

24

5 of 7 Catholic Sacraments, Traditions

INTRODUCTION

PREVIOUS chapters addressed some issues on Catholic teachings that make it a challenge for non-Catholics to evangelize and worship alongside Catholics. Chapters 24 to 28 conclude this review starting with Chapter 24 which addresses sacraments - with a primary focus on water baptism and confirmation - and traditions (page 330).

WATER BAPTISM AND CONFIRMATION

From the website link: www.catholic.org/prayers/sacrament.php, I copied the following on February 4, 2020. Formatting is mine. I added bracketed numbers (1), (2) etc. to facilitate review.

> ... The liturgical life of the Catholic Church revolves around the Eucharistic sacrifice and the sacraments. There are seven sacraments in the Church: Baptism, Confirmation, Eucharist, Penance, Anointing of the Sick, Matrimony, and Holy Orders. The purpose of the sacraments is to make people holy, to build up the body of Christ, and finally, to give worship to God; but being signs, they also have a teaching function. ... The Church Thus Teaches: There are **seven sacraments**. They were instituted by Christ and given to the Church to administer. **They are necessary for salvation (1)** .... Institution and **alteration of them is reserved to the Holy See** (2) ...
>
> Baptism
> Baptism, the **first and fundamental sacrament** and **the gate to the other sacraments (3)**, is the purifying and sanctifying sacrament of rebirth. **It is the means by which its recipients are incorporated into the church** (4) in a sacramental bond of unity.
>
> Confirmation
> By a signing with the gift of the Spirit, **confirmation enriches the baptized with the Holy Spirit, binding them more perfectly to the Church,** (5) and **strengthening them in their witness to Christ by word and deed (6)** and in their work to bring to its fullness the Body of Christ. **Confirmation is conferred through**

anointing with chrism and the laying on of hands. *(7)*

The above comments are a minuscule subset of Roman Catholic teachings on these topics. But I do believe they reveal some key issues.

Changes to Sacraments

24:1   Consider point (2). Neither God nor the Bible change. If the sacraments are from God, if the Roman Catholic church has the true teachings, if the Roman Catholic church is the one true church that started before the cross with Peter as its first head - and if God does not change - why would Catholic sacraments ever change? And thus, why the need for the change clause *'alteration of them is reserved to the Holy See'*?

Salvation and Water Baptism

The 7 Catholic Sacraments are water baptism, confirmation (which is centered around Baptism of the Holy Spirit), communion, penance, anointing of the sick, matrimony, and Holy Orders. Chapters 4, 6, 8 and 10 of **CEASED?** discussed issues related to salvation and being born again, and showed why none of the sacraments as per point (1) are required to be born again, to be initially saved, and to become a child of God. Consider these aspects related to water baptism:

- ❖ The original apostles and others gathered on resurrection Sunday evening were born again that night. Holy Spirit was breathed into them. While I believe they were water baptized at some point after that night, there is no specific mention of the apostles actually being water baptized.
- ❖ Individuals such as Cornelius, family and friends and the 12 disciples at Ephesus were baptized in water after they were born again and already had Holy Spirit in [en] them.
- ❖ Paul never once taught water baptism is required to be born again.
- ❖ Other than possibly Acts 2:38 which Chapter 10 in **CEASED?** shows most likely refers to Baptism in the Holy Spirit, Peter never stated a person needed water baptism to be born again.
- ❖ Philip the evangelist, was not an original apostle, but water baptized the eunuch in a body of water, and not with a few drops of water.
- ❖ Ananias, who was not an original apostle, baptized Saul/Paul in water.

24:2   Per point (4), water baptism: *"… is the means by which its recipients are incorporated into the church in a sacramental bond of unity"*. When a person is water baptized, the Bible does not say anything about water baptism incorporating a person into a church organization. However, the Bible does teach that when a person is born again, Holy Spirit automatically baptizes the new believer into the Body of Christ. Let me ask:

   i.   do we get water baptized to bind ourselves more perfectly to a church, or out of obedience to God's Word and for the blessings that God may have for us? and

   ii. what is to be our primary relationship here on earth - a church organization which has a limited life span - or God who is our Creator and Savior, and who we will be with in Heaven forever?

24: 5 Catholic Sacraments, Traditions

In other teachings, the Roman Catholic church teaches water baptism is only to be done by priests. However, God's Word says all believers are part of the royal priesthood.

- *1 Peter 2:5 you also, as living stones, are being built up as a spiritual house for a **holy priesthood**, to offer up spiritual sacrifices acceptable to God through Jesus Christ ... 9 But **you are a chosen race, a royal priesthood**, a **holy nation, a people for God's own possession**, ...*

24:3 Given 1 Peter 2:5 indicates all believers are priests, doesn't that mean all believers have the right and responsibility to baptize believers? And wouldn't that be consistent with Jesus's command that all believers are to make disciples and to baptize them? Something non-apostles Ananias did for Paul, and Philip did for the eunuch?

- *Matthew 28:19 Go therefore and **make disciples** of all the nations, **baptizing them** in the name of the Father and the Son and the Holy Spirit,*

24:4 Per point (3), water baptism is the gate to the other 6 sacraments. Chapter 4 of **CEASED?** explained why water baptism is not required for salvation.
  i. Given such an error, how good a gate is water baptism for Confirmation?
  ii. Do the issues surrounding water baptism raise concerns about the remaining 6 sacraments accessed through this gate?
  iii. Isn't Jesus the gate we should focus on?

- *John 10:9 I am **the door**; if anyone enters through Me, he will be saved, and will go in and out and find pasture. (NASB)*
- *John 10:9 Yes, I am **the gate**. Those who come in through me will be saved. They will come and go freely and will find good pastures. (NLT)*

Confirmation

24:5 Chapter 8 discussed why I view the second Roman Catholic sacrament, Confirmation, as being centered to a very large degree on and around the Baptism of the Holy Spirit. I repeat part of question 8:45: '... I conclude that Confirmation is primarily about Baptism of the Holy Spirit. If this conclusion is not correct, my question to Catholics is - where is Baptism of Holy Spirit covered in detail in Catholic teaching?'

24:6 Jesus's last instructions to His disciples before He ascended was for them to wait to be Baptized in the Holy Spirit. Why is such an important commandment from Jesus not specifically and clearly spelled out in the Catholic Catechism?

Information on Confirmation on pages 325-326 is provided again for your convenience.

*By a signing with the gift of the Spirit, **confirmation enriches the baptized with the Holy Spirit, binding them more perfectly to the Church**, (5) and **strengthening them in their witness to Christ by word and deed** (6) and in their work to bring to its fullness the Body of Christ. **Confirmation is conferred through anointing with chrism and the laying on of hands**. (7)*

Point (5) states that confirmation binds a person more perfectly to the Church. There certainly can be an emotional impact when one is powerfully touched by God as a result of Jesus Baptizing us in the Holy Spirit. However, the Bible doesn't say Baptism of the Holy Spirit is designed to bind us more perfectly to the church. The Bible is clear the Baptism of the Holy Spirit is intended, first and foremost, to give believers power to be witnesses. In so doing, it will most likely bring believers closer to God and to other believers as well, but those are secondary issues. Point (6) refers to witnessing in word and deed. If deeds corresponded to the power associated with the 9 Holy Spirit gifts, that would be great. However, given the main Roman Catholic church doesn't incorporate the 9 Holy Spirit gifts as a central part of their teachings on Confirmation, there seems to be a major gap in the deeds part of Roman Catholic teaching, and in witnessing.

Point (7) refers to the Baptism of the Holy Spirit occurring when a Catholic Bishop performs this baptism by laying on off hands and using chrism. No chrism is ever used in biblical Baptisms of the Holy Spirit. And while hands can be laid on a person as part of getting Baptized in the Holy Spirit, this is not always done as we see at Pentecost and again at Cornelius's house. We can ask for this Baptism ourselves, with or without a 'junior' or 'senior' believer present.

In terms of other aspects related to Catholic teaching on Baptism of the Holy Spirit;

- ❖ Catholic teaching states a person can only be Confirmed if they were water baptized properly. God's Word reveals 'proper' water baptism requires the person doing the baptizing to be born again, the person being water baptized to be born again, and the baptism to involve full immersion in water, as per Philip's baptism of the eunuch.
- ❖ Water baptism is not a requirement to receive the Baptism in the Holy Spirit. Individuals such as the ~120 at Pentecost and Cornelius, family and friends were all Baptized in the Holy Spirit before they were water baptized.
- ❖ Roman Catholic teaching states Confirmation seals a person with the Holy Spirit. The Bible teaches we're sealed with the Holy Spirit, not when we're Baptized in the Holy Spirit where Holy Spirit comes upon [epi] us, but when we're born again and Holy Spirit comes in [en] us.
- ❖ Roman Catholic teachings hold that Confirmation yields 7 gifts - wisdom, understanding, knowledge, fortitude or courage, counsel, piety or love, and fear of the Lord. The Bible does not attribute any of these 7 gifts to the Baptism of the Holy Spirit.
- ❖ I found Catholic teachings do not clearly distinguish between the in [en] and the upon [epi] experiences of the Holy Spirit. They are intermixed along with other issues.
- ❖ I also found notable differences in teachings between the mainline Catholic church and the Charismatic part of the Roman Catholic church on the 9 Holy Spirit gifts and the Baptism of the Holy Spirit. What is clear is that the Baptism of the Holy Spirit and the 9 Holy Spirit gifts that flow from this Baptism aren't a key focus of the mainline Roman Catholic church. This directly contradicts Jesus's last command in Acts 1:8.

24: 5 Catholic Sacraments, Traditions

❖ I found the Roman Catholic church has no official position on tongues, one of the 9 Holy Spirit gifts that believers can be given after being Baptized in the Holy Spirit.

Other Sacraments

As per Chapter 4 of **CEASED?**, the need to confess sins to a priest is largely based on John 20.

❑ *John 20:21 So Jesus said to them again, "Peace be with you; as the Father has sent Me, **I also send you.**" 22 And when He had said this, **He breathed on them** and said to them, **"Receive the Holy Spirit**. 23 **If you forgive** the sins of any, their sins have been forgiven them; if you retain the sins of any, they have been retained."*

When Jesus appeared to the apostles on resurrection Sunday evening, He stated He was sending them. He breathed on them, He told them to receive the Holy Spirit, and He told them to forgive. Catholic teachings contend this responsibility /authority to forgive was only given to the original apostles and their successors - Roman Catholic priests - through the sacrament of Holy Orders. Priests grant forgiveness to a person, not because the person committed serious sins against the priest himself, but for serious sins committed against any other person or against God. Such forgiveness is part of the sacrament of penance, confession or reconciliation.

If indeed Jesus only breathed on the apostles and only told the apostles to forgive, the above argument may - may - have merit. However, Chapter 6 of **CEASED?** (page 107) provides evidence there were ~120 people in attendance on resurrection Sunday evening - the apostles, the 2 believers Jesus met on the road to Emmaus, and the entire group described as *'those who were with them'*. Moreover, there were both men and women in attendance.

24:7 If Jesus was sending all of the ~120, breathed on all of the ~120 and told all of the ~120 (some of whom were women) to forgive, wouldn't that change the picture entirely? Wouldn't that mean Jesus was telling all believers to forgive, not just male apostles? And wouldn't that mean the function of forgiveness done by priests today is misguided?

If we study the Lord's prayer for guidance, we see it isn't an issue of person A (a priest) forgiving person B for sins person B committed against one or more third-parties - persons C, D, E etc. Jesus told His disciples they were to forgive anyone who sinned against them. In other words, the Lord's prayer is very clear that persons C, D and E are called to forgive person B.

❑ *Matthew 6:12 And forgive us our debts, as we also have forgiven our debtors.*

24:8 Given the above, why would John 20:23 be any different? I can't find any scriptures clearly stating otherwise - that Jesus only told the apostles to forgive and not the entire group of ~120. I can't find any scriptures stating Jesus told the apostles He was giving them the authority to forgive sins on His behalf, or on behalf of another person. I don't see any scriptures enabling a priest to forgive me for a wrong/sin I committed against you. You may not

CEASED?

want to forgive me now. Given that, isn't the forgiveness in John 20:23:
  i. about each of us forgiving all those who wronged/sinned against us; and not
  ii. apostles/priests forgiving the person who did wrong/committed sins (person B) on behalf of the person wronged/sinned against (you, me or persons C, D, E), or on behalf of God?

24:9 And doesn't that show the sacraments of Holy Orders and penance are flawed?

24:10 After 1,900 years since the New Testament books were written, Catholic teachings have many issues on the sacraments of water baptism, confirmation, and Holy Orders. Issues with Holy Orders brings into question the sacrament of penance. Chapter 4 raised many problems on the sacrament of communion. Given that, how solid is the house of Roman Catholic teachings given the many flaws and holes in these 5 sacraments?

TRADITIONS

Background

Traditions have been a topic of much debate. Let me throw my 2 cents (2.8 cents CAD) into the pot. My abbreviated understanding of Roman Catholic teachings on traditions is as follows:
  i. traditions were a gift from Jesus to the original apostles, and for all future generations;
  ii. traditions are key to Jesus being amongst us in the same way He was with the Apostles;
  iii. traditions are not in opposition to scripture: they complement and confirm one another;
  iv. there are capital 'T' traditions which are the official teachings handed down from the original apostles. Lower case 't' traditions are customs and of less significance; and
  v. traditions are to be adhered to as they help draw a person closer to God.

Traditions certainly have their place. Biblical traditions relevant today should be continued.

❑ *2 Thessalonians 2:15 So then, brethren, **stand firm and hold to the traditions** which you were taught, whether by word of mouth or by letter from us.*

24:11 However, for traditions which aren't Biblical, don't the following verses suggest we need to be very careful as to what traditions are followed?

❑ *Matthew 15:3 And He answered and said to them, **"Why do you yourselves transgress the commandment of God for the sake of your tradition?** ... 6 ... **And by this you invalidated the word of God for the sake of your tradition**.*

2 Groups of Traditions

In the first decades after the cross, the first Christians had none, then only a limited amount of the New Testament to read. Somewhere in the 4-6 decades after

24: 5 Catholic Sacraments, Traditions

the cross, the entire New Testament was written. Making copies of these early writings was time-consuming, and far slower than the technologies available today. Only a few people could read. Oral teaching was key. When it comes to traditions relevant to the New Covenant, few details are in the Bible. The Catholic church teaches, however, that these traditions were recorded by some of the early church fathers.

A key issue in my mind is how do the traditions carried out in ~30 AD when Jesus went to the cross, compare to the traditions followed in both Roman Catholic and non-Catholic churches today.

24:12 To that end, is it prudent to group traditions and their components into 1 of 2 groups:
1. current traditions that were in place when Jesus went to the cross, and which remain unchanged today; or
2. current traditions and portions of current traditions that weren't in place when Jesus went to the cross, but which were added or changed over time?

24:13 Given a yes to the above 2 groupings, wouldn't it be most prudent to only engage in traditions fitting into the first group? If not, why not?

24:14 Breaking Roman Catholic traditions into 2 groups may seem difficult, but should it be?
   i. Shouldn't the first group be extremely easy for Roman Catholics to identify by simply looking at the writings of those early church fathers who were discipled by the original apostles? If not, why not?
   ii. And if we can't identify what traditions or parts of traditions were occurring according to those early church fathers who were discipled by the original apostles, how do we know which traditions today are of God, and which aren't?

Traditions and Scriptures

God is also clear about not messing around with His Word.
- *Deuteronomy 4:2 You **shall not add to the word** which I am commanding you, nor take away from it, that you may keep the commandments of the Lord your God which I command you.*
- *Deuteronomy 12:32 **Whatever I command you, you shall be careful to do; you shall not add to nor take away from it.***
- *Galatians 1:8 But even **if we, or an angel from heaven, should preach to you a gospel contrary to what we have preached to you, he is to be accursed**! 9 As we have said before, so I say again now, **if any man is preaching to you a gospel contrary to what you received, he is to be accursed!***

24:15 The Catholic church teaches a combination of scriptures plus traditions handed down by the apostles represent the full teaching of Christ. The above scriptures are clear that we are not to add to or change the gospels, or any part of His Word. In other words, God's word is supreme. Doesn't that contradict the claim of the Catholic church in terms of how traditions

CEASED?

are to be viewed?

24:16 If today's capital 'T' traditions are viewed on par with the Bible, wouldn't it be reasonable to expect Holy Spirit would have inspired the details of these traditions to be written and canonized just as the New Testament was canonized? If not, why not?

Catholic Inventions

Francis Chan is a widely respected, though sometimes controversial, Protestant teacher who is currently viewed as 'friendly' towards the Roman Catholic church. I make this comment, not to suggest he agrees with everything about the Roman Catholic church, but to make it clear he is not a Catholic opposer. He doesn't have an axe to grind as it were. One of Francis's websites, www.juststopandthink.com has a list of 45 Roman Catholic 'inventions' available at the link:

www.juststopandthink.com/wp-content/uploads/2012/03/catholic-inventions.pdf

The list is from the book *"Roman Catholicism"* written by Loraine Boettner and published in 1962. I copied the inventions on February 15, 2020, then reproduced part of the list below in two sections. The year when the invention materialized is identified in brackets after the description.

A: Historical Events No Longer Applicable

One invention listed in Mr. Boettner's book that no longer applies today involves the Bible.

30. Bible forbidden to laymen, placed on the Index of Forbidden books by the council of Toulouse (1229 AD)

B: Aspects Valid Today

Some creations after the cross and listed in Mr. Boettner's book that still apply today include:

1. Prayers for the dead (300)
2. Making the sign of the cross (300)
4. Veneration of angels and dead saints, and use of images (375)
5. The Mass, as a daily celebration (394)
6. Beginning of the exaltation of Mary, term "Mother of God" first applied to her by the Council of Ephesus (431)
7. Priests began to dress differently from laymen (500)
9. The doctrine of Purgatory, established by Gregory I (593)
10. Latin Language, used in prayer and worship, imposed by Gregory I (600)
11. Prayers directed to Mary, dead saints and angels, about (600)
13. Kissing of the Pope's foot, began with Pope Constantine (709)
15. Worship of the cross, images, and relics, authorized (786)
16. Holy water mixed with a pinch of salt and blessed by a priest (850)
17. Worship of St. Joseph (890)
19. Baptism of bells, instituted by Pope John XIII (965)
20. Canonization of dead saints, first by Pope John XV (995)

24: 5 Catholic Sacraments, Traditions

22. The Mass, developed gradually as a sacrifice, attendance made obligatory in 11th century
23. Celibacy of the priesthood, decreed by Pope Gregory VII (1079)
24. The Rosary, mechanical praying with beads, invented by Peter the Hermit (1090)
28. Auricular (out loud) Confession of sins to a priest instead of to God, instituted by Pope Innocent III, in Lateral council (1215)
29. Adoration of the wafer (Host), decreed by Pope Honorius III (1220)
34. The doctrine of Seven Sacraments affirmed (1439)
35. The Ave Maria (Hail Mary) (part of last half finished 50 years later) (1508)
37. Tradition declared as equal authority with the Bible /Council of Trent (1545)
40. Immaculate Conception of the Virgin Mary, proclaimed by Pope Pius IX (1854)
44. Assumption of the Virgin Mary (bodily ascension into heaven shortly after her death), proclaimed by Pope Pius XII (1950)
45. Mary proclaimed Mother of the Church, by Pope Paul VI (1965)

24:17 The timeline of these events is certainly interesting as it shows the evolution of Catholic teachings such as how Mary went from being one of a ~120-person prayer group in Acts 1:14 in ~30AD to now being exalted as the Mother of God, and a host of other divine type titles. However, the long and short of it - at least to me - is this. What traditions were being followed when Jesus went to the cross that closely resemble the 45 items? I ask this because if these traditions weren't clearly followed at the time of the cross, how can they be viewed as anywhere close to being equal with God's Word?

24:18 On the basis the above items came into existence after the cross, doesn't their addition to what are considered God's teachings go directly against the teachings of Deuteronomy 4.2, Deuteronomy 12.32 and Galatians 1:8-9 shown just before question 24:15? If not, why not?

24:19 For traditions or portions of traditions which were either added or which are different from the traditions in place when Jesus went to the cross - on what basis can we be 100% confident that such things are of God?

24:20 If you're not 100% confident such items listed are of God, wouldn't it be prudent to avoid such activities, and go by what the Bible teaches?

24:21 On the basis the Catholic church places traditions on par with the Bible as per item #37, an issue arises as to what should rule if the tradition disagrees with the Bible. To me, the Bible should rule as there is no doubt it is God's Word which in the original Greek and Hebrew, is without error. In the case of a conflict between the Bible and a tradition, the tradition must be in error. But is that what the Roman Catholic church teaches? My understanding is that Catholic traditions usually rank ahead of God's Word. If that is the case even once, isn't that troublesome?

CEASED?

Is it About God, or Others

Figure 24:1 lists 10 of the many practices and activities currently going on in the Roman Catholic church. Before looking at the 10 items, let me ask.

24:22 Should any church, Roman Catholic or not, have any traditions where God isn't the primary beneficiary of attention and the recipient of all glory?

- 1 Corinthians 10:31 Whether, then, you eat or drink or whatever you do, **do all to the glory of God**.
- 1 Timothy 1:17 Now to the King eternal, immortal, invisible, the **only God, be honor and glory forever and ever**. Amen.
- Matthew 6:33 But **seek first His kingdom** and His righteousness, and all these things will be added to you.
- Matthew 6:9 "Pray, then, in this way: 'Our Father who is in heaven, Hallowed be Your name. 10 'Your kingdom come. **Your will be done**, On earth as it is in heaven. 11 'Give us this day our daily bread. 12 'And forgive us our debts, as we also have forgiven our debtors. 13 'And do not lead us into temptation, but deliver us from evil. For **Yours is the kingdom** and the power **and the glory forever**. Amen.

Figure 24:1 Ten Activities and Practices Occurring in Roman Catholic church

Item	Source		Primary focus on God or others?		Glory and Focus	
	Bible	Catholic Church	God	Others	All to God?	Shared?
1. Praying Lord's Prayer	x		x		x	
2. Praying the rosary/praying to Mary in general		x		x		x
3. Seeking 15 promises of rosary		x		x		x
4. Seeking 7 graces						
5. Praying to deceased saints		x		x		x
6. Kissing Pope's hand, feet of statues		x		x		x
7. Creation/attention given to graven images of saints		x		x		x
8. Preserving bones, blood, other parts of deceased saints for display after the cross		x		x		x
9. Unique robes & hats worn by Popes & priests		x		x		x
10. Titles such as 'His Holiness' or 'Mother Superior'		x		x		x

24:23   Apart from #1, how do any items from #2 through #10 bring all glory to

24: 5 Catholic Sacraments, Traditions

God? And if they don't bring all glory to God, shouldn't they be discontinued? If not, why not?

24:24 If you're a Roman Catholic, is there merit to studying the Bible for yourself to determine the parts of Catholic capital 'T' and small 't' traditions that are confirmed by the Bible and still relevant today? And is there merit to rejecting all traditions, and parts of traditions, not confirmed by the Bible?

Reliability of Source Documents for Today's Catholics

Based on my research, the Roman Catholic church claims teachings and information on traditions not found in the Bible are nonetheless of God for two key reasons:

1. the roots of the Roman Catholic church go back to the cross and the original apostles - notably Peter the first pope - which makes it the one true church; and
2. teachings of early church fathers, some of whom were discipled by the original apostles, wrote down the key information on the capital 'T' traditions that aren't found in the Bible.

CEASED? has shown, or will show in subsequent chapters, several issues which - from my perspective - show extremely serious gaps in Roman Catholic teaching. Major issues involve the Ten Commandments, graven images and idolatry, salvation and the in [en] experience. Other major issues are seen in 5 of the 7 sacraments - water baptism, confirmation (Baptism of the Holy Spirit), communion, Holy Orders and penance.

24:25 The above deficiencies in core Roman Catholic teachings can be identified because we can compare Roman Catholic teachings to the Bible, to God's Word which is without error. **IF** the writings of early church fathers are consistent with current Roman Catholic teachings, and **GIVEN** some core Catholic teachings have major errors:
   i. doesn't that mean some writings of the early church fathers are also in error; and
   ii. if so, how confident can we be other writings of early church fathers not verifiable by the Bible, but which are relied on by the Catholic church, aren't also in error?

24:26 On the other hand, if writings of the early church fathers aren't in error but Catholic teachings are in error, doesn't that mean there must be differences between the teachings of early church fathers and current Catholic teachings? And if so:
   i. why do Catholic teachings differ from these reliable early teachings; and
   ii. how could such errors exist given the millions of Catholic priests and scholars who have studied Catholic teachings over the centuries?

24:27 Per the section above on inventions, Mr. Boettner's book revealed that tradition was declared as having equal authority with the Bible by the Council of Trent in 1545. More than 1,500 years after Christ died, the Roman Catholic Church determines that traditions now rank equal to the

Bible. How can that massive of a change be God's doing? God does not change, but we're supposed to believe that for 1,500 years, it was God's will that traditions were not equal to God's Word, but thereafter, they were equal?

24:28 If there isn't 100% reliability of the accuracy on the writings of early church fathers or 100% reliability on how the Roman Catholic church interprets these writings, how can anyone put traditions on par with God's Word which is 100% without error?

24:29 The end result is this. When we look at current Roman Catholic traditions or the traditions of any Protestant denomination that are not supported by the Bible, how can one be 100% confident these traditions:
   i. have not changed from what they were like in the early church;
   ii. are of God and not a creation of mankind or an organization; and
   iii. haven't to some degree been influenced by satan, who after all, is a master counterfeiter, and the central figure in our spiritual battles.

❑ *Ephesians 6:12 For our struggle is not against flesh and blood, but against the rulers, against the powers, against the world forces of this darkness, against the spiritual forces of wickedness in the heavenly places.*

CLOSING POINT TO PONDER

24:30 God's Word is without error. If we're engaged in anything that potentially goes against His Word, against God's commands and instructions, aren't we playing with fire?

25

Peter and Mary

INTRODUCTION
PETER, successor Popes to Peter, and Mary have central roles in the Roman Catholic church. Chapter 25 addresses if such attention is biblical for Peter and Mary (page 344).

PETER - APOSTLE ONLY
or APOSTLE, ROCK AND POPE?

Many Protestants have reservations about Roman Catholic teachings relating to Peter being the first Pope, the earthly head of the church. Most Protestants don't agree that Peter, or any person who has held the position of Pope, was or is the head of the earthly church. We view Jesus as being the head of the earthly church.

The Rock
The cornerstone scripture suggesting Peter was the first Pope is Matthew 16:18.

❑ *Matthew 16:13 Now when Jesus came into the district of Caesarea Philippi, He was asking His disciples, "Who do people say that the Son of Man is?" 14 And they said, "Some say John the Baptist; and others, Elijah; but still others, Jeremiah, or one of the prophets." 15 He said to them, "But who do you say that I am?" 16 Simon Peter answered, "You are the Christ, the Son of the living God." 17 And Jesus said to him, "Blessed are **you, Simon Barjona**, because flesh and blood did not reveal this to you, but My Father who is in heaven. 18 I also **say to you that you are Peter**, and **upon this rock I will build My church**; and the gates of Hades will not overpower it.*

In the Greek, the word Peter means stone or rock. As a result, Roman Catholic teaching links Peter to the phrase *'upon this rock'*. Catholic teaching holds that changing Peter's name from Cephas to Peter occurred because Jesus was declaring Peter was to be the earthly head of the church - the first pope. He was the rock that Jesus could rely on. Some Protestants also believe Peter is the rock, but don't believe that label translates to Peter or any other person being designated as the head of the earthly church. Jesus was and remains the head of our earthly church.

Joseph Raymond notes in his 2006 article *"Simon, Cephas, Petros, Petra"*, that Peter's name before first meeting Christ was not Cephas, but Simon, the son of John. Simon is the English version of the Hebrew name Shimon which is derived from the

CEASED?

Hebrew word Sh'ma. Sh'ma means to listen, or hear and obey. Right after meeting Simon at the beginning of Jesus's earthly ministry, Jesus tells Simon that his name is to be changed to Cephas which means stone or rock.
- ❑ *John 1:42 He brought him to Jesus. Jesus looked at him and said, "**You are Simon the son of John; you shall be called Cephas**" (which is translated Peter).*

25:1 In Matthew 16:18 when Jesus told Peter his name was again changed, this time to Peter, there was no change in the meaning underlying Peter's name. So why the change from Cephas to Peter? Was it as simple as Greek was more widely spoken at the time, and changing Peter's name from Aramaic to Greek would help Peter share the gospel?

25:2 Even if there is a simple explanation to Peter's name change in Matthew 16:18 from Cephas to Peter, the issue nonetheless goes back to John 1 when the first change in Peter's name was made from Simon to Cephas. Why the change? Was it a prophetic statement that Peter was indeed the rock upon which God's church would be built?

What do the Other Gospels Say

If Peter is the rock upon which Christ's church would be built, that's an incredibly unique position that comes with much responsibility. Let's see what the gospels of Mark, Luke and John say about the matter.
- ❑ **Mark 8:27** *Jesus went out, along with His disciples, to the villages of Caesarea Philippi; and on the way He questioned His disciples, saying to them, "Who do people say that I am?" 28 They told Him, saying, "John the Baptist; and others say Elijah; but others, one of the prophets." 29 And He continued by questioning them, "**But who do you say that I am?**" Peter answered and said to Him, "**You are the Christ**." 30 **And He warned them to tell no one about Him**.*
- ❑ **Luke 9:18** *And it happened that while He was praying alone, the disciples were with Him, and He questioned them, saying, "Who do the people say that I am?" 19 They answered and said, "John the Baptist, and others say Elijah; but others, that one of the prophets of old has risen again." 20 And He said to them, "**But who do you say that I am?**" And Peter answered and said, "**The Christ of God**." 21 **But He warned them and instructed them not to tell this to anyone**,*
- ❑ **John:** *Nil*

In regards to the issue *"Who do you say that I am?"*, we find the following.
- ❖ In the book of John, nothing is said at all. No mention is made about the discussion of Peter's name change, the rock or that Jesus was the Christ.
- ❖ Both Mark and Luke describe Peter stating Jesus is Christ. However, neither of these books mention Peter's name change from Cephas to Peter, or refer to the rock upon which the church would be built.

25:3 Issues of significant importance are almost always mentioned in more than one book and/or more than once in the same book. This issue of Peter potentially being the rock - the head of the new church - is mentioned in only

25: Peter and Mary

one book, and only once in that book. If Peter was indeed the first Pope, wouldn't this significant and unique position amongst all believers warrant mention in more than the book of Matthew? Or at least mentioned more than once in Matthew?

25:4 While Paul wrote the most books in the New Testament, Luke wrote the most Greek words. Luke is viewed as being a thorough researcher and scholar. If Peter was indeed the first Pope and head of the church, isn't it likely Luke would have taken care to make this point crystal clear when he wrote Luke 9:20? If not, why would Luke (as well as Mark and John) ignore such a critical appointment?

25:5 Further, if such a critical appointment was only to be mentioned once, why wouldn't God make it more definitive in Matthew 16:18 by stating something akin to:
   i. *"... and you Peter, you will be the rock upon whom I will build my church?"*; or
   ii. *"... and I also say to you Peter, you will be the head of the church on earth. You and you alone will be delegated special authority from the Father, and you will be My Chief representative as will your successors"*?

Petros and Petra

In the Greek, nouns have gender. The Greek word *'petros'* [4074] is masculine while *'petra'* [G4073] is feminine. Peter, the man, is referred to using the word *petros*. The rock Jesus said He would build His church on was not *petros* - the Greek word used for Peter - but *petra*.

- ❑ *Matthew 16:18 I also say to you that you are **Peter [petros]**, and upon this **rock [petra]** I will build My church; and the gates of Hades will not overpower it."*

12 other Scriptures

Much has been written on petros and petra. Let me keep it short by looking at 12 scriptures. The first two involve Paul and Peter referring to Jesus. They both used the Greek word petra.

- ❑ *1 Peter 2:8 and A stone of stumbling and a **rock [petra]** of offense ...*
- ❑ *1 Corinthians 10:4 and all drank the same spiritual drink, for they were drinking from a spiritual **rock [petra]** which followed them; and the **rock [petra]** was Christ.*

25:6 Both Peter and Paul use petra when referencing Jesus as the rock. Doesn't this support the notion that Jesus was the rock on which the church would be built, and not Peter? If not, why not?

Here are 10 scriptures referring to Jesus as a stone, cornerstone or foundation.

- ❑ *Matthew 21:42 Jesus said to them, "Did you never read in the Scriptures, 'The **stone** which the builders rejected, This became the **chief corner stone**; This came about from the Lord, And it is marvelous in our eyes'?*
- ❑ *Mark 12:10 Have you not even read this Scripture: 'The **stone** which the builders rejected, This became the **chief corner stone**;*

CEASED?

- Luke 20:17 But Jesus looked at them and said, "What then is this that is written: 'The **stone** which the builders rejected, This became the **chief corner stone**'?
- Acts 4:11 He is the **stone** which was rejected by you, the builders, but which became the **chief corner stone**.
- Romans 9:33 just as it is written, "Behold, I lay in Zion a stone of stumbling and a **rock of offense**, And he who believes in Him will not be disappointed."
- 1 Corinthians 3:11 For no man can lay a **foundation** other than the one which is laid, which is Jesus Christ.
- Ephesians 2:20 having been built on the foundation of the apostles and prophets, Christ Jesus Himself being **the corner stone**,
- 1 Peter 2:6 ... "Behold, I lay in Zion a choice stone, a precious **corner stone**, And he who believes in Him will not be disappointed."
- 1 Peter 2:7 This precious value, then, is for you who believe; but for those who disbelieve, "The **stone** which the builders rejected, This became the **very corner stone**,"
- 2 Timothy 2:19 Nevertheless, the firm **foundation** of God stands ...

Whereas at least 12 scriptures refer to Jesus as a rock, stone, cornerstone or foundation, there isn't one other scripture identifying Peter as a unique rock, stone, cornerstone or foundation.

25:7 If the rock on which the church would be built was Peter, wouldn't we expect more scriptures referring to Peter as a rock of some kind, and clarifying he - not Jesus - was the rock - the foundation - on which the church was to be built?

I also found over 30 Old Testament scriptures where God is referred to as a rock including the following 4 verses.
- Psalm 18:2 The **Lord is my rock** ... **My God, my rock** ...
- 2 Samuel 22:3 **My God, my rock** ...
- Deuteronomy 32:4 "**The Rock!** His work is perfect ...
- Isaiah 26:4 ... For **in God the Lord, we have an everlasting Rock**.

Were the other Apostles Rocks as well

Consider the role that the apostles and prophets played.
- Ephesians 2:17 And He came and preached peace to you who were far away, and peace to those who were near; 18 for through Him we both have our access in one Spirit to the Father. 19 So then you are no longer strangers and aliens, but you are fellow citizens with the saints, and are of God's household, 20 **having been built on the foundation of the apostles and prophets**, **Christ Jesus Himself being the corner stone**, 21 in whom the whole building, being fitted together, is growing into a holy temple in the Lord, 22 in whom you also are being built together into a dwelling of God in the Spirit.

25:8 Doesn't Ephesians 2 show Peter, like the other apostles and prophets, was part of the church foundation while Jesus, is the cornerstone - the key rock of any foundation?

25: Peter and Mary

Keys, Binding and Loosing

Another key scripture Catholics cite as reason to believe Peter was the first Pope is the notion Peter was given the keys to the kingdom of heaven.

❑ *Matthew 16:19 I **will give you the keys of the kingdom of heaven** ...*

If we continue reading in Matthew 16:19, we find these keys relate to binding and loosing - a topic **CEASED?** touched on in Chapter 23 - where believers are to bring heaven to earth.

❑ *Matthew 16:19 I will give you the keys of the kingdom of heaven; and **whatever you bind on earth shall have been bound in heaven**, and **whatever you loose on earth shall have been loosed in heaven**.*

A couple of things. First, Peter was given the keys **OF** the kingdom of heaven, not the keys **TO** the kingdom of heaven. Second, just before Matthew 16:19, we learn Jesus was speaking not only to Peter, but to all His disciples.

❑ *Matthew 16:13 Now when Jesus came into the district of Caesarea Philippi, **He was asking His disciples**, "Who do people say that the Son of Man is?"*

This message that binding and loosing applied to all disciples was repeated in Matthew 18.

❑ *Matthew 18:1 ... **the disciples** came to Jesus ... "Who then is greatest in the kingdom of heaven?" ... 18 Truly I say to you, **whatever you bind on earth shall have been bound in heaven; and whatever you loose on earth shall have been loosed in heaven**.*

25:9 Since Matthew 16:13-19 and Matthew 18:1-18 show Jesus telling all the disciples they can bind and loose, doesn't this negate the argument that Peter, and Peter alone, had these keys of the kingdom of heaven and a special status amongst the apostles? And given Jesus was speaking to the disciples, doesn't this mean all believers - including you and me today - have the keys of the kingdom of heaven? If not, why not?

Who was the Greatest Apostle

Now consider how the other apostles viewed Peter. After the Last Supper which took place after the discussion in Matthew 16 where Jesus said *'upon this rock I will build my church'*, the disciples were wondering in Luke 22 who is greatest.

❑ *1 Peter 5:1 Therefore, I exhort the elders among you, as **your fellow elder and witness** of the sufferings of Christ, and a partaker also of the glory that is to be revealed.*

❑ *Luke 22:14 When the hour had come, He reclined at the table, and the apostles with Him. 15 And He said to them, "I have earnestly desired to eat this Passover with you before I suffer ... 24 And there arose also a **dispute among them as to which one of them was regarded to be greatest**.*

25:10 Doesn't 1 Peter 5 indicate Peter saw himself as an equal, and not as a superior elder?

25:11 Doesn't the fact the disciples were even discussing the issue of who was the greatest suggest there was no clearly designated leader?

CEASED?

25:12 If Peter was the first Pope, is it reasonable to expect Jesus would have made his appointment crystal clear to the other apostles? And if Peter was their leader, the other apostles would have to accept that reality and admit, perhaps reluctantly, it was Peter who was the greatest of them all?

Peter or Paul
Paul corrected Peter; Peter never corrected Paul.
- ❑ *Galatians 2:11 But when Cephas came to Antioch, I opposed him to his face, because he stood condemned.*

Figure 25:1 shows the frequency of mention of Paul and Peter in the 23 New Testament books other than the 4 Gospels.

Figure 25:1

Book	Peter	Saul + Paul
Acts Chapters 1-12	60	14 + 0 = 14
Acts Chapters 13-28	0	8 + 143 = 151
James		
Galatians *	3	4
1 Thessalonians *		3
2 Thessalonians *		2
1 Corinthians *		9
2 Corinthians *		7
Romans *		1
Ephesians *		2
Philippians *		
Philemon *		3
Colossians *		3
1 Timothy *		1
Titus *		1
1 Peter	1	
2 Timothy *		1
2 Peter	1	1
Hebrews		
Jude		
1 John		
2 John		
3 John		
TOTAL	**65**	**203**

* Written by Paul

We find Peter is referred to ~60 times in Acts compared to Paul's ~165 times (14+151). We also find Peter is not referred to once after Chapter 12 in Acts, and very little in the other books.

25:13 Is there a bias to the numbers because Paul wrote 13 books and Peter only wrote 2? Absolutely. But is the underlying bias there because Paul's

25: Peter and Mary

mandate was larger than Peter's since Paul was primarily charged with taking the gospel to the more populous and spiritually uneducated Gentiles, while Peter's mandate was primarily to the Jews?

❑ *Galatians 2:7 But on the contrary, seeing that I had been entrusted with the gospel to the uncircumcised, just as Peter had been to the circumcised.*

25:14   In addition, Luke who was the most prolific writer in the New Testament, traveled with Paul, not Peter. Paul's personal trials are written about at length; Peter's trials after the cross are documented in a very limited way. If there was an earthly head of the early church, doesn't the evidence suggest Paul and not Peter?

Personal Status

25:15   Jesus healed Peter's mother-in-law which indicates Peter was married. Some believers say this is reason to argue Peter would have been ineligible to be a Pope. However, given the Catholic church only adopted the practice of celibacy for priests in 1079 (item 23, page 333), that may explain why Peter could still have been the first pope. But doesn't the issue of a new celibacy requirement speak to an even larger issue? If celibacy for priests - as well as the other inventions on pages 332 and 333 - are truly of God, what Biblical evidence is there that God would wait many centuries after the cross before making a number of radical changes, one of which is requiring celibacy for priests?

❑ *Mark 1:30 Now Simon's mother-in-law was lying sick with a fever; and immediately they spoke to Jesus about her.*

So, Who is: 'Upon this rock I will build my church'

❑ *Matthew 16:18 I also say to you **that you are Peter**, and upon **this rock I will build My church**; and the gates of Hades will not overpower it.*

This issue of whether or not Peter is the rock on which the church would be built is an extremely important issue. To a large extent, the very existence of the Roman Catholic church depends on it. But if Peter is not the rock - the first pope - as suggested in **CEASED?**, does the Bible clearly state who is? Again, consider verses 13 through 16.

❑ *Matthew 16:13 Now when Jesus came into the district of Caesarea Philippi,* **He was asking His disciples, "Who do people say that the Son of Man is?"** *14 And they said, "Some say John the Baptist; and others, Elijah; but still others, Jeremiah, or one of the prophets." 15 He said to them, "But who do you say that I am?" 16* **Simon Peter answered, "You are the Christ, the Son of the living God."**

At the end of the dialogue about who Jesus is, Jesus acknowledges Peter is right, that Jesus is the Messiah. And it is Jesus, the Messiah, who is the rock on whom the church will be built.

CEASED?

To Recap Peter Being the First Pope

1. There is one scripture alluding to the notion Peter may - may - be the rock.
2. No other scripture mentions Peter as being the petra, the rock of the church.
3. At least 12 other scriptures refer specifically to Jesus as rock, cornerstone or foundation.
4. Peter and Paul both refer to Jesus as petra, the rock.
5. Peter, like the rest of the apostles and prophets, is described as part of the foundation of the church. By contrast, Jesus is the cornerstone which is the key rock in a foundation.
6. The apostles fought amongst themselves as to who was the greatest. Given they even discussed the issue shows Peter was not the leader.
7. Jesus told all His disciples, not just the apostles, they could bind and loose on earth what has already been bound and loosed in heaven. As a result, all Jesus's disciples have the keys of the kingdom of heaven, not just Peter and the apostles.
8. Paul is much more prevalent in the New Testament after the cross than Peter. Peter is non-existent in Acts after Acts 12. Paul took the gospel to the much more populous Gentiles. Paul rebuked Peter; Peter never rebuked Paul. Paul wrote ~13 books in the New Testament; Peter wrote 2. Paul's personal trials are written about at length; Peter's trials are mentioned in a minor way.
9. Jesus as the rock is consistent with who Jesus is, with what He did, and supported by at least 12 scriptures that reference Jesus as a rock, stone, foundation or cornerstone.

25:16 Who do you say is the rock on which the church will be built - sinful, human Peter who denied Christ or Holy, Almighty Jesus who redeemed Peter?

Successors to Peter

In my research, the Biblical evidence for Peter being the first head of the earthly church - the first Pope - is minimal, and dwarfed by evidence suggesting he was not. If you're Roman Catholic, do we you see why so many Protestants disagree that the position of Pope has merit, and why so many disagree Pope Francis is the earthly head of God's church? We believe Jesus is the head of the church, with the one true church being the overall body of believers, not an organization.

MARY: MORE THAN JESUS'S EARTHLY MOTHER?

Mary is revered within the Roman Catholic church. I get that. We're all thankful for her being the earthly mother of Jesus. If you're Roman Catholic, and find my research, questions and/or comments about Mary to be offensive, that's not my intent. If you do get offended, I am sorry, but I do request that you try to identify the root cause of the offense. For instance, are you simply tired of fighting the ongoing criticism from Protestants? Is it because my information and comments are false or misleading? Or is because the information herein has merit, contradicts your beliefs, and thereby poses one or more difficulties for you?

25: Peter and Mary

Why go to Mary - Intercessory Prayer

In my research on Mary, two of the primary reasons publicly stated by Catholics as to why they go to Mary are a) to honor her and b) to have Mary intercede for them.

In terms of interceding, the reasoning is that - since Mary is both the earthly mother of Jesus and someone who Roman Catholics view as having been sinless (Chapter 3 discusses this issue about Mary) and therefore more righteous than any other person who lived on earth besides Jesus - Mary is better able to influence Jesus. And because of her unique degree of influence, a person who comes to Mary can obtain a better result than if they went directly to Jesus.

In terms of honoring Mary as the earthly mother of Jesus Christ, I agree we should honor Mary. But I have a big 'but' in doing so. Let me explain my but. My Mom was a pretty darn good softball player in her youth. I remember playing catch with her when she was in her 50's and thinking - man, she's still got game. If I told you that my Mom was a professional softball player in her youth, that would not honor her. It would not honor her because that claim would be an exaggeration, and as such, it would be a lie. And by making such claims about my Mom, it would also suggest that somehow Mom was not good enough as she was. That would be a huge lie. I'm very proud of my Mom, and she was and is more than good enough. She's great in fact, and I have zero interest in exaggerating anything about her. Unless she gives me baking.

25:17   Lies come in many forms including exaggerations. If Mary is to be honored, isn't it vital that what we say and think about Mary are not exaggerations? If not, why not?

25:18   As a result, when we look at the many titles Roman Catholics place on Mary such as Mother of God, Spouse of the Spirit, Queen of Heaven, Queen of the Apostles, Queen of all Saints, Queen of Peace, Queen of Justice and the Ark of the New Covenant since she carried God's presence in her womb, don't we need to ensure that these and the dozens of other titles given to Mary are valid and appropriate, and not exaggerations?

Mary Has a Special Place

Elizabeth, the mother of John the Baptist, tells Mary how blessed she is among women.

- ❑ *Luke 1:41 When Elizabeth heard Mary's greeting, the baby leaped in her womb; and Elizabeth was filled with the Holy Spirit. 42 And she cried out with a loud voice and said, "__Blessed are you among women__, and __blessed is the fruit of your womb__!*

Elizabeth acknowledges Mary is the earthly mother of Elizabeth's Lord.

- ❑ *Luke 1:43 And how has it happened to me, that the __mother of my Lord__ would come to me? 44 For behold, when the sound of your greeting reached my ears, the baby leaped in my womb for joy. 45 And blessed is she who believed that there would be a fulfillment of what had been spoken to her by __the Lord__."*

25:19   Elizabeth seemed quite aware of the significance of Jesus. But if Mary was much more than the earthly mother of Jesus, isn't it rather significant that Elizabeth's interest was more focused on who Mary was carrying, and not on Mary herself?

Status & Role of Mary in the Roman Catholic church

Pope Francis's Perspective

In terms of the Roman Catholic church's view of Mary, consider the following that was copied verbatim on October 18, 2019 from the Vatican News website. Formatting is my doing.

(https://www.vaticannews.va/en/pope/news/2018-12/pope-new-year-s-day-mary-mother-god-let-us-be-amazed.html)

Pope at Mass: 'let us be amazed'
*Pope Francis says in his homily during the liturgy he celebrated in St Peter's Basilica on New Year's Day that we need to be amazed by Mary, the Mother of God, **allow her to gaze on us, embrace us and take us by the hand**.*

By Sr Bernadette Mary Reis, fsp
*Pope Francis took his cue for his homily for the Solemnity of Mary, Mother of God, from Luke's Gospel of the day which says that all were amazed by what the shepherds had to tell them. We should be **amazed today by the Mother of God**, he said, and **allow Mary to gaze on us, embrace us and take us by the hand**.*

Amazed by Mary
Mary is not only the Mother of God, *Pope Francis began,* **she also presents all of us "reborn to the Lord"**, *he said. The Church too, needs to be amazed, he continued, "at being the dwelling place of the living God, the Bride of the Lord,* **a Mother who gives birth to her children". It is Our Lady who "gives the Church the feel of home**", *the Pope said.*

Allow Mary to gaze on us
Whenever Mary gazes on us, *Pope Francis said* **"she does not see sinners but children"**. *By allowing her to gaze on us, we will see the reflection of God's beauty and heaven.* **Her gaze, he said, penetrates the darkest corner and rekindles hope**.

"As she gazes upon us, she says: **'Take heart, dear children; here I am, your Mother!'"**

It's clear Pope Francis (as well as previous Popes) and the Roman Catholic church in general, see Mary not only as the earthly mother of Jesus, but as the Mother of God. She is viewed as the Mother of all believers. She gives Catholics the feel of home. Mary gazes on all children of God. She takes our hands and presents individuals as *"reborn to the Lord"*. These kinds of activities, **IF** they are truly of God, should be something to honor and delight in by all believers.

25: Peter and Mary

25:20 Do Pope Francis's comments indicate:
  i. Pope Francis is asking Mary to pray along the lines of an intercessory prayer; or
  ii. Pope Francis expects Mary to behave supernaturally and will deliver the supernatural blessings herself? Blessings such as being able to:
     a. gaze on the billion+ Roman Catholics at the same time;
     b. take every Roman Catholic by the hand;
     c. present all Catholics as reborn to the Lord;
     d. give birth to her Catholic children;
     e. give the church the feel of home; and
     f. gaze in a way that penetrates the darkest corner facing a billion+ Catholics, and rekindles hope to all Catholics.

25:21 To me, it's clear that Pope Francis expects Mary is able to carry out a multitude of supernatural things, things that only God can deliver. As a result, don't the Pope's words indicate he believes Mary is effectively God? Even if he doesn't use words to that effect?

25:22 If your answer to the above question is *"No, Mary is not viewed as being God"*, then let me ask. Who else but God can do such things? What other saint(s) can perform such things not only for the Pope, but for hundreds of millions of other Roman Catholics - simultaneously? Where in the Bible did any saint, living or deceased, do such things?

The Pope refers to Mary as the Mother of God. Let me repeat this question from Chapter 1:

1:18 My related question is this. Mary is a creation of God. If God created Mary, how could Mary be the Mother of God? In other words, how can Mary be the Mother of the One who created her?

Medjugorje
Now consider a small village called Medjugorje in Bosnia-Herzegovina where since 1981, claims have been made that Mary has been appearing and giving messages to the world. While any apparitions and the messages from Medjugorje have not been fully approved by the Vatican, steps taken to date indicate the Vatican has effectively approved events at Medjugorje. Consider two messages from Mary that I copied verbatim from www.medjugorje.org on December 28, 2019.

*December 25, 2019 Message to Marija "**Dear children**! **I am carrying my Son Jesus to you**, for Him to bless you and reveal to you His love, which comes from Heaven. Your heart yearns for peace, of which there is less and less on earth. That is why people are far from God and souls are sick and heading towards spiritual death. **I am with you, little children, to lead you** on this way of salvation to which God calls you. **Thank you for having responded to my call**."*

*December 25, 2019 Message to Jakov: At the last daily apparition to Jakov Colo on September 12th, 1998, **Our Lady** told him that henceforth he would have one apparition a year, every December 25th, on Christmas Day. This is also how it was*

CEASED?

*this year. The apparition began at 2:25 pm and lasted 9 minutes. **<u>Our Lady came with little Jesus in her arms</u>**. **Through Jakov**, Our Lady gave the following message: "**<u>Dear children</u>**, today, on this day of grace, in a special way I am calling you to open your hearts and to implore Jesus to strengthen your faith. **<u>Children</u>**, through prayer with the heart, faith and works you will come to know what it means to live a sincere Christian life. Often times, **<u>children</u>**, darkness, pain and crosses overwhelm your hearts. Do not waver in faith and ask 'why' because you think that you are alone and abandoned. Instead, open your hearts, pray and believe firmly and then your heart will feel God's nearness and that God never abandons you - that He is beside you at every moment. Through prayer and faith, God will answer your every 'why' and transform your every pain, darkness and cross into light. Thank you."*

25:23   Don't the above comments:
    i.   show Mary is not praying to God on behalf of people, but rather show Mary is speaking to believers in a direct, personalized way as if she were on high, and all Roman Catholics are her children?
    ii. contradict/conflict with God's Word which says:
       a. believers are children of God;
       b. children of God are to be led by Holy Spirit, not a person; and
       c. God's Word and not another saint, is the light to our path?
    iii. confirm that the Roman Catholic church believes Mary is God? If you still believe the answer is no, consider this. The Bible teaches truly born-again believers are children of God. The Roman Catholic church teaches that Catholics are Mary's children. As a result, doesn't it follow that the Roman Catholic church must also believe Mary is God? Or, to put the issue another way, if Mary isn't God, how can she possibly be the mother of hundreds of millions of Catholics?

❑   *Romans 8:14 For all who are being led by the Spirit of God, these are sons of God.*
❑   *Psalm 119:105 Your word is a lamp to my feet And a light to my path.*

When I ask someone to pray for me, my friends pray in different ways such as the following.

"Father God, thank You for sending Jesus to earth. Thank You for the cross and for the tearing of the veil so that I can come to You directly. I lift up Don and ask Lord that You ... (pray for specific issue or issues). In addition Lord, I ask that You bless Don with an increased desire to spend time alone with You. Bless him with more hunger for Your Word. Speak to him through Your Word and other ways including other believers. Draw Don closer to You Lord, and reveal anything in his heart that isn't right and is hindering his walk with You Lord. It is my hope that Don seeks Your Kingdom first as he begins each day, and that he is led by Holy Spirit throughout each day. Jesus, I ask You baptize Don afresh with power and fire. Bring godly men into his life to guide and mentor him. Father God, I pray all this in the mighty name of Your Son Jesus. Amen and Amen."

25: Peter and Mary

25:24 When considering Mary's comments from Medjugorje, do they resemble words akin to intercessory prayer as per my example above? If you believe Mary's comments are intercessory in nature, how does that reconcile with the fact Mary is speaking to people, not God? Or how do words such as *"I am with you little children to lead you"*, and *"thank you for having responded to my call"* equate to intercessory prayer?

25:25 Who besides God can lead His little children? Or call out to them? And thus, if Roman Catholics believe the prayers of Pope Francis or the Medjugorje are true and can be relied upon, how can Catholics not believe Mary is God? And if she is not God, aren't these nothing but idle, feel-good words? Or potentially words of demonic origin?

25:26 Per question 25:23 iii, when Mary calls believers her children, couldn't Catholics only be viewed as Mary's children if she was God? When logic follows lines of *"because Mary is the earthly mother of Jesus, and because Jesus is God, that makes Mary the Mother of God"*, or *"because we're children of God, and because Mary is the Mother of God, that makes Mary our mother"*, isn't that kind of logic the same as saying *"because my brother is friends with John Q pro hockey player, I'm also friends with John Q pro hockey player"*?

Praying the Rosary

Website rosarycenter.org provides instructions on how to pray the rosary.
1. Make the Sign of the Cross and say the "Apostles' Creed"
2. Say the "Our Father"
3. Say **three "Hail Marys"** for Faith, Hope, and Charity
4. Say the "Glory Be"
5. Announce the First Mystery and then say the "Our Father"
6. Say **ten "Hail Marys"** while meditating on the Mystery
7. Say the "Glory Be" (**Optional:** Say the "O My Jesus" prayer requested by Mary at Fatima)
8. Announce the Next Mystery; then say the "Our Father" and repeat these steps (6 through 8) as you continue through the remaining Mysteries.
9. Say the closing prayers: the "**Hail Holy Queen**" and "Final Prayer"
10. Make the "Sign of the Cross".

25:27 I can't find mention of anything resembling the rosary in the Bible. Mr. Boettner's book shows the rosary was started by Peter the Hermit in 1090. If the message of the rosary is not in the Bible, how can the rosary be viewed as Biblical, and not an addition to God's Word? How can it not be considered an independent creation of the Catholic church?

25:28 Jesus is mentioned specifically by name or otherwise referred to hundreds of times after Pentecost. Mary isn't mentioned or referred to once after Pentecost. Yet in the core Roman Catholic prayer - the rosary - the situation is reversed. Mary has the dominant position, far more than Father God, Jesus and Holy Spirit. Isn't that rather unusual? Where did God make it clear the rosary with its focus on Mary are His doing, and not the

CEASED?

results of centuries of slow changes within the Roman Catholic church?

15 Promises of the Rosary

Website www.themostholyrosary.com provides insight into 15 promises that Mary commits to give to those who recite the rosary.

The Blessed Virgin Mary promised to Saint Dominic and to all who follow that "Whatever you ask in the Rosary will be granted." She left for all Christians Fifteen Promises to those who recite the Holy Rosary.

Imparted to Saint Dominic and Blessed Alan
1. Whoever shall faithfully serve me by the recitation of the Rosary, **shall receive signal graces**.
2. I promise **my special protection** and the **greatest graces** to all those who shall recite the Rosary.
3. The Rosary shall be a **powerful armor against hell**, it will **destroy vice**, **decrease sin**, and **defeat heresies**.
4. The Rosary will **cause virtue** and **good works to flourish**; it will **obtain for souls the abundant mercy of God**; it will **withdraw the hearts of men from the love of the world and its vanities**, and **will lift them to the desire for eternal things**. Oh, that **souls would sanctify themselves** by this means.
5. The soul which recommends itself to me by the recitation of the Rosary, **shall not perish**.
6. Whoever shall recite the Rosary devoutly, applying himself to the consideration of its sacred mysteries **shall never be conquered by misfortune**. **God will not chastise him** in His justice, **he shall not perish by an unprovided death**; if he be just he shall remain in the grace of God, and become worthy of eternal life.
7. Whoever shall have a true devotion for the Rosary **shall not die without the sacraments of the Church**.
8. Those who are faithful to recite the Rosary shall have during their life and at their death the **light of God and the plentitude of His graces**; at the **moment of death they shall participate in the merits of the saints in paradise**.
9. I shall **deliver from Purgatory** those who have been devoted to the Rosary.
10. The faithful children of the Rosary shall **merit a high degree of glory in Heaven**.
11. You **shall obtain all you ask of me** by the recitation of the Rosary.
12. All those who propagate the Holy Rosary **shall be aided by me in their necessities**.
13. I have obtained from my Divine Son that all the advocates of the Rosary **shall have for intercessors the entire celestial court during their life and at the hour of death**.
14. All who recite the Rosary **are my sons and daughters, and brothers and sisters of my only Son Jesus Christ**.
15. Devotion of my Rosary is **a great sign of predestination**.

25: Peter and Mary

25:29 Do the 15 promises of the rosary resemble blessings a person can expect to receive by going to Mary, and asking Mary to speak to God who will deliver the blessings? Or, are the 15 promises a list of blessings a person would expect Mary to deliver herself?

25:30 In other words, don't the 15 promises clearly show praying the rosary is not the same as an intercessory prayer, but is a prayer expecting Mary to deliver amazing blessings? If one argues Mary is not delivering these supernatural blessings, re-read promises such as #9 and #12. If Mary isn't delivering on the promises, who is 'I' and 'me'?

25:31 Or consider promise #2. How can a person believe Mary can offer them some of 'her special protection' unless they viewed Mary as God and capable of offering protection?

25:32 In these 15 promises, God is mentioned twice, Jesus once and neither Father God or Holy Spirit are referred to at all. When you read the promises, accolades and names attributed to Mary, doesn't this show the Roman Catholic church views Mary as God? And doesn't that mean the Catholic Godhead is not a triune God, but a four-member Godhead? And that Mary - not the Father, Jesus or Holy Spirit - is who Roman Catholics are taught to go to first?

25:33 I can't find anything in the Bible justifying that Mary has the **authority** or **ability** to deliver on the 15 promises of the rosary, or that she is able to gaze on us, embrace us, lead us by the hand and present all of us as reborn to the Lord. Again, I ask: how can Mary be expected to deliver on such promises if she isn't viewed as being God?

25:34 If you still believe Mary is not God nor is viewed as being God, I encourage you to read the 15 promises again with this question in mind.

"According to the rosary and its 15 promises, if one is faithful in reciting the rosary and encouraging others to do the same, does one need to do anything else, or seek anyone else, in their Christian walk?"

According to the rosary and the 15 promises, who does a person need most - Mary or Jesus?

25:35 And consider reading the 15 promises with this second question in mind.
Are the blessings associated with the 15 promises in the rosary more likely to arise from:
  i. *a personal relationship and time spent alone with Father God, Holy Spirit and Jesus, and spending time reading God's Word; or*
  ii. *being disciplined in completing a defined set of activities and recitation of specific words of prayer on a very regular basis that are focused on Mary?*

25:36 Is i. or ii. in 25:35 most likely to lead to the words: "*I never knew you; depart from me.*"
- Matthew 7:23 And then I will declare to them, '**I never knew you**; depart from Me, you who practice lawlessness.'

CEASED?

25:37 Without faith, without trust in God, it's impossible to please God. Don't the 15 promises of the Rosary cause a person to trust in the rosary instead of God? And because our trust is elsewhere, are we therefore unable to please God? And unless we're focused and abiding in Jesus, won't our heavenly fruit be virtually nil? And aren't we missing out on rewards from God because we're seeking someone other than God?

- ❏ *Hebrews 11:6 And **without faith it is impossible to please Him**, for he who comes to God must believe that He is and **that He is a rewarder of those who seek Him**.*
- ❏ *John 15:5 I am the vine, you are the branches; he who abides in Me and I in him, he bears much fruit, for **apart from Me you can do nothing**.*

25:38 If *the* Roman Catholic church insists Mary is not God, then Mary can't personally deliver on things that only God can deliver. And thus, I fail to see how Mary can deliver on the 15 promises of the rosary. On that basis, doesn't that mean Catholics earnestly praying the rosary and expecting Mary to deliver on these promises are praying in futility? And as a result, is there really any difference between:
  i. Roman Catholics praying the rosary or other prayers to Mary; and
  ii. individuals in other faiths who pray to false gods such as the goddess Artemis?

- ❏ *Acts 19:26 You see and hear that not only in Ephesus, but in almost all of Asia, this Paul has persuaded and turned away a considerable number of people, saying that gods made with hands are no gods at all. 27 Not only is there danger that this trade of ours fall into disrepute, but also that the temple of the great goddess Artemis be regarded as worthless and that she whom all of Asia and the world worship will even be dethroned from her magnificence." 28 When they heard this and were filled with rage, they began crying out, saying, "Great is Artemis of the Ephesians!"*

25:39 The Roman Catholic church, and thus Roman Catholics faithful to the church, believe that Mary can deliver on the 15 promises of the rosary. As such, once again I ask, doesn't any Catholic who prays the rosary effectively believe, whether they realize it or not, that Mary is able to deliver things that only God can deliver? Putting it another way, how can Roman Catholics have one belief that Mary can deliver the 15 promises of the rosary and a second belief that Mary is not God? Aren't these two beliefs mutually exclusive, and as such, doesn't one belief have to go? And if one belief has to go, what does that say about the overall reliability of Roman Catholic teachings?

Supernatural Abilities

There are over one billion individuals classified as Roman Catholics. Based on Mary taking an average of 1 minute per day to hear and process each Catholic's prayer, that means Mary would spend over 1 billion minutes per day with Roman Catholics. There are only 1,440 minutes in a day (60 minutes per hour * 24 hours

25: Peter and Mary

per day = 1,440). To spend 1 minute on each person, Mary would need to be simultaneously communicating (hearing, interceding) an average of 694,444 individuals at a time - around the clock 24/7 (1 billion / 1,440 = 694,444). And after 1 minute, Mary would have another 694,444 individuals, on average, to deal with.

You may feel the numbers are too high as only a portion of Catholics pray daily. You may feel they're too low as it takes ~15 minutes to recite the rosary. Numbers vary by time of day and time zone. There are many variables. But whatever number you feel is right, the point remains many Catholics are praying to Mary at the same time. On Sundays, in areas with heavy concentrations of Roman Catholics in the same time zone, there will be tens of millions of Catholics praying to Mary at the same time. Moreover, these Catholics aren't in one room, but spread around the globe.

25:40   For Mary to simultaneously communicate with millions of people from all over the world requires Mary to have God-like abilities. If not, how do we explain her abilities?

25:41   Does an argument akin to - *In heaven, there is no such thing as time and thus Mary has infinite time to answer such prayers in the future, the answers of which are brought back in time to today* - actually hold water? Or is it a theory designed to justify a belief?

25:42   If Mary is constantly dealing with prayers from all these people here on earth, how do you think Mary is enjoying her time in Heaven?

Power of God and Mary

Mary gathered with others in prayer in Acts 1:14.

❏   *Acts 1:13 When they had entered the city, they went up to the upper room where they were staying; that is, Peter and John and James and Andrew, Philip and Thomas, Bartholomew and Matthew, James the son of Alphaeus, and Simon the Zealot, and Judas the son of James. 14 These all with one mind were **continually devoting themselves to prayer**, along with the women, and **Mary the mother of Jesus**, and with His brothers.*

25:43   At Pentecost, followers of Christ were *'all together'* and *'all filled with the Holy Spirit'*. Given Mary was with the group in Acts 1:14, is there any reason to believe Mary wasn't part of the group at Pentecost? And thus, is there any reason to believe she wasn't Baptized with the Holy Spirit, just like all of the other ~120 who were present?

❏   *Acts 2:1 When the day of Pentecost had come, **they were all together** in one place ... 4 And they were **all filled with the Holy Spirit** and began to speak with other tongues, as the Spirit was giving them utterance.*

25:44   To start His ministry, Jesus was Baptized in the Holy Spirit where Holy Spirit came upon [epi] Him like a dove. Jesus did many signs and wonders. Paul and other believers were Baptized in the Holy Spirit, and performed many signs and wonders. Yet, not one miracle was said to be done through Mary. If Mary is now able to hear millions of prayers at the same time, isn't the lack of supernatural involvement in Mary's earthly life totally inconsistent with the supernatural involvement attributed to Mary today?

Jesus's View of Who is Blessed

Elizabeth, John the Baptist's mother, said Mary would be blessed. Luke 11 describes a woman exalting Mary and stating Mary is blessed. But does Jesus say Mary is to be blessed?

- ❏ Matthew 12:47 Someone said to Him, "Behold, Your mother and Your brothers are standing outside seeking to speak to You." 48 But Jesus answered the one who was telling Him and said, "**Who is My mother** and who are My brothers?" 49 And stretching out His hand toward His disciples, He said, "Behold My mother and My brothers! 50 **For whoever does the will of My Father who is in heaven, he is My brother and sister and mother**."
- ❏ Luke 8:19 And **His mother and brothers came to Him**, and they were unable to get to Him because of the crowd. 20 And it was reported to Him, "**Your mother** and Your brothers are standing outside, wishing to see You." 21 But He answered and said to them, "**My mother and My brothers are these who hear the word of God and do it**."
- ❏ Luke 11:27 While Jesus was saying these things, one of the women in the crowd raised her voice and said to Him, "**Blessed is the womb that bore You** and the breasts at which You nursed." 28 But He said, "**On the contrary, blessed are those who hear the word of God** and **observe it**."

25:45   Do any of the above scriptures show that Jesus wanted Mary to be held in an exalted position above any other person?

Consider the woman who poured the expensive perfume on Jesus's head. Jesus made sure her actions would be remembered.

- ❏ Matthew 26:7 a woman came to Him with an alabaster vial of very costly perfume, and she poured it on His head as He reclined at the table ... 13 Truly I say to you, wherever this gospel is preached in the whole world, what this woman has done will also be spoken of in memory of her."

25:46   I can't find any New Testament scriptures where Jesus or any apostle said or did anything to support the many titles given to Mary today. I also can't find any scriptures which show Mary would continue to be in the lives of living saints for centuries to come after she died. Isn't that inconsistent with the many titles given to Mary today?

New Testament Scriptures Involving Mary

As the issue of Mary is a big one, I suggest it's worth examining all New Testament references to Mary. If I missed any, I apologize. I organized the scriptures chronologically. The 6 occasions where Mary spoke are bolded and underlined.

Mary Prior to Conception

- ❏ **(1 of 20)** Matthew 1:16 Jacob was the father of Joseph the husband of Mary, by whom Jesus was born, who is called the Messiah 17 So all the generations from Abraham to David are fourteen generations; from David to the deportation to Babylon, fourteen generations; and from the deportation to Babylon to the Messiah, fourteen generations. 18 Now the birth of Jesus

25: Peter and Mary

Christ was as follows: when His mother Mary had been betrothed to Joseph, before they came together she was found to be with child by the Holy Spirit. 19 And Joseph her husband, being a righteous man and not wanting to disgrace her, planned to send her away secretly. 20 But when he had considered this, behold, an angel of the Lord appeared to him in a dream, saying, "Joseph, son of David, do not be afraid to take Mary as your wife; for the Child who has been conceived in her is of the Holy Spirit.

- ❏ *21 She will bear a Son; and you shall call His name Jesus, for He will save His people from their sins." 22 Now all this took place to fulfill what was spoken by the Lord through the prophet: 23 "Behold, the virgin shall be with child and shall bear a Son, and they shall call His name Immanuel," which translated means, "God with us."*

- ❏ *__(2 of 20)__ Luke 1:26 Now in the sixth month the angel Gabriel was sent from God to a city in Galilee called Nazareth, 27 to a virgin engaged to a man whose name was Joseph, of the descendants of David; and the virgin's name was Mary. 28 And coming in, he said to her, "Greetings, favored one! The Lord is with you." 29 But she was very perplexed at this statement, and kept pondering what kind of salutation this was. 30 The angel said to her, "Do not be afraid, Mary; for you have found favor with God. 31 And behold, you will conceive in your womb and bear a son, and you shall name Him Jesus. 32 He will be great and will be called the Son of the Most High; and the Lord God will give Him the throne of His father David; 33 and He will reign over the house of Jacob forever, and His kingdom will have no end." 34 Mary said to the angel, __"How can this be, since I am a virgin?"__ 35 The angel answered and said to her, "The Holy Spirit will come upon you, and the power of the Most High will overshadow you; and for that reason the holy Child shall be called the Son of God. 36 And behold, even your relative Elizabeth has also conceived a son in her old age; and she who was called barren is now in her sixth month. 37 For nothing will be impossible with God." 38 And Mary said, __"Behold, the bondslave of the Lord; may it be done to me according to your word."__ And the angel departed from her*

25:47 Do either of the above scriptures (1 and 2 of 20) suggest:
    i.   Mary was sinless;
    ii. Mary was more than the earthly mother of Jesus; or
    iii. Mary would play a key role filled with supernatural abilities after her death?
    iv. If so, what verse(s) and why?

Conception of Jesus to His Birth

- ❏ *__(3 of 20)__ Matthew 1:24 And Joseph awoke from his sleep and did as the angel of the Lord commanded him, and took Mary as his wife, 25 but kept her a virgin until she gave birth to a Son; and he called His name Jesus.*

- ❏ *__(4 of 20)__ Luke 1:39 Now at this time Mary arose and went in a hurry to the hill country, to a city of Judah, 40 and entered the house of Zacharias and greeted Elizabeth. 41 When Elizabeth heard Mary's greeting, the baby*

CEASED?

> leaped in her womb; and Elizabeth was filled with the Holy Spirit. 42 And she cried out with a loud voice and said, "Blessed are you among women, and blessed is the fruit of your womb! 43 And how has it happened to me, that the mother of my Lord would come to me? 44 For behold, when the sound of your greeting reached my ears, the baby leaped in my womb for joy. 45 And blessed is she who believed that there would be a fulfillment of what had been spoken to her by the Lord." 46 And Mary said: **"My soul exalts the Lord**, 47 **And my spirit has rejoiced in God my Savior**. 48 **For He has had regard for the humble state of His bondslave; For behold, from this time on all generations will count me blessed**.
> 49 **For the Mighty One has done great things for me; And holy is His name**. 50 **And His mercy is upon generation after generation Toward those who fear Him**. 51 "**He has done mighty deeds with His arm; He has scattered those who were proud in the thoughts of their heart**. 52 **He has brought down rulers from their thrones, And has exalted those who were humble**. 53 **He has filled the hungry with good things; And sent away the rich empty-handed**. 54 **He has given help to Israel His servant, In remembrance of His mercy**, 55 **As He spoke to our fathers, To Abraham and his descendants forever**." 56 And Mary stayed with her about three months, and then returned to her home.
>
> ❑ **(5 of 20)** Luke 2:4 Joseph also went up from Galilee, from the city of Nazareth, to Judea, to the city of David which is called Bethlehem, because he was of the house and family of David, 5 in order to register along with Mary, who was engaged to him, and was with child. 6 While they were there, the days were completed for her to give birth.

25:48   Do any of the above scriptures (3 to 5 of 20) suggest:
   i. Mary was sinless;
   ii. Mary was more than the earthly mother of Jesus; or
   iii. Mary would play a key role filled with supernatural abilities after her death?
   iv. If so, what verse(s) and why?

Matthew 1:25 **(3 of 20)** reminds us of the issue of Mary's eternal virginity. If you still believe Mary was a virgin forever, I copy the following from Chapter 3 of **CEASED?**

> In terms of Mary and Joseph having a sexless marriage, I find it rather interesting when I compare the NASB version to the Catholic Public Domain Version.
>
> ❑ Matthew 1:24 And Joseph awoke from his sleep and did as the angel of the Lord commanded him, and took Mary as his wife, 25 **but kept her a virgin until she gave birth to a Son**; and he called His name Jesus. (NASB)
>
> ❑ Matthew 1:24 Then Joseph, arising from sleep, did just as the Angel of the Lord had instructed him, and he accepted her as his wife. **And he knew her not, yet she bore her son, the firstborn**. And he called his name JESUS. (CPDV: Catholic Public Domain Version)

25: Peter and Mary

The Word 'Until'

The NASB version clearly states Mary and Joseph had physical intimacy, but not until after Jesus was born. The Catholic Public Domain Version states Mary and Joseph never had physical intimacy before or after Mary gave birth to Jesus. In the NASB translation, the English word 'until' is derived from the Greek word 'heos' [G2193] which Strong's defines as '1. til, until'.

> 3:20 The Catholic Public Domain Version changed God's Word when the translators took out the Greek word 'heos' by intentionally omitting the related English word 'until'. Isn't that a rather big omission? If the word until was put back into the Catholic Bible, it would say "... he knew her not until ..." instead of "... knew her not ...". Doesn't adding the word 'until' put a totally different perspective on a sexless Mary and Joseph marriage, a sinless Mary, and the whole Mother of God issue?

25:48   Omitting the word *'until'* effectively involves deleting the Greek word *'heos'* from God's Word. Regardless of the issue at hand, taking from God's word at any time is very troublesome. As it relates to Mary, I can't see how this omission from the Catholic Bible is by chance, or is an error. It is a necessary omission in order for the sexless marriage argument to hold up. If the word until is put back into the Catholic Bible, the impact on the elevated teachings of Mary are substantial. In fact, don't virtually all teachings on Mary crumble? And isn't what remains what Mary truly was - the earthly mother of Jesus?

Birth to Beginning of Jesus's Earthly Ministry

- ☐ **(6 of 20)** Luke 2:6 *While they were there, the days were completed for her to give birth. 7 And she gave birth to her firstborn son; and she wrapped Him in cloths, and laid Him in a manger, because there was no room for them in the inn.*
- ☐ **(7 of 20)** Matthew 2:11 *After coming into the house they saw the Child with Mary His mother; and they fell to the ground and worshiped Him ... 13 Now when they had gone, behold, an angel of the Lord appeared to Joseph in a dream and said, "Get up! Take the Child and His mother and flee to Egypt ... 14 So Joseph got up and took the Child and His mother while it was still night, and left for Egypt.*
- ☐ **(8 of 20)** Matthew 2:19 *But when Herod died, behold, an angel of the Lord appeared in a dream to Joseph in Egypt, and said, 20 "Get up, take the Child and His mother, and go into the land of Israel; for those who sought the Child's life are dead." 21 So Joseph got up, took the Child and His mother, and came into the land of Israel.*
- ☐ **(9 of 20)** Luke 2:18 *And all who heard it wondered at the things which were told them by the shepherds. 19 But Mary treasured all these things, pondering them in her heart.*
- ☐ **(10 of 20)** Luke 2:27 *And he came in the Spirit into the temple; and when the parents brought in the child Jesus, to carry out for Him the custom of the Law, 28 then he took Him into his arms, and blessed God, and said ... 33 And*

CEASED?

> *His father and mother were amazed at the things which were being said about Him. 34 And Simeon blessed them and said to Mary His mother, "Behold, this Child is appointed for the fall and rise of many in Israel, and for a sign to be opposed. 35 and a sword will pierce even your own soul - to the end that thoughts from many hearts may be revealed." 36 And there was a prophetess, Anna the daughter of Phanuel, of the tribe of Asher. She was advanced in years and had lived with her husband seven years after her marriage, 37 and then as a widow to the age of eighty-four. She never left the temple, serving night and day with fastings and prayers. 38 At that very moment she came up and began giving thanks to God, and continued to speak of Him to all those who were looking for the redemption of Jerusalem. 39 When they had performed everything according to the Law of the Lord, they returned to Galilee, to their own city of Nazareth.*

- ❑ ***(11 of 20)*** *Luke 2:41 Now His parents went to Jerusalem every year at the Feast of the Passover. 42 And when He became twelve, they went up there according to the custom of the Feast; 43 and as they were returning, after spending the full number of days, the boy Jesus stayed behind in Jerusalem. But His parents were unaware of it, 44 but supposed Him to be in the caravan, and went a day's journey; and they began looking for Him among their relatives and acquaintances. 45 When they did not find Him, they returned to Jerusalem looking for Him. 46 Then, after three days they found Him in the temple, sitting in the midst of the teachers, both listening to them and asking them questions. 47 And all who heard Him were amazed at His understanding and His answers. 48 When they saw Him, they were astonished; and His mother said to Him,* **"<u>Son, why have You treated us this way? Behold, Your father and I have been anxiously looking for You.</u>"** *49 And He said to them, "Why is it that you were looking for Me? Did you not know that I had to be in My Father's house?" 50 But they did not understand the statement which He had made to them. 51 And He went down with them and came to Nazareth, and He continued in subjection to them; and His mother treasured all these things in her heart.*

25:50 Do any of the above scriptures (6 to 11 of 20) suggest:
  i. Mary was sinless;
  ii. Mary was more than the earthly mother of Jesus; or
  iii. Mary would play a key role filled with supernatural abilities after her death?
  iv. If so, what verse(s) and why?

<u>Jesus's Earthly Ministry to Jesus's Arrest and Sentence</u>

- ❑ ***(12 of 20)*** *John 2:1 On the third day there was a wedding in Cana of Galilee, and the mother of Jesus was there; 2 and both Jesus and His disciples were invited to the wedding. 3 When the wine ran out, the mother of Jesus said to Him,* **"<u>They have no wine.</u>"** *4 And Jesus said to her, "Woman, what does that have to do with us? My hour has not yet come." 5 His mother said to the servants,* **"<u>Whatever He says to you, do it.</u>"** *... 12 After this He went down*

25: Peter and Mary

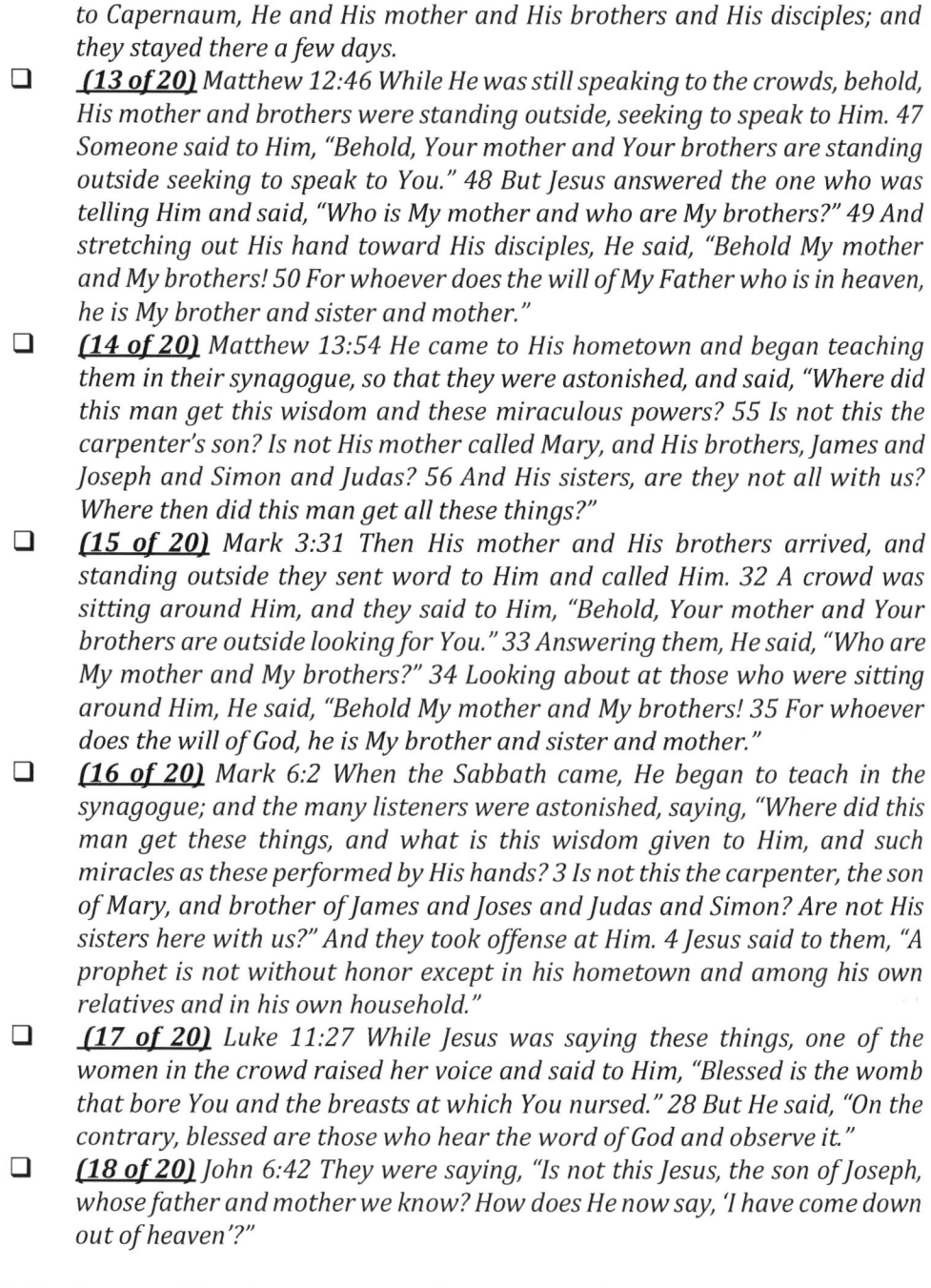

to Capernaum, He and His mother and His brothers and His disciples; and they stayed there a few days.

- ☐ **(13 of 20)** Matthew 12:46 While He was still speaking to the crowds, behold, His mother and brothers were standing outside, seeking to speak to Him. 47 Someone said to Him, "Behold, Your mother and Your brothers are standing outside seeking to speak to You." 48 But Jesus answered the one who was telling Him and said, "Who is My mother and who are My brothers?" 49 And stretching out His hand toward His disciples, He said, "Behold My mother and My brothers! 50 For whoever does the will of My Father who is in heaven, he is My brother and sister and mother."

- ☐ **(14 of 20)** Matthew 13:54 He came to His hometown and began teaching them in their synagogue, so that they were astonished, and said, "Where did this man get this wisdom and these miraculous powers? 55 Is not this the carpenter's son? Is not His mother called Mary, and His brothers, James and Joseph and Simon and Judas? 56 And His sisters, are they not all with us? Where then did this man get all these things?"

- ☐ **(15 of 20)** Mark 3:31 Then His mother and His brothers arrived, and standing outside they sent word to Him and called Him. 32 A crowd was sitting around Him, and they said to Him, "Behold, Your mother and Your brothers are outside looking for You." 33 Answering them, He said, "Who are My mother and My brothers?" 34 Looking about at those who were sitting around Him, He said, "Behold My mother and My brothers! 35 For whoever does the will of God, he is My brother and sister and mother."

- ☐ **(16 of 20)** Mark 6:2 When the Sabbath came, He began to teach in the synagogue; and the many listeners were astonished, saying, "Where did this man get these things, and what is this wisdom given to Him, and such miracles as these performed by His hands? 3 Is not this the carpenter, the son of Mary, and brother of James and Joses and Judas and Simon? Are not His sisters here with us?" And they took offense at Him. 4 Jesus said to them, "A prophet is not without honor except in his hometown and among his own relatives and in his own household."

- ☐ **(17 of 20)** Luke 11:27 While Jesus was saying these things, one of the women in the crowd raised her voice and said to Him, "Blessed is the womb that bore You and the breasts at which You nursed." 28 But He said, "On the contrary, blessed are those who hear the word of God and observe it."

- ☐ **(18 of 20)** John 6:42 They were saying, "Is not this Jesus, the son of Joseph, whose father and mother we know? How does He now say, 'I have come down out of heaven'?"

25:51 Do any of the above scriptures (12 to 18 of 20) suggest:
  i. Mary was sinless;
  ii. Mary was more than the earthly mother of Jesus; or
  iii. Mary would play a key role filled with supernatural abilities after her death?
  iv. If so, what verse(s) and why?

CEASED?

Death and Crucifixion of Christ
- ❑ ***(19 of 20)*** *John 19:25 Therefore the soldiers did these things. But standing by the cross of Jesus were His mother, and His mother's sister, Mary the wife of Clopas, and Mary Magdalene. 26 When Jesus then saw His mother, and the disciple whom He loved standing nearby, He said to His mother, "Woman, behold, your son!" 27 Then He said to the disciple, "Behold, your mother!" From that hour the disciple took her into his own household.*

25:52 Do the above scriptures (19 of 20) suggest:
    i. Mary was sinless;
    ii. Mary was more than the earthly mother of Jesus; or
    iii. Mary would play a key role filled with supernatural abilities after her death?
    iv. If so, what verse(s) and why?

After the Resurrection of Christ
- ❑ ***(20 of 20)*** *Acts 1:12 Then they returned to Jerusalem from the mount called Olivet, which is near Jerusalem, a Sabbath day's journey away. 13 When they had entered the city, they went up to the upper room where they were staying; that is, Peter and John and James and Andrew, Philip and Thomas, Bartholomew and Matthew, James the son of Alphaeus, and Simon the Zealot, and Judas the son of James. 14 These all with one mind were continually devoting themselves to prayer, along with the women, and Mary the mother of Jesus, and with His brothers. 15 At this time Peter stood up in the midst of the brethren (a gathering of about one hundred and twenty persons was there together), and said,*

25:53 The last specific reference to Mary in the Bible sees her gathered in a prayer meeting along with ~120 other followers of Christ. Does anything in Acts 1:12-15 suggest:
    i. Mary was sinless;
    ii. Mary was more than the earthly mother of Jesus; or
    iii. Mary would play a key role filled with supernatural abilities after her death?
    iv. If so, how?

25:54 If there is virtually nothing in the New Testament clearly showing:
    i. Mary was sinless;
    ii. Mary was more than the earthly mother of Jesus; or
    iii. Mary would play a key role filled with supernatural abilities after her death …

… Then how can we view Mary as sinless, as more than the earthly mother of Jesus, or as anyone who played another significant role in the lives of believers during her earthly life before the cross, after the cross, or in her life in heaven? Where does scripture show that Mary is doing anything

25: Peter and Mary

today beyond loving her time with Jesus and the other saints in heaven? And perhaps explaining one more time, what Jesus was like as a child.

Mary's Death

25:55 Mary's year of death is typically viewed as being in the 43-49AD range. If Mary is the Queen of Heaven, the Mother of God etc., wouldn't we expect to see her death mentioned in the Bible since almost every book in the New Testament was written after her death?

25:56 If Mary had a death and ascension different than normal, why don't we read of Mary's death and ascension as we do Enoch and Elijah?
- *Hebrews 11:5 By faith Enoch was taken up so that he would not see death; and he was not found because God took him up; for he obtained the witness that before his being taken up he was pleasing to God.*
- *2 Kings 2:11 As they were going along and talking, behold, there appeared a chariot of fire and horses of fire which separated the two of them. And Elijah went up by a whirlwind to heaven.*

25:57 One possible reason why her death would not be mentioned is if she died after all the books in the New Testament were written, and not before. When Jesus was born, Mary is typically viewed as being somewhere around 15 years of age. Jesus asked John to look after His mother. If anybody would have been personally inclined to write about Mary's death, wouldn't it have been John? When John finished writing the last of his 5 books somewhere in the 75-95AD time frame, Mary would have been 90-110 years old if she was still living. Is that likely? Thus, again, if Mary is the Queen of heaven, the Mother of God etc., wouldn't we expect to see her death at least mentioned by John, the person Jesus asked to look after her?

Prayers Involving Mary in the Bible

The original apostles asked Jesus to teach them one thing: how to pray. Jesus responded with:
- *Matthew 6:8 So do not be like them; for your Father knows what you need before you ask Him. 9 "Pray, then, in this way: **Our Father who is in heaven**, Hallowed be Your name. 10 'Your kingdom come. Your will be done, On earth as it is in heaven. 11 'Give us this day our daily bread. 12 'And forgive us our debts, as we also have forgiven our debtors. 13 'And do not lead us into temptation, but deliver us from evil. For Yours is the kingdom and the power and the glory forever. Amen.'*

25:58 Mary is not mentioned in this prayer. Isn't that a significant omission if Mary is the one to whom believers are to go to first? And inconsistent with the notion of the rosary?

25:59 Would the abundance of prayers to Mary today, and the total lack of prayers to Mary in the Bible, be understandable if praying to Mary was introduced by the Catholic church after the New Testament was written, such as in 600AD as per Mr. Boettner's book?

CEASED?

The only time we read of Mary being involved in prayer is in Acts 1 after the cross.
- ❏ *Acts 1:14 These all with one mind **were continually devoting themselves to prayer**, along with the women, and **Mary the mother of Jesus**, and with His brothers.*

25:60 Does Acts 1:14 indicate Mary had a more significant role in prayer, or in any other way, than any of the ~120 who were gathered with her in prayer?

25:61 And again, is there anything in the New Testament that supports:
   i. Mary is to have a major, supernatural, God-like role after her death;
   ii. the rosary prayer is of God; or
   iii. Mary is able to deliver on the 15 promises of the rosary?

Mary as Mediator

The English word *'mediator'* is derived from the Greek word *'mesites'* [G3316] which means in part, someone who intervenes between two other people, a reconciler, a medium of communication, an arbitrator. When we ask another believer to pray for us, we aren't asking them to mediate for us. The reason we don't ask them to mediate is because they can't mediate for us. The Bible is clear that Jesus is the only mediator between God and His daughters and sons.
- ❏ *1 Timothy 2:5 For there is one God, and **one mediator also between God and men, the man Christ Jesus**,*

25:62 Given Jesus sits at the right hand of Father God, and all authority was given to Jesus, is it surprising that Jesus is the only mediator between God and His sons and daughters?

25:63 Given 1 Timothy 2:5 says Jesus is the only mediator between God and men, on what scriptural basis is there to treat Mary or any other deceased saint as our mediator?

25:64 By calling Mary a mediator, isn't that exaggerating who she is and what she can do?

(Note: To clarify, living believers pray for us but they don't mediate for us. They intercede for us.)

Jesus and Mary after the Gospels

An extremely simplistic but fairly revealing way to consider the relative profile that Jesus and Mary should each have in our lives today is to count the number of references to Jesus and Mary in the New Testament. For the analysis in Figure 25:2, I used the NASB translation. For Jesus, I counted the number of references to *'Jesus'*, *'Jesus Christ'* or *'Christ'*. For Mary, I counted the number of unique references to *'Mary'*, to the *'mother of Jesus'* and to *'Jesus's parents'*.

25: Peter and Mary

Figure 25:2

	Total	4 Gospels	Acts	Other 22 NT Books
Jesus	1,281	702	80	499
Mary	29	28	1	0

After the gospels, there are 579 references to Jesus compared to 1 for Mary. This single reference to Mary occurs in Acts 1 when ~120 people were gathered in prayer.

- ❏ *Acts 1:14 These **all with one mind** were continually devoting themselves to prayer, **along with the women**, and **Mary the mother of Jesus**, and with His brothers. 15 At this time Peter stood up in the midst of the brethren (a gathering of about **one hundred and twenty persons** was there together), and said,*

25:65 If Mary was to play a prominent role in the Body of Christ in the 2,000+ years following the cross, doesn't the fact there is only one reference to Mary after the gospels seem unusually small?

25:66 In this meeting with believers who all had Holy Spirit in [en] them, Mary is praying with both male and female disciples. The only indication she is different is by the reference that she is the mother of Jesus. God's word doesn't say that anyone came to Mary for guidance, comfort, advice or help of any kind after the cross. She doesn't play a leadership role. She is not viewed as the Mother of God. If she was more than a regular human being, wouldn't the Bible make her supernatural nature, power and role evident at some point after Christ's resurrection and ascension? If not, why not?

25:67 If Mary was to play such a central role after the cross, isn't it unusual there is not one book in the New Testament that mentions a single word Mary spoke after the cross?

Other Women after Pentecost

In contrast to Mary not being mentioned after Pentecost, other women were mentioned.

- ❏ *Acts 21:8 On the next day we left and came to Caesarea, and entering the house of Philip the evangelist, who was one of the seven, we stayed with him. 9 Now this man had **four virgin daughters** who were prophetesses.*

- ❏ *Acts 18:24 Now a Jew named Apollos, an Alexandrian by birth, an eloquent man, came to Ephesus; and he was mighty in the Scriptures ... 26 and he began to speak out boldly in the synagogue. But when **Priscilla** and Aquila heard him, they took him aside and explained to him the way of God more accurately.*

- ❏ *Philippians 4:2 I urge **Euodia** and I urge **Syntyche** to live in harmony in the Lord. 3 Indeed, true companion, I ask you also to help these women who have shared my struggle in the cause of the gospel, together with Clement also and the rest of my fellow workers, whose names are in the book of life.*

- ❏ *Romans 16:1 I commend to you our sister **Phoebe**, who is a servant of the church which is at Cenchrea; 2 that you receive her in the Lord in a manner* *worthy of the saints, and that you help her in whatever matter she may have need of you; for she herself has also been a helper of many, and of myself as well.*

25:68 If Mary was to have a dominant role in the church after the cross, isn't it surprising that other women were shown as playing key roles after the cross, but Mary wasn't? Was it because the call on her life had been fulfilled, and going forward, God was using other women?

Other Disciples' View of Mary

In terms of how other disciples saw Mary, consider Stephen as he was being stoned.

❑ *Acts 7:54 Now when they heard this, they were cut to the quick, and they began gnashing their teeth at him. 55 But being full of the Holy Spirit, **he gazed intently into heaven and saw the glory of God, and Jesus standing at the right hand of God**; 56 and he said, **"Behold, I see the heavens opened up and the Son of Man standing at the right hand of God**." 57 But they cried out with a loud voice, and covered their ears and rushed at him with one impulse. 58 When they had driven him out of the city, they began stoning him; and the witnesses laid aside their robes at the feet of a young man named Saul. 59 They went on stoning Stephen as he called on the Lord and said, **"Lord Jesus, receive my spirit!"** 60 Then falling on his knees, he cried out with a loud voice, **"Lord, do not hold this sin against them!"** Having said this, he fell asleep.*

25:69 Stephen never sought or cried out to Mary. If Mary was to be our comforter, why wouldn't Stephen have reached out to her? While Mary is not even mentioned, Lori pointed out that Jesus - our true advocate and mediator - rose from His heavenly, seated position and stood for Stephen when He saw Stephen being stoned. What does that say about who is to be our focus?

25:70 If the case is made that Mary's role as a supernatural being started after Mary died and not before her death, on what scriptural basis can that point of view be substantiated?

If Mary was the Mother of God

25:71 If Mary is/was the supernatural Mother of God, why didn't she know about the birth of Jesus beforehand? And why wouldn't God tell her directly instead of using an angel to deliver the message?

❑ *Luke 1:26 Now in the sixth month the angel Gabriel was sent from God to a city in Galilee called Nazareth ... 29 **But she was very perplexed at this statement, and kept pondering what kind of salutation this was**. 30 The angel said to her, "**Do not be afraid, Mary; for you have found favor with God**.*

25:72 If Mary is/was the supernatural Mother of God, why was Mary so earthly minded as evidenced by her questioning how she - a virgin - could give

25: Peter and Mary

birth to Jesus, and then state she was a servant?
- *Luke 1:34 Mary said to the angel, "**How can this be, since I am a virgin?**" ... 38 And Mary said, "Behold, **the bondslave of the Lord**; may it be done to me according to your word." And the angel departed from her.*

25:73   If Mary is/was the supernatural Mother of God, why did Mary point people to Jesus, but Jesus never pointed people to Mary?
- *John 2:3 When the wine ran out, the mother of Jesus said to Him, "They have no wine." 4 And Jesus said to her, "**Woman**, what does that have to do with us? My hour has not yet come." 5 His mother said to the servants, "Whatever He says to you, do it."*

25:74   If Mary is/was the supernatural Mother of God, wouldn't we expect to see Jesus exalting Mary instead of calling her 'woman', the same term Jesus called other earthly women?

Jesus's words to Mary:
- *John 2:4 And Jesus said to her, "**Woman**, what does that have to do with us? My hour has not yet come."*
- *John 19:26 When Jesus then saw His mother, and the disciple whom He loved standing nearby, He said to His mother, "**Woman**, behold, your son!"*

Jesus's words to other women:
- *John 4:21 Jesus said to her, "**Woman**, believe Me, an hour is coming when neither in this mountain nor in Jerusalem will you worship the Father.*
- *Luke 13:12 When Jesus saw her, He called her over and said to her, "**Woman**, you are freed from your sickness."*

25:75   If Mary is/was the supernatural Mother of God, why do Catholics not baptize individuals in the name of the Father, Mary, Jesus and Holy Spirit?
- *Matthew 28:19 Go therefore and make disciples of all the nations, baptizing them in the name of the **Father** and the **Son** and the **Holy Spirit**,*

25:76   If Mary is/was the Mother of God, why did Jesus deny Mary's request to talk to Him?
- *Matthew 12:46 While He was still speaking to the crowds, behold, His mother and brothers were standing outside, seeking to speak to Him. 47 Someone said to Him, "Behold, Your mother and Your brothers are standing outside seeking to speak to You." 48 But Jesus answered the one who was telling Him and said, "**Who is My mother and who are My brothers?**" 49 And stretching out His hand toward His disciples, He said, "Behold My mother and My brothers! 50 **For whoever does the will of My Father who is in heaven, he is My brother and sister and mother.**"*

25:77   Doesn't Matthew 12 effectively put Mary on par with other believers? And even then, isn't she only on par with other believers if she does the will of God?

CEASED?

25:78 If Mary was the supernatural Mother of God and the one who provides comfort and other blessings such as protection, why is the Bible silent on that aspect of Mary but does tell us - in both the Old and New Testaments - that angels will do such things?
- *Psalm 91:11 For He will give His angels charge concerning you, To guard you in all your ways.*
- *Hebrews 1:14 Are they not all ministering spirits, sent out to render service for the sake of those who will inherit salvation?*
- *Luke 4:10 for it is written, 'He will command His angels concerning You to guard You,'*

25:79 Jesus mentioned He would send a helper/comforter/advocate (Holy Spirit), but never said there would be a supernatural comforter in addition to Holy Spirit, with one exception per question 25:78 - His ministering angels.
   i. The one who people go to for comfort and help shows who they have the most faith or trust in. Isn't Mary, not Holy Spirit, the comforter who the Catholic church teaches that people should go to first, and who many/most Catholics do go to first?
   ii. If Mary was to play the dominant role as a helper and comforter, isn't it surprising this critical role of Mary is not even mentioned in the Bible? But Holy Spirit in these roles is mentioned?
- *John 16:7 But I tell you the truth, it is to your advantage that I go away; for if I do not go away, **the Helper** will not come to you; but if I go, I **will send Him** to you.*
- *Acts 9:31 So the church throughout all Judea and Galilee and Samaria enjoyed peace, being built up; and going on in the fear of the Lord and **in the comfort of the Holy Spirit**, it continued to increase.*

25:80 If Mary was the supernatural Mother of God and the one who provides comfort, why didn't Jesus cry out to Mary instead of Father God when dying on the cross? Or at least call out to both Mary and Father God?
- *Matthew 27:46 About the ninth hour Jesus cried out with a loud voice, saying, "Eli, Eli, lama sabachthani?" that is, "My God, My God, why have You forsaken Me?"*

25:81 In the early church, Holy Spirit provided God's comfort. Believers prayed directly to God. Doesn't that show Mary was not front and center? And that while Mary was a person blessed to give birth to Jesus, she was otherwise no different than other believers?

Ark of the New Covenant

Another title attributed to Mary is she is the Ark of the New Covenant. In the Old Testament, the Ark housed the presence of God. In a similar way, Mary housed baby Jesus - i.e. God - in her womb. As a result, Mary is seen by the Roman Catholic church as the Ark of the New Covenant.

25: Peter and Mary

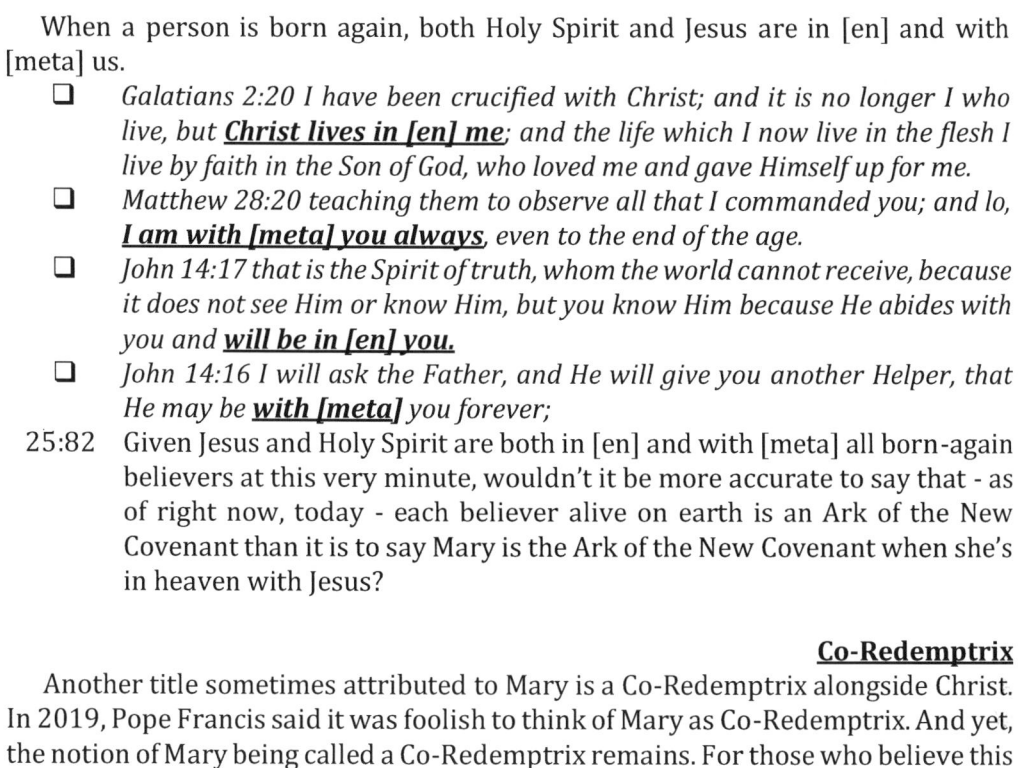

When a person is born again, both Holy Spirit and Jesus are in [en] and with [meta] us.
- Galatians 2:20 *I have been crucified with Christ; and it is no longer I who live, but **Christ lives in [en] me**; and the life which I now live in the flesh I live by faith in the Son of God, who loved me and gave Himself up for me.*
- Matthew 28:20 *teaching them to observe all that I commanded you; and lo, **I am with [meta] you always**, even to the end of the age.*
- John 14:17 *that is the Spirit of truth, whom the world cannot receive, because it does not see Him or know Him, but you know Him because He abides with you and **will be in [en] you.***
- John 14:16 *I will ask the Father, and He will give you another Helper, that He may be **with [meta] you** forever;*

25:82 Given Jesus and Holy Spirit are both in [en] and with [meta] all born-again believers at this very minute, wouldn't it be more accurate to say that - as of right now, today - each believer alive on earth is an Ark of the New Covenant than it is to say Mary is the Ark of the New Covenant when she's in heaven with Jesus?

Co-Redemptrix

Another title sometimes attributed to Mary is a Co-Redemptrix alongside Christ. In 2019, Pope Francis said it was foolish to think of Mary as Co-Redemptrix. And yet, the notion of Mary being called a Co-Redemptrix remains. For those who believe this title has merit, I have four questions.

25:83 When someone is a co-author, co-producer or co-coach, there is an inherent equivalence in their role. Mary never had her body mangled to pay the penalty for the sins of humanity, never shed her blood, never died on the cross and was not resurrected. She was never referred to as the Messiah or Savior. Besides giving birth and caring for Jesus in His younger years, what specific role did Mary play that warrants calling her our redeemer?

25:84 When Jesus told His disciples to partake of the bread and wine to remember Jesus, why didn't Jesus mention Mary should also be remembered if she was His Co-Redemptrix?
- Luke 22:19 *And when He had taken some bread and given thanks, He broke it and gave it to them, saying, "This is My body which is given for you; do this in remembrance of Me." 20 And in the same way He took the cup after they had eaten, saying, "This cup which is poured out for you is the new covenant in My blood.*

25:85 When Roman Catholics take communion, Jesus is sacrificed in an unbloody manner. If Mary was truly the Co-Redemptrix, why isn't she sacrificed as part of communion alongside Jesus?

25:86 If Mary is considered a Co-Redemptrix due to her close relationship with Jesus, then isn't there a case to be made that each of Father God and Holy Spirit are dramatically more 'deserving' than Mary of being labeled a Co-Redemptrix? Which they're not.

CEASED?

Mary the Creation

Dr. Scott Hahn is a Catholic scholar who converted to Roman Catholicism in 1986. Dr. Hahn gave the first annual Rosary Shrine Lecture (16 March 2018) at Holy Rosary Shrine in Belsize Park, London. His remarks are found on YouTube at the link: www.youtube.com/watch?v=Dn1tWuIoZsg. Starting at ~11 minutes, Dr. Hahn states the following about Mary:

> "She is in fact the **masterpiece of Christ**, the **redemptive artist**. What do I mean? Well, all of us are works in progress. Christ is the artist of my redemption and yours. And we entrust ourselves to Him. But if **we wanted to figure out how perfect His redemptive work was, we wouldn't see the perfection on any of us**. **But we would see it, as I mentioned before, in her**. And so, if you go to an art exhibit, a gallery, where you have an exhibition of a **famous painter**, all of his work. And if this artist happened to show up, **he wouldn't feel threatened or slighted in the least if instead of staring at him, you were looking at all of his works and spending the most time appreciating his masterpiece**. Just like every artist wants to really devote his talent and his time and energy to one great work, so the **Blessed Virgin Mary does not detract from the work of Christ**. She refracts the light of the world more perfectly than anyone. So the model disciple that we can all imitate, the Mother of God that we can see, as the one who bore Jesus to the world, and the masterpiece of Jesus Christ, the artist of our redemption."

Mary played an important and sometimes difficult role in being the earthly mother to Jesus. Mary was obedient and was willing to suffer the social consequences of being pregnant while not being married. Wonderful. However, Mary was not perfect.

1. Mary questioned God and expressed doubt when told she would be pregnant with Jesus.
   - ☐ Luke 1:30 The angel said to her, "Do not be afraid, Mary; for you have found favor with God. 31 And behold, you will conceive in your womb and bear a son, and you shall name Him Jesus ... 34 **Mary said to the angel, "How can this be, since I am a virgin**?"

2. Mary asked Jesus to deal with the wine at the wedding, a less than ideal time as Jesus's hour had not yet come.
   - ☐ John 2:3 When the wine ran out, the mother of Jesus said to Him, "They have no wine." 4 And Jesus said to her, "**Woman**, what does that have to do with us? **My hour has not yet come**."

3. Mary left Jerusalem without 12-year-old Jesus before returning to find Him 3 days later.
   - ☐ Luke 2:43 and as they were returning, after spending the full number of days, the **boy Jesus stayed behind** in Jerusalem. But His **parents were unaware** of it, 44 but supposed Him to be in the caravan, and **went a day's journey**; and they began looking for Him among their relatives and acquaintances. 45 When they did not find Him, they returned to Jerusalem looking for Him.

25: Peter and Mary

*46 Then, **after three days they found Him** in the temple, sitting in the midst of the teachers, both listening to them and asking them questions. 47 And all who heard Him were amazed at His understanding and His answers. 48 When they saw Him, they were astonished; and His mother said to Him, "Son, why have You treated us this way? Behold, Your father and I have been anxiously looking for You." 49 And He said to them, "**Why is it that you were looking for Me? Did you not know that I had to be in My Father's house**?" 50 **But they did not understand** the statement which He had made to them.*

25:87 Mary, the Catholic Mother of God, didn't understand what Jesus was saying. Is that a surprise if Mary's role wasn't Mother of God, but was limited to earthly mother of Jesus?

After Mary was born again resurrection Sunday evening (Chapter 6), we have one scripture referring to Mary's personal Christian walk. She was praying with ~120 others.

❑ *Acts 1:14 These all with one mind **were continually devoting themselves to prayer**, along with the women, and **Mary the mother of Jesus**, and with His brothers. 15 At this time Peter stood up in the midst of the brethren (a gathering of **about one hundred and twenty persons** was there together), and said,*

25:88 Prayer is a cornerstone of Christianity. In terms of modeling that aspect, Mary being in that prayer meeting is great. But so were ~120 others. In terms of Mary being the perfect role model of a disciple - a masterpiece in Dr. Hahn's words - is there anything in the above scriptures or any other New Testament scriptures that identifies Mary as being a better disciple than any of the other ~120 who were gathered? If so, what?

25:89 Followers of Christ are commanded to do many things. Various signs will indicate one is a believer. However, there is no mention of Mary doing any of the following:
1. sharing the gospel;
2. giving financially;
3. helping widows or orphans;
4. casting out demons;
5. healing the sick;
6. cleansing the lepers;
7. raising the dead;
8. forgiving and loving her enemies;
9. taking communion to remember what Jesus did; or
10. making disciples and baptizing them in water.

25:90 In terms of role models, Paul shared the gospel with incredible commitment and zeal, was beaten and imprisoned, stoned and left for dead, and was eventually martyred. Isn't he more of a role model than Mary? If we look at what the Bible teaches, how can we consider Mary the masterpiece of a disciple? The role model that we are to follow?

CEASED?

Romans 1:25 reveals one of my concerns for Catholics who agree with Dr. Hahn.
- *Romans 1:25 For they exchanged the truth of God for a lie, and worshiped and served the creature rather than the Creator, who is blessed forever. Amen*

25:91 Jesus is the creator; Mary is the creation. Dr. Hahn indicated Jesus would not mind us spending more time with His masterpiece which means less time is spent with Jesus. Doesn't that directly contradict the warning in Romans 1:25? One may argue that Mary is not a creature as per Romans 1:25, but isn't that playing with semantics? Isn't the principle the key? According to the Bible, I think Jesus would mind a great deal if we took our focus off Him and put undue attention on any of His creations. God is to be front and center, not in the background or off to the sidelines.

25:92 Dr. Hahn's teachings and other Catholic teachings all say the Catholic faith does not worship Mary or anyone else other than God. It reminds me of Hamlet where Shakespeare writes: *"The lady doth protest too much methinks"*. Claims are also commonly made that none of the prayers and activities involving Mary or deceased saints, statues and shrines, traditions etc. take away from Jesus. My question is: How can they not take away from Jesus? Without much effort, I found 85 references in the Bible telling us to seek God, but not one scripture stating we're to set our eyes on Mary or any other deceased saint. Doesn't that alone give reason to wonder why go to Mary?

25:93 When you think of Dr. Hahn's and other teachings, what do you believe?
    i. Does the focus on Mary, on other deceased saints and the many traditions involving priests a) take away from, b) have no effect on, or c) increase one's focus on Father God, Jesus and Holy Spirit?
    ii. By going to Mary and other deceased saints first, aren't God's creations being given attention and glory meant for our Creator?
    iii. In other words, do these activities give all glory to God as required by the Bible?

25:94 Consider a married couple. Instead of spending time with his wife, the husband spent most of his time communicating with her mother who would in turn communicate with his wife. What would that relationship look like? I think there might be a permanent dip in the couch from all his nights sleeping there … alone.

Capital "M" Mother of God, or small 'm' mother of God.

As mentioned before, Roman Catholic teachings state the Catholic church believes Mary is a creation of God, and that she is the earthly, small 'm' mother of Jesus. However, since Jesus is God, Mary also warrants being viewed as the capital 'M' Mother of God.

25:95 I see how the logic is created, but even if I were to buy into the logic (which I don't), why capitalize the 'M' in mother? By capitalizing the 'M', doesn't doing so effectively give Mary a divine status? If not, then why doesn't the

25: Peter and Mary

Roman Catholic church always - as in always - keep the 'm' small and say something like 'Mary, the earthly mother of God Jesus' to clarify she is not God, but Jesus was? Why take the chance of influencing others to think Mary is God or God-like when she isn't?

As mentioned in Chapter 1, when I was pondering this issue of Mary being the Mother of God, Holy Spirit reminded me of Matthew 22.
- ❑ *Matthew 22:41 Now while the Pharisees were gathered together, Jesus asked them a question: 42 "What do you think about the Christ, whose son is He?" They said to Him, "The son of David." 43 He said to them, "Then how does David in the Spirit call Him 'Lord,' saying, 44 'The Lord said to my Lord, "Sit at My right hand, Until I put Your enemies beneath Your feet"'? 45* **If David then calls Him 'Lord,' how is He his son***?" 46 No one was able to answer Him a word, nor did anyone dare from that day on to ask Him another question.*

Dr. Hahn and others view Mary as a masterpiece creation of God. We all have our views on what is a masterpiece but let me go back one more time to the question I asked in Chapter 1.

1:18 My related question is this. Mary is a creation of God. If God created Mary, how could Mary be the Mother of God? In other words, how can Mary be the Mother of the One who created her?

25:96 As a result, isn't calling Mary the capital 'M' Mother of God a major misrepresentation and exaggeration of who Mary was and is today - which is the mother of earthly Jesus?

25:97 Based on the information presented in **CEASED?** as well as from elsewhere, each Roman Catholic needs to decide if Mary is divine or not, is effectively God or not, and can deliver on the various things attributed to her (such as the 15 promises of the rosary), or not. If you're Roman Catholic and believe Mary is not God, and therefore can't deliver on all these promises that only God can deliver on, aren't the various titles given to Mary major exaggerations of who Mary was, and is today? And don't those exaggerations, associated accolades and statues of Mary dishonor her in a massive way?

Types and Shadows of Mary

Roman Catholic teachings that lead to the many titles bestowed on Mary are primarily driven by types and shadows in the Old Testament. Types and shadows are a person, event or thing in the Old Testament that foreshadows something significant in the New Testament. The bronze serpent made by Moses, for instance, was a foreshadowing of Jesus's death on the cross.
- ❑ *Numbers 21:6 The Lord sent fiery serpents among the people and they bit the people, so that many people of Israel died ... 8 Then the Lord said to Moses, "Make a fiery serpent, and set it on a standard; and it shall come about, that everyone who is bitten, when he looks at it, he will live." 9 And*

CEASED?

> *Moses made a bronze serpent and set it on the standard; and it came about, that if a serpent bit any man, when he looked to the bronze serpent, he lived.*

25:98 There was considerable foreshadowing in the Old Testament that support titles given to Jesus such as God, Savior and Messiah. One key difference between Mary and Jesus, however, is that I don't see one scripture in the New Testament that specifically confirms Mary's many titles in the Roman Catholic faith beyond Mary being a virgin who was blessed when she became the earthly mother of Jesus. Isn't that difference between Jesus and Mary an extremely massive issue?

25:99 And isn't it significant that while Paul proved Jesus was the Christ by looking at Old Testament scriptures, Paul was absolutely silent on Mary?

❑ *Acts 18:28 for he powerfully refuted the Jews in public, demonstrating by the Scriptures that Jesus was the Christ.*

The Great Exchange and Mary

Chapter 6 of **CEASED?** discusses some, but not all, of the many blessings received when we're born again. Some blessings are summarized in Figure 6:1, the Great Exchange, on pages 100-102. Figure 6:1 is reproduced below but amended to exclude the scriptural references. Figure 25:3 on page 373 is my attempt at creating a comparable summary for Mary based on the New Testament scriptures referencing Mary (pages 354-360). I didn't include potential references to Mary in the Old Testament. If they aren't confirmed in the New Testament, I struggle to see their value.

25:100 When we consider Figures 6:1 and 25:3 and everything else about Mary and Jesus, what New Testament scriptures give reason to take our eyes off Jesus and put them on Mary?

25:101 If the argument supporting Mary's elevated status is that we need to view Mary as she is seen and foreshadowed in the Old Testament, how valid or reliable are the foreshadowings in the Old Testament if they aren't confirmed in the New Testament?

To illustrate the difference between Mary and Jesus, consider Isaiah 53:7 - Jesus the lamb.

❑ *Isaiah 53:7 He was oppressed and He was afflicted, Yet He did not open His mouth; Like a lamb that is led to slaughter, And like a sheep that is silent before its shearers, So He did not open His mouth.*

25:102 The New Testament refers to Jesus as the lamb 30 times. Not one New Testament verse confirms, clearly suggests or connects Mary to Old Testament types and shadows such that Mary should be viewed as the capital "M" Mother of God, Spouse of the Spirit, Queen of Heaven, Queen of all Saints, Second Eve, Ark of the New Covenant, Mother of the Church etc. Not one. If these titles were valid, isn't it awfully surprising not to see any of these confirmed?

25: Peter and Mary

Figure 6:1 The Great Exchange with Jesus
(without scripture references)

What happened to Jesus?	What happened for us?
1. Enslaved in human flesh; earthly living challenges	Blessings in heavenly places
2. Tempted by devil	Works of devil destroyed for us Ability to resist/be free from sinning
3. Sold for price of a slave	Bought with blood of Jesus
4. Surrendered	Given spiritual authority
5. Captured due to sins of world	Delivered from sins of the world
6. Despised, shamed, tormented, mocked	God's glory, love, peace
7. Rejected by many Jews; abandoned by disciples	Acceptance/fellowship with God
8. Fulfilled law / made a curse	Free of the law; saved by grace
9. Did not sin; took on our sins	Freed from the penalty of our sins; forgiven, made righteous
10. Took our sorrows and griefs	Gladness and joy
11. Body was mangled	By His stripe(s), healed us
12. Forsaken/separated from God	Adopted as a child of God Christ in us Holy Spirit in us; leads us
13. Died thankless, cruel death	Eternal life/gift of salvation
14. Died to tear the veil	Direct access to God any time
15. Died in total poverty; nothing of earthly value left	Abundant life Heir of God/Joint heir with Jesus Citizen of heaven

Figure 25:3 Our Exchange with Mary

What happened to Mary?	What happened for us?
1. Gave birth/ looked after Jesus ❖ Matthew 1:23 ❖ Luke 2:7	Blessed to have our Savior born and cared for as a child
2. With Jesus when crucified ❖ John 19:27	Unknown, if any
3. Prayed with a group of ~120 ❖ Acts 1:14	Unknown, if any
4. No mention after Pentecost	Unknown, if any

To Recap Mary So Far

When we consider all the New Testament verses involving Mary, we find:
- ❖ The New Testament has many verses confirming Jesus is the Lamb, Messiah, Savior etc.

CEASED?

- No New Testament scripture confirms Mary as having any form of elevated position or ministry beyond being the earthly mother of Jesus.
- God did not communicate with Mary directly, but through an angel, an angel she feared.
- No person treated or spoke about Mary in a special way after the cross.
- No one came to Mary for prayer, guidance, a miracle such as a healing or a prophetic word, or help of any kind before, during, or after Jesus's earthly ministry. When Jesus turned water into wine at the wedding, Mary noticed the problem and initiated action. But no one came to her asking for help on the lack of wine.
- After the gospels, there is 1 reference to Mary and ~579 references to Jesus.
- Mary's spoken words are identified in 6 different situations. None of them indicate Mary is anything beyond an ordinary woman used by God wonderfully and importantly.
- Mary didn't die on the cross for us, shed no blood for us, and wasn't resurrected for us.
- The Bible does not say to remember Mary in any unique way, including communion.

25:103 Isn't there a rather big chasm between what the Bible teaches about Mary, and how Mary is viewed by the Roman Catholic church?

When did Exalting of Mary Begin

In the section on Traditions, I included several items referred to as inventions of the Catholic church. A partial list of items referring to Mary is as follows:

6. Beginning of the exaltation of Mary, the term "Mother of God" first applied to her by the Council of Ephesus (431 AD)
11. Prayers directed to Mary, dead saints and angels, about (600)
24. The Rosary, mechanical praying with beads, invented by Peter the Hermit (1090)
35. The Ave Maria (Hail Mary) (part of last half-finished 50 years later) (1508)
40. Immaculate Conception of the Virgin Mary, proclaimed by Pope Pius IX (1854)
44. Assumption of the Virgin Mary (bodily ascension into heaven shortly after her death), proclaimed by Pope Pius XII (1950)
45. Mary proclaimed Mother of the Church, by Pope Paul VI (1965)

25:104 Don't the above pieces of information show a progression of the role of Mary? Don't they explain how Mary could evolve from a person who was part of a ~120-person prayer group in Acts 1:14-15 to the exalted, God-like person she is portrayed to be by the Roman Catholic church today? And thus, doesn't all the information on Mary provide more reasons to be concerned about the reliability of other Roman Catholic church teachings that aren't supported by the Bible?

25:105 Furthermore, if you're Roman Catholic, can you see why Protestants such

25: Peter and Mary

as myself see Mary as blessed because she is the earthly mother of Jesus, but that virtually all the other titles bestowed on Mary are an exaggeration, and do not honor Mary but dishonor her?

25:106 When we consider Mary, doesn't it all come back to what is one's authority - the Bible or the Roman Catholic church's teachings?

But Mary has Blessed me

There are 2 spiritual kingdoms on earth, God's and satan's. All false religions are part of satan's kingdom. In spite of people pursuing false gods, our one and true God can and does send rain and blessings to both those who are in His kingdom, and those who are in satan's kingdom.

- *Matthew 5:44 But I say to you, love your enemies and pray for those who persecute you, 45 so that you may be sons of your Father who is in heaven; for He causes **His sun to rise on the evil and the good**, and **sends rain on the righteous and the unrighteous**.*

Individuals from false religions speak highly of their god(s) or goddesses, and of the benefits they receive. Members of false religions make claims of being blessed by their god(s). And they may be. After all, satan and his demons have supernatural powers. satan afflicted Job with boils. If he left Job and ended the affliction, this would have brought an instant, miraculous healing. The Bible shows various people with afflictions who were healed when demons were cast out.

25:107 satan is the father of lies. He is evil and hurts people. He distracts people from the truth by making a sin-filled life look desirable. Whatever it takes to keep people from the truth, satan will do it. We should recognize not all blessings experienced on earth are from God. Think of people who are rich or famous, and living the good life, but are on the road to hell. Don't you think satan may help some get richer, more famous and live an even better worldly life by giving them thoughts or information they couldn't know in the natural? And in so doing, isn't satan and his demons causing them to continue to believe lies such as they don't need God, or they have already found the one true god?

- *2 Corinthians 11:14 No wonder, for even Satan disguises himself as an angel of light.*

When individuals attribute blessings to Mary, such blessings could be from God. However, they can also be from satan and his army of demons. Consider my experience.

My Testimony

I loved my father a great deal. Soon after he died, I went to see a psychic. Even though I was not born again, I knew in my knower I shouldn't go. But I did. Before entering the psychic's house, I had been told to list questions about anyone I wanted to get information. I wrote down some questions about my dad and my cousin. The psychic knew nothing in advance. After pleasantries, I sat down. She started by describing two spirits that appeared behind me. Her description of their physical appearances closely resembled my dad and my cousin. Information shared by the psychic was private to Dad and I, or to my cousin and I. No one else could have known. I was shocked. The psychic was an extremely nice lady who said she loved to help people. I felt comforted. A couple of days later, however, I just knew what I witnessed was not of God. Later on, when I understood spiritual warfare and the demonic realm a bit better, I gained an entirely different perspective. The two spirits were demons and this precious woman was simply a pawn in the hands of the demonic world. What looked and felt so good was simply a sinister plan of the enemy, evil that was disguised and manifesting in goodness.

At His own initiative, God caused deceased saints Samuel, Moses and Elijah to appear with a very specific purpose.
- ❑ *1 Samuel 28:13 The king said to her, "Do not be afraid; but what do you see?" And the woman said to Saul, "I see a divine being coming up out of the earth." 14 He said to her, "What is his form?" And she said, "An old man is coming up, and he is wrapped with a robe." And Saul knew that it was Samuel, and he bowed with his face to the ground and did homage.*
- ❑ *Matthew 17:1 Six days later Jesus took with Him Peter and James and John his brother, and led them up on a high mountain by themselves. 2 And He was transfigured before them; and His face shone like the sun, and His garments became as white as light. 3 And behold, Moses and Elijah appeared to them, talking with Him.*

When Roman Catholics see manifestations of Mary such as Medjugorje or Lady Fatima in 1917, such manifestations are either from God or from satan. The Bible doesn't say believers will see manifestations of loved ones or any deceased saints. This may happen as God can do anything - except things that are contrary to His perfect nature such as lying. However, when God did send messages through one of His creations, He typically sent angels.
- ❑ *Psalm 91:11 For He will give His angels charge concerning you, To guard you in all your ways. 12 They will bear you up … That you do not strike your foot against a stone.*
- ❑ *Hebrews 1:14 Are they not all ministering spirits, sent out to render service for the sake of those who will inherit salvation?*

God's Word also forewarns us that while we're to cast out demons, we're also not to turn to individuals utilizing demons for their benefit.
- ❑ *Leviticus 19:31 Do not turn to mediums or spiritists; do not seek them out to be defiled by them. I am the Lord your God.*
- ❑ *Deuteronomy 18:10 There shall not be found among you anyone who makes his son or his daughter pass through the fire, one who uses **divination**, one who practices **witchcraft**, or one **who interprets omens,** or a **sorcerer**, 11 or one who casts a **spell**, or a **medium**, or a **spiritist**, or one who **calls up the dead**. 12 For whoever does these things is detestable to the Lord; and because of these detestable things the Lord your God will drive them out before you.*
- ❑ *2 Kings 21:6 He made his son pass through the fire, practiced witchcraft and*

25: Peter and Mary

used divination, and dealt with mediums and spiritists. He did much evil in the sight of the Lord provoking Him to anger.

25:108 Our eyes are to be on Jesus, our mediator, friend, Lord and Savior. We're to spend time alone with Him in our secret place, to read His Word, and to give all glory to God. Who do manifestations of Mary and other deceased saints tend to draw people closer to first:
   i.   to Mary and other deceased individuals; or
   ii. to Jesus?
25:109 Would satan want such manifestations to occur if they would help draw people's attention away from Jesus?
25:110 If one contends these manifestations are truly of God, on what Biblical grounds are such claims justifiable?

If you're Roman Catholic, I understand my comments may be very upsetting. But please consider the evidence. Do your own search for Bible scriptures that show these apparitions and ongoing manifestations of Mary are of God. And if these supernatural manifestations aren't of God, doesn't that mean they have to be from the kingdom of darkness? That's not something I say lightly because I recognize Mary has a special place in Roman Catholic hearts. She has a place in my heart too, but only as the earthly mother of Jesus. If you think she is more than that, I encourage you to go back and read all the New Testament scriptures on Mary starting on page 354 of **CEASED?**.

It may be helpful to remember the majority of people in this world don't believe in the Jesus of the Bible. So many of these people are wonderful, loving and kind people. They are devoted to their god(s) and/or goddess(es). But they are deceived. It breaks my heart to talk to them and hear them speak of their faith, and see their passion and devotion to it, when I know they have been deceived and their beliefs are wrong. Their god(s) and/or their goddess(es) are false. They are all from satan's kingdom. They are demonic. And because of that, shouldn't we speak honestly, with respect and in love - to them about the truths of Jesus and His Word, even if doing so might offend them?

In Summary

25:111 The name of Jesus is above all other names. When Protestants such as myself share the Good News and disciple believers, we want the name of Jesus to be exalted at all times. If you're Roman Catholic, can you see why so many non-Catholics like myself struggle with how Mary is exalted as she is, when there's no basis in the New Testament to do so? There are types and shadows in the Old Testament that you can argue are a foreshadowing, but without confirmation in the New Testament, how valid can these types and shadows be? There may be human logic, church history, church tradition or church teachings that seem to support the views and practices involving Mary, but if they aren't supported clearly by God's Word, how reliable can they be?
25:112 If one looks at Mary through the lens of her being a regular human who

CEASED?

was wonderfully used by God and nothing more, is there anything in the New Testament that would contradict that view? If so, what is it and why?

Another Jesus, Another God, Another Godhead

Individuals of the Mormon and JW faiths have a different Jesus and a different god than the Jesus and God of the Bible. These faiths claim they have the true Bible, and the true teachings. They ignore evidence of the Dead Sea Scrolls and Codex Sinaiticus that show the underlying Hebrew and Greek has not changed in any material way, and that the Protestant Bible hasn't been changed. They ignore other evidence such as Ivan Panin's work, and they fail to provide evidence showing their Bible is the only true Bible. The main reason for ignoring evidence is their blinding loyalty to their beliefs, beliefs typically gained from their parents.

A Different Catholic Godhead

The majority of people in the world believe in a god that is not true. Don't we have that issue in regards to Catholic teachings on Mary? If we examine the 15 promises of the rosary on page 350, who but God could deliver on the promises. The same website showing the 15 promises also states Mary grants seven graces. I copied this on June 3, 2020. Formatting is mine.

*The Blessed Virgin **Mary grants seven graces** to the souls who **honor her daily** by **saying seven Hail Mary's** and **meditating on her tears and dolors (sorrows).** The devotion was passed on by St. Bridget.*

HERE ARE THE SEVEN GRACES:
1. ***I will grant peace*** *to their families.*
2. ***They will be enlightened*** *about the divine mysteries.*
3. ***I will console them*** *in their pains and **I will accompany them in their work**.*
4. ***I will give them*** *as much as they ask for as long as it does not oppose the adorable will of my divine Son or the sanctification of their souls.*
5. ***I will defend them in their spiritual battles*** *with the infernal enemy and **I will protect them*** *at every instant of their lives.*
6. *I will **visibly help them at the moment of their death**, they will see the face of their Mother.*
7. ***I have obtained from my divine Son, that those who propagate this devotion to my tears and dolors, will be taken directly from this earthly life to eternal happiness*** *since all their sins will be forgiven and my Son and I will be their eternal consolation and joy.*

SEVEN SORROWS
1. The prophecy of Simeon. (St. Luke 2:34, 35)
2. The ***flight into Egypt***. (St. Matthew 2:13, 14)
3. The ***loss of the Child Jesus in the temple***. (St. Luke 2: 43-45)
4. The meeting of Jesus and Mary on the Way of the Cross.
5. The Crucifixion.
6. The taking down of the Body of Jesus from the Cross.
7. The burial of Jesus.

25: Peter and Mary

25:113 Mary, not God, is front and center in the 15 promises of the rosary and the 7 graces. Mary gives major supernatural blessings to those who serve and honor her, who meditate on her sorrows, and who are devoted to Mary and the rosary. If that isn't evidence of Mary being viewed as God, what is it?

25:114 Why aren't Catholics celebrating Jesus and all God has done for us instead of spending time on Mary's tears and sorrows? Why is Mary still crying over the fact that Joseph, herself and Jesus had to flee to Egypt? Why is Mary still in sorrow after more than 2,000 years - more than 730,000 days - since she and Joseph left 12-year old Jesus behind for 3 days in Jerusalem? Jesus wasn't fazed back then. No one in the New Testament - including Peter and Paul - was meditating on Mary's sorrows. So why are Roman Catholics dwelling on her sorrows today? And getting blessed for doing so?

25:115 If Mary is to be our role model and dwelling on sorrows forever is an example of how we're to live our lives, then shouldn't every parent be weeping their entire life over mistakes made in parenting our children?

❑ *Romans 15:13 Now may the God of hope fill you with all joy and peace in believing, so that you will abound in hope by the power of the Holy Spirit.*

25:116 Isn't this daily looking back and focusing on Mary a form of spiritual hijacking and/or bondage by keeping the eyes of Roman Catholics on Mary, and off of Jesus?

Personal Relationship

God created human beings for relationship with Him. After creating Adam and Eve, God walked and talked with them in the garden. God also spoke directly or indirectly through angels to many others including Noah, Abraham, Moses, Elijah, David, Daniel, Mary, Joseph and Saul/Paul.

Sin separated humans from God, but God provided a solution - Jesus's shed blood, death and resurrection. When Jesus died on the cross, the veil in the temple separating God from the ordinary person was torn. We can now have direct access to God. When John rested his head on Jesus's chest, it foreshadowed the Christian walk. Jesus, the Prince of Peace, is right here for each one of us to lay our heads on His shoulder.

From the moment we're born again, we can have an intimate relationship with God where Holy Spirit comes in [en] us. Jesus is with and in us. God is to be front and center in our lives. We are to seek God with no one in between. We're to glorify God, and only God, in all we say and do.

A commonly used visual representation of a believer's relationship with God is to think of a glass jar. When God is front and center, this relationship jar is filled with living water. Other people are to be in our lives, but God is to be first priority followed by family, then others. When people or things in our lives are put ahead of God - Father God, Jesus and Holy Spirit - they effectively steal God's space by displacing some of the living water in our God relationship jar, akin to what happens if we drop stones into a jar of regular water. In other words, God gets pushed out of

CEASED?

our relationship with Him when other people and things take some of God's rightful place in our lives.

25:115 Mary, deceased saints, graven images, priests and the Pope have major roles in the lives of Catholics. Aren't they displacing the presence of God in 'God relationship jars'?

CLOSING POINTS TO PONDER

When I first started dating Lori, I wasn't born again. Lori kept talking about having a personal relationship with Jesus. I didn't understand what she meant. Over time, I observed Lori and others talking about their experiences with God. Sometimes He spoke to them through His word. Sometimes a still small voice. Sometimes things would happen in their lives that could only be attributed to God. Over time, I realized God is not a far-off distant being. He is here with [para, meta], in [en] and sometimes [upon] His children. When we get to heaven, God's presence will be manifested in ways we can't imagine.

25:116 God wants a relationship with each one of us. Is it more likely that:
  i. God waits until we get to heaven before He has a close, personal, 2-way relationship with us; or
  ii. God wants a close, personal, 2-way relationship with us forever including the rest of our lives on earth and continuing on into heaven, with no one in between?

25:117 And if God doesn't speak directly, outside His Word, to anybody since the Bible was written, doesn't that mean He hasn't spoken to a person in over 1,900 years?

- ❏ *John 10:27 My sheep hear My voice, and I know them, and they follow Me; 28 and I give eternal life to them, and they will never perish; and no one will snatch them out of My hand.*
- ❏ *Job 33:14 "Indeed God speaks once, Or twice, yet no one notices it.*
- ❏ *Jeremiah 33:3 'Call to Me and I will answer you, and I will tell you great and mighty things, which you do not know.'*

26

Graven Images
Different Ten Commandments
Saints

INTRODUCTION

THERE are several sources of dispute between Roman Catholics and Protestants. Honoring deceased saints with statues and shrines, differing Ten Commandments, and praying to deceased saints are the three primary topics covered in Chapter 26.

  i. graven images of deceased saints (page 381);
 ii. different Ten Commandments (page 383); and
iii. praying to deceased saints (page 390).

GRAVEN IMAGES

The Roman Catholic church bought the Crystal Cathedral in 2012, completed a $72 million restoration, and re-opened it in July 2019. Featuring some 11,000 glass panes, it is apparently a beautiful building. The church has a 1,000-pound crucifix, a hand-painted mosaic of Lady of Guadalupe, and portraits of several deceased saints in the entryway. Relics from Korean, Vietnamese, Mexican and American martyrs as well as Pope John Paul II are encased in an altar. A 2-acre, outdoor shrine is being built in honor of Lady of La Vang. Is all this attention given to deceased saints appropriate? To start, consider the Bible says all glory is to go to God.

- ❏ *Ephesians 3:20 Now to Him who is able to do far more abundantly beyond all that we ask or think, according to the power that works within us, 21* **to Him be the glory** *in the church and in Christ Jesus to all generations forever and ever. Amen.*

As we saw earlier, King Herod took glory due to God and paid a heavy price.

- ❏ *Acts 12:23 And immediately an angel of the Lord struck* **him because he did not give God the glory***, and he was* **eaten by worms** *and died.*

Three apostles - Paul, Barnabas and Peter - responded quickly and decisively to any glory and accolades that people tried to give them.

- ❏ *Acts 14:12 And they began calling Barnabas, Zeus, and Paul, Hermes, because*

CEASED?

>*he was the chief speaker. 13 The priest of Zeus, whose temple was just outside the city, brought oxen and garlands to the gates, and wanted to offer sacrifice with the crowds. 14 But when the apostles Barnabas and Paul heard of it, **<u>they tore their robes and rushed out into the crowd, crying out</u>** 15 **<u>and saying, "Men, why are you doing these things? We are also men of the same nature as you</u>**, and preach the gospel to you that you should turn from these vain things to a living God, who made the heaven and the earth and the sea and all that is in them.*
> ❑ *Acts 10:25 When Peter entered, Cornelius met him, and fell at his feet and worshiped him. 26 But Peter raised him up, saying, "**<u>Stand up; I too am just a man</u>**."*

26:1 If Peter, Paul and Barnabas were alive today and saw pictures, shrines, statues or other physical artifacts of them. or in any way dedicated to them, would they:
  i. want them destroyed; or
  ii. maintained, embellished and increased in number and size?

26:2 If Peter, Paul and Barnabas were attending renovation meetings on the portraits, mosaic and the 2-acre shrine honor of Lady of La Vang for the Crystal Cathedral, would their reaction be i. or ii.?
  i. "NO! Nothing of the kind is to be built!"
  ii. "Awesome, and we must make sure such items are in every village, town and city in the world!"

26:3 If the likes of Peter, Paul and Barnabas would not support such items, should church leaders today be adding to the collection of millions of pictures, images, statues and other physical images currently in the Roman Catholic church - or destroying them?

26:4 If statues, shrines and artifacts were wanted by God, why doesn't His Word mention such items should be made to honor the likes of Adam, Eve, Noah, Abraham, Moses, Elijah, Joseph, David and Solomon from the Old Testament, and Mary and Joseph, Peter, John or Paul from the New Testament? God's Word gives no direction to make any statues, shrines or artifacts of any person. In fact, doesn't it say the opposite? So how do we justify all the graven images in the Roman Catholic church today?

In my research, I found Roman Catholic apologists acknowledge God said no graven images were to be made. However, I also usually found they move past this commandment by pointing to the cherubim created for the Ark of the Covenant, to the bronze serpent, and to the statues in Solomon's temple as justification that graven images can be created and actively used today.

26:5 While God gave instructions in the Old Testament for a few images to be made, isn't it significant God never gave instructions to make graven images of any person?

26:6 Do exceptions when God created images for specific purposes give the Catholic church a green light to make millions of graven images of deceased saints?

26: Ten Commandments, Images, Saints
DIFFERENT TEN COMMANDMENTS

One factor contributing to the controversy might be found in the Ten Commandments where the Roman Catholic church has a different list of commandments than do Protestant churches.

Catholic	**Protestant**
1: No other Gods Before Me; no graven images, likenesses, do do not bow down, nor worship	1: No Other Gods Before Me
	2: No graven images, likenesses, do not bow down to, nor worship
2: Do not take Lord's name in vain	3: Do not take Lord's name in vain
3: Keep the Sabbath	4: Keep the Sabbath
4: Honor Father and Mother	5: Honor Father and Mother
5: Do not kill	6: Do not kill
6: Do not commit adultery	7: Do not commit adultery
7: Do not steal	8: Do not steal
8: Do not bear false witness	9: Do not bear false witness
9: Do not covet neighbor's wife	10: Do not covet
10: Do not covet neighbor's goods	

Protestants and Roman Catholics both agree verse 3 is the 1st Commandment. We are not to have any other gods in our lives.
- *Exodus 20:1 Then God spoke all these words, saying, 2 "I am the Lord your God, who brought you out of the land of Egypt, out of the house of slavery. 3 "You shall have **no other gods** before Me.*

The Roman Catholic church views 'no carved images and likenesses' in Exodus 20:4-6 as part of the 1st Commandment. Protestants view these verses as representing a separate commandment.
- *Exodus 20:4 "**You shall not make** for yourself **an idol, or any likeness** of **what is in heaven above or on the earth beneath** or in the water under the earth. 5 You **shall not worship them** or serve them ... (NASB)*
- *Exodus 20:4 "You shall not make for yourself a **carved image** ... (ESV)*
- *Exodus 20:4 Thou shalt not make unto thee any **graven image** ... (KJV)*

The next point of disagreement is that the Roman Catholic church splits the issue of coveting in Exodus 20:17 into 2 Commandments - #9 and #10 - while Protestant churches view Exodus 20:17 as only one commandment, the 10th Commandment.
- *Exodus 20:17 "**You shall not covet** your **neighbor's house**; you shall not covet your **neighbor's wife** or his male servant or his female servant or his ox or his donkey or anything that belongs to your neighbor."*

Deuteronomy 5 also lists the Ten Commandments. Verse 21 deals with coveting and has one different item - field. It also lists the items in a slightly different order.
- *Deuteronomy 5:21 'You shall not covet your **neighbor's wife**, and you shall*

CEASED?

*not desire your **<u>neighbor's house, his field or his male servant or his female servant, his ox or his donkey or anything</u>** that belongs to your neighbor.'*

Exodus 20:17	**Deuteronomy 5:21**
1: House	1: Neighbor's Wife
2: Neighbor's Wife	2: House
3: Male Servant	**3: Field**
4: Female Servant	4: Male Servant
5: Ox	5: Female Servant
6: Donkey	6: Ox
7: Anything that is neighbor's	7: Donkey
	8: Anything that is neighbor's

26:7 Does the order of the items and groups of people suggest a priority? If, for instance, the neighbor's wife was worthy of its own commandment, shouldn't we expect to see 'neighbor's wife' listed first in both Exodus and Deuteronomy?

26:8 Given house is the first item in Exodus 20 and neighbor's wife is the first item in Deuteronomy 5, why wouldn't the 9th commandment be about coveting a neighbor's house as opposed to coveting a neighbor's wife?

26:9 Does the commandment 'do not covet a neighbor's wife' mean God is less worried about women coveting a neighbor's husband than He is about men coveting a neighbor's wife?

26:10 Is coveting a neighbor's husband, parents, uncle, aunt, nephew, niece, cousin or children part of the Catholic 9th or 10th Commandment, and why?

26:11 If the answer to the last two questions is the 9th Commandment deals with not coveting another person while the 10th Commandment deals with not coveting things, why doesn't Deuteronomy 5 list male servant and female servant immediately after neighbor's wife instead of after house and field? In other words, why are people and things intermixed in both Deuteronomy 5 and Exodus 20?

26:12 The Roman Catholic church teaches a key reason to have the 9th Commandment *of 'not coveting a wife'* is to emphasize we aren't to engage in sexual sin. No question, but isn't the issue of sexual immorality already covered with the Commandment that we're not to commit adultery, a commandment Jesus took to a new level in the New Testament?

❏ *Matthew 5:28 but I say to you that everyone who looks at a woman with lust for her has already committed adultery with her in his heart.*

26:13 Consider Romans 7:7 and 13:9. Don't both verses show that coveting is a principle telling us not to covet anyone, or anything?

❏ *Romans 7:7 What shall we say then? Is the Law sin? May it never be! On the contrary, I would not have come to know sin except through the Law; **<u>for I would not have known about coveting</u>** if the Law had not said, "**<u>You shall</u>***

26: Ten Commandments, Images, Saints

not covet." 8 *But sin, taking opportunity through the commandment, produced in **me coveting of every kind**; for apart from the Law sin is dead.*
❑ *Romans 13:9 For this, "You shall not commit adultery, You shall not murder, You shall not steal, **You shall not covet**," ...*

26:14 If you were sitting on a translation committee for a new version of the Bible discussing the Ten Commandments, would you recommend:
'A': combining Exodus 20:3-4 into one commandment and splitting Exodus 20:7 into two coveting commandments; or
'B': treating Exodus 20:3, 20:4 and 20:17 as three separate commandments?

'A'	**'B'**
1: No other Gods Before Me; no graven images, likenesses, do not bow down, nor worship	1: No Other Gods Before Me
	2: No graven images, likenesses, do not bow down to, nor worship
9: Do not covet neighbor's wife	10: Do not covet
10: Do not covet neighbor's goods	

If you choose 'A', what is your Biblical justification?

About Making Images and Likenesses

Images and likenesses, in my view, are a big deal. At the beginning of this section, I referred to the changes to the Crystal Cathedral. Recall Exodus 20:4 which states we're not to make an idol or any likeness of things in heaven or on earth.
❑ *Exodus 20:4 "You **shall not make** for yourself **an idol, or any likeness** of what is in **heaven above or on the earth** beneath or in the water under the earth. (NASB)*
❑ *Exodus 20:4 "You shall not make for yourself **a carved image**, or any likeness of anything that is in heaven above, or that is in the earth beneath, or that is in the water under the earth. (ESV)*

Isaiah reaffirms this command of God where no praise is to go to graven images.
❑ *Isaiah 42:8 I am the Lord, that is My name; **I will not give My glory to another, Nor My praise to graven images**.*

The English word praise is derived from the Hebrew word 'tehillah' [H8416] which Thayer defines in part as *'praise, song or hymn of praise, adoration, thanksgiving, act of general or public praise, renown or fame'.*

26:15 When we look at a statue, spend time mulling on a statue and the person it represents, speak or pray to a statue and/or the person it represents, or give thanks to the person the statue represents, aren't we giving praise? If not, why not, and what *'is'* going on?

CEASED?

Many Protestants read scriptures such as Exodus 20:4 and Isaiah 42:8 and think any statues, shrines or other artifacts of deceased saints or God Himself violates the 2nd commandment. Many of us see all of them as objects of idolatry.

Catholic teachings disagree and thus the Roman Catholic church has millions of statues, shrines and artifacts of individuals in their ~220,000 parishes around the world. A key reason justifying such items starts with the fact God had His followers make cherubim statues for the Holy of Holies for the Ark of the Covenant, various items in the temple built by Solomon, and the bronze serpent.

- ❏ *Exodus 25:18 You shall **make two cherubim** of hammered gold at the two ends of the mercy seat.*
- ❏ *1 Kings 6:35 He carved on it **cherubim, palm trees, and open flowers**; and he overlaid them with gold evenly applied on the engraved work.*
- ❏ *Numbers 21:8 Then the Lord said to Moses, "Make a **fiery serpent** [of bronze] and set it on a pole; and everyone who is bitten will live when he looks at it."*

The argument continues by stating that since God caused such images to be made, that gives Roman Catholics the right to make images as well.

26:16   The 5th or 6th Commandment says do not kill. However, God killed two believers, Ananias and Sapphira, for not giving all the proceeds from the sale of land. If we use the same logic in regards to justifying the creation of human images, does it hold that since God killed these people for their sins, we are justified in killing people today who sin? If this extension of logic isn't valid, how is the above logic on graven images valid?

26:17   If one still believes we can justify the creation and display of graven images based on what God did, then shouldn't we also be guided by what God actually desired to be made? And since none of the images, statues or artifacts that God commissioned were of a person or even God Himself, how can Catholics or any believer for that matter justify making and paying attention to graven images of people? Or of God Himself?

26:18   The images such as those for the Holy of Holies were made according to specific directions from God. Has God given specific, detailed directions in His Word to the Roman Catholic church for every one of the statues, shrines and artifacts of deceased saints within the Roman Catholic church and the homes of Roman Catholics?

Without the death, shed blood and resurrection of Jesus, all believers in current and previous generations would be unclean. All of our deeds would be like a filthy or polluted garment, a filthy rag. It is only because of God's grace and mercy, and what Jesus did for us are we made clean.

- ❏ *Isaiah 64:6 For all of us have become like one who is **unclean**, And all our righteous deeds are like a **filthy garment** ... (NASB)*
- ❏ *Isaiah 64:6 For we all have become like one who is [ceremonially] unclean [**like a leper**], And all our deeds of righteousness are like **filthy rags** ... (AMP)*
- ❏ *Isaiah 64:6 We have all become like one who is **unclean**, and all our*

26: Ten Commandments, Images, Saints

*righteous deeds are like a **polluted garment** ... (ESV)*

26:19 Why exalt any person who, in their own merits and strength, is not clean? Why not give all glory and attention to the One who made you, me and every other believer clean?

26:20 If one argues that having items such as statues, images and shrines help draw us closer to Christ in some way, then why didn't God cause this to happen for Biblical men and women such as Enoch, Noah, Abraham, Isaac, Jacob, Moses, Elijah, Elisha, David, Daniel, John the Baptist or Stephen - the first apostle martyred? And why didn't God make this crystal clear that we are to continue to do so going forward?

26:21 The papal ferula is the pastoral staff (akin to a rod or walking stick) used by Popes. At the top, there is a small sculpture of Jesus hanging on a cross. Bishops use crosiers, sticks with a top that is curved and features one or more of a variety of objects. There is no mention in the Bible of a single apostle, including Peter, having a papal ferula, crosier or other such objects. If the early apostles did not use these religious objects, what Biblical basis is there for any leader to use them today?

26:22 Items in the temple were limited, were used for specific purposes that enabled priests to approach God. These items were before the cross. Given Jesus is the living sacrifice, and believers are the temple where Holy Spirit resides, hasn't the situation changed from a religious service for God, to a personal relationship with God?

Carved Images

Exodus 20:4 in the NASB translation says we're not to make *'idols'*. KJV uses the phrase *'graven image'*. The ESV uses the phrase *'carved image'*.

- *Exodus 20:4 "You shall not make for **yourself an idol** ... (NASB)*
- *Exodus 20:4 Thou shalt not make unto thee any **graven image** ... (KJV)*
- *Exodus 20:4 "You shall not make for yourself a **carved image** ... (ESV)*

The English words *'idol'*, *'carved image'*, and *'graven image'* are derived from the Greek word *'pesel'* [H6459] which means an idol, image or carved image. Pesel is derived from the Greek word *'pasal'* [G6458] which means to cut, hew, quarry. When making a 3-dimensional object such as a statue or shrine, we could find ways to argue today's images are not cut, hewed, quarried or carved. Whatever way we seek to deal with this issue, the reality is they are objects created to be a central part of the Catholic faith, objects that are influencing hundreds of millions of people.

26:23 God never had a statue or shrine made of a person. The Bible does not say believers are to make physical images of any person including Jesus. When a physical image of a person such as Jesus on the papal ferula or a statue of a deceased saint is made, are you 100% confident that the making and/or subsequent speaking to or otherwise spending time with such objects isn't an act of disobedience, an act of idolatry, and thus an act of sin? And if so, what is your Biblical basis for that confidence?

CEASED?

If you still think graven images are ok, consider Leviticus 26.

- *Leviticus 26:1 You **shall not make for yourselves idols**, **nor shall you set up for** yourselves **an image or a sacred pillar**, **nor shall you place a figured stone** in your land **to bow down** to it; **for I am** the **Lord your God**.*

Now consider Deuteronomy 4. When God spoke to His people at Horeb, He gathered them so they would learn to fear God. That's rather attention getting isn't it? Per verse 12, God only spoke. God did not show His form. The reason God didn't show His form was because if He did show His form, per verses 15 through 19, the people would act corruptly and make graven images.

- *Deuteronomy 4:10 Remember the day you stood before the Lord your God at Horeb, when the Lord said to me, 'Assemble the people to Me, that I may let them hear My words so they **may learn to fear Me all the days they live on the earth**, and that they may teach their children.' 11 You came near and stood at the foot of the mountain, and the mountain burned with fire to the very heart of the heavens: darkness, cloud and thick gloom. 12 Then the Lord spoke to you from the midst of the fire; **you heard the sound of words, but you saw no form - only a voice**. 13 So He declared to you His covenant which He commanded you to perform, that is, the Ten Commandments; and He wrote them on two tablets of stone. 14 The Lord commanded me at that time to teach you statutes and judgments, that you might perform them in the land where you are going over to possess it. 15 "So watch yourselves carefully, **since you did not see any form on the day the Lord spoke to you at Horeb** from the midst of the fire, 16 **so that you do not act corruptly and make a graven image for yourselves in the form of any figure, the likeness of male or female, 17 the likeness of any animal that is on the earth, the likeness of any winged bird that flies in the sky, 18 the likeness of anything that creeps on the ground, the likeness of any fish that is in the water below the earth. 19 And beware not to lift up your eyes to heaven and see the sun and the moon and the stars, all the host of heaven, and be drawn away and worship them and serve them**, those which the Lord your God has allotted to all the peoples under the whole heaven. 20 But the Lord has taken you and brought you out of the iron furnace, from Egypt, to be a people for His own possession, as today.*

26:24 Don't Leviticus 26:1 and Deuteronomy 4 make it pretty darn clear:
    i. God took steps to ensure His people didn't make graven images: and
    ii. given God doesn't change, doesn't that mean believers aren't to make graven images of anything including statues and shrines today? Or am I missing something?

Pictures of Family

Another argument supporting the existence of Catholic graven images is that because we have pictures and memorabilia of friends and family, we are justified in having stained glass or other forms of graven images of deceased saints, or even God Himself.

26: Ten Commandments, Images, Saints

26:25 Isn't there a significant difference between a picture of a friend or family member, and a picture, statue or shrine of a deceased person we never knew, and who had no direct involvement with our family?

26:26 If taking and keeping of family pictures is used as justification for the creation of graven images, doesn't that put human reasoning above Biblical teachings?

26:27 For those who believe we should treat family pictures the same way we treat graven images, don't we have two basic choices:
  i. take what we believe is right for family pictures and use that to determine what to do with graven images of saints and God; or
  ii. study what the Bible says about graven images, then use that to help determine what to do for family pictures?

26:28 If the link between family pictures and graven images is that direct, shouldn't the direction be from the Bible to our lives, instead of our lives to the Bible? In other words, is it appropriate to justify actions in our Christian walk based on what happens in our personal lives or on the personal lives of others? Or should we take what God's Word says, and then apply what God's Word says to our personal lives?

26:29 If we try to justify graven images based on the fact we already have pictures and memorabilia of friends and family, I wonder to what extent this view is a heart issue of looking for ways to justify doing what we want or keeping what we have, as opposed to honoring and obeying God's command not to create such images. In other words, are such arguments effectively developed as a way to justify sin?

For what it's worth, I believe graven images are not ok, while pictures of family and friends are very much ok. Pictures of entertainment or sports stars on our walls at home are not ok.

Worshipping Images

God told Moses to create a bronze serpent so that anyone bitten by a serpent could simply look at the serpent and be healed. Later on, however, Hezekiah destroyed the statue because the people were burning incense to it. In other words, they were worshiping it.

- ❏ *Numbers 21:9 And **Moses made a bronze serpent** and set it on the standard; and it came about, that if a serpent bit any man, when he looked to the bronze serpent, he lived.*
- ❏ *2 Kings 18:4 He removed the high places and broke down the sacred pillars and cut down the Asherah. He also **broke in pieces the bronze serpent** that Moses had made, for until those days the sons of Israel **burned incense to it**; and it was called Nehushtan.*

From a starting point of looking at the bronze serpent - a foreshadowing of what Jesus would do on the cross - God's people moved from looking at the serpent to worshiping the serpent. The words in many Catholic teachings are clear that Catholics are not to worship people, statues or images, and rightfully so. However,

CEASED?

how many Catholics have gone from looking to worshipping?

- ❏ *Exodus 20:5 You shall not **worship** them or **serve** them; for I, the Lord your God, am a jealous God, visiting the iniquity of the fathers on the children, on the third and the fourth generations of those who hate Me, (NASB)*
- ❏ *Exodus 20:5 You shall **not bow down** to them or serve them, for I the Lord your God am a jealous God, visiting the iniquity of the fathers on the children to the third and the fourth generation of those who hate me, (ESV)*

The English word worship in verse 5 is derived from the Hebrew word 'shachah' [H7812] which Strong's defines in part as to '... bow down ... do reverence ... to stoop ... to worship.'

26:30 Many Popes have kneeled before statues of Mary and paid special homage. Many Catholics have kissed the feet of statues of deceased saints which has led to the feet on some of these statues to be worn down over time. Catholics bow down to the Pope.
    i. Aren't these and other acts of adoration and reverence to living and deceased saints a form of worship? If not, why not? And what are they if not acts of worship?
    ii. Are these actions somewhat similar to what was going on in 2 Kings which led to Hezekiah removing the high places, breaking down the sacred pillars and destroying the bronze serpent?

PRAYING TO DECEASED SAINTS

Deceased and Living in One Body

A Roman Catholic argument says Catholics who died and are in heaven are not only aware of what is happening on earth, they can hear prayers of living Catholics. Some teachings contend these deceased saints can also hear our thoughts. Moreover, they want to pray for living Catholics.

The logic behind this perspective is that since all followers of Christ are in one body, and the body is to be united with no divisions, then both deceased and living saints remain in the same Body of Christ today. And as such, deceased and living saints can communicate and help each other.

- ❏ *Romans 12:5 So we, who are many, **are one body in Christ**, and individually members one of another.*
- ❏ *1 Corinthians 12:25 so that there may **be no division in the body**, but that the members may have the same care for one another.*

What's Required

When we pray here on earth, we can think thoughts, pray very quietly, or we can speak out loud. Either way, God hears us. And how can He not? He is God, and Holy Spirit is in [en] us when we're truly born again. When we speak out loud, other people, angels and demonic forces can hear us, but only if they are in our presence or we're talking to another person(s) via some form of technology. As far as I know, there is no scripture indicating deceased saints can hear us, or know our thoughts. In contrast, God hears everything and even knows our thoughts. satan and/or one

26: Ten Commandments, Images, Saints

or more of his demons can get a good read on our thoughts not only because they can give us thoughts and see how we respond to them, they can also watch us and learn our views and see our reactions to conversations and events in our lives. However, I can't find any Bible verse indicating deceased saints have any such abilities to give thoughts, observe, or know thoughts of living saints.

26:31   When a person asks another living saint for prayer, there is direct contact either through face to face discussion or through other means such as telephone, texting, emails or via assorted apps. Isn't it a rather big assumption to believe that deceased saints, even though they are still part of the Body of Christ, can continue to hear prayers of living saints? And know the prayers we're thinking about, or are speaking very quietly? For deceased saints to hear us living saints and know the prayers we're thinking, wouldn't:
   i. their heavenly being (spirit and soul at least) need to be here on earth, and very close to us to hear our words, or if not, wouldn't they need a supernatural ability to hear us if they remain in heaven while we're here on earth; and
   ii. they need to have received a supernatural ability to know the prayers we're thinking of but not speaking out loud; and
   iii. they need to have received a supernatural ability to know who we are when we pray to them given most deceased individuals have no clue who any of us are; and
   iv. they need to have received a supernatural ability to hear not only from one person, but from hundreds, thousands or even millions of people at the same time? And can simultaneously communicate all these prayers to God? If not why not?

26:32   Given angels can only be in one place at a time, wouldn't the supernatural abilities for deceased saints need to be greater than angels in this regard? Consider one believer in Los Angeles and another in Brisbane. If two living saints are praying at the same time to the same deceased saint, how can the deceased saint hear both prayers at the same time - unless the deceased saint had God's omnipresent ability to be in more than one place at a time? Where is that found in the Bible?

26:33   I wonder if Holy Spirit ever wonders: *"I'm right here - in [en] and with [meta] you. Why not talk to me? And if you're not aware, I know the prayers you're going to say to Mary and other deceased saints before you even say them?"*

26:34   When we ask living saints to pray for us, they will often acknowledge they're doing so. If deceased saints can hear our prayers and know the prayers in our thoughts, then:
   i. shouldn't we be able to hear the saints in heaven speaking to us, and confirming they are praying for us? If not, why is it only a one-way communication?
   ii. I've seen arguments that we can hear deceased saints. Apparitions/visions of deceased saints are cited as examples of

CEASED?

deceased saints speaking to us. Consider two things. First, compared to the many billions/trillions of communications flowing annually from living saints to deceased saints, doesn't a very small number of apparitions from deceased saints seem radically disproportionate? Secondly, what's to say such apparitions are not demonic?

❑ *2 Corinthians 11:14 ... for even Satan disguises himself as an angel of light.*

26:35 There is no indication in the New Testament that any living saints prayed to dead saints after the cross. If praying to deceased saints was Biblical and of much benefit to followers of the resurrected Jesus, wouldn't it be reasonable to expect the Bible to show examples of living saints praying to deceased saints such as:
   i. Stephen while he was being martyred as per Acts 7;
   ii. apostles who were in jail and/or otherwise facing tough times; or
   iii. other believers who personally knew highly regarded disciples such as Stephen or the apostles before they died?

We don't find any examples of such prayers in the Bible.

More on this Two-Way Relationship

Consider the last part of 1 Corinthians 12:25.

❑ *1 Corinthians 12:25 so that there may be no division in the body, but that the members **may have the same care for one another**.*

26:36 If living saints are to have this ongoing relationship with deceased saints in heaven, how do we give the same care to someone in heaven as we do to living neighbors who we may give money, look after their sick child, or cut their lawn? Do saints in heaven need anything from us? Isn't God meeting all their needs?

26:37 Isn't there a dramatic difference between having a relationship with a person living on earth who speaks back to us, and a 'relationship' with another person who has died, is in heaven and we never hear from?

26:38 In Philippians 1, doesn't Paul indicate there is going to be a major difference between our life here on earth and in heaven?

❑ *Philippians 1:21 For to me, to live is Christ and to die is gain. 22 But if I am to live on in the flesh, this will mean fruitful labor for me; and I do not know which to choose. 23 But I am hard-pressed from both directions, having the desire to depart and be with Christ, for that is very much better; 24 yet to remain on in the flesh is more necessary for your sake.*

26:39 Paul loved his fellow believers. Is there anything in the New Testament that suggests Paul would continue to be praying for, watching over, or keeping in contact with the saints after he died? Is there any indication living saints could contact him after he died? Is there one example of another believer in the New Testament who said after the cross they would keep in contact with living saints after they died? I can't find it.

26: Ten Commandments, Images, Saints

Enhancing our Relationship with Jesus

26:40 Before we ask others to pray for us, should we pray to God first?
- ❑ *Matthew 6:33 But seek first His kingdom and His righteousness, and all these things will be added to you.*
- ❑ *Hebrews 4:16 Therefore let us draw near with confidence to the throne of grace, so that we may receive mercy and find grace to help in time of need.*

26:41 Believers are to pray for another. But if we're thinking about asking someone to pray for us, wouldn't it be wise to see if Holy Spirit wants us to ask them before doing so?
- ❑ *Romans 8:14 For all who are being led by the Spirit of God, these are sons of God.*
- ❑ *Matthew 6:9 "Pray, then, in this way: 'Our Father who is in heaven …*

26:42 When we pray to deceased saints instead of directly to Father God, Jesus or to Holy Spirit who is in [en] us when we're born again, how do such prayers enhance our personal closeness with God?

26:43 Do such prayers inherently show a lack of trust and faith in God by not going directly to God? And, if so, wouldn't we be displeasing God instead of pleasing Him?
- ❑ *Hebrews 11:6 And **without faith it is impossible to please Him**, for he who comes to God must believe that He is and that He is a rewarder of those who seek Him.*

Heavenly Life for Deceased Saints

Lori's mom, Joy, used to say, *"If I am aware of all the problems my family is having, it won't be heaven."*

26:44 As I understand heaven, it will be an amazing place of worship, joy, peace, fun, grandeur and holiness. Tears and worries and sadness and all the negative stuff of our earthly lives will be gone. If that is the case, wouldn't many of these prayers to deceased saints from humans living on earth today bring pain and sorrow to these deceased saints, and therefore take away from their enjoyment of heaven? If not, why not?
- ❑ *Revelation 21:4 and He will **wipe away every tear from their eyes**; and there will no longer be any death; there **will no longer be any mourning, or crying, or pain**; the first things have passed away."*

Lifting our prayers up

Another piece of the Roman Catholic view justifying praying to deceased saints in heaven is that they believe these deceased saints lift our prayers up to God.
- ❑ *Revelation 5:7 And He came and took the book out of the right hand of Him who sat on the throne. 8 When He had taken the book, the four living creatures and the twenty-four elders fell down before the Lamb, **each one holding a harp and golden bowls full of incense, which are the prayers of the saints**.*

CEASED?

26:45 The bowls the 24 elders hold up contain the prayers of the saints. It begs the question of what do these bowls, 24 elders and prayers actually mean.
  i. Did the 24 elders hear each prayer and supernaturally place each prayer in a bowl?
  ii. Are the prayers placed supernaturally in the bowls and the 24 elders deliver them to God, similar to how a FedEx driver delivers a package from one party to another but knows nothing about the contents of the package, nor has any right to know?
  iii. Are only the 24 elders involved in this process but no other believers? And if so, don't Catholics need to know the names of these 24 elders so they can pray primarily to the deceased saints who do the actual lifting up of prayers?
  iv. And if the lifting of prayers is not limited to just 24 elders, but to some other saints (yet not all saints), how does a Catholic know which saints are involved and should be prayed to?
  v. Or - are the bowls and 24 elders symbolic just as the 7 horns and 7 eyes of the Lamb are symbolic?

❑ *Revelation 5:6 And I saw ... a Lamb standing ... having seven horns and seven eyes,*

Saints in Heaven are more Righteous

Another Catholic argument for praying to deceased saints is based on James 5:16.

❑ *James 5:16 Therefore, confess your sins to one another, and pray for one another so that you may be healed.* **The effective prayer of a righteous man can accomplish much**.

26:46 The Catholic argument states that people in heaven are more righteous than followers of Christ here on earth, and thus their prayers have more impact or clout with God. But aren't followers of Christ all blood-bought children of God washed clean by Jesus's shed blood through His one-time sacrifice on the cross? Aren't we clean in God's eyes now?

26:47 But - if deceased saints have more influence - let me ask again. Why don't we see the early church praying to deceased saints, or see God's Word encouraging us to do so?

Praying to the Deceased in the Old Testament

Consider Deuteronomy 18:

❑ *Deuteronomy 18:10 There shall not be found among you anyone who makes his son or his daughter pass through the fire, one who uses divination, one who practices witchcraft, or one who interprets omens, or a sorcerer, 11 or one who casts a spell, or a medium, or a spiritist, or* **one who calls up the dead**. *12 For* **whoever does these things is detestable to the Lord;** *and because of these detestable things the Lord your God will drive them out before you.*

26:48 God doesn't change. Given God called it detestable in the Old Testament for anyone who called up the dead, wouldn't it still be detestable to try to speak to a deceased person today? If not, why not?

26: Ten Commandments, Images, Saints

Exalting Any Person

The Bible refers to saints frequently. Paul often writes to the saints.
- ❑ *Acts 9:13 But Ananias answered, "Lord, I have heard from many about this man, how much harm he did to **Your saints at Jerusalem**;*
- ❑ *Acts 9:32 ... he came down also to the **saints who lived at Lydda**.*
- ❑ *Acts 9:41 ... **and calling the saints and widows**, he presented her alive.*
- ❑ *Acts 26:10... **not only did I lock up many of the saints in prisons** ...*
- ❑ *Romans 8:27 and He who searches the hearts knows what the mind of the Spirit is, because He **intercedes for the saints** according to the will of God.*
- ❑ *Romans 12:13 contributing to the **needs of the saints**, practicing hospitality.*
- ❑ *Romans 15:25 but now, I am going to Jerusalem **serving the saints**.*
- ❑ *Romans 15:26 ... contribution for the poor among the **saints in Jerusalem**.*
- ❑ *1 Corinthians 1:2 ... at Corinth ... **saints by calling** ...*
- ❑ *2 Corinthians 1:1 ... **with all the saints who are throughout Achaia**:*
- ❑ *Ephesians 1:1 ... To **the saints who are at Ephesus** ...*
- ❑ *Ephesians 4:12 for **the equipping of the saints** for the work of service, to the building up of the body of Christ;*

26:49 Per the above:
   i. aren't all believers to be regarded as saints, and not a select few?
   ii. If only a few are saints as decided by the Catholic church, wouldn't that mean Paul's teachings were limited to the select few saints he addressed his writings to, which excludes virtually everybody who is alive today including you and me?

26:50 The only criteria I can find in God's Word that defines whether or not a person is a saint is that the person must be born again. I can't find evidence in the Bible supporting the Roman Catholic process and criteria used to determine whether or not a person is a saint? Can you?

26:51 When I raised this issue with a Catholic acquaintance, he admitted all believers are saints. Then he smiled and went on to say the Roman Catholic church has a few *"super saints"*. If you're Roman Catholic, do you think Peter and Paul would want to be thought of today as super saints? Didn't Paul say he was the least of all saints? And isn't the notion of a *"super saint"* contrary to scriptures that state all glory is to go to God?

I visited a church where pastors had titles such as the Holy John Doe and the Most Holy James Doe. I was dumbfounded. All of us are sinners. The only reason any of us are righteous is because of what Jesus did for us. As we live more holy and righteous day-to-day lives, it is only because of the transforming work God does in our hearts. We all sin, and as a result, isn't it inappropriate to give any person a title of Holy including the Pope's His Holiness, when no priest, pastor, deacon, elder, prophet, apostle, teacher, evangelist or leader is any more holy than the person sitting in the back pew? We need to show all people respect, but does any person in 'authority' deserve more respect or a holier designation than a person who cooks or cleans the washrooms? Titles are useful to help identify functions and roles, but to imply one

CEASED?

believer is holier than another is not only a major assumption, it is inconsistent with what the Body of Christ is all about.

Attention on Ungodly Things

In 2019, a statue of Moloch - the Canaanite deity that demanded the sacrifice of infants and small children - was placed in front of the Roman Colosseum to welcome visitors to an exhibition dedicated to an ancient rival of Rome, the city of Carthage. The colosseum is under the Vatican's control.

26:52   If Exodus 20:4 - do not make a graven image or likeness - was the 2nd commandment in Roman Catholic teachings, would there be fewer statues, pictures, shrines and other artifacts? And rejection of hideous statues such as the statue of Moloch?

26:53   Various businesses and Catholic ministries sell things such as bobbleheads of the Pope and deceased saints. What do you think Paul and Peter would say if they saw bobbleheads of them being sold? I wonder what Peter, Paul and Barnabas would say if they toured the 54 museums at the Vatican consisting of 1,400 rooms, chapels and galleries spread over 4.5 km and studied the 70,000+ pieces of art? Or what would Peter say if he knew people were spending time looking at what many Catholics and other Christians believe is his burial site in Rome?

26:54   In the latter stages of writing **CEASED?**, a 5.7 earthquake broke off the trumpet from a Mormon statue in Salt Lake City. A second 5.3 earthquake broke off the tip off a spire on a Catholic church in Croatia. A foreshadowing of God destroying idols?

It's about a Personal Relationship

Christianity is about having a personal relationship with God, both here on earth and continuing into heaven. God created us, not for a long-distance relationship, but a close and intimate relationship. To illustrate, consider person A who is married to B. Would B want A to speak to B directly, or to B's picture in the living room while B sits outside in the front yard watching the paint on the fence peel off? In some cases, such as when my wife Lori travels, I do look at her picture and I give thanks. (And no, I'm not thanking her for being away ... although ... I do have full control of the thermostat and fridge.) In our relationship with God, God is never away traveling. He is always here, as in right here. As per Chapter 6, when a person is born again and truly becomes a follower of Christ, Holy Spirit comes in [en] that person.

26:55   If we're truly born again and God is in us, is it more likely God:
   i. wants us to communicate directly with Him; or
   ii. wants us to look at a statue, idol or painting, and pray to that item or to another deceased saint who will speak to God on our behalf?

26:56   And if a person is not communicating with God - both speaking to and hearing from God through His word and other means - is there reason for that person:
   i. to change things so they have two-way communications with God; and/or
   ii. to be concerned they may not even be saved?

26: Ten Commandments, Images, Saints

Overall

26:57   Nowhere in the Bible are we told to create images, statues and shrines of any person, be it Father God, Jesus, Holy Spirit or any individuals in the Old or New Testament. Nowhere does the Bible tell us to pray to deceased persons or to bow down to statues or to pay ongoing homage towards them. All of those issues are tantamount to idolatry. God's Word tells us to seek the living God, not an image and likeness. We are to pray to God, not a person or object. Thus, if you're Roman Catholic, do you see why graven images, different Ten commandments and praying to deceased saints are major stumbling blocks preventing many non-Catholics from coming alongside a Roman Catholic and/or the Roman Catholic church?

Having said this, if Holy Spirit tells a Catholic and a Protestant to minister together, they need to obey. But they must both know they're hearing from God and not another voice. They need to avoid ministering together if the reason for doing so is pressure from one's family, one's church or other people, or enhancing one's personal profile or bank account.

Ultimate Authority

The issue of images and likeness brings us back to what is our ultimate authority - God and His Word, or the teachings and traditions of an organization. Catholic beliefs on graven images are based on Catholic teachings and traditions. They contradict God's Word, and as a result, agreement on this and many other issues is simply not feasible.

26:58   When we die or Jesus returns, we will each come face to face with God. Will God deal with us based on church teachings and traditions, or His Word?

CLOSING POINTS TO PONDER

Graven Images

26:59   No scripture in the New Testament says believers are to create images, statues, likenesses etc. of God or any person. Why would we make them and/or incorporate them into our lives today, especially when Almighty God is in [en] us after we're born again?

26:60   Peter, Paul and Barnabas all rejected any glory that people tried to give them. Wouldn't they scream and shout against the statues, images and artifacts of deceased saints created for the Crystal Cathedral? And to the creation and sale of bobbleheads by businesses and ministries? If not, why not. What has changed?

26:61   When God spoke to the people at Horeb, He didn't show His face because if He did, God knew they would make graven images and worship them. Isn't that a pretty clear message for us that we shouldn't have graven images either?

❏   *Leviticus 26:1 You shall **not make** for yourselves **idols**, **nor** shall you **set up** for yourselves an **image or a sacred pillar**, nor shall you **place a figured stone** in your land **to bow down** to it; **for I am** the **Lord your God**.*

CEASED?

- *Deuteronomy 4:10 Remember the day you stood before the Lord your God at Horeb ... may **learn to fear Me** all the days they live on the earth ... 12... you heard the sound of words, but **you saw no form - only a voice**. ... 15 ... since you did not see any form on the day the Lord spoke to you at Horeb from the midst of the fire, 16 **so that you do not act corruptly and make a graven image for yourselves in the form of any figure**, the **likeness of male or female**, 17 the likeness of **any animal** that is on the earth, the likeness of **any winged bird** that flies in the sky, 18 the likeness of **anything that creeps** on the ground, the likeness of **any fish** that is in the water below the earth. 19 And **beware not** to lift up your eyes to heaven and **see the sun** and the **moon** and the **stars**, all the host of heaven, and be drawn away and **worship them** and serve them ...*

26:63 And if there is any doubt, doesn't Deuteronomy 4:16 which says not to make *"the likeness of male or female"* eliminate all doubt?

Different Ten Commandments
26:64 God's Word is so rich and so complex. His Ten Commandments were a monumental gift to mankind. Each of us needs to make a choice on whether the Roman Catholic or Protestant Ten Commandments is the proper list, and why. What's your personal view?

Praying to Deceased Saints
26:65 God is alive. He is with and in believers, and for many, also upon them. God died for us out of His incredible love for mankind. His Great Exchange shows some, but by no means all, of the many blessings and gifts He makes available to mankind. God did so much for us because He wants relationship. If we don't go to Him directly, how much of a relationship can we build with God? How well can we know Him?

27

Has a New Temple Veil been Created?

INTRODUCTION

PRIOR to Jesus's death on the cross, the Jewish temple had a thick curtain - a veil - that separated the Holy of Holies from the rest of the temple. One priest went into the Holy of Holies once each year, and that was for the temporary atonement (forgiving, pardoning) of sins. When Jesus died on the cross, the veil was torn from top to bottom. There was no longer a barrier between God and people who wanted a relationship with Him. They could come directly to God 24/7. Chapter 27 addresses the issue of whether or not a new veil has been created between believers and God.

Organizational Perspectives

Figure 27:1 provides a simplistic organization chart of God's creations which consists of people, angels, demons and other creations such as the earth, moon, sun, birds, animals and plants.

Figure 27:1 God and His Creations

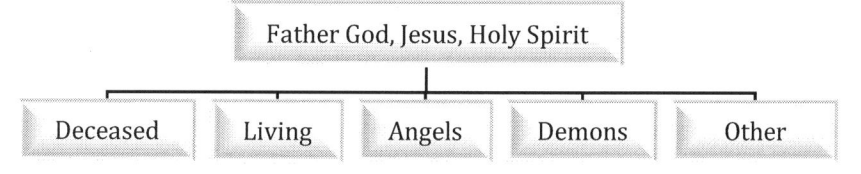

```
          Father God, Jesus, Holy Spirit
   ┌──────────┬──────────┬──────────┬──────────┐
 Deceased   Living    Angels    Demons     Other
```

If we look at the one component of people living today, we have a sub-organization chart as per Figure 27:2 with God at the top, under whom are 4 basic groups:
1. true born-again Christians;
2. individuals who think of themselves as Christians but who don't personally know the Jesus of the Bible;
3. individuals in false religions; and
4. individuals with other non-religious beliefs such as atheism.

CEASED?

Figure 27:2   God and People

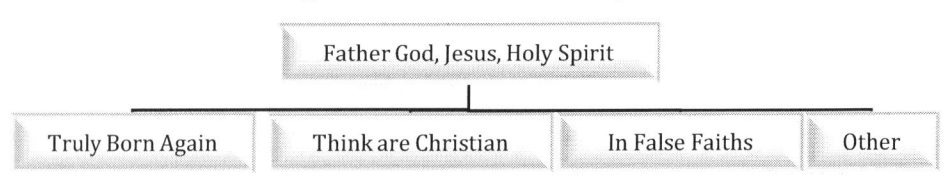

```
                    Father God, Jesus, Holy Spirit
      ┌──────────────────┬──────────────┬──────────────┐
 Truly Born Again   Think are Christian  In False Faiths   Other
```

I grieve for the latter 3 groups, all of whom will get a surprise when they come face to face with Jesus. The group who may get the biggest surprise, however, is group 2 - those who think they're Christian, but who aren't.
- ❏ *Matthew 7:23 And then I will declare to them, '**I never knew you; depart from Me**, you who practice lawlessness.'*

If we further limit the organization chart to truly born-again followers of Christ as per Figure 27:3, there are two levels in the entire chart. God and His children.

Figure 27:3   God and His Children

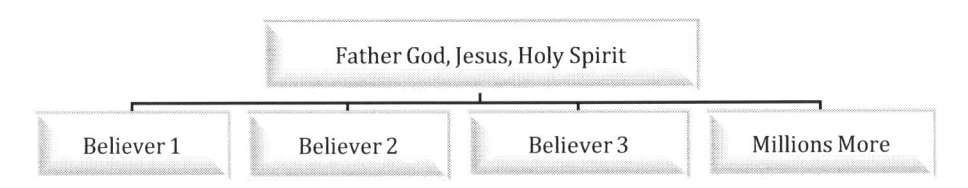

```
                    Father God, Jesus, Holy Spirit
      ┌──────────────┬──────────────┬──────────────┐
   Believer 1     Believer 2      Believer 3    Millions More
```

As mentioned in the Introduction, when Jesus died on the cross, the veil in the temple was torn from top to bottom. There was no longer a barrier between God and people who wanted a relationship with Him. We are blessed as sons and daughters of God, because we can enter God's presence directly at any time of day, on any and every day, and any number of times per day.
- ❏ *Matthew 27:51 And behold, **the veil of the temple was torn in two** from top to bottom; and the earth shook and the rocks were split.*
- ❏ *Psalm 100:4 **Enter His gates with thanksgiving** And **His courts with praise**. Give thanks to Him, bless His name.*
- ❏ *Hebrews 4:16 Therefore **let us draw near with confidence to the throne of grace**, so **that we may receive mercy and find grace** to help in time of need.*

Intercessory prayer
When other believers pray for me or mentor me, they are never between myself and God. They come alongside me. Holy Spirit is with [meta] and in [en] every believer as is Jesus. God is right here with us. Our walk with God is to be very intimate. Each of us is a child of God. God wants to speak to us directly, just like He did with Adam and Eve, and many other individuals in the Bible. We're all part of the Body of Christ with no person above or below another.

If you're Roman Catholic, and have read **CEASED?** so far, I congratulate you. Reading material that contradicts our beliefs is not easy.   Chapter 27 is no different.

27: A New Veil?

My question is:

27:1 Has the Catholic church effectively inserted itself between God and individual Catholics by means of the substantial roles and profile held by priests, Popes, Mary, and other deceased saints, and by various traditions and teachings? And in so doing, has the Catholic church created a new veil to replace the veil Jesus tore ~2,000 years ago?

Figure 27:4 A New Veil Between Roman Catholics and God?

```
                    Father God, Jesus, Holy Spirit
                                 |
              Pope          ─────┼─────          Mary
                                 |
             Priests        ─────┼─────     Deceased Saints
                                 |
           2 Baptisms       ─────┼─────     Other Sacraments
                                 |
           Traditions       ─────┼─────      Graven Images
                                 |
          Membership        ─────┼─────      Other Influences
                                 |
        ┌────────────┬───────────┴──────────┬─────────────┐
    Catholic 1   Catholic 2             Catholic 3    Millions of
                                                        others
```

Question 27:1 may seem far fetched, but if any person, activity, or thing comes between ourselves and Jesus, our personal relationship with Jesus is going to be hindered. Our relationship just won't be as close or personal. Let me briefly expand on each of the items listed in Figure 27:4.

1: Pope   Per Chapter 25 of **CEASED?**, the evidence supporting Peter as the rock upon whom Jesus will build the church is minimal. The evidence showing Jesus is the rock is extensive. Jesus is the head of the church here on earth. Followers are to look to Jesus, and to be led by Holy Spirit in all things including giving us revelations from God's Word. All believers have the keys of heaven. All believers can bind and loose. Titles such as 'His Holiness' attribute an elevated status or profile to the Pope, something Paul and Peter would have found unacceptable. Items such as special indulgences elevate the Pope's personal value to Catholics. And thus, when Jesus is replaced as the earthly head of the church by the Pope, aren't the Pope and the Roman Catholic church being inserted - to some extent - between believers and Jesus?

CEASED?

2: Mary

CEASED? provides extensive evidence showing Mary is viewed by the Roman Catholic church as if she is God. Mary is believed to be capable of simultaneously handling millions of prayers at the same time. She gives supernatural blessings of 7 graces and 15 promises of the rosary, but only to those Catholics who honor Mary, who are devoted to her, who day in and day out say the rosary, say 7 Hail Mary's, and who meditate on Mary's sorrows. Only God can deliver such blessings. Nothing in the Bible says Mary has been authority or the ability to do such things. As a born-again believer living on earth after the cross, she was given the same child of God authority as was given to other believers. No more and no less. When we're born again, Holy Spirit is in [en] us to guide and comfort us, not Mary. We're to seek God first; Catholics are taught to go to Mary first. Graven images such as statues of Mary are widespread in violation of God's commandments. Given all this, and more, isn't Mary and/or the Catholic church being inserted - to some extent - between believers and Jesus?

If you still believe Mary does not have God-like abilities, consider the following *'Prayer for Protection in Time of Pandemic'* provided by the Supreme Chaplain, Archbishop William Lori, Knights of Columbus Supreme Council. Knights of Columbus is a global, fraternal organization of Catholic men. This prayer was taken from a YouTube video (https://youtu.be/vD5Z1D1zwVQ) on April 9, 2020 in the midst of the COVID-19 pandemic. Formatting is mine.

> *"Oh **Mary, you** always brighten our path as a sign of salvation and of hope. We **entrust ourselves to you**, Health of the Sick. Who, at the Cross, took part in Jesus' pain while remaining steadfast in faith. O loving Mother, **you know what we need**, and we are confident you will provide for us as at Cana in Galilee. Intercede for us with your Son Jesus, the Divine Physician, for those who have fallen ill, for those who are vulnerable, and for those who have died. Intercede also for those charged with protecting the health and safety of others and for those who are tending to the sick and seeking a cure.*
>
> ***Help us, O Mother of Divine Love, to conform to the will** of the Father and to do as we are told by Jesus, who took upon himself our sufferings and carried our sorrows, so as to lead us, through the Cross, to the glory of the Resurrection. Amen. **Under thy protection we seek refuge**, O Holy Mother of God. In our needs, despise not our petitions but **deliver us always from all dangers**, O **glorious** and blessed Virgin. Amen.*

Only God can help a person conform to the will of the Father. Only God can protect and deliver Catholics from all dangers. If Mary is believed capable of doing such things, she is either God, or has unique authority far beyond that given to any other person or angel. Neither of those possibilities are supported by the Bible.

27: A New Veil?

3: Priests — On resurrection Sunday evening, Jesus told the apostles + the 2 disciples who Jesus met on the road to Emmaus + *'those who were with them'*, to forgive those who sinned against them. No priest or any other human can forgive us of our sins committed against a 3rd party, or forgive the sins of a 3rd party who sinned against us. The person sinned against must do the forgiving. Ananias, a non-apostle, baptized Paul in water. Philip, a non-apostle, baptized the eunuch in water. All believers are to make disciples and to baptize them in water, not just priests. All believers are encouraged to be Baptized in the Holy Spirit, a baptism that Jesus gives and not a priest or Bishop. All believers can take communion on their own if they desire, to remember what Jesus did. A priest is not required. When teachings state that priests are the only ones who can baptize a person in water, only priests can forgive mortal sins, only Bishops or their delegates can confirm a person so they can be Baptized in the Holy Spirit, only priests can lead communion, aren't the priests and the Roman Catholic church again being inserted - to some extent - between believers and Jesus?

When a person is on their deathbed and a priest or lay Eucharist minister issues last rites, communion is given. However, given any believer can lead communion, aren't priests, these lay eucharist ministers and the Catholic church again being inserted - to some extent - between believers and Jesus?

When leaders have titles stating greater holiness or superiority, don't such titles elevate leaders and again insert the leaders plus the Catholic church - to some extent - between lay Catholics and God?

4: Deceased Saints — Deceased saints were at one time part of the Body of Christ living on earth. They are now in heaven with Jesus and other saints. There is no scriptural basis to believe living Christians can or should try to speak with deceased saints. Deceased saints are no more righteous than living saints. Every saint is redeemed and cleansed by the death of Jesus, His shed blood and His resurrection. When believers pray to deceased saints to intervene for them, aren't these living saints trusting the deceased saints' relationships with Jesus more than their own personal relationship with Jesus? And thus, aren't these deceased saints and the Catholic church again being inserted - to some extent - between believers and Jesus?

The Bible is clear that all believers are saints. The only requirement to be a saint is to be born-again. The Roman Catholic church says otherwise. When it says it can determine who is and who isn't a saint, isn't the Roman Catholic church again inserting itself - to some extent - between believers and Jesus?

CEASED?

5: Two Baptisms	Water baptism is not required to be born again. Don't Roman Catholic teachings that water baptism is required to be born again, and that water baptism must be done by a priest, again insert priests and the Roman Catholic church - to some extent - between believers and Jesus?

Baptism of the Holy Spirit is separate from water baptism and isn't required to be born again. Don't Roman Catholic teachings that state one cannot be Baptized in the Holy Spirit (confirmed) unless one has been properly water baptized by a priest (not true), and that a Bishop or delegate gives this Baptism in the Holy Spirit (when Jesus is the one who does it) using chrism (which isn't biblical), again insert the Roman Catholic church - to some extent - between believers and Jesus?

Don't comments that water baptism *'is the means by which its recipients are incorporated into the church'* and that Baptism of the Holy Spirit/Confirmation *'enriches the baptized with the Holy Spirit, binding them more perfectly to the Church'* collectively indicate these two baptisms as conducted by priests and Bishops serve to connect the believer first and foremost to the Roman Catholic church? And thus, don't these comments confirm that these baptisms again insert the Roman Catholic church and church leadership - to some extent - between believers and Jesus? |
6: Other Sacraments	A key part of Catholic teachings involves 7 Sacraments, two of which are water baptism and Confirmation (Baptism of the Holy Spirit). Two others, Holy Orders and Penance, result in Catholics confessing mortal sins to priests who are authorized to forgive them. However, the scriptures used to support this forgiveness of mortal sins by Catholic priests alone, actually refer to all believers wherein all of us believers are to forgive anyone who sins against us - the same message that was given in the Lord's Prayer. A 5th sacrament, communion, is only to be led by Roman Catholic priests, which isn't what God intended. Any believer can take communion to remember who Christ is, and what Jesus did on the cross. Don't these sacraments once again insert the Roman Catholic church and its priests - to some extent - between believers and Jesus?
7: Traditions	Catholic teachings are partially based on the writings of early church fathers. They are also partly based on decisions of various magisteriums over the centuries that have led to new as well as revised traditions. Don't these various Catholicized traditions again insert the Roman Catholic church and its priests - to some extent - between believers and Jesus?
8: Graven Images	The Bible is clear we're not to make graven images. God never once commanded statues or shrines or any facsimiles to be made of any

27: A New Veil?

human being. When Catholics kneel in front of such statues, kiss the feet or hands of such items, pray to or gaze upon such items, haven't these graven images and the Catholic church that created them been inserted - to some extent - between believers and Jesus?

9: Member of Roman Catholic Church

When a person is born again, Holy Spirit comes in [en] the person. Holy Spirit automatically baptizes the individual into the Body of Christ, the church of God. Roman Catholic teachings are clear that a person must be a member of the Roman Catholic church to be saved, and to leave the Catholic church is the equivalent of committing a mortal sin. To get forgiveness for that mortal sin, one has to confess the sin to a Catholic priest. But given one has left the Catholic church, how likely is that? Doesn't that hook - the message of leaving the Roman Catholic church means one is going to hell - inherently instill a fear that, if you leave, you will never get to heaven? Isn't that messaging similar to what cults do in terms of reinforcing allegiance to their organization? And don't these messages once again insert the Roman Catholic church - to some extent - between the believer and Jesus?

10: Other Influences

Consider God's Word which is so rich, alive and active. It is amazing. It is truth. The Bible is God's love letter to mankind. Consider three items:
  i. In ~2008, Lori spent a weekend at a retreat managed by a Catholic nun. She was well educated, and clearly loved Jesus. God's presence was all over her. She told Lori that she was not allowed to have her own Bible until 1979.
  ii. The Council of Toulouse in 1229 A.D, stated: *"We prohibit laymen possessing copies of the Old and New Testament ... We forbid them most severely to have them in the popular vernacular."*
  iii. In the 16th century, the Council of Trent placed the Bible on its list of prohibited books. People could not read the Bible without a license from a bishop. The Council warned: *"If any one shall dare to read or keep in his possession that book, without such a license, he shall not receive absolution (from the punishment of sins) till he has given it up to his ordinary (bishop)."*

When the Catholic church inhibited access to God's Word in the past, didn't that create a dependence on the Catholic church? Didn't these actions serve to insert the Catholic church between the believer and Jesus? Don't masses in Latin - which still go on to some extent today, but which was the norm for all masses for ~400 years from ~1550 until the mid 1960's - also serve to insert the Roman Catholic church between the lay Catholic in the pew and Jesus who is the Word? If you say no, let me ask. What percentage of people in the pews knew what was being said? What percentage were totally dependent on the church for what to believe?

CEASED?

In addition to the 10 items mentioned in Figure 27:4, the Holy Spirit's indwelling (*the in [en] experience when we're born again*), power (*the upon [epi] when we're Baptized in the Holy Spirit*), and His 9 gifts also warrant consideration.

11: Holy Spirit Indwelling, Power, and 9 Gifts
Per Chapter 6 of **CEASED?**, Holy Spirit comes in us when we're born again. Jesus is also in us. Almighty God is in us. God had a personal, intimate relationship with Adam and Eve where He talked to them, and they talked to Him. God wants an intimate relationship with each one of us, a relationship involving two-way, one-on-one communications with no one in between. The Catholic church talks and teaches about Holy Spirit in many ways, but the notion of having a direct, intimate relationship with God involving ongoing two-way communication throughout each day is not central to Catholic teachings. The importance of this indwelling of God in a person is not a core teaching. Instead of focusing our intimacy on God, a great deal of such intimacy is reserved for Mary.

Jesus baptizes believers in the Holy Spirit. Holy Spirit then gives one or more of the 9 Holy Spirit gifts as He chooses. The gifts are often for the benefit of others, but they can also be for our own benefit. Whether we're the recipient or the delivery vehicle, these gifts will impact us personally. Operating in these gifts results in a closer intimacy between God and believers, not only because of the results we witness, but because they involve a direct connection between God and the person operating in the gift. Nobody is in between. It is always beneficial, exciting and fun to be used by God, and to see God's power in action in different ways. And when we see brothers and sisters being used through these gifts to heal or give a word of knowledge to another person, it's so cool, and reminds us of how powerful and loving our God truly is. These gifts draw a person closer to God. A church can facilitate, and equip the saints in the use of these gifts, but the church is not to be the prime beneficiary of these gifts.

As seen in **CEASED?**, the Baptism of the Holy Spirit and the 9 Holy Spirit gifts have never stopped since Pentecost, almost 2,000 years ago. John and Peter traveled to Samaria to ensure the new believers received these blessings. Paul's first priority for the 12 disciples at Ephesus was to ensure they were Baptized in the Holy Spirit. Paul encouraged the pursuit of the Holy Spirit gifts, especially prophecy but also tongues. And yet, today, the vast majority of Roman Catholics are not taught properly on the Baptism of the Holy Spirit, nor are they taught or encouraged to pursue the 9 Holy Spirit gifts.

Apart from an outpouring of the Holy Spirit in the 1960's which led to the birth of the Charismatic movement within the Roman Catholic church, the Holy Spirit gifts largely lay dormant within the Catholic

27: A New Veil?

church for ~ 17 to 20 centuries depending on one's view as to when the Catholic church started. Whenever it started, didn't this sidelining of the 9 Holy Spirit gifts from the main Catholic church for many centuries prevent the flow of valuable blessings from God associated with these gifts, blessings that create a closeness between believers and God with no one in between? As a result, doesn't this sidelining of the 9 Holy Spirit gifts for the vast majority of Roman Catholics today again serve to insert the Roman Catholic church and its priests - to some extent - between believers and Jesus?

27:2 When we consider all the items above, hasn't the Catholic church through its leaders and priests combined with the positioning of Mary at the center of the Catholic faith, effectively interjected itself between believers and God to an extremely large extent? And pushed Jesus to the background behind Mary and the church? And thus, hasn't the Roman Catholic church effectively created a new veil separating believers from God, where ordinary Catholics aren't to go directly to God, but to someone else?

Figure 27:5 includes Figure 27:4 as well as the indwelling of Holy Spirit, the Baptism of the Holy Spirit and the 9 Holy Spirit gifts which are sitting idle on the sidelines for hundreds of millions of Roman Catholics. Isn't it unfortunate to see the associated teachings and gifts available, but effectively unutilized?

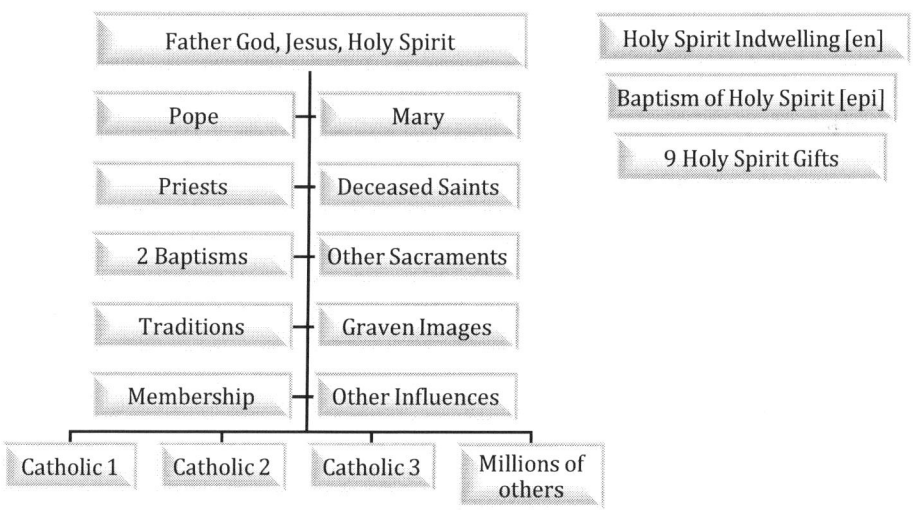

Figure 27:5 A New Veil Between Roman Catholics and God?

Left Branch	Right Branch
Father God, Jesus, Holy Spirit	
Pope	Mary
Priests	Deceased Saints
2 Baptisms	Other Sacraments
Traditions	Graven Images
Membership	Other Influences

Sidelined:
- Holy Spirit Indwelling [en]
- Baptism of Holy Spirit [epi]
- 9 Holy Spirit Gifts

Catholic 1 | Catholic 2 | Catholic 3 | Millions of others

Heaven on Earth

27:3 If you're Catholic, do the inserted 10 items help you walk in nearness to Jesus in a somewhat similar way you see yourself walking with Jesus in heaven? Or is your plan to walk closest with Mary, pope, priests and the Catholic church today, and then switch to Jesus after you get to heaven?

CEASED?

Still Not Sure?
27:4   If you still don't believe the Roman Catholic church has effectively inserted itself between people and God, consider this development during the COVID-19 crisis. In a mass that was live-streamed on March 20, 2020, Pope Francis taught that Catholics who can't make a personal confession to a priest can confess their sins directly to God. They should tell God the truth and ask for forgiveness with all their heart.
   i. If Catholics didn't already know they could go to God directly, and had not been instructed to do so as a normal part of their relationship with God, doesn't this confirm that the veil which was torn and removed by Jesus, has been replaced?
   ii. If Catholics don't believe they can go to God directly at any time to deal with sin issues, but need to come to the church, isn't that yet another major indicator the Catholic church has inserted itself between the individual Catholic and God?
27:5   Pope Francis also said once the pandemic recedes, Catholics need to go to confession.
   i. Isn't Pope Francis effectively saying going directly to God for confession is second best, and that it isn't enough?
   ii. Don't Pope Francis's statements show that he believes Jesus's one-time sacrifice on the cross was not enough? That more needs to be done, and *'the more to be done'* can only be done through the priests of the Roman Catholic church?

CLOSING POINTS TO PONDER

God is a jealous God. He doesn't want anyone or anything to come ahead of Him.
- *Exodus 20:5 You shall not worship them nor serve them; for I, the Lord your God, am a jealous (impassioned) God [**demanding what is rightfully and uniquely mine**] … (AMP)*

Picture Mom and Dad on the front deck of their home. They have two groups of children.

Group 1:
The parents are actively involved in the lives of this group of children. The parents talk with each child almost every day, and usually many times a day. Sometimes the parents talk a lot, and sometimes they listen a lot. Sometimes they say virtually nothing. The parents have an incredible Family Book that provides not only information on family history, but tremendous information on how their children can live more meaningful lives today, and what to expect when they die. Their children study this book, and love to share new revelations they find. These children are not perfect by any means, but their hearts continue to improve slowly but surely. Children typically help each other out. The children often disagree, and need some guidance and help to get their relationships restored. Sacrificing their time and other parts of their lives for the benefit of others is the norm for most of the children. However, no one is more important than their parents. When in doubt,

27: A New Veil?

children know to go to their parents first. And if the children mess up, they need to come clean with their parents, and seek forgiveness from whomever they wronged. In turn, they need to forgive those who wronged them.

The parents aren't pushovers. They don't tolerate certain things, and the boundaries between right and wrong are very clear. Their love for their children is unfathomable. And they have many treasures and blessings for their children. Some are for today, but their biggest inheritances are down the road at a time that is unknown to the children.

The children love to introduce their parents to their friends and neighbors. The children are excited to join their friends and neighbors in talking and spending time with their parents. The children are not jealous of any blessings given to their friends and neighbors by their parents. In fact, they are thankful for these blessings, and take special joy when they see their friends and neighbors spending time with their parents in a group, or one-on-one.

Group 2:

The parents have another group of children who have chosen a more distant relationship. These children do many good things for others, and know the importance of apologizing, seeking forgiveness and forgiving others. This second group of children also genuinely cares for each other, and for their friends and neighbors. They do a lot of good in their community, and in the world.

The parents watch this second group of children come and go. They hear their children talking, crying in tough times and laughing in great times, anguishing over difficult decisions, struggling with health issues, grieving over the loss of loved ones, and sometimes fighting each other. But their children seldom come to them directly for help. Instead, they go to other children, friends and neighbors whose love, wisdom and abilities are far less. Many times, comments to their parents are given indirectly through other children. When the children do speak directly to their parents, they do so in one-way conversations using words that aren't personal, but are taken from a list of standard messages. Often, the very same words are spoken day after day, after day, after day. Many gather together one day of the week out of respect for their parents, and a sense of duty.

The parents see the neighbors interact with their children - sometimes in good ways and sometimes in not so good ways. An influential male child tells the other children not to introduce their friends and neighbors to their parents.

Most children don't seek a two-way relationship with their parents, yet they expect their parents to deliver major blessings. One of the children has been elevated to where most children, friends and neighbors go to her and not the parents, because they believe she can do virtually everything her parents can do, but no other child can do. It's quite unfortunate, because she can't. Some children are given titles inferring they are better or somehow superior than other children, and even their friends and neighbors. They 'know best' and tell the remaining children what to believe. These 'leaders' have created a customized Family Book with various changes that suit the leaders' beliefs and preferences. These leaders have changed some family traditions and instituted several new traditions they feel are appropriate. Misalignment with their parents' views is often tolerated, and

CEASED?

sometimes encouraged. The parents sit and watch their children live their lives from a distance. Sadly, their children don't even know their parents on a one to one basis.

27:6 Which children will most likely receive the major blessings and inheritances from the parents?

27:7 I don't mean to be funny or sarcastic with the above story, but doesn't the group 2 scenario resemble the type of relationship that the Catholic church and some Protestant denominations have fostered by replacing a personal, 2-way relationship with God (group 1) with religious activities, and by inserting the church and leaders between laypeople and God (group 2)? Besides the Catholic church, how many Protestant churches claim they are the one true church, and have effectively inserted a veil with their church and leaders between laypeople and God? And if so, is there reason for many Catholics and Protestants to be concerned about Matthew 7:23?

❑ *Matthew 7:23 And then I will declare to them, 'I never knew you; depart from Me, you who practice lawlessness.'?*

28

Protestants & Roman Catholics Together?

INTRODUCTION

PREVIOUS chapters addressed some issues that can make it a challenge for both non-Catholics and Roman Catholics to evangelize and worship alongside each other. Chapter 28 concludes this review by addressing a few topics including:
1. should Catholics worship and evangelize alongside Protestants (page 411);
2. should Protestants worship and evangelize alongside Catholics (page 413);
3. should Protestants *'come home'* to the Roman Catholic church (page 419); and
4. God's warning to teachers (page 419).

As you go through Chapter 28, please know my heart is to reveal what God's Word says. I have tried to be objective and fair. If I made mistakes or failed in my goals, I apologize. What matters first and foremost is God's Word and His truths, not my opinions or views, or those of any other person or organization.

SHOULD CATHOLICS WORSHIP AND EVANGELIZE ALONGSIDE PROTESTANTS?

Discussions around the 11 items listed in Figure 27:5, in my view, show the Roman Catholic church has effectively inserted itself between Catholics and God. As a result of all these issues, and more that have not been addressed in **CEASED?**, I don't believe the major decision facing Catholics is whether or not to worship and evangelize alongside Protestants. If you're Catholic, I see the more fundamental decisions are the following:
- ❖ Is the Roman Catholic church teaching you the truth about God and His Word?
- ❖ Has the Roman Catholic church created a new veil between yourself and God?
- ❖ Is the Catholic church enhancing your personal relationship with Jesus and ensuring Jesus is 1st in your life, or is Mary and the church 1st and 2nd, with God in 3rd spot? And if God isn't 1st, aren't major changes necessary - now?
- ❑ *Colossians 1:18 He is also head of the body, the church; and He is the beginning, the firstborn from the dead, so that He Himself will come to have first place in everything.*

CEASED?

A big part of your decision will boil down to what is your authority - God's Word or Roman Catholic teachings and traditions, only part of which are based on God's Word.

Fear or Peace

A frequent comment from Roman Catholics is they aren't sure if they're saved or not. They're fearful on this issue. Isn't that surprising given the most frequent command in God's Word is that we're not to fear. Instead, when we're born again, we should experience God's peace.

- ❑ *Philippians 4:6 **Be anxious for nothing**, but in everything by prayer and supplication with thanksgiving **let your requests be made known to God**. 7 And **the peace of God**, which surpasses all comprehension, will guard your hearts and your minds in Christ Jesus.*
- ❑ *Romans 8:15 For you have not received a spirit of slavery leading to fear again, but you have received a spirit of adoption as sons by which we cry out, "Abba! Father!"*
- ❑ *2 Timothy 1:7 **for God gave us a spirit not of fear** but of power and love and self-control. (ESV)*

28:1 If you're Catholic, and have fears, would peace for you come from knowing:
    i. Jesus paid the penalty for **ALL** your sins through His one-time death on the cross and His associated shed blood and resurrection;
    ii. when born again, Holy Spirit comes in you, you're adopted as a child of God, you become a joint-heir, and you're seated in heavenly places;
    iii. when born again, you enter into a Great Exchange that makes you right with God and allows you to be in His presence 24/7 with Holy Spirit leading the way;
    iv. fear is from the enemy and when you're born again - as per Jimmy Evans's prayer on page 310 - you have authority over the spirit of fear and can deal with it.

28:2 Is fear there because you believe you should or need to be doing one or more things repeatedly to make you right with God? Things that are not in the Bible, but which were created by the Roman Catholic church such as:
    i. daily seeking Mary and praying the rosary; and
    ii. 15 promises of the rosary and 7 graces associated with Mary's sorrows; and
    iii. weekly going to mass and taking communion, and regularly confessing sins to priests.

28:3 And even if you do all that you think is needed, is there still fear your efforts won't be enough, and all you can hope for is that you might eventually get out of purgatory? But even then, that still might not be enough?

The Bible is clear that Jesus has dealt with the penalty for your all sins on the cross. I encourage you to study the New Testament yourself and try to find scriptural evidence that shows you are to pray to Mary, you are to recite the rosary, you are to expect that Mary can and will deliver on the 7 graces and the 15 promises of the rosary, and that you may/will go to purgatory upon your death but might/should/will get out of there eventually. Seek Biblical evidence that clearly backs Catholic teachings and counteracts the Biblical evidence that **CEASED?** provides concerning water baptism, confirmation and confessing to priests. I'm not saying I'm 100% right on all matters of faith I addressed herein. I may not be right, which is why you need to check out for yourself whether or not what I say is true, or is not true. My plea is for you to study the Bible for yourself. After all, it is your eternal destiny at stake. And as you study God's Word, please remember that it was Jesus who died for you, not Mary or a pope, priest or the Roman Catholic church.

SHOULD PROTESTANTS
WORSHIP AND EVANGELIZE ALONGSIDE CATHOLICS?

It should be clear I don't believe Protestants and Roman Catholics should come alongside each other. If you're Protestant and still inclined to do so, let me ask.

28:4 If someone you deeply care about - spouse, parent, child, sibling - is starting to seek after Jesus, would you want them going to a Roman Catholic seminary, or being taught and mentored by someone devoted to Roman Catholic teachings?

28:5 Would you share the stage and support a Catholic priest or apologist who was speaking on the merits of the Roman Catholic faith and would absolutely agrees on all the blessings of Mary, about the need for priests to forgive mortal sins, about the blessing of purgatory, about praying to deceased saints and creating statues of them? Would you want to join in communion led by a priest who calls down Jesus to be sacrificed one more time?

28:6 If you have any qualms at all about seeing a loved one either going to Roman Catholic seminary or becoming a Roman Catholic, then how can you in any way support the Roman Catholic church given the multitude of false teachings and emphasis on other individuals and things besides Father God, Jesus and Holy Spirit?

Consider a December 20, 2019 meeting with students at Rome's Pilo Albertelli classical secondary school. Pope Francis stated people of all faiths are children of God. God's Word, however, tells us that no person is a child of God until they are born again. Only then are we adopted into God's family.
- ❏ *John 1:12 But as many as received Him, to them **He gave the right to become children of God**, even to those who believe in His name,*
- ❏ *Ephesians 1:5 He predestined us to adoption as sons **through Jesus Christ to Himself**, according to the kind intention of His will,*

Pope Francis also said we should respect people of other faiths and not try to convert them to Christianity using words. In contrast, the Bible is clear that Jesus is the only way, and that we are to witness, to spread the Good News about Him, and to preach - to share the gospel in words.
- ❏ *John 14:6 Jesus said to him, "**I am the way**, and **the truth**, and **the life**; **no one** comes to the Father **but through Me**.*

CEASED?

- *Mark 16:15 And He said to them, "**Go into all the world and preach the gospel to all creation**,*
- *Romans 15:20 And **thus I aspired to preach the gospel**, not where Christ was already named, so that I would not build on another man's foundation; 21 but as it is written, "**They who had no news of Him shall see, And they who have not heard shall understand**."*

28:7 9 Holy Spirit gifts are key for sharing the gospel in words and power. Is it a coincidence:
    i. Pope Francis encourages Roman Catholics not to share the gospel; and
    ii. The mainline Roman Catholic church neither encourages the pursuit of the 9 Holy Spirit gifts, nor equips the vast majority of Catholics on how to use these gifts?

On February 4, 2019, Pope Francis as a representative of Roman Catholics and Grand Imam Ahmed Al-Tayebb of Al-Azhar University representing Muslims issued a joint declaration:

"in the name of God who has created all human beings equal in rights, duties and dignity."

In 1965, the Second Vatican Council approved Nostra Aetate, a declaration on relations with non-Christian religions. Part of it reads:

"The church also regards with esteem the Muslims. They adore the one God, living and subsisting in himself, merciful and all-powerful, the Creator of heaven and earth," although *"they do not acknowledge Jesus as God and regard him as only a prophet."*

28:8 Various articles written by Catholics talk of why we should understand and be open to the idea that Muslims and Christians worship the same God. The argument is based on the premise Christians and Muslims both worship the God of Abraham, Isaac and Jacob. However, how can it be so? Jesus is God. Islam teaches Jesus is a prophet. Our God is Father God, Jesus and Holy Spirit. Muslims worship Allah who is not the Father, Jesus and Holy Spirit. Whatever justification and rationale one wants to use, the truth is Christianity and Islam do not worship the same God. And aren't any efforts that encourage, support, rationalize or promote that view not only wrong, but dangerous? Doesn't supporting that teaching in any way, shape or form:
    i. contradict the truths of the Bible;
    ii. reinforce Pope Francis's comments that Christians don't need to share the gospel in words;
    iii. contribute to Muslims believing they know the truth, when they don't;
    iv. support the view that all will be saved - universal salvation - which is false;
    v. support the view there are many ways to heaven - which is false;
    vi. support the view that Jesus isn't the only way - which is false; and
    vii. make one wonder as to the real agenda behind these statements and

28: Protestants and Catholics Together?

actions of Pope Francis and previous popes before him?

28:9 Contrary to what Pope Francis says, God's Word tells us we are to preach the gospel and that Jesus - Jesus - is the only Way. And contrary to what Pope Francis says, God's Word is clear that the only people who are *'children of God'* are those who are born-again followers of Jesus.
   i. If you're Roman Catholic, whose instructions are you going to follow - God's Word or the Roman Catholic church's teachings?
   ii. If you say Roman Catholic teachings, what are you going to say to Jesus when you meet Him?

One last story. I've mentored a few young adults about the importance of digging for the truth when considering business deals and investments. In business deals, there are many wonderful people. There are also some unscrupulous people - people with kind or flattering words, but deceitful, self-serving hearts. Their sales pitch may sound great, but when one gets into the nitty-gritty details, the story often changes. In cases of fraud or corruption, the deception of the deal is usually surrounded by a great deal of truth. To illustrate my point, I often offer an unopened bottle of water, pop or juice. and ask if they would like it. The person typically says yes. When I tell them that I might have injected 10 drops of arsenic into the bottle, their desire for the drink changes.

28:10 Roman Catholics have done many good things. Fighting against abortion, feeding the poor, and emphasizing family are all so important. However, when teachings of salvation are in error, when a different Godhead is taught and when Jesus's one-time sacrifice on the cross is diluted, aren't these drops of arsenic to one's walk with Jesus?

For a multitude of reasons, I can't recommend Protestants evangelizing and worshipping alongside those who are Catholics or who support the Roman Catholic church and its teachings. I can't recommend another person attend or join the Roman Catholic church. And I am deeply concerned when I see Protestants supporting the Catholic church and/or signing agreements with the Roman Catholic church. My views are not held because I don't like Catholics. It's because there are such a multitude of significant issues that contradict or conflict with God's Word. And for me personally, the role Mary plays and the expectations that Mary can deliver things that only God can deliver, effectively puts Mary in a position of being God. And I can't recommend anybody get involved, or stay involved, with any group or organization that has a false God.

If you're Catholic, these comments may seem awfully offensive. But I would sooner you be mad at me now because I am speaking up, as opposed to being mad at me later when you realize you were led astray. It's vital to ignore the rhetoric that *"Mary is not God"*, and look at the evidence - the prayers of Pope Francis and others, the 7 graces, the rosary, the 15 promises of the rosary, the titles, the statues, the shrines, the accolades - and then compare all that to what the New Testament actually says about Mary. Nothing of note in the New Testament supports the supernatural, elevated role Mary currently holds within the Roman Catholic church.

CEASED?

Nothing. If this evidence doesn't alarm you, let me remind you that after resurrection Sunday, there is only one verse that mentions Mary. One. Mary's entire involvement role after Resurrection Sunday was that of a person in prayer, one of ~120 other believers gathered in prayer. After that, nothing more is specifically mentioned about Mary. Nothing.

- ❑ Acts 1:14 These all with one mind were continually devoting themselves to prayer, along with the women, and Mary the mother of Jesus, and with His brothers.

<u>Article by Nick Benson</u>
An article which was written by Nick Benson, dated April 23, 2020 and published during the COVID-19 pandemic, is reproduced below. The article was copied from a Catholic website at the link: https://www.thecatholicuniverse.com/bishops-of-us-and-canada-will-consecrate-their-nations-to-mary-on-1st-may/

Highlighting and formatting is mine. The word consecrate means to dedicate.

BISHOPS OF US AND CANADA WILL CONSECRATE THEIR NATIONS TO MARY ON 1ST MAY

*Archbishop Jose H. Gomez of Los Angeles, president of the US Conference of Catholic Bishops, has announced the US bishops will join the Canadian Conference of Catholic Bishops on 1st May in **<u>consecrating the two nations to the care of the Blessed Mother</u>** under the title '**<u>Mary, Mother of the Church</u>**'.*
*'This will give the Church the occasion to pray **<u>for Our Lady's continued protection</u>** of the vulnerable, **<u>healing of the unwell</u>** and **<u>wisdom for those who work to cure</u>** this terrible virus,' said Archbishop Gomez in a letter to the US bishops. **<u>Each year, the Church seeks the special intercession of the Mother of God</u>** during the month of May.*

*'This year, **<u>we seek the assistance of Our Lady</u>** all the more earnestly as we face together the effects of the global pandemic,' he said.*

This consecration reaffirms the bishops' previous consecrations of the United States to Mary. In 1792, the first bishop of the United States, Bishop John Carroll, consecrated the nation to Mary under the title Immaculate Conception, and in 1846, the bishops unanimously chose Mary under that title as the patroness of the nation.

In 1959, Cardinal Patrick O'Boyle of Washington again consecrated the United States to the Immaculate Heart of Mary. This was the year when construction of the National Shrine of the Immaculate Conception in Washington was completed. The national shrine was elevated to minor basilica status by St John Paul ll on 12th Octtober 1990. This was renewed by the US bishops on 11th November 2006

Archbishop Gomez will lead the prayer of reconsecration on 1st May at 3pm EDT (8pm UK time) and has invited the bishops to join in from their respective dioceses

28: Protestants and Catholics Together?

and asked them to extend the invitation to the faithful in their dioceses for their participation.

28:11 The Roman Catholic church believes Mary is able to care for the nations of Canada and the United States, protect the vulnerable, heal the sick and give wisdom to those seeking a cure for COVID-19. Every year, bishops seek assistance from Mary. None of those beliefs are supported in the New Testament. None. When Mary was still living on earth, she was not credited with doing one miracle involving the 9 Holy Spirit gifts including healing or any of the speaking gifts. Only Almighty God cares for nations. Only Almighty God protects, heals and gives supernatural wisdom that is implied or stated in this consecration of two nations. Again, I ask: How is it possible that Roman Catholics think Mary isn't God given the God-like expectations on her?

- *Acts 4:12 And there is salvation in no one else; for **there is no other name under heaven** that has been given among men by which we must be saved."*
- *Philippians 2:9 For this reason also, God highly exalted Him, **and bestowed on Him the name which is above every name**, 10 so that at the name of Jesus every knee will bow, of those who are in heaven and on earth and under the earth, 11 and that every tongue will confess that Jesus Christ is Lord, to the glory of God the Father.*
- *John 14:13 Whatever you ask **in My name**, that will I do, so that the Father may be glorified in the Son.*

28:12 Aren't there only two options each Catholic has to choose from in regards to Mary?
  i. **Acceptance and endorsement that Mary is God**: Mary can do all the things mentioned in **CEASED?** including delivering on the 15 promises of the rosary. And the 7 graces. Mary is God, and warrants all titles, homage and attention to her as the Roman Catholic church teaches. Or;
  ii. **Mother of Earthly Jesus only**: Mary is to be appreciated for giving birth and caring for Jesus during parts of His earthly life. However, Mary is not God, and she is one of many saints currently in heaven enjoying her time with God. Mary doesn't have the ability to meet the many supernatural expectations that Catholics and the Roman Catholic church have of her. The titles and accolades given to Mary today do not honor her, but in fact dishonor her, because they are extreme exaggerations of who Mary was back then, and is today. All such unwarranted titles are to be rejected, and all statues and shrines of her need to be destroyed.
  iii. What's your decision, and why?

28:13 In relation to these Bishops who consecrated the USA and Canada to Mary:
  i. Why did these Bishops go to Mary, and not to Jesus, to consecrate Canada and the United States and seek His help to care, protect, heal

CEASED?

      and give wisdom? After all, isn't Jesus God, and weren't all things created through Jesus?
- ii. Is Catholic trust in the Name of Jesus, or in the name of Mary?
- iii. If these Bishops are children of God and in leadership roles, they are to be led by Holy Spirit, to seek the Kingdom of God first, and to abide in Jesus. Do these consecrations line up with any of those 3 characteristics of a Christian?

- ❏ *Romans 8:14 For all who are being led by the Spirit of God, these are sons of God.*
- ❏ *Matthew 6:33 But seek first His kingdom and His righteousness, and all these things will be added to you.*
- ❏ *John 15:5 I am the vine, you are the branches; he who abides in Me and I in him, he bears much fruit, for apart from Me you can do nothing.*
- ❏ *John 15:6 If anyone does not abide in Me, he is thrown away as a branch and dries up; and they gather them, and cast them into the fire and they are burned.*

28:14   Would it be surprising if many believers wonder if these Bishops are being led by a spirit other than the Holy Spirit? Or if they are abiding in someone other than Jesus? And if they are not abiding in Jesus, how much good fruit will result from such a consecration?

I ask the above questions on Mary, the Bishops, Peter/Popes, Catholic traditions, sacraments, forgiveness of sins by priests, communion, graven images, 10 Commandments etc. with a heavy heart. I'm raising issues that conflict with long-held views that run deep in millions of hearts. I'm not dealing with opinions on what's the best cookie recipe or the best sport. I'm dealing with people's personal relationship with God or lack of it, not only for today but for the rest of their earthly lives and into eternity in heaven ... or hell. I take these issues very seriously and, again, it's not lay Catholics I have an issue with. It's the Roman Catholic teachings, traditions and practices that concern me greatly. God's Word is the one source of information that we know is true, and we must put it first as our source of truth above all else apart from hearing from God directly. Unfortunately, too many Roman Catholic teachings contradict or conflict with God's Word, which is why I can't support anyone attending or supporting the Roman Catholic church - unless one is led into the Catholic church by God to be a missionary.

And just so you know, I also won't recommend someone attend a Protestant church which doesn't have the Bible at the center of its teachings, where prayer is not emphasized, where there is a watered-down gospel, where universal salvation is taught, where sin is condoned or endorsed, where the focus is on earthly matters instead of heavenly matters, where sexual predators are given priority over victims, or where witchcraft and spiritual abuse/control are tolerated and perpetuated. That's just me. You have to make your own choice.

28: Protestants and Catholics Together?

SHOULD PROTESTANTS COME HOME TO THE CATHOLIC CHURCH

Roman Catholic teaching, which is not always shared fully, is that without being a member of the Catholic church, one is destined to hell. As a result, many Roman Catholics believe they need to help Protestants 'come home' to the Roman Catholic church to save us from hell.

The word catholic means universal. Most Protestants don't see the Roman Catholic church as the one, true universal church. We believe the one true church is not a formal organization per se, but the overall Body of Christ comprised of believers with Jesus as its head.

If I ask Protestants if they would consider joining a Mormon, JW or Bahai church, or even getting together occasionally to worship and evangelize alongside people of these faiths, the vast majority - thankfully - would say no. One of the key reasons for saying no is that these religions worship a different Jesus than our Jesus. They unfortunately worship a different God. While the Roman Catholic faith has the same Jesus as Protestants, the Catholic church effectively views and treats Mary as God. As a result, it has created a 4-person Godhead, and thus worships a different God than Protestants. Political correctness would say that is way too harsh a comment. But that's the reality, and when we're dealing with people's eternal lives, we can't afford to dance around the truth. For me, with Mary and the litany of other issues, how could I possibly recommend Protestants *'come home'* to a Catholic church? I can't.

The vast majority of Protestants don't see joining the Catholic church as going home. We would see it as going astray. Christianity, in its simplest form, is about having a personal relationship with God where the Father, Jesus and Holy Spirit are first and foremost in our lives. Instead of wondering about *'going home to the Catholic church'*, our thoughts are more along the lines of:

> *"How can a Roman Catholic, if truly born again and Holy Spirit is in [en] them, stay in the Roman Catholic church where so many issues contradict the Bible, where the church has inserted itself between individuals and God, where Baptism of the Holy Spirit and the 9 Holy Spirit gifts are largely sidelined, where idolatry is rampant, and where lay Catholics' personal relationships with Jesus - which is the essence of Christianity - is not facilitated but hindered, and placed third behind their relationships with Mary and the Roman Catholic church?"*

GOD'S WARNING TO TEACHERS

The Bible says all scripture is inspired by God.

❏ *2 Timothy 3:16 All Scripture is inspired by God and profitable for teaching, for reproof, for correction, for training in righteousness;*

God's Word is ... God's word. And those who teach what God has to say are held to a higher standard. It is best for them if they stay true to God's Word, or else they may ...

❏ *James 3:1 Let not many of you become teachers, my brethren, knowing that*

CEASED?

as such we will incur a stricter judgment.

For those who change the teachings of God, Paul says not once but twice, that teachers of a false gospel should be accursed.
- *Galatians 1:8 But even if we, or an angel from heaven, **should preach to you a gospel contrary to what we have preached to you, he is to be accursed**! 9 As we have said before, so **I say again now, if any man is preaching to you a gospel contrary to what you received, he is to be accursed**!*

Consider the gospel, the core of which is the death, shed blood, burial and resurrection of Jesus.
- *1 Corinthians 15:1 Now I make known to you, brethren, **the gospel** which I preached to you, which also you received, in which also you stand, 2 by which also you are saved, if you hold fast the word which I preached to you, unless you believed in vain. 3 For I delivered to you as of first importance what I also received, that **Christ died for our sins** according to the Scriptures, 4 and that **He was buried**, and that **He was raised on the third day** according to the Scriptures,*

28:15 I believe Roman Catholic teachings that Jesus's crucifixion was not a one-time provision to pay the penalty for all sins, and therefore must be sacrificed over and over again represents a false gospel. If I'm right, what are the consequences for all the Catholic priests, Catholic nuns and lay Catholics who have taught a false gospel?

A former acquaintance of mine decided to attend a Roman Catholic seminary to become a priest. Over a period of several weeks, we discussed several issues including the issue of a false gospel. He wasn't concerned if he learned something false, and then proceeded to teach others that same false teaching. His lack of concern came about because his priest said he wouldn't be held accountable.

28:16 When this man meets Jesus face to face one day, what is Jesus going to evaluate this young man on - God's Word or the priest's opinion?

28:17 When we share information that contradicts, adds to or deletes from, or in any way changes what the Bible teaches, are we playing spiritual poker with ourselves, and potentially influencing others to do the same?

28:18 Coming alongside a Roman Catholic to study God's Word is great, and highly recommended provided the focus is on God, and God's Word. God's Word is alive and active. It illuminates, and it will draw people to His truth. For Protestants involved in the ecumenical movement or who otherwise come alongside and embrace/support in one form or another the Roman Catholic church and its teachings - where God's Word is not held up as the ultimate authority - aren't these individuals also at risk of running afoul of Galatians 1:8-9 and James 3:1?

28:19 Would you want a young man you love to be mentored by that priest who would tell him not to worry if he engages in false teachings?

28: Protestants and Catholics Together?

CLOSING POINTS TO PONDER

In the introduction to **CEASED?** on page vii. my perspective on dealing with issues of Protestants and Catholics evangelizing and worshiping alongside each other was as follows:

First, how significant are the differences in key beliefs between Protestants and Roman Catholics, both Charismatic and non-Charismatic? And second, should these differences prevent individuals of these denominations from worshipping and evangelizing alongside each other, even in situations where both appear to have been Baptized in the Holy Spirit and operate in one or more of the 9 Holy Spirit gifts?

By no means does **CEASED?** provide a complete analysis of all the issues. I do hope, however, that **CEASED?** brought clarity to some. Much like the Cessationist vs Continuationist debate, the only way Protestants and Catholics can truly agree on matters of disagreement is if individuals:
1. are committed to seek the truth;
2. will admit they are wrong if wrong, and want to go where the truth leads;
3. and accept the Bible as their ultimate authority on matters of faith.

If you're Roman Catholic, I hope **CEASED?** has brought you increased revelations of God's Word. If I have said anything wrong or misleading in any way, I apologize. That's not my intent. Going forward, you have to decide whether or not the Catholic church is teaching you the truth, and is helping you to grow in your personal relationship with Jesus. Yes, the Roman Catholic church has roots going back many centuries. Exactly when is debatable, but there is no question it was long ago.

28:20 Consider for a moment the Roman Catholic church position that it goes back to the time of the cross. Given there are so many fundamental errors and issues surrounding the teachings and traditions of the Roman Catholic church, is it prudent to ignore such issues in order to stay loyal to the Roman Catholic church, and to stay true to family ties to the Catholic church? Or is most prudent to seek God and study His word for yourself, and as God leads you, to then go to a church or denomination where the truth of God's Word is pursued and taught, and where your personal relationship with Jesus is the first priority?

28:21 The Bible is clear individuals will do signs and wonders such as prophesying, casting out demons, and other miracles, but who won't get into heaven because they don't know Jesus on a personal basis. They are able to do amazing things, but only because they use the Name of Jesus. I wonder how many Charismatic Catholics and Protestants this applies to today. If we're engaged in such things but don't have an ongoing, 2-way, personal communication with Jesus going on, shouldn't we be worried? Shouldn't our first and immediate priority be to seek Jesus and get our relationship with Him established above all else?

❑ *Matthew 7:21 "**Not everyone** who says to Me, 'Lord, Lord,' **will enter the kingdom of heaven**, but he who does the will of My Father who is in heaven*

CEASED?

> *will enter. 22 Many will say to Me on that day, 'Lord, Lord, **did we not prophesy** in Your name, and in Your name **cast out demons**, and in Your name **perform many miracles?'** 23 And then I will declare to them, '**<u>I never knew you; depart from Me</u>**, you who practice lawlessness.'*

28:22   I suspect some individuals may still believe that Roman Catholic teachings must be true, and that the Roman Catholic church must be the one true church, because the Roman Catholic church has been around for so long.
  - i. If a teaching or organization has been around a long time, and that longevity means something must be true, wouldn't that mean the teachings of religions such as Hinduism which started in ~2,000 BC, Buddhism which started in ~500 BC, and Islam which started in ~600 AD, must all be true?
  - ii. However, given many of the teachings of these religions contradict each other as well as the teachings of the Bible and/or the Roman Catholic church, doesn't that mean some of these long-standing teachings must be wrong?
  - iii. As a result, given some of these long-standing religions must be in error, doesn't that invalidate the argument that because the Roman Catholic church has been around for so long, its teachings, traditions and other practices must be right?

The thought of leaving the Roman Catholic church may be difficult, especially if friends and family members don't understand the issues as you do, and may speak or behave unkindly towards you. However, please remember you're dealing with eternal matters here. Your strength to witness through words and actions could be the catalyst for friends, family members and others in the Roman Catholic community to also seek the truth in God's Word, and to cause them to make the Bible their final authority on matters of faith.

If you're a Roman Catholic priest or are otherwise employed by the Roman Catholic church, leaving the Catholic church presents even more challenges. I encourage you to seek God, and He will guide you as to what to do, and when. He loves it when we decide to pursue Him above all else. God can solve problems and move mountains you may think are impossible to solve or move. He is God after all. Open God's Word, and read how He rescued Israel time after time. And reach out to some local Protestants – or to Protestants who may not be so local.

For all Roman Catholics, regardless of your beliefs and decisions, I pray God radically blesses you with His truth, His love, His presence, and His power. One of the things Jesus came to during His earthly ministry was to reveal Father God. I pray you will get deep revelation of your heavenly Father's love for you. And thank you for reading **CEASED?**. I hope it benefitted you in some small way. And if you seek Protestant' teachings, there are many good teachers. Ask God to guide you. If you're not sure where to start, consider the teachers mentioned in the Suggested Resources section found at the end of **CEASED?.** They have many great teachings not only in their books and other materials for sale, but through free resources such as teachings on YouTube and their websites.

29

Leaders: A Crazy Request

THE Christian walk is an interesting one. We all have our unique quirks, giftings, desires, personalities, and a willingness to offer unsolicited advice that leaders are 'blessed' to have an opportunity to hear. Today's walk for leaders is challenging in ways that do not apply to us laypeople. Leaders, especially pastors, have so many demands often making it difficult to live a life where one's spouse and family are the first priority after Christ. Pastors often can't share personal, financial and relationship struggles out of fear of losing credibility and even their job. They often can't go to another pastor in town to talk about personal issues; I've been advised doing so is like going to the competition. Pastors are often expected to lead the way in living by faith. The result is they often work for relatively low salaries. Pastor's children often pay a significant price. To pastors, spouses and children, you have our thanks and prayers. May God bless you all.

But ... here's the deal. I firmly believe the Baptism in the Holy Spirit and the 9 Holy Spirit gifts/manifestations continue today. They have not ceased. For those Cessationists that now agree with me, several challenges await. One challenge is learning how to properly use the 9 Holy Spirit gifts in their personal Christian walk. Another challenge is equipping the saints they influence in their use of the Holy Spirit gifts. And for some, a third challenge may be how to reconcile with those whom they spoke and/or wrote about inappropriately in the past.

Prayer 1

If any of the above applies to you, I pray God blesses you, strengthens you, gives you wisdom, and draws you even closer to God Himself as you walk this journey. I also pray that brothers and sisters in Christ who are experienced in these gifts open their hearts, and share their experiences, knowledge and wisdom with you.

Prayer 2

Another prayer of mine is for leaders to gather together, not only for times of praise, worship, reconciliation, but for the equipping of leaders who are new to the Baptism of Holy Spirit and the 9 Holy Spirit gifts. This wouldn't be for Cessationists who wish to debate but for Cessationists who want to be equipped. Hopefully, they also wouldn't be gatherings for Charismatic leaders who wish to promote their profile or ministry. They wouldn't be for Roman Catholics to teach and argue their faith, or to look to give the Roman Catholic church credibility. It would be for Catholics who want to learn the truths of God's Word through Protestant eyes, and who are prepared to accept the fact that doing so may result in them leaving the Catholic church. Such gatherings are not about compromising God's Word, but to enable the full gospel to be shared in love, words and power.

CEASED?

I would love to see every leader's spouse be involved in such gatherings. A husband and wife are a team. While one may have a higher profile, the other spouse typically makes huge sacrifices while also playing an extremely key role in their spouse's more public ministry.

There are so many Christian leaders, and in the end, God will direct traffic of such gatherings and connections. My fleshly nature would love to see those mentioned in my Acknowledgments and Thanks section gather together along with other individuals from both the Continuationist and Cessationist camps I have become familiar with to a degree. Some of these individuals include:

John Arnott	Heidi Baker	Robert Breaker
Michael Brown	Michael Bullet	Candace Cameron Bure
Christine Caine	Kirk Cameron	G. Alexander Bryant
Randy Clark	Graham Cooke	Sarah Davis
Wayne Drain	David Demian	Sandro Di Sabatino
Jeff Durbin	Alf Dyck	Jonathan Evans
Tony Evans	Todd Friel	Jentezen Franklin
J.D. Greear	Craig Groeschel	Faytene Grasseschi
Derrick Hamre	Costi Hinn	Michael Houdmann
T.D. Jakes	Robert Jeffress	Mark Jobe
Steve Lawson	Max Lucado	John MacArthur
Joyce Meyer	Mario Murillo	Sam Owusu
Joel Osteen	Ante Pavkovic	Tom Pennington
Justin Peters	Cal Pierce	Chuck Pierce
Phil Robertson	Willie Robertson	Jennifer Rothschild
Sid Roth	Charles Stanley	Joni Eareckson Tada
Lana Vawser	Lance Wallnau	Sam Waldron
Paul Washer	Paula White	Ted N. C. Wilson
Andrew Wommack	Donna Wright	Sarah Young

If I haven't mentioned you above or at the beginning of **CEASED?**, please don't be thankful or offended; it may be as simple as I haven't heard of you - yet.

I'm well aware there are differing views on whether or not women should be teaching. If you strongly believe women should not be teaching God's Word, and should not be involved in such gatherings, I ask you to remember female teachers sacrifice much, they are God's daughters, and they have collectively brought a great deal of good fruit to life. And, you never know, there just might be a Priscilla and Aquila conversation awaiting you and/or your spouse that will bless you.

And if you're currently Roman Catholic, and you want to pursue more truths in God's Word and grow in your personal relationship with God, I encourage you to start spending some time alone with Him. Speak freely and candidly to Him, and listen. Ask Him to guide you. Read His word starting with John, Romans, Ephesians and Galatians. Reach out to Bible-teaching, Protestant churches gathering online, in church buildings, or in homes near you. Leaders and people attending these churches will bless you immensely. One way or another, God will lead you to quality Protestant teachers, or He will bring them to you.

May God bless and guide you all.

30

In Closing

IF after reading **CEASED?**, you still believe the 9 Holy Spirit gifts/manifestations and the Baptism of the Holy Spirit have ceased, consider the apostle Paul one last time. Paul was very clear he fully preached the gospel in words and power.

- ❏ *Romans 15:19 in the power of signs and wonders, in the power of the Spirit; so that from Jerusalem and round about as far as Illyricum I have fully preached the gospel of Christ.*

30:1 If the apostle Paul, and by extension, all other apostles and believers who were Baptized in the Holy Spirit in the Bible, needed the Baptism of the Holy Spirit and the 9 Holy Spirit gifts/manifestations, why wouldn't we still need them today?

30:2 Wouldn't the power of God through signs and wonders such as instantaneous healings or words of knowledge be of great help in sharing the Good News of Jesus today?

And again, consider the following scriptures:

- ❏ *Mark 16:15 And He said to them, "Go into all the world and preach the gospel to all creation.*
- ❏ *Mark 16:17 These signs will accompany those who have believed: in My name they will cast out demons, they will speak with new tongues; 18 they will pick up serpents, and if they drink any deadly poison, it will not hurt them; they will lay hands on the sick, and they will recover.*
- ❏ *Matthew 10:8 Heal the sick, raise the dead, cleanse the lepers, cast out demons. Freely you received, freely give.*
- ❏ *Matthew 28:19 Go therefore and make disciples of all the nations, baptizing them in the name of the Father and the Son and the Holy Spirit,*

30:3 Aren't all the above commands still applicable today? If you say no, why?

30:4 Within your own life and that of your church in the last 12 months, what are the counts of individuals who:
  i. were used by God to help others get immediate/miraculous physical healing;
  ii. cast out demons;
  iii. shared the gospel in words;
  iv. shared the gospel in words and power; and who
  v. water baptized others excluding relatives?

30:5 If your 'numbers' are low, isn't something missing? And if it isn't the Baptism in the Holy Spirit and the associated Holy Spirit gifts/manifestations, what is missing?

30:6 Are we actively engaged in the Great Commission, or are our churches just a holding pen for sheep?

To Other Believers

I've been a low-profile Christian who ministers to others in the background. I've been blessed by coming into contact with people who have helped me learn and grow in many different ways including educating me in the 9 Holy Spirit gifts/manifestations. Going forward, if you're new to the gifts/manifestations and you're not sure if you should pursue them, I encourage you to ask God what He wants you to do. From my perspective, it would be great if every believer was Baptized in the Holy Spirit and operated in the gifts as Holy Spirit distributes them. However, it's a personal choice and if you choose not to pursue such gifts, that's ok. And in so doing, you're no less and no more, a child of God than the believer who does engage in them. Whatever our choice, I pray believers will love, respect and support those who make a different choice.

Roman Catholics and Roman Catholic Charismatics

I have addressed some issues that are very close to the hearts of Roman Catholics. After reading my comments that conflict with Roman Catholic teachings, I hope you see that the basis for my concerns are centered on what the Bible teaches. The Bible is my ultimate authority, not any church teachings or traditions. Jesus, and not a church or organization, died for me. Holy Spirit is in [en] me as is Jesus. Jesus is my mediator, not another person. Jesus has already paid the one-time penalty for all my sins on the cross, not some of them. Jesus calls each believer into a personal relationship directly with Him. Anything or anyone that comes in between us can only hinder my relationship with Him in the same way my relationship with my spouse or children would be hindered if I primarily communicated with them through a third party. Thus, when I say that I have major struggles in worshipping or co-evangelizing alongside Roman Catholics, it's not because of you as an individual. I'm not questioning if you're a Christian. It is because too many key teachings are contradictory or out of alignment with Biblical teaching, and it is these incorrect teachings and unbiblical traditions that cause me to grieve for Roman Catholics. My prayer is for every Roman Catholic to be immersed in God's Word daily, and that God speaks directly to you. And if you believe the Bible is not accurate or that you aren't capable of reading it, those are lies from the pit of hell.

But to Leaders - It's Another Story

I believe in unity and don't like division within the Body of Christ. However, there are a few big howevers. Unity with compromise is fine if the compromise is a minor issue such as what color to paint the nursery. However, unity that compromises God's Word on key issues such as salvation is not acceptable. Unity that involves acceptance, endorsement and ignoring of sin is not acceptable. Unity that keeps

30: In Closing

problems quiet, takes away the voice of congregants, or in any away facilitates spiritual or other forms of abuse is not acceptable. Unity that undermines the Father, Jesus or Holy Spirit, the Bible, the cross, the shed blood of Christ, Christ's death, burial and resurrection, or the fact that Jesus is the only Way, is not acceptable.

When it comes to Baptism of the Holy Spirit and the 9 Holy Spirit gifts/manifestations in 1 Corinthians 12, I don't think the biggest stumbling blocks are over disagreement on scripture or compromise. I believe the biggest issues are heart issues including pride, arrogance, greed and perhaps most of all, loyalty to current beliefs over a commitment to seeking the truth in God's Word. Many concerns expressed by Cessationists are valid. However, I have also seen blanket statements and comments from Cessationists that are flat out wrong and misleading. Some comments and behaviors were appalling. And my guess is, there will be Cessationists whose first reaction will not be to sit back and try to determine if my points are valid, but rather will try to find a way to justify existing beliefs and discredit myself or the contents herein. If anything short of seeking the truth is not pursued ... well, that's just sad. And please, if I'm wrong on something in **CEASED?**, please share. I do want to know.

Due Respect

None of us know another person's heart and thus we often don't know whether or not a person has a personal relationship with God. Leaders and those who feel they are called to speak out against other teachers need to pray and seek guidance from God rather than automatically criticize, mock and demean. And when we do speak out, leaders have a responsibility to be accurate and fair. We need to refrain from only seeking the negative, from presenting biased evidence using selective videos and incidents, from making blanket statements based on a limited sample size, and from misrepresenting the other's point of view. The standard used should be God's standard, and nothing less. We also need to seek God's guidance before commenting on others who are learning to live the more supernatural life, a life that typically requires a different level of faith.

CEASED? presents a considerable amount of evidence and asks hundreds of questions. **CEASED?** is also not the be-all and end-all of information on this issue. However, I do suggest that Cessationist leaders who continue to teach that the Baptism of the Holy Spirit and 9 Holy Spirit gifts/manifestations have ceased, have a responsibility to explain where and why the key arguments against cessation in **CEASED?** are wrong. And to do so objectively with a mindset of leading those being influenced towards the truth, not to justify any long-held mindsets or teaching. Our focus has to be one of taking the love and truth of God to the lost and hurting, and anything short of honestly seeking the truth in God's worth is irresponsible.

Ok, I'm off my soapbox. May God bless you and your families with His presence not only today, but every day going forward.

Don

Suggested Resources

Books:
Neil Anderson	The Bondage Breaker
Francis Chan	Forgotten God
Randy Clark	The Spiritual Gifts Handbook
Lori Dixon	Soles Defining Souls
Jack Frost	Experiencing Father's Embrace
Gary Habermas, Michael Licona	The Case for the Resurrection of Jesus
Beth Moore	Breaking Free
Robert Morris	The Blessed Life
	Beyond Blessed
	The God I Never Knew
Bill Johnson	Face to Face with God
	When Heaven Invades Earth
Derek Prince	The Promise of Provision
	Experiencing God's Power
Chuck Smith	Living Water
George Spormont	Wigglesworth, A Man Who Walked with God
Lee Strobel	A Case for Christ
Kris Vallotton	Spirit Wars
	The Supernatural Ways of Royalty
Ravi Zacharias	Why Jesus?
	Jesus Among Other Gods

Information related to Cessationist vs Continuationist debate:
Michael L. Brown	Authentic Fire
John MacArthur	Strange Fire

Teachings and insights from 2 former Roman Catholics:
Mike Gendron	proclaimingthegospel.org
Fred Tarsitano	lighthascome.com

Scientific Evidence for God and His Word:
Jay Seegert	Thestartingpointproject.com
Ken Ham	Answersingenesis.org
Creation Ministries International	Creation.com
Institute for Creation Research	icr.org

About the Author

Don Dixon basically ignored the issue of faith for the first 45 years of his life. He spent the following 10 years in church where he came to know a fair amount about Jesus. However, he didn't begin a personal relationship with Jesus until tough times hit in his mid-fifties. During one of his darkest days, he cried out to Jesus. Jesus responded and Don was truly born again. A transformation in his whole being began, one aspect of which involved a different attitude towards sin. His transformation process was expedited a few months later when Don was Baptized in the Holy Spirit and Fire.

After decades in the large corporate world where the pursuit of money was his key goal, Don's primary desire now is to have an ever-improving relationship with God and his family, to share the Good News of Jesus, and to support his wife Lori in her ministry, part of which involves educating church leaders and believers on trauma. Lori is the author of *'Soles Defining Souls'*, a book based on real-world experiences of women hurt by other Christians and church leadership.

Don and Lori live near Vancouver, British Columbia, Canada.

Contact Me

FEEDBACK on any aspect of **CEASED?** is appreciated, especially if it shows where and why I'm wrong, or provides new perspectives, additional scriptures and/or questions that would help clarify issues. Please share through my website - www.ceased.ca. Thank you in advance for taking the time to share.

If your intent is just to attack, criticize, ridicule and/or make statements that aren't respectful, I won't validate such communications with a reply. I will, however, pray that God blesses you and your family in radical ways.

Blessings to you all.

- *Mark 16:15 And He said to them, "Go into all the world and preach the gospel to all creation ... 17 **These signs** will accompany those who have believed: in My name they will **cast out demons**, they will **speak with new tongues**; 18 they will pick up serpents, and if they drink any deadly poison, it will not hurt them; they will **lay hands on the sick, and they will recover.**"*

- *Acts 1:8 but **you will receive power** when the **Holy Spirit** has come **upon [epi] you**; and you shall be My witnesses both in Jerusalem, and in all Judea and Samaria, and even to the remotest part of the earth.*

- *1 Corinthians 14:1 Pursue love, yet **desire earnestly spiritual gifts**, but **especially** that you may **prophesy** ... 5 Now I wish that you all spoke in **tongues,** but even more that you would prophesy; and **greater is one who prophesies than one who speaks in tongues, unless he interprets** ...*

- *1 Corinthians 2:5 so that your **faith** would not rest on the wisdom of men, but **on the power of God.***

Manufactured by Amazon.ca
Bolton, ON